THE
POST-SYNODAL
APOSTOLIC
EXHORTATIONS
OF
JOHN PAUL II

Edited with Introductions
by J. Michael Miller, C.S.B.

Our Sunday Visitor Publishing Division
Our Sunday Visitor, Inc.
Huntington, Indiana 46750

The author and publisher are grateful to the Vatican Press, which provided the translations of the apostolic exhortations. With the exception of minor corrections, including modifications for the sake of consistency of style, the text remains unchanged from the official version. If any copyrighted materials have been inadvertently used in this work without proper credit being given in one manner or another, please notify Our Sunday Visitor in writing so that future printings of this work may be corrected accordingly.

International Standard Book Number: 0-87973-928-2
Library of Congress Catalog Card Number: 97-69354

Cover design by Monica Watts

PRINTED IN THE UNITED STATES OF AMERICA

928

Abbreviations of the Books of the Bible

Acts	Acts of the Apostles	Lk	Luke
Bar	Baruch	1 Mac	1 Maccabees
1 Chron	1 Chronicles	2 Mac	2 Maccabees
2 Chron	2 Chronicles	Mic	Micah
Col	Colossians	Mk	Mark
1 Cor	1 Corinthians	Mt	Matthew
2 Cor	2 Corinthians	Neh	Nehemiah
Dan	Daniel	Num	Numbers
Dt	Deuteronomy	1 Pet	1 Peter
Eccles	Ecclesiastes	2 Pet	2 Peter
Eph	Ephesians	Phil	Philippians
Ex	Exodus	Philem	Philemon
Ezek	Ezekiel	Prov	Proverbs
Gal	Galatians	Ps	Psalms
Gen	Genesis	Rev	Revelation
Heb	Hebrews	Rom	Romans
Hos	Hosea	1 Sam	1 Samuel
Is	Isaiah	2 Sam	2 Samuel
Jas	James	Sir	Sirach
Jer	Jeremiah	1 Thess	1 Thessalonians
Jn	John	2 Thess	2 Thessalonians
1 Jn	1 John	1 Tim	1 Timothy
2 Jn	2 John	2 Tim	2 Timothy
Jon	Jonah	Tit	Titus
Jos	Joshua	Tob	Tobit
Judg	Judges	Wis	Wisdom
1 Kg	1 Kings	Zech	Zechariah
Lam	Lamentations	Zeph	Zephaniah
Lev	Leviticus		

Other Abbreviations

AAS — *Acta Apostolicae Sedis.* Rome, 1909—.

CCL — *Corpus Christianorum. Series Latina.* Turnhout, 1953—.

CSCO — *Corpus Scriptorum Christianorum Orientalium.* Paris-Louvain, 1903—.

CSEL — *Corpus Scriptorum Ecclesiasticorum Latinorum.* Vienna, 1866—.

DS — Denzinger-Schönmetzer. Henry Denzinger and Adolf Schönmetzer, eds., *Enchiridion Symbolorum, Definitionum et Declarationum de Rebus Fidei et Morum.* 33rd ed. Freiburg im Breisgau, 1964.

PG — *Patrologia Graeca.* J. P. Migne, ed. Paris, 1857-1866. 162 volumes.

PL — *Patrologia Latina.* J. P. Migne, ed. Paris, 1844-1864. 221 volumes.

SCh — *Sources Chrétiennes.* Paris. 1941—.

Contents

Preface

Established in 1965, the Synod of Bishops has played a significant role in implementing the teachings and pastoral directives of the Second Vatican Council. Ordinary General Assemblies of the Synod now meet regularly in Rome, usually every three or four years. To date, Pope John Paul II has issued six post-synodal apostolic exhortations on the topics treated at these meetings. These exhortations, published about a year after the month-long gathering, have been instrumental in renewing the Church's life in the areas of catechesis, the family, penance and reconciliation, and with regard to the different states of life: the laity, the priesthood, and the consecrated life. Here, for the first time, these six papal documents, along with an introduction to each one, have been gathered together in a single volume. This book complements the collection of John Paul's twelve encyclicals previously published by Our Sunday Visitor, Inc. Together these two volumes make available the heart of the Pope's thought to the English-speaking world.

In post-synodal apostolic exhortations the Church's ordinary Magisterium is exercised in a unique, even novel, way. As a genre of papal document, they are theologically and pastorally innovative. Until now, these exhortations have not been given the attention they deserve. This collection aims to correct this neglect by stressing their importance to the Pope's ministry of teaching "the truth of the Gospel" (Gal 2:5). They also embody John Paul's conviction, expressed in his encyclical *Ut Unum Sint* (1995), of the need to find "a way of exercising the primacy which, while in no way renouncing what is essential to its mission, is nonetheless open to a new situation" (§95.2).

Post-synodal apostolic exhortations are the fruit of the collegial deliberations of the Synod of Bishops. As such they are in harmony with Vatican II's ecclesiology of communion and its teaching on the common responsibility of the whole Episcopal College for the "care of all the Churches" (2 Cor 11:28). More than encyclicals, post-synodal exhortations emphasize the Pope's role *within* the College of Bishops. As the Successor of Peter, he "receives" the Synod's recommendations in order to transmit them to the whole Church. In these six exhortations the Holy Father speaks in the name of his brother Bishops, uniting their witness in a single voice. For John Paul II, such a function belongs to his pastoral office as the center of the visible communion of the universal Church.

The definitive Latin version of post-synodal apostolic exhortations can be found in the Vatican's official journal of record, the *Acta Apostolicae Sedis*. Each translation in the present volume was approved by the Secretariat of

State and officially published by the Vatican Press. I have made only minimal changes in these texts, and then only in order to adapt the translation to the conventions of American spelling, capitalization, and punctuation. In addition, as a help to the reader, I have numbered sequentially the individual paragraphs of every document. Also, for the sake of consistency, I have adopted the editorial style of the Pope's most recent exhortations. This decision entailed changing the formatting of the earlier exhortations as well as considerable editing of the footnotes.

The indexes of scriptural quotations and principal themes of John Paul's encyclicals and post-synodal apostolic exhortations at the end of this volume should be particularly helpful to the reader. Both indexes are cumulative; the entries cover the Holy Father's twelve encyclicals published in the previous volume and the six exhortations of the present work. The biblical index lists the direct and indirect references to Scripture which I judged to be significant, either because the Pope relies on them to make a point or because he uses them in a fresh or unusual way. The subject index provides references to the main places where the Holy Father develops a particular theme. While not exhaustive, the indexes are meant to encourage further study of John Paul's thought.

Every book is a collaborative venture, and this one is certainly no exception. I am deeply indebted to all those who have helped me to bring this second volume of the Pope's principal writings to its conclusion. To my former colleagues in the English-language section of the Secretariat of State of the Holy See, I am especially grateful for their unfailing support and example of filial love for the Church. Likewise, I express my thanks to my students at the Pontifical Gregorian University in Rome who, through their enthusiasm for the teaching of Pope John Paul II, encouraged me to put together this volume of his post-synodal apostolic exhortations for a wider public. It is also a pleasure to express my heartfelt gratitude to all those who read and corrected the manuscript in its various stages: Miss Sharon Bychowski, of the University of Saint Thomas in Houston; Mother Ann Marie Kerper, F.S.E., in Rome; Monsignor Alan McCormack, of the Congregation for the Doctrine of the Faith; Father Joseph McLaughlin, S.S.E., of Saint Michael's College in Colchester, Vermont; Father P. Wallace Platt, C.S.B., of the Cardinal Flahiff Basilian Centre in Toronto; Father Richard J. Schiefen, C.S.B., of the University of Saint Thomas in Houston; and Father William Sheehan, C.S.B., of the Vatican Apostolic Library. Finally, I wish to thank James Manney and Henry O'Brien of Our Sunday Visitor, Inc., for their endless patience in editing this second volume of papal documents. Without the critical eye and suggestions of these friends and colleagues this collection would never have seen the light of day.

Introduction to the Post-Synodal Apostolic Exhortations

As the Successor of Peter, the Pope has a unique responsibility for teaching "the truth of the Gospel" (Gal 2:5) and guiding the faithful to live it. The Bishop of Rome is the primary guardian of the apostolic Tradition, which he recalls, restates, and confirms through his Magisterium. In the words of Pope John Paul II, the mission of Peter's Successor is "to establish and authoritatively confirm what the Church has received and believed from the beginning, what the Apostles taught, what Sacred Scripture and Christian Tradition have determined as the object of faith and the Christian norm of life."[1] Fulfilling Christ's promise that Peter's faith would not fail, God sustains the Pope's teaching ministry of confirming the faith of his brothers and sisters (cf. Lk 22:32).

In recent years, post-synodal apostolic exhortations have proved to be an effective instrument which the Pope has used to carry out his mission as the principal guarantor of the Church's obedience to revelation. While theologians have paid considerable attention to the teaching of papal encyclicals,[2] the same is not true for apostolic exhortations. Only very recently have they been mentioned in lists of the different kinds of papal statements, and then with little or no explanation of their origin, characteristics, or authority.[3]

---

[1] Address at the General Audience, March 10, 1993, *L'Osservatore Romano*, 11 (1993), 11.

[2] See J. Michael Miller, ed., *The Encyclicals of John Paul II* (Huntington: Our Sunday Visitor, Inc., 1996), 9-30.

[3] See, for example, J. T. Catoir, "Documents, papal," in the *New Catholic Encyclopedia,* vol. 4 (New York: McGraw-Hill Publishing Company, 1967), 946-947, which does not mention apostolic exhortations; Francis G. Morrisey, "Papal and Curial Pronouncements: Their Canonical Significance in light of the 1983 Code of Canon Law," *The Jurist,* 50 (1990), 102-125, dedicates a single paragraph to apostolic exhortations (106-107); Carlo Egger, "Documentorum Pontificiorum ratio et divisio hac nostra aetate," in Cleto Pavanetto, ed., *Elementa linguae et grammaticae latinae,* 3rd ed. (Rome: Salesianum Press, 1991), 168-173, makes only a passing reference to apostolic exhortations; Claudia Carlen, in *Papal Pronouncements — A Guide: 1740-1978,* vol. 1 (Ann Arbor: The Pierian Press, 1990), xiii, lists the apostolic exhortation in her classification of papal documents but adds only that it is "a more or less formal instruction given on a specific occasion." In his topology of papal statements, Giovanni Peduto merely says: "Apostolic Exhortations usually are universal in nature, but their subject matter is considered less important than an Encyclical's" ("A Guide to Various Papal Documents," *L'Osservatore Romano,* 41 [1993], 6). Neither Carlen nor Peduto even mentions *post-synodal* apostolic exhortations.

In 1939, to commemorate the consecration of twelve missionary Bishops, Pius XII (1939-1958) issued the first document labeled an "exhortation."[4] The same year he addressed an "apostolic exhortation" to priests and clerics serving in the military.[5] While the qualifier "apostolic" suggests a higher degree of papal teaching authority, the Pope gave no explanation for adding the adjective. During his pontificate, Pius XII published two more "apostolic exhortations,"[6] and two other documents simply called "exhortations."[7] His successor, John XXIII (1958-1963), was equally sparing in using this label; he issued only two "apostolic exhortations."[8]

Only with Paul VI (1963-1978) does the apostolic exhortation become a regular document of the ordinary papal Magisterium — that which does not propose doctrines *ex cathedra* or infallibly.[9] The Pope made two significant contributions in this regard. First, he fixed the nomenclature: from then on, all exhortations have been labeled as "apostolic." Second, he determined that this particular literary genre could be used to address the whole Church on important matters, though he attributed less doctrinal weight to apostolic exhortations than to encyclical letters. After the publication of *Humanae Vitae* in 1968, Paul VI did not write another encyclical, but his apostolic exhortations became more frequent. Perhaps the controversy provoked by his encyclical on human life deterred him from using the more authoritative genre. During the last ten years of his pontificate, however, Pope Paul published a number of apostolic exhortations, including several which had an influence on the Church's life equal to or greater than that of many papal encyclicals: *Evangelica Testificatio* (1971), on the renewal of religious life[10]; *Marialis Cultus*

---

[4] *AAS* 31 (1939), 595-598.

[5] *AAS* 31 (1939), 696-701.

[6] See the apostolic exhortation to the clergy of the world, on the spiritual perfection of priests (*AAS* 42 [1950], 657-702); and to the First International Congress of Teaching Sisters, on educating youth (*AAS* 43 [1951], 738-744).

[7] See the exhortation to people of Rome (*AAS* 44 [1952], 158-162); and to the Bishops of Italy, on the effects of television (*AAS* 46 [1954], 18-24).

[8] See the apostolic exhortation to the clergy, on the Divine Office and the Second Vatican Council (*AAS* 54 [1962], 66-75); and to the Bishops, on preparing for the Second Vatican Council (*AAS* 55 [1963], 440-441).

[9] See, for example, his four apostolic exhortations to the Bishops of the world on the occasion of the Second Vatican Council: on prayer and penance for its success (*AAS* 55 [1963], 729-733); on entreating prayers and penance for the unity of Christians (*AAS* 56 [1964], 183-188); before the opening of its fourth session (*AAS* 57 [1965], 689-693); and at its closing (*AAS* 57 [1965], 865-871).

[10] *AAS* 63 (1971), 497-526; translation in *L'Osservatore Romano*, 28 (1971), 5-10; and in *Origins*, 1 (1971), 130-139.

(1974), on devotion to the Blessed Virgin Mary[11]; *Paterna cum Benevolentia* (1974), on reconciliation within the Church[12]; and *Gaudete in Domino* (1975), on Christian joy.[13] His last one, *Evangelii Nuntiandi* (1975),[14] is really the first post-synodal apostolic exhortation, even though when it was issued, the term "post-synodal" was not yet used. Besides those published after the Synods, John Paul II, too, has written several apostolic exhortations: *Redemptionis Donum* (1984), to men and women Religious on their consecration in light of the mystery of the Redemption[15]; and *Redemptoris Custos* (1989), on the person and mission of Saint Joseph in the life of Christ and the Church.[16]

Apostolic exhortations generally entail a more restricted use of the Pope's ordinary Magisterium than do encyclicals. But as yet, there is no official or standard theological explanation for this specific kind of papal document. Two tentative conclusions, however, can be drawn. First, they are, as the name implies, chiefly "exhortative," even when the subject deals with issues of doctrinal significance. Second, the Pope does not write exhortations when he wants to teach on matters of faith or morals with the full force of his Petrine charism.

I. The Synod of Bishops

Post-synodal apostolic exhortations are papal documents which have their origin in the Synod of Bishops. The word "synod" comes from the Greek *synodos,* which means a "coming together." In the early Church, assemblies patterned on the apostolic council held in Jerusalem (cf. Acts 15:5-29) frequently met to make decisions about matters of crucial interest to the Christian community. Today's Synod of Bishops draws its inspiration from this ancient synodal activity and from the synodal government of the Eastern Churches, though it has specific characteristics. It is, then, a representative gathering of Bishops with the Pope who "make a journey together" to discuss vital pastoral questions.

---

[11] *AAS* 66 (1974), 113-168; translation in *L'Osservatore* Romano, 14 (1974), 1-9; and excerpts in *Origins,* 3 (1974), 633, 635-638.

[12] *AAS* 67 (1975), 5-23; translation in *L'Osservatore Romano,* 52 (1974), 1-4; and in *Origins,* 4 (1975), 449, 451-456.

[13] *AAS* 67 (1975), 289-322; translation in *L'Osservatore Romano,* 22 (1975), 1-7; and in *Origins,* 5 (1975), 1, 3-13.

[14] *AAS* 68 (1976), 5-76; translation in *L'Osservatore Romano,* 52 (1975), 1-6, 11-13; and excerpts in *Origins,* 5 (1976), 459-468.

[15] *AAS* 76 (1984), 513-546; translation in *L'Osservatore Romano,* 14 (1984), 1-5, 16; and in *Origins,* 13 (1984), 721, 723-731.

[16] *AAS* 82 (1990), 5-34; translation in *L'Osservatore Romano,* 44 (1989), 1-6; and in *Origins,* 19 (1990), 507-514.

In order to prolong the collegial experience which animated the Second Vatican Council, the Fathers recommended that a permanent body should be established which would express the Bishops' coresponsibility for the universal Church. Paul VI quickly responded to their request, and in 1965 set up the Synod of Bishops.[17]

According to the 1983 Code of Canon Law, which follows Paul VI's *motu proprio* of 1965 very closely, the Synod of Bishops has three purposes. First, it promotes closer unity between the Successor of Peter and the Successors of the Apostles by fostering the Bishops' collegial solicitude for issues affecting the universal Church. Second, the Synod assists the Pope in carrying out his primatial ministry. Bishops from throughout the world gather to advise him on how best to proclaim and explain matters of faith and morals, and to maintain and strengthen ecclesiastical unity. Third, the Synod of Bishops takes up questions pertaining to the Church's activity in the world, a pastoral duty which has become increasingly significant since the Second Vatican Council.[18]

Besides these stated canonical purposes, Synods in fact have other functions. They provide Bishops with a valuable forum in which they can discuss common pastoral problems. These Assemblies further knowledge on all sides and, if there is any misunderstanding, can help the Episcopal College to reach a common mind. The Synod of Bishops also affords the occasion for what Cardinal Joseph Ratzinger calls "mutual self-correction." The Assemblies allow the Bishops and the Pope a unique opportunity to engage in a frank exchange of views. Some critics have observed, however, that the Bishops' deferential attitude to the Pope curtails the freedom of synodal debate and limits their ability to offer him helpful advice.[19] In addition to fostering reciprocal correction, writes Ratzinger, Synods are meant to encourage and strengthen "the positive forces inside and outside the Church."[20]

Since the Second Vatican Council, the Church has frequently been described as a communion. This ecclesiology provides a key for describing the mutual relations between the Bishops and the Pope in their care of the universal Church. Consequently, the Synod of Bishops can also be situated in

---

[17] *Apostolica Sollicitudo*, AAS 57 (1965), 775-780; translation in *The Pope Speaks*, 10 (1965), 339-342.

[18] Code of Canon Law, canon 342.

[19] Thomas J. Reese, *Inside the Vatican: The Politics and Organization of the Catholic Church* (Cambridge, MA: Harvard University Press, 1996), 61.

[20] "The Structure and Tasks of the Synod of Bishops," in *Church, Ecumenism and Politics*, trans. Robert Nowell (New York: Crossroad Publishing Company, 1988), 61-62.

the mystery of the Church as a communion. Episcopal Synods, in fact, are signs and instruments of the structured communion of the College of Bishops and give life to that communion. According to John Paul II, "the Synod constitutes a unique experience on a universal basis of episcopal communion, which strengthens the sense of the universal Church and the sense of responsibility of the Bishops toward the universal Church and her mission, in affective and effective communion around Peter."[21]

The intimate connection between ecclesial communion and the Synod of Bishops has been pointed out by Cardinal Jan P. Schotte, Secretary General of the Synod of Bishops: "The collegiality which underlies the Synod of Bishops is not simply a juridico-disciplinary matter, rather it is a requirement of communion and actually fosters Church communion. . . . In this way, the Synod of Bishops is inserted into the life of the universal ecclesial communion as one of its moving forces and as one of its more important instruments."[22] In 1990, John Paul affirmed that, in the years after Vatican II, the Synod "immediately proved to be a special expression and instrument of ecclesial communion."[23] Later, in the post-synodal apostolic exhortation *Ecclesia in Africa* (1995), the Holy Father wrote: "The Synod of Bishops is an extremely beneficial instrument for fostering ecclesial communion. . . . the more the communion of the Bishops among themselves is strengthened, the more the communion of the Church as a whole is enriched" (§15). More than being a merely consultative body for practical matters, he added, the Synod helps the Church to move forward "by strengthening communion among her members, beginning with her Pastors" (§17.1).

As expressed by the Second Vatican Council, the Synod was to "bear testimony to the participation of all the Bishops in hierarchical communion in the care of the universal Church."[24] The synodal process reveals the relationship of "mutual interiority" between the universal Church, represented by the Pope, and the particular Churches, represented by their Bishops. Each local Church,

---

[21] Address at the Conclusion of the Eighth Ordinary General Assembly of the Synod of Bishops, October 27, 1990, *L'Osservatore Romano*, 45 (1990), 7.

[22] "The Synod of Bishops: A Permanent yet Adaptable Church Institution," *Studia Canonica*, 26 (1992), 295.

[23] Address to the Roman Curia, December 20, 1990, *L'Osservatore Romano*, 52 (1990), 2; see also his Homily at the Conclusion of the Synod of Bishops, Sixth Ordinary General Assembly, October 29, 1983, *L'Osservatore Romano*, 45 (November 7, 1983), 3: "The Synod of Bishops is a particularly precious manifestation of the episcopal collegiality of the Church, and one of its most effective instruments."

[24] Decree on the Bishops' Pastoral Office in the Church, *Christus Dominus*, 5.

as a realization of the one Church of Christ, is therefore present in every other local Church, with which it shares its own gifts. The Bishop of Rome ensures the convergence of these gifts toward the center, the See of Peter, so that they may flow from there to the other Churches. During the synodal Assemblies, Bishops carry out their mission of serving the universal Church. In fact, they "express their apostolic solidarity in a preeminent way through the Synod of Bishops."[25]

John Paul II is resolutely committed to the Synod of Bishops which, he says, was established by "a truly Providential act" of Paul VI and has matured in light of the Second Vatican Council. Speaking to the Council of the General Secretariat of the Synod of Bishops, he expressed a positive evaluation of the institution: "The experience of the post-conciliar period shows clearly in what noteworthy measure the synodal activity can set the pace for the pastoral life of the universal Church."[26] In a certain way, the Synod of Bishops can now be considered a necessary institution belonging to the Church's hierarchical structure. Addressing the Roman Curia in 1994, the Holy Father remarked: "For deciding issues of great importance there is need for a Synod, for a meeting of Pastors aided by experts who, through prayer and sharing experiences, are able to suggest useful operational techniques for that proclamation of the Gospel which is brought about by word and life."[27] In still stronger terms, in off-the-cuff remarks in Manila, he commented that "it is necessary to return to this experience, the synodal experience of the Church [of the first millennium]." John Paul also added that history might judge him to have been "the Pope of the Synod" or the "Synodal Pope."[28]

Instrument of collegiality

Episcopal Synods are collective gatherings that are an authentic "sign and instrument of the collegial spirit."[29] They embody the principle of episcopal collegiality taught by the Second Vatican Council. Synods let Bishops have a say in the pastoral government of the universal Church, and enable the Pope to carry out his ministry in a collegial way. Although the Bishop of Rome also relies on the College of Cardinals and the Roman Curia to help him to dis-

---

[25] John Paul II, *Ecclesia in Africa*, §132.

[26] Address to the Council of the General Secretariat of the Synod of Bishops, April 30, 1983, *L'Osservatore Romano*, 21 (1983), 9; see also *Dominum et Vivificantem*, §26.2.

[27] Address to the Roman Curia, December 22, 1994, *L'Osservatore Romano*, 1 (1995), 7.

[28] Remarks to the Sixth Plenary Assembly of the Federation of Asian Bishops' Conferences, January 15, 1995, *L'Osservatore Romano*, 4 (1995), 6.

[29] Synod of Bishops, Second Extraordinary General Assembly, "The Final Report," *L'Osservatore Romano*, 50 (1985), 8; and in *Origins*, 15 (1985), 448.

charge his ministry, he gives pride of place to the Synod of Bishops. The Code of Canon Law reflects this priority in its arrangement of the relevant canons: it treats the Synod of Bishops immediately after the College of Bishops, before the College of Cardinals.[30]

Collegiality allows for various degrees of intensity. In the fullest sense it belongs to the entire Episcopal College which, as the subject of supreme authority in the Church, is indivisible. Only when the College of Bishops acts as a corporate body can it engage in fully collegial acts. An Ecumenical Council, when all Bishops are gathered with the Pope, manifests *effective* collegiality in the strictest sense. Episcopal Synods enjoy less authority, since they cannot perform strictly collegial acts. A Synod is not a mini-Council but "an assembly of Bishops representing the Catholic episcopate."[31] In ordinary circumstances the Episcopal College addresses major ecclesial concerns through the Synod of Bishops. This latter body manifests *affective* collegiality, or the "collegial spirit," securing the fraternal bonds of solidarity between the Bishops and the Pope, and among the Bishops with one another.

John Paul II has frequently drawn attention to the connection between the Synod of Bishops and episcopal collegiality. Already in his first encyclical, the Pope referred to the Synod of Bishops as "a permanent organ of collegiality."[32] According to him, "the Synod constitutes a realization and an illustration of the collegial nature of the order of Bishops, of which the Second Vatican Council has, so to speak, come to a renewed awareness."[33] He is convinced that the Synod of Bishops provides a way for putting collegiality into practice. "Episcopal Synods, established after Vatican II, are meant," the Holy Father said, "to realize concretely the participation of the Episcopal College in the universal

---

[30] See the order of the Code of Canon Law: canons 331-335, on the Roman Pontiff; canons 336-341, on the College of Bishops; canons 342-348, on the Synod of Bishops; canons 349-359, on the College of Cardinals; and canons 360-361, on the Roman Curia.

[31] Schotte, "The Synod of Bishops," 290.

[32] *Redemptor Hominis,* §5.1.

[33] Address at the Conclusion of the Eighth Ordinary General Assembly of the Synod of Bishops, October 27, 1990, *L'Osservatore Romano,* 45 (1990), 7. See also his remark that in every Synod "the collegiality of the Bishops of the whole Church is expressed in a special way" (Letter to Priests for Holy Thursday 1991, §2); his statement that the Synod of Bishops is "a unique expression of the collegiality of the Bishops with the Pope" (Address to the Roman Curia, December 20, 1990, *L'Osservatore Romano,* 52 [1990], 2); and his observation that the Synod of Bishops is "the principal expression of collegiality, that is, to say, of the particular responsibility of Bishops as willed by the Council" (Address to the Second Plenary Meeting of the College of Cardinals, November 26, 1982, *L'Osservatore Romano,* 49 [1982], 6).

government of the Church."[34] For the Pope, the Synod "expresses collegiality in a highly intense way, even if it does not equal that achieved by the Council."[35]

The Synod opens possibilities for the Bishops' regular, disciplined, and collegial collaboration with the Successor of Peter. Repeatedly the Holy Father asserts that the Petrine ministry is meant to foster episcopal collegiality. Addressing the Council of the General Secretariat of the Synod of Bishops, he affirmed: "The Synod itself makes the intimate connection between collegiality and the primacy stand out: the task of the Successor of Peter is also service to the collegiality of the Bishops, and conversely the effective and affective collegiality of the Bishops is an important aid to the primatial Petrine service."[36]

The Pope's role

According to *Apostolica Sollicitudo*, the Synod of Bishops was to be closely associated with the papal office. This institution is, affirmed Paul VI, "directly and immediately subject to our power."[37] The 1983 Code of Canon Law adopted the same position, describing it as a body at the service of the Pope: "It is the role of the Synod of Bishops to discuss the questions on their agenda and to express their desires about them but not to resolve them or to issue decrees about them, unless the Roman Pontiff in certain cases has endowed the Synod with deliberative power, and, in this event, it is his role to ratify its deci-

---

[34] Address at the General Audience, October 7, 1992, *L'Osservatore Romano*, 41 (1992), 11.

[35] Address to the Council of the General Secretariat of the Synod of Bishops, April 30, 1983, *L'Osservatore Romano*, 21 (1983), 9.

[36] Address to the General Secretariat of the Synod of Bishops, April 30, 1983, *L'Osservatore Romano*, 21 (1983), 9. On another occasion, John Paul referred to the *"synodalitas effectiva"* of the Synod of Bishops (Address at the Conclusion of the Seventh Ordinary General Assembly of the Synod of Bishops, October 29, 1987, *L'Osservatore Romano*, 45 [1987], 2). Jan P. Schotte, too, has referred to the Synod of Bishops as "an instrument of effective and affective collegiality" (Presentation of the *Instrumentum Laboris* for the 1990 Synod, *L'Osservatore Romano*, 30 [1990], 8). Many theologians, however, avoid describing the Synod of Bishops as an instance of "effective" collegiality, reserving that designation for the whole College of Bishops when it exercises supreme power as a corporate body. There are disputed questions: whether a strictly collegial act always requires the use of supreme authority, and whether collegiality can admit of varying degrees of intensity. See J. Michael Miller, *The Shepherd and the Rock: Origins, Development, and Mission of the Papacy* (Huntington: Our Sunday Visitor, Inc., 1995), 240-241; and Charles M. Murphy, "Collegiality: An Essay Toward Better Understanding," *Theological Studies*, 46 (1985), 38-49.

[37] Introduction.

sions."[38] The Pope's key role at Assemblies is expressed by his prerogatives: he convokes it when and where he sees fit; he ratifies the choice of delegates and names his own appointees; he determines the topics for discussion, sets the agenda, presides at its sessions or appoints a delegate; and he can conclude, transfer, suspend, or dissolve it.[39]

According to John Paul II, "the Synod of Bishops responds to the needs of the Church when the Successor of Peter, with the aid of his brother Bishops, has to carry out tasks which emerge from his apostolic mandate as universal Shepherd, amid complex circumstances which are subject to continuing change."[40] The synodal Assembly meets *cum Petro* and *sub Petro* — with and under Peter's authority. "In relationship with the Successor of Peter the Synod finds not only the guarantee of unity both in the origin and carrying out of its work, but also the basis for its authoritativeness."[41] According to Ratzinger, the Synod of Bishops as an institution "derives its legal basis from the primacy,"[42] while at the same time it expresses the collegial nature of the Episcopal College.

It is now the custom for the Pope to attend all plenary sessions of the Synod. This practice confirms the Assembly's truly "collegial" nature, since the head of the Episcopal College is present in the Synod Hall with his brother Bishops. His presence symbolizes and guarantees the unity of the Assembly. John Paul II wishes to carry out his primatial ministry "in a strong 'framework' of collegiality."[43]

The Synod's function is preeminently advisory to the Holy Father. Its members express their opinions to the Bishop of Rome on matters that he has chosen to submit for their discussion. After being given the topic, the Bishops gather information, debate it, and then identify and judge a course of action. Since the Assembly is a consultative body, the Pope is free to accept or reject its advice. In this respect the Synod of Bishops is unlike an Ecumenical Council, which acts in a fully collegial way, or the synodal bodies of the Eastern Churches, which resolve problems and issue decrees on their own authority.

---

[38] Canon 343. The Code of Canons of the Eastern Churches says very little about the Synod of Bishops, merely listing it as a way in which the Bishops assist the Roman Pontiff "in exercising his office" (canon 46 §1).

[39] Code of Canon Law, canon 344.

[40] Address at the Conclusion of the Eighth Ordinary General Assembly of the Synod of Bishops, October 27, 1990, *L'Osservatore Romano,* 45 (1990), 7.

[41] John Paul II, Address to the Roman Curia, December 20, 1990, *L'Osservatore Romano,* 52/53 (1990), 2.

[42] "Structure and Tasks of the Synod of Bishops," 57.

[43] Address to the Roman Curia, June 28, 1980, *L'Osservatore Romano,* 28 (1980), 13.

Kinds of Synods

The 1983 Code of Canon Law lists three different kinds of Synods: ordinary, extraordinary, and special assemblies.

Ordinary Synods

Ordinary Synods now meet regularly in Rome, usually every three or four years, during the month of October. Nine of them took place between 1967 and 1997. Most Synod participants, who generally number just over two hundred,[44] are elected by Episcopal Conferences, according to a quota system based on their size. The Pope directly appoints fifteen percent of the voting membership, and the Union of Superiors General elects ten members from clerical religious Institutes. In addition, about thirty heads of the different departments of the Roman Curia are *ex officio* members of the Synod.[45] In 1971, lay experts were invited for the first time to take part in the Synod's preparatory stages and its fall meeting in Rome. Members of the laity, as well as consecrated men and women, are now routinely invited; so, too, are representatives of other Churches and Ecclesial Communities. While invited members can address the Synod Fathers and take part in discussions, they cannot vote.

The First Ordinary General Assembly met in 1967 and, in the wake of Vatican II, dealt with questions of doctrinal orthodoxy, the Code of Canon Law, seminaries, mixed marriages, and the liturgy. The Synod Fathers recommended the establishment of an International Theological Commission, approved the ten Guiding Principles which were to govern the revision of the Code of Canon Law, greater oversight of seminaries by Episcopal Conferences, and new regulations for mixed marriages. Paul VI acted on all five proposals.

The topics taken up by the Second Ordinary General Assembly were priesthood and justice. At its conclusion, the Synod issued two statements in its own name, though with Paul VI's approval: "The Ministerial Priesthood"[46] and "Justice in the World."[47] The Pope had these documents published in

---

[44] The number of voting members at each Ordinary General Assembly of the Synod of Bishops is given in parentheses after the year it met: 1967 (197), 1971 (210), 1974 (209), 1977 (204), 1980 (216), 1983 (221), 1987 (232), 1990 (238), 1994 (244). Since 1971, participants from Africa, Asia, and Latin America have formed the majority.

[45] Code of Canon Law, canon 346 §1.

[46] Translation in Austin Flannery, ed., *Vatican Council II: More Postconciliar Documents*, vol. 2 (Northport: Costello Publishing Company, 1982), 672-694; also in *L'Osservatore Romano*, 50 (1971), 1-4.

[47] Translation in Austin Flannery, ed., *Vatican Council II: More Postconciliar Documents*,

the Vatican's official journal, a practice not followed after the later Synods.[48]

In 1974, the topic for the third Synod was evangelization in the modern world. This subject came to have an enormous influence on the Church's life, no doubt due, at least in part, to the landmark apostolic exhortation, *Evangelii Nuntiandi* (1975), published by Pope Paul VI as the fruit of the Synod's deliberations.

The exhortations published after the Fourth to Ninth Ordinary General Assemblies are dealt with in the later chapters of this book. Each of these Synods treats either a particular pastoral question or a specific group of people in the Church, and after each the Pope issued an apostolic exhortation: catechesis (1977), *Catechesi Tradendae* (1979)[49]; the family (1980), *Familiaris Consortio* (1981)[50]; reconciliation and penance (1983), *Reconciliatio et Paenitentia* (1984)[51]; the laity (1987), *Christifideles Laici* (1988)[52]; the priesthood (1990), *Pastores Dabo Vobis* (1992)[53]; and the consecrated life (1994), *Vita Consecrata* (1996).[54] A Synod on the episcopacy is planned as part of the celebrations for the Jubilee Year 2000.

Extraordinary Synods

Besides convoking the now regularly-scheduled Synods, the Pope can call an extraordinary Synod if an urgent matter affecting the whole Church needs to be addressed. Unlike the meetings of ordinary Synods, for which Episcopal Conferences elect the majority of the delegates, the membership of an extraordinary Synod consists principally of presidents of the Conferences. Heads of the departments of the Roman Curia and representatives of clerical Institutes of consecrated life also attend. Except for these norms concerning membership, however, "the distinction between ordinary and extraordinary Synods is not precise."[55]

Between 1967 and 1997 two extraordinary Assemblies were held. In 1969, Paul VI called an extraordinary Synod to discuss the relation of the Episcopal Conferences to the Holy See and to one another, and the nature and exercise

---

vol. 2 (Northport: Costello Publishing Company, 1982), 695-710; also in *L'Osservatore Romano*, 50 (1971), 5-7.

[48] *"De Sacerdotio Ministeriali,"* AAS 63 (1971), 898-922; *"De Iustitia in Mundo,"* AAS 63 (1971), 923-942.

[49] AAS 71 (1979), 1277-1340.

[50] AAS 74 (1982), 81-191.

[51] AAS 77 (1985), 185-275.

[52] AAS 81 (1989), 393-521.

[53] AAS 84 (1992), 658-804.

[54] AAS 88 (1996), 377-486.

[55] Patrick Granfield, *The Limits of the Papacy* (New York: Crossroad Publishing Company, 1987), 88.

of collegiality. The Synod Fathers made three principal recommendations to the Pope: regular meetings of the Synod should be planned every two years (the practice was later changed to every three years); the Bishops should have input in determining the topic chosen for the Assembly; and a Council of the Synod, with twelve elected members (three each from Africa, the Americas, Asia and Oceania, and Europe) and three papal nominees, should be established. Paul VI immediately acted on the Fathers' proposals.

In 1985, John Paul II convened an extraordinary Synod to commemorate the twentieth anniversary of the closing of the Second Vatican Council. He hoped that at this meeting the Bishops would relive the Council's spirit of ecclesial communion, evaluate the implementation of the conciliar decrees, and foster the documents' reception among the faithful. Among the significant recommendations of the 1985 Synod was the Fathers' call for a catechism for the universal Church and a Code of Canon Law for the Oriental Churches. The former was published in 1992 as the *Catechism of the Catholic Church,* and the latter promulgated in 1990. At the end of this Synod and for the first time since 1971, the Bishops issued, with the Pope's consent, an official report of its proceedings.[56]

Special assemblies

If a particularly critical question arises which affects a local Church or region, the Pope can call a special assembly of the Synod of Bishops for the area concerned. Membership in special assemblies "consists of those who have been especially selected from the regions for which the Synod has been convoked."[57] Even though special assemblies deal with problems specific to a geographical area, they take up issues that can affect the Church throughout the world. They effectively demonstrate their bond with the universal Church by including some Bishops from other regions as voting members.

Since the promulgation of the Code of Canon Law in 1983, three special assemblies have been held.[58] In 1991, following the collapse of the Berlin Wall and in light of the new situation in eastern Europe, John Paul II called a

---

[56] Synod of Bishops, Second Extraordinary General Assembly, "Final Report," *L'Osservatore Romano*, 50 (1985), 6-9; and *Origins,* 15 (1985), 444-450.

[57] Code of Canon Law, canon 346 §3.

[58] The Dutch Synod (1980) and the Synod for the Ukraine (1980) both took place before the promulgation of the Code of Canon Law in 1983, which legislated the three types of Synod. In 1980, John Paul II referred to both of them as "particular Synods" (Address to the Roman Curia, July 28, 1980, *L'Osservatore Romano,* 28 [1980], 13). Theologians and canonists, however, generally prefer to describe the two Synods of 1980 as "particular sessions" of the Synod of Bishops. For his part, the General Secretary of the Synod of Bishops lists the Dutch Synod

Special Assembly for Europe of the Synod of Bishops. The Synod's work culminated in the publication of a Final Declaration in which the Fathers presented a program for the new evangelization of Europe and appealed for solidarity among its citizens.[59]

The Special Assembly for Africa, which met in 1994, followed at every stage the procedures of an ordinary Assembly. This was also evident in its concluding documents. The Bishops issued a Message to the People of God, and the Pope published the Special Assembly's results in a post-synodal apostolic exhortation, *Ecclesia in Africa* (1995).

In 1995, a Special Assembly for Lebanon met in Rome, and in 1997 the Holy Father signed, during his visit to Beirut, its follow-up apostolic exhortation, *Une nouvelle espérance pour le Liban.* In preparation for the third millennium, a Special Assembly for the Americas was held in 1997, and Special Assemblies were called for Asia and Oceania in 1998, and Europe in 1999.

Preparation and Meeting of the Synod

Since 1974, each Synod has dealt with a specific problem in the Church's life. Before the end of a synodal Assembly, the Fathers are polled for their suggestions about the next topic to be studied. Afterward, the Council of the General Secretariat of the Synod of Bishops consults Patriarchs of the Eastern Churches, Episcopal Conferences, heads of the dicasteries of the Roman Curia, and the Union of Superiors General for their proposals about a theme. According to synodal regulations, these submissions are to be guided by four norms. The topic must be: of interest to the whole People of God; capable of fostering the Church's growth; pastorally relevant yet with doctrinal implications; and a subject which lends itself to synodal discussion. After compiling the proposals, the Council submits to the Pope a list of topics accompanied by observations. The Holy Father chooses the theme of the next Synod and, consequently, the topic of the subsequent post-synodal apostolic exhortation.

While John Paul usually takes the advice which the Council offers him, on occasion he has either selected or modified the topic. For example, he expressly added to the 1980 Synod on the family an emphasis on its role in the modern world. Likewise, in 1983 the Pope changed the theme from the suggested "reconciliation and renewal" to "reconciliation and penance."[60] Since

---

among the special assemblies (Jan P. Schotte, Presentation of the *Lineamenta* for the Special Assembly for America of the Synod of Bishops, *L'Osservatore Romano,* 37 [1996], 8).

[59] Synod of Bishops, Special Assembly for Europe, "Final Declaration," *L'Osservatore Romano,* 51/52 (December 23/30, 1991), 3-4, 13-14.

[60] Reese, *Inside the Vatican,* 48.

the beginning of John Paul's pontificate, the subjects dealt with have reflected many of his long-standing pastoral concerns: the family and conjugal sexuality, the need for individual confession, the mission of the laity in the world, priestly formation and celibacy, and the renewal of the consecrated life.

Each Synod is a process which lasts at least four years, from the time of choosing a theme to the publication of the post-synodal apostolic exhortation. The entire synodal procedure is meant to be a "continuous process of prayer, reflection, verification, and orientation so as to deepen a sense of the Church's mission and to stimulate all the people of God to participate in this mission, each according to his or her state."[61] Such a demanding task involves extensive preparation. This entails gathering information and opinions in order to prepare a working document capable of guiding the Assembly's Roman phase. For the process to be successful the Bishops should come together only "after they have deeply reflected together with the people on the topic, so that what they bring to the Synod is really the input of the whole Church."[62] With each passing Synod, consultation has been broadened to include more and more groups.

According to established procedures, the synodal Assembly in Rome unfolds in three distinct phases, which together last for about a month. The first phase, of about a week, is devoted to the eight-minute interventions made to the whole Assembly by delegates of the Episcopal Conferences or by individual Bishops on their own. During this week the Synod Fathers hear the results of the local consultations, and a panoramic view of the pastoral and doctrinal issues in a worldwide framework. This listening and informative phase is followed by small-group discussion, which focuses on a series of questions drawn up for the participants on the basis of the individual interventions. These *circuli minores* meet for about a week in language groups which, with the help of experts, report their conclusions back to the full Assembly. The small groups then work on preparing a list of recommendations, which will eventually be submitted to the Pope. These *"propositiones"* are winnowed by a drafting committee, and then debated and voted on by all the Synod Fathers. During this last phase another drafting committee prepares the Synod's Final Message, which the Fathers also debate and vote on.

The synodal procedure favors suggestions which reflect a wide collegial consensus, and tends to eliminate minority views. According to Thomas P. Rausch, "the Synod process resembles a funnel which filters the diversity of opinions expressed on the floor down to the acceptable common denomina-

---

[61] Schotte, "The Synod of Bishops," 297.
[62] From an interview with Jan P. Schotte, cited in Reese, *Inside the Vatican,* 49.

tor."[63] In a similar vein, Cardinal Edward B. Clancy said at the 1990 Synod of Bishops: "The achievement of consensus in the propositions often results in a certain blandness, the repetition of general truth, and the elimination of ideas that are new and challenging. It is to be hoped that future Synods might provide greater scope for the prophetic voices among us to reach the ears of the Pope."[64]

II. Post-Synodal Apostolic Exhortations

Beginning in 1975, with the publication of *Evangelii Nuntiandi*, a new type of papal document came into being: the post-synodal apostolic exhortation. At a time when the formerly precise distinctions between different kinds of papal documents are now less carefully observed,[65] the post-synodal apostolic exhortation is an innovative genre of pontifical statement, one which contributes to finding "a way of exercising the primacy which, while in no way renouncing what is essential to its mission, is nonetheless open to a new situation."[66]

The origin of post-synodal apostolic exhortations lies in the synodal experience which had been maturing since the end of the Second Vatican Council. John Paul has said that "the Synod of Bishops has contributed in a most noteworthy manner to the implementation of the teachings and the doctrinal and pastoral directives of the Second Vatican Council in the life of the universal Church."[67] By implication, this contribution applies also to the final act of the Synod, the post-synodal apostolic exhortation, which sums up the whole synodal experience. It is a document whose purpose is to interpret, apply, and develop the achievements and reforms of Vatican II. The Holy Father has noted that the results of the Synod Fathers' discussion of pastoral and doctrinal questions are "produced in agreement with the Apostolic See," and "collected in documents which are disseminated everywhere."[68]

The Fathers at the first Assemblies of the Synod of Bishops never envi-

---

[63] Thomas P. Rausch, "The Synod of Bishops: Improving the Synod Process," *The Jurist*, 49 (1989), 254.

[64] John Paul II, Address at the Synod of Bishops, Eighth Ordinary General Assembly, October 1, 1990, *Catholic International*, 1 (1990), 236.

[65] It is puzzling, for example, that a document of such doctrinal importance as *Ordinatio Sacerdotalis* (1994) was issued as an apostolic letter, and not as an encyclical or apostolic constitution.

[66] John Paul II, *Ut Unum Sint* §95.2.

[67] Address to the Council of the General Secretariat of the Synod of Bishops, April 30, 1983, *L'Osservatore Romano*, 21 (1983), 9.

[68] Address at the General Audience, October 7, 1992, *L'Osservatore Romano*, 41 (1992), 11.

sioned that their discussions would be used as the basis of a later papal document. Paul VI's *Apostolica Sollicitudo* made no provision for any post-synodal publication, either by the Fathers or by the Pope. The Fathers at the 1971 Synod on justice and priestly ministry, however, issued two statements. But, it was later asked, by what authority did they write such documents?

This question was settled by the 1974 Synod on evangelization, the first one prepared and organized by the Council of the General Secretariat of the Synod of Bishops. When preparing a final document, as had been done at the end of the 1971 Synod, the Fathers reached an impasse. The majority of the Assembly rejected the proposal submitted for their approval by the committee charged with drawing up such a document. At the end of the Synod, wrote Peter Hebblethwaite, the Fathers "simply dumped a series of confused propositions in the papal lap and invited the Pope to sort them out."[69] Admitting their inability to compose a final document in the course of their meetings, the Fathers wrote in the closing Declaration: "We have preferred to offer the integral fruits of our exchange to the Holy Father with great confidence and simplicity, and to await a new impetus from him."[70]

That new impetus was the first post-synodal apostolic exhortation. While the Fathers may not have intended it, their failure to issue a statement fixed the pattern for subsequent Synods: the Pope would publish a document after its conclusion. During the Assembly of 1977, Bishop Wladyslaw Rubin, the Secretary General of the Synod of Bishops, suggested that "the final document could be prepared in such a way that what is submitted to the Pope could, with his permission, be published for the entire people of God."[71] By the end of that Synod, however, it was assumed that the Fathers would no longer even try to draw up and approve a lengthy final text. Whereas after the 1974 Synod the Fathers submitted to the Pope a narrative report on their deliberations, from 1977 onward their submission has taken the form of specific recommendations, along with the other documentation produced. Undoubtedly the practical impossibility of being able to write a suitable document during the course of month-long proceedings influenced the Holy Father to take the matter in hand.

In 1977, Philippe Delhaye, then Secretary of the International Theological

---

[69] "The Synod of Bishops," in Adrian Hastings, ed., *Modern Catholicism: Vatican II and After* (London: SPCK, 1991), 206.

[70] Synod of Bishops, Third Ordinary General Assembly, "Declaration of the Synodal Fathers," *L'Osservatore Romano*, 45 (1974), 3.

[71] "Summary of the Report on the Work of the General Secretariat and the Council of the Synod of Bishops 1974-1977," *L'Osservatore Romano*, 41 (1977), 5.

Commission, warned the Synod Fathers against imitating the Second Vatican Council's practice of composing documents: "The fact that Vatican II published such a large number is no reason for the Synods to be obsessed with composing numerous and long declarations every time." His advice was not taken. Nor was his accompanying suggestion that it would be better if the Synod were "to recall some principles, instead of wanting to write long treatises on theology and the apostolate."[72]

The first document which John Paul explicitly labeled a "post-synodal" apostolic exhortation was *Reconciliatio et Paenitentia* (1984). But, as we have seen, the apostolic exhortations published after the Synods of 1974, 1977, and 1980 can, in retrospect, also claim that designation. The term "post-synodal" was carefully chosen: the "post" is a reminder that the Assembly itself does not issue the exhortation; and the adjective "apostolic" explicitly affirms that the exhortation belongs to the papal Magisterium. By adding "post-synodal" to the title, the Holy Father suggests that he wishes to highlight the specifically collegial nature of this kind of apostolic exhortation: "Because of their collaborative nature, the documents resulting from recent Synods are expressly called 'post-synodal.'"[73]

Documentary Sources

Assemblies of the Synod of Bishops generate a wealth of documentation. Much of this comes from the Synod's preparatory stages, especially the initial outline for discussion, or *Lineamenta,* and the working document, or *Instrumentum Laboris,* which are produced at this time. The *Lineamenta* and *Instrumentum Laboris* were drafted for the first time for the 1974 Synod on evangelization, and today they are still the preparatory documents of every Assembly. During its meeting in Rome the Synod produces many more texts, including the moderator's opening and closing summaries, the participants' interventions in the Assembly Hall, the minutes of the small discussion groups, the Final Message to the People of God, and the *propositiones,* or recommendations, submitted to the Holy Father.

Papal contributions

John Paul readily acknowledges his debt to this vast documentation. He admits that in writing an exhortation he makes "abundant use of the docu-

---

[72] "Results and Prospects [of the Synod of Bishops]," *L'Osservatore Romano,* 35 (1977), 3.

[73] Address at the General Audience, October 7, 1992, *L'Osservatore Romano,* 41 (1992), 11.

ments left by the Synod."[74] But he also draws on material that he has prepared for the particular Synod, both before and during its meeting in Rome. This personal documentation includes the addresses often given before, during, and after the meeting of the Synod at the Wednesday general audience or the Sunday Angelus. For example, in the fall of 1979, John Paul began a five-year cycle of reflections on the Book of Genesis. These talks, he said, had as one of their aims "the purpose of accompanying, from afar, so to speak, the work of preparation for the Synod [on the family], not touching its subject directly, however, but turning our attention to the deep roots from which this subject springs."[75] The influence of these weekly reflections is evident in *Familiaris Consortio* (1981), even though they are never directly cited.

For the more recent Synods, John Paul has prepared mini-treatises on the theme under discussion. At the time of the 1987 Synod on the laity, instead of using the Wednesday general audience addresses, he relied on the shorter format of his Sunday Angelus reflections. Over eighteen Sundays he set the tone for the synodal Assembly and, at least indirectly, spelled out his thoughts for the subsequent post-synodal apostolic exhortation.[76] Again in 1990, the Pope used the Angelus format to convey his ideas on the Synod's theme, delivering twenty-seven short talks on priestly formation.[77] For the 1994 Synod, the Holy Father spoke on the consecrated life during his regular Wednesday catechesis. Beginning just before the Synod's opening, and continuing for over four months, John Paul gave a series of twenty addresses on the consecrated life.[78] This time he acknowledged his debt to these talks in his post-synodal document: "During the Synod, I also sought to offer the entire People of God a number of systematic talks on the consecrated life in the Church. In them I presented anew the teachings found in the texts of the Second Vatican Council, which was an enlightening point of reference for subsequent doctrinal developments and for the reflections of the Synod dur-

---

[74] *Catechesi Tradendae,* §4.1.

[75] Address at the General Audience, September 5, 1979, *L'Osservatore Romano,* 37 (1979), 1. See the collection of these talks: *Original Unity of Man and Woman* (Boston: St. Paul Editions, 1981); *Blessed Are the Pure in Heart* (Boston: St. Paul Editions, 1983); *Reflections on "Humanae Vitae"* (Boston: St. Paul Editions, 1984); and *The Theology of Marriage and Celibacy* (Boston: St. Paul Editions, 1986).

[76] See the Angelus talks from February 1, 1987 to October 18, 1987, published in *L'Osservatore Romano.*

[77] See the Angelus talks from December 17, 1989 to October 28, 1990, published in *L'Osservatore Romano.*

[78] See the addresses at the Wednesday General Audiences from September 28, 1994 to March 29, 1995, published in *L'Osservatore Romano.*

ing the busy weeks of its work."[79] Besides these non-synodal addresses, the Pope's homilies at the Synod's principal liturgies, as well as his opening and closing addresses to the Fathers, provide additional material that he later drew on.

"Lineamenta"

The greatest influence on the content of a post-synodal apostolic exhortation comes from the documents produced for and by the Synod of Bishops itself. Once the Pope has decided on the topic, the General Secretary calls upon various experts in the particular field to draft the *Lineamenta,* a document outlining the specific issues that need attention. It is reviewed by the Council of the General Secretariat, approved by the Pope, translated into various languages, and then distributed for official comments to the Episcopal Conferences, the Roman Curia, and the Union of Superiors General.[80] This preliminary document sets the synodal process in motion in the local Churches.

The purpose of the *Lineamenta* is to encourage the whole Church's participation by stimulating discussion, observations, and suggestions. Destined to be superseded, this outline is not an exhaustive treatment of the subject or a theological treatise. Nor is it meant to anticipate the Synod's possible conclusions or serve as the initial draft of a subsequent apostolic exhortation. Rather, the *Lineamenta* is intended to foster reflection and prayer, and to provide the Bishops and other interested parties with input. At the end of the preparatory document is a series of open-ended questions whose purpose is to structure the discussion at the grassroots level. They are deliberately framed in general terms, leaving local groups maximum freedom to express themselves.

Every recipient of the *Lineamenta* is expected to study them carefully. When a Bishop prepares his response, he is encouraged to consult others: diocesan and religious priests, women and men Religious, the laity, movements, associations, faculties of theology, and various diocesan councils. This process of consultation takes between six and nine months, after which the Bishop drafts his response, which he sends to the Episcopal Conference of which he is a member. The Conference then compiles the reactions and suggestions, and

---

[79] *Vita Consecrata,* §13.

[80] See the *Lineamenta* for the Synod on catechetics: *Origins,* 5 (1976), 741, 743-751; for the Synod on the family: *Origins,* 9 (1979), 113, 115-128; for the Synod on reconciliation and penance: *Origins,* 11 (1982), 565, 567-580; for the Synod on the laity: *Origins,* 14 (1985), 624-634; for the Synod on priestly formation: *Origins,* 19 (1989), 33, 35-46; and for the Synod on the consecrated life: *L'Osservatore Romano,* 48 (1992), 5-16, and *Origins,* 22 (1992), 433, 435-454.

sends them to the General Secretariat in Rome.[81] Departments of the Roman Curia and the Union of Superiors General also submit their recommendations, as do some individual Bishops.

"Instrumentum Laboris"

After sifting through the responses to the *Lineamenta*, the General Secretariat draws up, with the help of the Pre-Synodal Council of the Secretariat, the *Instrumentum Laboris*. It is put together after reading all the submissions, from which a selection of principal subjects is made. All relevant material is compiled into a text which organizes the reflections, experiences, and proposals sent to the General Secretariat. The working document also provides a kind of general summary of the Church's teaching on the Synod's theme, giving special attention to the contribution of the Second Vatican Council.[82] After the Pope approves the *Instrumentum Laboris*, it is translated and sent to the Synod participants. For the more recent Assemblies, John Paul has allowed the *Instrumentum Laboris* to be published in order to encourage widespread participation in the synodal process.

Although the *Instrumentum Laboris* is designed to help guide the Fathers' deliberations in Rome, during the Assembly they are free to amend, complete, or rewrite it. The document's usefulness to the synodal process depends on the quality of the responses received. Not a summary of the submissions, the *Instrumentum Laboris* is intended as a point of departure for discussion both before and during the synodal Assembly.

Despite the thoroughness of the *Instrumentum Laboris*, "this document should not be considered an anticipation of the conclusions of the Assem-

---

[81] The percentage of responses from the Episcopal Conferences varies considerably from one Synod to the next: 75 percent in 1974, 67 percent in 1977, 50 percent in 1980, 43 percent in 1983, 54 percent in 1987, 64 percent in 1990, and 65 percent in 1994 (Jan P. Schotte, Presentation of the *Instrumentum Laboris* for the 1990 Synod, *L'Osservatore Romano*, 30 [1990], 8; and Reese, *Inside the Vatican*, 52).

[82] See the *Instrumentum Laboris* for the Synod on the family: *Origins*, 10 (1980), 225, 227-233; for the Synod on the laity: *Origins*, 17 (1987), 1, 3-19; for the Synod on priestly formation: *Origins*, 20 (1990), 149, 151-168, and *L'Osservatore Romano*, 30 (1990), 1-14; for the Synod on the consecrated life: *L'Osservatore Romano*, 27 (1994), i-xii, and 28 (July 13, 1994), xiii-xxiv, and *Origins*, 24 (1994), 97, 99-138. A brief summary but not the full text of the *Instrumentum Laboris* for the Synod on catechesis was published in *L'Osservatore Romano*, 38 (1977), 5, 7. The *Instrumentum Laboris* for the Synod on penance and reconciliation was not published either in *L'Osservatore Romano* or *Origins*, but an unofficial translation was prepared by the Canadian Conference of Catholic Bishops (*Reconciliation and Penance in the Mission of the Church* [Ottawa, 1983]).

bly."[83] However, insofar as the working document incorporates the replies to the *Lineamenta,* it is a good gauge of the mind of the universal Church on the matter under discussion. John Paul considers the *Instrumentum Laboris* to be "a sign and builder of communion," since "it expresses the voice of the Church, and at the same time it fosters an exchange which enriches that voice in the common task."[84]

Messages to the People of God

To mark the end of the 1974 Synod on evangelization, the Fathers, who had failed to approve a longer document, issued a shorter final public Declaration.[85] In 1977, at the close of the Synod on catechesis, the Fathers published a brief statement which they entitled "Message to the People of God." All subsequent Synods have followed suit.[86] These messages, however, are not designed to settle matters or to be understood as decrees on the subject, since that is not the Synod's competency.[87] Nonetheless the Pope frequently cites or incorporates material from the Fathers' Messages to the People of God in his post-synodal apostolic exhortations.

"Propositiones"

Toward the end of the synodal Assembly, the Fathers vote on a series of *propositiones* to be sent to the Pope. These recommendations, whose number varies from Synod to Synod,[88] sum up the mind of the Fathers as it was ex-

---

[83] Jan P. Schotte, Presentation of the *Lineamenta* for the Special Assembly for America of the Synod of Bishops, September 3, 1996, *L'Osservatore Romano,* 37 (1996), 9.

[84] Letter to the Bishops on the Publication of the *Instrumentum Laboris* for the Synod of 1987, *L'Osservatore Romano,* 19 (1987), 18.

[85] See "Declaration of the Synodal Fathers," *L'Osservatore Romano,* 45 (1974), 3.

[86] See the "Message to the People of God" for the Synod on catechesis: *L'Osservatore Romano,* 44 (1977), 3, 5-6, and *Origins,* 7 (1977), 321, 323-328; for the Synod on the family: *L'Osservatore Romano,* 45 (1980), 6-7, and *Origins,* 10 (1980), 321, 323-325; for the Synod on reconciliation and penance: *L'Osservatore Romano,* 44 (1983), 4, and *Origins,* 13 (1983), 369, 371; for the Synod on the laity: *L'Osservatore Romano,* 44 (1987), 1, 11, and *Origins,* 17 (1987), 385, 387-389; for the Synod on priestly formation: *L'Osservatore Romano,* 44 (1990), 1-2, and *Origins,* 20 (1990), 349, 351-355; and for the Synod on the consecrated life: *L'Osservatore Romano,* 44 (1994), 6, and *Origins,* 24 (1994), 369, 371-374.

[87] Code of Canon Law, canon 343.

[88] The number of *propositiones* submitted to the Pope varies as follows: 34 for the 1977 Synod on catechesis; 43 for the 1980 Synod on the family; 63 for the 1983 Synod on reconciliation and penance; 54 for the 1987 Synod on the laity; 41 for the 1990 Synod on priestly formation; and 55 for the 1994 Synod on the consecrated life.

pressed in their discussion.[89] Unlike the *Lineamenta* and *Instrumentum Laboris*, the *propositiones* are fully "synodal," in that the Fathers draw them up. The *propositiones* are, so to speak, a primary goal of the Assembly's synodal journey, and their importance is confirmed by being voted on. As the final result of the Fathers' shared reflection, they manifest what Archbishop Jozef Tomko has called "synodal truth."[90] This official list of recommendations usually reflects the widespread consultation previously carried out in the local Churches.[91] It contains elements taken from the entire synodal process: from the *Lineamenta* to the final conclusions. In this way the Synod Fathers' consensus is communicated to the Pope, and they invite him to compose the final comprehensive statement of their deliberations. In *Christifideles Laici* (1988), for example, he writes: "The Synod Fathers made known to me their desires and requested that, at an opportune time, a conclusive papal document on the topic of the lay faithful be offered to the universal Church" (§2.11).[92]

The *propositiones* are not officially made public. Sometimes, however, they become known,[93] and their results compared to the later papal document.[94] It

---

[89] Cardinal Aloysio Lorscheider has expressed, however, some of the frustrations connected with formulating the *propositiones*. Many Bishops, he says, complain that "their recommendations are not faithfully recorded or followed up, especially when the recommendations refer to matters which are the subject of debate in the Church, or when they offend some people's key sensibilities" (Address at the Synod of Bishops, Eighth Ordinary General Assembly, October 1, 1990, *Catholic International*, 1 [1990], 223).

[90] Jozef Tomko, "A Retrospective Look at the 1983 Synod of Bishops," *L'Osservatore Romano*, 52 (1983), 4.

[91] On the other hand, Archbishop John R. Quinn has suggested that the Synod Fathers are intimidated by the presence of representatives of the Roman Curia in the Assembly Hall, and that "it is made clear that certain recommendations should not be made to the Pope at the conclusion of a Synod" ("Considering the Papacy," *Origins*, 26 [1996], 124).

[92] The first recommendation of the 1987 Synod stated: "Therefore the Synod Fathers ask the Holy Father to be willing to offer to the universal Church at an appropriate time a document on the vocation and mission of the laity in the Church and in the world" (*Origins*, 17 [1987], 500).

[93] See the *propositiones* from the 1980 Synod on the family: *The Tablet*, 235 (1981), 116-118, 141-142, 164-167; and those from the Synod on the laity: *Origins*, 17 (1987), 499-509. See also the official summary of the *propositiones* of the 1977 Synod: *L'Osservatore Romano*, 46 (1977), 6-7; of the 1983 Synod: *Origins*, 13 (1983), 371-373; and of the 1990 Synod: *Origins*, 20 (1990), 353-355.

[94] See the study of Jan Grootaers and Joseph A. Selling on the 1980 Synod. They conclude that 15 percent of *Familiaris Consortio* is taken from the Bishops' *propositiones*. Indeed, approximately half of the proposals are found in the final text in one form or another (*The 1980 Synod of Bishops "On the Role of the Family": An Exposition of the Event and an Analysis of Its Texts* [Louvain: Louvain University Press, 1983], 304, 333-338). See also the remarks of Jesús

is hard to assess the precise extent to which the Pope uses the Fathers' proposals and other materials in drawing up the post-synodal document. Patrick Granfield notes the difficulty in determining "how closely the apostolic exhortations accurately reflect the deliberations of the Synod — not an easy task considering the aura of secrecy that surrounds much of its proceedings."[95] With the passing of time, however, John Paul has directly cited the *propositiones* with increasing frequency. There are only three explicit references to the *propositiones* in *Catechesi Tradendae* (1979),[96] two in *Familiaris Consortio* (1982),[97] and five in *Reconciliatio et Paenitentia* (1984).[98] But there are 45 in *Christifideles Laici* (1988), 66 in *Pastores Dabo Vobis* (1992), and 67 in *Vita Consecrata* (1995). This trend reflects the Pope's desire to confirm how much he relies on the Fathers' official recommendations.

In fact, the Pope often acknowledges his extensive use of the material prepared for him by the Synod Fathers, which includes the *Lineamenta* and *Instrumentum Laboris,* the reports of the plenary sessions and of the small group meetings, the *propositiones,* and the input of the Council of the General Secretariat of the Synod. With the help of experts, this Council examines the Synod's conclusions and suggests how they could be implemented. It then gives the results of its consultations to the Holy Father. What does he do with them? After the Council presented him with the results of the Synod on the family, John Paul told the members: "We assure you that we will make use of them when we draw up a document on this matter."[99] And after the publica-

---

López-Gay on *Catechesi Tradendae* ("General Introduction to the Apostolic Exhortation *Catechesi Tradendae,*" in Cesare Bonivento, ed., *"Going, Teach . . .": Commentary on the Apostolic Exhortation "Catechesi Tradendae" of John Paul II* [Boston: St. Paul Editions, 1980], 84).

[95] Granfield, *The Limits of the Papacy,* 90.

[96] While not direct citations of the *propositiones,* there are 19 references to synodal teaching in *Catechesi Tradendae* (§§5.1, 14.2, 17, 18.1, 25.2, 29.2, 29.7, 33.2, 40.1, 43, 47.2, 51.2, 52, 55.1, 55.2, 61.3, 63.1, 70.2, 73.1).

[97] While not direct citations of the *propositiones,* there are 28 references to synodal teaching in *Familiaris Consortio* (§§7.2, 10.4, 17.4, 20.2, 20.6, 22.1, 22.2, 23.3, 24.4, 29.3, 31.3, 34.5, 39.3, 39.5, 43.4, 46.2, 46.3, 46.4, 52.2, 56.3, 61.2, 64.5, 72.2, 73.2, 77.7, 79, 84.1, 84.3).

[98] While not direct citations of the *propositiones,* there are 18 references to synodal teaching in *Reconciliatio et Paenitentia* (§§4.7, 4.11, 17.12, 17.16, 23.7, 23.8, 26.1, 26.2, 26.8, 28.1, 28.2, 29.6, 31.1, 33.2, 33.3, 34.1, 34.2, 34.4).

[99] Address to the Council of the General Secretariat of the Synod of Bishops, March 21, 1981, *L'Osservatore Romano* 15 (1981), 11. This is very similar to the remark of Paul VI at the end of the 1971 Synod: "On our side, we will examine them [*propositiones*] carefully, together with all the material that has been presented to us. Subsequently — acceding to the desire expressed by you — we will be happy to make known to the universal Church the points we consider most opportune" (October 29, 1977, *L'Osservatore Romano,* 45 [1977], 1).

tion of *Familiaris Consortio* (1981), he let it be known that he had kept his promise: "At the end of the Synod, I gathered up and developed its *propositiones*, taking also into account the suggestions made at the daily meetings in which I took part."[100] Speaking to the Fathers at the end of the 1987 Synod, the Pope agreed to gather "the wishes and the will clearly expressed by the Fathers," and to take into serious account "that sort of 'author's rights' that belong to the Synod itself."[101] Soon afterward, in an address to the Roman Curia, he again mentioned his obligation to be faithful to the Assembly's deliberations: "As with preceding Synods, it shall be my duty to follow the indications that have emerged during those unforgettable days."[102] Returning to the same point for a third time, the Holy Father expressed his thanks to the Council of the General Secretariat for the "synodal aid" which it provided. He assured them that he would study all the material "so that the whole wealth of the Synod itself will be reflected in my post-synodal document."[103] At the conclusion of the 1990 Synod on priestly formation, the Pope expressed his appreciation for the Fathers' contribution:

> The extensive consultation which the Synod structure allows for during every Assembly has never failed to yield results and decisions as well. Given the way they function, Synods are never able to immediately publish a document which takes on deliberative form. That notwithstanding, the post-synodal document takes its inspiration from and, one might say, contains what was planned out in common. It therefore can be asserted that a Synod's *proposals* indirectly assume the importance of *decisions.* For, when the Sovereign Pontiff publishes the corresponding document, he takes great care to express the full wealth of the reflections and discussion which led up to the synodal *Propositiones*, as well as the views of the synodal Assembly, as much as possible.[104]

John Paul makes a conscious effort to bring the whole synodal process to completion with a papal document which reflects the mind of the Synod.

---

[100] Address to the Roman Curia, December 22, 1981, *L'Osservatore Romano,* 3 (1982), 9.

[101] Address at the Conclusion of the Seventh Ordinary General Assembly of the Synod of Bishops, October 29, 1987, *L'Osservatore Romano,* 45 (1987), 1.

[102] Address to the Roman Curia, December 22, 1987, *L'Osservatore Romano,* 2 (1988), 7.

[103] Address to the Council of the General Secretariat of the Synod of Bishops, June 17, 1988, *L'Osservatore Romano,* 30 (1988), 4.

[104] Address at the Conclusion of the Eighth Ordinary General Assembly of the Synod of Bishops, October 27, 1990, *L'Osservatore Romano,* 45 (1990), 7.

Collegial Documents

As an instrument of ecclesial communion, the Synod of Bishops is "a unique expression of the collegiality of the Bishops with the Pope."[105] Moreover, when the Holy Father consigns to writing the fruit of the Synod's deliberations and proposals in a post-synodal apostolic exhortation, his document expresses the same collegiality evident during the synodal Assembly. In the introduction to *Christifideles Laici* (1988), John Paul remarks that his document "is not something in contradistinction to the Synod, but is meant to be a faithful and coherent expression of it, a fruit of collegiality" (§2.12). As no other papal document, post-synodal apostolic exhortations reflect a unique exercise of the Church's ordinary Magisterium, one which is both primatial and collegial.

The Bishop of Rome is not juridically bound to accept a Synod's *propositiones.* Even though canonically the recommendations are merely consultative, they nonetheless enjoy a large measure of moral authority. For John Paul, the vote of the Synod Fathers, "if morally unanimous, has a qualitative ecclesial weight which surpasses the merely formal aspect of the consultative vote."[106] In the same vein he adds: "It is therefore even more important that the documents, which appear after the Synod, reflect the common thought of the Synod Assembly and of the Pope who presides over it *ex officio.*"[107] Because the Holy Father wants his exhortations to be faithful summaries of the Synod's deliberations,[108] he is firmly committed to the principle that the document "will reflect what has emerged during the course of the Assembly."[109] The Pope treats the Synod Fathers' official proposals as an authoritative witness

---

[105] John Paul II, Address to the Roman Curia, December 20, 1990, *L'Osservatore Romano,* 52/53 (1990), 2.

[106] Address to the Council of the General Secretariat of the Synod of Bishops, April 30, 1983, *L'Osservatore Romano,* 21 (1983), 9.

[107] Address at the Conclusion of the Sixth Ordinary General Assembly of the Synod of Bishops, October 29, 1983, *L'Osservatore Romano,* 45 (1983), 3.

[108] John Paul has said, for example, that *Catechesi Tradendae* (1979) "sums up the wishes expressed at the Synod of Bishops" (Address to the Roman Curia, December 23, 1979, *L'Osservatore Romano,* 2 [1980], 12); and that *Familiaris Consortio* (1981) "sums up the wishes and experience of the Episcopates of the five continents, and is therefore a true expression of collegiality in the Church" (Address to the Roman Curia, December 22, 1981, *L'Osservatore Romano,* 3 [1982], 9).

[109] Homily at the Conclusion of the Synod of Bishops, Ninth Ordinary General Assembly, October 29, 1995, *L'Osservatore Romano,* 44 (1994), 1. See also his Homily at the Conclusion of the Synod of Bishops, Sixth Ordinary General Assembly, October 29, 1983, *L'Osservatore Romano,* 45 (1983), 3, in which he expresses the hope that the subsequent exhortation will gather "all the richness of the elements which emerged during the Synod . . . [and] will see that these concepts are adequately deepened."

to the life and faith of the whole Church. But, at the same time, he carefully avoids saying that the Fathers' proposals oblige him, leaving himself free to incorporate the Synod's views as he sees fit.

Post-synodal apostolic exhortations are therefore the outcome of two complementary factors: the vast collective input of the Bishops and the personal contribution of the Pope. In *Reconciliatio et Paenitentia* (1984), for example, John Paul declares his indebtedness to the Synod Fathers:

> The document . . . is also — and I wish to say this clearly as a duty to truth and justice — something produced by the Synod itself. For the contents of these pages come from the Synod. . . . Here we have the result of the joint work of the Fathers (§4.13).

According to the Pope, a post-synodal apostolic exhortation is "a fruit of collegiality,"[110] a response to what the Synod Fathers have asked him to do.

John Paul admits that he needs the Bishops' input in order to address doctrinal and pastoral issues in a relevant and convincing way. In *Evangelium Vitae* (1995), he had acknowledged that he asked the Bishops, "in the spirit of collegiality," to offer him "their cooperation" in drawing up the encyclical (§5.2). Although this kind of consultation is unusual in the case of encyclicals, it has become normative for post-synodal apostolic exhortations. In the latter documents the Pope can recast in a more global framework the counsel offered by the particular Churches. From their recommendations he draws up guidelines suitable for the whole Church. In this way the Synod is collectively involved in reaching decisions about major questions affecting Church life. For the Holy Father, this episcopal collaboration expresses collegiality. Post-synodal apostolic exhortations can therefore be considered as the end result of a truly "collegial endeavor."[111] In John Paul's mind, Synods significantly influence the formulation of his teaching in post-synodal apostolic exhortations.[112]

---

[110] *Christifideles Laici*, §2.12.

[111] John Paul II, *Ecclesia in Africa*, §1.4.

[112] For an opposing view, based on a comparison between *Familiaris Consortio* and the 43 *propositiones* which the Synod submitted to the Pope, see Grootaers and Selling, *The 1980 Synod of Bishops*, 257-296, 337-338, 342. See also James Dallen's remarks on *Reconciliatio et Paenitentia* (1984) which, he maintains, differs from the Synod's views on such matters as social sin, general absolution, and the pastoral care of alienated people in the Church: "It is not clear that the positions taken in the document are necessarily those which the bishops took, or reflect the importance given various themes in the Synod" ("*Reconciliatio et Paenitentia:* The Postsynodal Apostolic Exhortation," *Worship,* 59 [1985], 99). This is also the position of Rausch, "The Synod of Bishops," 255-256.

Post-synodal apostolic exhortations, besides providing the Successor of Peter with an instrument for exercising the particular charism of teaching that belongs to his office, are also a way for him to proclaim the mind of the Synod to the whole world. After the 1980 Synod, John Paul accepted the Fathers' request that he should be "a spokesman before humanity of the Church's lively care for the family and to give suitable indications for renewed pastoral effort in this fundamental sector of the life of man and of the Church."[113] In *Reconciliatio et Paenitentia* (1984), he mentions that he accepted, "as a serious and welcome duty" of his ministry, the task of drawing up a doctrinal pastoral message for the People of God based on the fruit of the Synod (cf. §4.12).

According to John Paul, the promulgation of a post-synodal apostolic exhortation is a way of "actuating in a particular matter the apostolic ministry"[114] with which he is entrusted. In fact, in these exhortations the Pope uses his Petrine charism in a novel way: by serving as a kind of arbiter or "clearing house" at the center of ecclesial communion. The way in which John Paul writes and issues his post-synodal apostolic exhortations reflects his understanding of the papal office as a ministry within, and at the service of (though not dependent on), the College of Bishops.

As a genre of papal document, post-synodal apostolic exhortations are theologically and pastorally innovative. They are perfectly in tune with Vatican II's ecclesiology of communion and its teaching on the common responsibility of the whole Episcopal College for the "care of all the churches" (2 Cor 11:28). More than encyclicals, post-synodal exhortations emphasize the Pope's role *within* the College of Bishops. In his exhortations he stresses that he is speaking in the name of his brother Bishops, giving them a single voice. The Successor of Peter "receives" the Synod's deliberations in order to transmit them to the whole Church. Such a function belongs to the Pope as the center of the visible communion of the universal Church. The Bishops fulfill their mission of witnessing to the faith of their local Churches within the worldwide communion through their representatives at the Synod. During the pontificate of John Paul II, the publication of post-synodal apostolic exhortations has opened up a new way for Bishops around the world to collaborate with the Bishop of Rome. The pastoral effectiveness of the Church's ordinary Magisterium is strengthened when it is articulated by the Pope in union with the Bishops in post-synodal apostolic exhortations. Collegial texts, which combine both synodal and papal contributions, are more likely to receive a hearing. Be-

---

[113] *Familiaris Consortio*, §2.3.
[114] *Familiaris Consortio*, §2.4.

cause they are produced with widespread cooperation, the faithful, who are increasingly aware of the importance of participation in building up the Church, are often better disposed to receive the teaching contained in post-synodal apostolic exhortations rather than that proposed without evident input from the laity or College of Bishops.

Audience

John Paul II addresses his post-synodal apostolic exhortations to the Church throughout the world: to her Bishops, clergy, and faithful. In the exhortations dealing with the family, laity, priesthood, and consecrated life, special mention is made of the particular group concerned, but never to the exclusion of others.

Unlike many of John Paul's encyclicals, which address "all men and women of good will" in the opening greeting,[115] none of his post-synodal apostolic exhortations do so. *Familiaris Consortio* (1981) includes a special appeal to "the young, who are beginning their journey toward marriage and family life" (§1.3); at the end, it urges "that every person of good will should endeavor to save and foster the values and requirements of the family" (§86.3). In *Reconciliatio et Paenitentia* (1984) the Holy Father mentions, though not in the salutation, that he is writing "also to all those who, whether they are believers or not, look to the Church with interest and sincerity" (§4.13). And in *Vita Consecrata* (1996), besides including the Bishops, priests, deacons, consecrated persons, and laity among those addressed, the Pope refers to "any others who might be interested" (§4.1). Despite some attention to a wider audience, post-synodal apostolic exhortations are primarily written for the Church's faithful.

Style

Like other papal and Vatican documents, post-synodal apostolic exhortations are known by the first two or three words of their Latin title — the *incipit*. The closing of the exhortations is stylized. It indicates the place of publication, "in Rome, at Saint Peter's,"[116] as well as the calendar date, the liturgical feast

---

[115] See especially the encyclicals which treat social questions at some length: *Redemptor Hominis* (1979), *Laborem Exercens* (1981), *Sollicitudo Rei Socialis* (1987), *Centesimus Annus* (1991), and *Evangelium Vitae* (1995).

[116] The only exceptions to this practice of promulgation in Rome are in the two post-synodal apostolic exhortations published after special assemblies of the Synod of Bishops: *Ecclesia in Africa* (1995): "Given at Yaoundé, in Cameroon"; and *Une nouvelle espérance pour le Liban* (1997): "Given at Beirut, on the occasion of my pastoral visit in Lebanon."

celebrated on the day of publication, and the year of the Pope's pontificate.

The authoritative version of a post-synodal apostolic exhortation is published in Latin in the Vatican's official organ, the *Acta Apostolicae Sedis.* The various language sections of the Secretariat of State are responsible for preparing or overseeing the approved translations,[117] usually made from an Italian draft, though the official text is the Latin.[118] These translations appear in Dutch, English, French, German, Polish, Portuguese, and Spanish.

Even though post-synodal apostolic exhortations strike a less personal note than encyclicals, due to the collegial cooperation involved in their preparation, they still bear John Paul's stamp and reflect his style. Above all they reflect a profoundly positive attitude. While fidelity to the truth demands that deviations and errors be pointed out, the Pope constantly seeks to confirm the good fruits of the Second Vatican Council, encourage new pastoral initiatives, and exhort those addressed. Often he includes very personal observations and remarks — a practice which has become more evident in later documents.

Some critics have observed that the consensual nature of the material sent to the Pope lends itself to making the post-apostolic exhortations bland rather than prophetic, exhaustive rather than incisive, tried and true rather than innovative. The post-synodal apostolic exhortations are said to lack the vivid and passionate language found in John Paul's major encyclicals. Others point out that the exhortations are often long and unwieldy compendia of established teaching on a given subject.[119] This approach, however, can be defended. Unlike scholarly works, whose purpose is to bring to light new insights, the exhortations express the received faith of the whole community. Each one is a kind of *vademecum* which aims to teach what is true in a way that enables the People of God to see why it is true.

Sacred Scripture

Following his usage in other papal documents, John Paul refers liberally to the Bible in his exhortations. Although he cites from a broad range of scrip-

---

[117] It seems, however, that on occasion certain translations betray another hand. The rather consistent use of inclusive language in the official translation of *Christifideles Laici,* for instance, stands out.

[118] The only exception to this is the post-synodal apostolic exhortation, *Une nouvelle espérance pour le Liban,* whose official version is the French text.

[119] As the following statistics show, the number of words in the post-synodal apostolic exhortations varies considerably. With the passing of time, there has been a tendency to increasing length: *Catechesi Tradendae* (20,000), *Familiaris Consortio* (35,000), *Reconciliatio et Paenitentia* (28,000), *Christifideles Laici* (40,000), *Pastores Dabo Vobis* (54,000), and *Vita Consecrata* (43,000).

tural texts, the Pope also shows a preference for certain books: above all the Gospels, especially John; Romans, 1 Corinthians, and Ephesians in the Pauline literature; and Genesis and the Psalms in the Old Testament.[120]

When the Holy Father cites Sacred Scripture in his post-synodal apostolic exhortations, he draws very little on the methods of contemporary biblical scholarship, despite his acknowledgment elsewhere of their importance.[121] His concern is not the original historical context or the stages of a text's formation. The Pope's purpose in citing Scripture is not to distinguish different authors or traditions, as in historical-critical exegesis, but to "sustain a unitary vision of the one God who speaks equally powerfully through every biblical witness."[122]

According to the Pope, the Bible is primarily a testimony to divine truth and love which must come alive and animate the Church of today. It is a collection of religious writings meant to inspire believers and the community of faith. The Holy Father stresses the Scriptures' unity and coherence as a witness to the whole of revelation. By no means does he limit the meaning of the Bible to an exclusively historical one, but he opens up its meaning for today. Indeed, it is always the religious and spiritual message that catches his interest and it is that message which he seeks to convey in his writings.

John Paul's approach might be called "catechetical exegesis." He recommends this approach in *Catechesi Tradendae* (1979), where he says that the Bible should be read "with the intelligence and heart of the Church . . . drawing inspiration from the two thousand years of the Church's reflection and life" (§27.2). This means that he reads Scripture and uses it in his documents in order to bring the word of God into the present. Typical of this desire to "actualize" the Bible is his reading of the call of Andrew and Peter recounted

---

[120] For the Pope's six post-synodal apostolic exhortations, the number of direct quotations from the biblical book is given first and the number of indirect references follows: Genesis (7-17), Exodus (1-3), Leviticus (0-4), Numbers (0-2), Deuteronomy (1-1), 2 Samuel (2-2), 1 Kings (0-2), Psalms (8-13), Wisdom (0-3), Sirach (0-3), Isaiah (2-7), Jeremiah (7-1), Ezekiel (1-4), Hosea (0-2), Joel (1-1), Jonah (1-0), Matthew (46-72), Mark (23-29), Luke (28-46), John (75-72), Acts (19-23), Romans (15-30), 1 Corinthians (23-22), 2 Corinthians (12-15), Galatians (9-7), Ephesians (24-32), Philippians (11-6), Colossians (5-12), 1 Thessalonians (1-0), 2 Thessalonians (0-3), 1 Timothy (6-7), 2 Timothy (3-6), Titus (0-5), Hebrews (9-11), James (1-3), 1 Peter (18-14), 1 John (10-13), and Revelation (5-8).

[121] See his Address to Members of the Biblical Commission, Pontifical Biblical Institute, and Diplomatic Corps, April 23, 1993, *L'Osservatore Romano,* 17 (1993), 3-4, 6.

[122] Terence Prendergast, " 'A Vision of Wholeness': A Reflection on the Use of Scripture in a Cross-section of Papal Writings," in John M. McDermott, ed., *The Thought of Pope John Paul II: A Collection of Essays and Studies* (Rome: Pontifical Gregorian University Press, 1993), 83.

in John's Gospel (cf. 1:35-42). In *Pastores Dabo Vobis,* the Pope says that John's narrative of the call of the two brothers "in some way is renewed constantly down the ages" (§34.4). The exhortations illustrate that John Paul's approach to Scripture is founded on *lectio divina.* His reading of the biblical texts is accompanied by reflection, meditation, prayer, and contemplation — the richness of which he strives to convey in his documents.

In several of his post-synodal apostolic exhortations the Holy Father often uses a particular rhetorical device. He presents a vivid biblical text from which he can draw observations and to which he frequently returns in the same document. For instance, in *Familiaris Consortio* (1981), John Paul relies heavily on selected passages from Genesis 1-3, Matthew 19:1-9, and Ephesians 5:21-33 to develop his understanding of conjugal love. *Reconciliatio et Paenitentia* (1984) draws on the parable of the prodigal son (Lk 15:11-32), with an emphasis on the older brother, to describe the meaning of sin and reconciliation. In *Christifideles Laici* (1988), the Pope invokes the Johannine image of the vine and the branches (15:1-7), and couples it with other similar references, in order to describe the laity's vocation and mission in the Church. *Pastores Dabo Vobis* (1992), as the title indicates, is structured around the scriptural image of the shepherd taken from the Old and New Testaments (cf. Jer 3:15; Jn 10:1-18), as well as Jesus' teaching in the synagogue at Nazareth (cf. Lk 4:16-22) and his call of the disciples (cf. Mk 3:13-15). In *Vita Consecrata* (1996), he uses the account of the Transfiguration (Mt 17:1-9) to describe the central truths of the consecrated life.

Tradition and Magisterium

Besides referring frequently to Sacred Scripture in his six post-synodal apostolic exhortations, John Paul often cites the Church Fathers and previous statements of the papal and conciliar Magisterium. He prefers to emphasize the continuity between the original revelation expressed in the deposit of faith and its unfolding in the Church's teaching, liturgy, theology, and life.

Post-synodal apostolic exhortations enable the Pope to make better known the teaching of the Second Vatican Council, "the great gift of the Spirit to the Church at the end of the second millennium."[123] His exhortations are an effective means for sustaining and implementing the Council's major orientations. In them the Holy Father routinely appeals to the documents of the Second

---

[123] John Paul II, *Tertio Millennio Adveniente,* §36.5.

Vatican Council, particularly *Lumen Gentium* and *Gaudium et Spes*.[124] Often the quotations are very lengthy. Referring explicitly to *Christifideles Laici* (1988), but equally applicable to the other exhortations as well, Cardinal Jan P. Schotte has defended the use of numerous long quotations. The Holy Father cites them, he said, to comply with the wish of the Council of the General Secretariat of the Synod: "They asked that ample excerpts of the Vatican II texts should be included not only because they fully retain their value, but because it cannot be taken for granted that the laity active and committed in the base ecclesial communities, in the parishes and in the associations have fully assimilated, or have always at hand, the conciliar teaching."[125] Taking their advice to heart, John Paul has written his three last post-synodal apostolic exhortations in such a way that each one furnishes a kind of updated commentary on a specific conciliar document: the Decree on the Apostolate of the Laity, *Apostolicam Actuositatem*, in *Christifideles Laici* (1988); the Decree on the Ministry and Life of Priests, *Presbyterorum Ordinis*, in *Pastores Dabo Vobis* (1990); and the Decree on the Appropriate Renewal of the Religious Life, *Perfectae Caritatis*, in *Vita Consecrata* (1996).

Authority

In the ordinary, or everyday, teaching of the papal Magisterium — in which the Bishop of Rome does not invoke his charism to teach infallibly or definitively — Petrine authority is expressed in varying degrees. These documents bear the authoritative weight which the Pope intends in each case. In some instances he attributes a very high degree of authority to a specific papal document. The formal authority of encyclicals, for example, is greater than that of post-synodal apostolic exhortations. Considering the particular way these exhortations are written, how authoritative does John Paul intend them to be?

A new document of the ordinary papal Magisterium

As a unique genre of official document, the post-synodal apostolic exhortation enjoys a specific kind of authority. Francis A. Sullivan lists five consid-

---

[124] In John Paul II's six post-synodal apostolic exhortations, *Lumen Gentium* is quoted directly or indirectly 97 times, and *Gaudium et Spes* 62 times. In the order of decreasing frequency the statistics for the other conciliar documents are given in parenthesis: *Presbyterorum Ordinis* (37), *Apostolicam Actuositatem* (30), *Perfectae Caritatis* (19), *Optatam Totius* (17), *Ad Gentes* (15), *Sacrosanctum Concilium* (12), *Gravissimum Educationis* (9), *Dei Verbum* (8), *Christus Dominus* (7), *Unitatis Redintegratio* (4), and *Dignitatis Humanae* (3). There are no references to *Nostra Aetate, Orientalium Ecclesiarum,* or *Inter Mirifica.*

[125] Presentation of the Document at the Press Conference, January 30, 1989, cited in Peter Coughlan, *The Hour of the Laity: Their Expanding Role* (Philadelphia: E. J. Dwyer, 1989), 5-6.

erations that must be taken into account in evaluating the level of authority entailed in any statement of the non-definitive ordinary Magisterium: who the teacher is, the audience addressed, the kind of document selected to express the teaching, the specific nature of the intervention (whether it directly treats matters pertaining to the deposit of faith), and the forcefulness of the language used.[126] These criteria can also be applied to post-synodal apostolic exhortations. In this way the degree of their authoritativeness can be clarified and, therefore, also the kind of assent due to them.

Post-synodal apostolic exhortations are issued by the Pope in his own name and are sealed with his authority. Nonetheless, as we have seen, John Paul consistently points out that these texts bear a profound collegial imprint. Because each exhortation is the fruit of a Synod's collaborative input, which the Successor of Peter confirms with his unique teaching charism, its authority is enhanced. In them the Bishops, as teachers endowed with divine authority in virtue of their episcopal ordination, make a contribution which serves to strengthen the Pope's voice.

As we have seen, post-synodal apostolic exhortations are a new genre of magisterial statement. They are not "papal" in exactly the same way that encyclicals, apostolic constitutions, and apostolic letters are. But neither are they "collegial" in the traditional sense, as are the decrees of Ecumenical Councils. Rather, these exhortations combine both elements. Because they appeal specifically to the Bishops' role in their composition, they are "collegial." At the same time, post-synodal apostolic exhortations, because they are issued by the Pope, are documents of the ordinary papal Magisterium. Thus they embody Vatican II's teaching on collegiality. Post-synodal apostolic exhortations demonstrate how the Petrine ministry can be carried out from within the College of Bishops.

Post-synodal apostolic exhortations have not been used to teach infallibly or definitively on matters of faith or morals. Other genres are more suited to that purpose. Rather, the exhortations echo received teaching, and treat more pastoral and practical concerns. None of the most authoritative statements of John Paul's pontificate have been issued in a post-synodal document. For these statements he has used the encyclical form, especially in *Veritatis Splendor* (1993) and *Evangelium Vitae* (1995), and the apostolic letter *Ordinatio Sacerdotalis* (1994).

The level of authoritativeness must be accurately assessed in each instance where Church teaching is involved. An examination of the language

---

[126] Francis A. Sullivan, *Creative Fidelity: Weighing and Interpreting Documents of the Magisterium* (New York: Paulist Press, 1996), 20-22.

used in apostolic exhortations confirms that a single document can contain different levels of authoritativeness. John Paul's repetition of the Church's teaching on contraception in *Familiaris Consortio* (cf. §32) or the need for individual confession in *Reconciliatio et Paenitentia* (cf. §31), for example, are more central to the hierarchy of truths than his reassertion of the doctrine on the superiority of virginity to marriage in *Vita Consecrata* (cf. §18.3). When a post-synodal apostolic exhortation invokes the Church's constant Tradition to emphasize its teaching on a certain subject, this carries more weight than when it provides pastoral directives.

Two conclusions on the level of authority of post-synodal apostolic exhortations can now be drawn. First, they are documents in which the Successor of Peter invokes his authority as the Church's chief teacher; issued in his name, these exhortations belong to the ordinary papal Magisterium.[127] Second, since these exhortations reflect the mind of the Synod of Bishops, this cooperation, far from diminishing their authority, actually increases their magisterial weight.[128]

Assent

In order to evaluate precisely the degree of assent called for by a post-synodal apostolic exhortation, the five considerations mentioned above should be taken into account. As Sullivan notes, in every instance "the response which a Catholic gives to such teaching [of the ordinary papal Magisterium] should be proportionate to the degree or authority that is exercised."[129] Not every exhortation nor every utterance within it is equally authoritative. Consequently, when describing the response to be given to the non-definitive teaching proposed, a post-synodal apostolic exhortation, a kind of "hierarchy of assent,"[130]

---

[127] While the adjective "papal" is theologically precise, John Paul himself, in alluding to the exhortation to be issued after the 1983 Synod, referred — perhaps deliberately — to "an appropriate document by the ordinary Magisterium of the Church" (Address to the Roman Curia, December 22, 1983, *L'Osservatore Romano*, 2 [1984], 4).

[128] In a similar case, the Holy See's official summary of *Evangelium Vitae* suggests that the encyclical's "great doctrinal authority" derives not only from its being an expression of the ordinary Magisterium of the Pope, but also, though in a partial way, of the Episcopal College. See "The Vatican's Summary of *Evangelium Vitae*," *Origins*, 24 (1995), 728.

[129] Sullivan, *Creative Fidelity*, 141.

[130] John P. Boyle, *Church Teaching Authority: Historical and Theological Studies* (Notre Dame: University of Notre Dame Press, 1995), 88. Boyle also sees the need to express with a fresh theological language the various kinds and degrees of acceptance due to authoritative teaching calling for the religious submission of mind and will (*Church Teaching Authority*, 168-169).

must be attended to. An individual's response will therefore reflect "the different levels of divine assistance"[131] involved in this exercise of papal authority.

The presumption is that the teaching in exhortations expresses a non-definitive exercise of the ordinary Magisterium: one which does not propose doctrine infallibly or definitively. The response called for is not the assent of divine and Catholic faith which is owed to what is taught as divinely revealed. Nor is the faithful Catholic called to give the firm acceptance due to a doctrine that is definitively proposed.

To the Pope's ordinary Magisterium the faithful owe what is called the "religious submission of will and intellect."[132] Catholics, therefore, are to give religious submission to the teaching of post-synodal apostolic exhortations. They are expected to accept what is *taught* in an exhortation and act in accordance with it. What the ordinary Magisterium proposes in this way has "a real, though not unconditional, claim on the assent of the faithful."[133]

Influence on the Church's Life

John Paul is convinced of the need for post-synodal texts which collect the Assembly's results: "We certainly need documents of this kind, which spring from the fruitful, and at times difficult, practical life of the Church, and which, conversely, give new growth to that same life."[134] Undoubtedly the greatest contribution of these exhortations to the Church's life has been to foster the ongoing implementation of the decrees of the Second Vatican Council. The encyclical *Dominum et Vivificantem* (1986) drew attention to the role of the Synod of Bishops in keeping the Council's initiatives alive. According to John Paul II, the deliberations of these Assemblies — and, we can add, the subsequent apostolic exhortations — "are to be carefully studied and evaluated, aiming as they do to ensure that the fruits of truth and love . . . become a lasting treasure of the People of God in its earthly pilgrimage down the centuries" (§26.2). Each exhortation issued after a meeting of

[131] Francis A. Sullivan, "The Theologian's Ecclesial Vocation and the 1990 CDF [Congregation for the Doctrine of the Faith] Instruction," *Theological Studies*, 52 (1991), 61.

[132] Second Vatican Ecumenical Council, Dogmatic Constitution on the Church *Lumen Gentium*, 25.

[133] Avery Dulles, *The Craft of Theology* (New York: Crossroad Publishing Company, 1992), 110.

[134] Address to the Council of the General Secretariat of the Synod of Bishops, December 16, 1979, *L'Osservatore Romano*, 1 (1979), 12.

the Synod of Bishops makes a specific contribution to the Holy Father's pastoral strategy of implementing Vatican II's doctrine and directives ever more fully. In fact, his exhortations have promoted a more fruitful application of the Council's teaching to areas of vital significance for the Church's life.

The influence of post-synodal apostolic exhortations varies considerably from one document to another. In order to determine the impact of a specific exhortation on the Church's life, two measures can be used: how frequently it is referred to in subsequent magisterial documents and how many follow-up statements it produces; and the extent of pastoral or other changes that can be linked to it.

In his encyclicals the Pope occasionally refers to the post-synodal apostolic exhortations. *Familiaris Consortio* (1980) is mentioned in five different encyclicals, and *Reconciliatio et Paenitentia* (1984) in four.[135] Curiously, the *Catechism of the Catholic Church* refers only infrequently to the four post-synodal apostolic exhortations published at the time of its release. Not surprisingly, it cites *Familiaris Consortio* (1981) the most often: fifteen times directly, and eleven indirectly. For *Catechesis Tradendae* (1979), the number of direct references is eight and indirect nine; for *Reconciliatio et Paenitentia* (1984), four and two; and for *Christifideles Laici,* three and one.

The Synods and the post-synodal apostolic exhortations have also led to other initiatives which have influenced ecclesial life. For example, after the 1980 Synod on the family, Pope John Paul II raised the rank of the Committee on the Family to the Pontifical Council on the Family. He also established the John Paul II Institute for Studies on Marriage and Family at the Pontifical Lateran University in Rome. And in 1983, following the Synod Fathers' request, the Vatican published the Charter of the Rights of the Family.[136] *Familiaris Consortio* also provided the inspiration for the Letter to the Bishops of the Catholic Church concerning the Reception of Holy Communion by Divorced and Remarried Members of the Faith, published by the Congregation of the Doctrine of the Faith in 1994.

After the 1987 Synod on the laity, the Holy Father wrote his apostolic

---

[135] The number of references, both direct and indirect, to the various encyclicals are given in parentheses: *Catechesi Tradendae*: *Redemptoris Missio* (2); *Familiaris Consortio*: *Sollicitudo Rei Socialis* (2), *Redemptoris Missio* (2), *Centesimus Annus* (2), *Veritatis Splendor* (2), *Evangelium Vitae* (5); *Reconciliatio et Paenitentia*: *Dominum et Vivificantem* (5), *Sollicitudo Rei Socialis* (2), *Centesimus Annus* (1), *Veritatis Splendor* (5); *Christifideles Laici*: *Redemptoris Missio* (8), *Centesimus Annus* (2). John Paul II never cites *Pastores Dabo Vobis* or *Vita Consecrata* in an encyclical.

[136] *L'Osservatore Romano*, 48 (1983), 3-4.

letter, *Mulieris Dignitatem* (1988), even before issuing *Christifideles Laici* (1988). Indeed, he wrote this letter because he wished "to respond to the desire of the Synodal Fathers."[137]

The 1990 Synod on priestly formation led to the publication of the Directory on the Ministry and Life of Priests by the Congregation of the Clergy in 1994. It also encouraged many Episcopal Conferences to update their programs of priestly formation. This was the case in the United States, where the Bishops issued a revised Program of Priestly Formation in 1993,[138] drawn up in light of the post-synodal apostolic exhortation *Pastores Dabo Vobis* (1992).

It must be admitted, however, that post-synodal apostolic exhortations have not received the attention they deserve. Both Synod Fathers and theologians have suggested a reason for this. They point out that there is insufficient time for the results of one Synod to be assimilated and a strategy set up for its implementation before the *Lineamenta* for the next one is released for discussion.[139] A greater interval between Synods would allow more time for study and application of the post-synodal apostolic exhortations in local Churches and parishes.

If the synodal process is a "journey made together" of the Bishops in union with the Pope, then it can also be said that its fruit, the post-synodal apostolic exhortation, is a "document written together." These exhortations express the ecclesiology of communion, which includes the principles of collegiality and primacy that have marked the Church's life since the Second Vatican Council. They furnish the People of God with authoritative teaching based on the Synod's proposals and authenticated by the Pope's judgment. As a new form of collegial document intimately linked to the Petrine ministry, post-synodal apostolic exhortations have proved to be an effective means of ensuring the pastoral vitality necessary for the Church to meet the pressing challenges of the third millennium. Their influence will surely grow in the years to come.

---

[137] Address to the Council of the General Secretariat of the Synod of Bishops, June 17, 1988, *L'Osservatore Romano,* 30 (1988), 4.

[138] See the fourth edition of the *Program of Priestly Formation,* issued by the National Conference of Catholic Bishops (Washington: United States Catholic Conference, 1993), revised in light of *Pastores Dabo Vobis.*

[139] See, for example, Aloysio Lorscheider, Address at the Synod of Bishops, Eighth Ordinary General Assembly, October 1, 1990, *Catholic International,* 1 (1990), 224; Joseph Cordeiro, Address at the Synod of Bishops, Eighth Ordinary General Assembly, October 1, 1990, *Catholic International,* 1 (1990), 229; and Edward B. Clancy, Address at the Synod of Bishops, Eighth Ordinary General Assembly, October 1, 1990, *Catholic International,* 1 (1990), 236. See also Rausch, "The Synod of Bishops," 256.

Catechesi Tradendae

Editor's Introduction

On October 16, 1979, the first anniversary of his election to the See of Peter, Pope John Paul II published *Catechesi Tradendae,* on catechesis in our time. He issued this inaugural apostolic exhortation "in response to the request which was expressly formulated by the Bishops at the end of the Fourth General Assembly of the Synod" (§4.1), which had met in the fall of 1977. Making abundant use of the synodal documents and the drafts prepared by Paul VI and John Paul I, the Holy Father wrote his exhortation "with a lively awareness of the primary responsibility that rests on him" as the Church's principal catechist (§16). In *Catechesi Tradendae,* John Paul provides a charter for a catechetical revival among the People of God.

The Pope confirms the Synod's view that the catechetical renewal after the Second Vatican Council is "a precious gift from the Holy Spirit to the Church of today" (§3.2). There are numerous indications that post-conciliar catechesis is a source of vitality for the Church, and he encourages a more widespread "catechetical awakening" (§72.9). A fresh impulse has been given to catechesis by the biblical movement, the increased involvement of the laity, developments in pedagogy, and new ways of thinking about the places and recipients of catechesis. At the same time, John Paul affirms that all changes in catechesis must be carefully evaluated in light of "the directives of the Magisterium" (§3.2).

The kerygmatic and anthropological movements were the two most significant theological trends that influenced the renewal of catechesis in the twentieth century. Dissatisfied with a doctrinal catechesis which concentrated almost exclusively on the knowledge of Christian truths and duties, the kerygmatic movement, which began before the Second World War, paid more attention to the heart. It focused on the proclamation of the Good News, which is Jesus Christ himself. More than a system of truths, Christianity is a message announced by heralds. On the positive side, the movement led to a renewal in the content of catechesis. It concentrated on the essential truths of revelation, a return to the Scriptures, an emphasis on the centrality of Christ, and the links between catechesis and liturgy. But, on the negative side, kerygmatic catechesis paid insufficient attention to the life-situation of those to whom the message was directed.

Beginning at the time of the Second Vatican Council, pastoral theologians interested in catechetics sought to correct the shortcomings of a kerygmatic catechesis. Their efforts led to the adoption of an anthropological approach to catechesis, one which took more into account the daily life and problems of those addressed. Consequently, the starting point of religious education is the human person, with his questions and concerns. Catechesis is a process by which individuals and groups interpret, live, and express their own situation in light of the Gospel. On the one hand, anthropological catechesis has made a lasting contribution to catechesis. Its emphasis on the need to embody the Christian message in the culture of the listener and on the intrinsic connection between faith and life has been widely accepted. On the other hand, the drawbacks of the approach, especially with regard to its content, have also become evident: the risk of substituting subjective experience for revealed truth, the omission of certain "difficult" doctrines, and the overemphasis on temporal activity at the expense of the spiritual life. Although *Catechesis Tradendae* alludes only indirectly to the kerygmatic and anthropological movements (cf. §§22, 25.1), their influence on the views of the Synod and the Pope is significant.

The tone of the exhortation is balanced. John Paul avoids extremes. For example, he accompanies his praise for creativity in catechesis with an appeal for "the required vigilance" (§4.2). As befits a document which reflects the Synod's pastoral orientation, the tone is serene, sometimes conversational, and often exhortative. The Pope steers clear of polemics and controversial questions. While he warns against doctrinal deviations, he never names those who criticize him. Convinced that the Petrine ministry should foster ecclesial unity, the Holy Father mediates between the conflicting, and sometimes contradictory, positions that emerged during the Synod debates. Rather than tackle still disputed questions, he confines his attention largely to concerns expressing a broad consensus.

The style of *Catechesi Tradendae* is not so personal as that of John Paul's first encyclical, *Redemptor Hominis*, published several months earlier. Even so, the apostolic exhortation still bears his characteristic stamp. In the introduction he mentions his long-standing personal interest in catechesis which, he says, "has always been a central care in my ministry as a priest and as a Bishop" (§4.1). As Archbishop of Cracow, Karol Wojtyla was a member of the Council of the Synod's General Secretariat which proposed the theme of the 1977 Synod to Paul VI. Later he worked on preparing the *Lineamenta* and *Instrumentum Laboris*. Wojtyla also took an active part in the synodal Assembly held in Rome, in October 1977. Building on this wealth of experience, John Paul was well equipped to shape the documentation and drafts that the

Fathers submitted to him. He took up his "apostolic charge" (§4.1) regarding catechetics with enthusiasm and succeeded in leaving his own mark on the document. The exhortation reflects the Christological focus of John Paul's teaching, his concern for joining orthodoxy with orthopraxy, and his solicitude for religious freedom.

For a Pope devoted to implementing the teaching and directives of the Second Vatican Council, it is not surprising that he cites conciliar documents more frequently than any other non-biblical source — more than twenty times. *Evangelii Nuntiandi* (1975), the fruit of the 1974 Synod of Bishops, is referred to nine times. Another of the Pope's sources is the General Catechetical Directory. Published by the Holy See in 1971, in response to an explicit mandate of Vatican II, the Directory systematically addresses the nature, content, and goals of catechesis. John Paul relies a great deal on the Directory, citing it eight times. Despite the importance of these magisterial documents, the New Testament far outstrips them as the major influence inspiring the whole apostolic exhortation. More than two-thirds of the 138 footnotes refer to biblical texts.

Summary

Besides its introduction and conclusion, *Catechesi Tradendae* contains nine chapters. For the most part, the exhortation moves logically and progressively, from the presentation of basic principles to pastoral applications. The introduction (§§1-4) states that catechesis is part of the Church's mission, outlines the contributions to catechetical renewal made by Paul VI and the 1977 Synod, and describes the exhortation's purpose. In chapter one, "We Have but One Teacher, Jesus Christ" (§§5-9), the Holy Father recalls that all catechetical efforts must focus on Christ. Chapter two, "An Experience as Old as the Church" (§§10-17), outlines a few salient points in the history of catechesis and draws from them lessons for the present. The third chapter, "Catechesis in the Church's Pastoral and Missionary Activity" (§§18-25), deals with the nature of catechesis, while the fourth chapter, "The Whole of the Good News Drawn from Its Source" (§§26-34), discusses the content of catechesis. Beginning in chapter five, "Everybody Needs To Be Catechized" (§§35-45), the exhortation describes the different groups to which catechesis is directed. Chapter six, "Some Ways and Means of Catechesis" (§§46-50), and chapter seven, "How To Impart Catechesis" (§§51-55), examine catechetical methodology and pedagogy. In chapter eight, "The Joy of Faith in a Troubled World" (§§56-61), the Holy Father considers today's difficulties in teaching the faith and treats further theological and methodological questions. The ninth chapter, "The Task Concerns Us All" (§§62-71), is a pressing appeal to the whole Church to assume responsibility for fostering catechetical renewal. In the conclusion (§§72-73), the Pope recalls the Holy Spirit's role as the interior Teacher and points to Mary as the mother and model of all catechists.

Christ and catechesis

According to *Catechesi Tradendae,* the principal aim of catechesis is "to put people not only in touch but in communion, in intimacy, with Jesus Christ" (§5.3). He is the one who brings them to the Father in the Spirit, enabling individuals to share in the life of the Trinity. At the heart of catechesis is Jesus of Nazareth, and "Christian living consists in following Christ, the *sequela Christi*" (§5.2).

A further proof of the Pope's Christocentric focus is his affirmation that "the primary and essential object of catechesis" (§5.3) is the fullness of the mystery of Christ: his person, his words of teaching, and his saving deeds — from the beginning of the Incarnation to the fulfillment of the Paschal Mystery. A close link exists between who Christ is, what he teaches, and what he does: "The whole of Christ's life was a continual teaching: his silences, his miracles, his gestures, his prayer, his love for people, his special affection for the little and the poor, his acceptance of the total sacrifice on the Cross for the Redemption of the world, and his Resurrection are the actualization of his word and the fulfillment of revelation" (§9.1). Christ does not teach a body of abstract truths to his disciples but communicates himself to them. Consequently, catechesis should pass on to others "the Truth that he communicates or, to put it more precisely, the Truth that he is" (§6).

John Paul also emphasizes that Christ, besides being the object of what is taught, is also the one who really teaches his followers. Christ himself is the Teacher who inspires catechists. During his public ministry, he taught with an authority which so astonished the crowds that they rightly called him "Teacher." Moreover, Jesus claimed to be a singular and unique Teacher, or Rabbi (cf. Mt 23:8; Jn 13:13-14). Today he continues to teach in the Christian community through the power of his Spirit.

It follows, then, that the catechist is "Christ's spokesman, enabling Christ to teach with his lips" (§6). Following the Master, every catechist should apply Jesus' words to himself or herself: "My teaching is not mine, but his who sent me" (Jn 7:16). Careful to avoid creating any confusion between personal opinion and the deposit of faith, catechists hand on to others the teaching which they themselves have received (cf. 1 Cor 11:23). Not only do they speak for

Christ but they also "must be very much aware of acting as a living, pliant instrument of the Holy Spirit" (§72.8).

Catechesis in the Church's history

Chapter two unfolds in two parts. The Holy Father begins with a series of reflections, inspired by different historical periods, on the various ways in which Christians have been introduced into the Church's life. After this overview, he draws three lessons which he applies to the contemporary situation.

Christ is certainly *the* Teacher, but he entrusted his Apostles with the mission of making disciples of all nations (cf. Mt 28:19). They were faithful to their assigned task, and the first communities were "devoted to the Apostles' teaching" (Acts 2:42). Almost from the beginning the Apostles invited others to share in the task of proclaiming the Gospel: deacons, "many others" (cf. Acts 15:35), including simple Christians who "went about preaching the Word" (Acts 8:4) and, finally, successors. This early teaching, or catechizing, of the Christian community was primarily oral, but soon some of it also came to be written down.

After treating the Church's catechetical mission in the apostolic age, the exhortation deals with two significant moments in the history of catechesis: the age of the Fathers in the fourth and fifth centuries and the period following the Council of Trent (1545-1563). The Fathers of the Church, most of whom were Bishops, catechized successfully by means of their oral teaching and written treatises. In response to the challenge of the Reformation, the Council of Trent gave an impetus to catechetical renewal by means of its decrees and constitutions. In the wake of the Council, religious instruction was organized, and the clergy were admonished to carry out their duty of catechizing. One of the greatest reforms was that promulgated by Pius V. In 1566, he issued the Roman Catechism, "which is a work of the first rank as a summary of Christian teaching and traditional theology for use by priests" (§13.1).

This thumbnail sketch of the history of two thousand years of catechetical experience leads John Paul to three conclusions. First, "the Church has always looked on catechesis as a sacred duty and an inalienable right" (§14.1). This duty falls primarily, but not exclusively, on pastors. Furthermore, every baptized person "has the right to receive from the Church instruction and education enabling him or her to enter on a truly Christian life" (§14.1, cf. §64). Repeating a constant theme of his Magisterium, the Holy Father affirms that the faithful have a fundamental human right to catechesis. Respect for religious freedom enables catechetical activity "to be carried out in favorable circumstances of time and place." It also makes possible "access to the mass media and suitable equipment" and assures that catechesis is given "without discrimination against parents, those receiving catechesis or those imparting it" (§14.2, cf. §§64, 69.3). Where the right to religious instruction is violated, the Pope calls upon States to remove all restraints on the freedom of religion.

Second, the Holy Father recalls that the internal life and missionary commitment of the Church are fostered when her pastoral care gives priority to catechetical instruction. He urges catechesis to become a primary aspect of the Church's mission of evangelization. The "best resources in people and energy, without sparing effort, toil or material means" (§15) should be devoted to catechetical initiatives.

Finally, John Paul draws a third conclusion. Every individual and group in the Church should accept its particular responsibility for catechesis: the Pope and Bishops, priests and Religious, parents and teachers, and men and women catechists. As in the past, the Church today should seek out and put into effect "new methods and new prospects for catechetical instruction" (§15).

Meaning and content of catechesis

According to the Holy Father, catechesis is "the teaching of Christian doctrine imparted, generally speaking, in an organic and systematic way, with a view to initiating the hearers into the fullness of Christian life" (§18.4). Without claiming to be exhaustive, the Pope describes four characteristics that belong to a definition of catechesis: its relation to evangelization, to a growth in knowledge, to the sacraments, and to Christian life in the Church and in the world. Each of these considerations sheds light on the nature of catechesis.

Evangelization focuses on the initial proclamation of the Gospel to people, a proclamation which leads individuals to faith and Baptism. For its part, catechesis aims more at "educating the true disciple of Christ by means of a deeper and more systematic knowledge of the Person and the message of our Lord Jesus Christ" (§19.1) . . . "to think like him, to judge like him, to act in conformity with his commandments" (§20.2). Catechesis is not the same as evangelization, but the two "integrate and complement each other" (§18.5). At least in theory, catechesis is directed at maturing the faith initially stirred up by evangelization. But, in pastoral practice, catechesis must often take on the task of "arousing it [faith] unceasingly with the help of grace, with opening the heart, with converting, and with preparing total adherence to Jesus Christ on the part of those who are still on the threshold of faith" (§19.2). Today's catechists cannot assume that those whom they are addressing have in fact already been evangelized. This is the situation of baptized children without any religious formation, unbaptized children attending catechetical instruction, and baptized adolescents wavering in their adherence to Christ.

Throughout *Catechesi Tradendae* the Pope restates the need for a systematic and organic catechesis. It is reflective study "that fundamentally distinguishes catechesis from all other ways of presenting the word of God" (§21.1). This methodical instruction must deal with all the essentials of the faith, foster an ever deeper knowledge of them, and promote the fullness of Christian living of those being catechized. Moreover, systematic catechesis has an apologetic purpose: it trains people "to make a defense to anyone who calls them to account for the hope that is in them" (§25.3).

Third, catechesis entails more than imparting sure knowledge of the faith. It is also "intrinsically linked with the whole of liturgical and sacramental activity" (§23.1). John Paul expresses this connection in two ways. On the one hand, authentic catechesis nourishes the initial seed of faith, preparing for a deeper sharing in the sacramental life of the Church, above all through the sacraments of initiation and the Eucharist. On the other hand, all liturgical celebrations have a catechetical dimension; they enlighten the mind as well as deepen divine life in the soul. In the Church's public worship God speaks to his people and nurtures their faith. Summarizing this link, the Pope writes: "Sacramental life is impoverished and very soon turns into hollow ritualism if it is not based on serious knowledge of the meaning of the sacraments, and catechesis becomes intellectualized if it fails to come alive in the sacramental practice" (§23.2).

Lastly, the exhortation rejects playing off orthodoxy against orthopraxy: true catechesis is aimed at deepening discipleship by fostering personal communion with Jesus and consistent Christian living. "Firm and well-thought-out convictions," it states, "lead to courageous and upright action" (§22.1). The ecclesial community should provide the kind of catechesis which sustains people in putting into practice in their daily lives what they have learned and inspires missionary dynamism.

In chapter four the Holy Father deals with the content of catechesis: its chief sources, essential components, and three principles regarding its integrity.

Catechesis "draws its content from the living source of the word of God transmitted in Tradition and the Scriptures" (§27.1). It is imbued with the outlook and spirit of the Bible, reading the scriptural texts "with the intelligence and heart of the Church" (§27.2). Such a reading is found in the Church's various Creeds which contain a synthetic catechetical expression of the handing down of God's word in the Tradition. The Pope singles out for special praise Paul VI's Creed of the People of God (1968), which summarizes the "essential elements of the Catholic faith" and is "a sure point of reference for the content of catechesis" (§28.2). Although John Paul provides no list of all the elements to be included in the content of a program of religious instruction, he specifically mentions Christology, ecclesiology, Christian anthropology, and the Church's moral and social teaching.

Chapter four's last sections take up three points concerning the individual's right "to receive 'the word of faith' not in mutilated, falsified or diminished form but whole and entire, in all its rigor and vigor" (§30.2). Above all, sound catechesis must present the entire deposit of faith; it neither rejects nor neglects any doctrine. Second, pedagogical methods suitable to ensuring integrity in teaching should be used. Lastly, catechesis today calls for an ecumenical dimension. This aspect fosters the desire for the unity of Christians, promotes respect for the faith of others, and encourages collaboration in catechesis. On the one hand, this practical cooperation with other Christians helps Catholics to affirm their own identity. But, on the other hand, it must never entail watering down doctrine to the lowest common denominator.

The catechized

Following the position taken by the Synod, *Catechesi Tradendae* affirms two principles concerning those to whom catechesis is directed. In the first place, "nobody in the Church of Jesus Christ should feel excused from receiving catechesis" (§45.3). The exhortation outlines five different stages of life, which extend from infancy to adulthood, and describes the characteristics of instruction suitable for each age group. Secondly, the relation between those who "give" and those who "receive" catechesis is complementary. Certainly adult Catholics have much to offer children and young people, but "they can also receive much from them for the growth of their own Christian lives" (§45.2).

By their word and witness of life, parents have an obligation to acquaint their children, beginning at a tender age, with "a simple and true presentation of the Christian faith" (§36). Preschoolers are to be introduced into a relationship with God as a loving and provident Father. School-age children require a catechesis that is "aimed at inserting him or her organically into the life of the Church, a moment that includes an immediate preparation for the celebration of the sacraments" (§37). Such a catechesis teaches all the mysteries of faith in a way intelligible to boys and girls and helps them to bear witness to their beliefs in their everyday lives.

According to John Paul, the catechesis offered to adolescents must be sensitive to their particular life-situation. Given the turmoil of these years, teenagers should be shown how Jesus is their "friend, guide and model, capable of being admired but also imitated" (§38). Catechists are to present

Jesus' saving message as the answer to the deep-seated questions of adolescents. For older teenagers and young men and women, catechesis ought to take into account that at this time in their lives they are engaged in making important decisions. The onset of maturity makes it possible for the Gospel to "be presented, understood and accepted as capable of giving meaning to life" (§39.1). For everyone, from infancy to maturity, catechesis is "a permanent school of the faith . . . a beacon lighting the path of the child, the adolescent and the young person" (§39.3).

Even though the theme of the 1977 Synod was directed mainly to "the catechesis of children and young people," John Paul believes that all Christians need to be catechized. It is a lifelong task. Indeed, catechesis is above all directed to adults, because they have "the greatest responsibilities and the capacity to live the Christian message in its fully developed form" (§43). Here, at the outset of his Pontificate, the Holy Father insists on the need for the ongoing formation of adults, a topic to which he frequently returns in his subsequent teaching. "For catechesis to be effective," he writes, "it must be permanent" (§43). Among the adults, he singles out for special attention those who are not yet evangelized, those who are from traditionally Christian areas or cultures but who lack education in the faith, and those who received a childhood catechesis but have drifted away from religious practice. Whereas the first group requires true evangelization, the latter two are the object of what the Pope will later refer to as the "new evangelization," a primary concern of the Church on the threshold of the third millennium.

Catechetical methods

Chapters six, seven, and eight consider current pastoral and theological questions concerning catechetical instruction. The exhortation describes the difficulties facing catechesis today, the basic principles of its methodology, the different ways of imparting it, and its relation to ideology, culture, popular piety, and theology.

The Holy Father briefly takes stock of the troubled and indifferent world in which catechesis takes place. The present state of affairs is marked by "hesitation, uncertainty and insipidity" (§56). Certain contemporary schools of philosophy and theology, because they present faith as if it were a kind of blindness rather than vision, promote this climate of uncertainty. To combat this false understanding of faith, catechists should provide "the simple but solid certainties" (§60.4) that will nourish assurance and conviction. Today's situation calls for a catechesis "which trains the young people and adults of our communities to remain clear and consistent in their faith, to affirm serenely their Christian and Catholic identity" (§57). It challenges catechists to be joyful and steadfast witnesses of the Gospel.

Efforts to find "the most suitable ways and means" for catechizing deserve encouragement. Up-to-date methods are needed to transmit a sturdy faith to future generations. While enthusiastically endorsing creative initiatives in catechetical pedagogy, the Pope proposes that all fresh undertakings should be guided by three norms. First, the presentation of the entire Christian message is never to be diluted by a method "harmful to the unity of the teaching of the one faith" (§51.2). Second, diversity of catechetical methods should be treasured as a sign of vitality and a resource to be exploited. In fact, different ages, degrees of spiritual development, social contexts, and cultural backgrounds "demand that catechesis should adopt widely differing methods for the attainment of its specific aim: education in the faith" (§51.1, cf. §47.2). Third, the "original pedagogy of the faith" (§58.1), which takes Christ the Teacher as its model, must be respected. This pedagogy makes use of, but does not simply imitate, methods taken from contemporary educational theory.

In the same three chapters, the Holy Father also comments on various practical ways of fostering a more effective catechesis. He writes optimistically about "the great possibilities" offered by the whole range of modern means of social communication (cf. §45.2). The Pope also lists different occasions whose catechetical potential can be taken advantage of: pilgrimages, parish missions, Bible-study groups, and meetings of ecclesial basic communities and associations of young people. In particular, he encourages youth groups to promote the "serious study of Christian doctrine" (§47.1) so as to fulfill their ecclesial mission better. The homily, too, has a specific catechetical role. Preaching centered on the scriptural readings assigned by the Church's official liturgy, John Paul says, should "familiarize the faithful with the whole of the mysteries of the faith and with the norms of Christian living" (§48). Catechesis will also be improved, the Pope believes, if memorization is judiciously used in catechetical instruction, especially of Jesus' words, important Bible passages, the ten commandments, the Creeds, liturgical texts, basic prayers, and key doctrines (cf. §55.2).

In its discussion of methodology, *Catechesi Tradendae* devotes most of its attention to catechetical materials. Many of these works are "a real treasure in the service of catechetical instruction," but others are "ambiguous and harmful to young people and to the life of the Church" (§49.1). The latter bewilder those being taught "either by deliberately or unconsciously omitting elements essential to the Church's faith, or by attributing excessive importance to certain themes at the expense of others, or, chiefly, by a rather horizontalist overall view out of keeping with the teaching of the Church's Magisterium" (§49.1). Bishops have the responsibility of correcting these errors. In agreement with the Holy See, they should prepare catechisms for local use that are faithful to the content of revelation and pedagogically sound.

John Paul also discusses the link between catechesis and ideology, culture, popular devotions, and theology. He points out the danger of mixing "catechetical teaching unduly with overt or masked ideological views, especially political and social ones, or with personal political options" (§52). If a catechist propagates any kind of temporal, social, or political "messianism," he or she is guilty of radically distorting the Christian message.

Culture has a profound influence on catechetical methods, an impact requiring further study which will enable the Church better to express the unsearchable riches of Christ (cf. Eph 3:8). Genuine catechesis must "take flesh" in the various cultures if it is to address its audience effectively. It is to bring "the power of the Gospel into the very heart of culture and cultures" (§53.1). For John Paul, fruitful inculturation must be guided by two principles. Christianity is not merely an idea but is rooted in historical events. On the one hand, the Gospel always remains tied in some way to the cultural expressions of the time and place of its origin and of its subsequent doctrinal development. Later generations cannot simply ignore the doctrinal formulations shaped by earlier Christians. On the other hand, Christ's message is transcendent; it has the power to transform and regenerate every culture which it encounters.

In keeping with his high regard for traditional religious piety, John Paul emphasizes the catechetical value of the valid elements of popular religiosity. The prayers and practices of this piety, when purified of unhealthy factors, can be profitably used "to help people advance toward knowledge of the mystery of Christ and of his message" (§54).

Lastly, the Pope describes the relation between catechesis and theology. He observes that, because "every stirring in the field of theology also has repercussions in that of catechesis" (§61.2), catechists should know and respect the difference between the Church's faith and theological opinions. By teaching the doctrine proposed by the Magisterium they avoid the confusion of "outlandish theories, useless questions and unproductive discussions" (§61.4).

Catechists and places of catechesis

Unlike the more discriminating tone of the previous three chapters on catechetical methods, chapter nine is more exhortative. It outlines the ways of implementing the Pope's call to confident action: "Yes, I wish to sow courage, hope and enthusiasm abundantly in the hearts of all those many diverse people who are in charge of religious instruction and training for life in keeping with the Gospel" (§62). The Holy Father inspires the various groups responsible for religious instruction — Bishops, priests, Religious, and laity — to commit themselves ever more zealously to the Church's catechetical mission, and then he describes the settings in which it takes place.

John Paul begins by reminding his brother Bishops that they have "the chief management of catechesis" (§63.3) in their local Churches. They have a fivefold task: fostering "a real passion for catechesis" (§63.3) among all their people; assuring the availability of competent personnel, suitable equipment, and financial resources; denouncing deviations and correcting errors; approving catechisms; and overseeing the formation of lay catechists. Together with the Pope, Bishops also bear a responsibility for the overall catechetical mission of the Church.

Priests, as the closest assistants of their Bishop, are also instructors in the faith. They are to provide "a well-organized and well-oriented catechetical effort" (§64) for the growth of the local ecclesial community entrusted to their pastoral care. For their part, men and women Religious should "dedicate as much as possible of what ability and means they have to the specific work of catechesis" (§65).

John Paul warmly encourages all the men and women who devote themselves to catechizing others, describing their work as "an eminent form of the lay apostolate" (§66.1). Even if their task is "not a formally instituted ministry" (§71.1), it is of utmost importance to the Church's life. Above all he praises the catechists in mission lands, recognizing their valuable contribution to the flourishing of the young Churches.

Next the Pope describes the four main settings where catechesis takes place. He offers encouragement and specific suggestions for improving its quality in parishes, families, schools, and ecclesial organizations. The parish community "must continue to be the prime mover and preeminent place for catechesis." It is still "a major point of reference for the Christian people, even for the non-practicing" (§67.2). In order to give a new impetus to parish catechesis, the Holy Father further asks that steps be taken to train parishioners for the catechetical apostolate.

In line with Pope John Paul's staunch promotion of the vocation and mission of the family, he points out its irreplaceable role in catechizing its members. This task is especially important where legislation prohibits or impedes religious instruction in the public sphere or where unbelief and secularism dominate social life. Parents are the primary catechists of their children. They carry out this ministry chiefly by the silent and powerful witness of their lives. But parents also fulfill their responsibility by explaining to their children the religious significance of the events of family life and by reinforcing the more methodical teaching received in the parish or at school. Family catechesis "precedes, accompanies and enriches all other forms of catechesis" (§68.2).

The Pope urges Catholic and public schools, as well as lay organizations, to assume responsibility for the Church's catechetical apostolate in ways appropriate to them. For their part, Catholic schools should integrate religious instruction into the students' overall curriculum, not restricting it to being merely one course isolated from the others. This integration, says the Holy Father, gives Catholic schools their special character: religious faith imbues the students' whole educational experience. It is the main reason why parents choose them for their children. In Catholic schools, the imparting of implicit and indirect religious education ought to complement scheduled times of explicit catechesis, not replace it.

Where Catholic children attend public schools, John Paul urges governments to respect their right to religious freedom. Public school children have the right to receive religious instruction, which "can be offered either by the school or in the setting of the school, or again with the framework of an agreement with the public authorities regarding school timetables, if catechesis takes place only in the parish or in another pastoral center" (§69.2).

Lastly, the Holy Father encourages lay associations, movements, and groups to provide ongoing catechesis for their members. Those who are actively engaged in temporal activities need further formation. "They will all accomplish their objectives better, and serve the Church better," he writes, "if they give an important place in their internal organization and their method of action to the serious religious training of their members" (§70.1).

Key Themes

Among the topics treated in *Catechesi Tradendae* three very significant ones stand out: the emphasis on Christ as the point of reference of all catechesis, the need for doctrinal integrity, and the importance of using pedagogical methods aimed at adapting catechesis to various listeners. Each theme reveals a specific dimension of the theological perspective and pastoral approach of John Paul II.

Christological vision

In all his writings the Pope stresses that Christ is the focal point of the Church's teaching and life. From its beginning, Christianity has had a

Christological focus. The exhortation's insistence on the absolute uniqueness of Christ, revealed by the Incarnation and Redemption, is an essential element of John Paul's Christocentric vision. Only in light of the Word made flesh can the mystery of God and the dignity and vocation of the human person be adequately understood. Jesus Christ is "the Teacher who reveals God to man and man to himself" (§9.2). He is the blueprint for humanity fashioned in the divine image (cf. Gen 1:26-27). Even though *Catechesis Tradendae* shows less intensity and poetic passion than *Redemptor Hominis* (1979), the encyclical's dominant theme — "the Redeemer of man, Jesus Christ, is the center of the universe and of history" (§1.1) — leaves a profound imprint on John Paul's first apostolic exhortation.

At the center of every catechetical initiative are the Person and teaching of Christ. The Holy Father forcefully endorses the Synod's conviction of "the Christocentricity of all authentic catechesis" (§5.1). Indeed, he insists that Jesus Christ is the object and subject of all catechesis. All religious instruction should be carried out in reference to Christ, making him more known and leading to a deeper love of him.

There is more to transmitting the faith to people than teaching its truths. According to the Pope, "the primary and essential object of catechesis . . . is 'the mystery of Christ'" (§5.3, cf. §§4.2, 20.2, 22.1), that is, God's saving plan fulfilled in his Son (cf. Eph 3:9, 18-19). The Christocentricity of catechesis entails both attachment to the Person of Christ and knowledge of his message. Catechesis has "the definitive aim" of putting those taught "in communion, in intimacy with Jesus Christ" (§5.3). It creates a bond which leads "to the love of the Father in the Spirit" (§6). Religious education brings people to a personal encounter with Jesus of Nazareth by making them his disciples. It inspires them to follow him, thus "initiating the hearers into the fullness of Christian life" (§18.4).

Besides fostering Christian discipleship, catechesis also teaches the whole truth about Christ, "the way, and the truth, and the life" (Jn 14:6). His Person and message are the heart of all catechetical activity. An individual, after having entrusted himself to Jesus in faith, "endeavors to know better this Jesus to whom he has entrusted himself: to know his 'mystery'" (§20.3). Catechists help people to deepen their knowledge of Christ by presenting the fullness of his teaching. According to John Paul, authentic catechesis entails an orderly and systematic presentation of God's revelation in Christ, "a revelation stored in the depths of the Church's memory and in Sacred Scripture, and constantly communicated from one generation to the next by a living, active *traditio*" (§22.3). The relationship between love of Christ and knowledge of his life-giving truth is dynamic. To teach doctrine without adherence to Christ is sterile, just as to foster adherence to Christ without doctrine leads to confusion.

The content of all catechetical programs must give pride of place to a sound Christology, one which emphasizes Christ's divinity as well as his humanity and affirms the spiritual dimension of his message. Programs should therefore clearly set forth the mysteries of the Incarnation, life and ministry of Jesus, Redemption, and his continuing presence in the Church through the sacraments (cf. §§29.2, 30.2, 35.2, 52, 54). This emphasis on the centrality of Christ in all catechetical instruction is evident in a question about pastoral responsibility which the Pope puts to the Bishops: "How are we to reveal Jesus Christ, God made man . . . his message, the plan of God that he has revealed, the call he addresses to each person, and the Kingdom that he wishes to establish in this world?"(§35.2).

For the Holy Father, the Gospel message responds to the deepest yearnings of the human heart. Speaking about youth, but evoking a principle applicable to everyone, he says that "in spite of appearances, these young people have within them, even though often in a confused way, not just a readiness or openness, but rather a real desire to know Jesus" (§40.1). Only the revelation of his Person and message can answer the difficulties and dilemmas facing people today. Jesus Christ is the definitive answer to humanity's religious and moral questions. To make his point more forcefully, the Pope cites *Redemptor Hominis* §10.1, where he had written: "The man who wishes to understand himself thoroughly — and not just in accordance with immediate, partial, often superficial, and even illusory standards and measures of his being — must come to Christ with his unrest and uncertainty, and even his weakness and sinfulness, his life and death. He must, so to speak, enter into Christ with all his own self, he must 'appropriate' Christ and assimilate the whole of the reality of the Incarnation and Redemption in order to find himself" (§61.5). Christ is the focal point of the Pope's vision.

A final way in which John Paul expresses his Christocentric vision is evident in his description of Christ as the "one" Teacher (cf. Mt 23:8). Not only is Jesus the object of catechesis, what is taught, but he is also its subject, the one who teaches. He alone can teach the truth he has received from the Father (cf. Jn 7:16). From Christ, through the mediation of the Church, the truth of the Gospel can reach everyone. Catechists, as teachers of the mystery of faith, are the Church's instruments which enable Christ to bring a share in the life of the Trinity to his people. The Pope also points out that the religious educator teaches Christ's message under the guidance of the Holy Spirit, who is the principal agent of the Church's catechetical mission. Catechesis, he writes, is "a work of the Holy Spirit, a work that he alone can initiate and sustain in the Church" (§72.6). Christ, working through the power of his Spirit, is the permanent goal, content, and point of reference of the Church's whole catechetical ministry.

Fullness of the faith

According to *Catechesi Tradendae,* the compromise or dilution of the doctrinal content of religious instruction is the most serious obstacle to catechetical renewal. The Pope's concern for orthodoxy reflects the unique responsibility of the Petrine ministry for defending and fostering the unity of faith. By his office, the Successor of Peter is obliged to ensure that the fullness of revealed truth is taught everywhere in the Church. Hence solicitude for a catechesis that is clear, unambiguous, and completely obedient to the revealed deposit of faith.

John Paul is particularly interested in recovering a sense of the wholeness, interior logic, and beauty of the Church's "symphony of faith." By stressing the integrity of her teaching, he hopes to overcome the confusion caused by opinions on faith, morals, and discipline which are at odds with the Magisterium. Accordingly, in *Catechesi Tradendae* the Pope vigorously exhorts catechists to teach Catholic doctrine integrally and systematically.

Even though the Holy Father does not dwell on the point, he is disturbed by the deficiencies that have crept into the catechetical renewal. "These limitations are particularly serious," he says, "when they endanger integrity of content" (§17). The exhortation provides no official list of specific errors to be combated. Nonetheless, the Pope does identify three areas of possible doctrinal distortion: first, a Christology which would "reduce Christ to his humanity alone or his message to no more than an earthly dimension" (§29.2); second, the use of "language that would result in altering the substance of the content of the Creed, under any pretext whatever, even a pretended scientific one" (§59.2); and third, an understanding of faith as "a seeking that never attains its object" (§61.2). As part of his pastoral strategy designed to minimize the influence of erroneous opinions, the Pope reminds the Bishops of their "thankless task of denouncing deviations and correcting errors" in catechesis (§63.3).

Few catechists deny Church doctrine outright. More frequently, they fail to present certain doctrines in their teaching. John Paul forcefully affirms that there is never sufficient reason for depriving the faithful of the fullness of the Gospel. They have the right to receive the Gospel in its integrity. He applies this principle of doctrinal integrity to ecumenism, pedagogical materials, and inculturation. Cooperation in catechetical initiatives with other Christians "must never mean a 'reduction' to a common minimum" (§33). Furthermore, the instructional materials used in passing on the mystery of Christ must avoid unsettling those being catechized "either by deliberately or unconsciously omitting elements essential to the Church's faith, or by attributing excessive importance to certain themes at the expense of others" (§49.2). Moreover, while the Gospel needs to be embodied in the world's various cultures, the Holy Father warns against accepting "an impoverishment of catechesis through a renunciation or obscuring of its message, by adaptations, even in language, that would endanger the 'precious deposit' of the faith, or by concessions in matters of faith or morals" (§53.5). Fidelity to divine revelation requires that religious educators never omit from their program any essential truth of faith.

Another threat to doctrinal integrity comes from catechists who teach "personal opinions and options as if they expressed Christ's teaching and the lessons of his life" (§6). Whenever catechists introduce political and social ideologies into their instruction, they compromise the Gospel, "to the point of obscuring it and putting it in second place or even using it to further their own ends" (§52). In addition, no catechist should "make a selection of what he considers important in the deposit of faith as opposed to what he considers unimportant, so as to teach the one and reject the other" (§30.2).

Also with his eye trained on doctrinal vigilance, John Paul discusses the relation between catechetics and theology. First of all, he praises many of the theological works written since the Second Vatican Council; they are "a real treasure in the service of catechetical instruction" (§49.1). But the Pope also laments that these positive initiatives have been accompanied by "articles and publications which are ambiguous and harmful to young people and the life of the Church" (§49.1). Catechists, he reminds us, receive their mission from the Church; they do not teach on their own authority. Consequently, educators in the faith should neither present theological opinions as certainties equivalent to Church teaching nor take sides in scholarly debates. The Holy Father admonishes catechists to "have the wisdom to pick from the field of theological research those points that can provide light for their own reflection and their teaching, drawing, like the theologians, from the true sources, in the light of the Magisterium" (§61.4, cf. §52).

Undoubtedly John Paul is concerned about doctrinal deviations in catechesis. But he prefers to concentrate his exhortatory remarks on what is positive: the marvelous "fullness" of the Church's faith. He encourages teaching doctrine in its integrity by emphasizing what belongs to sound catechesis. An integral religious education is marked by three characteristics. It illumines the whole of life; it is doctrinally complete; and it is taught in a systematic and orderly way.

A complete catechesis aims to initiate its recipients into "the fullness of Christian life" (§18.4), imbuing their whole humanity with the Gospel. Again and again the Pope teaches that catechesis involves "an integral Christian initiation, open to all the other factors of Christian life" (§21.2, cf. §33.1). It is a matter of mind and heart, of intellect and will. Orthodoxy and orthopraxy are complementary, since "Christianity is inseparably both" (§22.1). Faithfulness to the word of God entails fidelity to the full riches of Catholic teaching and to a life of discipleship. Divine revelation illumines "the whole of life with the light of the Gospel" (§22.3). A catechesis that is directed to the whole person ensures the integrity of teaching. Doctrine and life are inseparably linked.

A second of John Paul's concerns about the content of catechesis touches its completeness. According to him, every stage of teaching should communicate "the whole and not just a part of 'the words of eternal life' and the 'ways of life'" (§31). In a manner adapted to the recipient, an authentic catechetical program must take up all the mysteries of faith and norms of Christian living. Repeatedly he stresses that doctrine is to be taught "in all its dimensions" (§5.3), so that the instruction will be "sufficiently complete" (§21.2) and "whole and entire" (§30.2). Catechetical works, he writes, "must make a point of giving the whole message of Christ and his Church" (§49.2). And programs should be designed which will communicate "God's revelation in its entirety" (§58.2), including the Gospel's demanding moral norms and implications for social justice. Good catechesis, imparted by those who practice their faith, fosters serious commitment from its recipients.

The doctrinal integrity of catechesis also requires a systematic presentation of Church teaching (cf. §§18.4, 21.1, 21.3, 22.3, 26). According to the exhortation, catechesis must be "systematic, not improvised but programmed to reach a precise goal" (§21.2). The Pope fears that in certain quarters the orderly presentation of material is all too often neglected. Hence he makes a point of stressing the advantages of a systematic study of the truths of faith. Such study is necessary if catechesis is to succeed in stimulating the serious reflection which distinguishes it from other ways of presenting God's word.

Catechesis and culture

As a way of teaching the fullness of the faith, John Paul encourages catechists to use creative pedagogical methods suitable to religious education. The Church is ever attentive to imparting catechesis in ways attuned to those receiving instruction. In line with this openness, the Pope urges a catechetical renewal marked "by the revision of its methods, by the search for suitable language, and by the utilization of new means of transmitting the message" (§17). With this in mind, he mentions the importance of inculturation, an idea much discussed in contemporary philosophy and theology. A solid catechesis must deal with the vital connection between faith and culture.

Inculturation is born of the need for the Gospel message to sink its roots deeply "into the very heart of culture and cultures" (§53.1). From the beginning of Christianity, the teaching of the faith has been "adapted to the various situations of believers and the many different situations in which the Church finds herself" (§13.2). Catechists and teachers have always looked for the most appropriate ways of communicating the Gospel to their listeners. Today, too, their methods should be relevant to the "real life of the generation to which they are addressed," and catechists "must try to speak a language comprehensible to the generation in question" (§49.2). These "generations" which receive the message are various. They are conditioned by age, level of intellectual and spiritual maturity, but also — and this is especially relevant for the younger Churches throughout the world — by their social and cultural milieu. Catechesis, then, must "take flesh" in very different environments. This process of enfleshment, which seeks to make the Gospel more readily understandable so that it can be lived more deeply and explained to others more persuasively, is called "inculturation."

The doctrinal foundation of inculturation is the truth that, as Redeemer, Christ saves what he has assumed to himself. According to the Holy Father, those who transmit the faith must know the specific "culture" that they are addressing, learn its most significant expressions, and respect its particular values which can be placed at the service of the Gospel. Through their preaching, catechists should help their listeners "to bring forth from their own living tradition original expressions of Christian life, celebration and thought" (§53.1). In this way catechesis will enrich the Church's catholicity without endangering her unity.

A single warning note is sounded about the vital importance of embodying the Gospel in different cultures: inculturation is a process which, if not carefully supervised, could involve risks to the integrity of the faith. In order to minimize this danger, John Paul proposes two norms which should guide the inculturation of catechesis. First, he recalls that the Gospel is always heard by people already embedded in a particular culture. This was true when Christianity first took root in the Semitic culture of Jesus' day and, later, in the Greco-Roman world as well. For the Holy Father, "the Gospel message cannot be purely and simply isolated from the culture in which it was first inserted" or "from the cultures in which it has already been expressed down the centuries" (§53.2). Revealed truth reaches those being catechized today as a message already stamped by different cultures of the past. These cultures on occasion — as in the definitions of Ecumenical Councils — have authoritatively interpreted the Gospel. New cultural expressions of the Gospel cannot therefore simply bypass the Church's Tradition. Rather, "apostolic dialogue which inevitably becomes part of a certain dialogue of cultures" must take place (§53.2) as part of the arduous task of inculturation.

Second, while the Gospel is necessarily expressed in the culture of those who adhere to Christ, its message also transcends every particular cultural embodiment. Not only does the Gospel *receive* from the culture in which it is incarnated, it also *gives* to that culture. God's word has the power to purify and regenerate every culture. Thus, catechesis seeks to transform all peoples' authentic cultural values by integrating them into Christianity.

The Pope concludes his apostolic exhortation with a pressing appeal for the renewal of the "catechetical dynamism in the Church" (§72.10). He implores Mary to obtain this grace through her maternal intercession. As Jesus' mother, she was his catechist, forming him "in human knowledge of the Scriptures and of the history of God's plan for his people, and in adoration of the Father" (§73.1). As her Son's disciple, Mary was the first one catechized in the New Covenant, receiving from Jesus lessons that she pondered in her heart (cf. Lk 2:51). John Paul therefore describes Mary as "the mother and model of catechists" (§73.1), and asks that she intercede with the Holy Spirit to grant the Church a fresh enthusiasm in carrying out her catechetical mission.

* * *

Selected Bibliography

Bonivento, Cesare, ed. *"Going, Teach . . . ": Commentary on the Apostolic Exhortation "Catechesi Tradendae" of John Paul II.* Boston: St. Paul Editions, 1980.

Bradley, Robert, ed. *John Paul II, Catechist: A Commentary on "Catechesi Tradendae," the New Charter for Religious Education in Our Time.* Chicago: Franciscan Herald Press, 1980.

Brennan, Nano, and McKenna, Robert. "Catechesis in Our Time." *Doctrine and Life,* 31 (1980), 90-97.

Campbell, Anna S. "Toward a Systematic Catechesis: An Interpretation of *Catechesi Tradendae." Living Light,* 17 (1980), 311-320.

Collins, Barry. *Joyful Gift of the Spirit: A Commentary on "Catechesi Tradendae."* Sydney: Catholic Education Office, 1980.

Fitzsimmons, Mary A. "Systematic Catechesis in the RCIA." *Living Light,* 27 (1981), 321-326.

Oddi, Silvio. "Jesus Christ Is the Message." *L'Osservatore Romano,* 25 (1981), 3-5, 11.

Rubin, Wladyslaw. "Presentation at the Press Conference for the Publication of *Catechesi Tradendae." L'Osservatore Romano,* 45 (1979), 13.

Synod of Bishops, Fourth Ordinary General Assembly. *"Lineamenta." Origins,* 5 (1976), 741, 743-751.

Synod of Bishops, Fourth Ordinary General Assembly. "Message to the People of God." *L'Osservatore Romano,* 44 (1977), 3, 5-6; and *Origins,* 7 (1977), 321, 323-328.

Synod of Bishops, Fourth Ordinary General Assembly. "Summary of the *Instrumentum Laboris." L'Osservatore Romano,* 38 (1977), 5, 7.

APOSTOLIC EXHORTATION

CATECHESI TRADENDAE

OF HIS HOLINESS
POPE JOHN PAUL II
TO THE EPISCOPATE, THE CLERGY
AND THE FAITHFUL
OF THE ENTIRE CATHOLIC CHURCH
ON CATECHESIS IN OUR TIME

Catechesi Tradendae
Introduction

Christ's final command

1.1 The Church has always considered catechesis one of her primary tasks, for, before Christ ascended to his Father after his Resurrection, he gave the Apostles a final command — to make disciples of all nations and to teach them to observe all that he had commanded.[1] He thus entrusted them with the mission and power to proclaim to humanity what they had heard, what they had seen with their eyes, what they had looked upon and touched with their hands, concerning the Word of Life.[2] He also entrusted them with the mission and power to explain with authority what he had taught them, his words and actions, his signs and commandments. And he gave them the Spirit to fulfill this mission.

1.2 Very soon the name of catechesis was given to the whole of the efforts within the Church to make disciples, to help people to believe that Jesus is the Son of God, so that believing they might have life in his name,[3] and to educate and instruct them in this life and thus build up the Body of Christ. The Church has not ceased to devote her energy to this task.

Paul VI's solicitude

2 The most recent Popes gave catechesis a place of eminence in their pastoral solicitude. Through his gestures, his preaching, his authoritative interpretation of the Second Vatican Council (considered by him the great catechism of modern times), and through the whole of his life, my venerated Predecessor Paul VI served the Church's catechesis in a particularly exemplary fashion. On March 18, 1971, he approved the General Catechetical Directory prepared by the Sacred Congregation for the Clergy, a directory that is still the basic document for encouraging and guiding catechetical renewal throughout the Church. He set up the International Council for Catechesis in 1975. He defined in masterly fashion the role and significance of catechesis in the life and mission of the Church when he addressed the participants in the first International Catechetical Congress on September 25, 1971,[4] and he returned explicitly to the subject in his Apostolic Exhortation *Evangelii*

---

[1] Cf. Mt 28:19-20.
[2] Cf. 1 Jn 1:1.
[3] Cf. Jn 20:31.
[4] Cf. *AAS* 63 (1971), 758-764.

Nuntiandi.[5] He decided that catechesis, especially that meant for children and young people, should be the theme of the Fourth General Assembly of the Synod of Bishops,[6] which was held in October 1977 and which I myself had the joy of taking part in.

A fruitful Synod

3.1 At the end of that Synod the Fathers presented the Pope with a very rich documentation, consisting of the various interventions during the Assembly, the conclusions of the working groups, the Message that they had with his consent sent to the People of God,[7] and especially the imposing list of "Propositions" in which they expressed their views on a very large number of aspects of present-day catechesis.

3.2 The Synod worked in an exceptional atmosphere of thanksgiving and hope. It saw in catechetical renewal a precious gift from the Holy Spirit to the Church of today, a gift to which the Christian communities at all levels throughout the world are responding with a generosity and inventive dedication that win admiration. The requisite discernment could then be brought to bear on a reality that is very much alive, and it could benefit from great openness among the People of God to the grace of the Lord and the directives of the Magisterium.

Purpose of this Exhortation

4.1 It is in the same climate of faith and hope that I am today addressing this Apostolic Exhortation to you, Venerable Brothers and dear sons and daughters. The theme is extremely vast and the Exhortation will keep to only a few of the most topical and decisive aspects of it, as an affirmation of the happy results of the Synod. In essence, the Exhortation takes up again the reflections that were prepared by Pope Paul VI, making abundant use of the documents left by the Synod. Pope John Paul I, whose zeal and gifts as a catechist amazed us all, had taken them in hand and was preparing to publish them when he was suddenly called to God. To all of us he gave an example of

---

[5] Cf. (December 8, 1975), 44, 45-48, 54: *AAS* 68 (1976), 34-35, 35-38, 43.

[6] According to the Motu Proprio *Apostolica Sollicitudo* (September 15, 1965), the Synod of Bishops can come together in General Assembly, in Extraordinary Assembly or in Special Assembly. In the present Apostolic Exhortation the words "Synod," "Synod Fathers" and "Synod Hall" always refer, unless otherwise indicated, to the Fourth General Assembly of the Synod of Bishops on catechesis, held in Rome in October 1977.

[7] Cf. Synod of Bishops, Fourth Ordinary General Assembly, Message to the People of God (October 28, 1977): *L'Osservatore Romano* (English-language edition), November 3, 1977, 3, 5-6.

catechesis at once popular and concentrated on the essential, one made up of simple words and actions that were able to touch the heart. I am therefore taking up the inheritance of these two Popes in response to the request which was expressly formulated by the Bishops at the end of the Fourth General Assembly of the Synod and which was welcomed by Pope Paul VI in his closing speech.[8] I am also doing so in order to fulfill one of the chief duties of my apostolic charge. Catechesis has always been a central care in my ministry as a priest and as a Bishop.

4.2 I ardently desire that this Apostolic Exhortation to the whole Church should strengthen the solidity of the faith and of Christian living, should give fresh vigor to the initiatives in hand, should stimulate creativity — with the required vigilance — and should help to spread among the communities the joy of bringing the mystery of Christ to the world.

I

We Have but One Teacher, Jesus Christ

Putting into communion with the Person of Christ

5.1 The Fourth General Assembly of the Synod of Bishops often stressed the Christocentricity of all authentic catechesis. We can here use the word "Christocentricity" in both its meanings, which are not opposed to each other or mutually exclusive, but each of which rather demands and completes the other.

5.2 In the first place, it is intended to stress that at the heart of catechesis we find, in essence, a Person, the Person of Jesus of Nazareth, "the only Son from the Father . . . full of grace and truth,"[9] who suffered and died for us and who now, after rising, is living with us forever. It is Jesus who is "the way, and the truth, and the life,"[10] and Christian living consists in following Christ, the *sequela Christi.*

5.3 The primary and essential object of catechesis is, to use an expression dear to Saint Paul and also to contemporary theology, "the mystery of Christ." Catechizing is in a way to lead a person to study this mystery in all its dimensions: "to make all men see what is the plan of the mystery . . . comprehend with all the saints what is the breadth and length and height and depth . . . know the love of Christ which surpasses knowledge . . . (and be filled) with all the fullness of God."[11] It is therefore to reveal in the Person of Christ the whole

---

[8] Cf. (October 29, 1977): *AAS* 69 (1977), 633.

[9] Jn 1:14.

[10] Jn 14:6.

[11] Eph 3:9, 18-19.

of God's eternal design reaching fulfillment in that Person. It is to seek to understand the meaning of Christ's actions and words and of the signs worked by him, for they simultaneously hide and reveal his mystery. Accordingly, the definitive aim of catechesis is to put people not only in touch but in communion, in intimacy, with Jesus Christ: only he can lead us to the love of the Father in the Spirit and make us share in the life of the Holy Trinity.

Transmitting Christ's teaching

6 Christocentricity in catechesis also means the intention to transmit not one's own teaching or that of some other master, but the teaching of Jesus Christ, the Truth that he communicates or, to put it more precisely, the Truth that he is.[12] We must therefore say that in catechesis it is Christ, the Incarnate Word and Son of God, who is taught — everything else is taught with reference to him — and it is Christ alone who teaches — anyone else teaches to the extent that he is Christ's spokesman, enabling Christ to teach with his lips. Whatever be the level of his responsibility in the Church, every catechist must constantly endeavor to transmit by his teaching and behavior the teaching and life of Jesus. He will not seek to keep directed toward himself and his personal opinions and attitudes the attention and the consent of the mind and heart of the person he is catechizing. Above all, he will not try to inculcate his personal opinions and options as if they expressed Christ's teaching and the lessons of his life. Every catechist should be able to apply to himself the mysterious words of Jesus: "My teaching is not mine, but his who sent me."[13] Saint Paul did this when he was dealing with a question of prime importance: "I received from the Lord what I also delivered to you."[14] What assiduous study of the word of God transmitted by the Church's Magisterium, what profound familiarity with Christ and with the Father, what a spirit of prayer, what detachment from self must a catechist have in order that he can say: My teaching is not mine!"

Christ the Teacher

7.1 This teaching is not a body of abstract truths. It is the communication of the living mystery of God. The Person teaching it in the Gospel is altogether

---

[12] Cf. Jn 14:6.

[13] Jn 7:16. This is a theme dear to the Fourth Gospel: cf. Jn 3:34, 8:28, 12:49-50, 14:24, 17:8, 17:14.

[14] 1 Cor 11:23: the word "deliver" employed here by Saint Paul was frequently repeated in the Apostolic Exhortation *Evangelii Nuntiandi* (December 8, 1975) to describe the evangelizing activity of the Church; for example 4, 15, 78-79: *AAS* 68 (1976), 7, 13-15, 70-72.

superior in excellence to the "masters" in Israel, and the nature of his doctrine surpasses theirs in every way because of the unique link between what he says, what he does and what he is. Nevertheless, the Gospels clearly relate occasions when Jesus "taught." "Jesus began to do and teach"[15] — with these two verbs, placed at the beginning of the Book of the Acts, Saint Luke links and at the same time distinguishes two poles in Christ's mission.

7.2 Jesus taught. It is the witness that he gives of himself: "Day after day I sat in the temple teaching."[16] It is the admiring observation of the Evangelists, surprised to see him teaching everywhere and at all times, teaching in a manner and with an authority previously unknown: "Crowds gathered to him again; and again, as his custom was, he taught them"[17]; "and they were astonished at his teaching, for he taught them as one who had authority."[18] It is also what his enemies note for the purpose of drawing from it grounds for accusation and condemnation: "He stirs up the people, teaching throughout all Judaea, from Galilee even to this place."[19]

The one "Teacher"

8.1 One who teaches in this way has a unique title to the name of "Teacher." Throughout the New Testament, especially in the Gospels, how many times is he given this title of Teacher![20] Of course the Twelve, the other disciples, and the crowds of listeners call him "Teacher" in tones of admiration, trust and tenderness.[21] Even the Pharisees and the Sadducees, the Doctors of the Law, and the Jews in general do not refuse him the title: "Teacher, we wish to see a sign from you"[22]; "Teacher, what shall I do to inherit eternal life?"[23] But above all, Jesus himself at particularly solemn and highly significant moments calls himself Teacher: "You call me Teacher and Lord; and you are right, for so I am"[24]; and he proclaims the singularity, the uniqueness of his character as

---

[15] Acts 1:1.

[16] Mt 26:55; cf. Jn 18:20.

[17] Mk 10:1.

[18] Mk 1:22; cf. Mt 5:2, 11:1, 13:54, 22:16; Mk 2:13, 4:1, 6:2, 6:6; Lk 5:3, 5:17; Jn 7:14, 8:2, etc.

[19] Lk 23:5.

[20] In nearly fifty places in the four Gospels, this title, inherited from the whole Jewish tradition but here given a new meaning that Christ himself often seeks to emphasize, is attributed to Jesus.

[21] Cf. among others, Mt 8:19; Mk 4:38, 9:38, 10:35, 13:1; Jn 11:28.

[22] Mt 12:38.

[23] Lk 10:25; cf. Mt 22:16.

[24] Jn 13:13-14; cf. Mt 10:25, 26:18 and parallel passages.

Teacher: "You have one teacher,"[25] the Christ. One can understand why people of every kind, race and nation have for two thousand years in all the languages of the earth given him this title with veneration, repeating in their own ways the exclamation of Nicodemus: "We know that you are a teacher come from God."[26]

8.2 This image of Christ the Teacher is at once majestic and familiar, impressive and reassuring. It comes from the pen of the Evangelists and it has often been evoked subsequently in iconography since earliest Christian times,[27] so captivating is it. And I am pleased to evoke it in my turn at the beginning of these considerations on catechesis in the modern world.

Teaching through his life as a whole

9.1 In doing so, I am not forgetful that the majesty of Christ the Teacher and the unique consistency and persuasiveness of his teaching can only be explained by the fact that his words, his parables and his arguments are never separable from his life and his very being. Accordingly, the whole of Christ's life was a continual teaching: his silences, his miracles, his gestures, his prayer, his love for people, his special affection for the little and the poor, his acceptance of the total sacrifice on the Cross for the Redemption of the world, and his Resurrection are the actualization of his word and the fulfillment of revelation. Hence for Christians the crucifix is one of the most sublime and popular images of Christ the Teacher.

9.2 These considerations follow in the wake of the great traditions of the Church and they all strengthen our fervor with regard to Christ, the Teacher who reveals God to man and man to himself, the Teacher who saves, sanctifies and guides, who lives, who speaks, rouses, moves, redresses, judges, forgives, and goes with us day by day on the path of history, the Teacher who comes and will come in glory.

9.3 Only in deep communion with him will catechists find light and strength for an authentic, desirable renewal of catechesis.

---

[25] Mt 23:8. Saint Ignatius of Antioch takes up this affirmation and comments as follows: "We have received the faith; this is why we hold fast, in order to be recognized as disciples of Jesus Christ, our only Teacher" (*Epistola ad Magnesios*, 9, 2: *Patres Apostolici*, ed. F. X. Funk, I, 198).

[26] Jn 3:2.

[27] The portrayal of Christ as Teacher goes back as far as the Roman catacombs. It is frequently used in the mosaics of Romano-Byzantine art of the third and fourth centuries. It was to form a predominant artistic motif in the sculptures of the great Romanesque and Gothic cathedrals of the Middle Ages.

II

An Experience as Old as the Church

The mission of the Apostles

10.1 The image of Christ the Teacher was stamped on the spirit of the Twelve and of the first disciples, and the command "Go . . . and make disciples of all nations"[28] set the course for the whole of their lives. Saint John bears witness to this in his Gospel when he reports the words of Jesus: "No longer do I call you servants, for the servant does not know what his master is doing; but I have called you friends, for all that I have heard from my Father I have made known to you."[29] It was not they who chose to follow Jesus; it was Jesus who chose them, kept them with him, and appointed them even before his Passover, that they should go and bear fruit and that their fruit should remain.[30] For this reason he formally conferred on them after the Resurrection the mission of making disciples of all nations.

10.2 The whole of the Book of the Acts of the Apostles is a witness that they were faithful to their vocation and to the mission they had received. The members of the first Christian community are seen in it as "devoted to the Apostles' teaching and fellowship, to the breaking of bread and the prayers."[31] Without any doubt we find in that a lasting image of the Church being born of and continually nourished by the word of the Lord, thanks to the teaching of the Apostles, celebrating that word in the Eucharistic Sacrifice and bearing witness to it before the world in the sign of charity.

10.3 When those who opposed the Apostles took offense at their activity, it was because they were "annoyed because (the Apostles) were teaching the people"[32] and the order they gave them was not to teach at all in the name of Jesus.[33] But we know that the Apostles considered it right to listen to God rather than to men on this very matter.[34]

Catechesis in the apostolic age

11.1 The Apostles were not slow to share with others the ministry of apostleship.[35] They transmitted to their successors the task of teaching. They

---

[28] Mt 28:19.
[29] Jn 15:15.
[30] Cf. Jn 15:16.
[31] Acts 2:42.
[32] Acts 4:2.
[33] Cf. Acts 4:18, 5:28.
[34] Cf. Acts 4:19.
[35] Cf. Acts 1:25.

entrusted it also to the deacons from the moment of their institution: Stephen, "full of grace and power," taught unceasingly, moved by the wisdom of the Spirit.[36] The Apostles associated "many others" with themselves in the task of teaching,[37] and even simple Christians scattered by persecution "went about preaching the word."[38] Saint Paul was in a preeminent way the herald of this preaching, from Antioch to Rome, where the last picture of him that we have in Acts is that of a person "teaching about the Lord Jesus Christ quite openly."[39] His numerous letters continue and give greater depth to his teaching. The Letters of Peter, John, James and Jude are also, in every case, evidence of catechesis in the apostolic age.

11.2 Before being written down, the Gospels were the expression of an oral teaching passed on to the Christian communities, and they display with varying degrees of clarity a catechetical structure. Saint Matthew's account has indeed been called the catechist's Gospel, and Saint Mark's the catechumen's Gospel.

The Fathers of the Church

12.1 This mission of teaching that belonged to the Apostles and their first fellow workers was continued by the Church. Making herself day after day a disciple of the Lord, she earned the title of "Mother and Teacher."[40] From Clement of Rome to Origen,[41] the post-apostolic age saw the birth of remarkable works. Next we see a striking fact: some of the most impressive Bishops and pastors, especially in the third and fourth centuries considered it an important part of their episcopal ministry to deliver catechetical instructions and write treatises. It was the age of Cyril of Jerusalem and John Chrysostom, of Ambrose and Augustine, the age that saw the flowering, from the pen of numerous Fathers of the Church, of works that are still models for us.

12.2 It would be impossible here to recall, even very briefly, the catechesis

[36] Cf. Acts 6:8-10; cf. Philip catechizing the minister of the Queen of the Ethiopians: Acts 8:26-40.

[37] Cf. Acts 15:35.

[38] Acts 8:4.

[39] Acts 28:31.

[40] Cf. John XXIII, Encyclical Letter *Mater et Magistra* (May 15, 1961), intro.: *AAS* 53 (1961), 401: the Church is "mother" because by Baptism she unceasingly begets new children and increases God's family; she is "teacher" because she makes her children grow in the grace of their Baptism by nourishing their *sensus fidei* through instruction in the truths of faith.

[41] Cf., for example, the letter of Clement of Rome to the Church of Corinth, the *Didache*, the *Epistola Apostolorum*, the writings of Irenaeus of Lyons (*Demonstratio Apostolicae Praedicationis* and *Adversus Haereses*), of Tertullian (*De Baptismo*), of Clement of Alexandria (*Paedagogus*), of Cyprian (*Testimonia ad Quirinum*), of Origen (*Contra Celsum*), etc.

that gave support to the spread and advance of the Church in the various periods of history, in every continent, and in the widest variety of social and cultural contexts. There was indeed no lack of difficulties. But the word of the Lord completed its course down the centuries; it sped on and triumphed, to use the words of the Apostle Paul.[42]

Councils and missionary activity

13.1 The ministry of catechesis draws ever fresh energy from the Councils. The Council of Trent is a noteworthy example of this. It gave catechesis priority in its constitutions and decrees. It lies at the origin of the Roman Catechism, which is also known by the name of that Council and which is a work of the first rank as a summary of Christian teaching and traditional theology for use by priests. It gave rise to a remarkable organization of catechesis in the Church. It aroused the clergy to their duty of giving catechetical instruction. Thanks to the work of holy theologians such as Saint Charles Borromeo, Saint Robert Bellarmine and Saint Peter Canisius, it involved the publication of catechisms that were real models for that period. May the Second Vatican Council stir up in our time a like enthusiasm and similar activity!

13.2 The missions are also a special area for the application of catechesis. The People of God have thus continued for almost two thousand years to educate themselves in the faith in ways adapted to the various situations of believers and the many different circumstances in which the Church finds herself.

13.3 Catechesis is intimately bound up with the whole of the Church's life. Not only her geographical extension and numerical increase, but even more, her inner growth and correspondence with God's plan depend essentially on catechesis. It is worthwhile pointing out some of the many lessons to be drawn from the experiences in Church history that we have just recalled.

Catechesis as the Church's right and duty

14.1 To begin with, it is clear that the Church has always looked on catechesis as a sacred duty and an inalienable right. On the one hand, it is certainly a duty springing from a command given by the Lord and resting above all on those who in the New Covenant receive the call to the ministry of being pastors. On the other hand, one can likewise speak of a right: from the theological point of view every baptized person, precisely by reason of being baptized, has the right to receive from the Church instruction and education enabling him or her to enter on a truly Christian life; and from the viewpoint

---

[42] Cf. 2 Thess 3:1.

of human rights, every human being has the right to seek religious truth and adhere to it freely, that is to say, "without coercion on the part of individuals or of social groups and any human power," in such a way that in this matter of religion, "no one is to be forced to act against his or her conscience or prevented from acting in conformity to it."[43]

14.2 That is why catechetical activity should be able to be carried out in favorable circumstances of time and place, and should have access to the mass media and suitable equipment, without discrimination against parents, those receiving catechesis or those imparting it. At present this right is admittedly being given growing recognition, at least on the level of its main principles, as is shown by international declarations and conventions in which, whatever their limitations, one can recognize the desires of the consciences of many people today.[44] But the right is being violated by many States, even to the point that imparting catechesis, having it imparted, and receiving it become punishable offenses. I vigorously raise my voice in union with the Synod Fathers against all discrimination in the field of catechesis, and at the same time I again make a pressing appeal to those in authority to put a complete end to these constraints on human freedom in general and on religious freedom in particular.

Priority of this task

15 The second lesson concerns the place of catechesis in the Church's pastoral programs. The more the Church, whether on the local or the universal level, gives catechesis priority over other works and undertakings the results of which would be more spectacular, the more she finds in catechesis a strengthening of her internal life as a community of believers and of her external activity as a missionary Church. As the twentieth century draws to a close, the Church is bidden by God and by events — each of them a call from him — to renew her trust in catechetical activity as a prime aspect of her mission. She is bidden to offer catechesis her best resources in people and energy, without sparing effort, toil or material means, in order to organize it better and to train qualified personnel. This is no mere human calculation; it is an attitude of faith. And an attitude of faith always has reference to the faithfulness of God, who never fails to respond.

---

[43] Second Vatican Ecumenical Council, Declaration on Religious Freedom *Dignitatis Humanae*, 2: AAS 58 (1966), 930.

[44] Cf. United Nations Organization, The Universal Declaration of Human Rights (December 10, 1948), Article 18; The International Pact on Civil and Political Rights (December 16, 1966), Article 4; Final Act of the Conference on European Security and Cooperation, Paragraph VII.

Shared but differentiated responsibility

16 The third lesson is that catechesis always has been and always will be a work for which the whole Church must feel responsible and must wish to be responsible. But the Church's members have different responsibilities, derived from each one's mission. Because of their charge, Pastors have, at differing levels, the chief responsibility for fostering, guiding and coordinating catechesis. For his part, the Pope has a lively awareness of the primary responsibility that rests on him in this field: in this he finds reasons for pastoral concern but principally a source of joy and hope. Priests and Religious have in catechesis a preeminent field for their apostolate. On another level, parents have a unique responsibility. Teachers, the various ministers of the Church, catechists, and also organizers of social communications, all have in various degrees very precise responsibilities in this education of the believing conscience, an education that is important for the life of the Church and affects the life of society as such. It would be one of the best results of the General Assembly of the Synod that was entirely devoted to catechesis if it stirred up in the Church as a whole and in each sector of the Church a lively and active awareness of this differentiated but shared responsibility.

Continual balanced renewal

17 Finally, catechesis needs to be continually renewed by a certain broadening of its concept, by the revision of its methods, by the search for suitable language, and by the utilization of new means of transmitting the message. Renewal is sometimes unequal in value; the Synod Fathers realistically recognized, not only an undeniable advance in the vitality of catechetical activity and promising initiatives, but also the limitations or even "deficiencies" in what has been achieved to date.[45] These limitations are particularly serious when they endanger integrity of content. The Message to the People of God rightly stressed that "routine, with its refusal to accept any change, and improvisation, with its readiness for any venture, are equally dangerous" for catechesis.[46] Routine leads to stagnation, lethargy and eventual paralysis. Improvisation begets confusion on the part of those being given catechesis and, when these are children, on the part of their parents; it also begets all kinds of deviations, and the fracturing and eventually the complete destruction of unity. It is important for the Church to give proof today, as she has

---

[45] Cf. Synod of Bishops, Fourth Ordinary General Assembly, Message to the People of God (October 28, 1977), 1: *L'Osservatore Romano* (English-language edition), November 3, 1977, 3.

[46] Ibid., 6: loc. cit., 5.

done at other periods of her history, of evangelical wisdom, courage and fidelity in seeking out and putting into operation new methods and new prospects for catechetical instruction.

III

Catechesis in the Church's Pastoral and Missionary Activity

Catechesis as a stage in evangelization

18.1 Catechesis cannot be dissociated from the Church's pastoral and missionary activity as a whole. Nevertheless it has a specific character which was repeatedly the object of inquiry during the preparatory work and throughout the course of the Fourth General Assembly of the Synod of Bishops. The question also interests the public both within and outside the Church.

18.2 This is not the place for giving a rigorous formal definition of catechesis, which has been sufficiently explained in the General Catechetical Directory.[47] It is for specialists to clarify more and more its concept and divisions.

18.3 In view of uncertainties in practice, let us simply recall the essential landmarks — they are already solidly established in Church documents — that are essential for an exact understanding of catechesis and without which there is a risk of failing to grasp its full meaning and import.

18.4 All in all, it can be taken here that catechesis is an education of children, young people and adults in the faith, which includes especially the teaching of Christian doctrine imparted, generally speaking, in an organic and systematic way, with a view to initiating the hearers into the fullness of Christian life. Accordingly, while not being formally identified with them, catechesis is built on a certain number of elements of the Church's pastoral mission that have a catechetical aspect, that prepare for catechesis, or that spring from it. These elements are: the initial proclamation of the Gospel or missionary preaching through the kerygma to arouse faith, apologetics or examination of the reasons for belief, experience of Christian living, celebration of the sacraments, integration into the ecclesial community, and apostolic and missionary witness.

18.5 Let us first of all recall that there is no separation or opposition between catechesis and evangelization. Nor can the two be simply identified

---

[47] Sacred Congregation for the Clergy, General Catechetical Directory (April 11, 1971), 17-35: *AAS* 64 (1972), 110-118.

with each other. Instead, they have close links whereby they integrate and complement each other.

18.6 The Apostolic Exhortation *Evangelii Nuntiandi* of December 8, 1975, on evangelization in the modern world, rightly stressed that evangelization — which has the aim of bringing the Good News to the whole of humanity, so that all may live by it — is a rich, complex and dynamic reality, made up of elements, or one could say moments, that are essential and different from each other, and that must all be kept in view simultaneously.[48] Catechesis is one of these moments — a very remarkable one — in the whole process of evangelization.

Catechesis and the initial proclamation of the Gospel

19.1 The specific character of catechesis, as distinct from the initial conversion-bringing proclamation of the Gospel, has the twofold objective of maturing the initial faith and of educating the true disciple of Christ by means of a deeper and more systematic knowledge of the Person and the message of our Lord Jesus Christ.[49]

19.2 But in catechetical practice, this model order must allow for the fact that the initial evangelization has often not taken place. A certain number of children baptized in infancy come for catechesis in the parish without receiving any other initiation into the faith and still without any explicit personal attachment to Jesus Christ; they only have the capacity to believe placed within them by Baptism and the presence of the Holy Spirit; and opposition is quickly created by the prejudices of their non-Christian family background or of the positivist spirit of their education. In addition, there are other children who have not been baptized and whose parents agree only at a later date to religious education: for practical reasons, the catechumenal stage of these children will often be carried out largely in the course of the ordinary catechesis. Again, many preadolescents and adolescents who have been baptized and been given a systematic catechesis and the sacraments still remain hesitant for a long time about committing their whole lives to Jesus Christ, even though they do actually try to avoid religious education in the name of their freedom. Finally, even adults are not safe from temptations to doubt or to abandon their faith, especially as a result of their unbelieving surroundings. This means that "catechesis" must often concern itself not only with nourishing and teaching the faith, but also with arousing it

---

[48] Cf. Nos. 17-24: *AAS* 68 (1976), 17-22.

[49] Cf. Synod of Bishops, Fourth Ordinary General Assembly, Message to the People of God (October 28, 1977), 1: *L'Osservatore Romano* (English-language edition), November 3, 1977, 3.

unceasingly with the help of grace, with opening the heart, with converting, and with preparing total adherence to Jesus Christ on the part of those who are still on the threshold of faith. This concern will in part decide the tone, the language and the method of catechesis.

Specific aim of catechesis

20.1 Nevertheless, the specific aim of catechesis is to develop, with God's help, an as yet initial faith, and to advance in fullness and to nourish day by day the Christian life of the faithful, young and old. It is in fact a matter of giving growth, at the level of knowledge and in life, to the seed of faith sown by the Holy Spirit with the initial proclamation and effectively transmitted by Baptism.

20.2 Catechesis aims therefore at developing understanding of the mystery of Christ in the light of God's word, so that the whole of a person's humanity is impregnated by that word. Changed by the working of grace into a new creature, the Christian thus sets himself to follow Christ and learns more and more within the Church to think like him, to judge like him, to act in conformity with his commandments, and to hope as he invites us to.

20.3 To put it more precisely: within the whole process of evangelization, the aim of catechesis is to be the teaching and maturation stage, that is to say, the period in which the Christian, having accepted by faith the Person of Jesus Christ as the one Lord and having given him complete adherence by sincere conversion of heart, endeavors to know better this Jesus to whom he has entrusted himself: to know his "mystery," the Kingdom of God proclaimed by him, the requirements and promises contained in his Gospel message, and the paths that he has laid down for anyone who wishes to follow him.

20.4 It is true that being a Christian means saying "yes" to Jesus Christ, but let us remember that this "yes" has two levels: it consists in surrendering to the word of God and relying on it, but it also means, at a later stage, endeavoring to know better and better the profound meaning of this word.

Need for systematic catechesis

21.1 In his closing speech at the Fourth General Assembly of the Synod, Pope Paul VI rejoiced "to see how everyone drew attention to the absolute need for systematic catechesis, precisely because it is this reflective study of the Christian mystery that fundamentally distinguishes catechesis from all other ways of presenting the word of God."[50]

---

[50] Address at the Closing of the Synod of Bishops, Fourth Ordinary General Assembly (October 29, 1977): *AAS* 69 (1977), 634.

21.2 In view of practical difficulties, attention must be drawn to some of the characteristics of this instruction:

— it must be systematic, not improvised but programmed to reach a precise goal;

— it must deal with essentials, without any claim to tackle all disputed questions or to transform itself into theological research or scientific exegesis;

— it must nevertheless be sufficiently complete, not stopping short at the initial proclamation of the Christian mystery such as we have in the kerygma;

— it must be an integral Christian initiation, open to all the other factors of Christian life.

21.3 I am not forgetting the interest of the many different occasions for catechesis connected with personal, family, social and ecclesial life — these occasions must be utilized and I shall return to them in chapter VI — but I am stressing the need for organic and systematic Christian instruction, because of the tendency in various quarters to minimize its importance.

Catechesis and life experience

22.1 It is useless to play off orthopraxy against orthodoxy: Christianity is inseparably both. Firm and well-thought-out convictions lead to courageous and upright action; the endeavor to educate the faithful to live as disciples of Christ today calls for and facilitates a discovery in depth of the mystery of Christ in the history of salvation.

22.2 It is also quite useless to campaign for the abandonment of serious and orderly study of the message of Christ in the name of a method concentrating on life experience. "No one can arrive at the whole truth on the basis solely of some simple private experience, that is to say, without an adequate explanation of the message of Christ, who is 'the way, and the truth, and the life' (Jn 14:6)."[51]

22.3 Nor is any opposition to be set up between a catechesis taking life as its point of departure and a traditional doctrinal and systematic catechesis.[52] Authentic catechesis is always an orderly and systematic initiation into the revelation that God has given of himself to humanity in Christ Jesus, a revelation stored in the depths of the Church's memory and in Sacred Scripture, and constantly communicated from one generation to the next by a living, active *traditio.* This revelation is not, however, isolated from life or artificially juxtaposed to it. It is concerned with the ultimate meaning of life and it illu-

[51] Ibid.

[52] Sacred Congregation for the Clergy, General Catechetical Directory (April 11, 1971), 40, 46: *AAS* 64 (1972), 121, 124-125.

mines the whole of life with the light of the Gospel, to inspire it or to question it.

22.4 That is why we can apply to catechists an expression used by the Second Vatican Council with special reference to priests: "instructors (of the human being and his life) in the faith."[53]

Catechesis and sacraments

23.1 Catechesis is intrinsically linked with the whole of liturgical and sacramental activity, for it is in the sacraments, especially in the Eucharist, that Christ Jesus works in fullness for the transformation of human beings.

23.2 In the early Church, the catechumenate and preparation for the Sacraments of Baptism and the Eucharist were the same thing. Although in the countries that have long been Christian the Church has changed her practice in this field, the catechumenate has never been abolished; on the contrary, it is experiencing a renewal in those countries[54] and is abundantly practiced in the young missionary Churches. In any case, catechesis always has reference to the sacraments. On the one hand, the catechesis that prepares for the sacraments is an eminent kind, and every form of catechesis necessarily leads to the sacraments of faith. On the other hand, authentic practice of the sacraments is bound to have a catechetical aspect. In other words, sacramental life is impoverished and very soon turns into hollow ritualism if it is not based on serious knowledge of the meaning of the sacraments, and catechesis becomes intellectualized if it fails to come alive in the sacramental practice.

Catechesis and ecclesial community

24.1 Finally, catechesis is closely linked with the responsible activity of the Church and of Christians in the world. A person who has given adherence to Jesus Christ by faith and is endeavoring to consolidate that faith by catechesis needs to live in communion with those who have taken the same step. Catechesis runs the risk of becoming barren if no community of faith and Christian life takes the catechumen in at a certain stage of his catechesis. That is why the ecclesial community at all levels has a twofold responsibility with regard to catechesis: it has the responsibility of providing for the training of its members, but it also has the responsibility of welcoming them into an environment where they can live as fully as possible what they have learned.

24.2 Catechesis is likewise open to missionary dynamism. If catechesis is done well, Christians will be eager to bear witness to their faith, to hand it on

---

[53] Cf. Decree on the Ministry and Life of Priests *Presbyterorum Ordinis*, 6: *AAS* 58 (1966), 999.

[54] Cf. Rite of Christian Initiation of Adults.

to their children, to make it known to others, and to serve the human community in every way.

Catechesis in the wide sense necessary for maturity and strength of faith

25.1 Thus through catechesis the Gospel kerygma (the initial ardent proclamation by which a person is one day overwhelmed and brought to the decision to entrust himself to Jesus Christ by faith) is gradually deepened, developed in its implicit consequences, explained in language that includes an appeal to reason, and channeled toward Christian practice in the Church and the world. All this is no less evangelical than the kerygma, in spite of what is said by certain people who consider that catechesis necessarily rationalizes, dries up and eventually kills all that is living, spontaneous and vibrant in the kerygma. The truths studied in catechesis are the same truths that touched the person's heart when he heard them for the first time. Far from blunting or exhausting them, the fact of knowing them better should make them even more challenging and decisive for one's life.

25.2 In the understanding expounded here, catechesis keeps the entirely pastoral perspective with which the Synod viewed it. This broad meaning of catechesis in no way contradicts but rather includes and goes beyond a narrow meaning which was once commonly given to catechesis in didactic expositions, namely, the simple teaching of the formulas that express faith.

25.3 In the final analysis, catechesis is necessary both for the maturation of the faith of Christians and for their witness in the world: it is aimed at bringing Christians to "attain to the unity of the faith and of the knowledge of the Son of God, to mature manhood, to the measure of the stature of the fullness of Christ"[55]; it is also aimed at making them prepared to make a defense to anyone who calls them to account for the hope that is in them.[56]

IV

The Whole of the Good News Drawn from Its Source

Content of the message

26 Since catechesis is a moment or aspect of evangelization, its content cannot be anything else but the content of evangelization as a whole. The one

---

[55] Eph 4:13.
[56] Cf. 1 Pet 3:15.

message — the Good News of salvation — that has been heard once or hundreds of times and has been accepted with the heart, is in catechesis probed unceasingly by reflection and systematic study, by awareness of its repercussions on one's personal life — an awareness calling for ever greater commitment — and by inserting it into an organic and harmonious whole, namely, Christian living in society and the world.

The source

27.1 Catechesis will always draw its content from the living source of the word of God transmitted in Tradition and the Scriptures, for "Sacred Tradition and Sacred Scripture make up a single sacred deposit of the word of God, which is entrusted to the Church," as was recalled by the Second Vatican Council, which desired that "the ministry of the word — pastoral preaching, catechetics and all forms of Christian instruction . . . — (should be) healthily nourished and (should) thrive in holiness through the word of Scripture."[57]

27.2 To speak of Tradition and Scripture as the source of catechesis is to draw attention to the fact that catechesis must be impregnated and penetrated by the thought, the spirit and the outlook of the Bible and the Gospels through assiduous contact with the texts themselves; but it is also a reminder that catechesis will be all the richer and more effective for reading the texts with the intelligence and the heart of the Church and for drawing inspiration from the 2,000 years of the Church's reflection and life.

27.3 The Church's teaching, liturgy and life spring from this source and lead back to it, under the guidance of the Pastors and, in particular, of the doctrinal Magisterium entrusted to them by the Lord.

The Creed, an exceptionally important expression of doctrine

28.1 An exceptionally important expression of the living heritage placed in the custody of the Pastors is found in the Creed or, to put it more concretely, in the Creeds that at crucial moments have summed up the Church's faith in felicitous syntheses. In the course of the centuries an important element of catechesis was constituted by the *traditio Symboli* (transmission of the summary of the faith), followed by the transmission of the Lord's Prayer. This expressive rite has in our time been reintroduced into the initiation of cat-

---

[57] Dogmatic Constitution on Divine Revelation *Dei Verbum*, 10, 24: *AAS* 58 (1966), 822, 828-829; cf. Sacred Congregation for the Clergy, General Catechetical Directory (April 11, 1971), 45 (*AAS* 64 [1972], 124), where the principal and complementary sources of catechesis are well set out.

echumens.[58] Should not greater use be made of an adapted form of it to mark that most important stage at which a new disciple of Jesus Christ accepts with full awareness and courage the content of what will from then on be the object of his earnest study?

28.2 In the Creed of the People of God, proclaimed at the close of the nineteenth centenary of the martyrdom of the Apostles Peter and Paul, my Predecessor Paul VI decided to bring together the essential elements of the Catholic faith, especially those that presented greater difficulty or risked being ignored.[59] This is a sure point of reference for the content of catechesis.

Factors that must not be neglected

29.1 In the third chapter of his Apostolic Exhortation *Evangelii Nuntiandi,* the same Pope recalled "the essential content, the living substance" of evangelization.[60] Catechesis, too, must keep in mind each of these factors and also the living synthesis of which they are part.[61]

29.2 I shall therefore limit myself here simply to recalling one or two points.[62] Anyone can see, for instance, how important it is to make the child, the adolescent, the person advancing in faith understand "what can be known about God"[63]; to be able in a way to tell them: "What you worship as unknown, this I proclaim to you"[64]; to set forth briefly for them[65] the mystery of the Word of God become man and accomplishing man's salvation by his Passover, that is to say, through his Death and Resurrection, but also by his preaching, by the

---

[58] Cf. Rite of Christian Initiation of Adults, 25-26, 183-187.

[59] Cf. (June 30, 1968): *AAS* 60 (1968), 436-445. Besides these great professions of faith of the Magisterium, note also the popular professions of faith, rooted in the traditional Christian culture of certain countries; cf. what I said to the young people at Gniezno, June 3, 1979, regarding the Bogurodzica song-message: "This is not only a song: it is also a profession of faith, a symbol of the Polish Credo, it is a catechesis and also a document of Christian education. The principal truths of faith and the principles of morality are contained here. This is not only a historical object. It is a document of life. [It has even been called] 'the Polish catechism' ": *AAS* 71 (1979), 754.

[60] (December 8, 1975), 25: *AAS* 68 (1976), 23.

[61] Ibid., especially 26-39: loc. cit., 23-30. The "principal elements of the Christian message" are presented in a more systematic fashion in the General Catechetical Directory (April 11, 1971), 47-69 (*AAS* 64 [1972], 125-141), where one also finds the norm for the essential doctrinal content of catechesis.

[62] Consult also on this point the General Catechetical Directory (April 11, 1971), 37-46: *AAS* 64 (1972), 120-125.

[63] Rom 1:19.

[64] Acts 17:23.

[65] Cf. Eph 3:3.

signs worked by him, and by the sacraments of his permanent presence in our midst. The Synod Fathers were indeed inspired when they asked that care should be taken not to reduce Christ to his humanity alone or his message to no more than an earthly dimension, but that he should be recognized as the Son of God, the mediator giving us in the Spirit free access to the Father.[66]

29.3 It is important to display before the eyes of the intelligence and of the heart, in the light of faith, the sacrament of Christ's presence constituted by the mystery of the Church, which is an assembly of human beings who are sinners and yet have at the same time been sanctified and who make up the family of God gathered together by the Lord under the guidance of those whom "the Holy Spirit has made . . . guardians, to feed the Church of God."[67]

29.4 It is important to explain that the history of the human race, marked as it is by grace and sin, greatness and misery, is taken up by God in his Son Jesus, "foreshadowing in some way the age which is to come."[68]

29.5 Finally, it is important to reveal frankly the demands — demands that involve self-denial but also joy — made by what the Apostle Paul liked to call "newness of life,"[69] "a new creation,"[70] being in Christ,[71] and "eternal life in Christ Jesus,"[72] which is the same thing as life in the world but lived in accordance with the Beatitudes and called to an extension and transfiguration hereafter.

29.6 Hence the importance in catechesis of personal moral commitments in keeping with the Gospel and of Christian attitudes, whether heroic or very simple, to life and the world — what we call the Christian or evangelical virtues. Hence also, in its endeavor to educate faith, the concern of catechesis not to omit but to clarify properly realities such as man's activity for his integral liberation,[73] the search for a society with greater solidarity and fraternity, the fight for justice and the building of peace.

29.7 Besides, it is not to be thought that this dimension of catechesis is altogether new. As early as the patristic age, Saint Ambrose and Saint John Chrysostom — to quote only them — gave prominence to the social conse-

---

[66] Cf. Eph 2:18.

[67] Acts 20:28.

[68] Second Vatican Ecumenical Council, Pastoral Constitution on the Church in the Modern World *Gaudium et Spes,* 39: *AAS* 58 (1966), 1056-1057.

[69] Rom 6:4.

[70] 2 Cor 5:17.

[71] Cf. 2 Cor 5:17.

[72] Rom 6:23.

[73] Cf. Paul VI, Apostolic Exhortation *Evangelii Nuntiandi* (December 8, 1975), 30-38: *AAS* 68 (1976), 25-30.

quences of the demands made by the Gospel. Close to our own time, the catechism of Saint Pius X explicitly listed oppressing the poor and depriving workers of their just wages among the sins that cry to God for vengeance.[74] Since *Rerum Novarum* especially, social concern has been actively present in the catechetical teaching of the Popes and the Bishops. Many Synod Fathers rightly insisted that the rich heritage of the Church's social teaching should, in appropriate forms, find a place in the general catechetical education of the faithful.

Integrity of content

30.1 With regard to the content of catechesis, three important points deserve special attention today.

30.2 The first point concerns the integrity of the content. In order that the sacrificial offering of his or her faith[75] should be perfect, the person who becomes a disciple of Christ has the right to receive "the word of faith"[76] not in mutilated, falsified or diminished form but whole and entire, in all its rigor and vigor. Unfaithfulness on some point to the integrity of the message means a dangerous weakening of catechesis and putting at risk the results that Christ and the ecclesial community have a right to expect from it. It is certainly not by chance that the final command of Jesus in Matthew's Gospel bears the mark of a certain entireness: "All authority . . . has been given to me . . . make disciples of all nations . . . teaching them to observe all . . . I am with you always." This is why, when a person first becomes aware of "the surpassing worth of knowing Christ Jesus,"[77] whom he has encountered by faith, and has the perhaps unconscious desire to know him more extensively and better, "hearing about him and being taught in him, as the truth is in Jesus,"[78] there is no valid pretext for refusing him any part whatever of that knowledge. What kind of catechesis would it be that failed to give their full place to man's creation and sin; to God's plan of redemption and its long, loving preparation and realization; to the Incarnation of the Son of God; to Mary, the Immaculate One, the Mother of God, ever Virgin, raised body and soul to the glory of heaven, and to her role in the mystery of salvation; to the mystery of lawlessness at work in our lives[79] and the power of God freeing us from it; to the need for penance and asceticism; to the sacramental and liturgical actions; to the reality of the Eucharistic presence; to participation in divine life here and hereafter, and so on? Thus, no true cat-

---

[74] Cf. *Catechismo maggiore*, Part V, Chapter 6, 965-966.
[75] Cf. Phil 2:17.
[76] Rom 10:8.
[77] Phil 3:8.
[78] Cf. Eph 4:20-21.
[79] Cf. 2 Thess 2:7.

echist can lawfully, on his own initiative, make a selection of what he considers important in the deposit of faith as opposed to what he considers unimportant, so as to teach the one and reject the other.

By means of suitable pedagogical methods

31 This gives rise to a second remark. It can happen that in the present situation of catechesis, reasons of method or pedagogy suggest that the communication of the riches of the content of catechesis should be organized in one way rather than another. Besides, integrity does not dispense from balance and from the organic hierarchical character through which the truths to be taught, the norms to be transmitted, and the ways of Christian life to be indicated will be given the proper importance due to each. It can also happen that a particular sort of language proves preferable for transmitting this content to a particular individual or group. The choice made will be a valid one to the extent that, far from being dictated by more or less subjective theories or prejudices stamped with a certain ideology, it is inspired by the humble concern to stay closer to a content that must remain intact. The method and language used must truly be means for communicating the whole and not just a part of "the words of eternal life"[80] and the "ways of life."[81]

Ecumenical dimension of catechesis

32.1 The great movement, one certainly inspired by the Spirit of Jesus, that has for some years been causing the Catholic Church to seek with other Christian Churches or confessions the restoration of the perfect unity willed by the Lord, brings me to the question of the ecumenical character of catechesis. This movement reached its full prominence in the Second Vatican Council[82] and since then has taken on a new extension within the Church, as is shown concretely by the impressive series of events and initiatives with which everyone is now familiar.

32.2 Catechesis cannot remain aloof from this ecumenical dimension, since all the faithful are called to share, according to their capacity and place in the Church, in the movement toward unity.[83]

32.3 Catechesis will have an ecumenical dimension if, while not ceasing to teach that the fullness of the revealed truths and of the means of salvation

---

[80] Jn 6:69; cf. Acts 5:20, 7:38.

[81] Acts 2:28, quoting Ps 16:11.

[82] Cf. the entire Decree on Ecumenism *Unitatis Redintegratio: AAS* 57 (1965), 90-112.

[83] Cf. ibid., 5: loc. cit., 96; cf. also Second Vatican Ecumenical Council, Decree on the Church's Missionary Activity *Ad Gentes,* 15: *AAS* 58 (1966), 963-965; Sacred Congregation for the Clergy, General Catechetical Directory (April 11, 1971), 27: *AAS* 64 (1972), 115.

instituted by Christ is found in the Catholic Church,[84] it does so with sincere respect, in words and in deeds, for the Ecclesial Communities that are not in perfect communion with this Church.

32.4 In this context, it is extremely important to give a correct and fair presentation of the other Churches and Ecclesial Communities that the Spirit of Christ does not refrain from using as means of salvation; "moreover, some, even very many, of the outstanding elements and endowments which together go to build up and give life to the Church herself, can exist outside the visible boundaries of the Catholic Church."[85] Among other things this presentation will help Catholics to have both a deeper understanding of their own faith and a better acquaintance with and esteem for their other Christian brethren, thus facilitating the shared search for the way toward full unity in the whole truth. It should also help non-Catholics to have a better knowledge and appreciation of the Catholic Church and her conviction of being the "universal help toward salvation."

32.5 Catechesis will have an ecumenical dimension if, in addition, it creates and fosters a true desire for unity. This will be true all the more if it inspires serious efforts — including the effort of self-purification in the humility and the fervor of the Spirit in order to clear the ways — with a view not to facile irenics made up of omissions and concessions on the level of doctrine, but to perfect unity, when and by what means the Lord will wish.

32.6 Finally, catechesis will have an ecumenical dimension if it tries to prepare Catholic children and young people, as well as adults, for living in contact with non-Catholics, affirming their Catholic identity while respecting the faith of others.

Ecumenical collaboration in the field of catechesis

33.1 In situations of religious plurality, the Bishops can consider it opportune or even necessary to have certain experiences of collaboration in the field of catechesis between Catholics and other Christians, complementing the normal catechesis that must in any case be given to Catholics. Such experiences have a theological foundation in the elements shared by all Christians.[86] But the communion of faith between Catholics and other Christians is not complete and perfect; in certain cases there are even profound divergences. Consequently, this ecumenical collaboration is by its very nature limited: it must

---

[84] Cf. Second Vatican Ecumenical Council, Decree on Ecumenism *Unitatis Redintegratio,* 3-4: *AAS* 57 (1965), 92-96.

[85] Ibid., 3: loc. cit., 93.

[86] Cf. ibid.; cf. also Second Vatican Ecumenical Council, Dogmatic Constitution on the Church *Lumen Gentium,* 15: *AAS* 57 (1965), 19.

never mean a "reduction" to a common minimum. Furthermore, catechesis does not consist merely in the teaching of doctrine: it also means initiating into the whole of Christian life, bringing full participation in the sacraments of the Church. Therefore, where there is an experience of ecumenical collaboration in the field of catechesis, care must be taken that the education of Catholics in the Catholic Church should be well ensured in matters of doctrine and of Christian living.

33.2 During the Synod, a certain number of Bishops drew attention to what they referred to as the increasingly frequent cases in which the civil authority or other circumstances impose on the schools in some countries a common instruction in the Christian religion, with common textbooks, class periods, etc., for Catholics and non-Catholics alike. Needless to say, this is not true catechesis. But this teaching also has ecumenical importance when it presents Christian doctrine fairly and honestly. In cases where circumstances impose it, it is important that in addition a specifically Catholic catechesis should be ensured with all the greater care.

The question of textbooks dealing with the various religions

34 At this point another observation must be made on the same lines but from a different point of view. State schools sometimes provide their pupils with books that for cultural reasons (history, morals or literature) present the various religions, including the Catholic religion. An objective presentation of historical events, of the different religions and of the various Christian confessions can make a contribution here to better mutual understanding. Care will then be taken that every effort is made to ensure that the presentation is truly objective and free from the distorting influence of ideological and political systems or of prejudices with claims to be scientific. In any case, such schoolbooks can obviously not be considered catechetical works: they lack both the witness of believers stating their faith to other believers and an understanding of the Christian mysteries and of what is specific about Catholicism, as these are understood within the faith.

V

Everybody Needs To Be Catechized

The importance of children and the young

35.1 The theme designated by my Predecessor Paul VI for the Fourth General Assembly of the Synod of Bishops was: "Catechesis in our time, with special reference to the catechesis of children and young people." The increase in the number of young people is without doubt a fact charged with hope and at the same time with anxiety for a large part of the contemporary world. In certain countries, especially those of the Third World, more than half of the population is under twenty-five or thirty years of age. This means millions and millions of children and young people preparing for their adult future. And there is more than just the factor of numbers: recent events, as well as the daily news, tell us that, although this countless multitude of young people is here and there dominated by uncertainty and fear, seduced by the escapism of indifference or drugs, or tempted by nihilism and violence, nevertheless it constitutes in its major part the great force that amid many hazards is set on building the civilization of the future.

35.2 In our pastoral care we ask ourselves: how are we to reveal Jesus Christ, God made man, to this multitude of children and young people, reveal him not just in the fascination of a first fleeting encounter but through an acquaintance, growing deeper and clearer daily, with him, his message, the plan of God that he has revealed, the call he addresses to each person, and the Kingdom that he wishes to establish in this world with the "little flock"[87] of those who believe in him, a Kingdom that will be complete only in eternity? How are we to enable them to know the meaning, the import, the fundamental requirements, the law of love, the promises and the hopes of this Kingdom?

35.3 There are many observations that could be made about the special characteristics that catechesis assumes at the different stages of life.

Infants

36 One moment that is often decisive is the one at which the very young child receives the first elements of catechesis from its parents and the family surroundings. These elements will perhaps be no more than a simple revelation of a good and provident Father in heaven to whom the child learns to turn its heart. The very short prayers that the child learns to lisp will be the start of a loving dialogue with this hidden God whose word it will then begin to hear. I cannot insist too strongly on this early initiation by Christian parents in which the child's faculties are integrated into a living relationship with God. It is a work of prime importance. It demands great love and profound respect for the child who has a right to a simple and true presentation of the Christian faith.

---

[87] Lk 12:32.

Children

37 For the child there comes soon, at school and in church, in institutions connected with the parish or with the spiritual care of the Catholic or State school not only an introduction into a wider social circle, but also the moment for a catechesis aimed at inserting him or her organically into the life of the Church, a moment that includes an immediate preparation for the celebration of the sacraments. This catechesis is didactic in character, but is directed toward the giving of witness in the faith. It is an initial catechesis but not a fragmentary one, since it will have to reveal, although in an elementary way, all the principal mysteries of faith and their effects on the child's moral and religious life. It is a catechesis that gives meaning to the sacraments, but at the same time it receives from the experience of the sacraments a living dimension that keeps it from remaining merely doctrinal, and it communicates to the child the joy of being a witness to Christ in ordinary life.

Adolescents

38 Next comes puberty and adolescence, with all the greatness and dangers which that age brings. It is the time of discovering oneself and one's own inner world, the time of generous plans, the time when the feeling of love awakens, with the biological impulses of sexuality, the time of the desire to be together, the time of a particularly intense joy connected with the exhilarating discovery of life. But often it is also the age of deeper questioning, of anguished or even frustrating searching, of a certain mistrust of others and dangerous introspection, and the age sometimes of the first experiences of setbacks and of disappointments. Catechesis cannot ignore these changeable aspects of this delicate period of life. A catechesis capable of leading the adolescent to reexamine his or her life and to engage in dialogue, a catechesis that does not ignore the adolescent's great questions — self-giving, belief, love and the means of expressing it constituted by sexuality — such a catechesis can be decisive. The revelation of Jesus Christ as a friend, guide and model, capable of being admired but also imitated; the revelation of his message which provides an answer to the fundamental questions; the revelation of the loving plan of Christ the Savior as the incarnation of the only authentic love and as the possibility of uniting the human race — all this can provide the basis for genuine education in faith. Above all, the mysteries of the Passion and Death of Jesus, through which, according to Saint Paul, he merited his glorious Resurrection, can speak eloquently to the adolescent's conscience and heart and cast light on his first sufferings and on the suffering of the world that he is discovering.

The young

39.1 With youth comes the moment of the first great decisions. Although the young may enjoy the support of the members of their family and their friends, they have to rely on themselves and their own conscience and must ever more frequently and decisively assume responsibility for their destiny. Good and evil, grace and sin, life and death will more and more confront one another within them, not just as moral categories but chiefly as fundamental options which they must accept or reject lucidly, conscious of their own responsibility. It is obvious that a catechesis which denounces selfishness in the name of generosity, and which without any illusory over-simplification presents the Christian meaning of work, of the common good, of justice and charity, a catechesis on international peace and on the advancement of human dignity, on development, and on liberation, as these are presented in recent documents of the Church,[88] fittingly completes in the minds of the young the good catechesis on strictly religious realities which is never to be neglected. Catechesis then takes on considerable importance, since it is the time when the Gospel can be presented, understood and accepted as capable of giving meaning to life and thus of inspiring attitudes that would have no other explanation, such as self-sacrifice, detachment, forbearance, justice, commitment, reconciliation, a sense of the Absolute and the unseen. All these are traits that distinguish a young person from his or her companions as a disciple of Jesus Christ.

39.2 Catechesis thus prepares for the important Christian commitments of adult life. For example, it is certain that many vocations to the priesthood and religious life have their origin during a well-imparted catechesis in infancy and adolescence.

39.3 From infancy until the threshold of maturity, catechesis is thus a permanent school of the faith and follows the major stages of life, like a beacon lighting the path of the child, the adolescent and the young person.

The adaptation of catechesis for young people

40.1 It is reassuring to note that, during the Fourth General Assembly of the Synod and the following years, the Church has widely shared the concern about how to impart catechesis to children and young people. God grant that

---

[88] See, for example, Second Vatican Ecumenical Council, Pastoral Constitution on the Church in the Modern World *Gaudium et Spes*: *AAS* 58 (1966), 1025-1120; Paul VI, Encyclical Letter *Populorum Progressio* (March 26, 1967): *AAS* 59 (1967), 257-299; Apostolic Letter *Octogesima Adveniens* (May 14, 1971): *AAS* 63 (1971), 401-441; Apostolic Exhortation *Evangelii Nuntiandi* (December 8, 1975): *AAS* 68 (1976), 5-76.

the attention thus aroused will long endure in the Church's consciousness! In this way the Synod has been valuable for the whole Church by seeking to trace with the greatest possible precision the complex characteristics of present-day youth; by showing that these young persons speak a language into which the message of Jesus must be translated with patience and wisdom and without betrayal; by demonstrating that, in spite of appearances, these young people have within them, even though often in a confused way, not just a readiness or openness, but rather a real desire to know "Jesus . . . who is called Christ"[89]; and by indicating that if the work of catechesis is to be carried out rigorously and seriously, it is today more difficult and tiring than ever before, because of the obstacles and difficulties of all kinds that it meets; but it is also more consoling, because of the depth of the response it receives from children and young people. This is a treasure which the Church can and should count on in the years ahead.

40.2 Some categories of young people to whom catechesis is directed call for special attention because of their particular situation.

The handicapped

41 Children and young people who are physically or mentally handicapped come first to mind. They have a right, like others of their age, to know "the mystery of faith." The greater difficulties that they encounter give greater merit to their efforts and to those of their teachers. It is pleasant to see that Catholic organizations especially dedicated to young handicapped people contributed to the Synod a renewed desire to deal better with this important problem. They deserve to be given warm encouragement in this endeavor.

Young people without religious support

42 My thoughts turn next to the ever increasing number of children and young people born and brought up in a non-Christian or at least non-practicing home but who wish to know the Christian faith. They must be ensured a catechesis attuned to them, so that they will be able to grow in faith and live by it more and more, in spite of the lack of support or even the opposition they meet in their surroundings.

Adults

43 To continue the series of receivers of catechesis, I cannot fail to emphasize now one of the most constant concerns of the Synod Fathers, a concern imposed with vigor and urgency by present experiences throughout the world:

[89] Mt 1:16.

I am referring to the central problem of the catechesis of adults. This is the principal form of catechesis, because it is addressed to persons who have the greatest responsibilities and the capacity to live the Christian message in its fully developed form.[90] The Christian community cannot carry out a permanent catechesis without the direct and skilled participation of adults, whether as receivers or as promoters of catechetical activity. The world, in which the young are called to live and to give witness to the faith which catechesis seeks to deepen and strengthen, is governed by adults. The faith of these adults too should continually be enlightened, stimulated and renewed, so that it may pervade the temporal realities in their charge. Thus, for catechesis to be effective, it must be permanent, and it would be quite useless if it stopped short at the threshold of maturity, since catechesis, admittedly under another form, proves no less necessary for adults.

Quasi-catechumens

44 Among the adults who need catechesis, our pastoral missionary concern is directed to those who were born and reared in areas not yet Christianized, and who have never been able to study deeply the Christian teaching that the circumstances of life have at a certain moment caused them to come across. It is also directed to those who in childhood received a catechesis suited to their age but who later drifted away from all religious practice and as adults find themselves with religious knowledge of a rather childish kind. It is likewise directed to those who feel the effects of a catechesis received early in life but badly imparted or badly assimilated. It is directed to those who, although they were born in a Christian country or in sociologically Christian surroundings, have never been educated in their faith and, as adults, are really catechumens.

Diversified and complementary forms of catechesis

45.1 Catechesis is therefore for adults of every age, including the elderly — persons who deserve particular attention in view of their experience and their problems — no less than for children, adolescents and the young. We should also mention migrants, those who are bypassed by modern developments, those who live in areas of large cities which are often without churches, build-

---

[90] Cf. Second Vatican Ecumenical Council, Decree on the Bishops' Pastoral Office in the Church *Christus Dominus,* 14: *AAS* 58 (1966), 679; Decree on the Church's Missionary Activity *Ad Gentes,* 14: *AAS* 58 (1966), 962-963; Sacred Congregation for the Clergy, General Catechetical Directory (April 11, 1971), 20: *AAS* 64 (1972), 112; cf. also Rite of Christian Initiation of Adults.

ings and suitable organization, and other such groups. It is desirable that initiatives meant to give all these groups a Christian formation, with appropriate means (audio-visual aids, booklets, discussions, lectures), should increase in number, enabling many adults to fill the gap left by an insufficient or deficient catechesis, to complete harmoniously at a higher level their childhood catechesis, or even to prepare themselves enough in this field to be able to help others in a more serious way.

45.2 It is important also that the catechesis of children and young people, permanent catechesis, and the catechesis of adults should not be separate watertight compartments. It is even more important that there should be no break between them. On the contrary, their perfect complementarity must be fostered: adults have much to give to young people and children in the field of catechesis, but they can also receive much from them for the growth of their own Christian lives.

45.3 It must be restated that nobody in the Church of Jesus Christ should feel excused from receiving catechesis. This is true even of young seminarians and young Religious, and of all those called to the task of being pastors and catechists. They will fulfill this task all the better if they are humble pupils of the Church, the great giver as well as the great receiver of catechesis.

VI

Some Ways and Means of Catechesis

Communications media

46.1 From the oral teaching by the Apostles and the letters circulating among the Churches down to the most modern means, catechesis has not ceased to look for the most suitable ways and means for its mission, with the active participation of the communities and at the urging of the Pastors. This effort must continue.

46.2 I think immediately of the great possibilities offered by the means of social communication and the means of group communication: television, radio, the press, records, tape-recordings — the whole series of audio-visual means. The achievements in these spheres are such as to encourage the greatest hope. Experience shows, for example, the effect had by instruction given on radio or television, when it combines a high aesthetic level and rigorous fidelity to the Magisterium. The Church now has many opportunities for considering these questions — as, for instance, on Social Communications Days — and it is not necessary to speak of them at length here, in spite of their prime importance.

Utilization of various places, occasions and gatherings

47.1 I am also thinking of various occasions of special value which are exactly suitable for catechesis: for example, diocesan, regional or national pilgrimages, which gain from being centered on some judiciously chosen theme based on the life of Christ, of the Blessed Virgin or of the saints. Then there are the traditional missions, often too hastily dropped but irreplaceable for the periodic and vigorous renewal of Christian life — they should be revived and brought up to date. Again there are Bible-study groups, which ought to go beyond exegesis and lead their members to live by the word of God. Yet other instances are the meetings of ecclesial basic communities, insofar as they correspond to the criteria laid down in the Apostolic Exhortation *Evangelii Nuntiandi.*[91] I may also mention the youth groups that, under varying names and forms but always with the purpose of making Jesus Christ known and of living by the Gospel, are in some areas multiplying and flourishing in a sort of springtime that is very comforting for the Church: these include Catholic Action groups, charitable groups, prayer groups and Christian meditation groups. These groups are a source of great hope for the Church of tomorrow. But, in the name of Jesus, I exhort the young people who belong to them, their leaders, and the priests who devote the best part of their ministry to them: no matter what it costs, do not allow these groups — which are exceptional occasions for meeting others, and which are blessed with such riches of friendship and solidarity among the young, of joy and enthusiasm, of reflection on events and facts — do not allow them to lack serious study of Christian doctrine. If they do, they will be in danger — a danger that has unfortunately proved only too real — of disappointing their members and also the Church.

47.2 The catechetical endeavor that is possible in these various surroundings, and in many others besides, will have all the greater chance of being accepted and bearing fruit if it respects their individual nature. By becoming part of them in the right way, it will achieve the diversity and complementarity of approach that will enable it to develop all the riches of its concept, with its three dimensions of word, memorial and witness — doctrine, celebration and commitment in living — which the Synod Message to the People of God emphasized.[92]

The homily

48 This remark is even more valid for the catechesis given in the setting of the liturgy, especially at the Eucharistic assembly. Respecting the specific

---

[91] Cf. (December 8, 1975), 58: *AAS* 68 (1976), 46-49.

[92] Cf. Synod of Bishops, Fourth Ordinary General Assembly, Message to the People of God (October 27, 1977), 7-10: *L'Osservatore Romano* (English-language edition), November 3, 1977, 5.

nature and proper cadence of this setting, the homily takes up again the journey of faith put forward by catechesis, and brings it to its natural fulfillment. At the same time it encourages the Lord's disciples to begin anew each day their spiritual journey in truth, adoration and thanksgiving. Accordingly, one can say that catechetical teaching too finds its source and its fulfillment in the Eucharist, within the whole circle of the liturgical year. Preaching, centered upon the Bible texts, must then in its own way make it possible to familiarize the faithful with the whole of the mysteries of the faith and with the norms of Christian living. Much attention must be given to the homily: it should be neither too long nor too short; it should always be carefully prepared, rich in substance and adapted to the hearers, and reserved to ordained ministers. The homily should have its place not only in every Sunday and feast-day Eucharist, but also in the celebration of Baptisms, penitential liturgies, marriages and funerals. This is one of the benefits of the liturgical renewal.

Catechetical literature

49.1 Among these various ways and means — all the Church's activities have a catechetical dimension — catechetical works, far from losing their essential importance, acquire fresh significance. One of the major features of the renewal of catechetics today is the rewriting and multiplication of catechetical books taking place in many parts of the Church. Numerous very successful works have been produced and are a real treasure in the service of catechetical instruction. But it must be humbly and honestly recognized that this rich flowering has brought with it articles and publications which are ambiguous and harmful to young people and to the life of the Church. In certain places, the desire to find the best forms of expression or to keep up with fashions in pedagogical methods has often enough resulted in certain catechetical works which bewilder the young and even adults, either by deliberately or unconsciously omitting elements essential to the Church's faith, or by attributing excessive importance to certain themes at the expense of others, or, chiefly, by a rather horizontalist overall view out of keeping with the teaching of the Church's Magisterium.

49.2 Therefore, it is not enough to multiply catechetical works. In order that these works may correspond with their aim, several conditions are essential:

a) they must be linked with the real life of the generation to which they are addressed, showing close acquaintance with its anxieties and questionings, struggles and hopes;

b) they must try to speak a language comprehensible to the generation in question;

c) they must make a point of giving the whole message of Christ and his Church, without neglecting or distorting anything, and in expounding it they will follow a line and structure that highlights what is essential;

d) they must really aim to give to those who use them a better knowledge of the mysteries of Christ, aimed at true conversion and a life more in conformity with God's will.

Catechisms

50.1 All those who take on the heavy task of preparing these catechetical tools, especially catechism texts, can do so only with the approval of the Pastors who have the authority to give it, and taking their inspiration as closely as possible from the General Catechetical Directory, which remains the standard of reference.[93]

50.2 In this regard, I must warmly encourage Episcopal Conferences of the whole world to undertake, patiently but resolutely, the considerable work to be accomplished in agreement with the Apostolic See in order to prepare genuine catechisms which will be faithful to the essential content of revelation and up-to-date in method, and which will be capable of educating the Christian generations of the future to a sturdy faith.

50.3 This brief mention of ways and means of modern catechetics does not exhaust the wealth of suggestions worked out by the Synod Fathers. It is comforting to think that at the present time every country is seeing valuable collaboration for a more organic and more secure renewal of these aspects of catechetics. There can be no doubt that the Church will find the experts and the right means for responding, with God's grace, to the complex requirements of communicating with the people of today.

VII

How To Impart Catechesis

Diversity of methods

51.1 The age and the intellectual development of Christians, their degree of ecclesial and spiritual maturity and many other personal circumstances

---

[93] Cf. Sacred Congregation for the Clergy, General Catechetical Directory (April 11, 1971), 119-121, 134: *AAS* 64 (1972), 166-167, 172.

demand that catechesis should adopt widely differing methods for the attainment of its specific aim: education in the faith. On a more general level, this variety is also demanded by the social and cultural surrounding in which the Church carries out her catechetical work.

51.2 The variety in the methods used is a sign of life and a resource. That is how it was considered by the Fathers of the Fourth General Assembly of the Synod, although they also drew attention to the conditions necessary for that variety to be useful and not harmful to the unity of the teaching of the one faith.

At the service of revelation and conversion

52 The first question of a general kind that presents itself here concerns the danger and the temptation to mix catechetical teaching unduly with overt or masked ideological views, especially political and social ones, or with personal political options. When such views get the better of the central message to be transmitted, to the point of obscuring it and putting it in second place or even using it to further their own ends, catechesis then becomes radically distorted. The Synod rightly insisted on the need for catechesis to remain above one-sided divergent trends — to avoid "dichotomies" — even in the field of theological interpretation of such questions. It is on the basis of revelation that catechesis will try to set its course, revelation as transmitted by the universal Magisterium of the Church, in its solemn or ordinary form. This revelation tells of a creating and redeeming God, whose Son has come among us in our flesh and enters not only into each individual's personal history but into human history itself, becoming its center. Accordingly, this revelation tells of the radical change of man and the universe, of all that makes up the web of human life under the influence of the Good News of Jesus Christ. If conceived in this way, catechesis goes beyond every form of formalistic moralism, although it will include true Christian moral teaching. Chiefly, it goes beyond any kind of temporal, social or political "messianism." It seeks to arrive at man's innermost being.

The message embodied in cultures

53.1 Now a second question. As I said recently to the members of the Biblical Commission: "The term 'acculturation' or 'inculturation' may be a neologism, but it expresses very well one factor of the great mystery of the Incarnation."[94] We can say of catechesis, as well as of evangelization in gen-

---

[94] Cf. (April 26, 1979): *AAS* 71 (1979), 607.

eral, that it is called to bring the power of the Gospel into the very heart of culture and cultures. For this purpose, catechesis will seek to know these cultures and their essential components; it will learn their most significant expressions; it will respect their particular values and riches. In this manner it will be able to offer these cultures the knowledge of the hidden mystery[95] and help them to bring forth from their own living tradition original expressions of Christian life, celebration and thought. Two things must, however, be kept in mind.

53.2 On the one hand, the Gospel message cannot be purely and simply isolated from the culture in which it was first inserted (the biblical world or, more concretely, the cultural milieu in which Jesus of Nazareth lived), nor, without serious loss, from the cultures in which it has already been expressed down the centuries; it does not spring spontaneously from any cultural soil; it has always been transmitted by means of an apostolic dialogue which inevitably becomes part of a certain dialogue of cultures.

53.3 On the other hand, the power of the Gospel everywhere transforms and regenerates. When that power enters into a culture, it is no surprise that it rectifies many of its elements. There would be no catechesis if it were the Gospel that had to change when it came into contact with the cultures.

53.4 To forget this would simply amount to what Saint Paul very forcefully calls "emptying the Cross of Christ of its power."[96]

53.5 It is a different matter to take, with wise discernment, certain elements, religious or otherwise, that form part of the cultural heritage of a human group and use them to help its members to understand better the whole of the Christian mystery. Genuine catechists know that catechesis "takes flesh" in the various cultures and milieux: one has only to think of the peoples with their great differences, of modern youth, of the great variety of circumstances in which people find themselves today. But they refuse to accept an impoverishment of catechesis through a renunciation or obscuring of its message, by adaptations, even in language, that would endanger the "precious deposit" of the faith,[97] or by concessions in matters of faith or morals. They are convinced that true catechesis eventually enriches these cultures by helping them to go beyond the defective or even inhuman features in them, and by communicating to their legitimate values the fullness of Christ.[98]

[95] Cf. Rom 16:25; Eph 3:5.
[96] 1 Cor 1:17.
[97] Cf. 2 Tim 1:14.
[98] Cf. Jn 1:16; Eph 1:10.

The contribution of popular devotion

54 Another question of method concerns the utilization in catechetical instruction of valid elements in popular piety. I have in mind devotions practiced by the faithful in certain regions with moving fervor and purity of intention, even if the faith underlying them needs to be purified or rectified in many aspects. I have in mind certain easily understood prayers that many simple people are fond of repeating. I have in mind certain acts of piety practiced with a sincere desire to do penance or to please the Lord. Underlying most of these prayers and practices, besides elements that should be discarded, there are other elements which, if they were properly used, could serve very well to help people advance toward knowledge of the mystery of Christ and of his message: the love and mercy of God, the Incarnation of Christ, his redeeming Cross and Resurrection, the activity of the Spirit in each Christian and in the Church, the mystery of the hereafter, the evangelical virtues to be practiced, the presence of the Christian in the world, etc. And why should we appeal to non-Christian or even anti-Christian elements refusing to build on elements which, even if they need to be revised or improved, have something Christian at their root?

Memorization

55.1 The final methodological question the importance of which should at least be referred to — one that was debated several times in the Synod — is that of memorization. In the beginnings of Christian catechesis, which coincided with a civilization that was mainly oral, recourse was had very freely to memorization. Catechesis has since then known a long tradition of learning the principal truths by memorizing. We are all aware that this method can present certain disadvantages, not the least of which is that it lends itself to insufficient or at times almost non-existent assimilation, reducing all knowledge to formulas that are repeated without being properly understood. These disadvantages and the different characteristics of our own civilization have in some places led to the almost complete suppression — according to some, alas, the definitive suppression — of memorization in catechesis. And yet certain very authoritative voices made themselves heard on the occasion of the Fourth General Assembly of the Synod, calling for the restoration of a judicious balance between reflection and spontaneity, between dialogue and silence, between written work and memory work. Moreover certain cultures still set great value on memorization.

55.2 At a time when, in non-religious teaching in certain countries, more and more complaints are being made about the unfortunate consequences of disregarding the human faculty of memory, should we not attempt to put this faculty back into use in an intelligent and even an original way in catechesis, all the more since the celebration or "memorial" of the great events of the history of salvation require a precise knowledge of them? A certain memorization of the words of Jesus, of important Bible passages, of the ten commandments, of the formulas of profession of the faith, of the liturgical texts, of the essential prayers, of key doctrinal ideas, etc., far from being opposed to the dignity of young Christians, or constituting an obstacle to personal dialogue with the Lord, is a real need, as the Synod Fathers forcefully recalled. We must be realists. The blossoms, if we may call them that, of faith and piety do not grow in the desert places of a memory-less catechesis. What is essential is that the texts that are memorized must at the same time be taken in and gradually understood in depth, in order to become a source of Christian life on the personal level and the community level.

55.3 The plurality of methods in contemporary catechesis can be a sign of vitality and ingenuity. In any case, the method chosen must ultimately be referred to a law that is fundamental for the whole of the Church's life: the law of fidelity to God and of fidelity to man in a single loving attitude.

VIII
The Joy of Faith in a Troubled World

Affirming Christian identity

56 We live in a difficult world in which the anguish of seeing the best creations of man slip away from him and turn against him creates a climate of uncertainty.[99] In this world catechesis should help Christians to be, for their own joy and the service of all, "light" and "salt."[100] Undoubtedly this demands that catechesis should strengthen them in their identity and that it should continually separate itself from the surrounding atmosphere of hesitation, uncertainty and insipidity. Among the many difficulties, each of them a challenge for faith, I shall indicate a few in order to assist catechesis in overcoming them.

In an indifferent world

57 A few years ago, there was much talk of the secularized world, the post-Christian era. Fashion changes, but a profound reality remains. Christians

---

[99] Cf. John Paul II, Encyclical Letter *Redemptor Hominis* (March 4, 1979), 15-16: *AAS* 71 (1979), 286-295.

[100] Cf. Mt 5:13-16.

today must be formed to live in a world which largely ignores God or which — in religious matters, in place of an exacting and fraternal dialogue, stimulating for all — too often flounders in a debasing indifferentism, if it does not remain in a scornful attitude of "suspicion" in the name of the progress it has made in the field of scientific "explanations." To "hold on" in this world, to offer to all a "dialogue of salvation"[101] in which each person feels respected in his or her most basic dignity, the dignity of one who is seeking God, we need a catechesis which trains the young people and adults of our communities to remain clear and consistent in their faith, to affirm serenely their Christian and Catholic identity, to "see him who is invisible"[102] and to adhere so firmly to the absoluteness of God that they can be witnesses to him in a materialistic civilization that denies him.

With the original pedagogy of the faith

58.1 The irreducible originality of Christian identity has for corollary and condition no less original a pedagogy of the faith. Among the many prestigious sciences of man that are nowadays making immense advances, pedagogy is certainly one of the most important. The attainments of the other sciences — biology, psychology, sociology — are providing it with valuable elements. The science of education and the art of teaching are continually being subjected to review, with a view to making them better adapted or more effective, with varying degrees of success.

58.2 There is also a pedagogy of faith, and the good that it can do for catechesis cannot be overstated. In fact, it is natural that techniques perfected and tested for education in general should be adapted for the service of education in the faith. However, account must always be taken of the absolute originality of faith. Pedagogy of faith is not a question of transmitting human knowledge, even of the highest kind; it is a question of communicating God's revelation in its entirety. Throughout sacred history, especially in the Gospel, God himself used a pedagogy that must continue to be a model for the pedagogy of faith. A technique is of value in catechesis only to the extent that it serves the faith that is to be transmitted and learned; otherwise it is of no value.

Language suited to the service of the Credo

59.1 A problem very close to the preceding one is that of language. This is obviously a burning question today. It is paradoxical to see that, while mod-

---

[101] Cf. Paul VI, Encyclical Letter *Ecclesiam Suam* (August 6, 1964), III: *AAS* 56 (1964), 637-659.

[102] Cf. Heb 11:27.

ern studies, for instance in the field of communication, semantics and symbology, attribute extraordinary importance to language, nevertheless language is being misused today for ideological mystification, for mass conformity in thought and for reducing man to the level of an object.

59.2 All this has extensive influence in the field of catechesis. For catechesis has a pressing obligation to speak a language suited to today's children and young people in general and to many other categories of people — the language of students, intellectuals and scientists; the language of the illiterate or of people of simple culture; the language of the handicapped, and so on. Saint Augustine encountered this same problem and contributed to its solution for his own time with his well-known work *De Catechizandis Rudibus.* In catechesis as in theology, there is no doubt that the question of language is of the first order. But there is good reason for recalling here that catechesis cannot admit any language that would result in altering the substance of the content of the Creed, under any pretext whatever, even a pretended scientific one. Deceitful or beguiling language is no better. On the contrary, the supreme rule is that the great advances in the science of language must be capable of being placed at the service of catechesis so as to enable it really to "tell" or "communicate" to the child, the adolescent, the young people and adults of today the whole content of doctrine without distortion.

Research and certainty of faith

60.1 A more subtle challenge occasionally comes from the very way of conceiving faith. Certain contemporary philosophical schools, which seem to be exercising a strong influence on some theological currents and, through them, on pastoral practice, like to emphasize that the fundamental human attitude is that of seeking the infinite, a seeking that never attains its object. In theology, this view of things will state very categorically that faith is not certainty but questioning, not clarity but a leap in the dark.

60.2 These currents of thought certainly have the advantage of reminding us that faith concerns things not yet in our possession, since they are hoped for; that as yet we see only "in a mirror dimly"[103]; and that God dwells always in inaccessible light.[104] They help us to make the Christian faith not the attitude of one who has already arrived, but a journey forward as with Abraham. For all the more reason one must avoid presenting as certain things which are not.

60.3 However, we must not fall into the opposite extreme, as too often

---

[103] 1 Cor 13:12.
[104] Cf. 1 Tim 6:16.

happens. The Letter to the Hebrews says that "faith is the assurance of things hoped for, the conviction of things not seen."[105] Although we are not in full possession, we do have an assurance and a conviction. When educating children, adolescents and young people, let us not give them too negative an idea of faith — as if it were absolute non-knowing, a kind of blindness, a world of darkness — but let us show them that the humble yet courageous seeking of the believer, far from having its starting point in nothingness, in plain self-deception, in fallible opinions or in uncertainty, is based on the word of God who cannot deceive or be deceived, and is unceasingly built on the immovable rock of this word. It is the search of the Magi under the guidance of a star,[106] the search of which Pascal, taking up a phrase of Saint Augustine, wrote so profoundly: "You would not be searching for me, if you had not found me."[107]

60.4 It is also one of the aims of catechesis to give young catechumens the simple but solid certainties that will help them to seek to know the Lord more and better.

Catechesis and theology

61.1 In this context, it seems important to me that the connection between catechesis and theology should be well understood.

61.2 Obviously this connection is profound and vital for those who understand the irreplaceable mission of theology in the service of faith. Thus it is no surprise that every stirring in the field of theology also has repercussions in that of catechesis. In this period immediately after the Council, the Church is living through an important but hazardous time of theological research. The same must be said of hermeneutics with respect to exegesis.

61.3 Synod Fathers from all continents dealt with this question in very frank terms: they spoke of the danger of an "unstable balance" passing from theology to catechesis and they stressed the need to do something about this difficulty. Pope Paul VI himself had dealt with the problem in no less frank terms in the introduction to his Solemn Profession of Faith[108] and in the Apostolic Exhortation marking the fifth anniversary of the close of the Second Vatican Council.[109]

61.4 This point must again be insisted on. Aware of the influence that

---

[105] Heb 11:1.

[106] Cf. Mt 2:1-12.

[107] Blaise Pascal, *Le mystère de Jésus: Pensées,* 553.

[108] Paul VI, Solemn Profession of Faith (June 30, 1968), 4: *AAS* 60 (1968), 434.

[109] Paul VI, Apostolic Exhortation *Quinque Iam Anni* (December 8, 1970), I: *AAS* 63 (1971), 99.

their research and their statements have on catechetical instruction, theologians and exegetes have a duty to take great care that people do not take for a certainty what on the contrary belongs to the area of questions of opinion or of discussion among experts. Catechists for their part must have the wisdom to pick from the field of theological research those points that can provide light for their own reflection and their teaching, drawing, like the theologians, from the true sources, in the light of the Magisterium. They must refuse to trouble the minds of the children and young people, at this stage of their catechesis, with outlandish theories, useless questions and unproductive discussions, things that Saint Paul often condemned in his Pastoral Letters.[110]

61.5 The most valuable gift that the Church can offer to the bewildered and restless world of our time is to form within it Christians who are confirmed in what is essential and who are humbly joyful in their faith. Catechesis will teach this to them, and it will itself be the first to benefit from it: "The man who wishes to understand himself thoroughly — and not just in accordance with immediate, partial, often superficial, and even illusory standards and measures of his being — must come to Christ with his unrest and uncertainty, and even his weakness and sinfulness, his life and death. He must, so to speak, enter into Christ with all his own self, he must 'appropriate' Christ and assimilate the whole of the reality of the Incarnation and Redemption in order to find himself."[111]

IX

The Task Concerns Us All

Encouragement to all responsible for catechesis

62 Now, beloved Brothers and sons and daughters, I would like my words, which are intended as a serious and heartfelt exhortation from me in my ministry as Pastor of the universal Church, to set your hearts aflame, like the Letters of Saint Paul to his companions in the Gospel, Titus and Timothy, or like Saint Augustine writing for the deacon Deogratias, when the latter lost heart before his task as a catechist, a real little treatise on

---

[110] Cf. 1 Tim 1:3-7, 4:1-11; 2 Tim 2:14-18, 4:1-5; Tit 1:10-12; cf. also Paul VI, Apostolic Exhortation *Evangelii Nuntiandi* (December 8, 1975), 78: *AAS* 68 (1976), 70.

[111] John Paul II, Encyclical Letter *Redemptor Hominis* (March 4, 1979), 10: *AAS* 71 (1979), 274.

the joy of catechizing.[112] Yes, I wish to sow courage, hope and enthusiasm abundantly in the hearts of all those many diverse people who are in charge of religious instruction and training for life in keeping with the Gospel.

Bishops

63.1 To begin with, I turn to my brother Bishops: the Second Vatican Council has already explicitly reminded you of your task in the catechetical area,[113] and the Fathers of the Fourth General Assembly of the Synod have also strongly underlined it.

63.2 Dearly beloved Brothers, you have here a special mission within your Churches: you are beyond all others the ones primarily responsible for catechesis, the catechists *par excellence*. Together with the Pope, in the spirit of episcopal collegiality, you too have charge of catechesis throughout the Church. Accept therefore what I say to you from my heart.

63.3 I know that your ministry as Bishops is growing daily more complex and overwhelming. A thousand duties call you: from the training of new priests to being actively present within the lay communities, from the living, worthy celebration of the sacraments and acts of worship to concern for human advancement and the defense of human rights. But let the concern to foster active and effective catechesis yield to no other care whatever in any way. This concern will lead you to transmit personally to your faithful the doctrine of life. But it should also lead you to take on in your Diocese, in accordance with the plans of the Episcopal Conference to which you belong, the chief management of catechesis, while at the same time surrounding yourselves with competent and trustworthy assistants. Your principal role will be to bring about and maintain in your Churches a real passion for catechesis, a passion embodied in a pertinent and effective organization, putting into operation the necessary personnel, means and equipment, and also financial resources. You can be sure that if catechesis is done well in your local Churches, everything else will be easier to do. And needless to say, although your zeal must sometimes impose upon you the thankless task of denouncing deviations and correcting errors, it will much more often win for you the joy and consolation of seeing your Churches flourishing because catechesis is given in them as the Lord wishes.

---

[112] *De Catechizandis Rudibus: PL* 40, 310-347.

[113] Cf. Decree on the Bishops' Pastoral Office in the Church *Christus Dominus,* 14: *AAS* 58 (1966), 679.

Priests

64 For your part, priests, here you have a field in which you are the immediate assistants of your Bishops. The Council has called you "instructors in the faith"[114]; there is no better way for you to be such instructors than by devoting your best efforts to the growth of your communities in the faith. Whether you are in charge of a parish, or are chaplains to primary or secondary schools or universities, or have responsibility for pastoral activity at any level, or are leaders of large or small communities, especially youth groups, the Church expects you to neglect nothing with a view to a well-organized and well-oriented catechetical effort. The deacons and other ministers that you may have the good fortune to have with you are your natural assistants in this. All believers have a right to catechesis; all pastors have the duty to provide it. I shall always ask civil leaders to respect the freedom of catechetical teaching; but with all my strength I beg you, ministers of Jesus Christ: do not, for lack of zeal or because of some unfortunate preconceived idea, leave the faithful without catechesis. Let it not be said that "the children beg for food, but no one gives to them."[115]

Men and women Religious

65 Many Religious Institutes for men and women came into being for the purpose of giving Christian education to children and young people, especially the most abandoned. Throughout history, men and women Religious have been deeply committed to the Church's catechetical activity, doing particularly apposite and effective work. At a time when it is desired that the links between Religious and Pastors should be accentuated and consequently the active presence of Religious communities and their members in the pastoral projects of the local Churches, I wholeheartedly exhort you, whose Religious consecration should make you even more readily available for the Church's service, to prepare as well as possible for the task of catechesis according to the differing vocations of your Institutes and the missions entrusted to you, and to carry this concern everywhere. Let the communities dedicate as much as possible of what ability and means they have to the specific work of catechesis.

Lay catechists

66.1 I am anxious to give thanks in the Church's name to all of you, lay teachers of catechesis in the parishes, the men and the still more numerous

---

[114] Decree on the Ministry and Life of Priests *Presbyterorum Ordinis,* 6: *AAS* 58 (1966), 999.
[115] Lam 4:4.

women throughout the world, who are devoting yourselves to the Religious education of many generations. Your work is often lowly and hidden but it is carried out with ardent and generous zeal, and it is an eminent form of the lay apostolate, a form that is particularly important where for various reasons children and young people do not receive suitable Religious training in the home. How many of us have received from people like you our first notions of catechism and our preparation for the Sacrament of Penance, for our first Communion and Confirmation! The Fourth General Assembly of the Synod did not forget you. I join with it in encouraging you to continue your collaboration for the life of the Church.

66.2 But the term "catechists" belongs above all to the catechists in mission lands. Born of families that are already Christian or converted at some time to Christianity and instructed by missionaries or by another catechist, they then consecrate their lives, year after year, to catechizing children and adults in their own country. Churches that are flourishing today would not have been built up without them. I rejoice at the efforts made by the Sacred Congregation for the Evangelization of Peoples to improve more and more the training of these catechists. I gratefully recall the memory of those whom the Lord has already called to himself. I beg the intercession of those whom my Predecessors have raised to the glory of the altars. I wholeheartedly encourage those engaged in the work. I express the wish that many others may succeed them and that they may increase in numbers for a task so necessary for the missions.

In the parish

67.1 I now wish to speak of the actual setting in which all these catechists normally work. I am returning this time, taking a more overall view, to the "places" for catechesis, some of which have already been mentioned in chapter VI: the parish, the family, the school, organizations.

67.2 It is true that catechesis can be given anywhere, but I wish to stress, in accordance with the desire of very many Bishops, that the parish community must continue to be the prime mover and preeminent place for catechesis. Admittedly, in many countries the parish has been, as it were, shaken by the phenomenon of urbanization. Perhaps some have too easily accepted that the parish should be considered old-fashioned, if not doomed to disappear, in favor of more pertinent and effective small communities. Whatever one may think, the parish is still a major point of reference for the Christian people, even for the non-practicing. Accordingly, realism and wisdom demand that we continue along the path aiming to restore to the parish, as needed, more adequate structures and, above all a new impetus through the increasing integration into it of qualified, responsible and generous members. This being said, and taking into account the necessary diversity of places for catechesis (the parish as such, families taking in children and adolescents, chaplaincies for State schools, Catholic educational establishments, apostolic movements that give periods of catechesis, clubs open to youth in general, spiritual formation weekends, etc.), it is supremely important that all these catechetical channels should really converge on the same confession of faith, on the same membership of the Church, and on commitments in society lived in the same Gospel spirit: "one Lord, one faith, one baptism, one God and Father."[116] That is why every big parish or every group of parishes with small numbers has the serious duty to train people completely dedicated to providing catechetical leadership (priests, men and women Religious, and lay people), to provide the equipment needed for catechesis under all aspects, to increase and adapt the places for catechesis to the extent that it is possible and useful to do so, and to be watchful about the quality of the religious formation of the various groups and their integration into the ecclesial community.

67.3 In short, without monopolizing or enforcing uniformity, the parish remains, as I have said, the preeminent place for catechesis. It must rediscover its vocation, which is to be a fraternal and welcoming family home, where those who have been baptized and confirmed become aware of forming the People of God. In that home, the bread of good doctrine and the Eucharistic Bread are broken for them in abundance, in the setting of the one act of worship[117]; from that home they are sent out day by day to their apostolic mission in all the centers of activity of the life of the world.

In the family

68.1 The family's catechetical activity has a special character, which is in a sense irreplaceable. This special character has been rightly stressed by the Church, particularly by the Second Vatican Council.[118] Education in the faith

---

[116] Eph 4:5-6.

[117] Cf. Second Vatican Ecumenical Council, Constitution on the Sacred Liturgy *Sacrosanctum Concilium,* 35, 52: *AAS* 56 (1964), 109, 114; cf. also the General Instruction of the Roman Missal promulgated by a Decree of the Sacred Congregation of Rites (April 6, 1969), 33, and what has been said above in chapter VI concerning the homily.

[118] Since the High Middle Ages, Provincial Councils have insisted on the responsibility of parents in regard to education in the faith: cf. Sixth Council of Arles (813), Canon 19; Council of Mainz (813), Canons 45, 47; Sixth Council of Paris (829), Book 1, Chapter 7: Mansi, *Sacrorum Conciliorum Nova et Amplissima Collectio,* XIV, 62; 74; 542. Among the more recent documents

by parents, which should begin from the children's tenderest age,[119] is already being given when the members of a family help each other to grow in faith through the witness of their Christian lives, a witness that is often without words but which perseveres throughout a day-to-day life lived in accordance with the Gospel. This catechesis is more incisive when, in the course of family events (such as the reception of the sacraments, the celebration of great liturgical feasts, the birth of a child, a bereavement) care is taken to explain in the home the Christian or religious content of these events. But that is not enough: Christian parents must strive to follow and repeat, within the setting of family life, the more methodical teaching received elsewhere. The fact that these truths about the main questions of faith and Christian living are thus repeated within a family setting impregnated with love and respect will often make it possible to influence the children in a decisive way for life. The parents themselves profit from the effort that this demands of them, for in a catechetical dialogue of this sort each individual both receives and gives.

68.2 Family catechesis therefore precedes, accompanies and enriches all other forms of catechesis. Furthermore, in places where anti-religious legislation endeavors even to prevent education in the faith, and in places where widespread unbelief or invasive secularism makes real religious growth practically impossible, "the Church of the home"[120] remains the one place where children and young people can receive an authentic catechesis. Thus there cannot be too great an effort on the part of Christian parents to prepare for this ministry of being their own children's catechists and to carry it out with tireless zeal. Encouragement must also be given to the individuals or institutions that, through person-to-person contacts, through meetings, and through all kinds of pedagogical means, help parents to perform their task: the service they are doing to catechesis is beyond price.

of the Magisterium, note Pius XI, Encyclical Letter *Divini Illius Magistri* (December 31, 1929): *AAS* 22 (1930), 49-86; the many addresses and messages of Pius XII; and above all the texts of the Second Vatican Ecumenical Council: Dogmatic Constitution on the Church *Lumen Gentium,* 11, 35: *AAS* 57 (1965), 15, 40; Decree on the Apostolate of the Laity *Apostolicam Actuositatem,* 11, 30: *AAS* 58 (1966), 847, 860; Pastoral Constitution on the Church in the Modern World *Gaudium et Spes,* 52: *AAS* 58 (1966), 1073; and especially Declaration on Christian Education *Gravissimum Educationis,* 3: *AAS* 58 (1966), 731.

[119] Cf. Second Vatican Ecumenical Council, Declaration on Christian Education *Gravissimum Educationis,* 3: *AAS* 58 (1966), 731.

[120] Second Vatican Ecumenical Council, Dogmatic Constitution on the Church *Lumen Gentium,* 11: *AAS* 57 (1965), 16; cf. Decree on the Apostolate of the Laity *Apostolicam Actuositatem,* 11: *AAS* 58 (1966), 848.

At school

69.1 Together with and in connection with the family, the school provides catechesis with possibilities that are not to be neglected. In the unfortunately decreasing number of countries in which it is possible to give education in the faith within the school framework, the Church has the duty to do so as well as possible. This of course concerns first and foremost the Catholic school: it would no longer deserve this title if, no matter how much it shone for its high level of teaching in non-religious matters, there were justification for reproaching it for negligence or deviation in strictly religious education. Let it not be said that such education will always be given implicitly and indirectly. The special character of the Catholic school, the underlying reason for it, the reason why Catholic parents should prefer it, is precisely the quality of the religious instruction integrated into the education of the pupils. While Catholic establishments should respect freedom of conscience, that is to say, avoid burdening consciences from without by exerting physical or moral pressure, especially in the case of the religious activity of adolescents, they still have a grave duty to offer a religious training suited to the often widely varying religious situations of the pupils. They also have a duty to make them understand that, although God's call to serve him in spirit and truth, in accordance with the commandments of God and the precepts of the Church, does not apply constraint, it is nevertheless binding in conscience.

69.2 But I am also thinking of non-confessional and public schools. I express the fervent wish that, in response to a very clear right of the human person and of the family, and out of respect for everyone's religious freedom, all Catholic pupils may be enabled to advance in their spiritual formation with the aid of a religious instruction dependent on the Church, but which, according to the circumstances of different countries, can be offered either by the school or in the setting of the school, or again within the framework of an agreement with the public authorities regarding school timetables, if catechesis takes place only in the parish or in another pastoral center. In fact, even in places where objective difficulties exist, it should be possible to arrange school timetables in such a way as to enable the Catholics to deepen their faith and religious experience, with qualified teachers, whether priests or lay people.

69.3 Admittedly, apart from the school, many other elements of life help in influencing the mentality of the young, for instance, recreation, social background and work surroundings. But those who study are bound to bear the stamp of their studies, to be introduced to cultural or moral values within the atmosphere of the establishment in which they are taught, and to be faced with many ideas met with in school. It is important for catechesis to take full account of this effect of the school on the pupils, if it is to keep in touch with the other elements of the pupil's knowledge and education; thus the Gospel will impregnate the mentality of the pupils in the field of their learning, and the harmonization of their culture will be achieved in the light of faith. Accordingly, I give encouragement to the priests, Religious and lay people who are devoting themselves to sustaining these pupils' faith. This is moreover an occasion for me to reaffirm my firm conviction that to show respect for the Catholic faith of the young to the extent of facilitating its education, its implantation, its consolidation, its free profession and practice would certainly be to the honor of any government, whatever be the system on which it is based or the ideology from which it draws its inspiration.

Within organizations

70.1 Lastly, encouragement must be given to the lay associations, movements and groups, whether their aim is the practice of piety, the direct apostolate, charity and relief work, or a Christian presence in temporal matters. They will all accomplish their objectives better, and serve the Church better, if they give an important place in their internal organization and their method of action to the serious religious training of their members. In this way every association of the faithful in the Church has by definition the duty to educate in the faith.

70.2 This makes more evident the role given to the laity in catechesis today, always under the pastoral direction of their Bishops, as the Propositions left by the Synod stressed several times.

Training institutes

71.1 We must be grateful to the Lord for this contribution by the laity, but it is also a challenge to our responsibility as Pastors, since these lay catechists must be carefully prepared for what is, if not a formally instituted ministry, at the very least a function of great importance in the Church. Their preparation calls on us to organize special centers and institutes, which are to be given assiduous attention by the Bishops. This is a field in which diocesan, interdiocesan or national cooperation proves fertile and fruitful. Here also the material aid provided by the richer Churches to their poorer sisters can show the greatest effectiveness, for what better assistance can one Church give to another than to help it to grow as a Church with its own strength?

71.2 I would like to recall to all those who are working generously in the service of the Gospel, and to whom I have expressed here my lively encouragement, the instruction given by my venerated Predecessor Paul VI: "As evangelizers, we must offer . . . the image of people who are mature in faith and capable of finding a meeting-point beyond the real tensions, thanks to a shared, sincere and disinterested search for truth. Yes, the destiny of evangelization is certainly bound up with the witness of unity given by the Church. This is a source of responsibility and also of comfort."[121]

Conclusion

The Holy Spirit, the Teacher within

72.1 At the end of this Apostolic Exhortation, the gaze of my heart turns to him who is the principle inspiring all catechetical work and all who do this work — the Spirit of the Father and of the Son, the Holy Spirit.

72.2 In describing the mission that this Spirit would have in the Church, Christ used the significant words: "He will teach you all things, and bring to your remembrance all that I have said to you."[122] And he added: "When the Spirit of truth comes, he will guide you into all the truth . . . he will declare to you the things that are to come."[123]

72.3 The Spirit is thus promised to the Church and to each Christian as a teacher within, who, in the secret of the conscience and the heart, makes one understand what one has heard but was not capable of grasping: "Even now the Holy Spirit teaches the faithful," said Saint Augustine in this regard, "in accordance with each one's spiritual capacity. And he sets their hearts aflame with greater desire according as each one progresses in the charity that makes him love what he already knows and desire what he has yet to know."[124]

72.4 Furthermore, the Spirit's mission is also to transform the disciples into witnesses to Christ: "He will bear witness to me; and you also are witnesses."[125]

72.5 But this is not all. For Saint Paul, who on this matter synthesizes a theology that is latent throughout the New Testament, it is the whole of one's "being a Christian," the whole of the Christian life, the new life of the children of God, that constitutes a life in accordance with the Spirit.[126] Only the Spirit enables us to say to God: "Abba, Father."[127] Without the Spirit we cannot say:

---

[121] Apostolic Exhortation *Evangelii Nuntiandi* (December 8, 1975), 77: *AAS* 68 (1976), 69.
[122] Jn 14:26.
[123] Jn 16:13.
[124] *In Ioannis Evangelium Tractatus,* 97, 1: *PL* 35, 1877.
[125] Jn 15:26-27.
[126] Cf. Rom 8:14-17; Gal 4:6.
[127] Rom 8:15.

"Jesus is Lord."[128] From the Spirit come all the charisms that build up the Church, the community of Christians.[129] In keeping with this, Saint Paul gives each disciple of Christ the instruction: "Be filled with the Spirit."[130] Saint Augustine is very explicit: "Both (our believing and our doing good) are ours because of the choice of our will, and yet both are gifts from the Spirit of faith and charity."[131]

72.6 Catechesis, which is growth in faith and the maturing of Christian life toward its fullness, is consequently a work of the Holy Spirit, a work that he alone can initiate and sustain in the Church.

72.7 This realization, based on the text quoted above and on many other passages of the New Testament, convinces us of two things.

72.8 To begin with, it is clear that, when carrying out her mission of giving catechesis, the Church — and also every individual Christian devoting himself to that mission within the Church and in her name — must be very much aware of acting as a living, pliant instrument of the Holy Spirit. To invoke this Spirit constantly, to be in communion with him, to endeavor to know his authentic inspirations must be the attitude of the teaching Church and of every catechist.

72.9 Secondly, the deep desire to understand better the Spirit's action and to entrust oneself to him more fully — at a time when "in the Church we are living an exceptionally favorable season of the Spirit," as my Predecessor Paul VI remarked in his Apostolic Exhortation *Evangelii Nuntiandi*[132] — must bring about a catechetical awakening. For "renewal in the Spirit" will be authentic and will have real fruitfulness in the Church, not so much according as it gives rise to extraordinary charisms, but according as it leads the greatest possible number of the faithful, as they travel their daily paths, to make a humble, patient and persevering effort to know the mystery of Christ better and better, and to bear witness to it.

72.10 I invoke on the catechizing Church this Spirit of the Father and the Son, and I beg him to renew catechetical dynamism in the Church.

Mary, Mother and model of the disciple

73.1 May the Virgin of Pentecost obtain this for us through her intercession! By a unique vocation, she saw her Son Jesus "increase in wisdom and in

---

[128] 1 Cor 12:3.
[129] Cf. 1 Cor 12:4-11.
[130] Eph 5:18.
[131] *Retractationum Liber*, I, 23, 2: *PL* 32, 621.
[132] (December 8, 1975), 75: *AAS* 68 (1976), 66.

stature, and in favor."[133] As he sat on her lap and later as he listened to her throughout the hidden life at Nazareth, this Son, who was "the only Son from the Father," "full of grace and truth," was formed by her in human knowledge of the Scriptures and of the history of God's plan for his people, and in adoration of the Father.[134] She in turn was the first of his disciples. She was the first in time, because even when she found her adolescent Son in the Temple she received from him lessons that she kept in her heart.[135] She was the first disciple above all else because no one has been "taught by God"[136] to such depth. She was "both Mother and disciple," as Saint Augustine said of her, venturing to add that her discipleship was more important for her than her motherhood.[137] There are good grounds for the statement made in the Synod Hall that Mary is "a living catechism" and "the Mother and model of catechists."

73.2 May the presence of the Holy Spirit, through the prayers of Mary, grant the Church unprecedented enthusiasm in the catechetical work that is essential for her. Thus will she effectively carry out, at this moment of grace, her inalienable and universal mission, the mission given her by her Teacher: "Go therefore and make disciples of all nations."[138]

With my Apostolic Blessing.

Given in Rome, at Saint Peter's, on October 16, 1979, the second year of my Pontificate.

[133] Cf. Lk 2:52.
[134] Cf. Jn 1:14; Heb 10:5; Saint Thomas Aquinas, *Summa Theologiae,* III, q. 12, a. 2; III, q. 12, a. 3, ad 3.
[135] Cf. Lk 2:51.
[136] Cf. Jn 6:45.
[137] Cf. *Sermo* 25, 7: *PL* 46, 937-938.
[138] Mt 28:19.

Familiaris Consortio

Editor's Introduction

"The future of humanity passes by way of the family" (§86.2). More than any previous Pope, John Paul II has spoken passionately and at length about the family's irreplaceable role in ecclesial and social life. From the beginning of his Pontificate the Holy Father has insisted that the fabric of society and of the Church can be healed only by means of the family. On November 22, 1981, he published the apostolic exhortation *Familiaris Consortio*, on the role of the Christian family in the world. This document is a *"summa"* of the Church's teaching on the family's identity, decisive tasks, and pastoral care.

The 1980 Synod on the family was the first Assembly at which John Paul presided as Pope. This choice of topic was entirely fitting, since it reflected his long-standing philosophical and pastoral interest in marriage and the family. As a professor of ethics at Lublin and Archbishop of Cracow, he published widely in these areas, including *Love and Responsibility* (1960), a book on sexual ethics, and *The Jeweler's Shop* (1960), a play on the trials of married life. As Pope, he has addressed themes touching human sexuality, marriage, and family on countless occasions, most ardently and extensively during the International Year of the Family in 1994. Besides countless discourses, homilies, messages, reflections, and interventions through the different organs of the Holy See, John Paul also treated these topics in his Letter to Families *Gratissimam Sane* (1994) and in his Message for the 1994 World Day of Peace.

The Pope admits his great debt to the deliberations and proposals of the Synod Fathers as important sources of *Familiaris Consortio*. At the end of the Assembly, they asked him to be "a spokesman before humanity of the Church's lively care for the family and to give suitable indications for renewed pastoral effort in this fundamental sector of the life of man and of the Church" (§2.3). His apostolic exhortation is a personal synthesis of the Synod's "very valuable contribution of teaching and experience" (§2.4).

Almost every page of *Familiaris Consortio* reflects the Church's firm commitment to safeguard and foster family life. Opposing those who consider the family merely an historically contingent way of organizing social life, the Holy Father defends "the entire truth and the full dignity of marriage and the family" (§5.1). The Christian community gives these initiatives her support because the truth about their identity and mission belongs to the proclamation of the Gospel. Indeed, since the Church is "illuminated by the faith that gives her an understanding of all the truth concerning the great value of marriage and the family and their deepest meaning" (§3.1), she is well equipped to proclaim this "good news" boldly and joyfully to everyone.

According to the Pope, when the Church voices her concern for the family, she takes into account the needs of three different groups. First, she supports those who are already aware of the precious value of marriage and the family and are trying to live in accordance with the Church's teaching. Second, the Christian community strives to enlighten those who are uncertain, bewildered, or still searching for the truth about conjugal life and marriage. Third, the Church wishes to strengthen those who are in any way hindered from freely living their family life. This exhortation is designed to encourage and inspire "every person who wonders about the destiny of marriage and the family" (§1.2). The Church's teaching in these areas is relevant for all men and women of good will. John Paul singles out young people in a special way as privileged recipients of *Familiaris Consortio*. It presents them with new horizons and helps them to discover "the beauty and grandeur of the vocation to love and the service of life" (§1.3).

In keeping with the genre of post-synodal papal documents, the Pope is especially attentive to ensuring its pastoral character and exhortative tone. *Familiaris Consortio* is therefore neither a theoretical text nor an historical survey of the Magisterium's doctrine of marriage and the family. Rather, the exhortation betrays the calm security and optimism which stem from the Pope's confidence in the family, a confidence rooted in Christ as the inexhaustible source of grace for married couples. In clearly proposing the truth with all its demands, he encourages families to live according to God's plan. Even though the Holy Father unmasks errors which are eroding the essential values of marriage and the family, he is chiefly concerned with forming people's consciences in light of the truth revealed by creation and Redemption. His goal is to express persuasively theological principles and pastoral guidelines.

In *Familiaris Consortio,* John Paul relies on a variety of sources. From the Scriptures, he cites most frequently texts from Genesis 1-3 and Ephesians 5:21-33. As is always true in his writings, he sprinkles his exhortation with innumerable references to the documents of the Second Vatican Council, above all to the section on marriage in *Gaudium et Spes* (§§47-52), and to *Lumen Gentium* and *Apostolicam Actuositatem.* Also the Pope often quotes or refers to Paul VI's encyclical *Humanae Vitae* (1968), especially in his discussion of the transmission of life. And, for the first time in an apostolic exhortation, he cites directly from several of the proposals which the Fathers handed over to him at the end of their Assembly. In fact, *Familiaris Consortio* is a systematic synthesis of the Synod's conclusions, which were then given shape by John Paul's theological vision, pastoral concerns, and stylistic touches.

Summary

As well as its introduction and conclusion, the apostolic exhortation is tightly organized in four principal sections. Chapter one, "Bright Spots and Shadows for the Family Today" (§§4-10), describes the positive and negative aspects of the contemporary family. In chapter two, "The Plan of God for Marriage and the Family" (§§11-16), the Holy Father analyzes the nature of the family as a community of persons built on love. Chapter three, "The Role of the Christian Family" (§§17-64), is a thorough treatment of the family's mission. It explains the family's tasks in four subsections: forming a community of persons (§§18-27), serving life (§§28-41), participating in the development of society (§§42-48), and sharing in the life and mission of the Church (§§49-64). In chapter four, "Pastoral Care of the Family: Stages, Structures, Agents and Situations" (§§65-85), the Pope recommends that the Church undertake vigorous initiatives on behalf of families, especially those that are wounded in some way.

Evangelical discernment of the family's current situation

According to John Paul II, today's family is in crisis; it is "the object of numerous forces that seek to destroy it or in some way to deform it" (§3.4). If the Church is to challenge these destructive forces effectively, she must scrutinize the signs of the times which influence sexuality, marriage, and the family in this period of rapid social and cultural change.

Familiaris Consortio describes the positive and negative aspects of the family's present situation as "an interplay of light and darkness" (§6.5). Among the encouraging signs of Christ's saving grace at work in the family are a greater awareness of personal freedom and the value of interpersonal relationships, the promotion of women's dignity, and the increased concern for responsible procreation, the education of children, interfamily support, and the family's responsibility to society and the Church. Along with these bright spots, the Pope describes the shadows cast over family life, to which he devotes more attention. Included among the negative phenomena that bespeak a disturbing degradation of family values are the following: "a mistaken theoretical and practical concept of the independence of the spouses in relation to each other; serious misconceptions regarding the relationship of authority between parents and children; the concrete difficulties that the family itself experiences in the transmission of values; the growing number of divorces; the scourge of abortion; the ever more frequent recourse to sterilization; the appearance of a truly contraceptive mentality" (§6.2). Other shadows mentioned later in the exhortation include confusion about the meaning of human sexuality, the exploitation of women, "machismo," cohabitation without marriage, and recourse to civil marriage by Catholics. Each of these has a destructive effect on individuals and society.

As is customary, the Holy Father goes beyond a description of the particular situation to an analysis of the root of the sickness requiring a remedy. He diagnoses the fundamental cause of family breakdown as "a corruption of the idea and the experience of freedom, conceived not as a capacity for realizing the truth of God's plan for marriage and the family, but as an autonomous power of self-affirmation, often against others, for one's own selfish well-being" (§6.3). Liberal societies interpret freedom as the right to do whatever one wants. Moreover, the distorted notion of freedom which they promote feeds the view that the family is merely a group of autonomous individuals who come together out of self-interest. Here, as elsewhere in his writings, John Paul vigorously upholds his conviction that the exercise of authentic freedom is always yoked to the objective truth of creation and Redemption.

According to *Familiaris Consortio*, the Church is the steward of the truth about the family. She "knows the path by which the family can reach the heart of the deepest truth about itself" (§86.8). But the Church does not labor arrogantly or alone. She works along with all those who are seeking the truth, offering her evangelical discernment as "an orientation in order that the entire truth and the full dignity of marriage and the family may be preserved and realized" (§5.1).

This process of discernment, of which the apostolic exhortation is itself a striking example, is a task for Bishops and laity alike. In questions touching on marriage and family life, Christian spouses, in virtue of the Sacrament of Matrimony, have received a particular charism of discernment. This gift allows them to make a "unique and irreplaceable contribution to the elaboration of an authentic evangelical discernment in the various situations and cultures in which men and women live their marriage and their family life" (§5.5). While Bishops must dutifully listen to the voice of the laity's experience and prayer, it remains their responsibility to "examine and authoritatively judge" the genuineness of the insights of the lay faithful (§5.4). It is the doctrine of the hierarchical Magisterium on marriage and the family, the Holy Father maintains, "which is the one authentic guide for the People of God" (§31.4).

God's plan for the family founded on marriage

Before outlining the family's mission in society and in the Church, John Paul describes its identity as revealed in the plan of the Creator and Redeemer. In chapter two he develops a theological vision which traces the family's origin to the will of God. The divine design for marriage and the family is first expressed in creation and then fulfilled in the New and Eternal Covenant sealed by the blood of Christ.

Familiaris Consortio begins its presentation of the theology of the family with a consideration of "the original design of God for marriage and the family" (§10.4). Following the example of Christ, who referred to the "beginning" (cf. Mt 19:8), when God revealed his will for ordering conjugal and family life, the Pope takes us back to the creation of man and woman. This "beginning," the time before the disruption in human relations caused by original sin, sets forth the original truth of the family. Today, due to the mystery of the Redemption, families can once again live this "beginning" with the help of Christ's grace (cf. §§3.3, 13.2). Accordingly, "the family must go back to the 'beginning' of God's creative act, if it is to attain self-knowledge and self-realization" (§17.2). In that journey back to the "beginning" the family discovers that it is a community of love and life.

One of the Pope's favorite scriptural texts is Genesis 1:27: "God created man in his own image, in the image of God he created him; male and female he created them" (1:27). Human beings are called into existence *"through love"* and *"for love"* (§11.1). Bearing the divine image, their vocation is to act as God acts. That is, they are to love as he does and to give themselves to others as he does: "Love is therefore the fundamental and innate vocation of every human being" (§11.2). This call to love and be loved is at the heart of the spousal covenant which forms the wider community of the family. Conjugal love and marriage "are ordained to the procreation and education of children, in whom they find their crowning" (§14.1). When a couple give themselves to one another in marital relations, they give not just their body and spirit "but also the reality of children, who are a living reflection of their love, a permanent sign of conjugal unity and a living and inseparable synthesis of their being a father and a mother" (§14.2).

For the Holy Father, each human being is an incarnate spirit, a person with a body, who expresses and receives love through that body. He or she "is called to love in his unified totality. Love includes the human body, and the body is made a sharer in spiritual love" (§11.3). As male or female the human body has a "nuptial meaning" (§37.6). And conjugal love, the basis of marriage and the family, is willed by God himself. It, too, is to be lived according to his design established in the "beginning."

The Old Testament recounts that God revealed his love for Israel by forming a Covenant with his people. This communion of love is meaningfully expressed by the marriage covenant between husband and wife. "Their bond of love," writes the Holy Father, "becomes the image and the symbol of the Covenant which unites God and his people" (§12.2). Covenantal love is thus the model of the faithful and life-giving love to which spouses are called and on which marriage is built.

It is, however, the New and Eternal Covenant brought about by Christ's redemptive sacrifice on Calvary which fully discloses God's plan for marriage and the family: "In this sacrifice there is entirely revealed that plan which God has imprinted on the humanity of man and woman since their creation" (§13.3). This Covenant, which is sealed by the blood of the Cross, confirms the original truth about marriage. Christ is the Bridegroom who unites the Church to himself as his Bride (cf. Eph 5:21-33). By means of this union, he removes the "hardness of heart" (Mt 19:8) caused by sin and, in his Church, "makes man capable of realizing this truth in its entirety" (§13.2). God's plan for marriage, first revealed in creation, is now elevated to a sacrament of the New Covenant. The marriage of baptized spouses — "in the Lord" (1 Cor 7:39) — is "a real symbol" (§13.3) of Christ's faithful and eternal love for his Bride, the Church. The belonging of husband and wife to each other is "the real representation," writes the Pope, "of the very relationship of Christ with the Church" (§13.7, cf. §51.2). The love of Christ for the Church furnishes the interpretive key for the exhortation's later discussion of the specific characteristics of conjugal and family love as total, sacrificial, faithful, exclusive, and indissoluble.

John Paul ends the chapter on God's plan for marriage and the family with a section devoted to virginity and celibacy. The choice of renouncing marriage for the sake of the Kingdom, he says, is also a calling, an exalted but less common way for a believer, to live his or her vocation to love. Virginity presupposes a high regard for marriage: "When marriage is not esteemed, neither can consecrated virginity or celibacy exist" (§16.1). The Pope holds that virginity or celibacy "keeps alive in the Church a consciousness of the mystery of marriage and defends it from any reduction and impoverishment" (§16.4). Moreover, he reaffirms the Church's Tradition regarding "the superiority of this charism to that of marriage." This objective excellence, which is distinct from an individual's holiness of life, is based on "the wholly singular link which it has with the Kingdom of God" (§16.5). By their virginal way of life, celibates express the definitive value of the Kingdom and anticipate the world of future resurrection (cf. Mt 22:30).

Family as a community of persons

According to John Paul II, the family is a community of love and life which arises from the spousal covenant of marriage. It is the path taken by most people in living out their vocation to love. Thus, "the essence and role of the family are in the final analysis specified by love": the family "has *the mission to guard, reveal and communicate love,* and this is a living reflection of and a real sharing in God's love for humanity and the love of Christ the Lord for the Church his Bride" (§17.2). In order to foster this mission of love the family is called to assume four responsibilities. It must form a community of persons, serve life, contribute to the development of society, and share in the Church's life and mission.

The first task of the family is to live faithfully and foster the growth of its inner life as a true community of persons. This means that love must be the family's life-giving principle. Its growth and fulfillment as a community of persons depends on love. Only love between spouses and among family members can establish and sustain this institution as a community of persons.

Before defining the specific traits of the family community, *Familiaris Consortio* describes two characteristics of the communion between husband and wife on which it is founded. First, this communion is marked by a continual growth in the spouses' mutual self-giving, a sharing of their entire life-project together. Thus husband and wife progress toward "an ever richer union with each other on all levels — of the body, of the character, of the heart, of the intelligence and will, of the soul" (§19.3). The unity and exclusivity of conjugal communion is "radically contradicted by polygamy" (§19.4), a practice which contradicts God's original revealed plan for man and woman. Second, authentic spousal communion must be indissoluble. The divine design of creation, renewed by Christ's teaching and grace, requires that the foundation of the family rest on a bond that "participates truly in the irrevocable indissolubility that binds Christ to the Church his Bride, loved by him to the end" (§20.4). Divorce and a subsequent marital union deny the truth of the indissolubility of marriage.

Just as Christ's grace bestowed in the Sacrament of Matrimony raises the union of husband and wife to a higher level than that given in creation, so also does that sacramental grace enable the broader community of the family to be united in a deeper communion, one which perfects the natural bonds of love between its members. Following the teaching of the Second Vatican Council, the Holy Father describes the Christian family as a "domestic Church," or Church of the home, since it is "a specific revelation and realization of ecclesial communion" (§21.3). The family intensifies its life as a community of persons by enabling each member to give and receive love from the others, by fostering the spirit of sacrifice, generosity, self-giving, forgiveness, and especially by celebrating the Sacraments of Reconciliation and Eucharist.

John Paul also mentions several serious obstacles that prevent the family from becoming a community of persons which fosters the personal dignity of each of its members. This concern leads him to take up questions dealing with women and mothers, men and husbands, children, and the elderly.

As persons of equal dignity created in God's image and likeness, husband and wife form the primary human community. The Holy Father forcefully asserts, as a truth of revelation, "the equal dignity and responsibility of women with men" (§22.3). He resolutely condemns the mentality which treats women as "things" rather than "persons"; such an attitude produces the bitter fruits of contempt, slavery, pornography, prostitution, and other forms of degrading discrimination against women (cf. §24). For John Paul, "the true advancement of women requires that clear recognition be given to the value of their maternal and family role, by comparison with all other public roles and all other professions" (§23.2). The promotion of the family as a community of persons also demands a renewed theology of work, especially as it affects women. This theology entails the recognition of and respect for the irreplaceable value of women's work in the family. It also requires that wives and mothers not be compelled to work outside the home in order to make ends meet.

Husbands and fathers, too, are to foster family community in suitable ways. Each one must show "a profound respect for the equal dignity of his wife" (§25.3). Men should be intimately involved in family life, yet without becoming an oppressive presence. The Pope excoriates "machismo," which he defines as "a wrong superiority of male prerogatives which humiliates women and inhibits the development of healthy family relationships" (§25.4). The provision of a sound education for the children is among the father's chief tasks in ensuring the family's growth as a community of persons.

The exhortation also recalls that parents foster the family's identity as a community of persons by showing profound esteem for their children's personal dignity and respect for their rights. This attitude calls for the parents to show a tender love to offspring, especially when sick, suffering, or handicapped, and to assume responsibility for their children's material, emotional, educational, and spiritual welfare. Moreover, John Paul observes that children can "offer their own precious contribution to building up the family community and even to the sanctification of their parents" (§26.4). Finally, he notes the need, where it has been neglected, to treasure the essential contribution made by the elderly in forming the family as a community of persons.

Serving life: procreation and education

A frequent theme of John Paul's teaching, and one repeated here, is that of the family's fundamental task to serve life, to make present in history "the original blessing of the Creator" (§28.2). After God created man and woman in his own image, he ordered them to "be fruitful and multiply" (Gen 1:28). Consequently, from the "beginning," husband and wife are to share in God's love and power "through their free and responsible cooperation in transmitting the gift of human life" (§28.1). Spousal fruitfulness is a unique participation in, and prolongation of, God's creative love; children are "the fruit and the sign of conjugal love" (§28.3).

Since procreation is such a sacred reality, the Church staunchly defends and fosters the dignity of conjugal love in her teaching. She shows this vigilance because "doubt or error in the field of marriage or the family involves obscuring to a serious extent the integral truth about the human person" (§31.4). In keeping with the defense of an authentic Christian anthropology, a concern which marks his entire Pontificate, John Paul reaffirms the Church's teaching on conjugal sexuality, as proposed by the Second Vatican Council and Paul VI's encyclical *Humanae Vitae* (1968). Certainly the Church's pastoral practice must reckon with the contemporary social and cultural situation which often makes her teaching difficult to understand. But, despite today's widespread pessimism about the future, pursuit of selfish pleasure, and exaggerated fear of demographic increase, she must boldly make known her "prophetic proclamation" (§29.2) on the transmission of human life. Amid society's widespread confusion which falsifies or misinterprets the meaning of conjugal love, "the Church more urgently feels how irreplaceable is her mission of presenting sexuality as a value and task of the whole person, created male and female in the image of God" (§32.1). Central to her teaching is the conviction that the procreative and unitive meanings of sex cannot be deliberately separated without distorting the true significance of conjugal relations.

In *Familiaris Consortio*, the Holy Father deals at length with contraception, as we shall examine later in detail. With insights based on his personalist ethics he explains why it is intrinsically immoral, and why it strikes "at God's creation itself at the level of the deepest interaction of nature and person" (§32.6). The Pope also clarifies the difference between contraception and natural methods of regulating fertility and spells out the pastoral ramifications of the Church's teaching on responsible parenthood.

In matters of conjugal morality, the Church is inseparably Teacher and Mother. As Teacher, she proposes the full truth of the revealed moral norms received from her Lord. As Mother, she is "close to the many married couples who find themselves in difficulty over this important point of the moral life" (§33.3). The Church's pastoral approach to contraception is rooted in her conviction that the divine law on transmitting life fosters the true good of married love and family communion. When faced by a couple's lack of understanding and failures in practice, all those engaged in family ministry must present the moral norms governing responsible procreation clearly and forcefully. But, at the same time, they must also make a "tenacious and courageous effort to create and uphold all the human conditions — psychological, moral and spiritual — indispensable for understanding and living the moral value and norm" (§33.5). The whole Church community — Bishops, priests, Religious, parents, and families — ought to assume responsibility for instilling conviction about the truth of human sexuality and offering the practical help necessary which enables spouses to live their conjugal life in light of Christ's teaching.

Besides following the Church's norms on responsible procreation, serving life in the family also entails the duty of parents to pass on to their children the "fruits of moral, spiritual and supernatural life" (§28.4). Because they participate in God's creative activity, mothers and fathers have the task of educating their offspring. Providing an integral education is a spiritual prolongation of procreation. It completes the conjugal love of parents and brings it to fulfillment. Through the rearing of children a mother and father become "fully parents" (§39.4).

The Holy Father lists four characteristics of the parents' right and duty to educate their children. First and foremost, parental love is "the *animating principle* and therefore the *norm* inspiring and guiding all concrete educational activity" (§36.3). Second, the education of children is a constitutive element of being a mother and a father. Third, parents are the most important educators of their own children; their role is "original and primary with regard to the educational role of others" (§36.2). Fourth, the parents' educational mission is "irreplaceable and inalienable" (§36.2). When any other people or institutions share in their responsibility, as is the case in all modern societies, they must respect the principle of subsidiarity, which recognizes the parents' prevailing rights in this domain.

John Paul then describes the content of the human and Christian education of children. He encourages parents to "train their children in the essential values of human life" (§37.1). In this way they carry out the family's task of being "the first and fundamental school of social living" (§37.2). He especially points out the primary right and duty of parents to provide a "clear and delicate" sex education and a formation in chastity for their children (cf. §37.3). Their instruction in this realm should be based on "a knowledge of and respect for the moral norms" (§37.6).

Like the universal Church, the family is both mother and teacher, "called together by word and sacrament as the Church of the home" (§38.3). Through the consecration received in the Sacrament of Matrimony parents receive the vocation and grace of "building up the Church in their children" (§38.3, cf. §39.3). This mission requires them to "present to their children all the topics that are necessary for the gradual maturing of their personality from a Christian and ecclesial point of view" (§39.1). Parents are the first heralds of the Gospel for their children, whom they instruct chiefly by the living witness of their lives.

No doubt having totalitarian regimes in mind, the Pope maintains that "the right of parents to choose an education in conformity with their religious faith must be absolutely guaranteed" (§40.3). This is in accordance with the principle of subsidiarity, which acknowledges the parents' God-given right to be the principal educators of their own children. The State and the Church are obliged to help parents to carry out their educational mission, but not to replace them. Parents, for their part, must offer cooperation to school and ecclesial authorities.

Family's mission to society

John Paul is convinced that the family, as the first and basic cell of society, has a key role to play in revitalizing social life. It is "the first school of the social virtues that are the animating principle of the existence and development of society itself" (§42.2). He describes this educational role by pointing out the contribution that the family should make to society, and the contribution that society should make to the family.

Contemporary society is becoming depersonalized. Things, efficiency, and technique are often given more importance than persons. But, according to John Paul II, the family can stem this negative tide. In fact, it is "the most effective means for humanizing and personalizing society" (§43.4). As its life-giving nucleus, the family participates in developing society. Every social institution, every concern touching education, work, economics, culture, and politics is connected with this vital social cell. The family makes its "first and fundamental contribution to society" (§43.1) by living its own interior vocation: being a communion of persons.

It is in the family that a person first becomes aware of his or her unique dignity and learns what it means to love and to be loved. Here, where "respecting and fostering personal dignity in each and every one" is regarded "as the only basis for value" (§43.2), the social fabric is reinforced. Families offset the anonymity and impersonality of modern social life by recognizing the uniqueness of each member, age or "usefulness" notwithstanding. To the extent that the family promotes true communion among its members, it can serve as "the first and irreplaceable school of social life, and example and stimulus for the broader community relationships marked by respect, justice, dialogue and love" (§43.3).

By becoming more what it is — a community of persons — the family, either singly or in association, can effectively contribute to the development of social and cultural life. Furthermore, the Pope urges families to take an active part in the political arena. He invites them to assume their responsibility for transforming society by becoming protagonists of "family politics." This task leads them to be "the first to take steps to see that the laws and institutions of the State not only do not offend but support and positively defend the rights and duties of the family" (§44.5).

For its part, society should defend and foster the family, respecting its specific identity and inalienable duties. Again the Pope mentions the importance of subsidiarity. The State is never to usurp the family's role of attending to its needs, which it accomplishes either on its own or in association with other families. Political authority must respect the family's rightful autonomy and refrain from regulating its internal life. Rather, the State should "favor and encourage as far as possible responsible initiative by families" (§45.3). At the same time, public authorities should strive to ensure that families have the economic, social, educational, and cultural help needed for their own development. As a way of protecting the family against incursions and of reminding the State of its duties, the Pope promises that the Holy See will draw up a Charter of the Rights of the Family which it will then present to the relevant authorities (cf. §46). This Charter was issued in 1983.

Family's mission in and for the Church

Even more important than the family's social role is its ecclesial task. Through the Sacrament of Matrimony, the Christian family "is grafted into the mystery of the Church to such a degree as to become a sharer, in its own way, in the saving mission proper to the Church" (§49.4). The family, then, is a *saved* community that is also called to be a *saving* community. It has the vocation of building up the Kingdom of God precisely as a community of persons. In the Holy Father's words: "The family's sharing in the Church's mission should follow *a community pattern:* the spouses together *as a couple,* the parents and children *as a family,* must live their service to the Church and to the world" (§50.2). Following the traditional depiction of Christ as Prophet, Priest, and King, *Familiaris Consortio* describes the family's threefold mission as prophetic, priestly, and kingly.

The family fulfills its prophetic mission by being a believing and an evangelizing community. As a believing community, it welcomes the word of God faithfully and bears witness to it in daily life. The family is also called to be an evangelizing community. For John Paul, "the future of evangelization depends in great part on the Church of the home" (§52.2, cf. §65.3). This ministry of evangelization within the domestic Church first embraces the children, but it extends to any member of the family who lacks faith or practices it inconsistently. The family's prophetic task also commits it to sharing in the Church's duty to "preach the Gospel to the whole creation" (Mk 16:15). It carries this out by the luminous witness of family love, by working in mission territories, and by fostering missionary vocations among its members.

As a community in dialogue with God, the family discharges its priestly calling through sharing in the sacraments, offering the spiritual sacrifice of life, and prayer. "The Christian family," writes the Pope, *"is called to be sanctified and to sanctify the ecclesial community and the world"* (§55.3). The Sacrament of Matrimony "is the specific source and original means of sanctification for Christian married couples and families" (§56.1). It is an act of worship whose graces are conferred on husband and wife and, through them, on the children. The family also lives out its priestly mission by partaking in the Eucharist, through which "the different members of the Christian family become one body" (§57.2), and by accepting forgiveness in Reconciliation. Matrimony also gives family members "the grace and moral obligation of transforming their whole lives into a 'spiritual sacrifice'" (§56.5, cf. §59.1). Lastly, the family is sanctified by prayer offered in common or in private for its specific needs.

The family's kingly mission is expressed in its service of love toward God and neighbor. Just as Christ exercises his royal power by serving others (cf. Mk 10:45), so also does the Christian family. It participates in Christ's kingship by "sharing his spirit and practice of service to man" (§63.4). As a community of persons sustained by the grace of the Sacrament of Matrimony, the family should work to bring about "a more homelike or family dimension" (§64.2) in the Church and to promote the truly human advancement of society.

Stages in the pastoral care of the family

In chapter four of *Familiaris Consortio,* John Paul II urges the whole Church to accept the challenge of strengthening the pastoral care of the family, an activity which he considers "a real matter of priority" (§65.3). He systematically describes the stages, structures, agents, and difficult situations of this pastoral intervention. Not given to laying down prohibitions or formulating a set of rules, the Pope proceeds by enlightening and encouraging. He stresses that the family's pastoral care is guided by three principles. First, it fosters the family's foundation in its vocation to safeguard love, the basis of its stability and vitality. Second, family ministry reaches out to all families, whether Christian or not, above all to those in difficult or irregular situations. Third, wise pastoral initiatives take into account that the path to holiness is arduous and achieved step by step.

According to the Holy Father, the pastoral care of the family begins with the promotion of "better and more intensive programs of marriage preparation" (§66.2). While education for married life is first of all the family's responsibility, today's situation calls for the Church and society to play a role in this process as well. *Remote* preparation begins in the home during childhood. Through the primarily silent witness of parents, children learn about relationships, values, and the human and spiritual meaning of marriage. A more *proximate* preparation for marriage and family life is provided during the teenage years by catechesis and religious formation. When a couple is engaged to be married, there should be an intense period of *immediate* preparation. *Familiaris Consortio* compares this last period to a catechumenate. Its purpose is to lead the couple to "a deeper knowledge of the mystery of Christ and the Church, of the meaning of grace and of the responsibility of Christian marriage" (§66.8).

The wedding ceremony itself also deserves pastoral attention. Those responsible for preparing the couple are to ensure that the proposed marriage meets the Church's regulations regarding free consent, absence of impediments, the observance of canonical form, and the liturgical rite of the marriage itself. Provision should also be made for appropriate cultural adaptations of the liturgical celebration and the participation of the wider community. The Pope also takes up the sensitive problem presented by a couple who are non-practicing but wishes a sacramental marriage. He warns against being overly rigorous in this regard. In particular, when motives of a social nature play a large part, he cautions against laying down rigid criteria which would too readily lead to refusing a sacramental marriage. As long as the couple at least implicitly consent to what the Church intends by Matrimony, they should not be turned away. The sacrament is to be denied only when, in spite of all efforts, "engaged couples show that they reject explicitly and formally what the Church intends to do when the marriage of baptized persons is celebrated" (§68.7).

The Church's pastoral concern should also be evident after the wedding. All members of the local community are invited to help the newly married to live their new vocation. Christian spouses with experience in living the Sacrament of Matrimony faithfully are the most valuable mentors of young couples.

Structures and agents of pastoral care

"No plan for organized pastoral work, at any level," writes John Paul, "must ever fail to take into consideration the pastoral care of the family" (§70.2). To carry out this ministry the Church has at her disposal various structures and devoted workers. As a way of preparing some members of the community more specifically for the family apostolate, the Pope recommends that they receive a specialized formation, if possible in institutes set up for this purpose.

By virtue of the grace of Matrimony, families have a unique role in providing pastoral care for themselves and for other families. This mission is particularly effective when it is carried out in the various movements of spirituality, formation, and apostolate which have family care among their specific concerns. Christian families are also called to take part in non-ecclesial associations which safeguard and promote authentic family life.

Familiaris Consortio singles out six different groups that minister to the family: Bishops, priests and deacons, Religious, theologians, lay specialists, and professionals in the field of social communications. The local Bishop, of course, is the one "principally responsible in the Diocese for the pastoral care of the family" (§73.1). For him, this ministry must be a priority: "He must devote to it personal interest, care, time, personnel and resources, but above all personal support for the families and for all those who, in the various diocesan structures, assist him in the pastoral care of the family" (§73.1).

After a serious preparation for the family apostolate, priests and deacons assist families by celebrating the sacraments and preaching the truth. The Holy Father reminds the clergy that their teaching and advice must "always be in full harmony with the authentic Magisterium of the Church." This fidelity, he maintains, will enable "the People of God to gain a correct sense of the faith" which can then be applied to everyday life (§73.4). With the same concern for doctrinal orthodoxy, the Pope addresses theologians. He exhorts them to explain clearly and thoroughly the Church's teaching on the family and recalls that "the proximate and obligatory norm in the teaching of the faith — also concerning family matters — belongs to the hierarchical Magisterium" (§73.5, cf. §31.4).

The Pope appeals to men and women Religious to develop their apostolate on behalf of the family. Likewise, lay specialists in the various professions, whether individually or in associations, can support families by their professional services and advice. Lastly, he asks those involved in the field of social communications to make every effort to promote authentic family values in the media and to avoid presenting distorted ways of looking at the family which undermine its dignity and mission.

Pastoral care in difficult cases

Families in difficult situations deserve from the Church a "generous, intelligent and prudent pastoral commitment, modeled on the Good Shepherd" (§77.1). John Paul invites all those entrusted with pastoral responsibilities to help wounded families to experience Christ's love, the Church's maternal comfort, and God's mercy, a mercy which is never separated from the demands of truth. Among the situations requiring special pastoral care are mixed marriages, *de facto* free unions, common-law marriages, civil marriages, and divorce (which is dealt with at greater length in the following section).

According to the Pope, marriages between Catholics and other baptized persons need pastoral attention in at least three important areas. First, before the marriage, care must be taken to guarantee that the Catholic party will enjoy "the free exercise of the faith" and that he or she accepts the "obligation to ensure, as far as is possible, the Baptism and upbringing of the children in the Catholic faith" (§78.3). Second, pastors should help spouses in mixed marriages to respect each other's right to religious freedom. Neither partner is to pressure the other to change his or her beliefs or to put obstacles in the way of the other's religious practice. Third, those who prepare a couple for a mixed marriage are to be sensitive to its ecumenical implications. They should make a real effort "to establish cordial cooperation between the Catholic and the non-Catholic ministers from the time that preparations begin for the marriage and the wedding ceremony" (§78.8). Even more special pastoral assistance ought to be given to a couple when one of the partners is non-baptized.

The Holy Father begins his discussion of pastoral care in situations which are "irregular," in a religious sense and often in a civil sense as well, with trial marriages: what Americans usually call "living together." Drawing on his personalist philosophy, John Paul gives two reasons that explain why premarital sex harms the couple involved and undermines the family as a social and ecclesial institution.

First, the Pope observes that conjugal relations outside marriage entail "carrying out an 'experiment' with human beings, whose dignity demands that they should be always and solely the term [that is, end] of a self-giving love without limitations of time or of any other circumstance" (§80.1). For those living together without the commitment to marriage, their sexual relations, which are meant to express a total and irrevocable self-gift, are conditioned: they withhold the future from each other. By choosing not to be married, the gift of self expressed in their conjugal relations is incomplete. In an earlier section, the Holy Father makes the same point very clearly: "The total physical self-giving would be a lie if it were not the sign and fruit of a total personal self-giving, in which the whole person, including the temporal dimension, is present: if the person were to withhold something or reserve the possibility of deciding otherwise in the future, by this very fact he or she would not be giving totally" (§11.5). A counterfeit gift of self treats the other person as an object to be "used" and cannot express the true love found in marriage.

Second, for those who are baptized, conjugal relations are "a real symbol of the union of Christ and the Church" (§80.2), and this union of the Bridegroom with the Bride is eternal and permanent. Christ has covenanted himself forever to the Church for which he sacrificed himself (cf. Eph 5:25). Any way of living a conjugal relationship which is not coupled with a promise of lifelong fidelity suggests that Christ's union with his Bride is temporary. The "language" of a time-conditioned sign, which is what premarital relations are, implies something false about the divine Covenant.

Familiaris Consortio refers to *de facto* free unions as those which lack any religious or civil recognition. In the United States they are called common-law marriages. The exhortation outlines many reasons which lead couples to make this choice. These couples present the Church "with arduous pastoral problems" (§81.3) which the ecclesial community should strive to resolve. John Paul recommends two ways of doing this.

In order to inspire couples to regularize their situation, those in family ministry should seek them out, enlighten them patiently, and explain to them the value of Christian marriage and family life. When dealing with Catholics who have contracted a civil marriage, the Pope recommends that pastoral action should "make these people understand the need for consistency between their choice of life and the faith that they profess, and to try to do everything possible to induce them to regularize their situation in the light of

Christian principles" (§82.2). Second, he urges that pastors should promote "a campaign of prevention" (§81.4), which would foster a true sense of marriage and the family among the young.

As is customary, the Holy Father concludes his apostolic exhortation with an urgent appeal. While acknowledging the many difficulties encountered, he calls upon Christians and other people of good will to restore their confidence in the riches that the family "possesses by nature and grace, and in the mission that God has entrusted to it" (§86.6). Invoking the protection of the Holy Family of Nazareth, John Paul asks the Virgin Mary to give new life to the family by showing herself as "the Mother of 'the Church of the home' " (§86.13).

Key Themes

Familiaris Consortio is a document rich in doctrine and pastoral wisdom. From such wealth, this section treats three themes: one more strictly doctrinal, and two which touch pressing pastoral questions. In the first category is the exhortation's treatment of spousal communion and family community. This provides a kind of hermeneutical key to John Paul's bracing vision of marriage and family life. In the second category, which deals with questions that are more controversial and highlighted by the media, is his presentation of the Church's teaching and pastoral practice on contraception and divorce.

Spousal communion and family community

Among the doctrinal threads running through the apostolic exhortation is its teaching that the origin of the family lies in God's plan first revealed in creation and "interiorly ordained to fulfillment in Christ" (§3.3). This emphasis on the divine design for marriage and the family frequently takes him back to the "beginning," to the creation of man and woman. Adam and Eve were created in the image and likeness of God as male and female, as the first married couple (cf. Gen 1:26-27). Thus their creation as a couple imaged the Holy Trinity, which is itself a communion of divine Persons. Because spouses image the Triune God, they form "the first communion . . . and they are called to grow continually in their communion through day-to-day fidelity to their marriage promise of total mutual self-giving" (§19.1). This communion of husband and wife gives birth to the family as a community. In *Familiaris Consortio,* as throughout his teaching, John Paul underscores that a sound Christian anthropology must take into account the uniqueness of every individual and his or her fulfillment "through a sincere gift of self" (*Gaudium et Spes,* §24). The apostolic exhortation combines the person-centeredness of his philosophy with his emphasis on the value of communion and community as essential to human perfection.

For John Paul, the tensions and conflicts which shake the modern world are "caused by the violent clash of various kinds of individualism and selfishness" (§37.2). Such individualism exalts the isolated person in an absolute way, leaving little or no place for openness to others and communion with them. In order to combat an individualistic concept of freedom, which minimizes a person's inherently relational dimension and undermines the family, the Pope insists on a basic truth of Christian anthropology. Human beings find their fulfillment in interpersonal communion; they exist and act *with* others and *for* others. Moreover, only equal persons who address each other as an "I" and a "thou" can live in communion. Marriage, as the coming together of husband and wife in "one flesh" (Gen 2:24; Mt 19:6), expresses the most intimate communion possible between two persons and is the primary antidote to individualism.

Spousal communion is an image of the Trinity, which itself "lives a mystery of personal loving communion" (§11.2). This unity of divine Persons in communion reveals a profound truth about what it means for a man and a woman to be created in God's image as a couple. From the "beginning," the conjugal love of husband and wife embodies and fosters a true communion of persons. Each one exists for the other but, at the same time, the unique dignity of husband and wife is personally perfected. Just as God exists as a unity in communion, so also does the couple created in the Trinitarian likeness. Thus husband and wife are called to live in a way that mirrors for the world the communion of love that is God's inner life (cf. 1 Jn 4:16).

The marital communion of love and life is perfected when the spouses become parents. Their conjugal communion, their "one flesh," is "the foundation of the wider community of the family" (§14.1). The "I-thou" relationship of husband and wife is profoundly dynamic and moves toward the formation of a new "we." The family, then, is "a community of persons: of husband and wife, of parents and children, of relatives" (§18.1, cf. §21.1). It brings to fulfillment the relationship of communion between husband and wife, creating the first human society as a genuine community.

Within the Trinity the three Persons love one another in the intimate mystery of their divine life. Likewise, love is the inner principle which animates the family community. Because love is "the fundamental and innate vocation of every human being" (§11.2), writes the Pope, "the essence and role of the family are in the final analysis specified by love" (§17.2, cf. §64.2). He affirms emphatically: "*Without love the family cannot live, grow and perfect itself as a community of persons*" (§18.2, cf. §§21.4, 37.2). "Love is essentially a gift" (§14.2), and the family is the place where the "sincere gift of self" is made to others. It is a community of persons where each member, after the example of the parents who receive the "gift" of a child (cf. §21.5), exists for others, becoming a "gift" for them.

The family, as a community built on spousal communion, has specific responsibilities to the Church and society. John Paul affirms that its "first task is to live with fidelity the reality of communion in a constant effort to develop an authentic community of persons" (§18.1). In the family each person's dignity is regarded as the sole measure of value. The affirmation of the other as a person occurs only if the other is loved for his or her own sake; this love is shown and nourished first and foremost in the family. Because its members form a unique community of persons, "the family finds in love the source and the constant impetus for welcoming, respecting and promoting each one of its members in his or her lofty dignity as a person" (§22.1, cf. §43.2). Thus, the measure of a family's success in living as a community of persons is dependent on the degree to which the dignity of individual family members is fostered.

Precisely because it is a community of persons, the family strengthens the social fabric. As society's first vital cell, it enables the wider community to be permeated and enlivened by the interpersonal relationships which it nourishes. In this way social life is less likely to fall prey to "the risk of becoming more and more depersonalized and standardized and therefore inhuman and dehumanizing" (§43.5). The family, inspired by self-giving love, carries out its mission of being the basic school of social life. According to the Holy Father, this experience of communion and sharing in the home, "represents its first and fundamental contribution to society" (§43.1).

Likewise, the family community contributes to the mission in the Church. In the family, the love of God is first experienced, the art of loving learned, and the love of neighbor taught and practiced. The love between spouses and family members constitutes "the nucleus of the saving mission of the Christian family in the Church and for the Church" (§50.3). This way of life in the family, which is marked by that love characteristic of a true community of persons, enriches the wider ecclesial community. It gives the Church a more family-like quality and serves to develop "a more human and fraternal style of relationships" among the People of God (§64.2).

Contraception and responsible parenthood

The widespread practice of contraception raises serious pastoral difficulties. This problem must be confronted if the family is to flourish according to God's plan. In *Familiaris Consortio,* John Paul faces the challenge head-on.

He addresses the cultural situation which promotes contraception and a contraceptive mentality, confirms the Church's doctrine, endeavors to provide fresh and convincing reasons for this teaching, and offers pastoral guidance aimed at helping couples to live holy lives in conformity with the moral norms of conjugal chastity.

In many contemporary societies prosperity is joined to anguish and uncertainty about the future. An exaggerated fear of demographic increase influences many couples to limit the size of their family. Others, under the sway of selfishness, view children as an obstacle to their personal fulfillment. These attitudes all too often lead to perceiving new life "not as a blessing, but as a danger from which to defend oneself" (§6.4). When these fears are combined with today's emphasis on the individual's right to self-fulfillment and people's infatuation with absolute control over their own destiny, couples regard contraceptive sex as an answer to their difficulties. At the root of this contraceptive mentality, the Pope says, "is the absence in people's hearts of God, whose love alone is stronger than all the world's fears" (§30.2). At the same time, John Paul also recognizes that many people fail to see the moral gravity of contraception: "The teaching of the Church in our day is placed in a social and cultural context which renders it more difficult to understand and yet more urgent and irreplaceable for promoting the true good of men and women" (§30.1).

Despite the failure of many Catholics to understand and live the Church's teaching on conjugal chastity, the Holy Father reaffirms that this doctrine is well grounded and secure. The Church has received from Christ "the special mission of guarding and protecting the lofty dignity of marriage and the most serious responsibility of the transmission of human life" (§29.1). Her doctrine is based on obedience to the revealed truth. As Teacher, the Church proclaims the moral norm about the responsible transmission of human life. She is very aware of being "in no way the author or the arbiter of this norm" (§33.2). The Church's teaching, which excludes every form of contraception, is rooted in God's loving plan. Consequently, it responds to "the deepest demands of the human being created by God" and serves "that person's full humanity" (§34.2).

The authoritative teaching of the Church, which *Familiaris Consortio* reconfirms, has been clearly proposed by the Second Vatican Council (§§29.2, 31.2, 32.3), by Paul VI, especially in his encyclical *Humanae Vitae* (cf. §§29.1, 31.2, 34.4), and by the Synod Fathers (cf. §29.3). The core of this teaching is straightforward: each time a couple has marital relations both the unitive and the procreative meaning of the conjugal act must be respected. These two goods, the strengthening of interpersonal unity and love between the spouses and the openness to new life, cannot be willfully separated in any act of marital love. Contraception is defined as a conjugal act which is intentionally rendered unfruitful and, as such, is "intrinsically immoral" (§32.3). A husband and a wife, when they engage in contraceptive sex, make two decisions: to have marital relations and to act deliberately against the life-giving meaning of sex.

In order to shed light on the moral disorder of contraception, John Paul takes two approaches. First, he presents contraception as a couple's refusal to accept God's sovereignty over life. Those who contracept act "as 'arbiters' of the divine plan" (§32.4); they fail to respect that plan in which they are meant to be collaborators. Second, and this is more innovative, the Holy Father affirms that contraceptive sex also undermines the unitive meaning of sexual communion. To make his point, he refers to the "innate language" which conjugal relations are meant to express. Through their bodily union husband and wife are to embody "the total reciprocal self-giving" of one to the other (§32.4, cf. §§11.6, 28.3). Included in this total gift of self, which includes the gift of fertility, is the potential of gracing one's spouse with motherhood or fatherhood. Contraception, however, introduces "an objectively contradictory language, namely, that of not giving oneself totally to the other" (§32.4). Instead of accepting each other totally, spouses who contracept reject an integral aspect of the other — the power of love to be fruitful. In this instance, the Pope says that there is "a falsification of the inner truth of conjugal love" (§32.4). The gift of self, which should be total, is incomplete, even counterfeit. The sexual language spoken in contraceptive sex is a lie.

The Church's full teaching on the morality of conjugal life also includes the need for procreation in a responsible way. This requires couples to be faithful interpreters of God's plan. John Paul supports couples who choose natural methods of regulating their fertility. When, for serious reasons, a husband and wife limit conjugal relations to periods of infertility, they make no decision to act *against* the life-giving meaning of sex. Rather, they act as " 'ministers' of God's plan and they 'benefit from' their sexuality according to the original dynamism of 'total' self-giving, without manipulation or alteration" (§32.5). By accepting the natural rhythms of their fertility, such couples show themselves to be faithful stewards of the biological laws inscribed in the human person. This regulation of fertility, which is commonly called natural family planning, is anthropologically and morally different from contraceptive intercourse (cf. §32.6). For this reason, the Pope recommends that "every effort must be made to render such knowledge accessible to all married people and also to young adults before marriage, through clear, timely and serious instruction and education given by married couples, doctors and experts" (§33.7, cf. §§35.2, 72.3).

As befits the exhortatory nature of a post-synodal document, the Holy Father does more than teach "the true meaning of human sexuality" (§32.1). He also provides pastoral guidance to the many married couples who have difficulty in accepting and living this teaching. Often spouses find it hard not only to fulfill the moral norm governing conjugal sexuality but even to understand its value. The Pope seeks to lead couples to the conviction that "there can be no true contradiction between the divine law on transmitting life and that on fostering authentic married love" (§33.4).

In spite of the sacrifices very often entailed, married couples are called to accomplish the full moral good of conjugal love. Pastors of souls must gently guide the spouses to fulfill their vocation to holiness. As a point of departure, husbands and wives should be led to "recognize clearly the teaching of *Humanae Vitae* as indicating the norm for the exercise of their sexuality, and that they should endeavor to establish the conditions necessary for observing that norm" (§34.4). The Pope is particularly concerned lest husbands and wives think that the Church's prohibition of contraception is "merely an ideal to be achieved in the future." Rather, he admonishes, "they must consider it as a command of Christ the Lord to overcome difficulties with constancy" (§34.4).

In various ways the Church helps couples to live their marital chastity. She makes every effort to present the truth of her teaching with a single voice unmarred by dissent; she encourages theologians to explain the reasons for this doctrine more persuasively; she recalls the indispensable role of asceticism and sacrifice in every Christian life; she encourages couples to pray and receive the Sacraments of Reconciliation and the Eucharist; lastly, she offers couples practical help, especially by making the natural methods of regulating fertility more widely known.

Indissolubility and divorce

Another dark shadow on family life today is the growing number of divorces, even on the part of Catholics. Although the Church is pressured from all sides to compromise her teaching on the indissolubility of sacramental marriage, her service to humanity obliges her to hold steadfast to the Gospel she has received. In *Familiaris Consortio,* the Pope reaffirms the Church's teaching on divorce, explains why conjugal love requires the permanent covenant of marriage, and encourages the whole Church to develop a pastoral response to those who are divorced and remarried. In the face of a culture that widely rejects the indissolubility of marriage, he wishes to "reconfirm the good news of the definitive nature of that conjugal love that has in Christ its foundation and strength" (§20.2).

John Paul insists that the Church's teaching on the permanence of the marital covenant is neither an arbitrary divine law nor merely a matter of ecclesiastical discipline. The indissolubility of marriage is rooted "in the plan that God has manifested in his revelation" (§20.3, cf. §68.3). It is an ethical demand springing from the meaning of love and of conjugal life.

The Law of Moses allowed for divorce because of people's "hardness of heart" (Mt 19:8). It regulated a practice which contradicted the original truth of creation. Christ, however, "renews the first plan that the Creator inscribed in the hearts of man and woman" (§20.4). He offers a "new heart" (Ezek 36:26) which enables spouses to carry out his command: "What therefore God has joined together, let not man put asunder" (Mt 19:6). Rooted in creation and confirmed by Christ, the indissolubility of marriage fosters the true welfare of the family.

Love, especially conjugal love which touches the innermost being of the human person, is meant to be "total." For the sexual "language" of physical self-giving to be honest, nothing can be held back, including the possibility of deciding otherwise in the future. As the Pope says, "The gift of the body in the sexual relationship is a real symbol of the giving of the whole person" (§80.2, cf. §11.5). Here the "yes" to the other reaches out to embrace the "forever." Love is true only when it is definitive. The imposition of any temporal condition — "I will love you until . . ." — falsifies the total self-giving "spoken" in the act of marital love. Thus, the marital gift of one person to another, if it is to be authentic, must be irrevocable.

Already in the Old Covenant, the bond of marriage was "the image and the symbol of the Covenant which unites God with his people" (§12.2). God pledged himself never to break the solemn alliance he had made with his people. Moreover, he intended his ever-faithful love to be mirrored in the enduring love between husband and wife, created in his image and likeness. The full and definitive revelation of God's covenantal love, however, comes to fulfillment in the New Covenant. By assuming a human nature, the Word of God made a definitive gift of himself to humanity and accomplished its salvation on the Cross. At the same time, he gave a new meaning to the marriage of baptized persons. It is now "a real symbol of that New and Eternal Covenant sanctioned in the blood of Christ" (§13.3). The conjugal love of husband and wife is thus raised up to a new supernatural level, because it participates in "the spousal covenant of Christ with the Church" (§13.6, cf. §20.4).

Christ will never break the Eternal Covenant that binds him to his Bride, the Church. His love is enduring. Nor will the Church, despite her infidelities, ever abandon her Bridegroom and Lord. Likewise, Christian spouses, who share in the permanent alliance of the Bridegroom and the Bride, can never break their covenant relationship, as long as they are both alive. By the very fact of their sacramental marriage, husband and wife are integrated into the permanent relationship of Christ to the Church. It follows, therefore, that "Christian couples are called to participate truly in the irrevocable indissolubility that binds Christ to the Church his Bride, loved by him to the end" (§20.4). In virtue of the Sacrament of Marriage, baptized spouses are bound to one another in such a way that they really represent the enduring relationship of Christ with his Church. For the Church and the world they are a " 'sign' — a small and precious sign, sometimes also subjected to temptation, but always renewed — of the unfailing fidelity with which God and Jesus Christ love each and every human being" (§20.6, cf. §13.7).

While encouraging Christian couples to bear witness to the inestimable value of the indissolubility of marriage as the foundation of family life, the Holy Father also turns his attention to those who are separated, divorced, or divorced and remarried. Their sufferings place an urgent pastoral challenge before the Church. To them she shows herself as a merciful Mother. The ecclesial community must offer solidarity and practical help to those who are separated or divorced. John Paul especially praises those who, despite the hardship, remain faithful to the Church's teaching on the indissolubility of marriage, bearing witness to "fidelity and Christian consistency" (§83.3, cf. §20.6). Their painful situation places no obstacle to admission to the Church's full sacramental life.

Those who have divorced and remarried also have a claim on the Church's pastoral care. The Pope affirms that the Church "cannot abandon to their own devices those who have been previously bound by sacramental marriage and who have attempted a second marriage." Instead, he adds, she will make "untiring efforts to put at their disposal her means of salvation" (§84.1). Pastoral initiatives for those in irregular second marriages are to be guided by two principles. First, divorced and remarried individuals remain members of the Church. Second, because of their irregular situation, they lack the fullness of ecclesial communion which is signified by reception of the Holy Eucharist.

The Church remains deeply concerned about the spiritual well-being of her divorced and remarried members. Hence the Pope urges that every effort should be made lest they "consider themselves as separated from the Church, for as baptized persons they can, and indeed must, share in her life" (§84.3). The ecclesial community should welcome divorced and remarried Catholics with the charity of Christ, exhort them to trust in God's mercy, and prudently encourage them to take the necessary steps to reintegrate themselves fully into the Church's sacramental life.

John Paul also reaffirms the Church's traditional teaching and practice, which are based upon Sacred Scripture (cf. Mk 10:11-12), of not admitting to Eucharistic Communion divorced persons who have remarried. This norm is not intended as a punishment. Rather, as the Pope explains, it expresses an objective situation which makes it impossible for such persons to receive Holy Communion. "Their state and condition of life," he writes, "objectively contradict that union of love between Christ and the Church which is signified and effected by the Eucharist" (§84.4). The Holy Father also mentions a pastoral reason for the Church's practice. Admitting the divorced and remarried to the Eucharist could easily lead the faithful into error or confusion about the Church's doctrine on the indissolubility of marriage. Only if a divorced and remarried person is willing to live without conjugal relations can he or she be restored to full ecclesial and Eucharist Communion. In pastoral care respect for this norm is always to be followed out of fidelity to God, who "communicates the indissolubility of marriage as a fruit, a sign and a requirement of the absolutely faithful love that God has for man and that the Lord Jesus has for the Church" (§20.3).

In confirming the Church's teaching on the truth about marriage and the family, the Pope is safeguarding its holiness. *Familiaris Consortio* forcefully proclaims that the history of humanity and of salvation passes by way of the family. This path is well known to the Church; she has learned it "at the school of Christ and the school of history interpreted in the light of the Spirit" (§86.8).

* * *

Selected Bibliography

Anderson, Carl A., and Gribbin, William J., eds. *The Family in the Modern World: A Symposium on Pope John Paul II's "Familiaris Consortio."* Washington: The American Family Institute, 1982.

Arthadeva, Basil Mary. "The Notion of Graduality in *Familiaris Consortio.*" *Christ to the World,* 27 (1982), 250-256.

Bagiackas, Joseph. *A Lay Person's Guide to Pope John Paul II's Teaching on the Family in his "Letter to Families" and "Familiaris Consortio."* South Bend: Light to the Nations Press, 1994.

Castrillón, Darío. "The Family in the Magisterium of John Paul II." In Joseph

Bernardin, ed. *John Paul II: A Panorama of His Teachings.* New York: New City Press, 1988. 113-121.

Colombo, Carlo. "The Apostolic Exhortation and the Spirituality of the Family." *L'Osservatore Romano,* 37 (1982), 11.

Cox Huneeus, Francisco José. "Pastoral Care of the Family in the Light of *Familiaris Consortio.*" *L'Osservatore Romano,* 31 (1982), 4-5.

Gagnon, Edouard. "The Church Places Her Hope in the Christian Family." *L'Osservatore Romano,* 29 (1982), 4-6.

Grootaers, Jan, and Selling, Joseph A. *The 1980 Synod of Bishops "On the Role of the Family": An Exposition of the Event and an Analysis of Its Texts.* Louvain: Louvain University Press, 1983.

Hamlon, John S. *A Call to Families: Study Guide and Commentary for "Familiaris Consortio."* Collegeville: Human Life Center, 1984.

Hebblethwaite, Peter. "The Pope and the Family." *The Tablet,* 236 (1982), 29-30.

Hogan, Richard M., and LeVoir, John M. "John Paul II on Family and Sexuality." *International Review of Natural Family Planning,* 9 (Summer 1985), 144-167.

Hogan, Richard M., and LeVoir, John M. "A Commentary on the Apostolic Exhortation on the Family." In *Covenant of Love: John Paul II on Sexuality, Marriage and Family in the Modern World.* Garden City: Doubleday & Company, Inc., 1985. 125-223.

Hotchkin, John Francis. "*Familiaris Consortio* — New Light on Mixed Marriages." *One in Christ,* 22 (1986), 73-79.

Iannone, Joseph A., and Iannone, Mercedes. "The Educational Ministry of the Christian Family." *Living Light,* 21 (1985), 128-135.

Kelly, George. "Whither *Familiaris Consortio?*" *Homiletic and Pastoral Review,* 83 (October 1982), 9-16.

Knox, James. "Marriage and the Eucharist." *L'Osservatore Romano,* 36 (1982), 9, 12.

Maida, Adam Joseph. "Responsible Parenthood in the Writings of Pope Paul VI and Pope John Paul II." *Linacre Quarterly,* 55 (November 1988), 25-31.

Maestri, William F. *A Guide for the Study of "Familiaris Consortio": The Community of the Family.* Boston: Pauline Books & Media, 1995.

Martin, Diarmuid. "The Question of Inculturation." *L'Osservatore Romano,* 17 (1982), 10-11.

Mastroeni, Anthony, ed. *The Church at the Service of the Family.* Proceedings from the Sixteenth Convention of the Fellowship of Catholic Scholars, 1993. Steubenville: Franciscan University Editions, 1994.

Miller, J. Michael. "Revitalizing Society through the Family: Vision of John Paul II." *Faith & Reason,* 19 (1993), 309-325.

Miller, J. Michael. "The Family as Sacrament: Pope John Paul II's 'New Theology.'" *The Catholic Answer,* 4 (November-December 1990), 38-44.

Morneau, Robert F. "*Familiaris Consortio:* Themes and Theses." *Review for Religious,* 41 (1982), 481-494. Also published in *Themes and Theses of Six Recent Papal Documents: A Commentary.* New York: Alba House, 1985. 137-160.

Murphy, David T. "Recent Outlines for Sex Education: *Familiaris Consortio* and the Charter of the Rights of the Family." *Social Justice Review,* 77 (1986), 113-115.

O'Connor, Edward. "The Catholic Vision of the Family." *Homiletic and Pastoral Review,* 84 (December, 1983), 9-19.

Ratzinger, Joseph. "Marriage and the Family in God's Plan." *L'Osservatore Romano,* 28 (1982), 4.

Roach, Richard. "*Familiaris Consortio* and the Roots of Contemporary Anti-Catholicism." *International Review of Natural Family Planning,* 10 (Summer 1986), 142-147.

Ryan, Dermot. "Forming a Community of Persons in *Familiaris Consortio.*" *L'Osservatore Romano,* 14/15 (1982), 14-15.

Synod of Bishops, Fifth Ordinary General Assembly. *"Instrumentum Laboris."* *Origins,* 10 (1980), 225, 227-233.

Synod of Bishops, Fifth Ordinary General Assembly. *"Lineamenta."* *Origins,* 9 (1979), 113, 115-128.

Synod of Bishops, Fifth Ordinary General Assembly. "Message to Christian Families." *L'Osservatore Romano,* 45 (1980), 6-7; and *Origins,* 10 (1980), 321, 323-325.

Tettamanzi, Dionigi. "The Pastoral Care of the Family and Irregular Situations." *L'Osservatore Romano,* 35 (1982), 6-8.

Tomko, Jozef. "Comment on the Apostolic Exhortation on the Family." *L'Osservatore Romano,* 5 (1982), 11-12.

Wales, Seán. "The Pulpit and the Hearts — Thoughts on *Familiaris Consortio.*" *The Furrow,* 33 (1982), 556-563.

Wrenn, Michael J., ed. *John Paul II and the Family.* Chicago: Franciscan Herald Press, 1983.

APOSTOLIC EXHORTATION
FAMILIARIS CONSORTIO
OF HIS HOLINESS
POPE JOHN PAUL II
TO THE EPISCOPATE
TO THE CLERGY AND TO THE FAITHFUL
OF THE WHOLE CATHOLIC CHURCH
REGARDING THE ROLE
OF THE CHRISTIAN FAMILY
IN THE MODERN WORLD

Familiaris Consortio
Introduction

The Church at the service of the family

1.1 The family in the modern world, as much as and perhaps more than any other institution, has been beset by the many profound and rapid changes that have affected society and culture. Many families are living this situation in fidelity to those values that constitute the foundation of the institution of the family. Others have become uncertain and bewildered over their role or even doubtful and almost unaware of the ultimate meaning and truth of conjugal and family life. Finally, there are others who are hindered by various situations of injustice in the realization of their fundamental rights.

1.2 Knowing that marriage and the family constitute one of the most precious of human values, the Church wishes to speak and offer her help to those who are already aware of the value of marriage and the family and seek to live it faithfully, to those who are uncertain and anxious and searching for the truth, and to those who are unjustly impeded from living freely their family lives. Supporting the first, illuminating the second and assisting the others, the Church offers her services to every person who wonders about the destiny of marriage and the family.[1]

1.3 In a particular way the Church addresses the young, who are beginning their journey toward marriage and family life, for the purpose of presenting them with new horizons, helping them to discover the beauty and grandeur of the vocation to love and the service of life.

The Synod of 1980 in continuity with preceding Synods

2.1 A sign of this profound interest of the Church in the family was the last Synod of Bishops, held in Rome from September 26 to October 25, 1980. This was a natural continuation of the two preceding Synods:[2] the Christian family, in fact, is the first community called to announce the Gospel to the human person during growth and to bring him or her, through a progressive education and catechesis, to full human and Christian maturity.

2.2 Furthermore, the recent Synod is logically connected in some way as well with that on the ministerial priesthood and on justice in the modern

---

[1] Cf. Second Vatican Ecumenical Council, Pastoral Constitution on the Church in the Modern World *Gaudium et Spes,* 52.

[2] Cf. John Paul II, Homily at the Opening of the Synod of Bishops, Fifth Ordinary General Assembly (September 26, 1980), 2: *AAS* 72 (1980), 1008.

world. In fact, as an educating community, the family must help man to discern his own vocation and to accept responsibility in the search for greater justice, educating him from the beginning in interpersonal relationships, rich in justice and in love.

2.3 At the close of their Assembly, the Synod Fathers presented me with a long list of proposals in which they had gathered the fruits of their reflections, which had matured over intense days of work, and they asked me unanimously to be a spokesman before humanity of the Church's lively care for the family and to give suitable indications for renewed pastoral effort in this fundamental sector of the life of man and of the Church.

2.4 As I fulfill that mission with this Exhortation, thus actuating in a particular matter the apostolic ministry with which I am entrusted, I wish to thank all the members of the Synod for the very valuable contribution of teaching and experience that they made, especially through the *Propositiones,* the text of which I am entrusting to the Pontifical Council for the Family with instructions to study it so as to bring out every aspect of its rich content.

The precious value of marriage and of the family

3.1 Illuminated by the faith that gives her an understanding of all the truth concerning the great value of marriage and the family and their deepest meaning, the Church once again feels the pressing need to proclaim the Gospel, that is the "good news," to all people without exception, in particular to all those who are called to marriage and are preparing for it, to all married couples and parents in the world.

3.2 The Church is deeply convinced that only by the acceptance of the Gospel are the hopes that man legitimately places in marriage and in the family capable of being fulfilled.

3.3 Willed by God in the very act of creation,[3] marriage and the family are interiorly ordained to fulfillment in Christ[4] and have need of his graces in order to be healed from the wounds of sin[5] and restored to their "beginning,"[6] that is, to full understanding and the full realization of God's plan.

3.4 At a moment of history in which the family is the object of numerous forces that seek to destroy it or in some way to deform it, and aware that the well-being of society and her own good are intimately tied to the good of the

---

[3] Cf. Gen 1–2.

[4] Cf. Eph 5.

[5] Cf. Second Vatican Ecumenical Council, Pastoral Constitution on the Church in the Modern World *Gaudium et Spes,* 47; John Paul II, Letter to Bishops, Priests and Faithful *Appropinquat Iam* (August 15, 1980), 1: *AAS* 72 (1980), 791.

[6] Cf. Mt 19:4.

family,[7] the Church perceives in a more urgent and compelling way her mission of proclaiming to all people the plan of God for marriage and the family, ensuring their full vitality and human and Christian development, and thus contributing to the renewal of society and of the People of God.

I

Bright Spots and Shadows for the Family Today

The need to understand the situation

4.1 Since God's plan for marriage and the family touches men and women in the concreteness of their daily existence in specific social and cultural situations, the Church ought to apply herself to understanding the situations within which marriage and the family are lived today, in order to fulfill her task of serving.[8]

4.2 This understanding is, therefore, an inescapable requirement of the work of evangelization. It is, in fact, to the families of our times that the Church must bring the unchangeable and ever new Gospel of Jesus Christ, just as it is the families involved in the present conditions of the world that are called to accept and to live the plan of God that pertains to them. Moreover, the call and demands of the Spirit resound in the very events of history, and so the Church can also be guided to a more profound understanding of the inexhaustible mystery of marriage and the family by the circumstances, the questions and the anxieties and hopes of the young people, married couples and parents of today.[9]

4.3 To this ought to be added a further reflection of particular importance at the present time. Not infrequently ideas and solutions which are very appealing, but which obscure in varying degrees the truth and the dignity of the human person, are offered to the men and women of today, in their sincere and deep search for a response to the important daily problems that affect their married and family life. These views are often supported by the powerful and pervasive organization of the means of social communica-

---

[7] Cf. Second Vatican Ecumenical Council, Pastoral Constitution on the Church in the Modern World *Gaudium et Spes,* 47.

[8] Cf. John Paul II, Address to the Council of the General Secretariat of the Synod of Bishops (February 23, 1980): *Insegnamenti* III/1 (1980), 472-476.

[9] Cf. Second Vatican Ecumenical Council, Pastoral Constitution on the Church in the Modern World *Gaudium et Spes,* 4.

tion, which subtly endanger freedom and the capacity for objective judgment.

4.4 Many are already aware of this danger to the human person and are working for the truth. The Church, with her evangelical discernment, joins with them, offering her own service to the truth, to freedom and to the dignity of every man and every woman.

Evangelical discernment

5.1 The discernment effected by the Church becomes the offering of an orientation in order that the entire truth and the full dignity of marriage and the family may be preserved and realized.

5.2 This discernment is accomplished through the sense of faith,[10] which is a gift that the Spirit gives to all the faithful,[11] and is therefore the work of the whole Church according to the diversity of the various gifts and charisms that, together with and according to the responsibility proper to each one, work together for a more profound understanding and activation of the word of God. The Church, therefore, does not accomplish this discernment only through the Pastors, who teach in the name and with the power of Christ, but also through the laity: Christ "made them his witnesses and gave them understanding of the faith and the grace of speech (cf. Acts 2:17-18; Rev 19:10), so that the power of the Gospel might shine forth in their daily social and family life."[12] The laity, moreover, by reason of their particular vocation have the specific role of interpreting the history of the world in the light of Christ, inasmuch as they are called to illuminate and organize temporal realities according to the plan of God, Creator and Redeemer.

5.3 The "supernatural sense of faith,"[13] however, does not consist solely or necessarily in the consensus of the faithful. Following Christ, the Church seeks the truth, which is not always the same as the majority opinion. She listens to conscience and not to power, and in this way she defends the poor and the downtrodden. The Church values sociological and statistical research, when it proves helpful in understanding the historical context in which pasto-

---

[10] Cf. Second Vatican Ecumenical Council, Dogmatic Constitution on the Church *Lumen Gentium,* 12.

[11] Cf. 1 Jn 2:20.

[12] Second Vatican Ecumenical Council, Dogmatic Constitution on the Church *Lumen Gentium,* 35.

[13] Cf. Second Vatican Ecumenical Council, Dogmatic Constitution on the Church *Lumen Gentium,* 12; Sacred Congregation for the Doctrine of the Faith, Declaration in Defense of Catholic Doctrine on the Church *Mysterium Ecclesiae* (June 24, 1973), 2: *AAS* 65 (1973), 398-400.

ral action has to be developed and when it leads to a better understanding of the truth. Such research alone, however, is not to be considered in itself an expression of the sense of faith.

5.4 Because it is the task of the apostolic ministry to ensure that the Church remains in the truth of Christ and to lead her ever more deeply into that truth, the Pastors must promote the sense of the faith in all the faithful, examine and authoritatively judge the genuineness of its expressions, and educate the faithful in an ever more mature evangelical discernment.[14]

5.5 Christian spouses and parents can and should offer their unique and irreplaceable contribution to the elaboration of an authentic evangelical discernment in the various situations and cultures in which men and women live their marriage and their family life. They are qualified for this role by their charism or specific gift, the gift of the Sacrament of Matrimony.[15]

The situation of the family in the world today

6.1 The situation in which the family finds itself presents positive and negative aspects: the first are a sign of the salvation of Christ operating in the world; the second, a sign of the refusal that man gives to the love of God.

6.2 On the one hand, in fact, there is a more lively awareness of personal freedom and greater attention to the quality of interpersonal relationships in marriage, to promoting the dignity of women, to responsible procreation, to the education of children. There is also an awareness of the need for the development of interfamily relationships, for reciprocal spiritual and material assistance, the rediscovery of the ecclesial mission proper to the family and its responsibility for the building of a more just society. On the other hand, however, signs are not lacking of a disturbing degradation of some fundamental values: a mistaken theoretical and practical concept of the independence of the spouses in relation to each other; serious misconceptions regarding the relationship of authority between parents and children; the concrete difficulties that the family itself experiences in the transmission of values; the growing number of divorces; the scourge of abortion; the ever more frequent recourse to sterilization; the appearance of a truly contraceptive mentality.

6.3 At the root of these negative phenomena there frequently lies a corruption of the idea and the experience of freedom, conceived not as a capacity for realizing the truth of God's plan for marriage and the family, but as an au-

---

[14] Cf. Second Vatican Ecumenical Council, Dogmatic Constitution on the Church *Lumen Gentium,* 12; Dogmatic Constitution on Divine Revelation *Dei Verbum,* 12.

[15] Cf. John Paul II, Homily at the Opening of the Synod of Bishops, Fifth Ordinary General Assembly (September 26, 1980), 3: *AAS* 72 (1980), 1008.

tonomous power of self-affirmation, often against others, for one's own selfish well-being.

6.4 Worthy of our attention also is the fact that, in the countries of the so-called Third World, families often lack both the means necessary for survival, such as food, work, housing and medicine, and the most elementary freedoms. In the richer countries, on the contrary, excessive prosperity and the consumer mentality, paradoxically joined to a certain anguish and uncertainty about the future, deprive married couples of the generosity and courage needed for raising up new human life: thus life is often perceived not as a blessing, but as a danger from which to defend oneself.

6.5 The historical situation in which the family lives therefore appears as an interplay of light and darkness.

6.6 This shows that history is not simply a fixed progression toward what is better, but rather an event of freedom, and even a struggle between freedoms that are in mutual conflict, that is, according to the well-known expression of Saint Augustine, a conflict between two loves: the love of God to the point of disregarding self, and the love of self to the point of disregarding God.[16]

6.7 It follows that only an education for love rooted in faith can lead to the capacity of interpreting "the signs of the times," which are the historical expression of this twofold love.

The influence of circumstances on the consciences of the faithful

7.1 Living in such a world, under the pressures coming above all from the mass media, the faithful do not always remain immune from the obscuring of certain fundamental values, nor set themselves up as the critical conscience of family culture and as active agents in the building of an authentic family humanism.

7.2 Among the more troubling signs of this phenomenon, the Synod Fathers stressed the following, in particular: the spread of divorce and of recourse to a new union, even on the part of the faithful; the acceptance of purely civil marriage in contradiction to the vocation of the baptized to "be married in the Lord"; the celebration of the Marriage Sacrament without living faith, but for other motives; the rejection of the moral norms that guide and promote the human and Christian exercise of sexuality in marriage.

Our age needs wisdom

8.1 The whole Church is obliged to a deep reflection and commitment, so that the new culture now emerging may be evangelized in depth, true values

---

[16] Cf. *De Civitate Dei*, XIV, 28: *CSEL* 40, II, 56-57.

acknowledged, the rights of men and women defended, and justice promoted in the very structures of society. In this way the "new humanism" will not distract people from their relationship with God, but will lead them to it more fully.

8.2 Science and its technical applications offer new and immense possibilities in the construction of such a humanism. Still, as a consequence of political choices that decide the direction of research and its applications, science is often used against its original purpose, which is the advancement of the human person.

8.3 It becomes necessary, therefore, on the part of all, to recover an awareness of the primacy of moral values, which are the values of the human person as such. The great task that has to be faced today for the renewal of society is that of recapturing the ultimate meaning of life and its fundamental values. Only an awareness of the primacy of these values enables man to use the immense possibilities given him by science in such a way as to bring about the true advancement of the human person in his or her whole truth, in his or her freedom and dignity. Science is called to ally itself with wisdom.

8.4 The following words of the Second Vatican Council can therefore be applied to the problems of the family: "Our era needs such wisdom more than bygone ages if the discoveries made by man are to be further humanized. For the future of the world stands in peril unless wiser people are forthcoming."[17]

8.5 The education of the moral conscience, which makes every human being capable of judging and of discerning the proper ways to achieve self-realization according to his or her original truth, thus becomes a pressing requirement that cannot be renounced.

8.6 Modern culture must be led to a more profoundly restored covenant with divine Wisdom. Every man is given a share of such Wisdom through the creating action of God. And it is only in faithfulness to this covenant that the families of today will be in a position to influence positively the building of a more just and fraternal world.

Gradualness and conversion

9.1 To the injustice originating from sin — which has profoundly penetrated the structures of today's world — and often hindering the family's full realization of itself and of its fundamental rights, we must all set ourselves in opposition through a conversion of mind and heart, following Christ Crucified by denying our own selfishness: such a conversion cannot fail to have a beneficial and renewing influence even on the structures of society.

---

[17] Pastoral Constitution on the Church in the Modern World *Gaudium et Spes,* 15.

9.2 What is needed is a continuous, permanent conversion which, while requiring an interior detachment from every evil and an adherence to good in its fullness, is brought about concretely in steps which lead us ever forward. Thus a dynamic process develops, one which advances gradually with the progressive integration of the gifts of God and the demands of his definitive and absolute love in the entire personal and social life of man. Therefore an educational growth process is necessary, in order that individual believers, families and peoples, even civilization itself, by beginning from what they have already received of the mystery of Christ, may patiently be led forward, arriving at a richer understanding and a fuller integration of this mystery in their lives.

Inculturation

10.1 In conformity with her constant Tradition, the Church receives from the various cultures everything that is able to express better the unsearchable riches of Christ.[18] Only with the help of all the cultures will it be possible for these riches to be manifested ever more clearly, and for the Church to progress toward a daily more complete and profound awareness of the truth, which has already been given to her in its entirety by the Lord.

10.2 Holding fast to the two principles of the compatibility with the Gospel of the various cultures to be taken up and of communion with the universal Church, there must be further study, particularly by the Episcopal Conferences and the appropriate departments of the Roman Curia, and greater pastoral diligence so that this "inculturation" of the Christian faith may come about ever more extensively, in the context of marriage and the family as well as in other fields.

10.3 It is by means of "inculturation" that one proceeds toward the full restoration of the covenant with the Wisdom of God, which is Christ himself. The whole Church will be enriched also by the cultures which, though lacking technology, abound in human wisdom and are enlivened by profound moral values.

10.4 So that the goal of this journey might be clear and consequently the way plainly indicated, the Synod was right to begin by considering in depth the original design of God for marriage and the family: it "went back to the beginning," in deference to the teaching of Christ.[19]

---

[18] Cf. Eph 3:8; Second Vatican Ecumenical Council, Pastoral Constitution on the Church in the Modern World *Gaudium et Spes,* 44; Decree on the Church's Missionary Activity *Ad Gentes,* 15, 22.

[19] Cf. Mt 19:4-6.

II

The Plan of God for Marriage and the Family

Man, the image of the God who is love

11.1 God created man in his own image and likeness:[20] calling him to existence *through love,* he called him at the same time *for love.*

11.2 God is love[21] and in himself he lives a mystery of personal loving communion. Creating the human race in his own image and continually keeping it in being, God inscribed in the humanity of man and woman the vocation, and thus the capacity and responsibility, of love and communion.[22] Love is therefore the fundamental and innate vocation of every human being.

11.3 As an incarnate spirit, that is a soul which expresses itself in a body and a body informed by an immortal spirit, man is called to love in his unified totality. Love includes the human body, and the body is made a sharer in spiritual love.

11.4 Christian revelation recognizes two specific ways of realizing the vocation of the human person, in its entirety, to love: marriage and virginity or celibacy. Either one is, in its own proper form, an actuation of the most profound truth of man, of his being "created in the image of God."

11.5 Consequently, sexuality, by means of which man and woman give themselves to one another through the acts which are proper and exclusive to spouses, is by no means something purely biological, but concerns the innermost being of the human person as such. It is realized in a truly human way only if it is an integral part of the love by which a man and a woman commit themselves totally to one another until death. The total physical self-giving would be a lie if it were not the sign and fruit of a total personal self-giving, in which the whole person, including the temporal dimension, is present: if the person were to withhold something or reserve the possibility of deciding otherwise in the future, by this very fact he or she would not be giving totally.

11.6 This totality which is required by conjugal love also corresponds to the demands of responsible fertility. This fertility is directed to the generation of a human being, and so by its nature it surpasses the purely biological order and involves a whole series of personal values. For the harmonious growth of

[20] Cf. Gen 1:26-27.

[21] 1 Jn 4:8.

[22] Cf. Second Vatican Ecumenical Council, Pastoral Constitution on the Church in the Modern World *Gaudium et Spes,* 12.

these values a persevering and unified contribution by both parents is necessary.

11.7 The only "place" in which this self-giving in its whole truth is made possible is marriage, the covenant of conjugal love freely and consciously chosen, whereby man and woman accept the intimate community of life and love willed by God himself,[23] which only in this light manifests its true meaning. The institution of marriage is not an undue interference by society or authority, nor the extrinsic imposition of a form. Rather it is an interior requirement of the covenant of conjugal love which is publicly affirmed as unique and exclusive, in order to live in complete fidelity to the plan of God, the Creator. A person's freedom, far from being restricted by this fidelity, is secured against every form of subjectivism or relativism and is made a sharer in creative Wisdom.

Marriage and communion between God and people

12.1 The communion of love between God and people, a fundamental part of the revelation and faith experience of Israel, finds a meaningful expression in the marriage covenant which is established between a man and a woman.

12.2 For this reason the central word of revelation, "God loves his people," is likewise proclaimed through the living and concrete word whereby a man and a woman express their conjugal love. Their bond of love becomes the image and the symbol of the Covenant which unites God and his people.[24] And the same sin which can harm the conjugal covenant becomes an image of the infidelity of the people to their God: idolatry is prostitution,[25] infidelity is adultery, disobedience to the law is abandonment of the spousal love of the Lord. But the infidelity of Israel does not destroy the eternal fidelity of the Lord, and therefore the ever faithful love of God is put forward as the model of the relations of faithful love which should exist between spouses.[26]

Jesus Christ, Bridegroom of the Church, and the Sacrament of Matrimony

13.1 The communion between God and his people finds its definitive fulfillment in Jesus Christ, the Bridegroom who loves and gives himself as the Savior of humanity, uniting it to himself as his Body.

13.2 He reveals the original truth of marriage, the truth of the "begin-

---

[23] Cf. ibid., 48.

[24] Cf., for example, Hos 2:21; Jer 3:6-13; Is 54.

[25] Cf. Ezek 16:25.

[26] Cf. Hos 3.

ning,"[27] and, freeing man from his hardness of heart, he makes man capable of realizing this truth in its entirety.

13.3 This revelation reaches its definitive fullness in the gift of love which the Word of God makes to humanity in assuming a human nature, and in the sacrifice which Jesus Christ makes of himself on the Cross for his Bride, the Church. In this sacrifice there is entirely revealed that plan which God has imprinted on the humanity of man and woman since their creation[28]; the marriage of baptized persons thus becomes a real symbol of that New and Eternal Covenant sanctioned in the blood of Christ. The Spirit which the Lord pours forth gives a new heart, and renders man and woman capable of loving one another as Christ has loved us. Conjugal love reaches that fullness to which it is interiorly ordained, conjugal charity, which is the proper and specific way in which the spouses participate in and are called to live the very charity of Christ who gave himself on the Cross.

13.4 In a deservedly famous page, Tertullian has well expressed the greatness of this conjugal life in Christ and its beauty: "How can I ever express the happiness of the marriage that is joined together by the Church, strengthened by an offering, sealed by a blessing, announced by angels and ratified by the Father? . . . How wonderful the bond between two believers with a single hope, a single desire, a single observance, a single service! They are both brethren and both fellow-servants; there is no separation between them in spirit or flesh; in fact they are truly two in one flesh, and where the flesh is one, one is the spirit."[29]

13.5 Receiving and meditating faithfully on the word of God, the Church has solemnly taught and continues to teach that the marriage of the baptized is one of the seven sacraments of the New Covenant.[30]

13.6 Indeed, by means of Baptism, man and woman are definitively placed within the New and Eternal Covenant, in the spousal Covenant of Christ with the Church. And it is because of this indestructible insertion that the intimate community of conjugal life and love, founded by the Creator,[31] is elevated and assumed into the spousal charity of Christ, sustained and enriched by his redeeming power.

---

[27] Cf. Gen 2:24; Mt 19:5.

[28] Cf. Eph 5:32-33.

[29] *Ad Uxorem*, II, VIII, 6-8: *CCL* 1, 393.

[30] Cf. Ecumenical Council of Trent, Session XXIV, Teaching on the Sacrament of Marriage, Canon 1: Mansi, *Sacrorum Conciliorum Nova et Amplissima Collectio,* XXXIII, 149-150 (*DS* 1801).

[31] Cf. Second Vatican Ecumenical Council, Pastoral Constitution on the Church in the Modern World *Gaudium et Spes,* 48.

13.7 By virtue of the sacramentality of their marriage, spouses are bound to one another in the most profoundly indissoluble manner. Their belonging to each other is the real representation, by means of the sacramental sign, of the very relationship of Christ with the Church.

13.8 Spouses are therefore the permanent reminder to the Church of what happened on the Cross; they are for one another and for the children witnesses to the salvation in which the sacrament makes them sharers. Of this salvation event marriage, like every sacrament, is a memorial, actuation and prophecy: "As a memorial, the sacrament gives them the grace and duty of commemorating the great works of God and of bearing witness to them before their children. As actuation, it gives them the grace and duty of putting into practice in the present, toward each other and their children, the demands of a love which forgives and redeems. As prophecy, it gives them the grace and duty of living and bearing witness to the hope of the future encounter with Christ."[32]

13.9 Like each of the seven sacraments, so also marriage is a real symbol of the event of salvation, but in its own way. "The spouses participate in it as spouses, together, as a couple, so that the first and immediate effect of marriage (res et sacramentum) is not supernatural grace itself, but the Christian conjugal bond, a typically Christian communion of two persons because it represents the mystery of Christ's Incarnation and the mystery of his Covenant. The content of participation in Christ's life is also specific: conjugal love involves a totality, in which all the elements of the person enter — appeal of the body and instinct, power of feeling and affectivity, aspiration of the spirit and of will. It aims at a deeply personal unity, the unity that, beyond union in one flesh, leads to forming one heart and soul; it demands indissolubility and faithfulness in definitive mutual giving; and it is open to fertility (cf. Humanae Vitae, 9). In a word, it is a question of the normal characteristics of all natural conjugal love, but with a new significance which not only purifies and strengthens them, but raises them to the extent of making them the expression of specifically Christian values."[33]

Children, the precious gift of marriage

14.1 According to the plan of God, marriage is the foundation of the wider community of the family, since the very institution of marriage and conjugal

---

[32] John Paul II, Address to the Delegates of the Centre de Liaison des Équipes de Recherche (November 3, 1979), 3: Insegnamenti II/2 (1979), 1032.

[33] Ibid., 4: loc. cit., 1032.

love are ordained to the procreation and education of children, in whom they find their crowning.[34]

14.2 In its most profound reality, love is essentially a gift; and conjugal love, while leading the spouses to the reciprocal "knowledge" which makes them "one flesh,"[35] does not end with the couple, because it makes them capable of the greatest possible gift, the gift by which they become cooperators with God for giving life to a new human person. Thus the couple, while giving themselves to one another, give not just themselves but also the reality of children, who are a living reflection of their love, a permanent sign of conjugal unity and a living and inseparable synthesis of their being a father and a mother.

14.3 When they become parents, spouses receive from God the gift of a new responsibility. Their parental love is called to become for the children the visible sign of the very love of God, "from whom every family in heaven and on earth is named."[36]

14.4 It must not be forgotten, however, that, even when procreation is not possible, conjugal life does not for this reason lose its value. Physical sterility in fact can be for spouses the occasion for other important services to the life of the human person, for example, adoption, various forms of educational work, and assistance to other families and to poor or handicapped children.

The family, a communion of persons

15.1 In matrimony and in the family a complex of interpersonal relationships is set up — married life, fatherhood and motherhood, filiation and fraternity — through which each human person is introduced into the "human family" and into the "family of God," which is the Church.

15.2 Christian marriage and the Christian family build up the Church: for in the family the human person is not only brought into being and progressively introduced by means of education into the human community, but by means of the rebirth of Baptism and education in the faith the child is also introduced into God's family, which is the Church.

15.3 The human family, disunited by sin, is reconstituted in its unity by the redemptive power of the Death and Resurrection of Christ.[37] Christian

---

[34] Cf. Second Vatican Ecumenical Council, Pastoral Constitution on the Church in the Modern World *Gaudium et Spes,* 50.

[35] Cf. Gen 2:24.

[36] Eph 3:15.

[37] Cf. Second Vatican Ecumenical Council, Pastoral Constitution on the Church in the Modern World *Gaudium et Spes,* 78.

marriage, by participating in the salvific efficacy of this event, constitutes the natural setting in which the human person is introduced into the great family of the Church.

15.4 The commandment to grow and multiply, given to man and woman in the beginning, in this way reaches its whole truth and full realization.

15.5 The Church thus finds in the family, born from the sacrament, the cradle and the setting in which she can enter the human generations, and where these in their turn can enter the Church.

Marriage and virginity or celibacy

16.1 Virginity or celibacy for the sake of the Kingdom of God not only does not contradict the dignity of marriage but presupposes it and confirms it. Marriage and virginity or celibacy are two ways of expressing and living the one mystery of the Covenant of God with his people. When marriage is not esteemed, neither can consecrated virginity or celibacy exist; when human sexuality is not regarded as a great value given by the Creator, the renunciation of it for the sake of the Kingdom of heaven loses its meaning.

16.2 Rightly indeed does Saint John Chrysostom say: "Whoever denigrates marriage also diminishes the glory of virginity. Whoever praises it makes virginity more admirable and resplendent. What appears good only in comparison with evil would not be particularly good. It is something better than what is admitted to be good that is the most excellent good."[38]

16.3 In virginity or celibacy, the human being is awaiting, also in a bodily way, the eschatological marriage of Christ with the Church, giving himself or herself completely to the Church in the hope that Christ may give himself to the Church in the full truth of eternal life. The celibate person thus anticipates in his or her flesh the new world of the future resurrection.[39]

16.4 By virtue of this witness, virginity or celibacy keeps alive in the Church a consciousness of the mystery of marriage and defends it from any reduction and impoverishment.

16.5 Virginity or celibacy, by liberating the human heart in a unique way,[40] "so as to make it burn with greater love for God and all humanity,"[41] bears witness that the Kingdom of God and his justice is that pearl of great price which is preferred to every other value no matter how great, and hence must

[38] *On Virginity*, X: *PG* 48, 540.

[39] Cf. Mt 22:30.

[40] Cf. 1 Cor 7:32-35.

[41] Second Vatican Ecumenical Council, Decree on the Appropriate Renewal of the Religious Life *Perfectae Caritatis*, 12.

be sought as the only definitive value. It is for this reason that the Church, throughout her history, has always defended the superiority of this charism to that of marriage, by reason of the wholly singular link which it has with the Kingdom of God.[42]

16.6 In spite of having renounced physical fecundity, the celibate person becomes spiritually fruitful, the father and mother of many, cooperating in the realization of the family according to God's plan.

16.7 Christian couples therefore have the right to expect from celibate persons a good example and a witness of fidelity to their vocation until death. Just as fidelity at times becomes difficult for married people and requires sacrifice, mortification and self-denial, the same can happen to celibate persons, and their fidelity, even in the trials that may occur, should strengthen the fidelity of married couples.[43]

16.8 These reflections on virginity or celibacy can enlighten and help those who, for reasons independent of their own will, have been unable to marry and have then accepted their situation in a spirit of service.

III
The Role of the Christian Family

Family, become what you are

17.1 The family finds in the plan of God the Creator and Redeemer not only its *identity*, what it *is*, but also its *mission*, what it can and should *do*. The role that God calls the family to perform in history derives from what the family is; its role represents the dynamic and existential development of what it is. Each family finds within itself a summons that cannot be ignored, and that specifies both its dignity and its responsibility: family, *become* what you *are.*

17.2 Accordingly, the family must go back to the "beginning" of God's creative act, if it is to attain self-knowledge and self-realization in accordance with the inner truth not only of what it is but also of what it does in history. And since in God's plan it has been established as an "intimate community of life and love,"[44] the family has the mission to become more and more what it

---

[42] Cf. Pius XII, Encyclical Letter *Sacra Virginitas* (March 25, 1954), II: *AAS* 46 (1954), 174-175.

[43] Cf. John Paul II, Letter to Priests for Holy Thursday 1979 *Novo Incipiente* (April 8, 1979), 9: *AAS* 71 (1979), 410-411.

[44] Second Vatican Ecumenical Council, Pastoral Constitution on the Church in the Modern World *Gaudium et Spes*, 48.

is, that is to say, a community of life and love, in an effort that will find fulfillment, as will everything created and redeemed, in the Kingdom of God. Looking at it in such a way as to reach its very roots, we must say that the essence and role of the family are in the final analysis specified by love. Hence the family has *the mission to guard, reveal and communicate love,* and this is a living reflection of and a real sharing in God's love for humanity and the love of Christ the Lord for the Church his Bride.

17.3 Every particular task of the family is an expressive and concrete actuation of that fundamental mission. We must therefore go deeper into the unique riches of the family's mission and probe its contents, which are both manifold and unified.

17.4 Thus, with love as its point of departure and making constant reference to it, the recent Synod emphasized four general tasks for the family:

1) forming a community of persons;
2) serving life;
3) participating in the development of society;
4) sharing in the life and mission of the Church.

1. Forming a Community of Persons

Love as the principle and power of communion

18.1 The family, which is founded and given life by love, is a community of persons: of husband and wife, of parents and children, of relatives. Its first task is to live with fidelity the reality of communion in a constant effort to develop an authentic community of persons.

18.2 The inner principle of that task, its permanent power and its final goal is love: without love the family is not a community of persons and, in the same way, *without love the family cannot live, grow and perfect itself as a community of persons.* What I wrote in the Encyclical *Redemptor Hominis* applies primarily and especially within the family as such: "Man cannot live without love. He remains a being that is incomprehensible for himself, his life is senseless, if love is not revealed to him, if he does not encounter love, if he does not experience it and make it his own, if he does not participate intimately in it."[45]

18.3 The love between husband and wife and, in a "derivatory" and broader way, the love between members of the same family — between parents and children, brothers and sisters, and relatives and members of the household — is given life and sustenance by an unceasing inner dynamism leading the

[45] Encyclical Letter *Redemptor Hominis* (March 4, 1979), 10: *AAS* 71 (1979), 274.

family to ever deeper and more intense *communion,* which is the foundation and soul of the *community* of marriage and the family.

The indivisible unity of conjugal communion

19.1 The first communion is the one which is established and which develops between husband and wife: by virtue of the covenant of married life, the man and woman "are no longer two but one flesh"[46] and they are called to grow continually in their communion through day-to-day fidelity to their marriage promise of total mutual self-giving.

19.2 This conjugal communion sinks its roots in the natural complementarity that exists between man and woman, and is nurtured through the personal willingness of the spouses to share their entire life-project, what they have and what they are: for this reason such communion is the fruit and the sign of a profoundly human need. But in the Lord Christ, God takes up this human need, confirms it, purifies it and elevates it, leading it to perfection through the Sacrament of Matrimony: the Holy Spirit, who is poured out in the sacramental celebration, offers Christian couples the gift of a new communion of love that is the living and real image of that unique unity which makes of the Church the indivisible Mystical Body of the Lord Jesus.

19.3 The gift of the Spirit is a commandment of life for Christian spouses and at the same time a stimulating impulse so that every day they may progress toward an ever richer union with each other on all levels — of the body, of the character, of the heart, of the intelligence and will, of the soul[47] — revealing in this way to the Church and to the world the new communion of love, given by the grace of Christ.

19.4 Such a communion is radically contradicted by polygamy: this, in fact, directly negates the plan of God which was revealed from the beginning, because it is contrary to the equal personal dignity of men and women who in matrimony give themselves with a love that is total and therefore unique and exclusive. As the Second Vatican Council writes: "Firmly established by the Lord, the unity of marriage will radiate from the equal personal dignity of husband and wife, a dignity acknowledged by mutual and total love."[48]

---

[46] Mt 19:6; cf. Gen 2:24.

[47] Cf. John Paul II, Address to Married People, Kinshasa (May 3, 1980), 4: *AAS* 72 (1980), 426-427.

[48] Pastoral Constitution on the Church in the Modern World *Gaudium et Spes,* 49; cf. John Paul II, Address to Married People, Kinshasa (May 3, 1980), 4: *AAS* 72 (1980), 426-427.

An indissoluble communion

20.1 Conjugal communion is characterized not only by its unity but also by its indissolubility: "As a mutual gift of two persons, this intimate union, as well as the good of children, imposes total fidelity on the spouses and argues for an unbreakable oneness between them."[49]

20.2 It is a fundamental duty of the Church to reaffirm strongly, as the Synod Fathers did, the doctrine of the indissolubility of marriage. To all those who, in our times, consider it too difficult, or indeed impossible, to be bound to one person for the whole of life, and to those caught up in a culture that rejects the indissolubility of marriage and openly mocks the commitment of spouses to fidelity, it is necessary to reconfirm the good news of the definitive nature of that conjugal love that has in Christ its foundation and strength.[50]

20.3 Being rooted in the personal and total self-giving of the couple, and being required by the good of the children, the indissolubility of marriage finds its ultimate truth in the plan that God has manifested in his revelation: he wills and he communicates the indissolubility of marriage as a fruit, a sign and a requirement of the absolutely faithful love that God has for man and that the Lord Jesus has for the Church.

20.4 Christ renews the first plan that the Creator inscribed in the hearts of man and woman, and in the celebration of the Sacrament of Matrimony offers a "new heart": thus the couples are not only able to overcome "hardness of heart,"[51] but also and above all they are able to share the full and definitive love of Christ, the New and Eternal Covenant made flesh. Just as the Lord Jesus is the "faithful witness,"[52] the "yes" of the promises of God[53] and thus the supreme realization of the unconditional faithfulness with which God loves his people, so Christian couples are called to participate truly in the irrevocable indissolubility that binds Christ to the Church his Bride, loved by him to the end.[54]

20.5 The gift of the sacrament is at the same time a vocation and commandment for the Christian spouses, that they may remain faithful to each other forever, beyond every trial and difficulty, in generous obedience to the holy will of the Lord: "What therefore God has joined together, let not man put asunder."[55]

20.6 To bear witness to the inestimable value of the indissolubility and

[49] Second Vatican Ecumenical Council, Pastoral Constitution on the Church in the Modern World *Gaudium et Spes,* 48.

[50] Cf. Eph 5:25.

[51] Mt 19:8.

[52] Rev 3:14.

[53] Cf. 2 Cor 1:20.

[54] Cf. Jn 13:1.

[55] Mt 19:6.

fidelity of marriage is one of the most precious and most urgent tasks of Christian couples in our time. So, with all my Brothers who participated in the Synod of Bishops, I praise and encourage those numerous couples who, though encountering no small difficulty, preserve and develop the value of indissolubility: thus, in a humble and courageous manner, they perform the role committed to them of being in the world a "sign" — a small and precious sign, sometimes also subjected to temptation, but always renewed — of the unfailing fidelity with which God and Jesus Christ love each and every human being. But it is also proper to recognize the value of the witness of those spouses who, even when abandoned by their partner, with the strength of faith and of Christian hope have not entered a new union: these spouses too give an authentic witness to fidelity, of which the world today has a great need. For this reason they must be encouraged and helped by the pastors and the faithful of the Church.

The broader communion of the family

21.1 Conjugal communion constitutes the foundation on which is built the broader communion of the family, of parents and children, of brothers and sisters with each other, of relatives and other members of the household.

21.2 This communion is rooted in the natural bonds of flesh and blood, and grows to its specifically human perfection with the establishment and maturing of the still deeper and richer bonds of the spirit: the love that animates the interpersonal relationships of the different members of the family constitutes the interior strength that shapes and animates the family communion and community.

21.3 The Christian family is also called to experience a new and original communion which confirms and perfects natural and human communion. In fact the grace of Jesus Christ, "the first-born among many brethren,"[56] is by its nature and interior dynamism "a grace of brotherhood," as Saint Thomas Aquinas calls it.[57] The Holy Spirit, who is poured forth in the celebration of the sacraments, is the living source and inexhaustible sustenance of the supernatural communion that gathers believers and links them with Christ and with each other in the unity of the Church of God. The Christian family constitutes a specific revelation and realization of ecclesial communion, and for this reason too it can and should be called "the domestic Church."[58]

---

[56] Rom 8:29.

[57] *Summa Theologiae*, II-II, q. 14, a. 2, ad 4.

[58] Second Vatican Ecumenical Council, Dogmatic Constitution on the Church *Lumen Gentium,* 11; cf. Decree on the Apostolate of the Laity *Apostolicam Actuositatem,* 11.

21.4 All members of the family, each according to his or her own gift, have the grace and responsibility of building, day by day, the communion of persons, making the family "a school of deeper humanity":[59] this happens where there is care and love for the little ones, the sick, the aged; where there is mutual service every day; when there is a sharing of goods, of joys and of sorrows.

21.5 A fundamental opportunity for building such a communion is constituted by the educational exchange between parents and children,[60] in which each gives and receives. By means of love, respect and obedience toward their parents, children offer their specific and irreplaceable contribution to the construction of an authentically human and Christian family.[61] They will be aided in this if parents exercise their unrenounceable authority as a true and proper "ministry," that is, as a service to the human and Christian well-being of their children, and in particular as a service aimed at helping them acquire a truly responsible freedom, and if parents maintain a living awareness of the "gift" they continually receive from their children.

21.6 Family communion can only be preserved and perfected through a great spirit of sacrifice. It requires, in fact, a ready and generous openness of each and all to understanding, to forbearance, to pardon, to reconciliation. There is no family that does not know how selfishness, discord, tension and conflict violently attack and at times mortally wound its own communion: hence there arise the many and varied forms of division in family life. But, at the same time, every family is called by the God of peace to have the joyous and renewing experience of "reconciliation," that is, communion reestablished, unity restored. In particular, participation in the Sacrament of Reconciliation and in the banquet of the one Body of Christ offers to the Christian family the grace and the responsibility of overcoming every division and of moving toward the fullness of communion willed by God, responding in this way to the ardent desire of the Lord: "that they may be one."[62]

The rights and role of women

22.1 In that it is, and ought always to become, a communion and community of persons, the family finds in love the source and the constant impetus

---

[59] Second Vatican Ecumenical Council, Pastoral Constitution on the Church in the Modern World *Gaudium et Spes*, 52.

[60] Cf. Eph 6:1-4; Col 3:20-21.

[61] Cf. Second Vatican Ecumenical Council, Pastoral Constitution on the Church in the Modern World *Gaudium et Spes*, 48.

[62] Jn 17:21.

for welcoming, respecting and promoting each one of its members in his or her lofty dignity as a person, that is, as a living image of God. As the Synod Fathers rightly stated, the moral criterion for the authenticity of conjugal and family relationships consists in fostering the dignity and vocation of the individual persons, who achieve their fullness by sincere self-giving.[63]

22.2 In this perspective the Synod devoted special attention to women, to their rights and role within the family and society. In the same perspective are also to be considered men as husbands and fathers, and likewise children and the elderly.

22.3 Above all it is important to underline the equal dignity and responsibility of women with men. This equality is realized in a unique manner in that reciprocal self-giving by each one to the other and by both to the children which is proper to marriage and the family. What human reason intuitively perceives and acknowledges is fully revealed by the word of God: the history of salvation, in fact, is a continuous and luminous testimony of the dignity of women.

22.4 In creating the human race "male and female,"[64] God gives man and woman an equal personal dignity, endowing them with the inalienable rights and responsibilities proper to the human person. God then manifests the dignity of women in the highest form possible, by assuming human flesh from the Virgin Mary, whom the Church honors as the Mother of God, calling her the new Eve and presenting her as the model of redeemed woman. The sensitive respect of Jesus toward the women that he called to his following and his friendship, his appearing on Easter morning to a woman before the other disciples, the mission entrusted to women to carry the good news of the Resurrection to the Apostles — these are all signs that confirm the special esteem of the Lord Jesus for women. The Apostle Paul will say: "In Christ Jesus you are all children of God through faith. . . . There is neither Jew nor Greek, there is neither slave nor free, there is neither male nor female; for you are all one in Christ Jesus."[65]

Women and society

23.1 Without intending to deal with all the various aspects of the vast and complex theme of the relationships between women and society, and limiting these remarks to a few essential points, one cannot but observe that in the

---

[63] Cf. Second Vatican Ecumenical Council, Pastoral Constitution on the Church in the Modern World *Gaudium et Spes,* 24.

[64] Gen 1:27.

[65] Gal 3:26, 28.

specific area of family life a widespread social and cultural tradition has considered women's role to be exclusively that of wife and mother, without adequate access to public functions which have generally been reserved for men.

23.2 There is no doubt that the equal dignity and responsibility of men and women fully justifies women's access to public functions. On the other hand the true advancement of women requires that clear recognition be given to the value of their maternal and family role, by comparison with all other public roles and all other professions. Furthermore, these roles and professions should be harmoniously combined, if we wish the evolution of society and culture to be truly and fully human.

23.3 This will come about more easily if, in accordance with the wishes expressed by the Synod, a renewed "theology of work" can shed light upon and study in depth the meaning of work in the Christian life and determine the fundamental bond between work and the family, and therefore the original and irreplaceable meaning of work in the home and in rearing children.[66] Therefore the Church can and should help modern society by tirelessly insisting that the work of women in the home be recognized and respected by all in its irreplaceable value. This is of particular importance in education: for possible discrimination between the different types of work and professions is eliminated at its very root once it is clear that all people, in every area, are working with equal rights and equal responsibilities. The image of God in man and in woman will thus be seen with added luster.

23.4 While it must be recognized that women have the same right as men to perform various public functions, society must be structured in such a way that wives and mothers are *not in practice compelled* to work outside the home, and that their families can live and prosper in a dignified way even when they themselves devote their full time to their own family.

23.5 Furthermore, the mentality which honors women more for their work outside the home than for their work within the family must be overcome. This requires that men should truly esteem and love women with total respect for their personal dignity, and that society should create and develop conditions favoring work in the home.

23.6 With due respect to the different vocations of men and women, the Church must in her own life promote as far as possible their equality of rights and dignity: and this for the good of all, the family, the Church and society.

23.7 But clearly all of this does not mean for women a renunciation of their femininity or an imitation of the male role, but the fullness of true femi-

---

[66] Cf. John Paul II, Encyclical Letter *Laborem Exercens* (September 14, 1981), 19: *AAS* 73 (1981), 625.

nine humanity which should be expressed in their activity, whether in the family or outside of it, without disregarding the differences of customs and cultures in this sphere.

Offenses against women's dignity

24.1 Unfortunately the Christian message about the dignity of women is contradicted by that persistent mentality which considers the human being not as a person but as a thing, as an object of trade, at the service of selfish interest and mere pleasure: the first victims of this mentality are women.

24.2 This mentality produces very bitter fruits, such as contempt for men and for women, slavery, oppression of the weak, pornography, prostitution — especially in an organized form — and all those various forms of discrimination that exist in the fields of education, employment, wages, etc.

24.3 Besides, many forms of degrading discrimination still persist today in a great part of our society that affect and seriously harm particular categories of women, as for example childless wives, widows, separated or divorced women, and unmarried mothers.

24.4 The Synod Fathers deplored these and other forms of discrimination as strongly as possible. I therefore ask that vigorous and incisive pastoral action be taken by all to overcome them definitively so that the image of God that shines in all human beings without exception may be fully respected.

Men as husbands and fathers

25.1 Within the conjugal and family communion-community, the man is called upon to live his gift and role as husband and father.

25.2 In his wife he sees the fulfillment of God's intention: "It is not good that the man should be alone; I will make him a helper fit for him,"[67] and he makes his own the cry of Adam, the first husband: "This at last is bone of my bones and flesh of my flesh."[68]

25.3 Authentic conjugal love presupposes and requires that a man have a profound respect for the equal dignity of his wife: "You are not her master," writes Saint Ambrose, "but her husband; she was not given to you to be your slave, but your wife. . . . Reciprocate her attentiveness to you and be grateful to her for her love."[69] With his wife a man should live "a very special form of personal friendship."[70] As for the Christian, he is called upon to develop a new

---

[67] Gen 2:18.
[68] Gen 2:23.
[69] *Exameron*, V, 7, 19: *CSEL* 32, I, 154.
[70] Paul VI, Encyclical Letter *Humanae Vitae* (July 25, 1968), 9: *AAS* 60 (1968), 486.

attitude of love, manifesting toward his wife a charity that is both gentle and strong like that which Christ has for the Church.[71]

25.4 Love for his wife as mother of their children and love for the children themselves are for the man the natural way of understanding and fulfilling his own fatherhood. Above all where social and cultural conditions so easily encourage a father to be less concerned with his family or at any rate less involved in the work of education, efforts must be made to restore socially the conviction that the place and task of the father in and for the family is of unique and irreplaceable importance.[72] As experience teaches, the absence of a father causes psychological and moral imbalance and notable difficulties in family relationships, as does, in contrary circumstances, the oppressive presence of a father, especially where there still prevails the phenomenon of "machismo," or a wrong superiority of male prerogatives which humiliates women and inhibits the development of healthy family relationships.

25.5 In revealing and in reliving on earth the very fatherhood of God,[73] a man is called upon to ensure the harmonious and united development of all the members of the family: he will perform this task by exercising generous responsibility for the life conceived under the heart of the mother, by a more solicitous commitment to education, a task he shares with his wife,[74] by work which is never a cause of division in the family but promotes its unity and stability, and by means of the witness he gives of an adult Christian life which effectively introduces the children into the living experience of Christ and the Church.

The rights of children

26.1 In the family, which is a community of persons, special attention must be devoted to the children by developing a profound esteem for their personal dignity, and a great respect and generous concern for their rights. This is true for every child, but it becomes all the more urgent the smaller the child is and the more it is in need of everything, when it is sick, suffering or handicapped.

26.2 By fostering and exercising a tender and strong concern for every child that comes into this world, the Church fulfills a fundamental mission: for she is called upon to reveal and put forward anew in history the example

---

[71] Cf. Eph 5:25.

[72] Cf. John Paul II, Homily, Terni (March 19, 1981), 3-5: *AAS* 73 (1981), 268-271.

[73] Cf. Eph 3:15.

[74] Cf. Second Vatican Ecumenical Council, Pastoral Constitution on the Church in the Modern World *Gaudium et Spes,* 52.

and the commandment of Christ the Lord, who placed the child at the heart of the Kingdom of God: "Let the children come to me, and do not hinder them; for to such belongs the Kingdom of heaven."[75]

26.3 I repeat once again what I said to the General Assembly of the United Nations on October 2, 1979: "I wish to express the joy that we all find in children, the springtime of life, the anticipation of the future history of each of our present earthly homelands. No country on earth, no political system can think of its own future otherwise than through the image of these new generations that will receive from their parents the manifold heritage of values, duties and aspirations of the nation to which they belong and of the whole human family. Concern for the child, even before birth, from the first moment of conception and then throughout the years of infancy and youth, is the primary and fundamental test of the relationship of one human being to another. And so, what better wish can I express for every nation and for the whole of mankind, and for all the children of the world than a better future in which respect for human rights will become a complete reality throughout the third millennium, which is drawing near?"[76]

26.4 Acceptance, love, esteem, many-sided and united material, emotional, educational and spiritual concern for every child that comes into this world should always constitute a distinctive, essential characteristic of all Christians, in particular of the Christian family: thus children, while they are able to grow "in wisdom and in stature, and in favor with God and man,"[77] offer their own precious contribution to building up the family community and even to the sanctification of their parents.[78]

The elderly in the family

27.1 There are cultures which manifest a unique veneration and great love for the elderly: far from being outcasts from the family or merely tolerated as a useless burden, they continue to be present and to take an active and responsible part in family life, though having to respect the autonomy of the new family; above all they carry out the important mission of being a witness to the past and a source of wisdom for the young and for the future.

27.2 Other cultures, however, especially in the wake of disordered indus-

---

[75] Lk 18:16; cf. Mt 19:14; Mk 10:14.

[76] John Paul II, Address to the General Assembly of the United Nations (October 2, 1979), 21: *AAS* 71 (1979), 1159.

[77] Lk 2:52.

[78] Cf. Second Vatican Ecumenical Council, Pastoral Constitution on the Church in the Modern World *Gaudium et Spes,* 48.

trial and urban development, have both in the past and in the present set the elderly aside in unacceptable ways. This causes acute suffering to them and spiritually impoverishes many families.

27.3 The pastoral activity of the Church must help everyone to discover and to make good use of the role of the elderly within the civil and ecclesial community, in particular within the family. In fact, "the life of the aging helps to clarify a scale of human values; it shows the continuity of generations and marvelously demonstrates the interdependence of God's people. The elderly often have the charism to bridge generation gaps before they are made: how many children have found understanding and love in the eyes and words and caresses of the aging! And how many old people have willingly subscribed to the inspired word that the 'crown of the aged is their children's children' (Prov 17:6)!"[79]

2. Serving Life

1) THE TRANSMISSION OF LIFE

Cooperators in the love of God the Creator

28.1 With the creation of man and woman in his own image and likeness, God crowns and brings to perfection the work of his hands: he calls them to a special sharing in his love and in his power as Creator and Father, through their free and responsible cooperation in transmitting the gift of human life: "God blessed them, and God said to them, 'Be fruitful and multiply, and fill the earth and subdue it.' "[80]

28.2 Thus the fundamental task of the family is to serve life, to actualize in history the original blessing of the Creator — that of transmitting by procreation the divine image from person to person.[81]

28.3 Fecundity is the fruit and the sign of conjugal love, the living testimony of the full reciprocal self-giving of the spouses: "While not making the other purposes of matrimony of less account, the true practice of conjugal love, and the whole meaning of the family life which results from it, have this aim: that the couple be ready with stout hearts to cooperate with the love of the Creator and the Savior, who through them will enlarge and enrich his own family day by day."[82]

---

[79] John Paul II, Address to the Participants in the International Forum on Active Aging (September 5, 1980), 5: *Insegnamenti* III/2 (1980), 539.

[80] Gen 1:28.

[81] Cf. Gen 5:1-3.

[82] Second Vatican Ecumenical Council, Pastoral Constitution on the Church in the Modern World *Gaudium et Spes,* 50.

28.4 However, the fruitfulness of conjugal love is not restricted solely to the procreation of children, even understood in its specifically human dimension: it is enlarged and enriched by all those fruits of moral, spiritual and supernatural life which the father and mother are called to hand on to their children, and through the children to the Church and to the world.

The Church's teaching and norm, always old yet always new

29.1 Precisely because the love of husband and wife is a unique participation in the mystery of life and of the love of God himself, the Church knows that she has received the special mission of guarding and protecting the lofty dignity of marriage and the most serious responsibility of the transmission of human life.

29.2 Thus, in continuity with the living Tradition of the ecclesial community throughout history, the recent Second Vatican Council and the Magisterium of my Predecessor Paul VI, expressed above all in the Encyclical *Humanae Vitae,* have handed on to our times a truly prophetic proclamation, which reaffirms and reproposes with clarity the Church's teaching and norm, always old yet always new, regarding marriage and regarding the transmission of human life.

29.3 For this reason the Synod Fathers made the following declaration at their last Assembly: "This sacred Synod, gathered together with the Successor of Peter in the unity of faith, firmly holds what has been set forth in the Second Vatican Council (cf. *Gaudium et Spes,* 50) and afterwards in the Encyclical *Humanae Vitae,* particularly that love between husband and wife must be fully human, exclusive and open to new life (*Humanae Vitae,* 11, cf. 9, 12)."[83]

The Church stands for life

30.1 The teaching of the Church in our day is placed in a social and cultural context which renders it more difficult to understand and yet more urgent and irreplaceable for promoting the true good of men and women.

30.2 Scientific and technical progress, which contemporary man is continually expanding in his dominion over nature, not only offers the hope of creating a new and better humanity, but also causes ever greater anxiety

---

[83] *Propositio* 21. Section 11 of the Encyclical Letter *Humanae Vitae* (July 25, 1968) ends with the statement: "The Church, calling people back to the observance of the norms of the natural law, as interpreted by her constant doctrine, teaches that each and every marriage act must remain open to the transmission of life (*ut quilibet matrimonii usus ad vitam humanam pro-creandam per se destinatus permaneat)*": AAS 60 (1968), 488.

regarding the future. Some ask themselves if it is a good thing to be alive or if it would be better never to have been born; they doubt therefore if it is right to bring others into life when perhaps they will curse their existence in a cruel world with unforeseeable terrors. Others consider themselves to be the only ones for whom the advantages of technology are intended and they exclude others by imposing on them contraceptives or even worse means. Still others, imprisoned in a consumer mentality and whose sole concern is to bring about a continual growth of material goods, finish by ceasing to understand, and thus by refusing, the spiritual riches of a new human life. The ultimate reason for these mentalities is the absence in people's hearts of God, whose love alone is stronger than all the world's fears and can conquer them.

30.3 Thus an anti-life mentality is born, as can be seen in many current issues: one thinks, for example, of a certain panic deriving from the studies of ecologists and futurologists on population growth, which sometimes exaggerate the danger of demographic increase to the quality of life.

30.4 But the Church firmly believes that human life, even if weak and suffering, is always a splendid gift of God's goodness. Against the pessimism and selfishness which cast a shadow over the world, the Church stands for life: in each human life she sees the splendor of that "Yes," that "Amen," who is Christ himself.[84] To the "No" which assails and afflicts the world, she replies with this living "Yes," thus defending the human person and the world from all who plot against and harm life.

30.5 The Church is called upon to manifest anew to everyone, with clear and stronger conviction, her will to promote human life by every means and to defend it against all attacks, in whatever condition or state of development it is found.

30.6 Thus the Church condemns as a grave offense against human dignity and justice all those activities of governments or other public authorities which attempt to limit in any way the freedom of couples in deciding about children. Consequently, any violence applied by such authorities in favor of contraception or, still worse, of sterilization and procured abortion, must be altogether condemned and forcefully rejected. Likewise to be denounced as gravely unjust are cases where, in international relations, economic help given for the advancement of peoples is made conditional on programs of contraception, sterilization and procured abortion.[85]

---

[84] Cf. 2 Cor 1:19; Rev 3:14.

[85] Cf. Synod of Bishops, Fifth Ordinary General Assembly, Message to Christian Families in the Modern World (October 24, 1980), 5: *L'Osservatore Romano* (English-language edition), November 10, 1980, 6.

That God's design may be ever more completely fulfilled

31.1 The Church is certainly aware of the many complex problems which couples in many countries face today in their task of transmitting life in a responsible way. She also recognizes the serious problem of population growth in the form it has taken in many parts of the world and its moral implications.

31.2 However, she holds that consideration in depth of all the aspects of these problems offers a new and stronger confirmation of the importance of the authentic teaching on birth regulation reproposed in the Second Vatican Council and in the Encyclical *Humanae Vitae.*

31.3 For this reason, together with the Synod Fathers, I feel it is my duty to extend a pressing invitation to theologians, asking them to unite their efforts in order to collaborate with the hierarchical Magisterium and to commit themselves to the task of illustrating ever more clearly the biblical foundations, the ethical grounds and the personalistic reasons behind this doctrine. Thus it will be possible, in the context of an organic exposition, to render the teaching of the Church on this fundamental question truly accessible to all people of good will, fostering a daily more enlightened and profound understanding of it: in this way God's plan will be ever more completely fulfilled for the salvation of humanity and for the glory of the Creator.

31.4 A united effort by theologians in this regard, inspired by a convinced adherence to the Magisterium, which is the one authentic guide for the People of God, is particularly urgent for reasons that include the close link between Catholic teaching on this matter and the view of the human person that the Church proposes: doubt or error in the field of marriage or the family involves obscuring to a serious extent the integral truth about the human person, in a cultural situation that is already so often confused and contradictory. In fulfillment of their specific role, theologians are called upon to provide enlightenment and a deeper understanding, and their contribution is of incomparable value and represents a unique and highly meritorious service to the family and humanity.

In an integral vision of the human person and of his or her vocation

32.1 In the context of a culture which seriously distorts or entirely misinterprets the true meaning of human sexuality, because it separates it from its essential reference to the person, the Church more urgently feels how irreplaceable is her mission of presenting sexuality as a value and task of the whole person, created male and female in the image of God.

32.2 In this perspective the Second Vatican Council clearly affirmed that "when there is a question of harmonizing conjugal love with the responsible transmission of life, the moral aspect of any procedure does not depend solely on sincere intentions or on an evaluation of motives. It must be determined by *objective standards*. These, *based on the nature of the human person and his or her acts,* preserve the full sense of mutual self-giving and human procreation in the context of true love. Such a goal cannot be achieved unless the virtue of conjugal chastity is sincerely practiced."[86]

32.3 It is precisely by moving from "an integral vision of man and of his vocation, not only his natural and earthly, but also his supernatural and eternal vocation,"[87] that Paul VI affirmed that the teaching of the Church "is founded upon the inseparable connection, willed by God and unable to be broken by man on his own initiative, between the two meanings of the conjugal act: the unitive meaning and the procreative meaning."[88] And he concluded by reemphasizing that there must be excluded as intrinsically immoral "every action which, either in anticipation of the conjugal act, or in its accomplishment, or in the development of its natural consequences, proposes, whether as an end or as a means, to render procreation impossible."[89]

32.4 When couples, by means of recourse to contraception, separate these two meanings that God the Creator has inscribed in the being of man and woman and in the dynamism of their sexual communion, they act as "arbiters" of the divine plan and they "manipulate" and degrade human sexuality — and with it themselves and their married partner — by altering its value of "total" self-giving. Thus the innate language that expresses the total reciprocal self-giving of husband and wife is overlaid, through contraception, by an objectively contradictory language, namely, that of not giving oneself totally to the other. This leads not only to a positive refusal to be open to life but also to a falsification of the inner truth of conjugal love, which is called upon to give itself in personal totality.

32.5 When, instead, by means of recourse to periods of infertility, the couple respect the inseparable connection between the unitive and procreative meanings of human sexuality, they are acting as "ministers" of God's plan and they "benefit from" their sexuality according to the original dynamism of "total" self-giving, without manipulation or alteration.[90]

32.6 In the light of the experience of many couples and of the data pro-

---

[86] Pastoral Constitution on the Church in the Modern World *Gaudium et Spes,* 51.
[87] Encyclical Letter *Humanae Vitae* (July 25, 1968), 7: *AAS* 60 (1968), 485.
[88] Ibid., 12: loc. cit., 488-489.
[89] Ibid., 14: loc. cit., 490.
[90] Ibid., 13: loc. cit., 489.

vided by the different human sciences, theological reflection is able to perceive and is called to study further *the difference, both anthropological and moral,* between contraception and recourse to the rhythm of the cycle: it is a difference which is much wider and deeper than is usually thought, one which involves in the final analysis two irreconcilable concepts of the human person and of human sexuality. The choice of the natural rhythms involves accepting the cycle of the person, that is the woman, and thereby accepting dialogue, reciprocal respect, shared responsibility and self-control. To accept the cycle and to enter into dialogue means to recognize both the spiritual and corporal character of conjugal communion and to live personal love with its requirement of fidelity. In this context the couple comes to experience how conjugal communion is enriched with those values of tenderness and affection which constitute the inner soul of human sexuality, in its physical dimension also. In this way sexuality is respected and promoted in its truly and fully human dimension, and is never "used" as an "object" that, by breaking the personal unity of soul and body, strikes at God's creation itself at the level of the deepest interaction of nature and person.

The Church as Teacher and Mother for couples in difficulty

33.1 In the field of conjugal morality the Church is Teacher and Mother and acts as such.

33.2 As Teacher, she never tires of proclaiming the moral norm that must guide the responsible transmission of life. The Church is in no way the author or the arbiter of this norm. In obedience to the truth which is Christ, whose image is reflected in the nature and dignity of the human person, the Church interprets the moral norm and proposes it to all people of good will, without concealing its demands of radicalness and perfection.

33.3 As Mother, the Church is close to the many married couples who find themselves in difficulty over this important point of the moral life: she knows well their situation, which is often very arduous and at times truly tormented by difficulties of every kind, not only individual difficulties but social ones as well; she knows that many couples encounter difficulties not only in the concrete fulfillment of the moral norm but even in understanding its inherent values.

33.4 But it is one and the same Church that is both Teacher and Mother. And so the Church never ceases to exhort and encourage all to resolve whatever conjugal difficulties may arise without ever falsifying or compromising the truth: she is convinced that there can be no true contradiction between the divine law on transmitting life and that on fostering authentic married love.[91] Accordingly, the concrete pedagogy of the Church must always remain linked with her doctrine and never be separated from it. With the same conviction as my Predecessor, I therefore repeat: "To diminish in no way the saving teaching of Christ constitutes an eminent form of charity for souls."[92]

33.5 On the other hand, authentic ecclesial pedagogy displays its realism and wisdom only by making a tenacious and courageous effort to create and uphold all the human conditions — psychological, moral and spiritual — indispensable for understanding and living the moral value and norm.

33.6 There is no doubt that these conditions must include persistence and patience, humility and strength of mind, filial trust in God and in his grace, and frequent recourse to prayer and to the Sacraments of the Eucharist and of Reconciliation.[93] Thus strengthened, Christian husbands and wives will be able to keep alive their awareness of the unique influence that the grace of the Sacrament of Marriage has on every aspect of married life, including therefore their sexuality: the gift of the Spirit, accepted and responded to by husband and wife, helps them to live their human sexuality in accordance with God's plan and as a sign of the unitive and fruitful love of Christ for his Church.

33.7 But the necessary conditions also include in the knowledge of the bodily aspect and the body's rhythms of fertility. Accordingly, every effort must be made to render such knowledge accessible to all married people and also to young adults before marriage, through clear, timely and serious instruction and education given by married couples, doctors and experts. Knowledge must then lead to education in self-control: hence the absolute necessity for the virtue of chastity and for permanent education in it. In the Christian view, chastity by no means signifies rejection of human sexuality or lack of esteem for it: rather it signifies spiritual energy capable of defending love from the perils of selfishness and aggressiveness, and able to advance it toward its full realization.

33.8 With deeply wise and loving intuition, Paul VI was only voicing the experience of many married couples when he wrote in his Encyclical: "To dominate instinct by means of one's reason and free will undoubtedly requires ascetical practices, so that the affective manifestations of conjugal life may observe the correct order, in particular with regard to the observance of periodic continence. Yet this discipline which is proper to the purity of married couples, far from harming conjugal love, rather confers on it a higher human value. It demands continual effort, yet, thanks to its beneficent influ-

---

[91] Cf. Second Vatican Ecumenical Council, Pastoral Constitution on the Church in the Modern World *Gaudium et Spes,* 51.

[92] Paul VI, Encyclical Letter *Humanae Vitae* (July 25, 1968), 29: *AAS* 60 (1968), 501.

[93] Cf. ibid., 25: loc. cit., 498-499.

ence, husband and wife fully develop their personalities, being enriched with spiritual values. Such discipline bestows upon family life fruits of serenity and peace, and facilitates the solution of other problems; it favors attention for one's partner, helps both parties to drive out selfishness, the enemy of true love, and deepens their sense of responsibility. By its means, parents acquire the capacity of having a deeper and more efficacious influence in the education of their offspring."[94]

The moral progress of married people

34.1 It is always very important to have a right notion of the moral order, its values and its norms; and the importance is all the greater when the difficulties in the way of respecting them become more numerous and serious.

34.2 Since the moral order reveals and sets forth the plan of God the Creator, for this very reason it cannot be something that harms man, something impersonal. On the contrary, by responding to the deepest demands of the human being created by God, it places itself at the service of that person's full humanity with the delicate and binding love whereby God himself inspires, sustains and guides every creature toward its happiness.

34.3 But man, who has been called to live God's wise and loving design in a responsible manner, is an historical being who day by day builds himself up through his many free decisions; and so he knows, loves and accomplishes moral good by stages of growth.

34.4 Married people too are called upon to progress unceasingly in their moral life, with the support of a sincere and active desire to gain ever better knowledge of the values enshrined in and fostered by the law of God. They must also be supported by an upright and generous willingness to embody these values in their concrete decisions. They cannot, however, look on the law as merely an ideal to be achieved in the future: they must consider it as a command of Christ the Lord to overcome difficulties with constancy. "And so what is known as 'the law of gradualness' or step-by-step advance cannot be identified with 'gradualness of the law,' as if there were different degrees or forms of precept in God's law for different individuals and situations. In God's plan, all husbands and wives are called in marriage to holiness, and this lofty vocation is fulfilled to the extent that the human person is able to respond to God's command with serene confidence in God's grace and in his or her own will."[95] On the same lines, it is part of the Church's pedagogy that husbands

---

[94] Ibid., 21: loc. cit., 496.

[95] John Paul II, Homily at the Closing of the Synod of Bishops, Fifth Ordinary General Assembly (October 25, 1980), 8: *AAS* 72 (1980), 1083.

and wives should first of all recognize clearly the teaching of *Humanae Vitae* as indicating the norm for the exercise of their sexuality, and that they should endeavor to establish the conditions necessary for observing that norm.

34.5 As the Synod noted, this pedagogy embraces the whole of married life. Accordingly, the function of transmitting life must be integrated into the overall mission of Christian life as a whole, which without the Cross cannot reach the Resurrection. In such a context it is understandable that sacrifice cannot be removed from family life, but must in fact be wholeheartedly accepted if the love between husband and wife is to be deepened and become a source of intimate joy.

34.6 This shared progress demands reflection, instruction and suitable education on the part of the priests, Religious and lay people engaged in family pastoral work: they will all be able to assist married people in their human and spiritual progress, a progress that demands awareness of sin, a sincere commitment to observe the moral law, and the ministry of reconciliation. It must also be kept in mind that conjugal intimacy involves the wills of two persons, who are, however, called to harmonize their mentality and behavior: this requires much patience, understanding and time. Uniquely important in this field is unity of moral and pastoral judgment by priests, a unity that must be carefully sought and ensured, in order that the faithful may not have to suffer anxiety of conscience.[96]

34.7 It will be easier for married people to make progress if, with respect for the Church's teaching and with trust in the grace of Christ, and with the help and support of the pastors of souls and the entire ecclesial community, they are able to discover and experience the liberating and inspiring value of the authentic love that is offered by the Gospel and set before us by the Lord's commandment.

Instilling conviction and offering practical help

35.1 With regard to the question of lawful birth regulation, the ecclesial community at the present time must take on the task of instilling conviction and offering practical help to those who wish to live out their parenthood in a truly responsible way.

35.2 In this matter, while the Church notes with satisfaction the results achieved by scientific research aimed at a more precise knowledge of the rhythms of women's fertility, and while it encourages a more decisive and wide-ranging extension of that research, it cannot fail to call with renewed vigor on the responsibility of all — doctors, experts, marriage counselors,

[96] Cf. Paul VI, Encyclical Letter *Humanae Vitae* (July 25, 1968), 28: *AAS* 60 (1968), 501.

teachers and married couples — who can actually help married people to live their love with respect for the structure and finalities of the conjugal act which expresses that love. This implies a broader, more decisive and more systematic effort to make the natural methods of regulating fertility known, respected and applied.[97]

35.3 A very valuable witness can and should be given by those husbands and wives who through the joint exercise of periodic continence have reached a more mature personal responsibility with regard to love and life. As Paul VI wrote: "To them the Lord entrusts the task of making visible to people the holiness and sweetness of the law which unites the mutual love of husband and wife with their cooperation with the love of God, the author of human life."[98]

2) EDUCATION

The right and duty of parents regarding education

36.1 The task of giving education is rooted in the primary vocation of married couples to participate in God's creative activity: by begetting in love and for love a new person who has within himself or herself the vocation to growth and development, parents by that very fact take on the task of helping that person effectively to live a fully human life. As the Second Vatican Council recalled, "since parents have conferred life on their children, they have a most solemn obligation to educate their offspring. Hence, parents must be acknowledged as the first and foremost educators of their children. Their role as educators is so decisive that scarcely anything can compensate for their failure in it. For it devolves on parents to create a family atmosphere so animated with love and reverence for God and others that a well-rounded personal and social development will be fostered among the children. Hence, the family is the first school of those social virtues which every society needs."[99]

36.2 The right and duty of parents to give education is *essential,* since it is connected with the transmission of human life; it is *original and primary* with regard to the educational role of others, on account of the uniqueness of the loving relationship between parents and children; and it is *irreplaceable and*

---

[97] Cf. John Paul II, Address to the Delegates of the Centre de Liaison des Équipes de Recherche (November 3, 1979), 9: *Insegnamenti* II/2 (1979), 1035; see also Address to the Participants in the First Congress for the Family of Africa and Europe (January 15, 1981): *Insegnamenti* IV/1 (1981), 80-84.

[98] Encyclical Letter *Humanae Vitae* (July 25, 1968), 25: *AAS* 60 (1968), 499.

[99] Declaration on Christian Education *Gravissimum Educationis,* 3.

inalienable, and therefore incapable of being entirely delegated to others or usurped by others.

36.3 In addition to these characteristics, it cannot be forgotten that the most basic element, so basic that it qualifies the educational role of parents, is *parental love,* which finds fulfillment in the task of education as it completes and perfects its service of life: as well as being a *source,* the parents' love is also the *animating principle* and therefore the *norm* inspiring and guiding all concrete educational activity, enriching it with the values of kindness, constancy, goodness, service, disinterestedness and *self-sacrifice* that are the most precious fruit of love.

Educating in the essential values of human life

37.1 Even amid the difficulties of the work of education, difficulties which are often greater today, parents must trustingly and courageously train their children in the essential values of human life. Children must grow up with a correct attitude of freedom with regard to material goods, by adopting a simple and austere lifestyle and being fully convinced that "man is more precious for what he is than for what he has."[100]

37.2 In a society shaken and split by tensions and conflicts caused by the violent clash of various kinds of individualism and selfishness, children must be enriched not only with a sense of true justice, which alone leads to respect for the personal dignity of each individual, but also and more powerfully by a sense of true love, understood as sincere solicitude and disinterested service with regard to others, especially the poorest and those in most need. The family is the first and fundamental school of social living: as a community of love, it finds in self-giving the law that guides it and makes it grow. The self-giving that inspires the love of husband and wife for each other is the model and norm for the self-giving that must be practiced in the relationships between brothers and sisters and the different generations living together in the family. And the communion and sharing that are part of everyday life in the home at times of joy and at times of difficulty are the most concrete and effective pedagogy for the active, responsible and fruitful inclusion of the children in the wider horizon of society.

37.3 Education in love as self-giving is also the indispensable premise for parents called to give their children a clear and delicate *sex education.* Faced with a culture that largely reduces human sexuality to the level of something commonplace, since it interprets and lives it in a reductive and impoverished

---

[100] Second Vatican Ecumenical Council, Pastoral Constitution on the Church in the Modern World *Gaudium et Spes,* 35.

way by linking it solely with the body and with selfish pleasure, the educational service of parents must aim firmly at a training in the area of sex that is truly and fully personal: for sexuality is an enrichment of the whole person — body, emotions and soul — and it manifests its inmost meaning in leading the person to the gift of self in love.

37.4 Sex education, which is a basic right and duty of parents, must always be carried out under their attentive guidance, whether at home or in educational centers chosen and controlled by them. In this regard, the Church reaffirms the law of subsidiarity, which the school is bound to observe when it cooperates in sex education, by entering into the same spirit that animates the parents.

37.5 In this context *education for chastity* is absolutely essential, for it is a virtue that develops a person's authentic maturity and makes him or her capable of respecting and fostering the "nuptial meaning" of the body. Indeed Christian parents, discerning the signs of God's call, will devote special attention and care to education in virginity or celibacy as the supreme form of that self-giving that constitutes the very meaning of human sexuality.

37.6 In view of the close links between the sexual dimension of the person and his or her ethical values, education must bring the children to a knowledge of and respect for the moral norms as the necessary and highly valuable guarantee for responsible personal growth in human sexuality.

37.7 For this reason the Church is firmly opposed to an often widespread form of imparting sex information dissociated from moral principles. That would merely be an introduction to the experience of pleasure and a stimulus leading to the loss of serenity — while still in the years of innocence — by opening the way to vice.

The mission to educate and the Sacrament of Marriage

38.1 For Christian parents the mission to educate, a mission rooted, as we have said, in their participation in God's creative activity, has a new specific source in the Sacrament of Marriage, which consecrates them for the strictly Christian education of their children: that is to say, it calls upon them to share in the very authority and love of God the Father and Christ the Shepherd, and in the motherly love of the Church, and it enriches them with wisdom, counsel, fortitude and all the other gifts of the Holy Spirit in order to help the children in their growth as human beings and as Christians.

38.2 The Sacrament of Marriage gives to the educational role the dignity and vocation of being really and truly a "ministry" of the Church at the service of the building up of her members. So great and splendid is the educational ministry of Christian parents that Saint Thomas has no hesitation in comparing it with the ministry of priests: "Some only propagate and guard spiritual life by a spiritual ministry: this is the role of the Sacrament of Orders; others do this for both corporal and spiritual life, and this is brought about by the Sacrament of Marriage, by which a man and a woman join in order to beget offspring and bring them up to worship God."[101]

38.3 A vivid and attentive awareness of the mission that they have received with the Sacrament of Marriage will help Christian parents to place themselves at the service of their children's education with great serenity and trustfulness, and also with a sense of responsibility before God, who calls them and gives them the mission of building up the Church in their children. Thus in the case of baptized people, the family, called together by word and sacrament as the Church of the home, is both teacher and mother, the same as the worldwide Church.

First experience of the Church

39.1 The mission to educate demands that Christian parents should present to their children all the topics that are necessary for the gradual maturing of their personality from a Christian and ecclesial point of view. They will therefore follow the educational lines mentioned above, taking care to show their children the depths of significance to which the faith and love of Jesus Christ can lead. Furthermore, their awareness that the Lord is entrusting to them the growth of a child of God, a brother or sister of Christ, a temple of the Holy Spirit, a member of the Church, will support Christian parents in their task of strengthening the gift of divine grace in their children's souls.

39.2 The Second Vatican Council describes the content of Christian education as follows: "Such an education does not merely strive to foster maturity . . . in the human person. Rather, its principal aims are these: that as baptized persons are gradually introduced into a knowledge of the mystery of salvation, they may daily grow more conscious of the gift of faith which they have received; that they may learn to adore God the Father in spirit and in truth (cf. Jn 4:23), especially through liturgical worship; that they may be trained to conduct their personal life in true righteousness and holiness, according to their new nature (Eph 4:22-24), and thus grow to maturity, to the stature of the fullness of Christ (cf. Eph 4:13), and devote themselves to the upbuilding of the Mystical Body. Moreover, aware of their calling, they should grow accustomed to giving witness to the hope that is in them (cf. 1 Pet 3:15), and to promoting the Christian transformation of the world."[102]

---

[101] *Summa contra Gentiles,* IV, 58.
[102] Declaration on Christian Education *Gravissimum Educationis,* 2.

39.3 The Synod too, taking up and developing the indications of the Council, presented the educational mission of the Christian family as a true ministry through which the Gospel is transmitted and radiated, so that family life itself becomes an itinerary of faith and in some way a Christian initiation and a school of following Christ. Within a family that is aware of this gift, as Paul VI wrote, "all the members evangelize and are evangelized."[103]

39.4 By virtue of their ministry of educating, parents are, through the witness of their lives, the first heralds of the Gospel for their children. Furthermore, by praying with their children, by reading the word of God with them and by introducing them deeply through Christian initiation into the Body of Christ — both the Eucharistic and the ecclesial Body — they become fully parents, in that they are begetters not only of bodily life but also of the life that through the Spirit's renewal flows from the Cross and Resurrection of Christ.

39.5 In order that Christian parents may worthily carry out their ministry of educating, the Synod Fathers expressed the hope that a suitable *catechism for families* would be prepared, one that would be clear, brief and easily assimilated by all. The Episcopal Conferences were warmly invited to contribute to producing this catechism.

Relations with other educating agents

40.1 The family is the primary but not the only and exclusive educating community. Man's community aspect itself — both civil and ecclesial — demands and leads to a broader and more articulated activity resulting from well-ordered collaboration between the various agents of education. All these agents are necessary, even though each can and should play its part in accordance with the special competence and contribution proper to itself.[104]

40.2 The educational role of the Christian family therefore has a very important place in organic pastoral work. This involves a new form of cooperation between parents and Christian communities, and between the various educational groups and pastors. In this sense, the renewal of the Catholic school must give special attention both to the parents of the pupils and to the formation of a perfect educating community.

40.3 The right of parents to choose an education in conformity with their religious faith must be absolutely guaranteed.

---

[103] Apostolic Exhortation *Evangelii Nuntiandi* (December 8, 1975), 71: *AAS* 68 (1976), 60-61.

[104] Cf. Second Vatican Ecumenical Council, Declaration on Christian Education *Gravissimum Educationis,* 3.

40.4 The State and the Church have the obligation to give families all possible aid to enable them to perform their educational role properly. Therefore both the Church and the State must create and foster the institutions and activities that families justly demand, and the aid must be in proportion to the families' needs. However, those in society who are in charge of schools must never forget that the parents have been appointed by God himself as the first and principal educators of their children and that their right is completely inalienable.

40.5 But corresponding to their right, parents have a serious duty to commit themselves totally to a cordial and active relationship with the teachers and the school authorities.

40.6 If ideologies opposed to the Christian faith are taught in the schools, the family must join with other families, if possible through family associations, and with all its strength and with wisdom help the young not to depart from the faith. In this case the family needs special assistance from pastors of souls, who must never forget that parents have the inviolable right to entrust their children to the ecclesial community.

Manifold service to life

41.1 Fruitful married love expresses itself in serving life in many ways. Of these ways, begetting and educating children are the most immediate, specific and irreplaceable. In fact, every act of true love toward a human being bears witness to and perfects the spiritual fecundity of the family, since it is an act of obedience to the deep inner dynamism of love as self-giving to others.

41.2 For everyone this perspective is full of value and commitment, and it can be an inspiration in particular for couples who experience physical sterility.

41.3 Christian families, recognizing with faith all human beings as children of the same heavenly Father, will respond generously to the children of other families, giving them support and love not as outsiders but as members of the one family of God's children. Christian parents will thus be able to spread their love beyond the bonds of flesh and blood, nourishing the links that are rooted in the spirit and that develop through concrete service to the children of other families, who are often without even the barest necessities.

41.4 Christian families will be able to show greater readiness to adopt and foster children who have lost their parents or have been abandoned by them. Rediscovering the warmth of affection of a family, these children will be able to experience God's loving and provident fatherhood witnessed to by Christian parents, and they will thus be able to grow up with serenity and confidence in life. At the same time the whole family will be enriched with the spiritual values of a wider fraternity.

41.5 Family fecundity must have an unceasing "creativity," a marvelous fruit of the Spirit of God, who opens the eyes of the heart to discover the new needs and sufferings of our society and gives courage for accepting them and responding to them. A vast field of activity lies open to families: today, even more preoccupying than child abandonment is the phenomenon of social and cultural exclusion, which seriously affects the elderly, the sick, the disabled, drug addicts, ex-prisoners, etc.

41.6 This broadens enormously the horizons of the parenthood of Christian families: these and many other urgent needs of our time are a challenge to their spiritually fruitful love. With families and through them, the Lord Jesus continues to "have compassion" on the multitudes.

3. Participating in the Development of Society

The family as the first and vital cell of society

42.1 "Since the Creator of all things has established the conjugal partnership as the beginning and basis of human society," the family is "the first and vital cell of society."[105]

42.2 The family has vital and organic links with society, since it is its foundation and nourishes it continually through its role of service to life: it is from the family that citizens come to birth and it is within the family that they find the first school of the social virtues that are the animating principle of the existence and development of society itself.

42.3 Thus, far from being closed in on itself, the family is by nature and vocation open to other families and to society, and undertakes its social role.

Family life as an experience of communion and sharing

43.1 The very experience of communion and sharing that should characterize the family's daily life represents its first and fundamental contribution to society.

43.2 The relationships between the members of the family community are inspired and guided by the law of "free giving." By respecting and fostering personal dignity in each and every one as the only basis for value, this free giving takes the form of heartfelt acceptance, encounter and dialogue, disinterested availability, generous service and deep solidarity.

---

[105] Second Vatican Ecumenical Council, Decree on the Apostolate of the Laity *Apostolicam Actuositatem,* 11.

43.3 Thus the fostering of authentic and mature communion between persons within the family is the first and irreplaceable school of social life, and example and stimulus for the broader community relationships marked by respect, justice, dialogue and love.

43.4 The family is thus, as the Synod Fathers recalled, the place of origin and the most effective means for humanizing and personalizing society: it makes an original contribution in depth to building up the world, by making possible a life that is properly speaking human, in particular by guarding and transmitting virtues and "values." As the Second Vatican Council states, in the family "the various generations come together and help one another to grow wiser and to harmonize personal rights with the other requirements of social living."[106]

43.5 Consequently, faced with a society that is running the risk of becoming more and more depersonalized and standardized and therefore inhuman and dehumanizing, with the negative results of many forms of escapism — such as alcoholism, drugs and even terrorism — the family possesses and continues still to release formidable energies capable of taking man out of his anonymity, keeping him conscious of his personal dignity, enriching him with deep humanity and actively placing him, in his uniqueness and unrepeatability, within the fabric of society.

The social and political role

44.1 The social role of the family certainly cannot stop short at procreation and education, even if this constitutes its primary and irreplaceable form of expression.

44.2 Families therefore, either singly or in association, can and should devote themselves to manifold social service activities, especially in favor of the poor, or at any rate for the benefit of all people and situations that cannot be reached by the public authorities' welfare organization.

44.3 The social contribution of the family has an original character of its own, one that should be given greater recognition and more decisive encouragement, especially as the children grow up, and actually involving all its members as much as possible.[107]

44.4 In particular, note must be taken of the ever greater importance in our society of hospitality in all its forms, from opening the door of one's home and still more of one's heart to the pleas of one's brothers and sisters, to concrete efforts to ensure that every family has its own home, as the natural

[106] Pastoral Constitution on the Church in the Modern World *Gaudium et Spes,* 52.

[107] Cf. Second Vatican Ecumenical Council Decree on the Apostolate of the Laity *Apostolicam Actuositatem,* 11.

environment that preserves it and makes it grow. In a special way the Christian family is called upon to listen to the Apostle's recommendation: "Practice hospitality,"[108] and therefore, imitating Christ's example and sharing in his love, to welcome the brother or sister in need: "Whoever gives to one of these little ones even a cup of cold water because he is a disciple, truly, I say to you, he shall not lose his reward."[109]

44.5 The social role of families is called upon to find expression also in the form of *political intervention:* families should be the first to take steps to see that the laws and institutions of the State not only do not offend but support and positively defend the rights and duties of the family. Along these lines, families should grow in awareness of being "protagonists" of what is known as "family politics" and assume responsibility for transforming society; otherwise, families will be the first victims of the evils that they have done no more than note with indifference. The Second Vatican Council's appeal to go beyond an individualistic ethic therefore also holds good for the family as such.[110]

Society at the service of the family

45.1 Just as the intimate connection between the family and society demands that the family be open to and participate in society and its development, so also it requires that society should never fail in its fundamental task of respecting and fostering the family.

45.2 The family and society have complementary functions in defending and fostering the good of each and every human being. But society — more specifically the State — must recognize that "the family is a society in its own original right"[111] and so society is under a grave obligation in its relations with the family to adhere to the principle of subsidiarity.

45.3 By virtue of this principle, the State cannot and must not take away from families the functions that they can just as well perform on their own or in free associations; instead it must positively favor and encourage as far as possible responsible initiative by families. In the conviction that the good of the family is an indispensable and essential value of the civil community, the public authorities must do everything possible to ensure that families have all those aids — economic, social, educational, political and cultural assistance — that they need in order to face all their responsibilities in a human way.

---

[108] Rom 12:13.

[109] Mt 10:42.

[110] Cf. Pastoral Constitution on the Church in the Modern World *Gaudium et Spes,* 30.

[111] Second Vatican Ecumenical Council, Declaration on Religious Freedom *Dignitatis Humanae,* 5.

The charter of family rights

46.1 The ideal of mutual support and development between the family and society is often very seriously in conflict with the reality of their separation and even opposition.

46.2 In fact, as was repeatedly denounced by the Synod, the situation experienced by many families in various countries is highly problematical, if not entirely negative: institutions and laws unjustly ignore the inviolable rights of the family and of the human person; and society, far from putting itself at the service of the family, attacks it violently in its values and fundamental requirements. Thus the family, which in God's plan is the basic cell of society and a subject of rights and duties before the State or any other community, finds itself the victim of society, of the delays and slowness with which it acts, and even of its blatant injustice.

46.3 For this reason, the Church openly and strongly defends the rights of the family against the intolerable usurpations of society and the State. In particular, the Synod Fathers mentioned the following rights of the family:

— the right to exist and progress as a family, that is to say, the right of every human being, even if he or she is poor, to found a family and to have adequate means to support it;

— the right to exercise its responsibility regarding the transmission of life and to educate children;

— the right to the intimacy of conjugal and family life;

— the right to the stability of the bond and of the institution of marriage;

— the right to believe in and profess one's faith and to propagate it;

— the right to bring up children in accordance with the family's own traditions and religious and cultural values, with the necessary instruments, means and institutions;

— the right, especially of the poor and the sick, to obtain physical, social, political and economic security;

— the right to housing suitable for living family life in a proper way;

— the right to expression and to representation, either directly or through associations, before the economic, social and cultural public authorities and lower authorities;

— the right to form associations with other families and institutions, in order to fulfill the family's role suitably and expeditiously;

— the right to protect minors by adequate institutions and legislation from harmful drugs, pornography, alcoholism, etc.;

— the right to wholesome recreation of a kind that also fosters family values;

— the right of the elderly to a worthy life and a worthy death;

— the right to emigrate as a family in search of a better life.[112]

46.4 Acceding to the Synod's explicit request, the Holy See will give prompt attention to studying these suggestions in depth and to the preparation of a Charter of Rights of the Family, to be presented to the quarters and authorities concerned.

The Christian family's grace and responsibility

47.1 The social role that belongs to every family pertains by a new and original right to the Christian family, which is based on the Sacrament of Marriage. By taking up the human reality of the love between husband and wife in all its implications, the sacrament gives to Christian couples and parents a power and a commitment to live their vocation as lay people and therefore to "seek the Kingdom of God by engaging in temporal affairs and by ordering them according to the plan of God."[113]

47.2 The social and political role is included in the kingly mission of service in which Christian couples share by virtue of the Sacrament of Marriage, and they receive both a command which they cannot ignore and a grace which sustains and stimulates them.

47.3 The Christian family is thus called upon to offer everyone a witness of generous and disinterested dedication to social matters, through a "preferential option" for the poor and disadvantaged. Therefore, advancing in its following of the Lord by special love for all the poor, it must have special concern for the hungry, the poor, the old, the sick, drug victims and those who have no family.

For a new international order

48.1 In view of the worldwide dimension of various social questions nowadays, the family has seen its role with regard to the development of society extended in a completely new way: it now also involves cooperating for a new international order, since it is only in worldwide solidarity that the enormous and dramatic issues of world justice, the freedom of peoples and the peace of humanity can be dealt with and solved.

48.2 The spiritual communion between Christian families, rooted in a common faith and hope and given life by love, constitutes an inner energy that generates, spreads and develops justice, reconciliation, fraternity and peace

---

[112] Cf. *Propositio* 42.

[113] Second Vatican Ecumenical Council Dogmatic Constitution on the Church *Lumen Gentium,* 31.

among human beings. Insofar as it is a "small-scale Church," the Christian family is called upon, like the "large-scale Church," to be a sign of unity for the world and in this way to exercise its prophetic role by bearing witness to the Kingdom and peace of Christ, toward which the whole world is journeying.

48.3 Christian families can do this through their educational activity — that is to say by presenting to their children a model of life based on the values of truth, freedom, justice and love — both through active and responsible involvement in the authentically human growth of society and its institutions, and by supporting in various ways the associations specifically devoted to international issues.

4. Sharing in the Life and Mission of the Church

The family, within the mystery of the Church

49.1 Among the fundamental tasks of the Christian family is its ecclesial task: the family is placed at the service of the building up of the Kingdom of God in history by participating in the life and mission of the Church.

49.2 In order to understand better the foundations, the contents and the characteristics of this participation, we must examine the many profound bonds linking the Church and the Christian family and establishing the family as a "Church in miniature" *(Ecclesia domestica),*[114] in such a way that in its own way the family is a living image and historical representation of the mystery of the Church.

49.3 It is, above all, the Church as Mother that gives birth to, educates and builds up the Christian family, by putting into effect in its regard the saving mission which she has received from her Lord. By proclaiming the word of God, the Church reveals to the Christian family its true identity, what it is and should be according to the Lord's plan; by celebrating the sacraments, the Church enriches and strengthens the Christian family with the grace of Christ for its sanctification to the glory of the Father; by the continuous proclamation of the new commandment of love, the Church encourages and guides the Christian family to the service of love, so that it may imitate and relive the same self-giving and sacrificial love that the Lord Jesus has for the entire human race.

49.4 In turn, the Christian family is grafted into the mystery of the Church

---

[114] Cf. Second Vatican Ecumenical Council Dogmatic Constitution on the Church *Lumen Gentium,* 11; Decree on the Apostolate of the Laity *Apostolicam Actuositatem,* 11; John Paul II, Homily at the Opening of the Synod of Bishops, Fifth Ordinary General Assembly (September 26, 1980), 3: *AAS* 72 (1980), 1008.

to such a degree as to become a sharer, in its own way, in the saving mission proper to the Church: by virtue of the sacrament, Christian married couples and parents "in their state and way of life have their own special gift among the People of God."[115] For this reason they not only *receive* the love of Christ and become a *saved* community, but they are also called upon to *communicate* Christ's love to their brethren, thus becoming a *saving* community. In this way, while the Christian family is a fruit and sign of the supernatural fecundity of the Church, it stands also as a symbol, witness and participant of the Church's motherhood.[116]

A specific and original ecclesial role

50.1 The Christian family is called upon to take part actively and responsibly in the mission of the Church in a way that is original and specific, by placing itself, in what it is and what it does as an "intimate community of life and love," at the service of the Church and of society.

50.2 Since the Christian family is a community in which the relationships are renewed by Christ through faith and the sacraments, the family's sharing in the Church's mission should follow *a community pattern:* the spouses together *as a couple,* the parents and children *as a family,* must live their service to the Church and to the world. They must be "of one heart and soul"[117] in faith, through the shared apostolic zeal that animates them, and through their shared commitment to works of service to the ecclesial and civil communities.

50.3 The Christian family also builds up the Kingdom of God in history through the everyday realities that concern and distinguish its *state of life.* It is thus in *the love between husband and wife and between the members of the family* — a love lived out in all its extraordinary richness of values and demands: totality, oneness, fidelity and fruitfulness [118] — that the Christian family's participation in the prophetic, priestly and kingly mission of Jesus Christ and of his Church finds expression and realization. Therefore, love and life constitute the nucleus of the saving mission of the Christian family in the Church and for the Church.

50.4 The Second Vatican Council recalls this fact when it writes: "Families

---

[115] Second Vatican Ecumenical Council, Dogmatic Constitution on the Church *Lumen Gentium,* 11.

[116] Cf. ibid., 41.

[117] Acts 4:32.

[118] Cf. Paul VI, Encyclical Letter *Humanae Vitae* (July 25, 1968), 9: *AAS* 60 (1968), 486-487.

will share their spiritual riches generously with other families too. Thus the Christian family, which springs from marriage as a reflection of the loving Covenant uniting Christ with the Church, and as a participation in that Covenant will manifest to all people the Savior's living presence in the world, and the genuine nature of the Church. This the family will do by the mutual love of the spouses, by their generous fruitfulness, their solidarity and faithfulness, and by the loving way in which all the members of the family work together."[119]

50.5 Having laid the *foundation* of the participation of the Christian family in the Church's mission, it is now time to illustrate its *substance in reference to Jesus Christ as prophet, priest and king* — three aspects of a single reality — by presenting the Christian family as 1) a believing and evangelizing community, 2) a community in dialogue with God, and 3) a community at the service of man.

1) THE CHRISTIAN FAMILY AS A BELIEVING AND EVANGELIZING COMMUNITY

Faith as the discovery and admiring awareness of God's plan for the family

51.1 As a sharer in the life and mission of the Church, which listens to the word of God with reverence and proclaims it confidently,[120] *the Christian family fulfills its prophetic role by welcoming and announcing the word of God:* it thus becomes more and more each day a believing and evangelizing community.

51.2 Christian spouses and parents are required to offer "the obedience of faith."[121] They are called upon to welcome the word of the Lord which reveals to them the marvelous news — the Good News — of their conjugal and family life sanctified and made a source of sanctity by Christ himself. Only in faith can they discover and admire with joyful gratitude the dignity to which God has deigned to raise marriage and the family, making them a sign and meeting place of the loving Covenant between God and man, between Jesus Christ and his Bride, the Church.

51.3 The very preparation for Christian marriage is itself a journey of faith. It is a special opportunity for the engaged to rediscover and deepen the faith received in Baptism and nourished by their Christian upbringing. In this way they come to recognize and freely accept their vocation to follow Christ and to serve the Kingdom of God in the married state.

---

[119] Pastoral Constitution on the Church in the Modern World *Gaudium et Spes,* 48.

[120] Cf. Second Vatican Ecumenical Council, Dogmatic Constitution on Divine Revelation *Dei Verbum,* 1.

[121] Rom 16:26.

51.4 The celebration of the Sacrament of Marriage is the basic moment of the faith of the couple. This sacrament, in essence, is the proclamation in the Church of the Good News concerning married love. It is the word of God that "reveals" and "fulfills" the wise and loving plan of God for the married couple, giving them a mysterious and real share in the very love with which God himself loves humanity. Since the sacramental celebration of marriage is itself a proclamation of the word of God, it must also be a "profession of faith" within and with the Church, as a community of believers, on the part of all those who in different ways participate in its celebration.

51.5 This profession of faith demands that it be prolonged in the life of the married couple and of the family. God, who called the couple *to* marriage, continues to call them *in* marriage.[122] In and through the events, problems, difficulties and circumstances of everyday life, God comes to them, revealing and presenting the concrete "demands" of their sharing in the love of Christ for his Church in the particular family, social and ecclesial situation in which they find themselves.

51.6 The discovery of and obedience to the plan of God on the part of the conjugal and family community must take place in "togetherness," through the human experience of love between husband and wife, between parents and children, lived in the Spirit of Christ.

51.7 Thus the little domestic Church, like the greater Church, needs to be constantly and intensely evangelized: hence its duty regarding permanent education in the faith.

The Christian family's ministry of evangelization

52.1 To the extent in which the Christian family accepts the Gospel and matures in faith, it becomes an evangelizing community. Let us listen again to Paul VI: "The family, like the Church, ought to be a place where the Gospel is transmitted and from which the Gospel radiates. In a family which is conscious of this mission, all the members evangelize and are evangelized. The parents not only communicate the Gospel to their children, but from their children they can themselves receive the same Gospel as deeply lived by them. And such a family becomes the evangelizer of many other families, and of the neighborhood of which it forms part."[123]

52.2 As the Synod repeated, taking up the appeal which I launched at Puebla, the future of evangelization depends in great part on the Church of

---

[122] Cf. Paul VI, Encyclical Letter *Humanae Vitae* (July 25, 1968), 25: *AAS* 60 (1968), 498.

[123] Apostolic Exhortation *Evangelii Nuntiandi* (December 8, 1975), 71: *AAS* 68 (1976), 60-61.

the home.[124] This apostolic mission of the family is rooted in Baptism and receives from the grace of the Sacrament of Marriage new strength to transmit the faith, to sanctify and transform our present society according to God's plan.

52.3 Particularly today, the Christian family has a special vocation to witness to the Paschal Covenant of Christ by constantly radiating the joy of love and the certainty of the hope for which it must give an account: "The Christian family loudly proclaims both the present virtues of the Kingdom of God and the hope of a blessed life to come."[125]

52.4 The absolute need for family catechesis emerges with particular force in certain situations that the Church unfortunately experiences in some places: "In places where anti-religious legislation endeavors even to prevent education in the faith, and in places where widespread unbelief or invasive secularism makes real religious growth practically impossible, 'the Church of the home' remains the one place where children and young people can receive an authentic catechesis."[126]

Ecclesial service

53.1 The ministry of evangelization carried out by Christian parents is original and irreplaceable. It assumes the characteristics typical of family life itself, which should be interwoven with love, simplicity, practicality and daily witness.[127]

53.2 The family must educate the children for life in such a way that each one may fully perform his or her role according to the vocation received from God. Indeed, the family that is open to transcendent values, that serves its brothers and sisters with joy, that fulfills its duties with generous fidelity, and is aware of its daily sharing in the mystery of the glorious Cross of Christ, becomes the primary and most excellent seedbed of vocations to a life of consecration to the Kingdom of God.

53.3 The parents' ministry of evangelization and catechesis ought to play a part in their children's lives also during adolescence and youth, when the children, as often happens, challenge or even reject the Christian faith re-

---

[124] Cf. Address at the Opening of the Third General Assembly of the Bishops of Latin America (January 28, 1979), IV, a: AAS 71 (1979), 204.

[125] Second Vatican Ecumenical Council, Dogmatic Constitution on the Church Lumen Gentium, 35.

[126] John Paul II, Apostolic Exhortation Catechesi Tradendae (October 16, 1979), 68: AAS 71 (1979), 1334.

[127] Cf. ibid., 36: loc. cit., 1308.

ceived in earlier years. Just as in the Church the work of evangelization can never be separated from the sufferings of the apostle, so in the Christian family parents must face with courage and great interior serenity the difficulties that their ministry of evangelization sometimes encounters in their own children.

53.4 It should not be forgotten that the service rendered by Christian spouses and parents to the Gospel is essentially an ecclesial service. It has its place within the context of the whole Church as an evangelized and evangelizing community. Insofar as the ministry of evangelization and catechesis of the Church of the home is rooted in and derives from the one mission of the Church and is ordained to the upbuilding of the one Body of Christ,[128] it must remain in intimate communion and collaborate responsibly with all the other evangelizing and catechetical activities present and at work in the ecclesial community at the diocesan and parochial levels.

To preach the Gospel to the whole creation

54.1 Evangelization, urged on within by irrepressible missionary zeal, is characterized by a universality without boundaries. It is the response to Christ's explicit and unequivocal command: "Go into all the world and preach the Gospel to the whole creation."[129]

54.2 The Christian family's faith and evangelizing mission also possesses this catholic missionary inspiration. The Sacrament of Marriage takes up and reproposes the task of defending and spreading the faith, a task that has its roots in Baptism and Confirmation,[130] and makes Christian married couples and parents witnesses of Christ "to the end of the earth,"[131] missionaries, in the true and proper sense, of love and life.

54.3 A form of missionary activity can be exercised even within the family. This happens when some member of the family does not have the faith or does not practice it with consistency. In such a case the other members must give him or her a living witness of their own faith in order to encourage and support him or her along the path toward full acceptance of Christ the Savior.[132]

54.4 Animated in its own inner life by missionary zeal, the Church of the home is also called to be a luminous sign of the presence of Christ and of his

---

[128] Cf. 1 Cor 12:4-6; Eph 4:12-13.

[129] Mk 16:15.

[130] Second Vatican Ecumenical Council, Dogmatic Constitution on the Church *Lumen Gentium,* 11.

[131] Acts 1:8.

[132] Cf. 1 Pet 3:1-2.

love for those who are "far away," for families who do not yet believe, and for those Christian families who no longer live in accordance with the faith that they once received. The Christian family is called to enlighten "by its example and its witness . . . those who seek the truth."[133]

54.5 Just as at the dawn of Christianity Aquila and Priscilla were presented as a missionary couple,[134] so today the Church shows forth her perennial newness and fruitfulness by the presence of Christian couples and families who dedicate at least a part of their lives to working in missionary territories, proclaiming the Gospel and doing service to their fellowman in the love of Jesus Christ.

54.6 Christian families offer a special contribution to the missionary cause of the Church by fostering missionary vocations among their sons and daughters[135] and, more generally, "by training their children from childhood to recognize God's love for all people."[136]

2) THE CHRISTIAN FAMILY AS A COMMUNITY IN DIALOGUE WITH GOD

The Church's sanctuary in the home

55.1 The proclamation of the Gospel and its acceptance in faith reach their fullness in the celebration of the sacraments. The Church which is a believing and evangelizing community is also a priestly people invested with the dignity and sharing in the power of Christ the High Priest of the New and Eternal Covenant.[137]

55.2 The Christian family too is part of this priestly people which is the Church. By means of the Sacrament of Marriage, in which it is rooted and from which it draws its nourishment, the Christian family is continuously vivified by the Lord Jesus and called and engaged by him in a dialogue with God through the sacraments, through the offering of one's life, and through prayer.

55.3 This is the *priestly role* which the Christian family can and ought to exercise in intimate communion with the whole Church, through the daily

---

[133] Second Vatican Ecumenical Council, Dogmatic Constitution on the Church *Lumen Gentium,* 35; cf. Decree on the Apostolate of the Laity *Apostolicam Actuositatem,* 11.

[134] Cf. Acts 18; Rom 16:3-4.

[135] Cf. Second Vatican Ecumenical Council, Decree on the Church's Missionary Activity *Ad Gentes,* 39.

[136] Second Vatican Ecumenical Council, Decree on the Apostolate of the Laity *Apostolicam Actuositatem,* 30.

[137] Cf. Second Vatican Ecumenical Council, Dogmatic Constitution on the Church *Lumen Gentium,* 10.

realities of married and family life. In this way the Christian family *is called to be sanctified and to sanctify the ecclesial community and the world.*

Marriage as a sacrament of mutual sanctification and an act of worship

56.1 The Sacrament of Marriage is the specific source and original means of sanctification for Christian married couples and families. It takes up again and makes specific the sanctifying grace of Baptism. By virtue of the mystery of the Death and Resurrection of Christ, of which the spouses are made part in a new way by marriage, conjugal love is purified and made holy: "This love the Lord has judged worthy of special gifts, healing, perfecting and exalting gifts of grace and of charity."[138]

56.2 The gift of Jesus Christ is not exhausted in the actual celebration of the Sacrament of Marriage, but rather accompanies the married couple throughout their lives. This fact is explicitly recalled by the Second Vatican Council when it says that Jesus Christ "abides with them so that, just as he loved the Church and handed himself over on her behalf, the spouses may love each other with perpetual fidelity through mutual self-bestowal. . . . For this reason, Christian spouses have a special sacrament by which they are fortified and receive a kind of consecration in the duties and dignity of their state. By virtue of this sacrament, as spouses fulfill their conjugal and family obligations, they are penetrated with the Spirit of Christ, who fills their whole lives with faith, hope and charity. Thus they increasingly advance toward their own perfection, as well as toward their mutual sanctification, and hence contribute jointly to the glory of God."[139]

56.3 Christian spouses and parents are included in the universal call to sanctity. For them this call is specified by the sacrament they have celebrated and is carried out concretely in the realities proper to their conjugal and family life.[140] This gives rise to the grace and requirement of an authentic and profound *conjugal and family spirituality* that draws its inspiration from the themes of creation, Covenant, Cross, Resurrection, and sign, which were stressed more than once by the Synod.

56.4 Christian marriage, like the other sacraments, "whose purpose is to sanctify people, to build up the Body of Christ, and finally, to give worship to

---

[138] Second Vatican Ecumenical Council, Pastoral Constitution on the Church in the Modern World *Gaudium et Spes,* 49.

[139] Ibid., 48.

[140] Cf. Second Vatican Ecumenical Council, Dogmatic Constitution on the Church *Lumen Gentium,* 41.

God,"[141] is in itself a liturgical action glorifying God in Jesus Christ and in the Church. By celebrating it, Christian spouses profess their gratitude to God for the sublime gift bestowed on them of being able to live in their married and family lives the very love of God for people and that of the Lord Jesus for the Church, his Bride.

56.5 Just as husbands and wives receive from the sacrament the gift and responsibility of translating into daily living the sanctification bestowed on them, so the same sacrament confers on them the grace and moral obligation of transforming their whole lives into a "spiritual sacrifice."[142] What the Council says of the laity applies also to Christian spouses and parents, especially with regard to the earthly and temporal realities that characterize their lives: "As worshipers leading holy lives in every place, the laity consecrate the world itself to God."[143]

Marriage and the Eucharist

57.1 The Christian family's sanctifying role is grounded in Baptism and has its highest expression in the Eucharist, to which Christian marriage is intimately connected. The Second Vatican Council drew attention to the unique relationship between the Eucharist and marriage by requesting that "marriage normally be celebrated within the Mass."[144] To understand better and live more intensely the graces and responsibilities of Christian marriage and family life, it is altogether necessary to rediscover and strengthen this relationship.

57.2 The Eucharist is the very source of Christian marriage. The Eucharistic Sacrifice, in fact, represents Christ's Covenant of love with the Church, sealed with his blood on the Cross.[145] In this sacrifice of the New and Eternal Covenant, Christian spouses encounter the source from which their own marriage covenant flows, is interiorly structured and continuously renewed. As a representation of Christ's sacrifice of love for the Church, the Eucharist is a fountain of charity. In the Eucharistic gift of charity the Christian family finds the foundation and soul of its "communion" and its "mission": by partaking in

---

[141] Second Vatican Ecumenical Council, Constitution on the Sacred Liturgy *Sacrosanctum Concilium,* 59.

[142] Cf. 1 Pet 2:5; Second Vatican Ecumenical Council, Dogmatic Constitution on the Church *Lumen Gentium,* 34.

[143] Second Vatican Ecumenical Council, Dogmatic Constitution on the Church *Lumen Gentium,* 34.

[144] Constitution on the Sacred Liturgy *Sacrosanctum Concilium,* 78.

[145] Cf. Jn 19:34.

the Eucharistic bread, the different members of the Christian family become one body, which reveals and shares in the wider unity of the Church. Their sharing in the Body of Christ that is "given up" and in his Blood that is "shed" becomes a never-ending source of missionary and apostolic dynamism for the Christian family.

The sacrament of conversion and reconciliation

58.1 An essential and permanent part of the Christian family's sanctifying role consists in accepting the call to conversion that the Gospel addresses to all Christians, who do not always remain faithful to the "newness" of the Baptism that constitutes them "saints." The Christian family too is sometimes unfaithful to the law of baptismal grace and holiness proclaimed anew in the Sacrament of Marriage.

58.2 Repentance and mutual pardon within the bosom of the Christian family, so much a part of daily life, receive their specific sacramental expression in Christian Penance. In the Encyclical *Humanae Vitae,* Paul VI wrote of married couples: "And if sin should still keep its hold over them, let them not be discouraged, but rather have recourse with humble perseverance to the mercy of God, which is abundantly poured forth in the Sacrament of Penance."[146]

58.3 The celebration of this sacrament acquires special significance for family life. While they discover in faith that sin contradicts not only the Covenant with God, but also the covenant between husband and wife and the communion of the family, the married couple and the other members of the family are led to an encounter with God, who is "rich in mercy,"[147] who bestows on them his love which is more powerful than sin,[148] and who reconstructs and brings to perfection the marriage covenant and the family communion.

Family prayer

59.1 The Church prays for the Christian family and educates the family to live in generous accord with the priestly gift and role received from Christ the High Priest. In effect, the baptismal priesthood of the faithful, exercised in the Sacrament of Marriage, constitutes the basis of a priestly vocation and mission for the spouses and family by which their daily lives are transformed into

---

[146] (July 25, 1968), 25: *AAS* 60 (1968), 499.

[147] Eph 2:4.

[148] Cf. John Paul II, Encyclical Letter *Dives in Misericordia* (November 30, 1980), 13: *AAS* 72 (1980), 1218-1219.

"spiritual sacrifices acceptable to God through Jesus Christ."[149] This transformation is achieved not only by celebrating the Eucharist and the other sacraments and through offering themselves to the glory of God, but also through a life of prayer, through prayerful dialogue with the Father, through Jesus Christ, in the Holy Spirit.

59.2 Family prayer has its own characteristic qualities. It is prayer offered *in common,* husband and wife together, parents and children together. Communion in prayer is both a consequence of and a requirement for the communion bestowed by the Sacraments of Baptism and Matrimony. The words with which the Lord Jesus promises his presence can be applied to the members of the Christian family in a special way: "Again I say to you, if two of you agree on earth about anything they ask, it will be done for them by my Father in heaven. For where two or three are gathered in my name, there am I in the midst of them."[150]

59.3 Family prayer has for its very own object *family life itself,* which in all its varying circumstances is seen as a call from God and lived as a filial response to his call. Joys and sorrows, hopes and disappointments, births and birthday celebrations, wedding anniversaries of the parents, departures, separations and homecomings, important and far-reaching decisions, the death of those who are dear, etc. — all of these mark God's loving intervention in the family's history. They should be seen as suitable moments for thanksgiving, for petition, for trusting abandonment of the family into the hands of their common Father in heaven. The dignity and responsibility of the Christian family as the domestic Church can be achieved only with God's unceasing aid, which will surely be granted if it is humbly and trustingly petitioned in prayer.

Educators in prayer

60.1 By reason of their dignity and mission, Christian parents have the specific responsibility of educating their children in prayer, introducing them to gradual discovery of the mystery of God and to personal dialogue with him: "It is particularly in the Christian family, enriched by the grace and the office of the Sacrament of Matrimony, that from the earliest years children should be taught, according to the faith received in Baptism, to have a knowledge of God, to worship him and to love their neighbor."[151]

---

[149] 1 Pet 2:5.

[150] Mt 18:19-20.

[151] Second Vatican Ecumenical Council, Declaration on Christian Education *Gravissimum Educationis,* 3; cf. John Paul II, Apostolic Exhortation *Catechesi Tradendae* (October 16, 1979), 36: *AAS* 71 (1979), 1308.

60.2 The concrete example and living witness of parents is fundamental and irreplaceable in educating their children to pray. Only by praying together with their children can a father and mother — exercising their royal priesthood — penetrate the innermost depths of their children's hearts and leave an impression that the future events in their lives will not be able to efface. Let us again listen to the appeal made by Paul VI to parents: "Mothers, do you teach your children the Christian prayers? Do you prepare them, in conjunction with the priests, for the sacraments that they receive when they are young: Confession, Communion and Confirmation? Do you encourage them when they are sick to think of Christ suffering, to invoke the aid of the Blessed Virgin and the saints? Do you say the family rosary together? And you, fathers, do you pray with your children, with the whole domestic community, at least sometimes? Your example of honesty in thought and action, joined to some common prayer, is a lesson for life, an act of worship of singular value. In this way you bring peace to your homes: *Pax huic domui.* Remember, it is thus that you build up the Church."[152]

Liturgical prayer and private prayer

61.1 There exists a deep and vital bond between the prayer of the Church and the prayer of the individual faithful, as has been clearly reaffirmed by the Second Vatican Council.[153] An important purpose of the prayer of the domestic Church is to serve as the natural introduction for the children to the liturgical prayer of the whole Church, both in the sense of preparing for it and of extending it into personal, family and social life. Hence the need for gradual participation by all the members of the Christian family in the celebration of the Eucharist, especially on Sundays and feast days, and of the other sacraments, particularly the sacraments of Christian initiation of the children. The directives of the Council opened up a new possibility for the Christian family when it listed the family among those groups to whom it recommends the recitation of the Divine Office in common.[154] Likewise, the Christian family will strive to celebrate at home, and in a way suited to the members, the times and feasts of the liturgical year.

61.2 As preparation for the worship celebrated in Church, and as its prolongation in the home, the Christian family makes use of private prayer, which presents a great variety of forms. While this variety testifies to the

---

[152] Address at General Audience (August 11, 1976): *Insegnamenti* XIV (1976), 640.
[153] Cf. Constitution on the Sacred Liturgy *Sacrosanctum Concilium,* 12.
[154] Cf. General Instruction on the Liturgy of the Hours, 27.

extraordinary richness with which the Spirit vivifies Christian prayer, it serves also to meet the various needs and life-situations of those who turn to the Lord in prayer. Apart from morning and evening prayers, certain forms of prayer are to be expressly encouraged, following the indications of the Synod Fathers, such as reading and meditating on the word of God, preparation for the reception of the sacraments, devotion and consecration to the Sacred Heart of Jesus, the various forms of veneration of the Blessed Virgin Mary, grace before and after meals, and observance of popular devotions.

61.3 While respecting the freedom of the children of God, the Church has always proposed certain practices of piety to the faithful with particular solicitude and insistence. Among these should be mentioned the recitation of the rosary: "We now desire, as a continuation of the thought of our Predecessors, to recommend strongly the recitation of the family rosary. . . . There is no doubt that . . . the rosary should be considered as one of the best and most efficacious prayers in common that the Christian family is invited to recite. We like to think, and sincerely hope, that when the family gathering becomes a time of prayer the rosary is a frequent and favored manner of praying."[155] In this way authentic devotion to Mary, which finds expression in sincere love and generous imitation of the Blessed Virgin's interior spiritual attitude, constitutes a special instrument for nourishing loving communion in the family and for developing conjugal and family spirituality. For she who is the Mother of Christ and of the Church is in a special way the Mother of Christian families, of domestic Churches.

Prayer and life

62.1 It should never be forgotten that prayer constitutes an essential part of Christian life, understood in its fullness and centrality. Indeed, prayer is an important part of our very humanity: it is "the first expression of man's inner truth, the first condition for authentic freedom of spirit."[156]

62.2 Far from being a form of escapism from everyday commitments, prayer constitutes the strongest incentive for the Christian family to assume and comply fully with all its responsibilities as the primary and fundamental cell of human society. Thus the Christian family's actual participation in the Church's life and mission is in direct proportion to the fidelity and intensity of

---

[155] Paul VI, Apostolic Exhortation *Marialis Cultus* (February 2, 1974), 52, 54: *AAS* 66 (1974), 160, 161.

[156] John Paul II, Address at the Mentorella Shrine (October 29, 1978): *Insegnamenti* I (1978), 78-79.

the prayer with which it is united with the fruitful vine that is Christ the Lord.[157]

62.3 The fruitfulness of the Christian family in its specific service to human advancement, which of itself cannot but lead to the transformation of the world, derives from its living union with Christ, nourished by the liturgy, by self-oblation and by prayer.[158]

3) THE CHRISTIAN FAMILY AS A COMMUNITY AT THE SERVICE OF MAN

The new commandment of love

63.1 The Church, a prophetic, priestly and kingly people, is endowed with the mission of bringing all human beings to accept the word of God in faith, to celebrate and profess it in the sacraments and in prayer, and to give expression to it in the concrete realities of life in accordance with the gift and new commandment of love.

63.2 The law of Christian life is to be found not in a written code, but in the personal action of the Holy Spirit who inspires and guides the Christian. It is the "law of the Spirit of life in Christ Jesus":[159] "God's love has been poured into our hearts through the Holy Spirit who has been given to us."[160]

63.3 This is true also for the Christian couple and family. Their guide and rule of life is the Spirit of Jesus poured into their hearts in the celebration of the Sacrament of Matrimony. In continuity with Baptism in water and the Spirit, marriage sets forth anew the evangelical law of love, and with the gift of the Spirit engraves it more profoundly on the hearts of Christian husbands and wives. Their love, purified and saved, is a fruit of the Spirit acting in the hearts of believers and constituting, at the same time, the fundamental commandment of their moral life to be lived in responsible freedom.

63.4 Thus, the Christian family is inspired and guided by the new law of the Spirit and, in intimate communion with the Church, the kingly people, it is called to exercise its "service" of love toward God and toward its fellow human beings. Just as Christ exercises his royal power by serving us,[161] so also the Christian finds the authentic meaning of his participation in the king-

---

[157] Cf. Second Vatican Ecumenical Council, Decree on the Apostolate of the Laity *Apostolicam Actuositatem,* 4.

[158] Cf. John Paul I, Address to a Group of Bishops from the United States of America on Their *ad Limina* Visit (September 21, 1978): *AAS* 70 (1978), 767.

[159] Rom 8:2.

[160] Rom 5:5.

[161] Cf. Mk 10:45.

ship of his Lord in sharing his spirit and practice of service to man. "Christ has communicated this power to his disciples that they might be established in royal freedom and that by self-denial and a holy life they might conquer the reign of sin in themselves (cf. Rom 6:12). Further, he has shared this power so that by serving him in their fellow human beings they might through humility and patience lead their brothers and sisters to that King whom to serve is to reign. For the Lord wishes to spread his Kingdom by means of the laity also, a Kingdom of truth and life, a Kingdom of holiness and grace, a Kingdom of justice, love and peace. In this Kingdom, creation itself will be delivered out of its slavery to corruption and into the freedom of the glory of the children of God (cf. Rom 8:21)."[162]

To discover the image of God in each brother and sister

64.1 Inspired and sustained by the new commandment of love, the Christian family welcomes, respects and serves every human being, considering each one in his or her dignity as a person and as a child of God.

64.2 It should be so especially between husband and wife and within the family, through a daily effort to promote a truly personal community, initiated and fostered by an inner communion of love. This way of life should then be extended to the wider circle of the ecclesial community of which the Christian family is a part. Thanks to love within the family, the Church can and ought to take on a more homelike or family dimension, developing a more human and fraternal style of relationships.

64.3 Love, too, goes beyond our brothers and sisters of the same faith since "everybody is my brother or sister." In each individual, especially in the poor, the weak, and those who suffer or are unjustly treated, love knows how to discover the face of Christ, and discover a fellow human being to be loved and served.

64.4 In order that the family may serve man in a truly evangelical way, the instructions of the Second Vatican Council must be carefully put into practice: "That the exercise of such charity may rise above any deficiencies in fact and even in appearance, certain fundamentals must be observed. Thus, attention is to be paid to the image of God in which our neighbor has been created, and also to Christ the Lord to whom is really offered whatever is given to a needy person."[163]

64.5 While building up the Church in love, the Christian family places

---

[162] Second Vatican Ecumenical Council, Dogmatic Constitution on the Church *Lumen Gentium*, 36.

[163] Decree on the Apostolate of the Laity *Apostolicam Actuositatem*, 8.

itself at the service of the human person and the world, really bringing about the "human advancement" whose substance was given in summary form in the Synod's Message to Families: "Another task for the family is to form persons in love and also to practice love in all its relationships, so that it does not live closed in on itself, but remains open to the community, moved by a sense of justice and concern for others, as well as by a consciousness of its responsibility toward the whole of society."[164]

IV

Pastoral Care of the Family: Stages, Structures, Agents and Situations

1. Stages of Pastoral Care of the Family

The Church accompanies the Christian family on its journey through life

65.1 Like every other living reality, the family too is called upon to develop and grow. After the preparation of engagement and the sacramental celebration of marriage, the couple begin their daily journey toward the progressive actuation of the values and duties of marriage itself.

65.2 In the light of faith and by virtue of hope, the Christian family too shares, in communion with the Church, in the experience of the earthly pilgrimage toward the full revelation and manifestation of the Kingdom of God.

65.3 Therefore, it must be emphasized once more that the pastoral intervention of the Church in support of the family is a matter of urgency. Every effort should be made to strengthen and develop pastoral care for the family, which should be treated as a real matter of priority, in the certainty that future evangelization depends largely on the domestic Church.[165]

65.4 The Church's pastoral concern will not be limited only to the Christian families closest at hand; it will extend its horizons in harmony with the Heart of Christ, and will show itself to be even more lively for families in general and for those families in particular which are in difficult or irregular

---

[164] Cf. Synod of Bishops, Fifth Ordinary General Assembly, Message to Christian Families in the Modern World (October 24, 1980), 12: *L'Osservatore Romano* (English-language edition), November 10, 1980, 6.

[165] Cf. John Paul II, Address at the Opening of the Third General Assembly of the Bishops of Latin America (January 28, 1979), IV, 1a: *AAS* 71 (1979), 204.

situations. For all of them the Church will have a word of truth, goodness, understanding, hope and deep sympathy with their sometimes tragic difficulties. To all of them she will offer her disinterested help so that they can come closer to that model of a family which the Creator intended from "the beginning" and which Christ has renewed with his redeeming grace.

65.5 The Church's pastoral action must be progressive, also in the sense that it must follow the family, accompanying it step by step in the different stages of its formation and development.

Preparation for marriage

66.1 More than ever necessary in our times is preparation of young people for marriage and family life. In some countries it is still the families themselves that, according to ancient customs, ensure the passing on to young people of the values concerning married and family life, and they do this through a gradual process of education or initiation. But the changes that have taken place within almost all modern societies demand that not only the family but also society and the Church should be involved in the effort of properly preparing young people for their future responsibilities. Many negative phenomena which are today noted with regret in family life derive from the fact that, in the new situations, young people not only lose sight of the correct hierarchy of values but, since they no longer have certain criteria of behavior, they do not know how to face and deal with the new difficulties. But experience teaches that young people who have been well prepared for family life generally succeed better than others.

66.2 This is even more applicable to Christian marriage, which influences the holiness of large numbers of men and women. The Church must therefore promote better and more intensive programs of marriage preparation, in order to eliminate as far as possible the difficulties that many married couples find themselves in, and even more in order to favor positively the establishing and maturing of successful marriages.

66.3 Marriage preparation has to be seen and put into practice as a gradual and continuous process. It includes three main stages: remote, proximate and immediate preparation.

66.4 *Remote preparation* begins in early childhood, in that wise family training which leads children to discover themselves as being endowed with a rich and complex psychology and with a particular personality with its own strengths and weaknesses. It is the period when esteem for all authentic human values is instilled, both in interpersonal and in social relationships, with all that this signifies for the formation of character, for the control and right use of one's inclinations, for the manner of regarding and meeting people of the opposite sex, and so on. Also necessary, especially for Christians, is solid spiritual and catechetical formation that will show that marriage is a true vocation and mission, without excluding the possibility of the total gift of self to God in the vocation to the priestly or religious life.

66.5 Upon this basis there will subsequently and gradually be built up the *proximate preparation,* which — from the suitable age and with adequate catechesis, as in a catechumenal process — involves a more specific preparation for the sacraments, as it were, a rediscovery of them. This renewed catechesis of young people and others preparing for Christian marriage is absolutely necessary in order that the sacrament may be celebrated and lived with the right moral and spiritual dispositions. The religious formation of young people should be integrated, at the right moment and in accordance with the various concrete requirements, with a preparation for life as a couple. This preparation will present marriage as an interpersonal relationship of a man and a woman that has to be continually developed, and it will encourage those concerned to study the nature of conjugal sexuality and responsible parenthood, with the essential medical and biological knowledge connected with it. It will also acquaint those concerned with correct methods for the education of children, and will assist them in gaining the basic requisites for well-ordered family life, such as stable work, sufficient financial resources, sensible administration, notions of housekeeping.

66.6 Finally, one must not overlook preparation for the family apostolate, for fraternal solidarity and collaboration with other families, for active membership in groups, associations, movements and undertakings set up for the human and Christian benefit of the family.

66.7 The *immediate preparation* for the celebration of the Sacrament of Matrimony should take place in the months and weeks immediately preceding the wedding, so as to give a new meaning, content and form to the so-called premarital enquiry required by canon law. This preparation is not only necessary in every case, but is also more urgently needed for engaged couples that still manifest shortcomings or difficulties in Christian doctrine and practice.

66.8 Among the elements to be instilled in this journey of faith, which is similar to the catechumenate, there must also be a deeper knowledge of the mystery of Christ and the Church, of the meaning of grace and of the responsibility of Christian marriage, as well as preparation for taking an active and conscious part in the rites of the marriage liturgy.

66.9 The Christian family and the whole of the ecclesial community should feel involved in the different phases of the preparation for marriage, which have been described only in their broad outlines. It is to be hoped that the Episcopal Conferences, just as they are concerned with appropriate initiatives to help engaged couples to be more aware of the seriousness of their choice and also to help pastors of souls to make sure of the couples' proper dispositions, so they will also take steps to see that there is issued a *Directory for the Pastoral Care of the Family.* In this they should lay down, in the first place, the minimum content, duration and method of the "preparation courses," balancing the different aspects — doctrinal, pedagogical, legal and medical — concerning marriage, and structuring them in such a way that those preparing for marriage will not only receive an intellectual training but will also feel a desire to enter actively into the ecclesial community.

66.10 Although one must not underestimate the necessity and obligation of the immediate preparation for marriage — which would happen if dispensations from it were easily given — nevertheless such preparation must always be set forth and put into practice in such a way that omitting it is not an impediment to the celebration of marriage.

The celebration

67.1 Christian marriage normally requires a liturgical celebration expressing in social and community form the essentially ecclesial and sacramental nature of the conjugal covenant between baptized persons.

67.2 Inasmuch as it is a *sacramental action of sanctification,* the celebration of marriage — inserted into the liturgy, which is the summit of the Church's action and the source of her sanctifying power[166] — must be *per se* valid, worthy and fruitful. This opens a wide field for pastoral solicitude, in order that the needs deriving from the nature of the conjugal covenant, elevated into a sacrament, may be fully met, and also in order that the Church's discipline regarding free consent, impediments, the canonical form and the actual rite of the celebration may be faithfully observed. The celebration should be simple and dignified, according to the norms of the competent authorities of the Church. It is also for them — in accordance with concrete circumstances of time and place and in conformity with the norms issued by the Apostolic See[167] — to include in the liturgical celebration such elements proper to each culture which serve to express more clearly the profound human and religious significance of the marriage contract, provided that

---

[166] Cf. Second Vatican Ecumenical Council, Constitution on the Sacred Liturgy *Sacrosanctum Concilium,* 10.

[167] Cf. Rite of Marriage, 17.

such elements contain nothing that is not in harmony with Christian faith and morality.

67.3 Inasmuch as it is a *sign,* the liturgical celebration should be conducted in such a way as to constitute, also in its external reality, a proclamation of the word of God and a profession of faith on the part of the community of believers. Pastoral commitment will be expressed here through the intelligent and careful preparation of the Liturgy of the Word and through the education to faith of those participating in the celebration and, in the first place, the couple being married.

67.4 Inasmuch as it is a *sacramental action of the Church,* the liturgical celebration of marriage should involve the Christian community, with the full, active and responsible participation of all those present, according to the place and task of each individual: the bride and bridegroom, the priest, the witnesses, the relatives, the friends, the other members of the faithful, all of them members of an assembly that manifests and lives the mystery of Christ and his Church. For the celebration of Christian marriage in the sphere of ancestral cultures or traditions, the principles laid down above should be followed.

Celebration of marriage and evangelization of non-believing baptized persons

68.1 Precisely because in the celebration of the sacrament very special attention must be devoted to the moral and spiritual dispositions of those being married, in particular to their faith, we must here deal with a not infrequent difficulty in which the pastors of the Church can find themselves in the context of our secularized society.

68.2 In fact, the faith of the person asking the Church for marriage can exist in different degrees, and it is the primary duty of pastors to bring about a rediscovery of this faith and to nourish it and bring it to maturity. But pastors must also understand the reasons that lead the Church also to admit to the celebration of marriage those who are imperfectly disposed.

68.3 The Sacrament of Matrimony has this specific element that distinguishes it from all the other sacraments: it is the sacrament of something that was part of the very economy of creation; it is the very conjugal covenant instituted by the Creator "in the beginning." Therefore the decision of a man and a woman to marry in accordance with this divine plan, that is to say, the decision to commit by their irrevocable conjugal consent their whole lives in indissoluble love and unconditional fidelity, really involves, even if not in a fully conscious way, an attitude of profound obedience to the will of God, an attitude which cannot exist without God's grace. They have thus already begun what is in a true and proper sense a journey toward salvation, a journey which the celebration of the sacrament and the immediate preparation for it can complement and bring to completion, given the uprightness of their intention.

68.4 On the other hand it is true that in some places engaged couples ask to be married in church for motives which are social rather than genuinely religious. This is not surprising. Marriage, in fact, is not an event that concerns only the persons actually getting married. By its very nature it is also a social matter, committing the couple being married in the eyes of society. And its celebration has always been an occasion of rejoicing that brings together families and friends. It therefore goes without saying that social as well as personal motives enter into the request to be married in church.

68.5 Nevertheless, it must not be forgotten that these engaged couples, by virtue of their Baptism, are already really sharers in Christ's marriage Covenant with the Church, and that, by their right intention, they have accepted God's plan regarding marriage and therefore at least implicitly consent to what the Church intends to do when she celebrates marriage. Thus, the fact that motives of a social nature also enter into the request is not enough to justify refusal on the part of pastors. Moreover, as the Second Vatican Council teaches, the sacraments by words and ritual elements nourish and strengthen faith:[168] that faith toward which the married couple are already journeying by reason of the uprightness of their intention, which Christ's grace certainly does not fail to favor and support.

68.6 As for wishing to lay down further criteria for admission to the ecclesial celebration of marriage, criteria that would concern the level of faith of those to be married, this would above all involve grave risks. In the first place, the risk of making unfounded and discriminatory judgments; secondly, the risk of causing doubts about the validity of marriages already celebrated, with grave harm to Christian communities, and new and unjustified anxieties to the consciences of married couples; one would also fall into the danger of calling into question the sacramental nature of many marriages of brethren separated from full communion with the Catholic Church, thus contradicting ecclesial Tradition.

68.7 However, when in spite of all efforts, engaged couples show that they reject explicitly and formally what the Church intends to do when the marriage of baptized persons is celebrated, the pastor of souls cannot admit them to the celebration of marriage. In spite of his reluctance to do so, he has the

[168] Cf. Constitution on the Sacred Liturgy *Sacrosanctum Concilium*, 59.

duty to take note of the situation and to make it clear to those concerned that, in these circumstances, it is not the Church that is placing an obstacle in the way of the celebration that they are asking for, but themselves.

68.8 Once more there appears in all its urgency the need for evangelization and catechesis before and after marriage, effected by the whole Christian community, so that every man and woman that gets married celebrates the Sacrament of Matrimony not only validly but also fruitfully.

Pastoral care after marriage

69.1 The pastoral care of the regularly established family signifies, in practice, the commitment of all the members of the local ecclesial community to helping the couple to discover and live their new vocation and mission. In order that the family may be ever more a true community of love, it is necessary that all its members should be helped and trained in their responsibilities as they face the new problems that arise, in mutual service, and in active sharing in family life.

69.2 This holds true especially for young families, which, finding themselves in a context of new values and responsibilities, are more vulnerable, especially in the first years of marriage, to possible difficulties, such as those created by adaptation to life together or by the birth of children. Young married couples should learn to accept willingly, and make good use of, the discreet, tactful and generous help offered by other couples that already have more experience of married and family life. Thus, within the ecclesial community — the great family made up of Christian families — there will take place a mutual exchange of presence and help among all the families, each one putting at the service of others its own experience of life, as well as the gifts of faith and grace. Animated by a true apostolic spirit, this assistance from family to family will constitute one of the simplest, most effective and most accessible means for transmitting from one to another those Christian values which are both the starting point and goal of all pastoral care. Thus young families will not limit themselves merely to receiving, but in their turn, having been helped in this way, will become a source of enrichment for other longer established families, through their witness of life and practical contribution.

69.3 In her pastoral care of young families, the Church must also pay special attention to helping them to live married love responsibly in relationship with its demands of communion and service to life. She must likewise help them to harmonize the intimacy of home life with the generous shared work of building up the Church and society. When children are born and the married couple becomes a family in the full and specific sense, the Church will still remain close to the parents in order that they may accept their children and love them as a gift received from the Lord of life, and joyfully accept the task of serving them in their human and Christian growth.

2. Structures of Family Pastoral Care

Pastoral activity is always the dynamic expression of the reality of the Church, committed to her mission of salvation. Family pastoral care too — which is a particular and specific form of pastoral activity — has as its operative principle and responsible agent the Church herself, through her structures and workers.

The ecclesial community and in particular the parish

70.1 The Church, which is at the same time a saved and a saving community, has to be considered here under two aspects: as universal and particular. The second aspect is expressed and actuated in the diocesan community, which is pastorally divided up into lesser communities, of which the parish is of special importance.

70.2 Communion with the universal Church does not hinder but rather guarantees and promotes the substance and originality of the various particular Churches. These latter remain the more immediate and more effective subjects of operation for putting the pastoral care of the family into practice. In this sense every local Church and, in more particular terms, every parochial community, must become more vividly aware of the grace and responsibility that it receives from the Lord in order that it may promote the pastoral care of the family. No plan for organized pastoral work, at any level, must ever fail to take into consideration the pastoral care of the family.

70.3 Also to be seen in the light of this responsibility is the importance of the proper preparation of all those who will be more specifically engaged in this kind of apostolate. Priests and men and women Religious, from the time of their formation, should be oriented and trained progressively and thoroughly for the various tasks. Among the various initiatives I am pleased to emphasize the recent establishment in Rome, at the Pontifical Lateran University, of a Higher Institute for the study of the problems of the family. Institutes of this kind have also been set up in some Dioceses. Bishops should see to it that as many priests as possible attend specialized courses there before taking on parish responsibilities. Elsewhere, formation courses are periodically held at Higher Institutes of theological and pastoral studies. Such initiatives should be encouraged, sustained, increased in number, and of course are also open to lay people who intend to use their professional skills (medical, legal, psychological, social or educational) to help the family.

The family

71.1 But it is especially necessary to recognize the unique place that, in this field, belongs to the mission of married couples and Christian families, by virtue of the grace received in the sacrament. This mission must be placed at the service of the building up of the Church, the establishing of the Kingdom of God in history. This is demanded as an act of docile obedience to Christ the Lord. For it is he who, by virtue of the fact that marriage of baptized persons has been raised to a sacrament, confers upon Christian married couples a special mission as apostles, sending them as workers into his vineyard, and, in a very special way, into this field of the family.

71.2 In this activity, married couples act in communion and collaboration with the other members of the Church, who also work for the family, contributing their own gifts and ministries. This apostolate will be exercised in the first place within the families of those concerned, through the witness of a life lived in conformity with the divine law in all its aspects, through the Christian formation of the children, through helping them to mature in faith, through education to chastity, through preparation for life, through vigilance in protecting them from the ideological and moral dangers with which they are often threatened, through their gradual and responsible inclusion in the ecclesial community and the civil community, through help and advice in choosing a vocation, through mutual help among family members for human and Christian growth together, and so on. The apostolate of the family will also become wider through works of spiritual and material charity toward other families, especially those most in need of help and support, toward the poor, the sick, the old, the handicapped, orphans, widows, spouses that have been abandoned, unmarried mothers and mothers-to-be in difficult situations who are tempted to have recourse to abortion, and so on.

Associations of families for families

72.1 Still within the Church, which is the subject responsible for the pastoral care of the family, mention should be made of the various groupings of members of the faithful in which the mystery of Christ's Church is in some measure manifested and lived. One should therefore recognize and make good use of — each one in relationship to its own characteristics, purposes, effectiveness and methods — the different ecclesial communities, the various groups and the numerous movements engaged in various ways, for different reasons and at different levels, in the pastoral care of the family.

72.2 For this reason the Synod expressly recognized the useful contribution made by such associations of spirituality, formation and apostolate. It will be their task to foster among the faithful a lively sense of solidarity, to favor a manner of living inspired by the Gospel and by the faith of the Church, to form consciences according to Christian values and not according to the standards of public opinion, to stimulate people to perform works of charity for one another and for others with a spirit of openness which will make Christian families into a true source of light and a wholesome leaven for other families.

72.3 It is similarly desirable that, with a lively sense of the common good, Christian families should become actively engaged, at every level, in other non-ecclesial associations as well. Some of these associations work for the preservation, transmission and protection of the wholesome ethical and cultural values of each people, the development of the human person, the medical, juridical and social protection of mothers and young children, the just advancement of women and the struggle against all that is detrimental to their dignity, the increase of mutual solidarity, knowledge of the problems connected with the responsible regulation of fertility in accordance with natural methods that are in conformity with human dignity and the teaching of the Church. Other associations work for the building of a more just and human world; for the promotion of just laws favoring the right social order with full respect for the dignity and every legitimate freedom of the individual and the family, on both the national and international level; for collaboration with the school and with the other institutions that complete the education of children, and so forth.

3. Agents of the Pastoral Care of the Family

As well as the family, which is the object but above all the subject of pastoral care of the family, one must also mention the other main agents in this particular sector.

Bishops and priests

73.1 The person principally responsible in the Diocese for the pastoral care of the family is the Bishop. As father and Pastor, he must exercise particular solicitude in this clearly priority sector of pastoral care. He must devote to it personal interest, care, time, personnel and resources, but above all personal support for the families and for all those who, in the various diocesan structures, assist him in the pastoral care of the family. It will be his particular care to make the Diocese ever more truly a "diocesan family," a model and source of hope for the many families that belong to it. The setting up of the Pontifical Council for the Family is to be seen in this light: to be a sign of the importance that I attribute to pastoral care for the family in the world, and at the same time to be an effective instrument for aiding and promoting it at every level.

73.2 The Bishops avail themselves especially of the priests, whose task — as the Synod expressly emphasized — constitutes an essential part of the Church's ministry regarding marriage and the family. The same is true of deacons to whose care this sector of pastoral work may be entrusted.

73.3 Their responsibility extends not only to moral and liturgical matters but to personal and social matters as well. They must support the family in its difficulties and sufferings, caring for its members and helping them to see their lives in the light of the Gospel. It is not superfluous to note that from this mission, if it is exercised with due discernment and with a truly apostolic spirit, the minister of the Church draws fresh encouragement and spiritual energy for his own vocation too and for the exercise of his ministry.

73.4 Priests and deacons, when they have received timely and serious preparation for this apostolate, must unceasingly act toward families as fathers, brothers, pastors and teachers, assisting them with the means of grace and enlightening them with the light of truth. Their teaching and advice must therefore always be in full harmony with the authentic Magisterium of the Church, in such a way as to help the People of God to gain a correct sense of the faith, to be subsequently applied to practical life. Such fidelity to the Magisterium will also enable priests to make every effort to be united in their judgments, in order to avoid troubling the consciences of the faithful.

73.5 In the Church, the Pastors and the laity share in the prophetic mission of Christ: the laity do so by witnessing to the faith by their words and by their Christian lives; the Pastors do so by distinguishing in that witness what is the expression of genuine faith from what is less in harmony with the light of faith; the family, as a Christian community, does so through its special sharing and witness of faith. Thus there begins a dialogue also between pastors and families. Theologians and experts in family matters can be of great help in this dialogue, by explaining exactly the content of the Church's Magisterium and the content of the experience of family life. In this way the teaching of the Magisterium becomes better understood and the way is opened to its progressive development. But it is useful to recall that the proximate and obligatory norm in the teaching of the faith — also concerning family matters — belongs to the hierarchical Magisterium. Clearly defined relationships between theologians, experts in family matters and the Magisterium are of no little assistance for the correct understanding of the faith and for promoting — within the boundaries of the faith — legitimate pluralism.

Men and women Religious

74.1 The contribution that can be made to the apostolate of the family by men and women Religious and consecrated persons in general finds its primary, fundamental and original expression precisely in their consecration to God. By reason of this consecration, "for all Christ's faithful Religious recall that wonderful marriage made by God, which will be fully manifested in the future age, and in which the Church has Christ for her only Spouse,"[169] and they are witnesses to that universal charity which, through chastity embraced for the Kingdom of heaven, makes them ever more available to dedicate themselves generously to the service of God and to the works of the apostolate.

74.2 Hence the possibility for men and women Religious, and members of Secular Institutes and other institutes of perfection, either individually or in groups, to develop their service to families, with particular solicitude for children, especially if they are abandoned, unwanted, orphaned, poor or handicapped. They can also visit families and look after the sick; they can foster relationships of respect and charity toward one-parent families or families that are in difficulties or are separated; they can offer their own work of teaching and counseling in the preparation of young people for marriage, and in helping couples toward truly responsible parenthood; they can open their own houses for simple and cordial hospitality, so that families can find there the sense of God's presence and gain a taste for prayer and recollection, and see the practical examples of lives lived in charity and fraternal joy as members of the larger family of God.

74.3 I would like to add a most pressing exhortation to the heads of institutes of consecrated life to consider — always with substantial respect for the proper and original charism of each one — the apostolate of the family as one of the priority tasks, rendered even more urgent by the present state of the world.

Lay specialists

75 Considerable help can be given to families by lay specialists (doctors, lawyers, psychologists, social workers, consultants, etc.) who either as individuals or as members of various associations and undertakings offer their contribution of enlightenment, advice, orientation and support. To these people one can well apply the exhortations that I had the occasion to address to the Confederation of Family Advisory Bureaus of Christian Inspiration: "Yours is a commitment that well deserves the title of mission, so noble are the aims

---

[169] Second Vatican Ecumenical Council, Decree on the Appropriate Renewal of the Religious Life *Perfectae Caritatis,* 12.

that it pursues, and so determining, for the good of society and the Christian community itself, are the results that derive from it. . . . All that you succeed in doing to support the family is destined to have an effectiveness that goes beyond its own sphere and reaches other people too and has an effect on society. The future of the world and of the Church passes through the family."[170]

Recipients and agents of social communications

76.1 This very important category in modern life deserves a word of its own. It is well known that the means of social communication "affect, and often profoundly, the minds of those who use them, under the affective and intellectual aspect and also under the moral and religious aspect," especially in the case of young people.[171] They can thus exercise a beneficial influence on the life and habits of the family and on the education of children, but at the same time they also conceal "snares and dangers that cannot be ignored."[172] They could also become a vehicle — sometimes cleverly and systematically manipulated, as unfortunately happens in various countries of the world — for divisive ideologies and distorted ways of looking at life, the family, religion and morality, attitudes that lack respect for man's true dignity and destiny.

76.2 This danger is all the more real inasmuch as "the modern life style — especially in the more industrialized nations — all too often causes families to abandon their responsibility to educate their children. Evasion of this duty is made easy for them by the presence of television and certain publications in the home, and in this way they keep their children's time and energies occupied."[173] Hence "the duty . . . to protect the young from the forms of aggression they are subjected to by the mass media," and to ensure that the use of the media in the family is carefully regulated. Families should also take care to seek for their children other forms of entertainment that are more wholesome, useful and physically, morally and spiritually formative, "to develop and use to advantage the free time of the young and direct their energies."[174]

76.3 Furthermore, because the means of social communication, like the

---

[170] Address to the Confederation of Family Advisory Bureaus of Christian Inspiration (November 29, 1980), 3-4: *Insegnamenti* III/2 (1980), 1453-1454.

[171] Paul VI, Message for the 1969 World Social Communications Day (April 7, 1969): *AAS* 61 (1969), 455.

[172] John Paul II, Message for the 1980 World Social Communications Day (May 1, 1980): *Insegnamenti* III/1 (1980), 1042.

[173] John Paul II, Message for the 1981 World Social Communications Day (May 10, 1981), 5: *Insegnamenti* IV/1 (1981), 1207.

[174] Cf. ibid.

school and the environment, often have a notable influence on the formation of children, parents as recipients must actively ensure the moderate, critical, watchful and prudent use of the media, by discovering what effect they have on their children and by controlling the use of the media in such a way as to "train the conscience of their children to express calm and objective judgments, which will then guide them in the choice or rejection of programs available."[175]

76.4 With equal commitment parents will endeavor to influence the selection and the preparation of the programs themselves, by keeping in contact — through suitable initiatives — with those in charge of the various phases of production and transmission. In this way they will ensure that the fundamental human values that form part of the true good of society are not ignored or deliberately attacked. Rather they will ensure the broadcasting of programs that present in the right light family problems and their proper solution. In this regard my venerated Predecessor Paul VI wrote: "Producers must know and respect the needs of the family, and this sometimes presupposes in them true courage, and always a high sense of responsibility. In fact they are expected to avoid anything that could harm the family in its existence, its stability, its balance and its happiness. Every attack on the fundamental value of the family — meaning eroticism or violence, the defense of divorce or of antisocial attitudes among young people — is an attack on the true good of man."[176]

76.5 I myself, on a similar occasion, pointed out that families "to a considerable extent need to be able to count on the good will, integrity and sense of responsibility of the media professionals — publishers, writers, producers, directors, playwrights, newsmen, commentators and actors."[177] It is therefore also the duty of the Church to continue to devote every care to these categories, at the same time encouraging and supporting Catholics who feel the call and have the necessary talents, to take up this sensitive type of work.

4. Pastoral Care of the Family in Difficult Cases

Particular circumstances

77.1 An even more generous, intelligent and prudent pastoral commitment, modeled on the Good Shepherd, is called for in the case of families

---

[175] Paul VI, Message for the 1969 World Social Communications Day (April 7, 1969): *AAS* 61 (1969), 456.

[176] Ibid.

[177] Message for the 1980 World Social Communications Day (May 1, 1980): *Insegnamenti* III/1 (1980), 1044.

which, often independently of their own wishes and through pressures of various other kinds, find themselves faced by situations which are objectively difficult.

77.2 In this regard it is necessary to call special attention to certain particular groups which are more in need not only of assistance but also of more incisive action upon public opinion and especially upon cultural, economic and juridical structures, in order that the profound causes of their needs may be eliminated as far as possible.

77.3 Such for example are the families of migrant workers; the families of those obliged to be away for long periods, such as members of the armed forces, sailors and all kinds of itinerant people; the families of those in prison, of refugees and exiles; the families in big cities living, practically speaking, as outcasts; families with no home; incomplete or single-parent families; families with children that are handicapped or addicted to drugs; the families of alcoholics; families that have been uprooted from their cultural and social environment or are in danger of losing it; families discriminated against for political or other reasons; families that are ideologically divided; families that are unable to make ready contact with the parish; families experiencing violence or unjust treatment because of their faith; teenage married couples; the elderly, who are often obliged to live alone with inadequate means of subsistence.

77.4 *The families of migrants,* especially in the case of manual workers and farm workers, should be able to find a homeland everywhere in the Church. This is a task stemming from the nature of the Church, as being the sign of unity in diversity. As far as possible these people should be looked after by priests of their own rite, culture and language. It is also the Church's task to appeal to the public conscience and to all those in authority in social, economic and political life, in order that workers may find employment in their own regions and homelands, that they may receive just wages, that their families may be reunited as soon as possible, be respected in their cultural identity and treated on an equal footing with others, and that their children may be given the chance to learn a trade and exercise it, as also the chance to own the land needed for working and living.

77.5 A difficult problem is that of the family which is *ideologically divided.* In these cases particular pastoral care is needed. In the first place it is necessary to maintain tactful personal contact with such families. The believing members must be strengthened in their faith and supported in their Christian lives. Although the party faithful to Catholicism cannot give way, dialogue with the other party must always be kept alive. Love and respect must be freely shown, in the firm hope that unity will be maintained. Much also depends on the relationship between parents and children. Moreover, ideologies which are alien to the faith can stimulate the believing members of the family to grow in faith and in the witness of love.

77.6 Other difficult circumstances in which the family needs the help of the ecclesial community and its pastors are: the children's adolescence, which can be disturbed, rebellious and sometimes stormy; the children's marriage, which takes them away from their family; lack of understanding or lack of love on the part of those held most dear; abandonment by one of the spouses, or his or her death, which brings the painful experience of widowhood, or the death of a family member, which breaks up and deeply transforms the original family nucleus.

77.7 Similarly, the Church cannot ignore the time of old age, with all its positive and negative aspects. In old age married love, which has been increasingly purified and ennobled by long and unbroken fidelity, can be deepened. There is the opportunity of offering to others, in a new form, the kindness and the wisdom gathered over the years, and what energies remain. But there is also the burden of loneliness, more often psychological and emotional rather than physical, which results from abandonment or neglect on the part of children and relations. There is also suffering caused by ill-health, by the gradual loss of strength, by the humiliation of having to depend on others, by the sorrow of feeling that one is perhaps a burden to one's loved ones, and by the approach of the end of life. These are the circumstances in which, as the Synod Fathers suggested, it is easier to help people understand and live the lofty aspects of the spirituality of marriage and the family, aspects which take their inspiration from the value of Christ's Cross and Resurrection, the source of sanctification and profound happiness in daily life, in the light of the great eschatological realities of eternal life.

77.8 In all these different situations let prayer, the source of light and strength and the nourishment of Christian hope, never be neglected.

Mixed marriages

78.1 The growing number of mixed marriages between Catholics and other baptized persons also calls for special pastoral attention in the light of the directives and norms contained in the most recent documents of the Holy See and in those drawn up by the Episcopal Conferences, in order to permit their practical application to the various situations.

78.2 Couples living in a mixed marriage have special needs, which can be put under three main headings.

78.3 In the first place, attention must be paid to the obligations that faith imposes on the Catholic party with regard to the free exercise of the faith and the consequent obligation to ensure, as far as is possible, the Baptism and upbringing of the children in the Catholic faith.[178]

78.4 There must be borne in mind the particular difficulties inherent in the relationships between husband and wife with regard to respect for religious freedom: this freedom could be violated either by undue pressure to make the partner change his or her beliefs, or by placing obstacles in the way of the free manifestation of these beliefs by religious practice.

78.5 With regard to the liturgical and canonical form of marriage, Ordinaries can make wide use of their faculties to meet various necessities.

78.6 In dealing with these special needs, the following points should be kept in mind:

— In the appropriate preparation for this type of marriage, every reasonable effort must be made to ensure a proper understanding of Catholic teaching on the qualities and obligations of marriage, and also to ensure that the pressures and obstacles mentioned above will not occur.

— It is of the greatest importance that, through the support of the community, the Catholic party should be strengthened in faith and positively helped to mature in understanding and practicing that faith, so as to become a credible witness within the family through his or her own life and through the quality of love shown to the other spouse and the children.

78.7 Marriages between Catholics and other baptized persons have their own particular nature, but they contain numerous elements that could well be made good use of and developed, both for their intrinsic value and for the contribution that they can make to the ecumenical movement. This is particularly true when both parties are faithful to their religious duties. Their common Baptism and the dynamism of grace provide the spouses in these marriages with the basis and motivation for expressing their unity in the sphere of moral and spiritual values.

78.8 For this purpose, and also in order to highlight the ecumenical importance of mixed marriages which are fully lived in the faith of the two Christian spouses, an effort should be made to establish cordial cooperation between the Catholic and the non-Catholic ministers from the time that preparations begin for the marriage and the wedding ceremony, even though this does not always prove easy.

78.9 With regard to the sharing of the non-Catholic party in Eucharistic

---

[178] Cf. Paul VI, Motu Proprio *Matrimonia Mixta,* 4-5: *AAS* 62 (1970), 257-259; John Paul II, Address to the Participants in the Plenary Meeting of the Secretariat for Promoting Christian Unity (November 13, 1981): *Insegnamenti* IV/2 (1981), 628-631.

Communion, the norms issued by the Secretariat for Promoting Christian Unity should be followed.[179]

78.10 Today in many parts of the world marriages between Catholics and non-baptized persons are growing in numbers. In many such marriages the non-baptized partner professes another religion, and his beliefs are to be treated with respect, in accordance with the principles set out in the Second Vatican Council's Declaration *Nostra Aetate* on relations with non-Christian religions. But in many other such marriages, particularly in secularized societies, the non-baptized person professes no religion at all. In these marriages there is a need for Episcopal Conferences and for individual Bishops to ensure that there are proper pastoral safeguards for the faith of the Catholic partner and for the free exercise of his faith, above all in regard to his duty to do all in his power to ensure the Catholic Baptism and education of the children of the marriage. Likewise the Catholic must be assisted in every possible way to offer within his family a genuine witness to the Catholic faith and to Catholic life.

Pastoral action in certain irregular situations

79 In its solicitude to protect the family in all its dimensions, not only the religious one, the Synod of Bishops did not fail to take into careful consideration certain situations which are irregular in a religious sense and often in the civil sense too. Such situations, as a result of today's rapid cultural changes, are unfortunately becoming widespread also among Catholics with no little damage to the very institution of the family and to society, of which the family constitutes the basic cell.

a) TRIAL MARRIAGES

80.1 A first example of an irregular situation is provided by what are called "trial marriages," which many people today would like to justify by attributing a certain value to them. But human reason leads one to see that they are unacceptable, by showing the unconvincing nature of carrying out an "experiment" with human beings, whose dignity demands that they should be always and solely the term of a self-giving love without limitations of time or of any other circumstance.

80.2 The Church, for her part, cannot admit such a kind of union, for further and original reasons which derive from faith. For, in the first place, the gift of the body in the sexual relationship is a real symbol of the giving of the whole person: such a giving, moreover, in the present state of things cannot

---

[179] Instruction *In Quibus Rerum Circumstantiis* (June 15, 1972): *AAS* 65 (1973), 616-619.

take place with full truth without the concourse of the love of charity, given by Christ. In the second place, marriage between two baptized persons is a real symbol of the union of Christ and the Church, which is not a temporary or "trial" union but one which is eternally faithful. Therefore between two baptized persons there can exist only an indissoluble marriage.

80.3 Such a situation cannot usually be overcome unless the human person, from childhood, with the help of Christ's grace and without fear, has been trained to dominate concupiscence from the beginning and to establish relationships of genuine love with other people. This cannot be secured without a true education in genuine love and in the right use of sexuality, such as to introduce the human person in every aspect, and therefore the bodily aspect too, into the fullness of the mystery of Christ.

80.4 It will be very useful to investigate the causes of this phenomenon, including its psychological and sociological aspect, in order to find the proper remedy.

b) DE FACTO FREE UNIONS

81.1 This means unions without any publicly recognized institutional bond, either civil or religious. This phenomenon, which is becoming ever more frequent, cannot fail to concern pastors of souls, also because it may be based on widely varying factors, the consequences of which may perhaps be containable by suitable action.

81.2 Some people consider themselves almost forced into a free union by difficult economic, cultural or religious situations, on the grounds that, if they contracted a regular marriage, they would be exposed to some form of harm, would lose economic advantages, would be discriminated against, etc. In other cases, however, one encounters people who scorn, rebel against or reject society, the institution of the family and the social and political order, or who are solely seeking pleasure. Then there are those who are driven to such situations by extreme ignorance or poverty, sometimes by a conditioning due to situations of real injustice, or by a certain psychological immaturity that makes them uncertain or afraid to enter into a stable and definitive union. In some countries, traditional customs presume that the true and proper marriage will take place only after a period of cohabitation and the birth of the first child.

81.3 Each of these elements presents the Church with arduous pastoral problems, by reason of the serious consequences deriving from them, both religious and moral (the loss of the religious sense of marriage seen in the light of the Covenant of God with his people; deprivation of the grace of the sacrament; grave scandal), and also social consequences (the destruction of the concept of the family; the weakening of the sense of fidelity, also toward society; possible psychological damage to the children; the strengthening of selfishness).

81.4 The pastors and the ecclesial community should take care to become acquainted with such situations and their actual causes, case by case. They should make tactful and respectful contact with the couples concerned, and enlighten them patiently, correct them charitably and show them the witness of Christian family life, in such a way as to smooth the path for them to regularize their situation. But above all there must be a campaign of prevention, by fostering the sense of fidelity in the whole moral and religious training of the young, instructing them concerning the conditions and structures that favor such fidelity, without which there is no true freedom; they must be helped to reach spiritual maturity and enabled to understand the rich human and supernatural reality of marriage as a sacrament.

81.5 The People of God should also make approaches to the public authorities, in order that the latter may resist these tendencies which divide society and are harmful to the dignity, security and welfare of the citizens as individuals, and they must try to ensure that public opinion is not led to undervalue the institutional importance of marriage and the family. And since in many regions young people are unable to get married properly because of extreme poverty deriving from unjust or inadequate social and economic structures, society and the public authorities should favor legitimate marriage by means of a series of social and political actions which will guarantee a family wage, by issuing directives ensuring housing fitting for family life and by creating opportunities for work and life.

c) CATHOLICS IN CIVIL MARRIAGES

82.1 There are increasing cases of Catholics who, for ideological or practical reasons, prefer to contract a merely civil marriage, and who reject or at least defer religious marriage. Their situation cannot of course be likened to that of people simply living together without any bond at all, because in the present case there is at least a certain commitment to a properly defined and probably stable state of life, even though the possibility of a future divorce is often present in the minds of those entering a civil marriage. By seeking public recognition of their bond on the part of the State, such couples show that they are ready to accept not only its advantages but also its obligations. Nevertheless, not even this situation is acceptable to the Church.

82.2 The aim of pastoral action will be to make these people understand the need for consistency between their choice of life and the faith that they profess, and to try to do everything possible to induce them to regularize their situation in the light of Christian principles. While treating them with great charity and bringing them into the life of the respective communities, the pastors of the Church will regrettably not be able to admit them to the sacraments.

d) SEPARATED OR DIVORCED PERSONS WHO HAVE NOT REMARRIED

83.1 Various reasons can unfortunately lead to the often irreparable breakdown of valid marriages. These include mutual lack of understanding and the inability to enter into interpersonal relationships. Obviously, separation must be considered as a last resort, after all other reasonable attempts at reconciliation have proved vain.

83.2 Loneliness and other difficulties are often the lot of separated spouses, especially when they are the innocent parties. The ecclesial community must support such people more than ever. It must give them much respect, solidarity, understanding and practical help, so that they can preserve their fidelity even in their difficult situation; and it must help them to cultivate the need to forgive which is inherent in Christian love, and to be ready perhaps to return to their former married life.

83.3 The situation is similar for people who have undergone divorce, but, being well aware that the valid marriage bond is indissoluble, refrain from becoming involved in a new union and devote themselves solely to carrying out their family duties and the responsibilities of Christian life. In such cases their example of fidelity and Christian consistency takes on particular value as a witness before the world and the Church. Here it is even more necessary for the Church to offer continual love and assistance, without there being any obstacle to admission to the sacraments.

e) DIVORCED PERSONS WHO HAVE REMARRIED

84.1 Daily experience unfortunately shows that people who have obtained a divorce usually intend to enter into a new union, obviously not with a Catholic religious ceremony. Since this is an evil that, like the others, is affecting more and more Catholics as well, the problem must be faced with resolution and without delay. The Synod Fathers studied it expressly. The Church, which was set up to lead to salvation all people and especially the baptized, cannot abandon to their own devices those who have been previously bound by sacramental marriage and who have attempted a second marriage. The Church will therefore make untiring efforts to put at their disposal her means of salvation.

84.2 Pastors must know that, for the sake of truth, they are obliged to exercise careful discernment of situations. There is in fact a difference between those who have sincerely tried to save their first marriage and have been unjustly abandoned, and those who through their own grave fault have destroyed a canonically valid marriage. Finally, there are those who have entered into a second union for the sake of the children's upbringing, and who are sometimes subjectively certain in conscience that their previous and irreparably destroyed marriage had never been valid.

84.3 Together with the Synod, I earnestly call upon pastors and the whole community of the faithful to help the divorced, and with solicitous care to make sure that they do not consider themselves as separated from the Church, for as baptized persons they can, and indeed must, share in her life. They should be encouraged to listen to the word of God, to attend the Sacrifice of the Mass, to persevere in prayer, to contribute to works of charity and to community efforts in favor of justice, to bring up their children in the Christian faith, to cultivate the spirit and practice of penance and thus implore, day by day, God's grace. Let the Church pray for them, encourage them and show herself a merciful Mother, and thus sustain them in faith and hope.

84.4 However, the Church reaffirms her practice, which is based upon Sacred Scripture, of not admitting to Eucharistic Communion divorced persons who have remarried. They are unable to be admitted thereto from the fact that their state and condition of life objectively contradict that union of love between Christ and the Church which is signified and effected by the Eucharist. Besides this, there is another special pastoral reason: if these people were admitted to the Eucharist, the faithful would be led into error and confusion regarding the Church's teaching about the indissolubility of marriage.

84.5 Reconciliation in the Sacrament of Penance, which would open the way to the Eucharist, can only be granted to those who, repenting of having broken the sign of the Covenant and of fidelity to Christ, are sincerely ready to undertake a way of life that is no longer in contradiction to the indissolubility of marriage. This means, in practice, that when, for serious reasons, such as for example the children's upbringing, a man and a woman cannot satisfy the obligation to separate, they "take on themselves the duty to live in complete continence, that is, by abstinence from the acts proper to married couples."[180]

84.6 Similarly, the respect due to the Sacrament of Matrimony, to the couples themselves and their families, and also to the community of the faithful, forbids any pastor, for whatever reason or pretext even of a pastoral na-

---

[180] John Paul II, Homily at the Closing of the Synod of Bishops, Fifth Ordinary General Assembly (October 25, 1980), 7: *AAS* 72 (1980), 1082.

ture, to perform ceremonies of any kind for divorced people who remarry. Such ceremonies would give the impression of the celebration of a new sacramentally valid marriage, and would thus lead people into error concerning the indissolubility of a validly contracted marriage.

84.7 By acting in this way, the Church professes her own fidelity to Christ and to his truth. At the same time she shows motherly concern for these children of hers, especially those who, through no fault of their own, have been abandoned by their legitimate partner.

84.8 With firm confidence she believes that those who have rejected the Lord's command and are still living in this state will be able to obtain from God the grace of conversion and salvation, provided that they have persevered in prayer, penance and charity.

Those without a family

85.1 I wish to add a further word for a category of people whom, as a result of the actual circumstances in which they are living, and this often not through their own deliberate wish, I consider particularly close to the Heart of Christ and deserving of the affection and active solicitude of the Church and of pastors.

85.2 There exist in the world countless people who unfortunately cannot in any sense claim membership of what could be called in the proper sense a family. Large sections of humanity live in conditions of extreme poverty, in which promiscuity, lack of housing, the irregular nature and instability of relationships and the extreme lack of education make it impossible in practice to speak of a true family. There are others who, for various reasons, have been left alone in the world. And yet for all of these people there exists a "good news of the family."

85.3 On behalf of those living in extreme poverty, I have already spoken of the urgent need to work courageously in order to find solutions, also at the political level, which will make it possible to help them and to overcome this inhuman condition of degradation.

85.4 It is a task that faces the whole of society but in a special way the authorities, by reason of their position and the responsibilities flowing therefrom, and also families, which must show great understanding and willingness to help.

85.5 For those who have no natural family the doors of the great family which is the Church — the Church which finds concrete expression in the diocesan and the parish family, in ecclesial basic communities and in movements of the apostolate — must be opened even wider. No one is without a family in this world: the Church is a home and family for everyone, especially those who "labor and are heavy laden."[181]

Conclusion

86.1 At the end of this Apostolic Exhortation my thoughts turn with earnest solicitude:

to you, married couples, to you, fathers and mothers of families;

to you, young men and women, the future and the hope of the Church and the world, destined to be the dynamic central nucleus of the family in the approaching third millennium;

to you, venerable and dear Brothers in the Episcopate and in the priesthood, beloved sons and daughters in the religious life, souls consecrated to the Lord, who bear witness before married couples to the ultimate reality of the love of God;

to you, upright men and women, who for any reason whatever give thought to the fate of the family.

86.2 *The future of humanity passes by way of the family.*

86.3 It is therefore indispensable and urgent that every person of good will should endeavor to save and foster the values and requirements of the family.

86.4 I feel that I must ask for a particular effort in this field from the sons and daughters of the Church. Faith gives them full knowledge of God's wonderful plan: they therefore have an extra reason for caring for the reality that is the family in this time of trial and of grace.

86.5 They must *show the family special love.* This is an injunction that calls for concrete action.

86.6 Loving the family means being able to appreciate its values and capabilities, fostering them always. Loving the family means identifying the dangers and the evils that menace it, in order to overcome them. Loving the family means endeavoring to create for it an environment favorable for its development. The modern Christian family is often tempted to be discouraged and is distressed at the growth of its difficulties; it is an eminent form of love to give it back its reasons for confidence in itself, in the riches that it possesses by nature and grace, and in the mission that God has entrusted to it. "Yes indeed, the families of today must be called back to their original position. They must follow Christ."[182]

86.7 Christians also have the mission of *proclaiming with joy and conviction the Good News about the family,* for the family absolutely needs to hear

---

[181] Mt 11:28.
[182] John Paul II, Letter *Appropinquat Iam* (August 15, 1980), 1: *AAS* 72 (1980), 791.

ever anew and to understand ever more deeply the authentic words that reveal its identity, its inner resources and the importance of its mission in the city of God and in that of man.

86.8 The Church knows the path by which the family can reach the heart of the deepest truth about itself. The Church has learned this path at the school of Christ and the school of history interpreted in the light of the Spirit. She does not impose it but she feels an urgent need to propose it to everyone without fear and indeed with great confidence and hope, although she knows that the Good News includes the subject of the Cross. But it is through the Cross that the family can attain the fullness of its being and the perfection of its love.

86.9 Finally, I wish to call on all Christians to *collaborate cordially and courageously* with all people of good will who are serving the family in accordance with their responsibilities. The individuals and groups, movements and associations in the Church which devote themselves to the family's welfare, acting in the Church's name and under her inspiration, often find themselves side by side with other individuals and institutions working for the same ideal. With faithfulness to the values of the Gospel and of the human person and with respect for lawful pluralism in initiatives, this collaboration can favor a more rapid and integral advancement of the family.

86.10 And now, at the end of my pastoral message, which is intended to draw everyone's attention to the demanding yet fascinating roles of the Christian family, I wish to invoke the protection of the Holy Family of Nazareth.

86.11 Through God's mysterious design, it was in that family that the Son of God spent long years of a hidden life. It is therefore the prototype and example for all Christian families. It was unique in the world. Its life was passed in anonymity and silence in a little town in Palestine. It underwent trials of poverty, persecution and exile. It glorified God in an incomparably exalted and pure way. And it will not fail to help Christian families — indeed, all the families in the world — to be faithful to their day-to-day duties, to bear the cares and tribulations of life, to be open and generous to the needs of others, and to fulfill with joy the plan of God in their regard.

86.12 Saint Joseph was "a just man," a tireless worker, the upright guardian of those entrusted to his care. May he always guard, protect and enlighten families.

86.13 May the Virgin Mary, who is the Mother of the Church, also be the Mother of "the Church of the home." Thanks to her motherly aid, may each Christian family really become a "little Church" in which the mystery of the Church of Christ is mirrored and given new life. May she, the Handmaid of the

Lord, be an example of humble and generous acceptance of the will of God. May she, the Sorrowful Mother at the foot of the Cross, comfort the sufferings and dry the tears of those in distress because of the difficulties of their families.

86.14 May Christ the Lord, the Universal King, the King of Families, be present in every Christian home as he was at Cana, bestowing light, joy, serenity and strength. On the solemn day dedicated to his kingship I beg of him that every family may generously make its own contribution to the coming of his Kingdom in the world — "a Kingdom of truth and life, a Kingdom of holiness and grace, a Kingdom of justice, love, and peace,"[183] toward which history is journeying.

86.15 I entrust each family to him, to Mary, and to Joseph. To their hands and their hearts I offer this Exhortation: may it be they who present it to you, venerable Brothers and beloved sons and daughters, and may it be they who open your hearts to the light that the Gospel sheds on every family!

86.16 I assure you all of my constant prayers and I cordially impart the Apostolic Blessing to each and every one of you, in the name of the Father, and of the Son, and of the Holy Spirit.

Given in Rome, at Saint Peter's, on November 22, the Solemnity of Our Lord Jesus Christ, Universal King, in the year 1981, the fourth of my Pontificate.

[183] The Roman Missal, Preface of Christ the King.

Reconciliatio et Paenitentia

Editor's Introduction

"Repent, and believe in the Gospel" (Mk 1:15). In the opening paragraph of his *Reconciliatio et Paenitentia,* Pope John Paul II cites Jesus' words and invites all people to "accept the good news of love, of adoption as children of God and hence of brotherhood" (§1.1). The Pope's third post-synodal apostolic exhortation, published on December 2, 1984, treats "reconciliation and penance in the mission of the Church today," the theme discussed at the Sixth Ordinary General Assembly of the Synod of Bishops held in 1983. In this document the Holy Father continues his teaching on the mystery of Redemption, presenting Jesus as the Reconciler of a shattered world. He urges the Church and the world to "discover and travel the path of penance, the only path that can lead it to full reconciliation" (§35.7).

The Pope deals with the theme of reconciliation and penance so as to revive in the Church a deeper awareness of the mission proclaimed by the Apostle Paul: "God . . . through Christ reconciled us to himself and gave us the ministry of reconciliation. . . . We beseech you on behalf of Christ, be reconciled to God" (2 Cor 5:18, 20). Christianity is a religion of reconciliation. It liberates humanity from the chains of sin and, beginning in each human heart, leads to the renewal of society. Already in his second encyclical, *Dives in Misericordia* (1980), the Holy Father turned his attention to conversion as fundamental to Christian existence. In *Reconciliatio et Paenitentia,* John Paul admits that he took up his subject following "an interior impulse which . . . was obeying both an inspiration from on high and the appeals of humanity" (§4.3). As well as establishing that the topic of the 1983 Synod of Bishops would be reconciliation and penance, he also decided that 1983 would be celebrated as a Jubilee Year of the Redemption. Even though his decision to commemorate the 1,950th anniversary of Christ's saving Death and Resurrection by a special Holy Year emerged after choosing the Synod's theme, the two initiatives complete each other. Both suited the Pope's desire to foster among people a deeper sense of sin, a greater acceptance of the fruits of the Redemption, and a renewal in the practice of sacramental Penance.

The deep-seated alienation which spawns countless divisions in the world greatly troubles John Paul II. The world needs reconciliation and longs for it. So does the Church. The Pope endorses Pius XII's observation that "the sin of the century is the loss of the sense of sin" (§18.3). In contemporary culture this situation is accompanied by a loss of the sense of God and an obscuring of the moral conscience. In the Church, John Paul is concerned about trends which minimize the personal nature of sin, misinterpret social sin, disregard the distinction between mortal and venial sin, and propose erroneous views of "grave" sin and the fundamental option. Also in the background are decisive pastoral problems: dissent from the Church's moral teaching, the need for a revitalized penitential discipline, the decline in the practice of confession, the loss of zeal by many priests for hearing confessions, the unauthorized use of general absolution. Each of these finds an echo in *Reconciliatio et Paenitentia.*

More than in his previous two post-synodal apostolic exhortations, John Paul explicitly recalls the contribution which the Synod Fathers made to its composition. While unquestionably a papal document — "a serious and welcome duty of my ministry" (§4.12) — *Reconciliatio et Paenitentia* depends heavily on the Synod's input. The Pope says that "the contents of these pages come from the Synod: from its remote and immediate preparation, from the *Instrumentum Laboris,* from the interventions in the Synod Hall and the *circuli minores,* and especially from the sixty-three propositions" (§4.13). He specifically acknowledges the influential role played by the Council of the General Secretariat of the Synod. It digested the Synod's documentation and then suggested to him "the lines considered most suitable for the preparation of the present document" (§4.13). In several instances John Paul invokes the Fathers' authority to explain or buttress his position on specific issues: for example, the distinction between mortal and venial sin (§17.12), the existence of intrinsically evil acts (§17.12), practical pastoral action in favor of penance and reconciliation (§23.7) and on catechesis and confession as the Church's principal means of promoting them (§26.1), the importance of priests' hearing confessions (§29.6), and general absolution (§33.2). This reliance of Peter's Successor on the Synod of Bishops shows the extent to which *Reconciliatio et Paenitentia* is the result of a truly collegial reflection. In this document he assumes the role of being the spokesman for his brother Bishops.

Despite the close collaboration of others, the post-synodal apostolic exhortation still bears the unmistakable imprint of John Paul's particular interests in the theme: concern for the deep-seated divisions in the world and in the Church, insistence on the personal nature of reconciliation and sacramental Penance, encouragement of priests to be zealous confessors, readiness to implement the Second Vatican Council's directives on Penance in light of the Church's broader Tradition, especially as expressed at the Council of Trent (1545-1563), and conviction that only God can satisfy man's desire for reconciliation. The exhortation's language seems less vivid and passionate than that of his encyclicals — a fact probably due to the numerous authors who lent a hand to its composition. As is now customary, the Holy Father speaks in the first person on various occasions, especially when confirming a synodal recommendation.

In *Reconciliatio et Paenitentia,* John Paul cites extensively from the conciliar and papal Magisterium, especially from Vatican II's *Gaudium et Spes* and *Lumen Gentium.* But he also frequently refers to the chapters and canons from the Council of Trent's Decree on Penance. Another important source of the Pope's thought is the *Ordo Paenitentiae,* or Rite of Penance. Paul VI promulgated this document in 1973 to reform the ritual of the Sacrament of Reconciliation in light of the Fathers' request at Vatican II. The new Rite, John Paul says, "made its own the whole of the teaching brought together by the Council of Trent . . . in order to translate it faithfully into terms more in keeping with the context of our own time" (§30.3).

The numerous references to these various ecclesial sources are, however, less important than his appeals to Scripture. More than half of the document's 207 footnotes refer to the Bible. Noteworthy, too, is the Pope's reliance on the methods and conclusions of contemporary historical-critical method. He uses philology (§21.1, note 68), syntaxis (§20.1, note 105), and elements of form criticism (§20.1) to explain some important points. The Holy Father also introduces uncharacteristic distinctions such as "Saint Paul's Christology" (§7.2) and "a long sapiential passage drawing from the Exodus tradition" (§29.1). He even cites the authority of biblical scholars to support his views (§§20.1, 20.4). Also innovative, and in keeping with the personal emphasis that he wishes to give to reconciliation and penance, is the place given to great biblical figures. Each one dramatizes a particular aspect of sin, conversion, and reconciliation: Cain (§§15.2, 31.14), David (§§13.2, 23.2, 31.14), the prodigal son (§§5-6, 13.2, 29.6, 31.8, 31.10, 31.14), the merciful father (§§5.2, 5.3, 6.2, 6.3, 10.3, 31.14), and Christ the Reconciler (§§7, 10.6-7, 20, 26.3). Like many other papal documents, *Reconciliatio et Paenitentia* "actualizes" certain biblical narratives in light of present-day experiences. For instance, in the parable of the prodigal son (Lk 15:11-32) every person is considered to be both the younger and the older son (§§5.3, 6.2). And in the account of the tower of Babel (Gen 1:1-11), the Pope concludes that "the tragedy of humanity today, as indeed of every period in history, consists precisely in its similarity to the experience of Babel" (§13.7).

John Paul, besides writing his exhortation for "the sons and daughters of the Church," envisions a wider audience. He intends it for "all those who, whether they are believers or not, look to the Church with interest and sincerity" (§4.13). Indeed, the Holy Father is convinced that "every institution or organization concerned with serving people and saving them in their fundamental dimensions must closely study reconciliation, in order to grasp more fully its meaning and significance, and in order to draw the necessary practical conclusions" (§4.1). Consequently, "the message and ministry of penance are addressed to all men and women, because all need conversion and reconciliation" (§13.4).

Summary

As well as having an introduction and conclusion, *Reconciliatio et Paenitentia* has three main chapters, each with several subsections. The introduction (§§1-4) describes the divisions of the modern world, humanity's desire for reconciliation, and the Synod's contribution to the post-synodal apostolic exhortation. In chapter one, "Conversion and Reconciliation: the Church's Task and Commitment" (§§5-12), the Pope affirms that the Church's mission is to work for the conversion of hearts. Chapter two, "The Love That Is Greater Than Sin" (§§13-22), deals with sin as the radical cause of the wounds which mar the relationships of individuals with themselves, God, neighbor, and creation. In light of God's mercy, it also discusses the nature and gravity of sin, and its personal and social dimensions. With a more pastoral eye, John Paul then turns in chapter three, "The Pastoral Ministry of Penance and Reconciliation" (§§23-34), to the means which the Church uses to foster reconciliation. His concluding chapter (§35) contains a final appeal for unity and conversion of heart.

A shattered world yearning for reconciliation

At the outset of his exhortation, the Holy Father sketches the contemporary situation, which portrays "the existence of many deep and painful divisions" (§1.5) in the world and in the Church. He laments the increasingly acute rifts between individuals, between individuals and groups, and between larger groups themselves. Among "the painful social phenomena of our time" (§2.2) he includes the rivalry between blocs of nations, torture, terrorism, the arms race, class division, ideological conflict, economic and political polarization, unfair distribution of the world's resources and of the assets of civilization, tribalism, discrimination, and the trampling of basic human rights, especially the right to life and to religious freedom. Of equal concern to the Pope are the divisions among Christians and within the Church herself. Not only do Christians lack full communion, but "the Church today is experiencing within herself sporadic divisions among her own members" (§2.3, cf. §§9, 25.8).

Despite this picture of a broken world and wounded Church, John Paul musters his characteristic optimism. The human heart cries out for fulfillment. Beneath the troubled waters he sees "an unmistakable desire among people of good will and true Christians to mend the divisions, to heal the wounds and to reestablish at all levels, an essential unity" (§3.1). The signs of division are accompanied by "the no less eloquent and significant signs of reconciliation" (§4.2). Although the word "reconciliation" may not be used, the desire for it is "without a shadow of doubt a fundamental driving force in our society" (§3.1). If the Church is to heal social and ecclesial divisions, she must discern their cause and apply the necessary remedy. For the Holy Father, reconciliation with God, self, and others can result only if the infected source of division is confronted: "that original wound which is the root of all other wounds: namely, sin" (§3.1).

Parable of reconciliation

The Pope uses the parable of the prodigal son (Lk 15:11-32) to explain the process of conversion and reconciliation. Above all the parable reveals God as a Father "rich in mercy" (Eph 2:4), who is always ready to forgive. Again and again John Paul repeats that "reconciliation is a *gift of God,* an *initiative on his part*" (§7.1, cf. §§4.9, 5.4, 6.3, 10.1, 10.4, 31.16). The Church too, then, must ensure that her "mission of reconciliation is the initiative, full of compassionate love and mercy, of that God who is love" (§10.1).

At the same time, the parable reveals man to himself. The Pope points out that each brother, in a different way, distances himself from his father's love and causes a rift with him. "This prodigal son is man — every human being: bewitched by the temptation to separate himself from his father in order to lead his own independent existence" (§5.3). In his desire to be forgiven, the younger son represents every sinner who recognizes his error and seeks to return to the father whom he has offended, confident that he will be restored to friendship. The older son is also "every human being" (§6.2). His selfishness divides the brothers and in this way represents "the story of the human family" (§6.3). He, too, needs a profound change of heart. The parable of the sinful brothers and the loving father enables the Church to grasp "her mission of working, in imitation of the Lord, for the conversion of hearts and for the reconciliation of people with God and with one another" (§6.4).

Christ and the Church as reconcilers

God's initiative in reconciling us to himself is made concrete in his Son, "Christ the Redeemer, the Reconciler and the Liberator of man from sin in all its forms" (§7.1, cf. §10.4). His Paschal Mystery is the cause of reconciliation. More specifically, the cause of reconciliation is the mystery of the Cross, "the loftiest drama in which Christ perceives and suffers to the greatest possible extent the tragedy of the division of man from God" (§7.7). Its vertical crossbeam symbolizes the fruit of Redemption as reconciliation between God and humanity and its horizontal crossbeam, reconciliation between people. The Cross and Resurrection free people from sin and elevate them to communion with the Trinity.

Because Christ's reconciling work lives on in the Church, she "must strive above all to bring all people to full reconciliation" (§8.4). As his Body and Bride, the Church shares in her Lord's ministry of reconciliation. By means of the Church Christ's redemptive act radiates throughout the world. This ecclesial ministry is carried out first of all by those ordained to be ministers of reconciliation *in persona Christi,* but also by the whole community of believers. According to John Paul, the Church's central task is "reconciling people: with God, with themselves, with neighbor, with the whole of creation" (§8.5).

Just as the Church cannot evangelize successfully until she is evangelized, so she cannot be a force for reconciliation unless she is first reconciled within herself. If reconciled, she can bear convincing, if silent, witness to reconciliation before the world. The Church is the great sacrament of reconciliation, "that is to say, the sign and means of reconciliation" (§11.1). In the face of divisions among Catholics, the Holy Father recalls that everyone "must try to be united in what is essential for Christian faith and life, in accordance with the ancient maxim: in what is doubtful, freedom; in what is necessary, unity; in all things, charity" (§9.3). John Paul also affirms that the Church must seek the restoration of unity among all Christians, as well as promote the "dialogue of salvation" (§9.5) with all men and women of good will. In every instance authentic reconciliation demands obedience to the truth. "The Church," writes the Pope, "promotes reconciliation *in the truth,* knowing well that neither reconciliation nor unity is possible outside or in opposition to the truth" (§9.6).

The ecclesial community fulfills her mission of reconciliation in various ways. First, she proclaims the message of conversion and reconciliation. As John Paul says, "the Church carries on the proclamation of reconciliation which Christ caused to echo through the villages of Galilee and all Palestine and does not cease to invite all humanity to be converted and to believe in the Good News" (§10.6). Before the whole world she untiringly condemns sin, preaches the need for conversion, and invites people to accept reconciliation. The Church proclaims her message "with clarity and tenacity in season and out of season" (§23.5). Besides preaching, the community's pastoral activity includes "all the activities whereby the Church, through each and every one of her members — Pastors and faithful, at all levels and in all spheres, and with all the means at her disposal, words and actions, teaching and prayer — leads people individually or as groups to true penance and thus sets them on the path to full reconciliation" (§23.6): the intercessory prayer of the saints, catechesis, and especially the celebration of the sacraments, above all the Sacrament of Penance.

Mystery of sin

After describing the good news of the divine gift of reconciliation, the Pope takes up the radical cause of every rupture between individuals and God, and among themselves: sin. There can be no conversion or reconciliation unless the need for forgiveness is first recognized.

Citing the First Letter of John (1:8-9, 3:20), the Holy Father makes two significant assertions about the human condition. On the one hand, personal and social sin are "an integral part of the truth about man" (§13.1). The Church intervenes to help bring about this awareness, enabling each person to acknowledge "*being a sinner,* capable of sin and inclined to commit sin" (§13.2). This humble recognition is the first and essential step in the long process of conversion. On the other hand, this situation of universal guilt must also take into account a divine dimension: "the love that is greater than sin." Human sin must therefore be viewed as "countered by the truth of divine love, which is just, generous and faithful, and which reveals itself above all in forgiveness and redemption" (§13.1).

John Paul invokes the biblical account of the tower of Babel to illuminate what he calls "the mystery of sin": the dark and hidden power at work in individuals which leads them away from eternal life. The narrative tells of the attempt to build a society without God, even if not in direct opposition to him. Whereas the first sin in Eden entailed an act of direct disobedience, the sin of Babel involved the neglect of God. "In the story of Babel *the exclusion of God* is presented not so much under the aspect of opposition to him as of forgetfulness and indifference toward him, as if God were of no relevance in the sphere of man's joint projects" (§14.2). In each case God's sovereignty over human life is denied, and a rupture occurs between the person and God.

Babel and Eden show that sin is a suicidal act, "an act of disobedience by a creature who rejects, at least implicitly, the very one from whom he came and who sustains him in life" (§15.4). Refusal to submit to God's sovereignty destroys man's "internal balance" and "almost inevitably causes damage to the fabric of his relationship with others and with the created world" (§15.4). Every sin opens a double wound in the sinner: in himself and in relationships with his neighbor. Consequently, it calls for the twofold healing of reconciliation — at the personal and social level.

Personal and social sin

Throughout *Reconciliatio et Paenitentia* John Paul emphasizes that "sin, in the proper sense, is always a *personal act,* since it is an act of freedom on the part of an individual person, and not properly of a group or community" (§16.1). Undoubtedly, numerous external factors or internal factors can influence or condition individuals in their moral choices. If powerful enough, they may diminish freedom and therefore responsibility or guilt. But these social, cultural, and psychological factors cannot abolish the truth that sin is a product of the freedom proper to an individual's human dignity.

The exhortation discusses "social" sin at greater length, describing three legitimate meanings given to the concept. First, because of the supernatural solidarity of all people, "every sin has repercussions on the entire ecclesial body and the whole human family" (§16.5). No matter how private or hidden, each sin stains the Church's holiness and diminishes the world's social harmony. Second, some sins directly attack social life, the love due to others: "They are an offense against God because they are offenses against one's neighbor" (§16.6). Third, social sin refers to the disordered relationships between different human communities, when these relationships are based on injustice, conflict, or the denial of human dignity. John Paul carefully points out that these skewed relationships are more precisely referred to as a social "evil." In fact, sinful structures and situations always result from "the accumulation and concentration of many *personal* sins" (§16.9). The Pope cautions against thinking of social institutions or structures as subjects of moral acts, as if they themselves were sinful rather than evil. He adds that "if one speaks of *social sin* here, the expression obviously has an analogical meaning" (§16.7).

Mortal and venial sin

At some length *Reconciliatio et Paenitentia* examines the gravity of sin: the classical distinction between mortal and venial sin. John Paul is disturbed by this subject and he returns to it later in his 1993 encyclical *Veritatis Splendor* (§§69-70). The reason for his preoccupation is twofold. Some contemporary moral theologians seem to suggest that it is nearly impossible for a practicing Christian to commit a mortal sin which severs divine life in the soul. Others introduce the concept of "grave" sin. Such a sin has serious spiritual consequences, they maintain, but it does not break an individual's relationship with God. To combat these mistaken opinions, the Pope reaffirms the Church's traditional teaching on the difference between mortal and venial sin. His thorough treatment includes its foundations in Scripture, Tradition, and the Magisterium.

Already the Old Testament testifies to a distinction between different kinds of sin. For some sins, the penalty could be death, while for others, especially those committed through ignorance, forgiveness could be obtained by making a sacrificial offering. In the New Testament, the Pope notes, two passages refer directly to serious sins. The First Letter of John (5:16-17) distinguishes between "a sin *which leads to death*" and "a sin *which does not lead to death*" (§17.4). Matthew's Gospel refers to a "blasphemy against the Holy Spirit" that "will not be forgiven" (12:31). For the Holy Father, Scripture provides the basis for the Church's distinction between sins that bring about spiritual death and those that do not.

It was, however, Saint Thomas Aquinas "who was to formulate in the clearest possible terms the doctrine which became constant in the Church" (§17.8) concerning the definition of, and distinction between, mortal and venial sins. Thomas analyzed this difference from three perspectives. First, mortal sin deprives the sinner of the supernatural life of charity, of friendship with God, while venial sin harms that relationship. Second, mortal sin, if unforgiven, leads to eternal punishment, whereas venial sin does not. Third, from the point of view of its matter, mortal sin is "sin whose object is grave matter and which is also committed with full knowledge and deliberate consent" (§17.12). Venial sin, on the other hand, entails a choice that is not considered gravely disordered or one committed with less than full knowledge of its evil or consent of the will.

The Pope uses the distinction between mortal and venial sins to draw four further conclusions. Invoking the Synod's authority, he reaffirms that some acts are intrinsically morally evil because of their freely chosen matter: "There exist acts which, *per se* and in themselves, independently of circumstances, are always seriously wrong by reason of their object. These acts, if carried out with sufficient awareness and freedom, are always gravely sinful" (§17.12, cf. §18.7). John Paul then mentions that some Synod Fathers proposed to classify sins in a threefold way: as venial, grave, or mortal. They understood "grave" sins to be those whose matter is objectively serious but lack the moral agent's full awareness and freedom. On the one hand, the Pope agrees that the category of "grave" sin can serve to highlight the scale of seriousness among sins.

But, on the other hand, nothing can compromise the teaching that "there is no middle way between life and death" (§17.16), between mortal and venial sin. Third, the Holy Father reminds his readers that venial sin is to be neither ignored nor regarded "as a sin of little importance" (§17.13). Consequently, he gives a fresh impetus to celebrating sacramental Penance "for venial sins alone, as is borne out by a centuries-old doctrinal tradition and practice" (§32.6). Lastly, the Pope cautions against an interpretation of the "fundamental option" which would minimize the moral significance of individual acts. Here he specifically rejects the opinion that mortal sin can be reduced to an act of a person's fundamental option, when this is limited to an act which explicitly and formally shows contempt for God or one's neighbor. He insists, rather, that "the fundamental orientation can be radically changed by individual acts" (§17.17).

Loss of the sense of sin

After outlining a theology of sin, Pope John Paul treats the pastoral problem presented by the modern world's loss of the sense of sin. His purpose in this section is clear: "The restoration of a *proper sense of sin* is the first way of facing the grave spiritual crisis looming over man today" (§18.11). Only if we grasp the reasons for this loss can a healthy sense of sin be restored, one which can open to conversion and reconciliation.

The Pope is convinced that an authentic sense of sin "is rooted in man's moral conscience and is as it were its thermometer" (§18.2). In today's world, unfortunately, the moral conscience is being deadened. This eclipse is accompanied by an obscuring of the sense of God "and as a result, with the loss of this decisive inner point of reference, the sense of sin is lost" (§18.3). The loss of the sense of sin is therefore a consequence of the prior loss, even the denial, of the sense of God. "To sin," the Pope writes, "is also to live as if he did not exist, to eliminate him from one's daily life" (§18.9). Four reasons account for the contemporary loss of the sense of sin in society.

First there is secularism. It excludes God and the transcendent from the dynamic life of society. By striving to build a world without God, secularism interprets sin as "what offends man" (§18.5). It sees "errors and faults only in the context of society" (§18.9), with no reference to God. A second reason for today's diminished sense of sin derives from an erroneous evaluation based on some findings of psychology, sociology, and cultural anthropology. Each of these human sciences has led many to doubt whether they are personally responsible for their actions or even whether they can sin. Third, contemporary ethical theories which derive from historical relativism weaken people's sensitivity to the gravity of sin. These theories not only deny intrinsically evil acts but also attenuate personal responsibility for evil. Lastly, the true sense of sin disappears in society when people erroneously identify it "with a morbid feeling of guilt, or with the mere transgression of legal norms and precepts" (§18.8).

John Paul maintains that society alone cannot be blamed for today's loss of the sense of sin. Within the Church certain trends favor the same view. He mentions, for example, that past attitudes to sin — seeing it everywhere, stressing fear of eternal punishment, and severity in correcting erroneous consciences — have been replaced by new exaggerations: not recognizing sin anywhere, preaching a God who does not punish sin, and respecting conscience to the point of ignoring the moral truth. The Pope adds another reason. Many people are now confused "by differences of opinions and teachings in theology, preaching, catechesis and spiritual direction *on serious and delicate questions of Christian morals*" (§18.10). Lastly, John Paul casts some blame for the loss of a healthy sense of sin on "certain deficiencies in the practice of sacramental Penance" (§18.10): failure to maintain the balance between the personal and social-ecclesial dimensions of sin, and routine ritualism in sacramental celebration.

Despite its power, sin is not the protagonist, still less the victor, in God's saving plan. Within the dynamism of history, the mystery of divine mercy will conquer the mystery of sin. John Paul builds on a verse of Paul's First Letter to Timothy — "great indeed, we confess, is the mystery of our religion (*mysterium pietatis*)" (3:16) — to convince his readers about the greatness of divine mercy. According to the Pope, this "mystery of our religion" (*mysterium pietatis*) is the whole saving plan of Christ's life, Death and Resurrection for us. This mystery is God's infinite loving kindness toward us: a mercy "capable of penetrating to the hidden roots of our iniquity, in order to evoke in the soul a movement of conversion, in order to redeem it and set it on course toward reconciliation" (§20.3). At the same time, this mystery of divine mercy beckons a human response: "The *loving kindness of God* toward the Christian must be matched by the *piety of the Christian* toward God" (§21.1).

Dialogue and reconciliation

In the third chapter of his exhortation, the Pope discusses the practical dimensions of the Church's pastoral ministry of penance and reconciliation. A fundamental presupposition governs his presentation: "What is *pastoral* is not opposed to what is *doctrinal*. Nor can pastoral action prescind from doctrinal content, from which in fact it draws its substance and real validity" (§26.2).

For him, dialogue, catechesis, and the sacraments are the primary means that the Church has at her disposal to foster reconciliation.

John Paul II follows the Second Vatican Council and Paul VI in proposing dialogue as a way for the Church to carry out her mission to the Church and the world. This "dialogue of salvation" — in the words of Paul VI in his encyclical *Ecclesiam Suam* (1964) — "is aimed above all at the rebirth of individuals, through interior conversion and repentance, but always with profound respect for consciences and with patience and at the step-by-step pace indispensable for modern conditions" (§25.4). In typical Wojtylan fashion, the Pope reminds his readers of the basic principle underlying all authentic dialogue. It does not begin with indifference to the truth, but "from a presentation of the truth, offered in a calm way, with respect for the intelligence and consciences of others. The dialogue of reconciliation can never replace or attenuate the proclamation of the truth of the Gospel" (§25.15). The Church engages in dialogue at three levels: within herself, with other Christians, and with the world.

First of all, the Holy Father calls for "permanent and renewed dialogue within the Catholic Church herself" (§25.7). This dialogue contributes to overcoming internal tensions which could become factors of division. The Pope warns especially against following subjective views and divisive ideological choices in theology and pastoral practice. His solution to division is an appeal to everyone to seek the truth "in the divine word itself and in the authentic interpretation of that word provided by the Magisterium of the Church" (§25.8). Internal dialogue likewise serves the Church's credibility and effectiveness in the world.

While the perseveration of open and sincere dialogue can help to secure reconciliation within the Catholic Church, such dialogue must also be directed to other Churches and Ecclesial Communities. John Paul expresses his commitment to ecumenical dialogue with other Christians as a means of achieving the full communion which all long for. Such a dialogue must be frank, clear in presenting positions, and faithful to the Magisterium. It should proceed "without facile optimism but also without distrust and without hesitation or delays" (§25.10). The Church is called to be a witness to reconciliation in her internal life and a servant of reconciliation for others.

In the world, the Church likewise works for reconciliation by fostering the method of dialogue. At the international level, the Holy See uses, and encourages others to use, dialogue as a way of resolving conflicts. At the local level, the Church carries out her reconciling activity in the world through Bishops and Episcopal Conferences, and especially through the lay faithful. Lay men and women "are called upon to engage directly in dialogue or to work for dialogue aimed at reconciliation" (§25.14).

Catechesis and sacraments

Pastors also discharge their pastoral ministry of penance and reconciliation by providing a catechesis suitably adapted to the audience addressed. Catechesis on reconciliation should be grounded in the Bible, especially in Jesus' teaching. After this biblical catechesis, a theological catechesis should follow. This latter synthesis "will also integrate the elements of psychology, sociology and the other human sciences which can serve to clarify situations, describe problems accurately, and persuade listeners or readers to make concrete resolutions" (§26.3).

In their catechesis on penance, John Paul reminds pastors to stress three points. First, an effective catechesis emphasizes the importance of conversion, the necessary precondition of reconciliation. Sinners are to recognize their situation of sinfulness and to turn away from it. Second, a catechesis on penance entails showing the need for repentance. Thus, "a good catechesis will show how repentance, just like conversion, is far from being a superficial feeling but a real overturning of the soul" (§26.5). Finally, catechesis should also point out that penance involves the external expression of the interior attitudes of conversion and repentance. This is "doing penance." Above all, it means "to reestablish the balance and harmony broken by sin, to change direction even at the cost of sacrifice" (§26.6).

Besides stressing these three themes in their catechesis, pastors should give due attention to the importance of the Church's penitential discipline and the proper formation of conscience. In addition, John Paul mentions the need to treat the following topics in their catechesis on penance: a healthy sense of sin, the meaning of temptation, the value of fasting and almsgiving, the four last things (death, judgment, heaven, and hell), and the contribution of the Church's social teaching to reconciliation in human relationships.

Before treating the Sacrament of Penance in detail, the Holy Father briefly explains how "each sacrament, over and above its own proper grace, is also a sign of penance and reconciliation" (§27.2). Baptism effectively brings about reconciliation with God by the forgiveness of sins, while Confirmation signifies and accomplishes "a greater conversion of heart" (§27.4). As the renewal of the Sacrifice of the Cross, the Eucharist is an efficacious sign of community reconciliation. Holy Orders provides for ministers of reconciliation. In Matrimony, the couple and family share in Christ's victory over the disintegrating forces of conflict and become an effective sign of "the reconciled and reconciling Church for a world reconciled in all its structures and institutions" (§27.8). For its part, Anointing of the Sick is a sign of definitive conversion to the Lord and full reconciliation with God.

Doctrinal convictions

John Paul devotes a long section of his apostolic exhortation specifically to the Sacrament of Penance. In light of today's crisis in the understanding and practice of the sacrament, he summarizes its doctrine, the respective roles of the confessor and penitent, and the three forms of its liturgical celebration.

In line with the judgment of the Synod Fathers, the Pope affirms that the Sacrament of Reconciliation is in crisis. He hopes that, by clarifying the reasons for this crisis, a positive solution will be found. The same factors which contribute to the lessening of the sense of sin also undermine the practice of sacramental confession. In addition, however, negative influences come from within the Church, especially "the sometimes widespread idea that one can obtain forgiveness directly from God, even in a habitual way, without approaching the Sacrament of Reconciliation" (§28.3). To meet this challenge, the Pope reaffirms the Church's convictions of faith about this sacrament "which represents and at the same time accomplishes penance and reconciliation" (§28.1).

Even in the Old Testament, God is described as compassionate and ready to forgive sins. In the New Testament, Jesus is not only merciful but also has the power to forgive sins, a power which he confers on his Apostles (cf. Jn 20:22). They received this authority from Jesus as a power they could transmit to their successors in the apostolic ministry. Thus there developed among Christians "the certainty that the Lord Jesus himself instituted and entrusted to the Church . . . a special sacrament for the forgiveness of sins committed after Baptism" (§30.1). God, through the Holy Spirit, forgives sins when the Church absolves penitents by means of her official ministers. In taking account of the sacrament's historical development, the Pope invokes the classical distinction between its unchanging "substance" and its changing forms of celebration. Speaking of Penance, John Paul says that "*with regard to the substance of the sacrament* there has always remained firm and unchanged in the consciousness of the Church *the certainty* that, by the will of Christ, forgiveness is offered to each individual by means of sacramental absolution given by the ministers of Penance" (§30.2).

The first conviction of faith deals with the divine institution of Penance as the sacrament of forgiveness. Christ himself left it as a gift for his Church. A second conviction affirms that "for a Christian *the Sacrament of Penance is the ordinary way* of obtaining forgiveness and the remission of serious sin committed after Baptism" (§31.2, cf. §§32.2, 33.2). Even though God's mercy extends beyond the sacramental sign of Reconciliation, Christ provides this specific means of forgiveness. It would be foolish and presumptuous to disregard his will in this regard. John Paul's third dogmatic conviction is that Penance is "a kind of *judicial action*" (§31.3). Today this notion is often obscured in favor of the more accessible idea that Reconciliation is directed to spiritual healing. While accepting this healing role, the Pope still insists that Penance remains a kind of tribunal, even though "a tribunal of mercy" wherein the minister judges and heals.

The confessor

As healer and judge, the confessor is "a figure of God the Father welcoming and forgiving the one who returns" (§31.11). When the priest pronounces the words of absolution, at that very moment "the Trinity becomes present in order to blot out sin and restore innocence" (§31.11). Sacramental absolution is a visible and effective sign of the divine intervention which imparts to the penitent the salvation won by Christ's Paschal Mystery.

According to John Paul, the power given to ordained ministers to forgive sins is "one of the most awe-inspiring innovations of the Gospel" (§29.3). In countless discourses and documents he exhorts priests to be frequent penitents and willing confessors. Moreover, he often praises as models of priestly zeal the saints who were "apostles of the confessional" (§29.9). The ministers of Reconciliation thus enjoy a certain "grandeur." Acting *in persona Christi,* they make Christ present as "the *brother of man,* the merciful High Priest, faithful and compassionate, the Shepherd intent on finding the lost sheep" (§29.5). When celebrating the Sacrament of Penance priests are totally at Christ's disposal; they speak and act only with the power received through the Church.

In his treatment of confessors, the Pope is especially exhortative. Hearing confessions, he writes, "is undoubtedly the most difficult and sensitive, the most exhausting and demanding ministry of the priest, but also one of the most beautiful and consoling" (§29.6). Above all, priests have the duty of hearing confessions willingly, since the faithful have "an inviolable and inalienable right" to individual confession (§33.3). The Pope explains the qualities, training, and spiritual practices necessary for priests if they are to be protagonists of the renewal in the celebration of the Sacrament of Penance called for by the Second Vatican Council.

In order to minister effectively, the confessor needs the human qualities of "prudence, discretion, discernment and a firmness tempered by gentleness and kindness" (§29.7). Careful preparation is also necessary, especially the serious study of theology and the human sciences and training in dialogue and dealing with people in a pastoral way. More importantly, confessors must have the spiritual qualities necessary for a fruitful ministry: a deep life of prayer, practice of the theological and moral virtues, obedience to the will of God, love for the Church, and docility to the Magisterium. Those who have seriously embarked on the path of Christian perfection can best lead others on the same journey.

Above all, John Paul believes that a good confessor approaches Reconciliation frequently and devoutly. "If a priest were no longer to go to confession or properly confess his sins," the Pope writes, "his *priestly being* and his *priestly action* would feel its effects very soon, and this would also be noticed by the community of which he was the pastor" (§31.18). Moreover, the Holy Father thinks that a priest's regular experience of the sacramental grace of Penance can become an incentive for others. As a beneficiary of mercy he is more likely to encourage the faithful to celebrate the sacrament frequently and "to arrange *special times for the celebration of the sacrament*" (§32.8).

In deference to the Synod's wishes, the Holy Father briefly treats the pastoral care of two "delicate cases" — the divorced and remarried and priests living in irregular unions. When dealing with these and similar situations, he reminds priests to take into account two important principles. First, confessors, aware that the Church always seeks the conversion of sinners, should show compassion, mercy, and patience. Second, they should safeguard "truth and consistency, whereby the Church does not agree to call good evil and evil good" (§34.2). Confessors can celebrate Penance only for those with the required dispositions, including a firm purpose of amendment. If these dispositions are lacking, then the ministers of Reconciliation must encourage those seeking forgiveness to seek divine mercy in non-sacramental ways, such as by prayer, fasting, and almsgiving.

The penitent

John Paul examines the three acts of the penitent who undergoes the journey of interior conversion through the work of the Holy Spirit: contrition, confession, and satisfaction. Together these acts are considered the sacramental sign of Reconciliation.

Reconciliatio et Paenitentia defines contrition as "a clear and decisive rejection of the sin committed, together with a resolution not to commit it again, out of the love which one has for God and which is reborn with repentance"

(§31.8). This contrition is "the beginning and the heart of *conversion*" (§31.8). It is a "drawing near to the holiness of God, a rediscovery of one's true identity, which has been upset and disturbed by sin, a liberation in the very depth of self and thus a regaining of lost joy" (§31.9). The validity of sacramental Penance depends on the penitent's heartfelt contrition. Essential to this interior attitude of sorrow is the admission of personal sinfulness, a recognition made possible by an examination of conscience. In this examination one's acts or omissions are compared sincerely and calmly, without anxious psychological introspection, "with the interior moral law, with the evangelical norms proposed by the Church, with Jesus Christ himself, who is our Teacher and Model of life, and with the heavenly Father, who calls us to goodness and perfection" (§31.7).

The personal confession of sins to a priest also forms part of the sacramental sign of Reconciliation. "A sincere and complete confession of sins," writes the Pope, "is inherent in the very nature of the sacrament" (§31.5). Penance is "a sign of the meeting of the sinner with the mediation of the Church in the person of the minister; a sign of the person's revealing of self as a sinner in the sight of God and the Church, of facing his own sinful condition in the eyes of God" (§31.10). Far more than a gesture of psychological self-liberation, the auricular confession of sins is a solemn liturgical act. The recounting of one's sins enables the confessor to be the penitent's spiritual judge and healer.

The penitent's third and final act, now performed after absolution, is called satisfaction or penance. According to the Pope, the penance assigned by the confessor consists of "acts of worship, charity, mercy or reparation" suited to the penitent's specific situation; it should "not be reduced to mere formulas to be recited" (§31.12). Certainly these simple and humble acts are not a price paid for the forgiveness obtained. Rather, they are a sign of the penitent's personal commitment to a new life of holiness. Doing penance after absolution reminds the pardoned sinner of two important truths. Like all suffering, the specified "physical and spiritual mortification" can serve to unite a person more closely with Christ's Passion. Furthermore, the penance also reminds him that, even after sacramental forgiveness, there still remains to be overcome "a dark area, due to the wound of sin, to the imperfection of love in repentance, to the weakening of the spiritual faculties" (§31.12).

Liturgical celebration of Penance

The exhortation treats in some detail the three liturgical forms prescribed by the Church for the celebration of Penance: reconciliation of individual penitents, reconciliation of many penitents with individual confession and individual absolution, and reconciliation of many penitents with general confession and general absolution. Whereas the first two rites are usual ways of celebrating Reconciliation, general absolution "is exceptional in character . . . [and] is regulated by a special discipline" (§32.2).

John Paul could not be more explicit about the need to maintain the practice of individual confession. It is "the only normal and ordinary way of celebrating the sacrament, and it cannot and must not be allowed to fall into disuse or be neglected" (§32.2, cf. §33.2). He favors this form because it embodies faithfulness to the will of Christ who instituted the sacrament of forgiveness, respects the Church's perennial Tradition and practice, and highlights the specifically personal dimension of the penitential process. Individual confession emphasizes the penitent's concrete situation: the desire for reconciliation with God and the need for assistance in one's spiritual life.

When individual confession is celebrated with others in a liturgical rite, it safeguards the personal value of Penance. At the same time, this second rite stresses "the ecclesial character of conversion and reconciliation" (§32.4). It vividly recalls that reconciliation with God also entails reconciliation with the Church. Because this form maintains individual confession and absolution, it can be considered a normal and ordinary way of celebrating the sacrament. The Pope notes that it is particularly meaningful for the different liturgical seasons and for special events. But the Holy Father adds a cautionary note. He admonishes priests to choose the form of celebration in light of "the true spiritual good of the faithful, in obedience to the penitential discipline of the Church" and not for "situational and subjective reasons" (§32.5).

John Paul is profoundly troubled by the increasingly irregular practice of general confession and absolution. To combat what he regards as a serious spiritual danger, the Pope insists that the liturgical and canonical norms which regulate this third form of celebration "must be accepted and applied in such a way as to avoid any sort of arbitrary interpretation" (§33.1). Throughout his treatment the Pope stresses that the use of general confession and absolution is limited to exceptional circumstances of grave necessity. He also includes an admonition: the Church's doctrine and discipline on Reconciliation is "not our property" but is always to be served "in truth" (§33.4).

Reconciliatio et Paenitentia ends with a call to the "unity of spirit" mentioned by Peter in his First Letter (3:8). John Paul entrusts his appeal of penance and reconciliation to the Father who is "rich in mercy," to the Son "made man as our Redeemer and Reconciler," and to the Holy Spirit who is the "source of unity and peace" (§35.4). The Pope expresses the hope that his exhortation will bear abundant fruit, and he turns to the Immaculate Heart of Mary "that through her intercession humanity may discover and travel the path of penance, the only path that can lead it to full reconciliation" (§35.7).

Key Themes

Among the most significant contributions of John Paul II's teaching is his development of a Christian anthropology: "the truth about man, a truth that is revealed to us in its fullness and depth in Christ" (*Dives in Misericordia,* §1.2). Essential to the truth of the human person is his or her absolute uniqueness. In *Redemptor Hominis,* the Pope writes: "We are not dealing with the 'abstract' man, but the real, 'concrete,' 'historical' man. We are dealing with 'each' man, for each one is included in the mystery of the Redemption and with each one Christ has united himself for ever through this mystery" (§13.3). In the Word made flesh, individuals enjoy their dignity as free and responsible moral agents. Their freely chosen acts make them who they are. It is not surprising, therefore, that this view of the human person marks *Reconciliatio et Paenitentia.* Indeed, the Holy Father's treatment of the intimately personal nature of sin, conversion, reconciliation, the meaning of social sin, and his preoccupation with general absolution are all solidly grounded in his anthropology.

Personal nature of sin, conversion, and reconciliation

A reverence for the inalienable dignity of the human person is at the heart of John Paul's Christian anthropology. His pastoral objective is to foster human dignity in all its dimensions, a project which includes a correct understanding of freedom and responsibility. Here, as in all his writings, the Pope maintains that people must preserve their moral responsibility and freedom if they are to safeguard and foster authentic human dignity. Thus, if light is to be shed on the dynamic of the Holy Father's thought, the personal character of sin and reconciliation need to be understood.

The Pope, like John in his First Letter, believes that "if we say we have no sin, we deceive ourselves, and the truth is not in us" (1:8). Sin, John Paul says, is "an integral part of the truth about man" (§13.1); it is an essential dimension of personhood. People can and do act against God, the ultimate end of their existence. Through a conscious and free act of will, a person "can change course and go in a direction opposed to God's will, separating himself from God (*aversio a Deo*), rejecting loving communion with him, detaching himself from the life-principle which God is" (§17.14).

Because people are free, they can perform truly human acts and therefore have the ability to sin. In a person's capacity to misuse the gift of freedom — to sin — the Pope sees a confirmation of human dignity. Sin, he writes, "is a product of man's freedom" (§14.1); it is "an act of freedom on the part of an individual person" (§16.1). Any ideology or theory which disregards this truth of individual freedom and responsibility meets with his staunch resistance. Of course, the Holy Father believes that internal and external factors and circumstances can attenuate an individual's degree of subjective guilt for a particular action, but they can never deny the existence of sin or justify it. He adamantly affirms not only that sin exists but that it proceeds from human freedom. According to John Paul, to reject these truths "would be to deny the person's dignity and freedom, which are manifested — even though in a negative and disastrous way — also in this responsibility for sin committed. Hence there is nothing so personal and untransferable in each individual as merit for virtue or responsibility for sin" (§16.1). Even the abuse of freedom, then, confirms human dignity. Sin itself emphasizes the personal responsibility and human dignity which the Pope so vigorously defends.

The preservation of human dignity demands that individuals take responsibility for the sins they freely commit, an act which sets them on the path of conversion. Each sinner must be able to say, "I have sinned against the Lord" (2 Sam 12:13). Reluctant as contemporary people are to recognize their mistakes, they must do so if they are to have that "knowledge of self" (§13.4) necessary to those seeking reconciliation. The words appropriate to acceptance of responsibility are "I repent" or "I am sorry": "Against you, you alone, have I sinned and done what is evil in your sight" (Ps 51:4).

If sin is personal for John Paul, so too, then, is conversion. "*To acknowledge one's sin,* indeed — penetrating still more deeply into the consideration of one's own personhood — *to recognize oneself as being a sinner,* capable of sin and inclined to commit sin, is the essential first step in returning to God" (§13.2). Conversion requires the acknowledgment of one's sin. Throughout his exhortation, the Holy Father points out that the same person who freely sins can also freely repent. He believes that this recognition is necessary if "the conversion of heart of every individual, of his or her return to God" (§4.11, cf. §§4.12, 13.4, 26.4) is to happen. The path to reconciliation can only be trod by those who have first walked the way of personal conversion and repentance.

Just as conversion is a personal experience that occurs in the depths of the human heart, so also is reconciliation; it "takes place in people's hearts and minds" (§4.7). While the Cross and Resurrection accomplish the reconciliation of humanity, making it available to all, each individual shares in the Paschal Mystery by personally appropriating the fruits of Redemption. Sin, which begins as "a *wound* in man's inmost self" (§2.4), first affects an individual's relationship with God. Inevitably, however, sin brings about further ruptures "within the various circles of a person's life" (§13.5).

Each of these divisions requires the healing of the divine gift of reconciliation. Underlining the profoundly interpersonal dynamics of sin and reconciliation, the Pope teaches that the "first and fundamental reconciliation" (§6.3) is the one which restores the sinner to filial friendship with God. He emphasizes that "the most precious result of the forgiveness obtained in the Sacrament of Penance consists in reconciliation with God, which takes place in the inmost heart of the son who was lost and found again" (§31.15). Just as sin spreads out in concentric circles, so also does the work of reconciliation. John Paul frequently recalls that reconciliation with God, which is always primary, is always accompanied by other reconciliations which repair the breaches caused by sin. When a person is forgiven, he "is reconciled with himself in his inmost being, where he regains his own true identity. He is reconciled with his brethren whom he has in some way attacked and wounded. He is reconciled with the Church. He is reconciled with all creation" (§31.15, cf. §§4.5, 26.15).

In *Reconciliatio et Paenitentia,* the Pope also emphasizes the personal nature of sin in several less direct ways. First, he draws on biblical images of individuals — from Adam and Eve, Cain and Abel, David, the prodigal son and merciful father — to reinforce his teaching that conversion from sin and divine reconciliation first of all heal the relationship between a person and God. Second, throughout his discussion of the Sacrament of Penance the Holy Father stresses the *personal* interchange between the confessor and the penitent. The confessor must know the penitent's state of soul if he is to be an effective judge and healer. For his part, the penitent must acknowledge and confess his sins if he is to be absolved and healed. Indeed, the confession of sins must be individual precisely because "sin is a deeply personal matter" (§31.10). All told, John Paul's teaching on the personal dimension of sin, conversion, and reconciliation is yet another way in which he defends the responsibility and freedom, and ultimately the immeasurable dignity, of the human person created in God's image and likeness.

Social sin

Human freedom, personal sin, and interior conversion are essential elements of John Paul's anthropology. At the same time they shed light on his view that the Church works to change unjust structures and situations primarily by appealing to the constant need for interior conversion. In his apostolic exhortation, the Pope squarely faces the theological and pastoral ramifications of "social" sin, a term frequently used at the 1983 Synod. He clearly distinguishes three meanings of "social" sin, the last of which merits his particular attention.

In the first place, sin is social because "by virtue of human solidarity which is as mysterious and intangible as it is real and concrete, each individual's sin in some way affects others" (§16.5). Every sin, even the most seemingly private, has repercussions on the Church and the human family. Drawing on many examples from Sacred Scripture, John Paul concludes that "man's rupture with God leads tragically to divisions between brothers" (§15.1) and damages his relationship with the created world. According to the Pope, the reason for this disorder lies in what he calls the "communion of sin." This supernatural solidarity of sinners is the reverse side of the profound mystery of the communion of saints which binds God's People together such that the holiness of one benefits others. Likewise, every sinner is united with all others. Through his sin, an individual drags down not only himself but also those to whom he is linked in God's saving plan.

Second, some sins can be considered "social" in another way. These social sins are direct attacks against the love of neighbor. Such sins, either of commission or omission, can be committed by an individual against another individual or against the community, or by the community against an individual. Here the Pope includes offenses against a person's human rights — especially the right to life, freedom of religion, and workers' rights — and sins against the common good.

Third, social sin "refers to the relationships between the various human communities" (§16.7) which violate God's plan. This meaning, made popular by Latin American liberation theology, is the most controversial, and John Paul carefully distinguishes an acceptable from an unacceptable sense. He accepts that human sinfulness and guilt frequently express themselves in various human communities and institutional structures. These, in turn, influence people living in them and lead to even further violations of God's will. The condemnation of unjust social, economic, and political situations is a constant of papal teaching. Nonetheless, the Holy Father, strictly speaking, does not consider such situations, whether the class struggle or the military confrontation of world blocs, as social *sin*. Instead, he refers to these situations or structures as a social *evil*. The Pope adds an important clarification for those who fail to make his distinction: "If one speaks of *social sin* here, the expression obviously has an analogical meaning" (§16.7). Social sin, therefore, is a term used to express an ethical judgment on a situation or structure, but it cannot be considered "sin" in the strict and proper sense.

The reasons which lead John Paul to affirm the analogical meaning of social sin in these cases is based on his anthropology. He reminds his readers that evil situations are caused by acts of individual freedom. Accordingly, the Pope warns against a minimizing of human freedom which would replace the responsibility of the moral conscience with blame laid at the doors of "some vague entity or anonymous collectivity, such as the situation, the system, society, structures, or institutions" (§16.8). Only individual persons are subjects of moral acts and thus capable of sinning; situations, structures, or institutions are not. John Paul insists that social evil — or social sin "by analogy" — always stems from an individual's abuse of freedom. An unjust situation is, he writes, "the result of the accumulation and concentration of many *personal sins*" (§16.9). At the heart of every situation or network of sin "are always to be found sinful people" (§16.11).

Changing the innumerable structures of social evil which plague the world can therefore come about only if people's hearts are converted. Neither legislation nor force of arms can do this. Evil structures are caused and maintained by people who make free moral decisions. Rather than excusing such individuals from their responsibility, the Pope challenges them to recognize their personal complicity in the vast and seemingly anonymous institutions and webs of oppression. He makes a forceful "appeal to the consciences of all, so that each may shoulder his or her responsibility seriously and courageously in order to change those disastrous conditions and intolerable situations" (§16.7). The Holy Father's teaching on social sin secures human dignity and opens the way to greater social justice because it reminds us that institutions and structures, while they embody disorder and sinfulness, nonetheless owe their origin and continuance to the free choices of responsible individuals.

Individual confession and general absolution

The specific pastoral question at the 1983 Synod of Bishops which drew the most media attention was undoubtedly general absolution. In their interventions many of the Synod Fathers called for fewer restrictions surrounding the third form of liturgical celebration outlined in the Rite of Penance: general absolution without individual confession of sins. Ten years of experience with the 1973 Rite led many of them to believe that a renewal in sacramental practice would come about by making this form of communal celebration more widely available. John Paul, however, disagrees. He takes an unequivocal stand in favor of individual confession and absolution as the only "normal and ordinary way of celebrating the sacrament" (§32.2). His reasons are founded on fidelity to divine revelation and on the anthropology contained in it.

A crucial question concerns the Church's power over the administration of the sacraments. Does this power extend to allowing general absolution to be considered an ordinary way of celebrating it? For centuries, pastoral practice has permitted, in certain circumstances, the granting of absolution without individual confession. This is allowed, for example, in dealing with the deaf or penitents without access to a confessor who speaks their language. In such instances, they have a clear will to confess their sins, even though auricular confession is impossible. During the two World Wars permission to grant absolution without prior individual confession was extended to cover the situation of large groups — troops before going into battle. Absolution was offered without prior individual confession, and the practice came to be called "general absolution." Since the Second Vatican Council, the Magisterium has declared in the Pastoral Norms (1972) issued by the Congregation for the Doctrine of the Faith, in the Rite of Penance (1973), and in the Code of Canon Law (1983) that, apart from wars, other situations might arise in which collective absolution without individual confession could be pastorally justified.

The Church, therefore, allows for general absolution in principle. It is a lawful practice which does not exceed the "power of the keys" given to forgive sins in the Sacrament of Penance. Nonetheless, the Pope decisively teaches that this practice must be interpreted in the correct theological light and practiced with due pastoral safeguards. John Paul explicitly invokes "*fidelity* to the will of the Lord Jesus, transmitted by the doctrine of the Church . . . [and] the unchanged teaching which the Church has derived from the most ancient Tradition" (§33.2) as the reason underlying his position. This teaching, which has been codified in her disciplinary laws, is clear: "The individual and integral confession of sins with individual absolution constitutes the *only ordinary way* in which the faithful who are conscious of serious sin are reconciled with God and with the Church" (§33.2). The obligation to confess mortal sins to a priest is postponed by general absolution; it is not eliminated. Consequently, obedience to divine revelation requires that general absolution be granted only if two conditions are met.

First, the Pope insists that priests are to give general absolution only "in cases of grave necessity" (§33.3). According to the Code of Canon Law, this situation occurs when there is no time to hear individual confessions, when either the danger of death is imminent or there are so many penitents that they would be deprived of the sacrament for a lengthy period of time (Canon 961). John Paul reminds Bishops of their serious obligation to respect the law and practice of the Church in this regard. They are not to leave to pastors or the faithful the decision about which form of celebration to use. He especially cautions that "the exceptional use of the third form of celebration must never lead to a lesser regard for, still less an abandonment of, the ordinary forms, nor must it lead to this form being considered an alternative to the other two forms" (§33.3). Second, the Holy Father recalls the doctrinal truth that can never be compromised: *Every serious sin must always be stated,* with its determining circumstances, *in an individual confession*" (§33.2). As a consequence of this doctrine, he states that "the obligation to make an individual confession of serious sins before again having recourse to another general absolution" must be made clear to the penitents (§33.3).

More indirectly, in his presentation of individual confession, John Paul provides more reasons for limiting general absolution to truly exceptional circumstances. These reasons all bear on the Pope's distrust of certain collectivist tendencies in modern thought and practice and his desire to highlight the dignity of the human person.

As beings who live in time and history, persons can discover their own identity only when they abandon their own sinful past and open themselves to conversion. In this process of conversion the sacramental confession of sins is a necessary step, one which renews communion with God and others. Individual confession is "a sign of the person's revealing of self as a sinner in the sight of God and the Church, of facing his own sinful condition in the eyes of God" (§31.10). Indeed, there is nothing "more personal and intimate" than Reconciliation, where "the sinner stands alone before God with his sin, repentance and trust" (§31.14). It is therefore understandable why "the *confession of sins* must ordinarily be individual not collective, just as sin is a deeply personal matter" (§31.10). For the Pope, the celebration of communal confession and general absolution can obscure the radically personal nature of conversion and reconciliation celebrated in the Sacrament of Penance. While the support of the ecclesial community can contribute a great deal to penitential practice, the community can never be a substitute for the individual, who must personally place his guilt and trust in God's hands.

The Holy Father's remarks on the confessor's important role in Penance also clarify his judicious approach to general absolution. First of all, the confessor is a judge who has "to evaluate both the seriousness of the sins and the repentance of the penitent" (§31.10). Likewise, he is a healer who "must acquaint himself with the condition of the sick person in order to treat and heal him" (§31.10). As both a tribunal of mercy and a place of spiritual healing, Reconciliation requires "a knowledge of the sinner's heart in order to be able to judge and absolve, to cure and heal" (§31.5). Moreover, the confessor, who acts *in persona Christi* in granting absolution, assures not only the Church's presence but also the personal nature of the encounter. He also guarantees, through hearing the individual confession, offering counsel and spiritual direction, and requiring an appropriate penance, that "the sacramental celebration [will] correspond more closely to the concrete situation of the penitent" (§32.3). According to John Paul, individual confession is the ordinary sacramental way for the Church to accomplish her mission of working for the conversion of hearts and the reconciliation of people with God and one another.

* * *

Selected Bibliography

Allard, Henry. "*Reconciliatio et Paenitentia*: A Comment." *Clergy Review*, 70 (1985), 200-203.

Bagiackas, Joseph. *A Lay Person's Guide to Pope John Paul II's Teaching on the Sacrament of Penance in his Exhortation "Reconciliatio et Paenitentia."* South Bend: Light to the Nations Press, 1994.

Bozell, L. Brent. "The Politics of Sin." *Homiletic and Pastoral Review*, 86 (January 1986), 54-57.

Corderio, Joseph. "Reconciliation and Penance for a Ruptured World." *L'Osservatore Romano*, 12 (1985), 6.

Dallen, James. "Church Authority and the Sacrament of Penance: The Synod of Bishops." *Worship*, 58 (1984), 194-214.

Dallen, James. "*Reconciliatio et Paenitentia*: The Postsynodal Apostolic Exhortation." *Worship*, 59 (1985), 98-116.

Ratzinger, Joseph. "The Celebration of the Sacrament with General Absolution." *L'Osservatore Romano*, 32 (1985), 11.

Synod of Bishops, Sixth Ordinary General Assembly. "*Instrumentum Laboris.*" Ottawa: Canadian Conference of Catholic Bishops, 1982.

Synod of Bishops, Sixth Ordinary General Assembly. "*Lineamenta.*" *Origins*, 11 (1982), 565, 567-580.

Synod of Bishops, Sixth Ordinary General Assembly. "Message to the People of God." *L'Osservatore Romano*, 44 (1983), 4; and *Origins*, 13 (1983), 369, 371.

POST-SYNODAL

APOSTOLIC EXHORTATION

RECONCILIATIO ET PAENITENTIA

OF

JOHN PAUL II

TO THE BISHOPS

CLERGY AND FAITHFUL

ON RECONCILIATION AND PENANCE

IN THE MISSION OF THE CHURCH TODAY

Reconciliatio et Paenitentia
Introduction

Origin and meaning of the document

1.1 To speak of reconciliation and penance is, for the men and women of our time, an invitation to rediscover, translated into their own way of speaking, the very words with which our Savior and Teacher Jesus Christ began his preaching: "Repent, and believe in the Gospel,"[1] that is to say, accept the good news of love, of adoption as children of God and hence of brotherhood.

1.2 Why does the Church put forward once more this subject and this invitation?

1.3 The concern to know better and to understand modern man and the contemporary world, to solve their puzzle and reveal their mystery, to discern the ferments of good and evil within them, has long caused many people to direct at man and the world a questioning gaze. It is the gaze of the historian and sociologist, philosopher and theologian, psychologist and humanist, poet and mystic: above all, it is the gaze, anxious yet full of hope, of the pastor.

1.4 In an exemplary fashion this is shown on every page of the important Pastoral Constitution of the Second Vatican Council *Gaudium et Spes* on the Church in the Modern World, particularly in its wide-ranging and penetrating introduction. It is likewise shown in certain documents issued through the wisdom and charity of my esteemed Predecessors, whose admirable Pontificates were marked by the historic and prophetic event of that Ecumenical Council.

1.5 In common with others, the pastor too can discern among the various unfortunate characteristics of the world and of humanity in our time the existence of many deep and painful divisions.

A shattered world

2.1 These divisions are seen in the relationships between individuals and groups, and also at the level of larger groups: nations against nations, and blocs of opposing countries, in a headlong quest for domination. At the root of this alienation it is not hard to discern conflicts which, instead of being resolved through dialogue, grow more acute in confrontation and opposition.

2.2 Careful observers, studying the elements that cause division, discover reasons of the most widely differing kinds: from the growing disproportion

[1] Mk 1:15.

between groups, social classes and countries, to ideological rivalries that are far from dead; from the opposition between economic interests to political polarization; from tribal differences to discrimination for social and religious reasons. Moreover, certain facts that are obvious to all constitute as it were the pitiful face of the division of which they are the fruit, and demonstrate its seriousness in an inescapably concrete way. Among the many other painful social phenomena of our times one can note:

— the trampling upon the basic rights of the human person, the first of these being the right to life and to a worthy quality of life, which is all the more scandalous in that it coexists with a rhetoric never before known on these same rights;

— hidden attacks and pressures against the freedom of individuals and groups, not excluding the freedom which is most offended against and threatened: the freedom to have, profess and practice one's own faith;

— the various forms of discrimination: racial, cultural, religious, etc.;

— violence and terrorism;

— the use of torture and unjust and unlawful methods of repression;

— the stockpiling of conventional or atomic weapons, the arms race with the spending on military purposes of sums which could be used to alleviate the undeserved misery of peoples that are socially and economically depressed;

— an unfair distribution of the world's resources and of the assets of civilization, which reaches its highest point in a type of social organization whereby the distance between the human conditions of the rich and the poor becomes ever greater.[2] The overwhelming power of this division makes the world in which we live a world shattered[3] to its very foundations.

2.3 Moreover, the Church — without identifying herself *with* the world or being *of* the world — is *in* the world and is engaged *in dialogue with the world*.[4] It is therefore not surprising if one notices in the structure of the Church herself repercussions and signs of the division affecting human society. Over and above the divisions between the Christian Communions that have afflicted her for centuries, the Church today is experiencing within herself sporadic divisions among her own members, divisions caused by differing views

---

[2] Cf. John Paul II, Address at the Opening of the Third General Assembly of the Bishops of Latin America (January 28, 1979): *AAS* 71 (1979), 198-204.

[3] The idea of a "shattered world" is seen in the works of numerous contemporary writers, both Christian and non-Christian, witnesses of man's condition in this tormented period of history.

[4] Cf. Pastoral Constitution on the Church in the Modern World *Gaudium et Spes,* 3, 43, 44; Decree on the Ministry and Life of Priests *Presbyterorum Ordinis,* 12; Paul VI, Encyclical Letter *Ecclesiam Suam* (August 6, 1964): *AAS* 56 (1964), 609-659.

or options in the doctrinal and pastoral field.[5] These divisions too can at times seem incurable.

2.4 However disturbing these divisions may seem at first sight, it is only by a careful examination that one can detect their root: it is to be found in a *wound* in man's inmost self. In the light of faith we call it sin: beginning with *original sin,* which all of us bear from birth as an inheritance from our first parents, to the sin which each one of us commits when we abuse our own freedom.

Longing for reconciliation

3.1 Nevertheless, that same inquiring gaze, if it is discerning enough, detects in the very midst of division an unmistakable desire among people of good will and true Christians to mend the divisions, to heal the wounds and to reestablish at all levels, an essential unity. This desire arouses in many people a real longing for reconciliation even in cases where there is no actual use of this word.

3.2 Some consider reconciliation as an impossible dream which ideally might become the lever for a true transformation of society. For others, it is to be gained by arduous efforts and therefore a goal to be reached through serious reflection and action. Whatever the case, the longing for sincere and consistent reconciliation is without a shadow of doubt a fundamental driving force in our society, reflecting an irrepressible desire for peace. And it is as strongly so as the factors of division, even though this is a paradox.

3.3 But reconciliation cannot be less profound than the division itself. The longing for reconciliation, and reconciliation itself, will be complete and effective only to the extent that they reach — in order to heal it — that original wound which is the root of all other wounds: namely, sin.

The Synod's view

4.1 Therefore, every institution or organization concerned with serving people and saving them in their fundamental dimensions must closely study reconciliation, in order to grasp more fully its meaning and significance, and in order to draw the necessary practical conclusions.

---

[5] At the very beginning of the Church, the Apostle Paul wrote with words of fire about division in the body of the Church, in the famous passage 1 Cor 1:10-16. Years later, Saint Clement of Rome was also to write to the Corinthians, to condemn the wounds inside that community: cf. *Letter to the Corinthians,* 3-6, 57: *Patres Apostolici,* ed. Funk, I, 103-109, 171-173. We know that from the earliest Fathers onward Christ's seamless robe, which the soldiers did not divide, became an image of the Church's unity: cf. Saint Cyprian, *De Ecclesiae Catholicae Unitate,* 7: CCL 3/1, 254-255; Saint Augustine, *In Ioannis Evangelium Tractatus,* 118, 4: CCL 36, 656-657; Saint Bede the Venerable, *In Marci Evangelium Expositio,* IV, 15: CCL 120, 630;

4.2 The Church of Jesus Christ could not fail to make this study. With the devotion of a Mother and the understanding of a Teacher, she earnestly and carefully applies herself to detecting in society not only the signs of division but also the no less eloquent and significant signs of the quest for reconciliation. For she knows that she especially has been given the ability, and assigned the mission, to make known the true and profoundly religious meaning of reconciliation and its full scope. She is thereby already helping to clarify the essential terms of the question of unity and peace.

4.3 My Predecessors constantly preached reconciliation, and invited to reconciliation the whole of humanity and every section and portion of the human community that they saw wounded and divided.[6] And I myself, by an interior impulse which — I am certain — was obeying both an inspiration from on high and the appeals of humanity, decided to emphasize the subject of reconciliation and to do this in two ways, each of them solemn and exacting. In the first place, by convoking the Sixth General Assembly of the Synod of Bishops; in the second place, by making reconciliation the center of the Jubilee Year called to celebrate the 1,950th anniversary of the Redemption.[7] Having to assign a theme to the Synod, I found myself fully in accord with the one suggested by many of my Brothers in the Episcopate, namely, the fruitful theme of *reconciliation* in close connection with the theme of *penance*.[8]

4.4 The term and the very concept of *penance* are very complex. If we link

---

In Lucae Evangelium Expositio, VI, 23: *CCL* 120, 403; *In Sancti Ioannis Evangelium Expositio,* 19: *PL* 92, 911-912.

[6] The Encyclical Letter *Pacem in Terris* (April 11, 1963), John XXIII's spiritual testament, is often considered a "social document" and even a "political message," and in fact it is, if these terms are understood in their broadest sense. As is evident more than twenty years after its publication, the document is in fact more than a strategy for the peaceful coexistence of people and nations; it is a pressing reminder of the higher values without which peace on earth becomes a mere dream. One of these values is precisely that of reconciliation among people, and John XXIII often referred to this subject. With regard to Paul VI, it will suffice to recall that in calling the Church and the world to celebrate the Holy Year of 1975, he wished "renewal and reconciliation" to be the central idea of that important event. Nor can one forget the catechesis which he devoted to this key theme, also in explaining the Jubilee itself.

[7] As I wrote in the Bull of Indiction of the Jubilee Year of the Redemption: "This special time, when all Christians are called upon to realize more profoundly their vocation to reconciliation with the Father in the Son, will only reach its full achievement if it leads to a fresh commitment by each and every person to the service of reconciliation, not only among all the disciples of Christ but also among all men and women": Bull *Aperite Portas Redemptori* (January 6, 1983), 3: *AAS* 75 (1983), 93.

[8] The theme of the Synod was, more precisely, "Reconciliation and Penance in the Mission of the Church."

penance with the *metánoia* which the Synoptics refer to, it means the inmost change of heart under the influence of the word of God and in the perspective of the Kingdom.[9] But *penance* also means *changing one's life* in harmony with the change of heart, and in this sense *doing penance* is completed by *bringing forth fruits worthy of penance:*[10] it is one's whole existence that becomes penitential, that is to say, directed toward a continuous striving for what is better. But *doing penance* is something authentic and effective only if it is translated into *deeds and acts of penance.* In this sense, *penance* means, in the Christian theological and spiritual vocabulary, *asceticism,* that is to say, the *concrete daily effort* of a person, supported by God's grace, to lose his or her own life for Christ as the only means of gaining it[11]; an effort to put off the *old man* and put on the *new*[12]; an effort to overcome in oneself what is *of the flesh* in order that what is *spiritual*[13] may prevail; a continual effort to rise from the things of *here below* to the things of *above,* where Christ is.[14] Penance is therefore *a conversion that passes from the heart to deeds,* and then to the Christian's whole life.

4.5 In each of these meanings *penance* is closely connected with *reconciliation,* for reconciliation with God, with oneself and with others implies overcoming that radical break which is sin. And this is achieved only through the interior transformation or *conversion* which bears fruit in a person's life through acts of penance.

4.6 The basic document of the Synod (also called the *Lineamenta*), which was prepared with the sole purpose of presenting the theme while stressing certain fundamental aspects of it, enabled the ecclesial communities throughout the world to reflect for almost two years on these aspects of a question — that of conversion and reconciliation — which concerns everyone. It also enabled them to draw from it a fresh impulse for the Christian life and apostolate. That reflection was further deepened in the more immediate preparation for the work of the Synod, thanks to the *Instrumentum Laboris* which was sent in due course to the Bishops and their collaborators. After that, the Synod Fathers, assisted by all those called to attend the actual sessions, spent a whole month assiduously dealing with the theme itself and with the numerous and varied questions connected with it. There emerged from the discussions, from

[9] Cf. Mt 4:17; Mk 1:15.
[10] Cf. Lk 3:8.
[11] Cf. Mt 16:24-26; Mk 8:34-36; Lk 9:23-25.
[12] Eph 4:23-24.
[13] Cf. 1 Cor 3:1-20.
[14] Cf. Col 3:1-2.

the common study and from the diligent and accurate work done, a large and precious treasure which the final *Propositiones* sum up in their essence.

4.7 The Synod's view does not ignore the acts of reconciliation (some of which pass almost unobserved in their daily ordinariness) which, though in differing degrees, serve to resolve the many tensions, to overcome the many conflicts and to conquer the divisions both large and small, by restoring unity. But the Synod's main concern was to discover, in the depth of these scattered acts, the hidden root — reconciliation so to speak "at the source," which takes place in people's hearts and minds.

4.8 The Church's charism and likewise her unique nature vis-à-vis reconciliation, at whatever level it needs to be achieved, lie in the fact that she always goes back to that reconciliation at the source. For by reason of her essential mission, the Church feels an obligation to go to the roots of that original wound of sin, in order to bring healing and to reestablish, so to speak, an equally original reconciliation which will be the effective principle of all true reconciliation. This is the reconciliation which the Church had in mind and which she put forward through the Synod.

4.9 Sacred Scripture speaks to us of this reconciliation, inviting us to make every effort to attain it.[15] But Scripture also tells us that it is above all a merciful gift of God to humanity.[16] The history of salvation — the salvation of the whole of humanity, as well as of every human being of whatever period — is the wonderful history of a reconciliation: the reconciliation whereby God, as Father, in the Blood and the Cross of his Son made man, reconciles the world to himself and thus brings into being a new family of those who have been reconciled.

4.10 Reconciliation becomes necessary because there has been the break of sin from which derive all the other forms of break within man and about him. Reconciliation therefore, in order to be complete, necessarily requires liberation from sin, which is to be rejected in its deepest roots. Thus a close internal link unites *conversion* and *reconciliation*. It is impossible to split these two realities or to speak of one and say nothing of the other.

4.11 The Synod at the same time spoke about the reconciliation of the whole human family and of the conversion of the heart of every individual, of his or her return to God: it did so because it wished to recognize and proclaim the fact that there can be no union among people without an internal change in each individual. *Personal conversion* is the necessary path to *harmony be-*

---

[15] "We beseech you on behalf of Christ, be reconciled to God": 2 Cor 5:20.

[16] "We also rejoice in God through our Lord Jesus Christ, through whom we have now received our reconciliation": Rom 5:11; cf. Col 1:20.

tween individuals.[17] When the Church proclaims the good news of reconciliation, or proposes achieving it through the sacraments, she is exercising a truly prophetic role, condemning the evils of man in their infected source, showing the root of divisions and bringing hope in the possibility of overcoming tensions and conflict and reaching brotherhood, concord and peace at all levels and in all sections of human society. She is changing an historical condition of hatred and violence into a civilization of love. She is offering to everyone the evangelical and sacramental principle of that reconciliation at the source, from which comes every other gesture or act of reconciliation, also at the social level.

4.12 It is this reconciliation, the result of conversion, which is dealt with in the present Apostolic Exhortation. For, as happened at the end of the three previous Assemblies of the Synod, this time too the Fathers who had taken part presented the conclusions of the Synod's work to the Bishop of Rome, the universal Pastor of the Church and the Head of the College of Bishops, in his capacity as President of the Synod. I accepted, as a serious and welcome duty of my ministry, the task of drawing from the enormous abundance of the Synod in order to offer to the People of God, as the fruit of the same Synod, a doctrinal and pastoral message on the subject of *penance and reconciliation.* In the first part I shall speak of the Church in the carrying out of her mission of reconciliation, in the work of the conversion of hearts in order to bring about a renewed embrace between man and God, man and his brother, man and the whole of creation. In the second part there will be indicated the radical cause of all wounds and divisions between people, and in the first place between people and God: namely, sin. Afterward I shall indicate the means that enable the Church to promote and encourage full reconciliation between people and God and, as a consequence, of people with one another.

4.13 The document which I now entrust to the sons and daughters of the Church and also to all those who, whether they are believers or not, look to the Church with interest and sincerity, is meant to be a fitting response to

---

[17] The Second Vatican Ecumenical Council noted in the Pastoral Constitution on the Church in the Modern World *Gaudium et Spes,* 10: "The dichotomy affecting the modern world is, in fact, a symptom of the deeper dichotomy that is in man himself. He is the meeting point of many conflicting forces. In his condition as a created being he is subject to a thousand shortcomings, but feels untrammeled in his inclinations and destined for a higher form of life. Torn by a welter of anxieties he is compelled to choose between them and repudiate some among them. Worse still, feeble and sinful as he is, he often does the very thing he hates and does not do what he wants (cf. Rom 7:14ff). And so he feels himself divided, and the result is a host of discords in social life."

what the Synod asked of me. But it is also — and I wish to say this clearly as a duty to truth and justice — something produced by the Synod itself. For the contents of these pages come from the Synod: from its remote and immediate preparation, from the *Instrumentum Laboris,* from the interventions in the Synod Hall and the *circuli minores,* and especially from the sixty-three propositions. Here we have the result of the joint work of the Fathers, who included the representatives of the Eastern Churches, whose theological, spiritual and liturgical heritage is so rich and venerable, also with regard to the subject that concerns us here. Furthermore, it was the Council of the Synod Secretariat which evaluated, in two important sessions, the results and orientations of the Synod Assembly just after it had ended, which highlighted the dynamics of the already mentioned *Propositiones,* and which then indicated the lines considered most suitable for the preparation of the present document. I am grateful to all those who did this work, and, in fidelity to my mission, I wish here to pass on the elements from the doctrinal and pastoral treasure of the Synod which seem to me providential for people's lives at this magnificent yet difficult moment in history.

4.14 It is appropriate — and very significant — to do this while there remains fresh in people's minds the memory of the Holy Year, which was lived in the spirit of penance, conversion and reconciliation. May this Exhortation, entrusted to my Brothers in the Episcopate and to their collaborators, the priests and deacons, to men and women Religious, and to all men and women of upright conscience, be a means of purification, enrichment and deepening in personal faith. May it also be a leaven capable of encouraging the growth in the midst of the world of peace and brotherhood, hope and joy — values which spring from the Gospel as it is accepted, meditated upon and lived day by day after the example of Mary, Mother of our Lord Jesus Christ, through whom it pleased God to reconcile all things to himself.[18]

I

Conversion and Reconciliation: The Church's Task and Commitment

1. A Parable of Reconciliation

5.1 At the beginning of this Apostolic Exhortation there comes into my mind that extraordinary passage in Saint Luke, the deeply religious as well as

---

[18] Cf. Col 1:19-20.

human substance of which I have already sought to illustrate in a previous document.[19] I refer to the parable of the prodigal son.[20]

From the brother who was lost . . .

5.2 "There was a man who had two sons; the younger of them said to his father, 'Father, give me the share of property that falls to me,' " says Jesus as he begins the dramatic story of that young man: the adventurous departure from his father's house, the squandering of all his property in a loose and empty life, the dark days of exile and hunger, but even more of lost dignity, humiliation and shame and then nostalgia for his own home, the courage to go back, the father's welcome. The father had certainly not forgotten his son, indeed he had kept unchanged his affection and esteem for him. So he had always waited for him, and now he embraces him and he gives orders for a great feast to celebrate the return of him who was dead, and is alive; "he was lost, and is found."

5.3 This prodigal son is man — every human being: bewitched by the temptation to separate himself from his father in order to lead his own independent existence; disappointed by the emptiness of the mirage which had fascinated him; alone, dishonored, exploited when he tries to build a world all for himself; sorely tried, even in the depths of his own misery, by the desire to return to communion with his father. Like the father in the parable, God looks out for the return of his child, embraces him when he arrives and orders the banquet of the new meeting with which the reconciliation is celebrated.

5.4 The most striking element of the parable is the father's festive and loving welcome of the returning son: it is a sign of the mercy of God, who is always willing to forgive. Let us say at once: reconciliation is principally a *gift of the heavenly Father.*

. . . to the brother who stayed at home

6.1 But the parable also brings into the picture the elder brother, who refuses to take his place at the banquet. He rebukes his younger brother for his dissolute wanderings and he rebukes his father for the welcome given to the prodigal son while he himself, a temperate and hard-working person, faithful to father and home, has never been allowed — he says — to have a celebration with his friends. This is a sign that he does not understand the father's good-

---

[19] Cf. John Paul II, Encyclical Letter *Dives in Misericordia* (November 30, 1980), 5-6: *AAS* 72 (1980), 1193-1199.

[20] Cf. Lk 15:11-32.

ness. To the extent that this brother, too sure of himself and his own good qualities, jealous and haughty, full of bitterness and anger, is not converted and is not reconciled with his father and brother, the banquet is not yet fully the celebration of a reunion and rediscovery.

6.2 Man — every human being — is also this elder brother. Selfishness makes him jealous, hardens his heart, blinds him and shuts him off from other people and from God. The loving kindness and mercy of the father irritate and enrage him; for him the happiness of the brother who has been found again has a bitter taste.[21] From this point of view he too needs to be converted in order to be reconciled.

6.3 The parable of the prodigal son is above all the story of the inexpressible love of a Father — God — who offers to his son when he comes back to him the gift of full reconciliation. But when the parable evokes, in the figure of the elder son, the selfishness which divides the brothers, it also becomes the story of the human family: it describes our situation and shows the path to be followed. The prodigal son, in his anxiety for conversion, to return to the arms of his father and to be forgiven, represents those who are aware of the existence in their inmost hearts of a longing for reconciliation at all levels and without reserve, and who realize with an inner certainty that this reconciliation is possible only if it derives from a first and fundamental reconciliation — the one which brings a person back from distant separation to filial friendship with God, whose infinite mercy is clearly known. But if the parable is read from the point of view of the other son, it portrays the situation of the human family, divided by forms of selfishness. It throws light on the difficulty involved in satisfying the desire and longing for one reconciled and united family. It therefore reminds us of the need for a profound transformation of hearts through the rediscovery of the Father's mercy and through victory over misunderstanding and over hostility among brothers and sisters.

6.4 In the light of this inexhaustible parable of the mercy that wipes out sin, the Church takes up the appeal that the parable contains and grasps her mission of working, in imitation of the Lord, for the conversion of hearts and for the reconciliation of people with God and with one another — these being two realities that are intimately connected.

---

[21] In the Old Testament, the Book of Jonah is a wonderful anticipation and figure of this aspect of the parable. Jonah's sin is that he was "displeased . . . exceedingly and he was angry" because God is "a gracious God and merciful, slow to anger, and abounding in steadfast love, and repentest of evil." His sin is also that of pitying a castor oil plant "which came into being in a night and perished in a night" and not understanding that the Lord pities Nineveh (Jon 4:1-2, 10).

2. At the Sources of Reconciliation

In the light of Christ the Reconciler

7.1 As we deduce from the parable of the prodigal son, reconciliation is a *gift of God,* an *initiative on his part.* But our faith teaches us that this initiative takes concrete form in the mystery of Christ the Redeemer, the Reconciler and the Liberator of man from sin in all its forms. Saint Paul likewise does not hesitate to sum up in this task and function the incomparable mission of Jesus of Nazareth, the Word and the Son of God made man.

7.2 We too can start with this *central mystery of the economy of salvation,* the key to Saint Paul's Christology. "If while we were enemies we were reconciled to God by the death of his Son," writes Saint Paul, "much more, now that we are reconciled, shall we be saved by his life. Not only so, but we also rejoice in God through our Lord Jesus Christ, through whom we have now received our reconciliation."[22] Therefore, since "God was in Christ reconciling the world to himself," Paul feels inspired to exhort the Christians of Corinth: "Be reconciled to God."[23]

7.3 This mission of reconciliation through death on the Cross is spoken of in another terminology by the Evangelist John, when he observes that Christ had to die "to gather into one the children of God who are scattered abroad."[24]

7.4 But it is once more Saint Paul who enables us to broaden our vision of Christ's work to cosmic dimensions, when he writes that in Christ the Father has reconciled to himself all creatures, those in heaven and those on earth.[25] It can rightly be said of Christ the Redeemer that "in the time of wrath he was taken in exchange"[26] and that, if he is "our peace,"[27] he is also our reconciliation.

7.5 With every good reason his Passion and Death, sacramentally renewed in the Eucharist, are called by the Liturgy the "sacrifice of reconciliation":[28] reconciliation with God and with the brethren, since Jesus teaches that fraternal reconciliation must take place before the sacrifice is offered.[29]

7.6 Beginning with these and other significant passages in the New Testament, we can therefore legitimately relate all our reflections on the whole mis-

---

[22] Cf. Rom 5:10-11; cf. Col 1:20-22.
[23] 2 Cor 5:18, 20.
[24] Jn 11:52.
[25] Cf. Col 1:20.
[26] Cf. Sir 44:17.
[27] Eph 2:14.
[28] Eucharistic Prayer 3.
[29] Cf. Mt 5:23-24.

sion of Christ to his mission as the one who reconciles. Thus there must be proclaimed once more the Church's belief in Christ's redeeming act, in the Paschal Mystery of his Death and Resurrection, as the cause of man's reconciliation, in its twofold aspect of liberation from sin and communion of grace with God.

7.7 It is precisely before the sad spectacle of the divisions and difficulties in the way of reconciliation *between people* that I invite all to look to the *mysterium Crucis* as the loftiest drama in which Christ perceives and suffers to the greatest possible extent the tragedy of the division of man from God, so that he cries out in the words of the Psalmist: "My God, my God, why have you forsaken me?"[30] and at the same time accomplishes our reconciliation. With our eyes fixed on the mystery of Golgotha we should be reminded always of that *"vertical" dimension* of division and reconciliation concerning the relationship between man and God, a dimension which in the eyes of faith always prevails over the *"horizontal" dimension,* that is to say, over the reality of division between people and the need for reconciliation between them. For we know that reconciliation between people is and can only be the fruit of the redemptive act of Christ, who died and rose again to conquer the kingdom of sin, to reestablish the Covenant with God and thus break down the dividing wall[31] which sin had raised up between people.

The reconciling Church

8.1 But, as Pope Saint Leo said, speaking of Christ's Passion, "Everything that the Son of God did and taught for the reconciliation of the world we know not only from the history of his past actions, but we experience it also in the effectiveness of what he accomplishes in the present."[32] We experience the reconciliation which he accomplished in his humanity in the efficacy of the sacred mysteries which are celebrated by his Church, for which he gave his life and which he established as the sign and also the means of salvation.

8.2 This is stated by Saint Paul, when he writes that God has given to Christ's Apostles a share in his work of reconciliation. He says: "God . . . gave us the ministry of reconciliation . . . and the message of reconciliation."[33]

8.3 To the hands and lips of the Apostles, his messengers, the Father has mercifully entrusted a *ministry of reconciliation,* which they carry out in a singular way, by virtue of the power to act *"in persona Christi."* But the message of

---

[30] Mt 27:46; Mk 15:34; Ps 22:2.
[31] Cf. Eph 2:14-16.
[32] *Tractatus* 63 (*De Passione Domini,* 12), 6: *CCL* 138/A, 386.
[33] 2 Cor 5:18-19.

reconciliation has also been entrusted to the whole community of believers, to the whole fabric of the Church, that is to say, the task of doing everything possible to witness to reconciliation and to bring it about in the world.

8.4 It can be said that the Second Vatican Council too, in defining the Church as a "sacrament — a sign and instrument, that is, of communion with God and of unity among all people," and in indicating as the Church's function that of obtaining "full unity in Christ" for the "people of the present day . . . drawn ever more closely together by social, technical and cultural bonds,"[34] recognized that the Church must strive above all to bring all people to full reconciliation.

8.5 In intimate connection with Christ's mission, one can therefore sum up the Church's mission, rich and complex as it is, as being her central task of reconciling people: with God, with themselves, with neighbor, with the whole of creation; and this in a permanent manner since, as I said on another occasion, "the Church is also by her nature always reconciling."[35]

8.6 The Church is reconciling inasmuch as she proclaims the message of reconciliation, as she has always done throughout her history, from the Apostolic Council of Jerusalem[36] down to the latest Synod and the recent Jubilee of the Redemption. The originality of this proclamation is in the fact that for the Church *reconciliation* is closely linked with conversion of heart: this is the necessary path to understanding among human beings.

8.7 The Church is also reconciling inasmuch as she shows man the paths and offers the means for reaching this fourfold reconciliation. The paths are precisely those of conversion of heart and victory over sin, whether this latter is selfishness or injustice, arrogance or exploitation of others, attachment to material goods or the unrestrained quest for pleasure. The means are those of faithful and loving attention to God's word; personal and community prayer; and in particular the sacraments, true signs and instruments of reconciliation, among which there excels, precisely under this aspect, the one which we are rightly accustomed to call the Sacrament of Reconciliation or Penance, and to which we shall return later on.

The reconciled Church

9.1 My venerable Predecessor Paul VI commendably highlighted the fact that the Church, in order to evangelize, must begin by showing that she her-

---

[34] Dogmatic Constitution on the Church *Lumen Gentium,* 1.

[35] Homily, Liverpool (May 30, 1982), 3: *Insegnamenti* V/2 (1982), 1992: "The Church is also by her nature always reconciling, handing on to others the gift that she herself has received, the gift of having been forgiven and made one with God."

[36] Cf. Acts 15:2-33.

self has been evangelized, that is to say, that she is open to the full and complete proclamation of the Good News of Jesus Christ in order to listen to it and put it into practice.[37] I too, by bringing together in one document the reflections of the Fourth General Assembly of the Synod, have spoken of a Church that is catechized to the extent that she carries out catechesis.[38]

9.2 I now do not hesitate to resume the comparison, insofar as it applies to the theme I am dealing with, in order to assert that the Church, if she is to be *reconciling,* must begin by being a *reconciled Church.* Beneath this simple and indicative expression lies the conviction that the Church, in order ever more effectively to proclaim and propose reconciliation to the world, must become ever more genuinely a community of disciples of Christ (even though it were only "the little flock" of the first days), united in the commitment to be continually converted to the Lord and to live as new people in the spirit and practice of reconciliation.

9.3 To the people of our time, so sensitive to the proof of concrete living witness, the Church is called upon to give an example of reconciliation particularly within herself. And for this purpose we must all work to bring peace to people's minds, to reduce tensions, to overcome divisions and to heal wounds that may have been inflicted by brother on brother when the contrast of choices in the field of what is optional becomes acute; and on the contrary we must try to be united in what is essential for Christian faith and life, in accordance with the ancient maxim: in what is doubtful, freedom; in what is necessary, unity; in all things, charity.

9.4 It is in accordance with this same criterion that the Church must conduct her ecumenical activity. For in order to be completely reconciled, she knows that she must continue the quest for unity among those who are proud to call themselves Christians but who are separated from one another, also as Churches or Communions, and from the Church of Rome. The latter seeks a unity which, if it is to be the fruit and expression of true reconciliation, is meant to be based neither upon a disguising of the points that divide nor upon compromises which are as easy as they are superficial and fragile. Unity must be the result of a true conversion of everyone, the result of mutual forgiveness, of theological dialogue and fraternal relations, of prayer and of complete docility to the action of the Holy Spirit, who is also the *Spirit of reconciliation.*

---

[37] Cf. Apostolic Exhortation *Evangelii Nuntiandi* (December 8, 1975), 13: *AAS* 68 (1976), 12-13.

[38] Cf. John Paul II, Apostolic Exhortation *Catechesi Tradendae* (October 16, 1979), 24: *AAS* 71 (1979), 1297.

9.5 Finally, in order that the Church may say that she is completely reconciled, she feels that it is her duty to strive ever harder, by promoting the "dialogue of salvation,"[39] to bring the Gospel to those vast sections of humanity in the modern world that do not share her faith, but even, as a result of growing secularism, keep their distance from her and oppose her with cold indifference, when they do not actually hinder and persecute her. She feels the duty to say once more to everyone in the words of Saint Paul: "Be reconciled to God."[40]

9.6 At any rate, the Church promotes reconciliation *in the truth,* knowing well that neither reconciliation nor unity is possible outside or in opposition to the truth.

3. God's Initiative and the Church's Ministry

10.1 The Church, as a reconciled and reconciling community, cannot forget that at the source of her gift and mission of reconciliation is the initiative, full of compassionate love and mercy, of that God who is love[41] and who out of love created human beings[42]; and he created them so that they might live in friendship with him and in communion with one another.

Reconciliation comes from God

10.2 God is faithful to his eternal plan even when man, under the impulse of the Evil One[43] and carried away by his own pride, abuses the freedom given to him in order to love and generously seek what is good, and refuses to obey his Lord and Father. God is faithful even when man, instead of responding with love to God's love, opposes him and treats him like a rival, deluding himself and relying on his own power, with the resulting break of relationship with the one who created him. In spite of this transgression on man's part, *God remains faithful in love.* It is certainly true that the story of the Garden of Eden makes us think about the tragic consequences of rejecting the Father, which becomes evident in man's inner disorder and in the breakdown of harmony between man and woman, brother and brother.[44] Also significant is the Gospel parable of the two brothers who, in different ways, distance themselves from their father and cause a rift between them. Refusal of God's fa-

---

[39] Cf. Paul VI, Encyclical Letter *Ecclesiam Suam* (August 6, 1964): *AAS* 56 (1964), 609-659.
[40] 2 Cor 5:20.
[41] Cf. 1 Jn 4:8.
[42] Cf. Wis 11:23-26; Gen 1:27; Ps 8:4-8.
[43] Cf. Wis 2:24.
[44] Cf. Gen 3:12-24, 4:1-16.

therly love and of his loving gifts is always at the root of humanity's divisions.

10.3 But we know that God, "rich in mercy,"[45] like the father in the parable, does not close his heart to any of his children. He waits for them, looks for them, goes to meet them at the place where the refusal of communion imprisons them in isolation and division. He calls them to gather about his table in the joy of the feast of forgiveness and reconciliation.

10.4 This initiative on God's part is made concrete and manifest in the redemptive act of Christ, which radiates through the world by means of the ministry of the Church.

10.5 For, according to our faith, the Word of God became flesh and came to dwell in the world; he entered into the history of the world, summing it up and recapitulating it in himself.[46] He revealed to us that God is love, and he gave us the "new commandment" of love,[47] at the same time communicating to us the certainty that the path of love is open for all people, so that the effort to establish universal brotherhood is not a vain one.[48] By conquering through his death on the Cross evil and the power of sin, by his loving obedience he brought salvation to all and became "reconciliation" for all. In him God reconciled man to himself.

10.6 The Church carries on the proclamation of reconciliation which Christ caused to echo through the villages of Galilee and all Palestine[49] and does not cease to invite all humanity to be converted and to believe in the Good News. She speaks in the name of Christ, making her own the appeal of Saint Paul which we have already recalled: "We are ambassadors for Christ, God making his appeal through us. We beseech you on behalf of Christ, be reconciled to God."[50]

10.7 Those who accept this appeal enter into the economy of reconciliation and experience the truth contained in that other affirmation of Saint Paul, that Christ "is our peace, who has made us both one, and has broken down the dividing wall of hostility . . . , so making peace" that he "might reconcile us both to God."[51] This text directly concerns the overcoming of the religious division between Israel — as the Chosen People of the Old Testament — and the other peoples, all called to form part of the New Covenant. Nevertheless it

---

[45] Eph 2:4.

[46] Cf. Eph 1:10.

[47] Jn 13:34.

[48] Cf. Second Vatican Ecumenical Council, Pastoral Constitution on the Church in the Modern World *Gaudium et Spes*, 38.

[49] Cf. Mk 1:15.

[50] 2 Cor 5:20.

[51] Eph 2:14-16.

contains the affirmation of the new spiritual universality desired by God and accomplished by him through the sacrifice of his Son, the Word made man, without limits or exclusions of any sort, for all those who are converted and who believe in Christ. We are all therefore called to enjoy the fruits of this reconciliation desired by God: every individual and every people.

The Church, the great sacrament of reconciliation

11.1 The Church has the mission of proclaiming this reconciliation and as it were of being its sacrament in the world. The Church is the *sacrament,* that is to say, the sign and means of reconciliation in different ways, which differ in value but which all come together to obtain what the divine initiative of mercy desires to grant to humanity.

11.2 She is a sacrament in the first place by her very existence as a reconciled community which witnesses to and represents in the world the work of Christ.

11.3 She is also a sacrament through her service as the custodian and interpreter of Sacred Scripture, which is the Good News of reconciliation inasmuch as it tells each succeeding generation about God's loving plan and shows to each generation the paths to universal reconciliation in Christ.

11.4 Finally she is a sacrament by reason of the seven sacraments which, each in its own way, "make the Church."[52] For since they commemorate and renew Christ's Paschal Mystery, all the sacraments are a source of life for the Church, and in the Church's hands they are means of conversion to God and of reconciliation among people.

Other means of reconciliation

12.1 The mission of reconciliation is proper to the whole Church, also and especially to that Church which has already been admitted to the full sharing in divine glory with the Virgin Mary, the angels and the saints, who contemplate and adore the thrice-holy God. The Church in heaven, the Church on earth and the Church in purgatory are mysteriously united in this cooperation with Christ in reconciling the world to God.

12.2 The first means of this salvific action is that of prayer. It is certain that the Blessed Virgin, Mother of Christ and of the Church,[53] and the saints who have now reached the end of their earthly journey and possess God's

---

[52] Cf. Saint Augustine, *De Civitate Dei,* XXII, 17: *CCL* 48, 835-836; Saint Thomas Aquinas, *Summa Theologiae,* III, q. 64, a. 2, ad 3.

[53] Cf. Paul VI, Address at the Closing of the Third Session of the Second Vatican Ecumenical Council (November 21, 1964): *AAS* 56 (1964), 1015-1018.

glory, sustain by their intercession their brethren who are on pilgrimage through the world, in the commitment to conversion, to faith, to getting up again after every fall, to acting in order to help the growth of communion and peace in the Church and in the world. In the mystery of the Communion of Saints universal reconciliation is accomplished in its most profound form, which is also the most fruitful for the salvation of all.

12.3 There is yet another means: that of preaching. The Church, since she is the disciple of the one Teacher Jesus Christ, in her own turn, as Mother and Teacher untiringly exhorts people to reconciliation. And she does not hesitate to condemn the evil of sin, to proclaim the need for conversion, to invite and ask people to "let themselves be reconciled." In fact, this is her prophetic mission in today's world, just as it was in the world of yesterday. It is the same mission as that of her Teacher and Head, Jesus. Like him, the Church will always carry out this mission with sentiments of merciful love and will bring to all people those words of forgiveness and that invitation to hope which come from the Cross.

12.4 There is also the often so difficult and demanding means of pastoral action aimed at bringing back every individual — whoever and wherever he or she may be — to the path, at times a long one, leading back to the Father in the communion of all the brethren.

12.5 Finally there is the means of witness, which is almost always silent. This is born from a twofold awareness on the part of the Church: that of being in herself "unfailingly holy,"[54] but also the awareness of the need to go forward and "daily be further purified and renewed, against the day when Christ will present her to himself in all her glory without spot or wrinkle," for, by reason of her sins, sometimes "the radiance of the Church's face shines less brightly" in the eyes of those who behold her.[55] This witness cannot fail to assume two fundamental aspects. The first aspect is that of being the sign of that universal charity which Jesus Christ left as an inheritance to his followers, as a proof of belonging to his Kingdom. The second aspect is translation into ever new manifestations of conversion and reconciliation both within the Church and outside her, by the overcoming of tensions, by mutual forgiveness, by growth in the spirit of brotherhood and peace which is to be spread throughout the world. By this means the Church will effectively be able to work for the creation of what my Predecessor Paul VI called the "civilization of love."

---

[54] Second Vatican Ecumenical Council, Dogmatic Constitution on the Church *Lumen Gentium*, 39.

[55] Second Vatican Ecumenical Council, Decree on Ecumenism *Unitatis Redintegratio*, 4.

II

The Love That Is Greater Than Sin

The tragedy of man

13.1 In the words of Saint John the Apostle, "if we say we have no sin, we deceive ourselves, and the truth is not in us. If we confess our sins, he is faithful and just and will forgive our sins."[56] Written at the very dawn of the Church, these inspired words introduce better than any other human expression the theme of sin, which is intimately connected with that of reconciliation. These words present the question of sin in its human dimension: sin as an integral part of the truth about man. But they immediately relate the human dimension to its divine dimension, where sin is countered by the truth of divine love, which is just, generous and faithful, and which reveals itself above all in forgiveness and redemption. Thus Saint John also writes a little further on that "whatever accusations (our conscience) may raise against us, God is greater than our conscience."[57]

13.2 *To acknowledge one's sin*, indeed — penetrating still more deeply into the consideration of one's own personhood — *to recognize oneself as being a sinner*, capable of sin and inclined to commit sin, is the essential first step in returning to God. For example, this is the experience of David, who "having done what is evil in the eyes of the Lord" and having been rebuked by the Prophet Nathan,[58] exclaims: "For I know my transgressions, and my sin is ever before me. Against you, you alone, have I sinned and done what is evil in your sight."[59] Similarly, Jesus himself puts the following significant words on the lips and in the heart of the prodigal son: "Father, I have sinned against heaven and before you."[60]

13.3 In effect, to become reconciled with God presupposes and includes detaching oneself consciously and with determination from the sin into which one has fallen. It presupposes and includes, therefore, *doing penance* in the fullest sense of the term: repenting, showing this repentance, adopting a real attitude of repentance — which is the attitude of the person who starts out on the road of return to the Father. This

---

[56] 1 Jn 1:8-9.

[57] 1 Jn 3:20; cf. my reference to this passage in my Address at the General Audience (March 14, 1984), 3: *Insegnamenti* VII/1 (1984), 683.

[58] Cf. 2 Sam 11-12.

[59] Ps 51:3-4.

[60] Lk 15:18, 21.

is a general law and one which each individual must follow in his or her particular situation. For it is not possible to deal with sin and conversion only in abstract terms.

13.4 In the concrete circumstances of sinful humanity, in which there can be no conversion without the acknowledgment of one's own sin, the Church's ministry of reconciliation intervenes in each individual case with a precise penitential purpose. That is, the Church's ministry intervenes in order to bring the person to the "knowledge of self" — in the words of Saint Catherine of Siena[61] — to the rejection of evil, to the reestablishment of friendship with God, to a new interior ordering, to a fresh ecclesial conversion. Indeed, even beyond the boundaries of the Church and the community of believers, the message and ministry of penance are addressed to all men and women, because all need conversion and reconciliation.[62]

13.5 In order to carry out this penitential ministry adequately, we shall have to evaluate the consequences of sin with "eyes enlightened"[63] by faith. These consequences of sin are the reasons for division and rupture, not only within each person, but also within the various circles of a person's life: in relation to the family, to the professional and social environment, as can often be seen from experience; it is confirmed by the passage in the Bible about the city of Babel and its tower.[64] Intent on building what was to be at once a symbol and a source of unity, those people found themselves more scattered than before, divided in speech, divided among themselves, incapable of consensus and agreement.

13.6 Why did the ambitious project fail? Why did "the builders labor in vain"?[65] They failed because they had set up as a sign and guarantee of the unity they desired a work of their own hands alone, and had forgotten the action of the Lord. They had attended only to the horizontal dimension of work and social life, forgetting the vertical dimension by which they would have been rooted in God, their Creator and Lord, and would have been directed toward him as the ultimate goal of their progress.

13.7 Now it can be said that the tragedy of humanity today, as indeed of every period in history, consists precisely in its similarity to the experience of Babel.

---

[61] Cf. *Lettere,* Florence, 1970, I, 3-4; *Il Dialogo della Divina Providenza*, Rome, 1980, *passim.*
[62] Cf. Rom 3:23-26.
[63] Cf. Eph 1:18.
[64] Cf. Gen 11:1-9.
[65] Cf. Ps 127:1.

1. The Mystery of Sin

14.1 If we read the passage in the Bible on the city and tower of Babel in the new light offered by the Gospel, and if we compare it with the other passage on the fall of our first parents, we can draw from it valuable elements for an understanding of the *mystery of sin.* This expression, which echoes what Saint Paul writes concerning the *mystery of evil,*[66] helps us to grasp the obscure and intangible element hidden in sin. Clearly, sin is a product of man's freedom. But deep within its human reality there are factors at work which place it beyond the merely human, in the border area where man's conscience, will and sensitivity are in contact with the dark forces which, according to Saint Paul, are active in the world almost to the point of ruling it.[67]

Disobedience to God

14.2 A first point which helps us to understand sin emerges from the biblical narrative on the building of the tower of Babel: the people sought to build a city, organize themselves into a society and to be strong and powerful *without God,* if not precisely *against God.*[68] In this sense the story of the first sin in Eden and the story of Babel, in spite of notable differences in content and form, have one thing in common: in both there is an *exclusion of God,* through direct opposition to one of his commandments, through an act of rivalry, through the mistaken pretension of being "like him."[69] In the story of Babel *the exclusion of God* is presented not so much under the aspect of opposition to him as of forgetfulness and indifference toward him, as if God were of no relevance in the sphere of man's joint projects. But in both cases *the relationship to God* is severed with violence. In the case of Eden there appears in all its seriousness and tragic reality that which constitutes the ultimate essence and darkness of sin: *disobedience to God,* to his law, to the moral norm that he has given man, inscribing it in his heart and confirming and perfecting it through revelation.

14.3 *Exclusion of God, rupture with God, disobedience to God:* throughout the history of mankind this has been and is, in various forms, sin. It can go as

[66] Cf. 2 Thess 2:7.

[67] Cf. Rom 7:7-25; Eph 2:2, 6:12.

[68] The terminology used in the Septuagint Greek translation and in the New Testament for "sin" is significant. The most common term for sin is *hamartía,* with its various derivatives. It expresses the concept of offending more or less gravely against a norm or law, or against a person or even a divinity. But sin is also called *adikía,* and the concept here is of acting unjustly. The Bible also speaks of *parábasis* (transgression), *asébeia* (impiety) and other concepts. They all convey the image of sin.

[69] Gen 3:5: "And you will be like God, knowing good and evil"; cf. Gen 3:22.

far as a very *denial* of God and his existence: this is the phenomenon called *atheism.*

14.4 It is the *disobedience* of a person who, by a free act, does not acknowledge God's sovereignty over his or her life, at least at that particular moment in which he or she transgresses God's law.

Division between brothers

15.1 In the biblical narratives mentioned above, man's rupture with God leads tragically to divisions between brothers.

15.2 In the description of the "first sin," the rupture with Yahweh simultaneously breaks the bond of friendship that had united the human family. Thus the subsequent pages of *Genesis* show us the man and the woman as it were pointing an accusing finger at each other.[70] Later we have the brother hating his brother and finally taking his life.[71]

15.3 According to the Babel story, the result of sin is the shattering of the human family, already begun with the first sin and now reaching its most extreme form on the social level.

15.4 No one wishing to investigate the mystery of sin can ignore this link between cause and effect. As a rupture with God, sin is an act of disobedience by a creature who rejects, at least implicitly, the very one from whom he came and who sustains him in life. It is therefore a suicidal act. Since by sinning man refuses to submit to God, his internal balance is also destroyed and it is precisely within himself that contradictions and conflicts arise. Wounded in this way, man almost inevitably causes damage to the fabric of his relationship with others and with the created world. This is an objective law and an objective reality, verified in so many ways in the human psyche and in the spiritual life, as well as in society, where it is easy to see the signs and effects of internal disorder.

15.5 The mystery of sin is composed of this twofold wound which the sinner opens in himself and in his relationship with his neighbor. Therefore one can speak of *personal* and *social* sin: from one point of view, every sin is *personal;* from another point of view, every sin is *social,* insofar as and because it also has social repercussions.

Personal sin and social sin

16.1 Sin, in the proper sense, is always a *personal act,* since it is an act of freedom on the part of an individual person, and not properly of a group or

---

[70] Cf. Gen 3:12.
[71] Cf. Gen 4:2-16.

community. This individual may be conditioned, incited and influenced by numerous and powerful external factors. He may also be subjected to tendencies, defects and habits linked with his personal condition. In not a few cases such external and internal factors may attenuate, to a greater or lesser degree, the person's freedom and therefore his responsibility and guilt. But it is a truth of faith, also confirmed by our experience and reason, that the human person is free. This truth cannot be disregarded in order to place the blame for individuals' sins on external factors such as structures, systems or other people. Above all, this would be to deny the person's dignity and freedom, which are manifested — even though in a negative and disastrous way — also in this responsibility for sin committed. Hence there is nothing so personal and untransferable in each individual as merit for virtue or responsibility for sin.

16.2 As a personal act, sin has its first and most important consequences in the *sinner himself:* that is, in his relationship with God, who is the very foundation of human life; and also in his spirit, weakening his will and clouding his intellect.

16.3 At this point we must ask what was being referred to by those who, during the preparation of the Synod and in the course of its actual work, frequently spoke of *social sin.*

16.4 The expression and the underlying concept in fact have various meanings.

16.5 To speak of *social sin* means in the first place to recognize that, by virtue of human solidarity which is as mysterious and intangible as it is real and concrete, each individual's sin in some way affects others. This is the other aspect of that solidarity which on the religious level is developed in the profound and magnificent mystery of the *Communion of Saints,* thanks to which it has been possible to say that "every soul that rises above itself, raises up the world."[72] To this *law of ascent* there unfortunately corresponds the *law of descent.* Consequently one can speak of a *communion of sin,* whereby a soul that lowers itself through sin drags down with itself the Church and, in some way, the whole world. In other words, there is no sin, not even the most intimate and secret one, the most strictly individual one, that exclusively concerns the person committing it. With greater or lesser violence, with greater or lesser harm, every sin has repercussions on the entire ecclesial body and the whole human family. According to this first meaning of the term, every sin can undoubtedly be considered as *social* sin.

16.6 Some sins, however, by their very matter constitute a direct attack on

---

[72] The expression from the French writer Elisabeth Leseur, *Journal et pensées de chaque jour*, Paris, 1918, 31.

one's neighbor and, more exactly, in the language of the Gospel, against one's brother or sister. They are an offense against God because they are offenses against one's neighbor. These sins are usually called *social sins,* and this is the second meaning of the term. In this sense *social* sin is sin against love of neighbor, and in the law of Christ it is all the more serious in that it involves the second commandment, which is "like unto the first."[73] Likewise, the term *social* applies to every sin against justice in interpersonal relationships, committed either by the individual against the community or by the community against the individual. Also *social* is every sin against the rights of the human person, beginning with the right to life and including the life of the unborn, or against a person's physical integrity. Likewise *social* is every sin against others' freedom, especially against the supreme freedom to believe in God and adore him; *social* is every sin against the dignity and honor of one's neighbor. Also *social* is every sin against the common good and its exigencies in relation to the whole broad spectrum of the rights and duties of citizens. The term *social* can be applied to sins of commission or omission — on the part of political, economic or trade union leaders, who though in a position to do so, do not work diligently and wisely for the improvement and transformation of society according to the requirements and potential of the given historic moment; as also on the part of workers who through absenteeism or non-cooperation fail to ensure that their industries can continue to advance the well-being of the workers themselves, of their families and of the whole of society.

16.7 The third meaning of *social sin* refers to the relationships between the various human communities. These relationships are not always in accordance with the plan of God, who intends that there be justice in the world, and freedom and peace between individuals, groups and peoples. Thus the class struggle, whoever the person who leads it or on occasion seeks to give it a theoretical justification, is a *social evil.* Likewise, obstinate confrontation between blocs of nations, between one nation and another, between different groups within the same nation — all this too is a *social evil.* In both cases one may ask whether moral responsibility for these evils, and therefore sin, can be attributed to any person in particular. Now it has to be admitted that realities and situations such as those described, when they become generalized and reach vast proportions as social phenomena, almost always become anonymous, just as their causes are complex and not always identifiable. Hence if one speaks of *social sin* here, the expression obviously has an analogical meaning. However, to speak even analogically of *social sins* must not cause us to underestimate the responsibility of the individuals involved. It is meant to be

---

[73] Cf. Mt 22:39; Mk 12:31; Lk 10:27-28.

an appeal to the consciences of all, so that each may shoulder his or her responsibility seriously and courageously in order to change those disastrous conditions and intolerable situations.

16.8 Having said this in the clearest and most unequivocal way, one must add at once that there is one meaning sometimes given to *social sin* that is not legitimate or acceptable even though it is very common in certain quarters today.[74] This usage contrasts *social sin* and *personal sin,* not without ambiguity, in a way that leads more or less unconsciously to the watering down and almost the abolition of *personal* sin, with the recognition only of *social* guilt and responsibilities. According to this usage, which can readily be seen to derive from non-Christian ideologies and systems — which have possibly been discarded today by the very people who formerly officially upheld them — practically every sin is a social sin, in the sense that blame for it is to be placed not so much on the moral conscience of an individual but rather on some vague entity or anonymous collectivity, such as the situation, the system, society, structures, or institutions.

16.9 Whenever the Church speaks of *situations* of sin, or when she condemns as *social sins* certain situations or the collective behavior of certain social groups, big or small, or even of whole nations and blocs of nations, she knows and she proclaims that such cases of *social sin* are the result of the accumulation and concentration of many *personal sins.* It is a case of the very personal sins of those who cause or support evil or who exploit it; of those who are in a position to avoid, eliminate or at least limit certain social evils but who fail to do so out of laziness, fear or the conspiracy of silence, through secret complicity or indifference; of those who take refuge in the supposed impossibility of changing the world; and also of those who sidestep the effort and sacrifice required, producing specious reasons of a higher order. The real responsibility, then, lies with individuals.

16.10 A situation — or likewise an institution, a structure, society itself — is not in itself the subject of moral acts. Hence a situation cannot in itself be good or bad.

16.11 At the heart of every *situation of sin* are always to be found sinful people. So true is this that even when such a situation can be changed in its structural and institutional aspects by the force of law, or — as unfortunately more often happens — by the law of force, the change in fact proves to be incomplete, of short duration, and ultimately vain and ineffective — not to say

---

[74] Cf. Sacred Congregation for the Doctrine of the Faith, Instruction on Certain Aspects of the Theology of Liberation *Libertatis Nuntius* (August 6, 1984), IV, 14-15: *AAS* 76 (1984), 885-886.

counterproductive — if the people directly or indirectly responsible for that situation are not converted.

Mortal and venial

17.1 But here we come to a further dimension in the mystery of sin, one on which the human mind has never ceased to ponder: the question of its gravity. It is a question which cannot be overlooked and one which the Christian conscience has never refused to answer. *Why* and *to what degree* is sin a serious matter in the offense it commits against God and in its effects on man? The Church has a teaching on this matter which she reaffirms in its essential elements, while recognizing that it is not always easy in concrete situations to define clear and exact limits.

17.2 Already in the Old Testament, individuals guilty of several kinds of sins — sins committed deliberately,[75] the various forms of impurity,[76] idolatry,[77] the worship of false gods[78] — were ordered to be "taken away from the people," which could also mean to be condemned to death.[79] Contrasted with these were other sins, especially sins committed through ignorance, that were forgiven by means of a sacrificial offering.[80]

17.3 In reference also to these texts, the Church has for centuries spoken of *mortal* sin and *venial* sin. But it is above all the New Testament that sheds light on this distinction and these terms. Here there are many passages which enumerate and strongly reprove sins that are particularly deserving of condemnation.[81] There is also the confirmation of the Decalogue by Jesus himself.[82] Here I wish to give special attention to two passages that are significant and impressive.

17.4 In a text of his First Letter, Saint John speaks of a sin *which leads to death (pros thánaton),* as opposed to a sin *which does not lead to death (mè pros thánaton).*[83] Obviously, the concept of *death* here is a spiritual death. It is a question of the loss of the true life or "eternal life," which for John is knowledge of the Father and the Son,[84] and communion and intimacy with them. In

---

[75] Cf. Num 15:30.
[76] Cf. Lev 18:26-30.
[77] Cf. Lev 19:4.
[78] Cf. Lev 20:1-7.
[79] Cf. Ex 21:17.
[80] Cf. Lev 4:2–5:26; Num 15:22-29.
[81] Cf. Mt 5:28, 6:23, 12:31-32, 15:19; Mk 3:28-30; Rom 1:29-31, 13:13; Jas 4.
[82] Cf. Mt 5:17, 15:1-10; Mk 10:19; Lk 18:20.
[83] Cf. 1 Jn 5:16-17.
[84] Cf. Jn 17:3.

that passage the sin *that leads to death* seems to be the denial of the Son,[85] or the worship of false gods.[86] At any rate, by this distinction of concepts John seems to wish to emphasize the incalculable seriousness of what constitutes the very essence of sin, namely the rejection of God. This is manifested above all in *apostasy* and *idolatry:* repudiating faith in revealed truth and making certain created realities equal to God, raising them to the status of idols or false gods.[87] But in this passage the Apostle's intention is also to underline the certainty that comes to the Christian from the fact of having been "born of God" through the coming of the Son: the Christian possesses a power that preserves him from falling into sin; God protects him, and "the evil one does not touch him." If he should sin through weakness or ignorance, he has confidence in being forgiven, also because he is supported by the joint prayer of the community.

17.5 In another passage of the New Testament, namely in Saint Matthew's Gospel,[88] Jesus himself speaks of a "blasphemy against the Holy Spirit" that "will not be forgiven" by reason of the fact that in its manifestation it is an obstinate refusal to be converted to the love of the Father of mercies.

17.6 Here of course it is a question of extreme and radical manifestations: rejection of God, rejection of his grace, and therefore opposition to the very source of salvation[89] — these are manifestations whereby a person seems to exclude himself voluntarily from the path of forgiveness. It is to be hoped that very few persist to the end in this attitude of rebellion or even defiance of God. Moreover, God in his merciful love is greater than our hearts, as Saint John further teaches us,[90] and can overcome all our psychological and spiritual resistance. So that, as Saint Thomas writes, "considering the omnipotence and mercy of God, no one should despair of the salvation of anyone in this life."[91]

17.7 But when we ponder the problem of a rebellious will meeting the infinitely just God, we cannot but experience feelings of salutary "fear and trembling," as Saint Paul suggests.[92] Moreover, Jesus' warning about the sin "that will not be forgiven" confirms the existence of sins which can bring down on the sinner the punishment of "eternal death."

---

[85] Cf. 1 Jn 2:22.

[86] Cf. 1 Jn 5:21.

[87] Cf. 1 Jn 5:16-21.

[88] Cf. Mt 12:31-32.

[89] Cf. Saint Thomas Aquinas, *Summa Theologiae,* II-II, q. 14, aa. 1-8.

[90] Cf. 1 Jn 3:20.

[91] *Summa Theologiae,* II-II, q. 14, a. 3, ad 1.

[92] Cf. Phil 2:12.

17.8 In the light of these and other passages of Sacred Scripture, Doctors and theologians, spiritual teachers and pastors have divided sins into *mortal* and *venial.* Saint Augustine, among others, speaks of *letalia* or *mortifera crimina,* contrasting them with *venialia, levia* or *quotidiana.*[93] The meaning which he gives to these adjectives was to influence the successive Magisterium of the Church. After him, it was Saint Thomas who was to formulate in the clearest possible terms the doctrine which became constant in the Church.

17.9 In defining and distinguishing between *mortal* and *venial* sins, Saint Thomas and the theology of sin that has its source in him could not be unaware of the biblical reference and therefore of the concept of spiritual death. According to Saint Thomas, in order to live spiritually man must remain in communion with the supreme principle of life, which is God, since God is the ultimate end of man's being and acting. Now sin is a disorder perpetrated by man against this life-principle. And when "through sin, the soul commits a disorder that reaches the point of turning away from its ultimate end — God — to which it is bound by charity, then the sin is mortal; on the other hand, whenever the disorder does not reach the point of a turning away from God, the sin is venial."[94] For this reason venial sin does not deprive the sinner of sanctifying grace, friendship with God, charity, and therefore eternal happiness, whereas just such a deprivation is precisely the consequence of mortal sin.

17.10 Furthermore, when sin is considered *from the point of view of the punishment* it merits, for Saint Thomas and other Doctors *mortal* sin is the sin which, if unforgiven, leads to eternal punishment; whereas *venial* sin is the sin that merits merely temporal punishment (that is, a partial punishment which can be expiated on earth or in purgatory).

17.11 Considering sin from the point of view of its *matter,* the ideas of death, of radical rupture with God, the Supreme Good, of deviation from the path that leads to God or interruption of the journey toward him (which are all ways of defining mortal sin) are linked with the idea of the gravity of sin's objective content. Hence, in the Church's doctrine and pastoral action, *grave* sin is in practice identified with *mortal* sin.

17.12 Here we have the core of the Church's traditional teaching, which was reiterated frequently and vigorously during the recent Synod. The Synod in fact not only reaffirmed the teaching of the Council of Trent concerning the

---

[93] Cf. *De Spiritu et Littera,* 28: CSEL 60, 202-203; *Enarratio in Psalmum 39,* 22: CCL 38, 441; *Enchiridion ad Laurentium de Fide et Spe et Caritate,* XIX, 71: CCL 46, 88; *In Ioannis Evangelium Tractatus,* 12, 3, 14: CCL 36, 129.

[94] Saint Thomas Aquinas, *Summa Theologiae,* I-II, q. 72, a. 5.

existence and nature of *mortal* and *venial* sins,[95] but it also recalled that *mortal* sin is sin whose object is grave matter and which is also committed with full knowledge and deliberate consent. It must be added — as was likewise done at the Synod — that some sins are *intrinsically* grave and mortal by reason of their matter. That is, there exist acts which, *per se* and in themselves, independently of circumstances, are always seriously wrong by reason of their object. These acts, if carried out with sufficient awareness and freedom, are always gravely sinful.[96]

17.13 This doctrine, based on the Decalogue and on the preaching of the Old Testament, and assimilated into the *kerygma* of the Apostles and belonging to the earliest teaching of the Church, and constantly reaffirmed by her to this day, is exactly verified in the experience of the men and women of all times. Man knows well by experience that, along the road of faith and justice which leads to the knowledge and love of God in this life and toward perfect union with him in eternity, he can cease to go forward or can go astray, without abandoning the way of God; and in this case there occurs *venial sin.* This, however, must never be underestimated, as though it were automatically something that can be ignored, or regarded as "a sin of little importance."

17.14 For man also knows, through painful experience, that by a conscious and free act of his will he can change course and go in a direction opposed to God's will, separating himself from God *(aversio a Deo)*, rejecting loving communion with him, detaching himself from the life-principle which God is, and consequently choosing *death.*

17.15 With the whole Tradition of the Church, we call *mortal sin* the act by which man freely and consciously rejects God, his law, the Covenant of love that God offers, preferring to turn in on himself or to some created and finite reality, something contrary to the divine will *(conversio ad creaturam).* This can occur in a direct and formal way in the sins of idolatry, apostasy and atheism; or in an equivalent way, as in every act of disobedience to God's commandments in a grave matter. Man perceives that this disobedience to God destroys the bond that unites him with his life-principle: it is a *mortal sin,* that is, an act which gravely offends God and ends in turning against man himself with a dark and powerful force of destruction.

[95] Cf. Ecumenical Council of Trent, Session VI, Decree on Justification *Cum Hoc Tempore,* Chapter 2 and Canons 23, 25, 27: *Conciliorum Oecumenicorum Decreta,* Ed. Istituto per le Scienze Religiose, 3rd ed., Bologna, 1973, 671 and 680-681 (*DS* 1522, and 1573, 1575, 1577).

[96] Cf. Ecumenical Council of Trent, Session VI, Decree on Justification *Cum Hoc Tempore,* Chapter 15: *Conciliorum Oecumenicorum Decreta,* Ed. Istituto per le Scienze Religiose, 3rd ed., Bologna, 1973, 677 (*DS* 1544).

17.16 During the Synod Assembly some Fathers proposed a threefold distinction of sins, classifying them as *venial, grave* and *mortal.* This threefold distinction might illustrate the fact that there is a scale of seriousness among grave sins. But it still remains true that the essential and decisive distinction is between sin which destroys charity, and sin which does not kill the supernatural life: there is no middle way between life and death.

17.17 Likewise, care will have to be taken not to reduce mortal sin to an act of *"fundamental option"* — as is commonly said today — against God, intending thereby an explicit and formal contempt for God or neighbor. For mortal sin exists also when a person knowingly and willingly, for whatever reason, chooses something gravely disordered. In fact, such a choice already includes contempt for the divine law, a rejection of God's love for humanity and the whole of creation: the person turns away from God and loses charity. Thus the fundamental orientation can be radically changed by individual acts. Clearly there can occur situations which are very complex and obscure from a psychological viewpoint, and which have an influence on the sinner's subjective culpability. But from a consideration of the psychological sphere one cannot proceed to the construction of a theological category, which is what the "fundamental option" precisely is, understanding it in such a way that it objectively changes or casts doubt upon the traditional concept of mortal sin.

17.18 While every sincere and prudent attempt to clarify the psychological and theological mystery of sin is to be valued, the Church nevertheless has a duty to remind all scholars in this field of the need to be faithful to the word of God that teaches us also about sin. She likewise has to remind them of the risk of contributing to a further weakening of the sense of sin in the modern world.

The loss of the sense of sin

18.1 Over the course of generations, the Christian mind has gained from the Gospel as it is read in the ecclesial community a fine sensitivity and an acute perception of the *seeds of death* contained in sin, as well as a sensitivity and an acuteness of perception for identifying them in the thousand guises under which sin shows itself. This is what is commonly called the *sense of sin.*

18.2 This sense is rooted in man's moral conscience and is as it were its thermometer. It is linked to the *sense of God,* since it derives from man's conscious relationship with God as his Creator, Lord and Father. Hence, just as it is impossible to eradicate completely the sense of God or to silence the conscience completely, so the sense of sin is never completely eliminated.

18.3 Nevertheless, it happens not infrequently in history, for more or less lengthy periods and under the influence of many different factors, that the moral conscience of many people becomes seriously clouded. "Have we the right idea of conscience?" — I asked two years ago in an address to the faithful — "Is it not true that modern man is threatened by an eclipse of conscience? By a deformation of conscience? By a numbness or 'deadening' of conscience?"[97] Too many signs indicate that such an eclipse exists in our time. This is all the more disturbing in that conscience, defined by the Council as "the most secret core and sanctuary of a man,"[98] is "strictly related to human *freedom*. . . . For this reason conscience, to a great extent, constitutes the basis of man's interior dignity and, at the same time, of his relationship to God."[99] It is inevitable therefore that in this situation there is an obscuring also of the *sense of sin,* which is closely connected with the moral conscience, the search for truth and the desire to make a responsible use of freedom. When the conscience is weakened the *sense of God* is also obscured, and as a result, with the loss of this decisive inner point of reference, the sense of sin is lost. This explains why my Predecessor Pius XII one day declared, in words that have almost become proverbial, that "the sin of the century is the loss of the sense of sin."[100]

18.4 Why has this happened in our time? A glance at certain aspects of contemporary culture can help us to understand the progressive weakening of the sense of sin, precisely because of the crisis of conscience and crisis of the sense of God already mentioned.

18.5 "Secularism" is by nature and definition a movement of ideas and behavior which advocates a humanism totally without God, completely centered upon the cult of action and production and caught up in the heady enthusiasm of consumerism and pleasure-seeking, unconcerned with the danger of "losing one's soul." This secularism cannot but undermine the sense of sin. At the very most, sin will be reduced to what offends man. But it is precisely here that we are faced with the bitter experience which I already alluded to in my first Encyclical, namely, that man can build a world without God, but this world will end by turning against him.[101] In fact, God is the origin and the supreme end of man, and man carries in himself a divine seed.[102]

---

[97] Angelus (March 14, 1982), 3: *Insegnamenti* V/1 (1982), 861.

[98] Pastoral Constitution on the Church in the Modern World *Gaudium et Spes,* 16.

[99] John Paul II, Angelus (March 14, 1982), 1: *Insegnamenti* V/1 (1982), 860.

[100] Radio Message to the National Catechetical Congress of the United States of America in Boston (October 26, 1946): *Discorsi e Radiomessaggi* VIII (1946), 288.

[101] Cf. Encyclical Letter *Redemptor Hominis* (March 4, 1979), 15: *AAS* 71 (1979), 286-289.

[102] Cf. Second Vatican Ecumenical Council, Pastoral Constitution on the Church in the Modern World *Gaudium et Spes,* 3; cf. 1 Jn 3:9.

Hence it is the reality of God that reveals and illustrates the mystery of man. It is therefore vain to hope that there will take root a sense of sin against man and against human values, if there is no sense of offense against God, namely the true sense of sin.

18.6 Another reason for the disappearance of the sense of sin in contemporary society is to be found in the errors made in evaluating certain findings of the human sciences. Thus on the basis of certain affirmations of psychology, concern to avoid creating feelings of guilt or to place limits on freedom leads to a refusal ever to admit any shortcoming. Through an undue extrapolation of the criteria of the science of sociology, it finally happens — as I have already said — that all failings are blamed upon society, and the individual is declared innocent of them. Again, a certain cultural anthropology so emphasizes the undeniable environmental and historical conditioning and influences which act upon man that it reduces his responsibility to the point of not acknowledging his ability to perform truly human acts and therefore his ability to sin.

18.7 The sense of sin also easily declines as a result of a system of ethics deriving from a certain historical relativism. This may take the form of an ethical system which relativizes the moral norm, denying its absolute and unconditional value, and as a consequence denying that there can be intrinsically illicit acts independent of the circumstances in which they are performed by the subject. Herein lies a real "overthrowing and downfall of moral values," and "the problem is not so much one of ignorance of Christian ethics," but ignorance "rather of the meaning, foundations and criteria of the moral attitude."[103] Another effect of this ethical turning upside down is always such an attenuation of the notion of sin as almost to reach the point of saying that sin does exist but no one knows who commits it.

18.8 Finally the sense of sin disappears, when — as can happen in the education of youth, in the mass media and even in education within the family — it is wrongly identified with a morbid feeling of guilt, or with the mere transgression of legal norms and precepts.

18.9 The loss of the sense of sin is thus a form or consequence of the *denial of God:* not only in the form of atheism but also in the form of secularism. If sin is the breaking off of one's filial relationship to God in order to situate one's life outside of obedience to him, then to sin is not merely to deny God. To sin is also to live as if he did not exist, to eliminate him from one's daily life. A model of society which is mutilated or distorted in one sense or

---

[103] John Paul II, Address to the Bishops of the Eastern Region of France on Their *ad Limina* Visit (April 1, 1982), 2: *Insegnamenti* V/1 (1982), 1081.

another, as is often encouraged by the mass media, greatly favors the gradual loss of the sense of sin. In such a situation the obscuring or weakening of the sense of sin comes from several sources: from a rejection of any reference to the transcendent in the name of the individual's aspiration to personal independence; from acceptance of ethical models imposed by general consensus and behavior, even when condemned by the individual conscience; from the tragic social and economic conditions that oppress a great part of humanity, causing a tendency to see errors and faults only in the context of society; finally and especially, from the obscuring of the notion of God's fatherhood and dominion over man's life.

18.10 Even in the field of the thought and life of the Church certain trends inevitably favor the decline of the sense of sin. For example, some are inclined to replace exaggerated attitudes of the past with other exaggerations: from seeing sin everywhere they pass to not recognizing it anywhere; from too much emphasis on the fear of eternal punishment they pass to preaching a love of God that excludes any punishment deserved by sin; from severity in trying to correct erroneous consciences they pass to a kind of respect for conscience which excludes the duty of telling the truth. And should it not be added that the *confusion* caused in the consciences of many of the faithful by differences of opinions and teachings in theology, preaching, catechesis and spiritual direction *on serious and delicate questions of Christian morals* ends by diminishing the true sense of sin almost to the point of eliminating it altogether? Nor can certain deficiencies in the practice of sacramental Penance be overlooked. These include the tendency to obscure the ecclesial significance of sin and of conversion and to reduce them to merely personal matters; or vice versa, the tendency to nullify the personal value of good and evil and to consider only their community dimension. There also exists the danger, never totally eliminated, of routine ritualism that deprives the sacrament of its full significance and formative effectiveness.

18.11 The restoration of a *proper sense of sin* is the first way of facing the grave spiritual crisis looming over man today. But the sense of sin can only be restored through a *clear reminder of the unchangeable principles of reason and faith* which the moral teaching of the Church has always upheld.

18.12 There are good grounds for hoping that a healthy sense of sin will once again flourish, especially in the Christian world and in the Church. This will be aided by sound catechetics, illuminated by the biblical theology of the Covenant, by an attentive listening and trustful openness to the Magisterium of the Church, which never ceases to enlighten consciences, and by an ever more careful practice of the Sacrament of Penance.

2. "*Mysterium Pietatis*"

19.1 In order to understand sin we have had to direct our attention to its nature as made known to us by the revelation of the economy of salvation: this is the *mysterium iniquitatis*. But in this economy sin is not the main principle, still less the victor. Sin fights against another active principle which — to use a beautiful and evocative expression of Saint Paul — we can call the *mysterium* or *sacramentum pietatis*. Man's sin would be the winner and in the end destructive, God's salvific plan would remain incomplete or even totally defeated, if this *mysterium pietatis* were not made part of the dynamism of history in order to conquer man's sin.

19.2 We find this expression in one of Saint Paul's *Pastoral Letters*, the *First Letter to Timothy*. It appears unexpectedly, as if by an exuberant inspiration. The Apostle had previously devoted long paragraphs of his message to his beloved disciple to an explanation of the meaning of the ordering of the community (the liturgical order and the related hierarchical one). Next he had spoken of the role of the heads of the community, before turning to the conduct of Timothy himself in "the Church of the living God, the pillar and bulwark of the truth." Then at the end of the passage, suddenly but with a profound purpose he evokes the element which gives meaning to everything that he has written: *"Great indeed, we confess, is the mystery of our religion."*[104]

19.3 Without in the least betraying the literal sense of the text, we can broaden this magnificent theological insight of Saint Paul into a more complete vision of the role which the truth proclaimed by him plays in the economy of salvation: "Great indeed," we repeat with him, "is the mystery of our religion," because it conquers sin.

19.4 But what is the meaning of this expression, in Paul's mind?

It is Christ himself

20.1 It is profoundly significant that when Paul presents this *mysterium pietatis* he simply transcribes, without making a grammatical link with what he has just written,[105] three lines of a *Christological hymn* which — in the opinion of authoritative scholars — was used in the Greek-speaking Christian communities.

---

[104] 1 Tim 3:15-16.

[105] The text presents a certain difficulty, since the relative pronoun which opens the literal translation does not agree with the neuter *mysterion*. Some later manuscripts have adjusted the text in order to correct the grammar. But it was Paul's intention merely to put next to what he had written a venerable text which for him was fully explanatory.

20.2 In the words of that hymn, full of theological content and rich in noble beauty, those first-century believers professed their faith in the mystery of Christ, whereby:

— he was made manifest in the reality of human flesh and was constituted by the Holy Spirit as the Just One who offers himself for the unjust;

— he appeared to the angels, having been made greater than them, and he was preached to the nations, as the bearer of salvation;

— he was believed in, in the world, as the one sent by the Father, and by the same Father assumed into heaven, as Lord.[106]

20.3 The mystery or sacrament of *pietas,* therefore, is the very mystery of Christ. It is, in a striking summary, the mystery of the Incarnation and Redemption, of the full Passover of Jesus, the Son of God and Son of Mary: the mystery of his Passion and Death, of his Resurrection and glorification. What Saint Paul in quoting the phrases of the hymn wished to emphasize was that *this mystery is the hidden vital principle* which makes the Church the house of God, the pillar and bulwark of the truth. Following the Pauline teaching, we can affirm that this same *mystery of God's infinite loving kindness toward us* is capable of penetrating to the hidden roots of our iniquity, in order to evoke in the soul a movement of conversion, in order to redeem it and set it on course toward reconciliation.

20.4 Saint John too, undoubtedly referring to this mystery, but in his own characteristic language which differs from Saint Paul's, was able to write that "anyone born of God does not sin, but he who was born of God keeps him, and the evil one does not touch him."[107] In this Johannine affirmation there is an indication of hope, based on the divine promises: the Christian has received the guarantee and the necessary strength not to sin. It is not a question therefore of a sinlessness acquired through one's own virtue or even inherent in man, as the Gnostics thought. It is a result of God's action. In order not to sin the Christian has knowledge of God, as Saint John reminds us in this same passage. But a little before he had written: "No one born of God commits sin; for God's seed abides in him."[108] If by "God's seed" we understand, as some commentators suggest, Jesus the Son of God, then we can say that in order not to sin, or in order to gain freedom from sin, the Christian has within

---

[106] The early Christian community expresses its faith in the crucified and glorified Christ, whom the angels adore and who is the Lord. But the striking element of this message remains the phrase "manifested in the flesh": that the eternal Son of God became man is the "great mystery."

[107] 1 Jn 5:18-19.

[108] 1 Jn 3:9.

himself the presence of Christ and the mystery of Christ, which is the mystery of God's loving kindness.

The effort of the Christian

21.1 But there is another aspect to the *mysterium pietatis:* the *loving kindness of God* toward the Christian must be matched by the *piety of the Christian* toward God. In this second meaning of the word, piety *(eusébeia)* means precisely the conduct of the Christian who responds to God's fatherly loving kindness with his own filial piety.

21.2 In this sense too we can say with Saint Paul that "great indeed is the mystery of our religion." In this sense too *piety,* as a force for conversion and reconciliation, confronts iniquity and sin. In this case too the essential aspects of the mystery of Christ are the object of *piety* in the sense that the Christian accepts the mystery, contemplates it and draws from it the spiritual strength necessary for living according to the Gospel. Here too one must say that "no one born of God commits sin"; but the expression has an imperative sense: sustained by the mystery of Christ as by an interior source of spiritual energy, the Christian, being a child of God, is warned not to sin, and indeed receives the commandment not to sin but to live in a manner worthy of "the house of God, that is the Church of the living God."[109]

Toward a reconciled life

22.1 Thus the word of Scripture, as it reveals to us the *mystery of pietas,* opens the intellect to conversion and reconciliation, understood not as lofty abstractions but as concrete Christian values to be achieved in our daily lives.

22.2 Deceived by the loss of the sense of sin and at times tempted by an illusion of sinlessness which is not at all Christian, the people of today too need to listen again to Saint John's admonition, as addressed to each one of them personally: "If we say we have no sin, we deceive ourselves, and the truth is not in us,"[110] and indeed "the whole world is in the power of the evil one."[111] Every individual therefore is invited by the voice of divine truth to examine realistically his or her conscience, and to confess that he or she has been brought forth in iniquity, as we say in the *Miserere* Psalm.[112]

22.3 Nevertheless, though threatened by fear and despair, the people of

---

[109] 1 Tim 3:15.
[110] 1 Jn 1:8.
[111] 1 Jn 5:19.
[112] Cf. Ps 51:5.

today can feel uplifted by the divine promise which opens to them the hope of full reconciliation.

22.4 The mystery of *pietas,* on God's part, is that mercy in which our Lord and Father — I repeat it again — is infinitely rich.[113] As I said in my Encyclical on the subject of divine mercy,[114] it is *a love more powerful than sin, stronger than death.* When we realize that God's love for us does not cease in the face of our sin or recoil before our offenses, but becomes even more attentive and generous; when we realize that this love went so far as to cause the Passion and Death of the Word made flesh who consented to redeem us at the price of his own blood, then we exclaim in gratitude: "Yes, the Lord is rich in mercy," and even: "The Lord *is* mercy."

22.5 The mystery of *pietas* is the path opened by divine mercy to a reconciled life.

III

The Pastoral Ministry
of Penance and Reconciliation

Promoting penance and reconciliation

23.1 To evoke conversion and penance in man's heart and to offer him the gift of reconciliation is the specific mission of the Church as she continues the redemptive work of her divine Founder. It is not a mission which consists merely of a few theoretical statements and the putting forward of an ethical ideal unaccompanied by the energy with which to carry it out. Rather it seeks to express itself in precise ministerial functions, directed toward a concrete practice of penance and reconciliation.

23.2 We can call this ministry, which is founded on and illumined by the principles of faith which we have explained, and which is directed toward precise objectives and sustained by adequate means, *the pastoral activity of penance and reconciliation.* Its point of departure is the Church's conviction that man, to whom every form of pastoral activity is directed but principally that of penance and reconciliation, is the man marked by sin whose striking image is to be found in King David. Rebuked by the Prophet Nathan, David faces squarely his own iniquity and confesses: "I have sinned against the

---

[113] Cf. Eph 2:4.

[114] Cf. Encyclical Letter *Dives in Misericordia* (November 30, 1980), 8, 15: *AAS* 72 (1980), 1203-1207, 1231.

Lord,"[115] and proclaims: "I know my transgressions, and my sin is ever before me."[116] But he also prays: "Purge me with hyssop, and I shall be clean; wash me, and I shall be whiter than snow,"[117] and he receives the response of the divine mercy: "The Lord has put away your sin; you shall not die."[118]

23.3 The Church thus finds herself face to face with man — with the whole human world — wounded by sin and affected by sin in the innermost depths of his being. But at the same time he is moved by an unrestrainable desire to be freed from sin and, especially if he is a Christian, he is aware that the *mystery of pietas*, Christ the Lord, is already acting in him and in the world by the power of the Redemption.

23.4 The Church's reconciling role must therefore be carried out in accordance with that intimate link which closely connects the forgiveness and remission of the sin of each person with the fundamental and full reconciliation of humanity which took place with the Redemption. This link helps us to understand that, since sin is the active principle of division — division between man and the nature created by God — only conversion from sin is capable of bringing about a profound and lasting reconciliation wherever division has penetrated.

23.5 I do not need to repeat what I have already said about the importance of this "ministry of reconciliation,"[119] and of the pastoral activity whereby it is carried out, in the Church's consciousness and life. This pastoral activity would be lacking an essential aspect of its being and failing in an indispensable function if the "message of reconciliation"[120] were not proclaimed with clarity and tenacity in season and out of season, and if the gift of reconciliation were not offered to the world. But it is worth repeating that the importance of the ecclesial service of reconciliation extends beyond the confines of the Church to the whole world.

23.6 To speak of *the pastoral activity of penance and reconciliation*, then, is to refer to all the tasks incumbent on the Church, at all levels, for their promotion. More concretely, to speak of this pastoral activity is to evoke all the activities whereby the Church, through each and every one of her members — Pastors and faithful, at all levels and in all spheres, and with all the means at her disposal, words and actions, teaching and prayer — leads people indi-

---

[115] 2 Sam 12:13.
[116] Ps 51:3.
[117] Ps 51:7.
[118] 2 Sam 12:13.
[119] Cf. 2 Cor 5:18.
[120] Cf. 2 Cor 5:19.

vidually or as groups to true penance and thus sets them on the path to full reconciliation.

23.7 The Fathers of the Synod, as representatives of their brother Bishops and as leaders of the people entrusted to them, concerned themselves with the most practical and concrete elements of this pastoral activity. And I am happy to echo their concerns by associating myself with their anxieties and hopes, by receiving the results of their research and experiences, and by encouraging them in their plans and achievements. May they find in this part of the present Apostolic Exhortation the contribution which they themselves made to the Synod, a contribution the usefulness of which I wish to extend, through these pages, to the whole Church.

23.8 I therefore propose to call attention to the essentials of *the pastoral activity of penance and reconciliation* by emphasizing, with the Synod Assembly, the following two points:

1. The means used and the paths followed by the Church in order to promote penance and reconciliation.

2. The Sacrament *par excellence* of Penance and Reconciliation.

1. The Promotion of Penance and Reconciliation: Ways and Means

24 In order to promote penance and reconciliation, the Church has at her disposal two principal means which were entrusted to her by her Founder himself: catechesis and the sacraments. Their use has always been considered by the Church as fully in harmony with the requirements of her salvific mission and at the same time as corresponding to the requirements and spiritual needs of people in all ages. This use can be in forms and ways both old and new, among which it will be a good idea to remember in particular what we can call, in the expression of my Predecessor Paul VI, *the method of dialogue.*

Dialogue

25.1 For the Church, dialogue is in a certain sense a means and especially a way of carrying out her activity in the modern world.

25.2 The Second Vatican Council proclaims that "the Church, by virtue of her mission to shed on the whole world the radiance of the Gospel message, and to unify under one Spirit all people . . . stands forth as a sign of that fraternal solidarity which allows honest dialogue and invigorates it." The Council adds that the Church should be capable of "establishing an ever more fruitful dialogue among all those who compose the one People of God,"[121] and also of "establishing a dialogue with human society."[122]

25.3 My Predecessor Paul VI devoted to dialogue a considerable part of his first Encyclical *Ecclesiam Suam,* in which he describes it and significantly characterizes it as the *dialogue of salvation.*[123]

25.4 The Church in fact uses the method of dialogue in order the better to lead people — both those who through Baptism and the profession of faith acknowledge their membership of the Christian community and also those who are outside — to conversion and repentance, along the path of a profound renewal of their own consciences and lives, in the light of the mystery of the Redemption and salvation accomplished by Christ and entrusted to the ministry of his Church. Authentic dialogue, therefore, is aimed above all at the rebirth of individuals, through interior conversion and repentance, but always with profound respect for consciences and with patience and at the step-by-step pace indispensable for modern conditions.

25.5 Pastoral dialogue aimed at reconciliation continues to be today a fundamental task of the Church in different spheres and at different levels.

25.6 The Church in the first place promotes an *ecumenical dialogue,* that is, with Churches and Ecclesial Communities which profess faith in Christ, the Son of God and only Savior. She also promotes dialogue with the other communities of people who are seeking God and wish to have a relationship of communion with him.

25.7 At the basis of this dialogue with the other Churches and Christian Communities and with the other religions, and as a condition of her credibility and effectiveness, there must be a sincere effort of permanent and renewed dialogue within the Catholic Church herself. She is aware that, by her nature, she is the *sacrament of the universal communion of charity*[124]; but she is equally aware of the tensions within her, tensions which risk becoming factors of division.

25.8 The heartfelt and determined invitation which was already extended by my Predecessor in preparation for the 1975 Holy Year[125] is also valid at the

---

[121] Pastoral Constitution on the Church in the Modern World *Gaudium et Spes,* 92.

[122] Decree on the Bishops' Pastoral Office in the Church *Christus Dominus,* 13; cf. Declaration on Christian Education *Gravissimum Educationis,* 8; Decree on the Church's Missionary Activity *Ad Gentes,* 11-12.

[123] Cf. Encyclical Letter *Ecclesiam Suam* (August 6, 1964), III: *AAS* 56 (1964), 639-659.

[124] Second Vatican Ecumenical Council, Dogmatic Constitution on the Church *Lumen Gentium,* 1, 9, 13.

[125] Paul VI, Apostolic Exhortation *Paterna Cum Benevolentia* (December 8, 1974): *AAS* 67 (1975), 5-23.

present moment. In order to overcome conflicts and to ensure that normal tensions do not prove harmful to the unity of the Church, we must all apply to ourselves the word of God; we must relinquish our own subjective views and seek the truth where it is to be found, namely in the divine word itself and in the authentic interpretation of that word provided by the Magisterium of the Church. In this light, listening to one another, respect, refraining from all hasty judgments, patience, the ability to avoid subordinating the faith which unites to the opinions, fashions and ideological choices which divide — these are all qualities of a dialogue within the Church which must be persevering, open and sincere. Obviously dialogue would not have these qualities and would not become a factor of reconciliation if the Magisterium were not heeded and accepted.

25.9 Thus actively engaged in seeking her own internal communion, the Catholic Church can address an appeal for reconciliation to the other Churches with which there does not exist full communion, as well as to the other religions and even to all those who are seeking God with a sincere heart. This she has been doing for some time.

25.10 In the light of the Council and of the Magisterium of my Predecessors, whose precious inheritance I have received and am making every effort to preserve and put into effect, I can affirm that the Catholic Church at every level is committed to frank ecumenical dialogue, without facile optimism but also without distrust and without hesitation or delays. The fundamental laws which she seeks to follow in this dialogue are, on the one hand, the conviction that only a spiritual ecumenism — namely an ecumenism founded on common prayer and in a common docility to the one Lord — enables us to make a sincere and serious response to the other exigencies of ecumenical action.[126] The other law is the conviction that a certain facile irenicism in doctrinal and especially dogmatic matters could perhaps lead to a form of superficial and short-lived coexistence, but it could not lead to that profound and stable communion which we all long for. This communion will be reached at the hour willed by divine Providence. But in order to reach it, the Catholic Church, for her part, knows that she must be open and sensitive to all "the truly Christian endowments from our common heritage which are to be found among our separated brethren"[127]; but she also knows that she must likewise base a frank and constructive dialogue upon a clarity regarding her own positions, and upon fidelity and consistency with the faith trans-

---

[126] Cf. Second Vatican Ecumenical Council, Decree on Ecumenism *Unitatis Redintegratio,* 7-8.

[127] Ibid., 4.

mitted and defined in accordance with the perennial tradition of her Magisterium. Notwithstanding the threat of a certain defeatism, and despite the inevitable slowness which rashness could never correct, the Catholic Church continues with all other Christian brethren to seek the paths to unity, and with the followers of the other religions she continues to seek to have sincere dialogue. May this interreligious dialogue lead to the overcoming of all attitudes of hostility, distrust, mutual condemnation and even mutual invective, which is the precondition for encounter at least in faith in one God and in the certainty of eternal life for the immortal soul. May the Lord especially grant that ecumenical dialogue will also lead to a sincere reconciliation concerning everything that we already have in common with the other Christian Churches: faith in Jesus Christ, the Son of God made man, our Savior and Lord; a listening to the word; the study of revelation and the Sacrament of Baptism.

25.11 To the extent to which the Church is capable of generating active harmony — unity in variety — within herself, and of offering herself as a witness to and humble servant of reconciliation with the other Churches and Ecclesial Communities and the other religions, she becomes, in the expressive definition of Saint Augustine, a *"reconciled world."*[128] Then she will be able to be a sign of reconciliation in the world and for the world.

25.12 The Church is aware of the extreme seriousness of the situation created by the forces of division and war, which today constitute a grave threat not only to the balance and harmony of nations but to the very survival of humanity, and she feels it her duty to offer and suggest her own unique collaboration for the overcoming of conflicts and the restoration of concord.

25.13 It is a complex and delicate dialogue of reconciliation in which the Church is engaged, especially through the work of the *Holy See* and its different *organisms.* The Holy See already endeavors to intervene with the leaders of nations and the heads of the various international bodies, or seeks to associate itself with them, conduct a dialogue with them and encourage them to dialogue with one another, for the sake of reconciliation in the midst of the many conflicts. It does this not for ulterior motives or hidden interests — since it has none — but "out of a humanitarian concern,"[129] placing its institutional structure and moral authority, which are altogether unique, at the service of concord and peace. It does this in the conviction that as "in war two parties rise against one another" so "in the question of peace there are also

---

[128] *Sermo* 96, 7: *PL* 38, 588.

[129] John Paul II, Address to Members of the Diplomatic Corps Accredited to the Holy See (January 15, 1983), 4, 6, 11: *AAS* 75 (1983), 376, 378-379, 381.

necessarily two parties which must know how to commit themselves," and in this "one finds the true meaning of a dialogue for peace."[130]

25.14 The Church engages in dialogue for reconciliation also through the Bishops in the competency and responsibility proper to them, either individually in the direction of their respective local Churches or united in their Episcopal Conferences, with the collaboration of the priests and of all those who make up the Christian communities. They truly fulfill their task when they promote this indispensable dialogue and proclaim the human and Christian need for reconciliation and peace. In communion with their Pastors, the laity, who have as "their own field of evangelizing activity . . . the vast and complicated world of politics, society . . . economics . . . (and) international life,"[131] are called upon to engage directly in dialogue or to work for dialogue aimed at reconciliation. Through them too the Church carries out her reconciling activity. Thus the fundamental presupposition and secure basis for any lasting renewal of society and for peace between nations lies in the regeneration of hearts through conversion and penance.

25.15 It should be repeated that, on the part of the Church and her members, dialogue, whatever form it takes (and these forms can be and are very diverse, since the very concept of dialogue has an analogical value), can never begin from an attitude of indifference to the truth. On the contrary, it must begin from a presentation of the truth, offered in a calm way, with respect for the intelligence and consciences of others. The dialogue of reconciliation can never replace or attenuate the proclamation of the truth of the Gospel, the precise goal of which is conversion from sin and communion with Christ and the Church. It must be at the service of the transmission and realization of that truth through the means left by Christ to the Church for the pastoral activity of reconciliation, namely catechesis and penance.

Catechesis

26.1 In the vast area in which the Church has the mission of operating through dialogue, *the pastoral ministry of penance and reconciliation* is directed to the members of the body of the Church principally through an adequate *catechesis* concerning the two distinct and complementary realities to which the Synod Fathers gave a particular importance and which they emphasized in some of the concluding *Propositiones:* these are pen-

---

[130] John Paul II, Homily at the Mass for the 16th World Day of Peace (January 1, 1983), 6: *Insegnamenti* VI/1 (1983), 7.

[131] Paul VI, Apostolic Exhortation *Evangelii Nuntiandi* (December 8, 1975), 70: *AAS* 68 (1976), 59-60.

ance and reconciliation. Catechesis is therefore the first means to be used.

26.2 At the basis of the Synod's very opportune recommendation is a fundamental presupposition: what is *pastoral* is not opposed to what is *doctrinal.* Nor can pastoral action prescind from doctrinal content, from which in fact it draws its substance and real validity. Now, if the Church is the "pillar and bulwark of the truth"[132] and is placed in the world as Mother and Teacher, how could she neglect the task of teaching the truth which constitutes a path of life?

26.3 From the pastors of the Church one expects, first of all, *catechesis on reconciliation.* This must be founded on the teaching of the Bible, especially the New Testament, on the need to rebuild the Covenant with God in Christ the Redeemer and Reconciler. And, in the light of this new communion and friendship, and as an extension of it, it must be founded on the teaching concerning the need to be reconciled with one's brethren, even if this means interrupting the offering of the sacrifice.[133] Jesus strongly insists on this theme of fraternal reconciliation: for example, when he invites us to turn the other cheek to the one who strikes us, and to give our cloak too to the one who has taken our coat,[134] or when he instills the law of forgiveness: forgiveness which each one receives in the measure that he or she forgives,[135] forgiveness to be offered even to enemies,[136] forgiveness to be granted seventy times seven times,[137] which means in practice without any limit. On these conditions, which are realizable only in a genuinely evangelical climate, it is possible to have a true reconciliation between individuals, families, communities, nations and peoples. From these biblical data on reconciliation there will naturally derive a *theological catechesis,* which in its synthesis will also integrate the elements of psychology, sociology and the other human sciences which can serve to clarify situations, describe problems accurately, and persuade listeners or readers to make concrete resolutions.

26.4 The pastors of the Church are also expected to provide *catechesis on penance.* Here too the richness of the biblical message must be its source. With regard to penance this message emphasizes particularly its value for *conversion,* which is the term that attempts to translate the word in the Greek text, *metánoia,*[138] which literally means to allow the spirit *to be overturned* in

---

[132] 1 Tim 3:15.
[133] Cf. Mt 5:23-24.
[134] Cf. Mt 5:38-40.
[135] Cf. Mt 6:12.
[136] Cf. Mt 5:43-48.
[137] Cf. Mt 18:21-22.
[138] Cf. Mk 1:4, 1:15; Mt 3:2, 4:17; Lk 3:8.

order to make it *turn toward* God. These are also the two fundamental elements which emerge from the parable of the son who was lost and found: his "coming to himself"[139] and his decision to return to his father. There can be no reconciliation unless these attitudes of conversion come first, and catechesis should explain them with concepts and terms adapted to people's various ages and their differing cultural, moral and social backgrounds.

26.5 This is a first value of penance and it extends into a second: penance also means *repentance.* The two meanings of *metánoia* appear in the significant instruction given by Jesus: "If your brother repents (= returns to you), forgive him; and if he sins against you seven times in the day, and turns to you seven times and says, 'I repent,' you must forgive him."[140] A good catechesis will show how repentance, just like conversion, is far from being a superficial feeling but a real overturning of the soul.

26.6 A third value is contained in penance, and this is the movement whereby the preceding attitudes of conversion and repentance are manifested externally: this is *doing penance.* This meaning is clearly perceptible in the term *metánoia,* as used by John the Baptist in the texts of the Synoptics.[141] *To do penance* means, above all, to reestablish the balance and harmony broken by sin, to change direction even at the cost of sacrifice.

26.7 A catechesis on penance, therefore, and one that is as complete and adequate as possible, is absolutely essential at a time like ours, when dominant attitudes in psychology and social behavior are in such contrast with the threefold value just illustrated. Contemporary man seems to find it harder than ever to recognize his own mistakes and to decide to retrace his steps and begin again after changing course. He seems very reluctant to say "I repent" or "I am sorry." He seems to refuse instinctively, and often irresistibly, anything that is penance in the sense of a sacrifice accepted and carried out for the correction of sin. In this regard I would like to emphasize that *the Church's penitential discipline,* even though it has been mitigated for some time, cannot be abandoned without grave harm both to the interior life of individual Christians and of the ecclesial community, and also to their capacity for missionary influence. It is not uncommon for non-Christians to be surprised at the negligible witness of true penance on the part of Christ's followers. It is clear, however, that Christian penance will only be authentic if it is inspired by love and not by mere fear; if it consists in a serious effort to crucify the "old man" so that the "new" can be born by the power of Christ; if it takes as its model

---

[139] Cf. Lk 15:17.
[140] Lk 17:3-4.
[141] Cf. Mt 3:2; Mk 1:2-6; Lk 3:1-6.

Christ, who though he was innocent chose the path of poverty, patience, austerity and, one can say, the penitential life.

26.8 As the Synod recalled, the pastors of the Church are also expected to provide *catechesis on conscience and its formation.* This too is a very relevant topic, in view of the fact that, in the upheavals to which our present culture is subjected, this interior sanctuary, man's innermost self, his conscience, is too often attacked, put to the test, confused and obscured. Valuable guidelines for a wise catechesis on conscience can be found both in the Doctors of the Church and in the theology of the Second Vatican Council, and especially in the documents on the Church in the modern world[142] and on religious liberty.[143] Along these same lines, Pope Paul VI often reminded us of the nature and role of conscience in our life.[144] I myself, following his footsteps, miss no opportunity to throw light on this most lofty element of man's greatness and dignity,[145] this "sort of *moral sense* which leads us to discern what is *good* and what is *evil* . . . like an inner eye, a visual capacity of the spirit, able to guide our steps along the path of good." And I have reiterated the need to form one's conscience, lest it become "a force which is destructive of the true humanity of the person, rather than that holy place where God reveals to him his true good."[146]

26.9 On other points too, of no less relevance for reconciliation, one looks to the pastors of the Church for catechesis.

26.10 On the *sense of sin,* which, as I have said, has become considerably weakened in our world.

26.11 On *temptation* and *temptations:* the Lord Jesus himself, the Son of God, "who in every respect has been tempted as we are, yet without sin,"[147] allowed himself to be tempted by the Evil One[148] in order to show that, like himself, his followers too would be subjected to temptation, and in order to

---

[142] Cf. Pastoral Constitution on the Church in the Modern World *Gaudium et Spes,* 8, 16, 19, 26, 41, 48.

[143] Cf. Declaration on Religious Freedom, *Dignitatis Humanae,* 2, 3, 4.

[144] Cf. among many others the Addresses at the General Audiences: (March 28, 1973): *Insegnamenti* XI (1973), 294-296; (August 8, 1973): *Insegnamenti* XI (1973), 772-775; (November 7, 1973): *Insegnamenti* XI (1973), 1054-1056; (March 13, 1974): *Insegnamenti* XII (1974), 230-232; (May 8, 1974): *Insegnamenti* XII (1974), 402-404; (February 12, 1975): *Insegnamenti* XIII (1975), 290-292; (July 13, 1977): *Insegnamenti* XV (1977), 710-712.

[145] Cf. Angelus (March 17, 1982): *Insegnamenti* V/1 (1982), 860-861.

[146] Cf. Address at the General Audience (August 17, 1983), 1-3: *Insegnamenti* VI/2 (1983), 256-257.

[147] Heb 4:15.

[148] Cf. Mt 4:1-11; Mk 1:12-13; Lk 4:1-13.

show how one should behave when subjected to temptation. For those who beseech the Father not to be tempted beyond their own strength[149] and not to succumb to temptation,[150] and for those who do not expose themselves to occasions of sin, being subjected to temptation does not mean that they have sinned; rather it is an opportunity for growing in fidelity and consistency through humility and watchfulness.

26.12 Catechesis is also expected on *fasting:* this can be practiced in old forms and new, as a sign of conversion, repentance and personal mortification and, at the same time, as a sign of union with Christ Crucified and of solidarity with the starving and suffering.

26.13 Catechesis on *almsgiving:* this is a means of making charity a practical thing, by sharing what one possesses with those suffering the consequences of poverty.

26.14 Catechesis on the *intimate connection* which links the overcoming of divisions in the world with perfect communion with God and among people, which is the eschatological purpose of the Church.

26.15 Catechesis on the *concrete circumstances* in which reconciliation has to be achieved (in the family, in the civil community, in social structures) and particularly catechesis on the *four reconciliations* which repair the four fundamental rifts: reconciliation of man with God, with self, with the brethren and with the whole of creation.

26.16 Nor can the Church omit, without serious mutilation of her essential message, a constant catechesis on what the traditional Christian language calls the four *last things of man:* death, judgment (universal and particular), hell and heaven. In a culture which tends to imprison man in the earthly life at which he is more or less successful, the pastors of the Church are asked to provide a catechesis which will reveal and illustrate with the certainties of faith what comes after the present life: beyond the mysterious gates of death, an eternity of joy in communion with God or the punishment of separation from him. Only in this eschatological vision can one realize the exact nature of sin and feel decisively moved to penance and reconciliation.

26.17 Pastors who are zealous and creative never lack opportunities for imparting this broad and varied catechesis, taking into account the different degrees of education and religious formation of those to whom they speak. Such opportunities are often given by the biblical readings and the rites of the Mass and the sacraments, as also by the circumstances of their celebration. For the same purpose many initiatives can be taken such as sermons, lec-

[149] Cf. 1 Cor 10:13.
[150] Cf. Mt 6:13; Lk 11:4.

tures, discussions, meetings, courses of religious education, etc., as happens in many places. Here I wish to point out in particular the importance and effectiveness of the old-style *popular missions* for the purposes of such catechesis. If adapted to the peculiar needs of the present time, such missions can be, today as yesterday, a useful instrument of religious education also regarding penance and reconciliation.

26.18 In view of the great relevance of reconciliation based on conversion in the delicate field of human relationships and social interaction at all levels, including the international level, catechesis cannot fail to inculcate the valuable contribution of *the Church's social teaching*. The timely and precise teaching of my Predecessors from Pope Leo XIII onward, to which was added the substantial contribution the Pastoral Constitution *Gaudium et Spes* of the Second Vatican Council and the contributions of the different Episcopates elicited by various circumstances in their respective countries, has made up an ample and solid body of doctrine. This regards the many different needs inherent in the life of the human community, in relationships between individuals, families, groups in their different spheres, and in the very constitution of a society that intends to follow the moral law, which is the foundation of civilization.

26.19 At the basis of this social teaching of the Church there is obviously to be found the vision which the Church draws from the word of God concerning the rights and duties of individuals, the family and the community; concerning the value of liberty and the nature of justice; concerning the primacy of charity; concerning the dignity of the human person and the exigencies of the common good, to which politics and the economy itself must be directed. Upon these fundamental principles of the social Magisterium, which confirm and repropose the universal dictates of reason and of the conscience of peoples, there rests in great part the hope for a peaceful solution to many social conflicts and, in short, the hope for universal reconciliation.

The sacraments

27.1 The second divinely instituted means which the Church offers for the pastoral activity of penance and reconciliation is constituted by the *sacraments.*

27.2 In the mysterious dynamism of the sacraments, so rich in symbolism and content, one can discern one aspect which is not always emphasized: each sacrament, over and above its own proper grace, is also a sign of penance and reconciliation. Therefore in each of them it is possible to relive these dimensions of the spirit.

27.3 Baptism is of course a salvific washing which, as Saint Peter says, is effective "not as a removal of dirt from the body but as an appeal to God for a clear conscience."[151] It is death, burial and resurrection with the dead, buried and risen Christ.[152] It is a gift of the Holy Spirit through Christ.[153] But this essential and original constituent of Christian Baptism, far from eliminating the penitential element already present in the Baptism which Jesus himself received from John "to fulfill all righteousness,"[154] in fact enriches it. In other words, it is a fact of conversion and of reintegration into the right order of relationships with God, of reconciliation with God, with the elimination of the original stain and the consequent introduction into the great family of the reconciled.

27.4 Confirmation likewise, as a ratification of Baptism and together with Baptism a sacrament of initiation, in conferring the fullness of the Holy Spirit and in bringing the Christian life to maturity, signifies and accomplishes thereby a greater conversion of the heart and brings about a more intimate and effective membership of the same assembly of the reconciled, which is the Church of Christ.

27.5 The definition which Saint Augustine gives of the Eucharist as *"sacramentum pietatis, signum unitatis, vinculum caritatis"*[155] clearly illustrates the effects of personal sanctification *(pietas)* and community reconciliation *(unitas* and *caritas)* which derive from the very essence of the Eucharistic mystery as an unbloody renewal of the Sacrifice of the Cross, the source of salvation and of reconciliation for all people.

27.6 However, it must be remembered that the Church, guided by faith in this great Sacrament, teaches that no Christian who is conscious of grave sin can receive the Eucharist before having obtained God's forgiveness. This we read in the Instruction *Eucharisticum Mysterium* which, duly approved by Paul VI, fully confirms the teaching of the Council of Trent: "The Eucharist is to be offered to the faithful also 'as a remedy, which frees us from daily faults and preserves us from mortal sin' and they are to be shown the fitting way of using the penitential parts of the liturgy of the Mass. The person who wishes to receive Holy Communion is to be reminded of the precept: 'Let a man examine himself' (1 Cor 11:28). And the Church's custom shows that such an examination is necessary, because no one who is conscious of being in mortal

---

[151] 1 Pet 3:21.
[152] Cf. Rom 6:3-4; Col 2:12.
[153] Cf. Mt 3:11; Lk 3:16; Jn 1:33; Acts 1:5, 11:16.
[154] Cf. Mt 3:15.
[155] *In Ioannis Evangelium Tractatus,* 26, 13: *CCL* 36, 266.

sin, however contrite he may believe himself to be, is to approach the Holy Eucharist without having first made a sacramental confession. If this person finds himself in need and has no means of going to confession, he should first make an act of perfect contrition."[156]

27.7 The Sacrament of Orders is intended to give to the Church the pastors who, besides being teachers and guides, are called to be witnesses and workers of unity, builders of the family of God, and defenders and preservers of the communion of this family against the sources of division and dispersion.

27.8 The Sacrament of Matrimony, the exaltation of human love under the action of grace, is a sign of the love of Christ for the Church. But it is also a sign of the victory which Christ grants to couples in resisting the forces which deform and destroy love, in order that the family born from this sacrament may be a sign also of the reconciled and reconciling Church for a world reconciled in all its structures and institutions.

27.9 Finally, the Anointing of the Sick, in the trial of illness and old age and especially at the Christian's final hour, is a sign of definitive conversion to the Lord and of total acceptance of suffering and death as a penance for sins. And in this is accomplished supreme reconciliation with the Father.

27.10 However, among the sacraments there is one which, though it has often been called the Sacrament of *Confession* because of the accusation of sins which takes place in it, can more appropriately be considered by antonomasia the *Sacrament of Penance,* as it is in fact called. And thus it is *the sacrament of conversion and reconciliation.* The recent Synod particularly concerned itself with this sacrament because of its importance with regard to reconciliation.

2. The Sacrament of Penance and Reconciliation

28.1 In all its phases and at all its levels, the Synod considered with the greatest attention that sacramental sign which represents and at the same time accomplishes penance and reconciliation. This sacrament in itself certainly does not contain all possible ideas of conversion and reconciliation. From the very beginning, in fact, the Church has recognized and used many and varying forms of penance. Some are liturgical or paraliturgical and include the penitential act in the Mass, services of atonement and pilgrimages; others are of an ascetical character, such as fasting. But of all such acts none is more significant, more divinely efficacious or more lofty and at the same time easily accessible as a rite than the Sacrament of Penance.

---

[156] Sacred Congregation of Rites, Instruction on the Worship of the Eucharistic Mystery *Eucharisticum Mysterium* (May 25, 1967), 35: *AAS* 59 (1967), 560-561.

28.2 From its preparatory stage, and then in the numerous interventions during the sessions, in the group meetings and in the final *Propositiones,* the Synod took into account the statement frequently made, with varying nuances and emphases, namely: *the Sacrament of Penance is in crisis.* The Synod took note of this crisis. It recommended a more profound catechesis, but it also recommended a no less profound analysis of a theological, historical, psychological, sociological and juridical character of penance in general and of the Sacrament of Penance in particular. In all of this the Synod's intention was to clarify the reasons for the crisis and to open the way to a positive solution, for the good of humanity. Meanwhile, from the Synod itself the Church has received a clear confirmation of its faith regarding the sacrament which gives to every Christian and to the whole community of believers the certainty of forgiveness through the power of the redeeming blood of Christ.

28.3 *It is good to renew and reaffirm this faith* at a moment when it might be weakening, losing something of its completeness or entering into an area of shadow and silence, threatened as it is by the negative elements of the above-mentioned crisis. For the Sacrament of Confession is indeed being undermined, on the one hand by the obscuring of the moral and religious conscience, the lessening of a sense of sin, the distortion of the concept of repentance, and the lack of effort to live an authentically Christian life. And on the other hand it is being undermined by the sometimes widespread idea that one can obtain forgiveness directly from God, even in a habitual way, without approaching the Sacrament of Reconciliation. A further negative influence is the routine of a sacramental practice sometimes lacking in fervor and real spontaneity, deriving perhaps from a mistaken and distorted idea of the effects of the sacrament.

28.4 It is therefore appropriate to recall the principal aspects of this *great sacrament.*

"Whose sins you shall forgive"

29.1 The Books of the Old and New Testament provide us with the first and fundamental fact concerning the Lord's mercy and forgiveness. In the Psalms and in the preaching of the Prophets, the name *merciful* is perhaps the one most often given to the Lord, in contrast to the persistent cliché whereby the God of the Old Testament is presented above all as severe and vengeful. Thus in the Psalms there is a long sapiential passage drawing from the Exodus tradition, which recalls God's kindly action in the midst of his people. This action, though represented in an anthropomorphic way, is perhaps one of the most eloquent Old Testament proclamations of the divine mercy. Suffice it to quote the verse: "Yet he, being compassionate, forgave their iniquity and did not destroy them; he restrained his anger often, and did not stir up all his wrath. He remembered that they were but flesh, a wind that passes and comes not again."[157]

29.2 In the fullness of time, the Son of God, coming as the Lamb who *takes away* and *bears upon himself* the sin of the world,[158] appears as the one who has the power both to judge[159] and to forgive sins,[160] and who has come not to condemn but to forgive and save.[161]

29.3 Now this power to "forgive sins" Jesus confers, through the Holy Spirit, upon ordinary men, themselves subject to the snare of sin, namely his Apostles: "Receive the Holy Spirit. Whose sins you shall forgive, they are forgiven; whose sins you shall retain, they are retained."[162] This is one of the most awe-inspiring innovations of the Gospel! He confers this power on the Apostles also as something which they can transmit — as the Church has understood it from the beginning — to their successors, charged by the same Apostles with the mission and responsibility of continuing their work as proclaimers of the Gospel and ministers of Christ's redemptive work.

29.4 Here there is seen in all its grandeur the figure of the minister of the Sacrament of Penance, who by very ancient custom is called the confessor.

29.5 Just as at the altar where he celebrates the Eucharist and just as in each one of the sacraments, so the priest, as the minister of Penance, acts *"in persona Christi."* The Christ whom he makes present and who accomplishes the mystery of the forgiveness of sins is the Christ who appears as the *brother of man*,[163] the merciful High Priest, faithful and compassionate,[164] the Shepherd intent on finding the lost sheep,[165] the Physician who heals and com-

---

[157] Ps 78:38-39.

[158] Cf. Jn 1:29; Is 53:7-12.

[159] Cf. Jn 5:27.

[160] Cf. Mt 9:2-7; Lk 5:18-25, 7:47-49; Mk 2:3-12.

[161] Cf. Jn 3:17.

[162] Jn 20:22; Mt 18:18; cf. also, as regards Peter, Mt 16:19. Blessed Isaac of Stella in one of his talks emphasizes the full communion of Christ with the Church in the forgiveness of sins: "The Church can forgive nothing without Christ, and Christ does not wish to forgive anything without the Church. The Church can forgive nothing except to a penitent, that is to say, to a person whom Christ has touched with his grace: Christ does not wish to consider anything forgiven in a person who despises the Church": *Sermo* 11 (*In Dominica II Post Epiphaniam,* 1): *PL* 194, 1729.

[163] Cf. Mt 12:49-50; Mk 3:33-34; Lk 8:20-21; Rom 8:29: "the firstborn among many brethren."

[164] Cf. Heb 2:17, 4:15.

[165] Cf. Mt 18:12-13; Lk 15:4-6.

forts,[166] the one Master who teaches the truth and reveals the ways of God,[167] the Judge of the living and the dead,[168] who judges according to the truth and not according to appearances.[169]

29.6 This is undoubtedly the most difficult and sensitive, the most exhausting and demanding ministry of the priest, but also one of the most beautiful and consoling. Precisely for this reason and with awareness also of the strong recommendation of the Synod, I will never grow weary of exhorting my brothers, the Bishops and priests, to the faithful and diligent performance of this ministry.[170] Before the consciences of the faithful, who open up to him with a mixture of fear and trust, the confessor is called to a lofty task which is one of service to penance and human reconciliation. It is a task of learning the weaknesses and falls of those faithful people, assessing their desire for renewal and their efforts to achieve it, discerning the action of the Holy Spirit in their hearts, imparting to them a forgiveness which God alone can grant, "celebrating" their reconciliation with the Father, portrayed in the parable of the prodigal son, reinstating these redeemed sinners in the ecclesial community with their brothers and sisters, and paternally admonishing these penitents with a firm, encouraging and friendly "Do not sin again."[171]

29.7 For the effective performance of this ministry, the confessor must necessarily have *human qualities* of prudence, discretion, discernment and a firmness tempered by gentleness and kindness. He must likewise have a serious and careful preparation, not fragmentary but complete and harmonious, in the different branches of theology, pedagogy and psychology, in the methodology of dialogue, and above all in a living and communicable knowledge of the word of God. But it is even more necessary that he should live an intense and genuine spiritual life. In order to lead others along the path of Christian perfection the minister of Penance himself must *first* travel this path. More by actions than by long speeches he must give proof of real experience of lived prayer, the practice of the theological and moral virtues of the Gospel, faithful obedience to the will of God, love of the Church and docility to her Magisterium.

29.8 All this fund of human gifts, Christian virtues and pastoral capabilities has to be worked for and is only acquired with effort. Every priest must be

[166] Cf. Lk 5:31-32.
[167] Cf. Mt 22:16.
[168] Cf. Acts 10:42.
[169] Cf. Jn 8:16.
[170] Cf. Address to the Penitentiaries of the Roman Patriarchal Basilicas and to the Priest Confessors at the Closing of the Jubilee of the Redemption (July 9, 1984): *Insegnamenti* VII/2 (1984), 63-69.
[171] Jn 8:11.

trained for the ministry of sacramental Penance from his years in the seminary, not only through the study of dogmatic, moral, spiritual and pastoral theology (which are simply parts of a whole), but also through the study of the human sciences, training in dialogue and especially in how to deal with people in the pastoral context. He must then be guided and looked after in his first activities. He must always ensure his own improvement and updating by means of permanent study. What a wealth of grace, true life and spiritual radiation would be poured out on the Church if every priest were careful never to miss, through negligence or various excuses, the appointment with the faithful in the confessional, and if he were even more careful never to go to it unprepared or lacking the necessary human qualities and spiritual and pastoral preparation!

29.9 In this regard I cannot but recall with devout admiration those extraordinary apostles of the confessional such as Saint John Nepomucene, Saint John Vianney, Saint Joseph Cafasso and Saint Leopold of Castelnuovo, to mention only the best-known confessors whom the Church has added to the list of her saints. But I also wish to pay homage to the innumerable host of holy and almost always anonymous confessors to whom is owed the salvation of so many souls who have been helped by them in conversion, in the struggle against sin and temptation, in spiritual progress and, in a word, in achieving holiness. I do not hesitate to say that even the great canonized saints are generally the fruit of those confessionals, and not only the saints but also the spiritual patrimony of the Church and the flowering of a civilization permeated with the Christian spirit! Praise then to this silent army of our brothers who have served well and serve each day the cause of reconciliation through the ministry of sacramental Penance!

The sacrament of forgiveness

30.1 From the revelation of the value of this ministry and power to forgive sins, conferred by Christ on the Apostles and their successors, there developed in the Church an awareness of the *sign of forgiveness,* conferred through the Sacrament of Penance. It is the certainty that the Lord Jesus himself instituted and entrusted to the Church — as a gift of his goodness and loving kindness[172] to be offered to all — a special sacrament for the forgiveness of sins committed after Baptism.

30.2 The practice of this sacrament, as regards its celebration and form, has undergone a long process of development as is attested to by the most ancient sacramentaries, the documents of Councils and Episcopal Synods,

[172] Cf. Tit 3:4.

the preaching of the Fathers and the teaching of the Doctors of the Church. But *with regard to the substance of the sacrament* there has always remained firm and unchanged in the consciousness of the Church *the certainty* that, by the will of Christ, forgiveness is offered to each individual by means of sacramental absolution given by the ministers of Penance. It is a certainty reaffirmed with particular vigor both by the Council of Trent[173] and by the Second Vatican Council: "Those who approach the Sacrament of Penance obtain pardon from God's mercy for the offenses committed against him, and are, at the same time, reconciled with the Church which they have wounded by their sins and which by charity, by example and by prayer works for their conversion."[174] And as an *essential element of faith* concerning the value and purpose of Penance it must be reaffirmed that our Savior Jesus Christ instituted in his Church the Sacrament of Penance so that the faithful who have fallen into sin after Baptism might receive grace and be reconciled with God.[175]

30.3 The Church's faith in this sacrament involves certain other fundamental truths which cannot be disregarded. The sacramental rite of Penance, in its evolution and variation of actual forms, has always preserved and highlighted these truths. When it recommended a reform of this rite, the Second Vatican Council intended to ensure that it would express these truths even more clearly,[176] and this has come about with the new *Rite of Penance.*[177] For the latter has made its own the whole of the teaching brought together by the Council of Trent, transferring it from its particular historical context (that of a resolute effort to clarify doctrine in the face of the serious deviations from the Church's genuine teaching), in order to translate it faithfully into terms more in keeping with the context of our own time.

Some fundamental convictions

31.1 The truths mentioned above, powerfully and clearly confirmed by the Synod and contained in the *Propositiones,* can be summarized in the following

---

[173] Cf. Session XIV, *De Sacramento Paenitentiae,* Chapter 1 and Canon 1: *Conciliorum Oecumenicorum Decreta,* Ed. Istituto per le Scienze Religiose, 3rd ed., Bologna, 1973, 703-704, 711 (*DS* 1668-1670, 1701).

[174] Dogmatic Constitution on the Church *Lumen Gentium,* 11.

[175] Cf. Ecumenical Council of Trent, Session XIV, *De Sacramento Paenitentiae,* Chapter 1 and Canon 1: *Conciliorum Oecumenicorum Decreta,* Ed. Istituto per le Scienze Religiose, 3rd ed., Bologna, 1973, 703-704, 711 (*DS* 1668-1670, 1701).

[176] Cf. Constitution on the Sacred Liturgy *Sacrosanctum Concilium,* 72.

[177] Cf. *Rituale Romanum ex Decreto Sacrosancti Concilii Oecumenici Vaticani II Instauratum, Auctoritate Pauli VI Promulgatum: Ordo Paenitentiae,* Vatican Polyglot Press, 1974.

convictions of faith, to which are connected all the other affirmations of the Catholic doctrine on the Sacrament of Penance.

31.2 The first conviction is that for a Christian *the Sacrament of Penance is the ordinary way* of obtaining forgiveness and the remission of serious sin committed after Baptism. Certainly, the Savior and his salvific action are not so bound to a sacramental sign as to be unable in any period or area of the history of salvation to work outside and above the sacraments. But in the school of faith we learn that the same Savior desired and provided that the simple and precious sacraments of faith would ordinarily be the effective means through which his redemptive power passes and operates. It would therefore be foolish, as well as presumptuous, to wish arbitrarily to disregard the means of grace and salvation which the Lord has provided and, in the specific case, to claim to receive forgiveness while doing without the sacrament which was instituted by Christ precisely for forgiveness. The renewal of the rites carried out after the Council does not sanction any illusion or alteration in this direction. According to the Church's intention, it was and is meant to stir up in each one of us a *new impulse* toward the renewal of our interior attitude; toward a deeper understanding of the nature of the Sacrament of Penance; toward a reception of the sacrament which is more filled with faith, not anxious but trusting; toward a more frequent celebration of the sacrament which is seen to be completely filled with the Lord's merciful love.

31.3 The second conviction concerns *the function of the Sacrament of Penance* for those who have recourse to it. According to the most ancient traditional idea, the sacrament is a kind of *judicial action;* but this takes place before a tribunal of mercy rather than of strict and rigorous justice, which is comparable to human tribunals only by analogy,[178] namely insofar as sinners reveal their sins and their condition as creatures subject to sin; they commit themselves to renouncing and combating sin, accept the punishment (*sacramental penance*) which the confessor imposes on them and receive absolution from him.

31.4 But as it reflects on the function of this sacrament, the Church's consciousness discerns in it, over and above the character of judgment in the sense just mentioned, a *healing of a medicinal* character. And this is linked to

---

[178] The Ecumenical Council of Trent uses the attenuated expression "ad instar actus iudicialis": Session XIV, *De Sacramento Paenitentiae,* Chapter 6: *Conciliorum Oecumenicorum Decreta,* Ed. Istituto per le Scienze Religiose, 3rd ed., Bologna, 1973, 707 (*DS* 1685), in order to emphasize the difference from human tribunals. The new Rite of Penance makes reference to this function, Nos. 6b and 10a.

the fact that the Gospel frequently presents Christ as healer,[179] while his redemptive work is often called, from Christian antiquity, *medicina salutis.* "I wish to heal, not accuse," Saint Augustine said, referring to the exercise of the pastoral activity regarding penance,[180] and it is thanks to the medicine of confession that the experience of sin does not degenerate into despair.[181] The *Rite of Penance* alludes to this healing aspect of the sacrament,[182] to which modern man is perhaps more sensitive, seeing as he does in sin the element of error but even more the element of weakness and human frailty.

31.5 Whether as a tribunal of mercy or a place of spiritual healing, under both aspects the sacrament requires a knowledge of the sinner's heart in order to be able to judge and absolve, to cure and heal. Precisely for this reason the sacrament involves, on the part of the penitent, a sincere and complete confession of sins. This therefore has a raison d'être not only inspired by ascetical purposes (as an exercise of humility and mortification), but one that is inherent in the very nature of the sacrament.

31.6 The third conviction, which is one that I wish to emphasize, concerns *the realities or parts* which make up the sacramental sign of forgiveness and reconciliation. Some of these realities are *acts of the penitent,* of varying importance but each indispensable either for the validity, the completeness or the fruitfulness of the sign.

31.7 First of all, an indispensable condition is the rectitude and clarity of the *penitent's conscience.* People cannot come to true and genuine repentance until they realize that sin is contrary to the ethical norm written in their inmost being[183]; until they admit that they have had a personal and responsible experience of this contrast; until they say not only that "sin exists" but also "I have sinned"; until they admit that sin has introduced a division into their consciences, which then pervades their whole being and separates them from God and from their brothers and sisters. The sacramental sign of this clarity

---

[179] Cf. Lk 5:31-32: "Those who are well have no need of a physician, but those who are sick" concluding: "I have . . . come to call . . . sinners to repentance"; Lk 9:2: "And he sent them out to preach the Kingdom of God and to heal." The image of Christ the Physician takes on new and striking elements if we compare it with the figure of the Servant of Yahweh, of whom the Book of Isaiah prophesies that "he has borne our griefs and carried our sorrows" and that "with his stripes we are healed" (Is 53:4-5).

[180] *Sermo* 82, 8: *PL* 38, 511.

[181] Saint Augustine, *Sermo* 352, 3, 8-9: *PL* 39, 1558-1559.

[182] Cf. *Ordo Paenitentiae,* 6c.

[183] Even the pagans recognized the existence of "divine" moral laws which have "always" existed and which are written in the depths of the human heart; cf. Sophocles (*Antigone,* verses 450-460) and Aristotle (*Rhetoric,* Book I, Chapter 15, 1375a-b).

of conscience is the act traditionally called the *examination of conscience,* an act that must never be one of anxious psychological introspection, but a sincere and calm comparison with the interior moral law, with the evangelical norms proposed by the Church, with Jesus Christ himself, who is our Teacher and Model of life, and with the heavenly Father, who calls us to goodness and perfection.[184]

31.8 But the essential act of Penance, on the part of the penitent, is *contrition,* a clear and decisive rejection of the sin committed, together with a resolution not to commit it again,[185] out of the love which one has for God and which is reborn with repentance. Understood in this way, *contrition* is therefore the beginning and the heart of *conversion,* of that evangelical *metánoia* which brings the person back to God like the prodigal son returning to his father, and which has in the Sacrament of Penance its visible sign and which perfects attrition. Hence "upon this contrition of heart depends the truth of penance."[186]

31.9 While reiterating everything that the Church, inspired by God's word, teaches about *contrition,* I particularly wish to emphasize here just one aspect of this doctrine. It is one that should be better known and considered. *Conversion* and *contrition* are often considered under the aspect of the undeniable demands which they involve and under the aspect of the mortification which they impose for the purpose of bringing about a radical change of life. But we do well to recall and emphasize the fact that *contrition* and *conversion* are even more a drawing near to the holiness of God, a rediscovery of one's true identity, which has been upset and disturbed by sin, a liberation in the very depth of self and thus a regaining of lost joy, the joy of being saved,[187] which the majority of people in our time are no longer capable of experiencing.

31.10 We therefore understand why, from the earliest Christian times, in line with the Apostles and with Christ, the Church has included in the sacramental sign of Penance *the confession of sins.* This latter takes on such im-

---

[184] On the role of conscience see what I said at the General Audience (March 14, 1984), 3: *Insegnamenti* VII/1 (1984), 683.

[185] Cf. Ecumenical Council of Trent, Session XIV, *De Sacramento Paenitentiae,* Chapter 4: *Conciliorum Oecumenicorum Decreta,* Ed. Istituto per le Scienze Religiose, 3rd ed., Bologna, 1973, 705 (*DS* 1676-1677). Of course, in order to approach the Sacrament of Penance it is sufficient to have attrition, or imperfect repentance, due more to fear than to love. But in the sphere of the sacrament, the penitent, under the action of the grace that he receives, *"ex attrito fit contritus,"* since Penance really operates in the person who is well disposed to conversion in love; cf. Ecumenical Council of Trent, ibid.: loc. cit., 705 (*DS* 1678).

[186] *Ordo Paenitentiae,* 6c.

[187] Cf. Ps 51:12.

portance that for centuries the usual name of the sacrament has been and still is that of *Confession.* The confession of sins is required, first of all, because the sinner must be known by the person who in the sacrament exercises *the role of judge.* He has to evaluate both the seriousness of the sins and the repentance of the penitent; he also exercises *the role of healer,* and must acquaint himself with the condition of the sick person in order to treat and heal him. But the individual confession also has the value of a *sign:* a sign of the meeting of the sinner with the mediation of the Church in the person of the minister; a sign of the person's revealing of self as a sinner in the sight of God and the Church, of facing his own sinful condition in the eyes of God. The confession of sins therefore cannot be reduced to a mere attempt at psychological self-liberation, even though it corresponds to that legitimate and natural need, inherent in the human heart, to open oneself to another. It is a liturgical act, solemn in its dramatic nature, yet humble and sober in the grandeur of its meaning. It is the act of the prodigal son who returns to his Father and is welcomed by him with the kiss of peace. It is an act of honesty and courage. It is an act of entrusting oneself, beyond sin, to the mercy that forgives.[188] Thus we understand why the *confession of sins* must ordinarily be individual not collective, just as sin is a deeply personal matter. But at the same time this confession in a way forces sin out of the secret of the heart and thus out of the area of pure individuality, emphasizing its social character as well, for through the minister of Penance it is the ecclesial community, which has been wounded by sin, that welcomes anew the repentant and forgiven sinner.

31.11 The other essential stage of the Sacrament of Penance this time belongs to the confessor as judge and healer, a figure of God the Father welcoming and forgiving the one who returns: this is *the absolution.* The words which express it and the gestures that accompany it in the old and in the new *Rite of Penance* are significantly *simple in their grandeur.* The sacramental formula "I absolve you . . . " and the imposition of the hand and the sign of the Cross made over the penitent show that *at this moment* the contrite and converted sinner comes into contact with the power and mercy of God. It is the moment at which, in response to the penitent, the Trinity becomes present in order to blot out sin and restore innocence. And the saving power of the Pas-

---

[188] I had occasion to speak of these fundamental aspects of penance at the General Audiences: (May 19, 1982), 2: *Insegnamenti* V/2 (1982), 1758-1759; (February 28, 1979): *Insegnamenti* II (1979), 475-478; (March 21, 1984): *Insegnamenti* VII/1 (1984), 720-722. See also the norms of the Code of Canon Law concerning the place for administering the sacrament and concerning confessionals (Canon 964 § 2-3).

sion, Death and Resurrection of Jesus is also imparted to the penitent as the "mercy stronger than sin and offense," as I defined it in my Encyclical *Dives in Misericordia*. God is always the one who is principally offended by sin — *"tibi soli peccavi!"* — and God alone can forgive. Hence the absolution that the priest, the minister of forgiveness, though himself a sinner, grants to the penitent, is the effective sign of the intervention of the Father in every absolution and the sign of the "resurrection" from "spiritual death" which is renewed each time that the Sacrament of Penance is administered. Only faith can give us certainty that *at that moment* every sin is forgiven and blotted out by the mysterious intervention of the Savior.

31.12 Satisfaction is the final act which crowns the sacramental sign of Penance. In some countries the act which the forgiven and absolved penitent agrees to perform after receiving absolution is called precisely the *penance.* What is the meaning of this *satisfaction* that one makes or the *penance* that one performs? Certainly it is not a price that one pays for the sin absolved and for the forgiveness obtained: no human price can match what is obtained, which is the fruit of Christ's precious blood. Acts of satisfaction — which, while remaining simple and humble, should be made to express more clearly all that they signify — mean a number of valuable things: they are the sign *of the personal commitment* that the Christian has made to God, in the sacrament, to begin a new life (and therefore they should not be reduced to mere formulas to be recited, but should consist of acts of worship, charity, mercy or reparation). They include the idea that the pardoned sinner is able to join his own physical and spiritual mortification — which has been sought after or at least accepted — to the Passion of Jesus who has obtained the forgiveness for him. They remind us that even after absolution there remains in the Christian a dark area, due to the wound of sin, to the imperfection of love in repentance, to the weakening of the spiritual faculties. It is an area in which there still operates an infectious source of sin which must always be fought with mortification and penance. This is the meaning of the humble but sincere act of satisfaction.[189]

31.13 There remains to be made a brief mention of *other important convictions* about the Sacrament of Penance.

31.14 First of all, it must be emphasized that nothing is more personal and intimate than this sacrament, in which the sinner stands alone before God with his sin, repentance and trust. No one can repent in his place or ask forgiveness in his name. There is a certain solitude of the sinner in his sin,

---

[189] I dealt with this subject concisely at the General Audience (March 7, 1984): *Insegnamenti* VII/1 (1984), 631-633.

and this can be seen dramatically represented in Cain with sin "crouching at his door," as the *Book of Genesis* says so effectively, and with the distinctive mark on his forehead[190]; in David, admonished by the Prophet Nathan[191]; or in the prodigal son when he realizes the condition to which he has reduced himself by staying away from his father and decides to return to him.[192] Everything takes place between the individual alone and God. But at the same time one cannot deny the social nature of this sacrament, in which the whole Church — militant, suffering and glorious in heaven — comes to the aid of the penitent and welcomes him again into her bosom, especially as it was the whole Church which had been offended and wounded by his sin. As the minister of Penance, the priest, by virtue of his sacred office, appears as the witness and representative of this ecclesial nature of the sacrament. The individual nature and ecclesial nature are two complementary aspects of the sacrament which the progressive reform of the Rite of Penance, especially that contained in the *Ordo Paenitentiae* promulgated by Paul VI, has sought to emphasize and to make more meaningful in its celebration.

31.15 Secondly, it must be emphasized that the most precious result of the forgiveness obtained in the Sacrament of Penance consists in reconciliation with God, which takes place in the inmost heart of the son who was lost and found again, which every penitent is. But it has to be added that this reconciliation with God leads, as it were, to other reconciliations which repair the breaches caused by sin. The forgiven penitent is reconciled with himself in his inmost being, where he regains his own true identity. He is reconciled with his brethren whom he has in some way attacked and wounded. He is reconciled with the Church. He is reconciled with all creation.

31.16 As a result of an awareness of this, at the end of the celebration there arises in the penitent a sense of gratitude to God for the gift of divine mercy received, and the Church invites the penitent to have this sense of gratitude.

31.17 Every confessional is a special and blessed place from which, with divisions wiped away, there is born new and uncontaminated a reconciled individual — a reconciled world!

31.18 Lastly, I particularly wish to speak of one *final consideration,* one which concerns all of us priests, who are the ministers of the Sacrament of Penance.[193] The priest's celebration of the Eucharist and administration of the

---

[190] Cf. Gen 4:7, 15.

[191] Cf. 2 Sam 12.

[192] Cf. Lk 15:17-21.

[193] Cf. Second Vatican Ecumenical Council, Decree on the Ministry and Life of Priests *Presbyterorum Ordinis*, 18.

other sacraments, his pastoral zeal, his relationship with the faithful, his communion with his brother priests, his collaboration with his Bishop, his life of prayer — in a word, the whole of his priestly existence, suffers an inexorable decline if by negligence or for some other reason he fails to receive the Sacrament of Penance at regular intervals and in a spirit of genuine faith and devotion. If a priest were no longer to go to confession or properly confess his sins, his *priestly being* and his *priestly action* would feel its effects very soon, and this would also be noticed by the community of which he was the pastor.

31.19 But I also add that even in order to be a good and effective minister of Penance the priest needs to have recourse to the source of grace and holiness present in this sacrament. We priests, on the basis of our personal experience, can certainly say that the more careful we are to receive the Sacrament of Penance and to approach it frequently and with good dispositions, the better we fulfill our own ministry as confessors and ensure that our penitents benefit from it. And on the other hand this ministry would lose much of its effectiveness if in some way we were to stop being good penitents. Such is *the internal logic* of this great sacrament. It invites all of us priests of Christ to pay renewed attention to our personal confession.

31.20 Personal experience in its turn becomes and must become *today* an incentive for the diligent, regular, patient and fervent exercise of the sacred ministry of Penance, to which we are committed by the very fact of our priesthood and our vocation as pastors and servants of our brothers and sisters. Also with this present Exhortation I therefore address an earnest invitation to all the priests of the world, especially to my Brothers in the Episcopacy and to pastors of souls, an invitation to make every effort to encourage the faithful to make use of this sacrament. I urge them to use all possible and suitable means to ensure that the greatest possible number of our brothers and sisters receive the "grace that has been given to us" through Penance for the reconciliation of every soul and of the whole world with God in Christ.

Forms of celebration

32.1 Following the suggestions of the Second Vatican Council, the *Ordo Paenitentiae* provided three rites which, while always keeping intact the essential elements, make it possible to adapt the celebration of the Sacrament of Penance to particular pastoral circumstances.

32.2 The first form — *reconciliation of individual penitents* — is the only normal and ordinary way of celebrating the sacrament, and it cannot and must not be allowed to fall into disuse or be neglected. The second form — *reconciliation of a number of penitents with individual confession and absolu-*

tion — even though in the preparatory acts it helps to give greater emphasis to the community aspects of the sacrament, is the same as the first form in the culminating sacramental act, namely, individual confession and individual absolution of sins. It can thus be regarded as equal to the first form as regards the normality of the rite. The third form, however — *reconciliation of a number of penitents with general confession and absolution* — is exceptional in character. It is therefore not left to free choice but is regulated by a special discipline.

32.3 The first form makes possible a highlighting of the more personal — and essential — aspects which are included in the penitential process. The dialogue between penitent and confessor, the sum of the elements used (the biblical texts, the choice of the forms of "satisfaction," etc.) make the sacramental celebration correspond more closely to the concrete situation of the penitent. The value of these elements is perceived when one considers the different reasons that bring a Christian to sacramental Penance: a need for personal reconciliation and readmission to friendship with God by regaining the grace lost by sin; a need to check one's spiritual progress and sometimes a need for a more accurate discernment of one's vocation; on many other occasions a need and a desire to escape from a state of spiritual apathy and religious crisis. Thanks then to its individual character, the first form of celebration makes it possible to link the Sacrament of Penance with something which is different but readily linked with it: I am referring to *spiritual direction.* So it is certainly true that personal decision and commitment are clearly signified and promoted in this first form.

32.4 The second form of celebration, precisely by its specific dimension, highlights certain aspects of great importance: the word of God listened to in common has a remarkable effect as compared to its individual reading, and better emphasizes the ecclesial character of conversion and reconciliation. It is particularly meaningful at various seasons of the liturgical year and in connection with events of special pastoral importance. The only point that needs mentioning here is that for celebrating the second form there should be an adequate number of confessors present.

32.5 It is therefore natural that the criteria for deciding which of the two forms of celebration to use should be dictated not by situational and subjective reasons but by a desire to secure the true spiritual good of the faithful, in obedience to the penitential discipline of the Church.

32.6 We shall also do well to recall that, for a balanced spiritual and pastoral orientation in this regard, great importance must continue to be given to teaching the faithful also to make use of the Sacrament of Penance for venial sins alone, as is borne out by a centuries-old doctrinal tradition and practice.

32.7 Though the Church knows and teaches that venial sins are forgiven in other ways too — for instance, by acts of sorrow, works of charity, prayer, penitential rites — she does not cease to remind everyone of the special usefulness of the sacramental moment for these sins too. The frequent use of the sacrament — to which some categories of the faithful are in fact held — strengthens the awareness that even minor sins offend God and harm the Church, the Body of Christ. Its celebration then becomes for the faithful "the occasion and the incentive to conform themselves more closely to Christ and to make themselves more docile to the voice of the Spirit."[194] Above all it should be emphasized that the grace proper to the sacramental celebration has a great remedial power and helps to remove the very roots of sin.

32.8 Attention to the actual celebration,[195] with special reference to the importance of the word of God which is read, recalled and explained, when this is possible and suitable, to the faithful and with them, will help to give fresh life to the practice of the sacrament and prevent it from declining into a mere formality and routine. The penitent will be helped rather to discover that he or she is living a salvific event, capable of inspiring fresh life and giving true peace of heart. This careful attention to the celebration will also lead the individual churches to arrange *special times for the celebration of the sacrament.* It will also be an incentive to teaching the faithful, especially children and young people, to accustom themselves to keeping to these times, except in cases of necessity, when the parish priest must always show a ready willingness to receive whoever comes to him.

Celebration of the sacrament with general absolution

33.1 The new liturgical regulation and, more recently, the *Code of Canon Law,*[196] specify the conditions which make it lawful to use "the rite of reconciliation of a number of penitents with general confession and absolution." The norms and regulations given on this point, which are the result of mature and balanced consideration, must be accepted and applied in such a way as to avoid any sort of arbitrary interpretation.

33.2 It is opportune to reflect more deeply on the reasons which order the celebration of Penance in one of the first two forms and permit the use of the third form. First of all, there is the reason of *fidelity* to the will of the Lord Jesus, transmitted by the doctrine of the Church, and also the reason of *obe-*

---

[194] *Ordo Paenitentiae,* 7b.
[195] Cf. ibid., 17.
[196] Canons 961-963.

dience to the Church's laws. The Synod repeated in one of its *Propositiones* the unchanged teaching which the Church has derived from the most ancient Tradition, and it repeated the law with which she has codified the ancient penitential practice: the individual and integral confession of sins with individual absolution constitutes the *only ordinary way* in which the faithful who are conscious of serious sin are reconciled with God and with the Church. From this confirmation of the Church's teaching it is clear that *every serious sin must always be stated,* with its determining circumstances, *in an individual confession.*

33.3 Then there is a reason of the pastoral order. While it is true that, when the conditions required by canonical discipline occur, use may be made of the third form of celebration, it must not be forgotten that *this form cannot become an ordinary one,* and it cannot and must not be used — as the Synod repeated — except "in cases of grave necessity." And there remains unchanged the obligation to make an individual confession of serious sins before again having recourse to another general absolution. The Bishop therefore, who is the only one competent in his own Diocese to assess whether the conditions actually exist which Canon Law lays down for the use of the third form, will give this judgment *with a grave obligation on his own conscience,* with full respect for the law and practice of the Church, and also taking into account the criteria and guidelines agreed upon — on the basis of the doctrinal and pastoral considerations explained above — with the other members of the Episcopal Conference. Equally, it will always be a matter of genuine pastoral concern to lay down and guarantee the conditions that make recourse to the third form capable of producing the spiritual fruits for which it is meant. The exceptional use of the third form of celebration must never lead to a lesser regard for, still less an abandonment of, the ordinary forms, nor must it lead to this form being considered an alternative to the other two forms. It is not in fact left to the freedom of pastors and the faithful to choose from among these forms the one considered most suitable. It remains the obligation of pastors to facilitate for the faithful the practice of integral and individual confession of sins, which constitutes for them not only a duty but also an inviolable and inalienable right, besides being something needed by the soul. For the faithful, the use of the third form of celebration involves the obligation of following all the norms regulating its exercise, including that of not having recourse again to general absolution before a normal integral and individual confession of sins, which must be made as soon as possible. Before granting absolution the priest must inform and instruct the faithful about this norm and about the obligation to observe it.

33.4 With this reminder of the doctrine and the law of the Church I wish to instill into everyone the lively sense of responsibility which must guide us when we deal with sacred things like the sacraments, which are not our property, or like consciences, which have a right not to be left in uncertainty and confusion. The sacraments and consciences, I repeat, are sacred, and both require that we serve them in truth.

33.5 This is the reason for the Church's law.

Some more delicate cases

34.1 I consider it my duty to mention at this point, if very briefly, a pastoral case that the Synod dealt with — insofar as it was able to do so — and which it also considered in one of the *Propositiones.* I am referring to certain situations, not infrequent today, affecting Christians who wish to continue their sacramental religious practice, but who are prevented from doing so by their personal condition, which is not in harmony with the commitments freely undertaken before God and the Church. These are situations which seem particularly delicate and almost inextricable.

34.2 Numerous interventions during the Synod, expressing the general thought of the Fathers, emphasized the coexistence and mutual influence of two equally important principles in relation to these cases. The first principle is that of compassion and mercy, whereby the Church, as the continuer in history of Christ's presence and work, not wishing the death of the sinner but that the sinner should be converted and live,[197] and careful not to break the bruised reed or to quench the dimly burning wick,[198] ever seeks to offer, as far as possible, the path of return to God and of reconciliation with him. The other principle is that of truth and consistency, whereby the Church does not agree to call good evil and evil good. Basing herself on these two complementary principles, the Church can only invite her children who find themselves in these painful situations to approach the divine mercy by other ways, not, however, through the Sacraments of Penance and the Eucharist, until such time as they have attained the required dispositions.

34.3 On this matter, which also deeply torments our pastoral hearts, it seemed my precise duty to say clear words in the Apostolic Exhortation *Familiaris Consortio,* as regards the case of the divorced and remarried,[199] and likewise the case of Christians living together in an irregular union.

[197] Cf. Ezek 18:23.
[198] Cf. Is 42:3; Mt 12:20.
[199] Cf. Apostolic Exhortation *Familiaris Consortio* (November 22, 1981), 84: *AAS* 74 (1982), 184-186.

34.4 At the same time, and together with the Synod, I feel that it is my clear duty to urge the ecclesial communities, and especially the Bishops, to provide all possible assistance to those priests who have fallen short of the grave commitments which they undertook at their ordination and who are living in irregular situations. None of these brothers of ours should feel abandoned by the Church.

34.5 For all those who are not at the present moment in the objective conditions required by the Sacrament of Penance, the Church's manifestations of maternal kindness, the support of acts of piety apart from sacramental ones, a sincere effort to maintain contact with the Lord, attendance at Mass and the frequent repetition of acts of faith, hope, charity and sorrow made as perfectly as possible, can prepare the way for full reconciliation at the hour that Providence alone knows.

Concluding Expression of Hope

35.1 At the end of this document, I hear echoing within me and I desire to repeat to all of you the exhortation which the first Bishop of Rome, at a critical hour of the beginning of the Church, addressed "to the exiles of the dispersion . . . chosen and destined by God the Father . . . : Have unity of spirit, sympathy, love of the brethren, a tender heart and a humble mind."[200] The Apostle urged: "Have unity of spirit." But he immediately went on to point out the sins against harmony and peace which must be avoided: "Do not return evil for evil or reviling for reviling; but on the contrary bless, for to this you have been called, that you may obtain a blessing." And he ended with a word of encouragement and hope: "Who is there to harm you if you are zealous for what is right?"[201]

35.2 At an hour of history which is no less critical, I dare to join my exhortation to that of the Prince of the Apostles, the first to occupy this See of Rome as a witness to Christ and as Pastor of the Church, and who here "presided in charity" before the entire world. In communion with the Bishops who are the successors of the Apostles, and supported by the collegial reflection that many of them, meeting in the Synod, devoted to the topics and problems of reconciliation, I too wish to speak to you with the same spirit of the fisherman of Galilee when he said to our brothers and sisters in the faith, distant in time but so closely linked in heart: "Have unity of spirit. . . . Do not return evil for evil. . . . Be zealous for what is right."[202] And he added:

[200] Cf. 1 Pet 1:1-2, 3:8.
[201] 1 Pet 3:9, 13.
[202] 1 Pet 3:8, 9, 13.

"It is better to suffer for doing right, if that should be God's will, than for doing wrong."[203]

35.3 This Exhortation is completely permeated by words which Peter had heard from Jesus himself, and by ideas which formed part of his "Good News": the new commandment of love of neighbor; the yearning for and commitment to unity; the beatitudes of mercy and patience in persecution for the sake of justice; the repaying of evil with good; the forgiveness of offenses; the love of enemies. In these words and ideas is the original and transcendent synthesis of the Christian ethic or, more accurately and more profoundly, of the spirituality of the New Covenant in Jesus Christ.

35.4 I entrust to the Father, rich in mercy, I entrust to the Son of God, made man as our Redeemer and Reconciler, I entrust to the Holy Spirit, source of unity and peace, this call of mine, as father and Pastor, to penance and reconciliation. May the Most Holy and Adorable Trinity cause to spring up in the Church and in the world the small seed which at this hour I plant in the generous soil of many human hearts.

35.5 In order that in the not too distant future abundant fruits may come from it, I invite you all to join me in turning to Christ's Heart, the eloquent sign of the divine mercy, the "propitiation for our sins," "our peace and reconciliation,"[204] that we may draw from it an interior encouragement to hate sin and to be converted to God, and find in it the divine kindness which lovingly responds to human repentance.

35.6 I likewise invite you to turn with me to the Immaculate Heart of Mary, Mother of Jesus, in whom "is effected the reconciliation of God with humanity . . . , is accomplished the work of reconciliation, because she has received from God the fullness of grace in virtue of the redemptive sacrifice of Christ."[205] Truly, Mary has been associated with God, by virtue of her divine motherhood, in the work of reconciliation.[206]

35.7 Into the hands of this Mother, whose *fiat* marked the beginning of that "fullness of time" in which Christ accomplished the reconciliation of humanity with God, to her Immaculate Heart — to which we have repeatedly entrusted the whole of humanity, disturbed by sin and tormented by so many tensions and conflicts — I now in a special way entrust this intention: that

---

[203] 1 Pet 3:17.

[204] Litany of the Sacred Heart; cf. 1 Jn 2:2; Eph 2:14; Rom 3:25, 5:11.

[205] John Paul II, Address at the General Audience (December 7, 1983), 2: *Insegnamenti* VI/2 (1983), 1264.

[206] Cf. John Paul II, Address at the General Audience (January 4, 1984): *Insegnamenti* VII/1 (1984), 16-18.

through her intercession humanity may discover and travel the path of penance, the only path that can lead it to full reconciliation.

35.8 To all of you who in a spirit of ecclesial communion in obedience and faith[207] receive the indications, suggestions and directives contained in this document and seek to put them into living pastoral practice, I willingly impart my Apostolic Blessing.

Given in Rome, at Saint Peter's, on December 2, the First Sunday of Advent, in the year 1984, the seventh of my Pontificate.

[207] Cf. Rom 1:5, 16:26.

Christifideles Laici

Editor's Introduction

"I have always been very aware of the urgent need for the *apostolate of the laity* in the Church. When the Second Vatican Council spoke of the vocation and mission of lay people in the Church and the world, I rejoiced: what the Council was teaching corresponded to the convictions which had guided my activity ever since the first years of my priestly ministry." So wrote Pope John Paul II in his memoir on the fiftieth anniversary of his ordination, *Gift and Mystery* (1996). In *Christifideles Laici*, published on December 30, 1988, he exercised his authority as the Successor of Peter to teach on a subject of fundamental pastoral concern: the laity's dignity and mission. This exhortation aims to foster "a deeper awareness among all the faithful of the gift and responsibility they share, both as a group and as individuals, in the communion and mission of the Church" (§2.13). *Christifideles Laici* charts the laity's path for the third millennium.

Accepting the recommendation of the different constituencies consulted, the Pope fixed the theme for the Seventh Ordinary Assembly of the Synod of Bishops: "the vocation and the mission of the lay faithful in the Church and in the world twenty years after the Second Vatican Council." Set to meet in 1986, this Assembly was postponed for a year, since John Paul scheduled an Extraordinary Synod for 1985 to celebrate, examine, and promote the application of Vatican II on the twentieth anniversary of its closing. The Seventh Ordinary Assembly of the Synod of Bishops convened in Rome in the fall of 1987 and, like the 1985 Extraordinary Synod, it emphasized the need to translate Vatican II's rich theory on the lay vocation into pastoral initiatives.

Post-conciliar theology and practice raise certain questions about the laity which the Pope wishes to address. Since the Council, many signs indicate that the Holy Spirit is renewing the Church and fostering "new aspirations toward holiness and the participation of so many lay faithful" (§2.8). He also mentions situations in the Church relatively unknown at the time of Vatican II: "the ministries and Church services entrusted at present and in the future to the lay faithful, the growth and spread of new 'movements' alongside other group forms of lay involvement, and the place and role of women both in the Church and in society" (§2.10). Besides these positive phenomena, disturbing shadows appear on the horizon. John Paul points out two dangers to which lay people today succumb: "the temptation of being so strongly interested in Church services and tasks that some fail to become actively engaged in their responsibilities in the professional, social, cultural and political world; and the temptation of legitimizing the unwarranted separation of faith from life, that is, a separation of the Gospel's acceptance from the actual living of the Gospel in various situations in the world" (§2.9). In the course of his post-synodal document the Holy Father takes up these two issues.

An accurate interpretation of *Christifideles Laici* requires that both its pastoral and doctrinal dimensions be considered. The exhortation's purpose is, however, chiefly a pressing appeal to the whole Church that she should come to a deeper understanding of the lay vocation and put this understanding into practice. John Paul sees his exhortation as confirming the Synod's message: "the *lay faithful's hearkening to the call of Christ the Lord to work in his vineyard,* to take an active, conscientious and responsible part in the mission of the Church *in this great moment in history*" (§3.1). This pastoral mobilization has a solid and well-developed doctrinal base, which is profoundly ecclesiological. In fact, the document's doctrinal foundation derives largely from the Final Report of the 1985 Synod, which provides the framework for the first three chapters of *Christifideles Laici*. Like the Final Report, the exhortation discusses the vocation and mission of the lay faithful in light of the Church as mystery, communion, and mission.

In keeping with the document's exhortatory nature, the Pope's tone strikes a note of urgency and hope. Repeatedly he warns that the current state of affairs in the Church and the world "calls with a particular urgency for the action of the lay faithful," and adds: *"It is not permissible for anyone to remain idle"* (§3.2). He frequently cites the words of Jesus: "You go into my vineyard too" (Mt 20:4). At the same time, the exhortation is suffused with John Paul's characteristic hope, founded on confidence in God's unfailing care for the Church. Despite innumerable adverse situations, the Church is not overcome, "because the Holy Spirit, who gives her life, sustains her in her mission" (§7.2). Moreover, Jesus Christ the Redeemer is the hope of humanity; he himself is *"the 'Good News' and the bearer of joy"* for mankind (§7.5).

A noteworthy point of style in this papal document is the use of "horizontal" inclusive language in the English translation. This editorial decision has affected the translations of all conciliar and papal documents. One notices, too, that the exhortation usually refers to "women and men," rather than "men and women," when speaking of the lay faithful (cf. §51.4).

The stylistic unity and theological force of *Christifideles Laici* depend on the biblical images which structure the document: the Johannine image of the vine and the branches (Jn 15:1-5), and the Synoptic image of the laborers in the vineyard (Mt 20:1-16). The vine is both Christ and the Church, and the disciples are the branches grafted on the vine which are to bear fruit. The vineyard is the world to be transformed, and the laborers are, for the most part, the lay faithful. All told, there are 156 references to the Bible in the exhortation, but quotations from the Gospels of John and Matthew, where these images are found, are the most frequent.

The Second Vatican Council is also an important source of the Pope's thought. Its teaching, he writes, had "prophetic significance" (§2.10) and it is still capable of enlightening and guiding today's situation. The Council's contribution, "with its rich doctrinal, spiritual and pastoral patrimony," is an ever valid reflection "on the nature, dignity, spirituality, mission and responsibility of the lay faithful" (§2.5). In *Christifideles Laici,* the Pope follows the way already marked out by the Synod Fathers, who were guided by conciliar teaching and wished to translate its "rich 'theory' on the lay state . . . into authentic Church 'practice'" (§2.10). He cites Vatican II with even more than his usual frequency — seventy-one times — showing a preference for *Lumen Gentium, Gaudium et Spes,* and *Apostolicam Actuositatem,* the Decree on the Apostolate of the Laity, which is particularly relevant to the exhortation's subject matter. The long citations result in a compendium of contemporary Church teaching on the lay faithful. His constant appeals to authoritative conciliar texts reveal the extent to which the Holy Father regards his post-synodal text as yet one more step in implementing the Second Vatican Council.

More than in previous exhortations, the Pope refers to the *propositiones,* or recommendations, of the Synod Fathers; he cites them directly thirty-one times, and indirectly eighteen times. This ample use of the Synod's proposals is in keeping with John Paul's expressed intention of incorporating all the richness of the Synod's deliberations into his document. He intends *Christifideles Laici* to be "not something in contradistinction to the Synod, but . . . a faithful and coherent expression of it, a fruit of collegiality" (§2.12).

While the Holy Father addresses his post-synodal apostolic exhortation to each member of the Church personally, the more specific audience he has in mind is the lay faithful. He instructs and exhorts them throughout. The special attention paid to the laity continues the pattern established at the Synodal Assembly, which had sixty lay "auditors," non-voting participants who could be consulted and who could, when invited, address the Synod. The post-synodal text, therefore, reflects their input as well. The Pope directs his words to lay men and women who "are personally called by the Lord, from whom they receive a mission on behalf of the Church and the world" (§2.4).

Summary

Christifideles Laici is divided into seven sections: an introduction, five main chapters, and a concluding appeal and prayer. The heading of each of the five principal chapters refers to a relevant biblical passage, drawn from the image of the vine and branches or of the vineyard. The first three chapters, which discuss the lay faithful in light of the Church as mystery, vocation, communion, and mission, are more doctrinal than the last two, which are more expressly exhortatory.

In the introduction (§§1-7), the Pope makes his initial plea for a more active laity, outlines the pressing challenges posed by the world to the Church, and proposes Jesus as the hope for humanity. Chapter one, "The Dignity of the Lay Faithful in the Church as Mystery" (§§8-17), explains the sacramental basis of the laity's lofty vocation, describes their mission, with special emphasis on its secular nature, and confirms their call to holiness. Chapter two, "The Participation of the Lay Faithful in the Life of the Church as Communion" (§§18-31), first summarizes the ecclesiology of communion, following the Final Report of the 1985 Synod very closely, and then takes up the role of ministries and charisms in the Church, the relationship of the particular Church to the universal Church, and the ecclesial role of the new lay movements and associations. In chapter three, "The Coresponsibility of the Lay Faithful in the Church as Mission" (§§32-44), the Pope describes the Church as a missionary communion in which the laity are to "bear fruit" (Jn 15:16). They fulfill their mission of transforming the world by proclaiming the Gospel and serving individuals and society. The Holy Father encourages the different groups of laborers in the vineyard to accomplish their mission and suggests a pastoral response to their needs in chapter four, "Good Stewards of God's Varied Grace" (§§45-56). In chapter five, "The Formation of the Lay Faithful" (§§57-63), John Paul encourages the laity to grow in the understanding of their vocation through a process of a total and integrated formation. He concludes with a final appeal for committed lay people and a prayer for Mary's intercession.

Signs of the times

As in many of his writings, the Pope turns a watchful eye on the current world situation as a backdrop to his discussion. In *Christifideles Laici* he describes the vineyard into which the householder sends the laborers. The signs of the times, which come to light "through the historic events of the Church and humanity" (§3.5), point to three emerging social trends. Each of these signs poses a serious threat to Christianity but, at the same time, each also reveals something positive and encouraging.

A very serious problem today is secularism, a way of thinking and acting which is founded on theoretical or, more often, practical atheism. Secularism is responsible for the spiritual impoverishment of individuals and whole communities. Those under its sway "cut the religious roots that are in their hearts; they forget God, or simply retain him without meaning in their lives, or outrightly reject him, and begin to adore various 'idols' of the contemporary world" (§4.1). But, despite the secularists' attempts, they cannot completely smother the need for religion. John Paul affirms that people today continue to bear witness to the restlessness of the human heart. Only God can satisfy this yearning, the signs of which are "an openness to a spiritual and transcendent outlook toward life, the renewed interest in religious research, the return to a sense of the sacred and to prayer, and the demand for freedom to call upon the name of the Lord" (§4.3).

The frequent degradation of the human person and violations of his or her rights also characterize the modern world. John Paul asserts that men and women are often manipulated and enslaved by those who are stronger. These powerful forces can have many different names — "an ideology, economic power, political and inhumane systems, scientific technocracy or the intrusiveness of the mass media" (§5.2) — and they may lead to abuses of human rights. The Pope insists that "the *sacredness of the human person* cannot be obliterated" (§5.4). Many people are now more conscious of human dignity, becoming ever more aware that the person is a free and responsible "subject" and not an "object" to be used. Furthermore, new forms of authentic humanism sustain and foster human dignity.

Lastly, the Holy Father draws attention to the various kinds of conflict buffeting contemporary society: the "fatal opposition of persons, groups, categories, nations and blocs of nations" which "takes the form of violence, of terrorism, and of war" (§6.1). But a sign of hope also appears on this horizon. People still long for the "inestimable good of *peace* in justice" (§6.2), and many are working to achieve this goal in a professional or volunteer capacity. Therefore, even though the vineyard of the world is convulsed with problems, that same vineyard manifests signs of openness to Christ's saving truth.

Identity and dignity of the lay faithful

John Paul defines the lay state in light of the mystery of the People of God as the vine and the branches. Christ is the "true vine" (Jn 15:1), but the Church, united to him as his Body and Bride, is also portrayed in the Scriptures as the vine. The faithful are grafted on this vine, which is Christ and/or the Church, the source of their life and fruitfulness. Consequently, the Pope affirms that "only *from inside the Church's mystery of communion is the 'identity' of the lay faithful made known,* and their fundamental dignity revealed" (§8.6).

According to *Christifideles Laici,* who the laity *are* can be adequately explained only if one acknowledges the extraordinary dignity they receive in Baptism. The "radical newness of the Christian life" (§10) comes from this sacrament. Through Baptism individuals enter into a personal relationship with each of the divine Persons. They become "children loved by the Father, members incorporated into Christ and his Church, living and holy temples of the Spirit" (§64.4, cf. §10). First, then, the sacrament of rebirth brings the gift of adopted sonship: "With Baptism we become *children of God in his only-begotten Son, Jesus Christ"* (§11.3). Second, it incorporates believers into Christ's Body, the Church. Not only is every disciple intimately united to Jesus, but he or she is also linked in a vital communion with other believers. This unity among Christians, says the Pope, is "an image and extension of that mystical *communion* that binds the Father to the Son and the Son to the Father in the bond of love, the Holy Spirit" (§12.3). Lastly, the baptized receive an outpouring of the Holy Spirit, thus becoming temples of his presence and sharers in "the mission of Jesus as the Christ, the Savior-Messiah" (§13.3).

The Holy Father emphasizes the dignity of lay people all the more when he confirms Vatican II's teaching that, on a par with clergy and Religious, their primary vocation is to live their call to holiness. It is a call which comes from Baptism itself, from the gift of being in communion with Christ and the Church. This charge entrusted to everyone, including each and every lay person, is not a simple moral exhortation. Rather, it is an *"undeniable requirement arising from the mystery of the Church"* (§16.2) which is the sign and instrument of holiness. The obligation to imitate Christ arises from one's baptismal consecration. A life of holiness is "the greatest testimony of the dignity conferred on a disciple of Christ" (§16.1).

Like all members of the Church, the laity are first of all new "beings" through their share in divine life. Having been created anew by grace, they are to express this dignity in deeds. Their vocation to holiness is *"intimately connected to mission* and to the responsibility entrusted to the lay faithful in the Church and in the world" (§17.2). Here Pope John Paul follows the traditional order of reflection. Just as action follows being, so does his discussion of the laity's mission follow that of their identity. To describe the specific mission of lay people, which manifests "the grace and dignity coming from Baptism" (§14.2), the Pope uses the framework found in *Lumen Gentium* (§§34-36) and his encyclical *Redemptor Hominis* (§§19-21). These documents depict the mission of the lay faithful as a participation in Christ's threefold mission as Priest, Prophet, and King. Since many passages of *Christifideles Laici* rely on this schematic triad as a principle of organization, the exhortation summarizes its essential elements at the outset. Lay men and women share in Christ's priestly mission primarily by joining themselves to his sacrifice "in the offering they make of themselves and their daily activities" (§14.5). They participate in his prophetic mission by accepting the Gospel in faith and bearing witness to it in word and deed. The lay faithful exercise their kingly mission by engaging in spiritual combat against sin and serving others in charity and justice.

The lay vocation is distinguished from the ministerial priesthood and consecrated life by the "secular character" which particularly belongs to it (§15.6). God calls the laity to continue Christ's redemptive work in the world — the place in which they receive their vocation to holiness. "Baptism does not take them from the world at all" but keeps them in it (§15.8). Here they are sanctified by working to renew the temporal order according to God's design.

Ecclesial communion

The Church as a communion — of each individual personally with Christ, and of all together with him, and thus also with one another — is key to John Paul's ecclesiology, just as it was to the Fathers at Vatican II and at the Extraordinary Synod of 1985. The Pope uses the metaphor of the vine and the branches to describe the laity's mission in the Church. Through Baptism the clergy, Religious, and lay faithful are all taken into a living and life-giving communion with Christ. This communion of each person with Jesus has "the unity of the Son with the Father in the gift of the Holy Spirit, as its model and source" (§18.3). From this vertical communion with the Triune God flows the horizontal communion that the baptized have with one another: all are branches of the one vine, Christ. Communion in the Church thus has the invisible dimension of an intimate union with the Trinity and other human beings; and a visible dimension of communion in the teaching of the Apostles, the sacraments, and the hierarchical ministry.

For the Holy Father, ecclesial communion is "organic," analogous to that of a living body. He follows Saint Paul's teaching on the Mystical Body of Christ very closely (cf. 1 Cor 12:12-30; Rom 12:4-5). Within this one Body, in which all share a common dignity, there is "a *diversity* and a *complementarity* of vocations and states in life, of ministries, of charisms and responsibilities" (§20.1). Everyone is consecrated by Baptism and Confirmation, but lay life, ordained ministry, and consecrated life express their vocation and mission distinctly. Each member is linked to the whole Body and offers his or her unique contribution to its functioning. Unity in diversity is preserved by the Holy Spirit, who is "the constant and never-ending source of communion in the Church" (§19.5).

Ministries and charisms

Guided by the Holy Spirit, the Church is constantly being built up by the various gifts lavished upon her. Adhering to the teaching of the Second Vatican Council, which is itself rooted in Pauline doctrine, the Pope distinguishes between the stable ministries and the various charisms and, within the Church's ministerial constitution, between the ministries which derive from Holy Orders and the ministries which derive from Baptism and Confirmation.

Even though in *Christifideles Laici* the ministries conferred by Holy Orders are not John Paul's main concern, he discusses them briefly. These ministries — diaconate, priesthood, and episcopacy — give the recipients "the authority and sacred power to serve the Church, acting *in persona Christi Capitis* (in the person of Christ, the Head), and to gather her in the Holy Spirit through the Gospel and the sacraments" (§22.1, cf. §23.3). The Holy Father maintains that these ordained ministries express "a participation in the priesthood of Jesus Christ that is different, not simply in degree but in essence, from the participation given to all the lay faithful through Baptism and Confirmation" (§22.2, cf. §§23.7, 23.12). At the same time, intended as they are as a grace for the entire Church, these ministries serve the royal priesthood of all the faithful.

In a way proper to their state, lay men and women, by carrying out certain ministries, share in the priestly, prophetic, and kingly mission of Christ and the Church. Not derived from Holy Orders, these lay ministries, offices, and roles have their *"foundation in the Sacraments of Baptism and Confirmation,* indeed, for a good many of them, *in the Sacrament of Matrimony"* (§23.2). An essential difference exists between ordained and lay ministries, one founded on the difference between the ministerial and the common priesthood. John Paul resolutely holds to this distinction in theory and practice. At the core of his view of the laity is respect for the unique dignity of their vocation precisely as lay. He resists any suggestion that it be assimilated to, or absorbed by, the clerical state. "The various ministries, offices and roles that the lay faithful can legitimately fulfill in the liturgy, in the transmission of the faith, and in the pastoral structure of the Church," the Pope writes, "ought to be exercised *in conformity with their specific lay vocation,* which is different from that of the sacred ministry" (§23.9). Consequently, any ministries carried out by lay people, including those traditionally associated with the pastoral ministry of the clergy, are entrusted to them in virtue of their Baptism.

Besides bestowing these diverse ministries, the Holy Spirit further enriches the Church with numerous charisms freely given to lay men and women. What are these charisms? "Whether they be exceptional and great or simple and ordinary, the charisms are *graces of the Holy Spirit that have,* directly or indirectly, *a usefulness for the ecclesial community,* ordered as they are to the building up of the Church, to the well-being of humanity and to the needs of the world" (§24.2). The Holy Father mentions that both the individual recipient and the Church as a whole should acknowledge these gifts of the Spirit gratefully. He also declares that every charism must be exercised in communion with the Bishop, and that ecclesiastical authority must carefully discern their authenticity (cf. 1 Thess 5:12, 19-21). These provisions ensure that all the charisms will "work together, in their diversity and complementarity, for the common good" (§24.6).

The Diocese and the parish

The laity effectively build ecclesial communion in their particular Church or Diocese and in their parish. According to John Paul, they carry out their mission in the particular Church to which they belong by taking part in Diocesan Pastoral Councils, Diocesan Synods, and Local Councils and by collaborating with national or regional Episcopal Conferences. At the same time, he encourages the lay faithful to cultivate a " 'catholic' spirit" (§25.4). This spirit will enable them to develop a strong sense of the *"primordial bond"* which links their particular Church to all other Churches and the universal Church (cf. §25.3).

While always having a universal dimension and outreach, the ecclesial community has its "most immediate and visible expression in the *parish. . . .* It is the *Church living in the midst of the homes of her sons and daughters"* (§26.1). Certainly the Church is also present and effective in places and organizations other than the parish. Even so, the Pope exhorts lay women and men "to be ever more convinced of the special meaning that their commitment to the apostolate takes on in their parish" (§27.3). As a theological reality founded on the Eucharist, the parish is a vital community of faith nourished by the complementary ministries of clergy and laity. The Holy Father expresses the hope that the parish will adhere to "its fundamental vocation and mission, that is, to be a 'place' in the world for the community of believers to gather together as a 'sign' and 'instrument' of the vocation of all to communion; in a word, to be a house of welcome to all and a place of service to all" (§27.6).

Lay associations and movements

Christifideles Laici describes two different ways in which the laity foster the Church's life of communion: as individuals and as members of lay associations, movements, or groups. First of all, the exhortation emphasizes the distinct identity and responsibility of the individual Christian. Called personally by God, each one is "entrusted with a unique task which cannot be done by another and which is to be fulfilled for the good of all" (§28.4). Every lay person promotes ecclesial communion by exercising an apostolate in his or her everyday life in the world.

In this exhortation, however, the Pope concentrates more on the lay faithful working together in associations, movements, or groups than on individual apostolates. The 1987 Synod of Bishops devoted considerable attention to these new movements, which were still relatively insignificant at the time of the Second Vatican Council. Even though lay associations such as confraternities and third orders have contributed to the Church's life for many centuries, recent decades have witnessed "*a new era of group endeavors* of the lay faithful" (§29.2). Formed to promote the spiritual life and/or apostolic work, these associations, movements, and groups include, for example, L'Arche communities, the Catholic Women's League, Cursillo, the Focolari Movement, the Knights of Columbus, and the Neocatechumenal Way. They differ considerably from one another "in their external structures, in their procedures and training methods, and in the fields in which they work" (§29.3). Some new ecclesial movements, while primarily lay, are also open in various ways to clergy and Religious. The Pope regards these new associations and movements as a true gift to the Church. For many Christians, he writes, they are a precious help "in remaining faithful to the demands of the Gospel and to the commitment to the Church's mission and the apostolate" (§29.4). They are true signs and instruments of organic ecclesial communion.

In order to ensure that these new lay groups, some of which have only tenuous links to the local parish, will build up Church communion, avoid rivalry among themselves, and respect episcopal authority, John Paul lays down two fundamental principles. First, the lay faithful are free to form groups whose purpose is in harmony with the Church's life of communion and her mission. This freedom of association is "a true and proper right that is not derived from any kind of 'concession' by authority, but flows from the Sacrament of Baptism" (§29.7). Second, the rightful freedom of these groups is to "be acknowledged and guaranteed by ecclesial authority and always and only to be exercised in Church communion" (§29.8).

These two principles lead the Pope to formulate five "criteria of ecclesiality" for evaluating an association of the lay faithful. The members of new movements and associations can use the criteria to determine whether they are carrying out their mission effectively, and Bishops can use them in discerning a group's ecclesial authenticity. The guidelines are designed to ensure that associations of the lay faithful remain united to the Bishops and develop pastoral programs in collaboration with them. John Paul regards the criteria as a checklist which can nourish cooperation between lay groups and the Pastors responsible for encouraging them and granting them official recognition.

First, the primary objective of a lay association must be a concern for the holiness of its members. They are to foster "growth toward the fullness of Christian life and the perfection of charity" (§30.2). Second, groups are to profess the Catholic faith "in its total content" and "in obedience to the Church's Magisterium" (§30.3). Third, while lay associations enjoy a certain legitimate autonomy from ecclesiastical authority, they are to bear witness to a *strong and authentic communion*" with the Successor of Peter and Pastor of the particular Church (§30.3). Members express this communion through their "loyal readiness to embrace the doctrinal teachings and pastoral initiatives of both Pope and Bishop" (§30.4). Fourth, lay associations are to share in the Church's apostolic endeavors, especially in today's task of re-evangelization. Lastly, in keeping with the secular character of the lay vocation, the groups and movements should foster their members' commitment to be present in the world, at the service of the integral dignity of the human person. Whether an association lives by these guidelines can be verified by examining "the *actual fruits* that various group forms show in their organizational life and the works they perform" (§30.7).

Mission to communion

Ecclesial communion is dynamic, reaching outward to embrace others. When authentically lived, the life of Church communion is "a *sign* for all the world and a compelling *force* that will lead persons to faith in Christ" (§31.8). Those living in communion with Christ and the Church are like branches on the vine: they are required to bear fruit (cf. Jn 15:5). The fruit of their communion shows itself in their resolute commitment to the Church's mission in the world. For Pope John Paul, "*communion represents both the source and the fruit of mission: communion gives rise to mission and mission is accomplished in communion*" (§32.4). From their experience of communion, lay men and women are equipped to bring the Good News to the whole world.

Compelled by a sense of urgency, the Holy Father issues a stirring challenge to the lay faithful. They are to accept responsibility for proclaiming the

Gospel, a task for which they are prepared by the sacraments of initiation and the various gifts of the Holy Spirit. They carry out this prophetic role in two different spheres of life. Above all, the Holy Father insists on the need for the re-evangelization of whole societies or sectors within them. "Without doubt," he says, "a mending of the Christian fabric of society is urgently needed in all parts of the world" (§34.3). The laity help to bring the Gospel to societies traditionally Christian by bearing witness to "how the Christian faith constitutes the only fully valid response . . . to the problems and hopes that life poses to every person and society" (§34.4). Besides working within their own surroundings, the lay faithful are also called to evangelize the world which does not yet know Christ. John Paul urges lay people to go, if possible, to mission territories and also to foster vocations for the missions in their families and communities. Through the testimony of their example and action the laity respond to the Lord's call to "preach the Gospel to the whole creation" (Mk 16:15).

Serving the person

In addition to her mission of evangelizing explicitly, the Church has the vocation of advancing the true good of each person and all humanity. This call is rooted "in the extraordinary and profound fact that 'through the Incarnation the Son of God has united himself in some fashion to every person' [*Gaudium et Spes*, §22]" (§36.2). The lay faithful serve the person by fostering human dignity, defending the inviolable right to life, and promoting religious freedom.

Fittingly, given the Pope's innumerable appeals and initiatives on behalf of human dignity, he asks the laity to take up this challenge: "*To rediscover and make others rediscover the inviolable dignity of every human person*" (§37.1). The promotion of the dignity of the person is the most important contribution which lay men and women can render to the human family. To help them understand the significance of their responsibility, John Paul explains what he means by human dignity. Only men and women are "persons," that is, intelligent and free beings and, "precisely for this reason, the 'center and summit' of all that exists on the earth" (§37.2). Every person without exception has inestimable worth, since he or she is created in God's image, redeemed by Christ's blood, and destined for a life of eternal communion with the Holy Trinity. Human dignity is thus based on what a person "is," and not on what he or she "has." It is an individual's most precious possession. Consequently, "the human being is *always a value as an individual,* and as such demands being considered and treated as a person and never, on the contrary, considered and treated as an object to be used, or as a means, or as a thing" (§37.5). The lay faithful have the vocation of affirming the grandeur of the human person and proclaiming that "every violation of the personal dignity of the human being cries out in vengeance to God and is an offense against the Creator" (§37.4).

The laity also serve the person by defending and promoting the inherent, universal, and inviolable rights of every human being, rights founded on their personal dignity. Foremost among these is *"the right to life,* the most basic and fundamental right and the condition for all other personal rights" (§38.2). In the face of a "culture of death," the lay faithful are charged with fostering respect and love for each individual *"in every phase of* development, from conception until natural death; and *in every condition,* whether healthy or sick, whole or handicapped, rich or poor" (§38.3). The Pope points especially to the need for the laity to respond to the new challenges posed by technology and bioethics.

Lastly, and quite characteristically, John Paul turns his attention as well to religious freedom. He believes that the effective recognition of this right "is among the highest goods and the most serious duties of every people that truly wishes to assure the good of the person and society" (§39.1). This right, the Pope observes, is all too frequently violated. Many of the lay faithful suffer persecution, marginalization, and even martyrdom for the sake of their faith. Their suffering and death constitute "the summit of the apostolic life among Christ's disciples" (§39.2). For this convincing testimony the whole Church is grateful.

Serving society through the family and works of charity

Besides serving individual persons, the lay faithful's kingly mission entails serving society. They carry out their first duty to society by safeguarding and fostering marriage and the family. To discharge this mission effectively they must first of all be convinced "of the unique and irreplaceable value that the family has in the development of society and the Church" (§40.4). Armed with this conviction, they can promote the family's role as society's basic cell, the cradle of life and love, and the primary school of " 'humanization' for the person and society" (§40.6). Lay men and women, therefore, contribute to social life chiefly by ensuring that the family is a true community of persons which enlivens its own members and the wider community. Their stable and loving families have an irreplaceable value for the general welfare of society; they guarantee its harmony, freedom, and prosperity. Especially today, when threatened by attempts to lessen the stability and importance of the family, lay people should strive to make the family aware of its identity and role in society, so that it might become an ever "more *active and responsible place* for proper growth and proper participation in social life" (§40.7).

As well as forming and fostering strong and responsible families, the lay faithful also contribute to society through their charitable works. Acts of charity for the good of one's neighbor are the ordinary way in which the laity, whether individually or in groups, show their coresponsibility for the Church's mission to the world. The performance of the spiritual and corporal works of mercy, whether in a traditional or contemporary form, is a fundamental way for them to "exercise and manifest their participation in the kingship of Christ" (§41.3).

Serving society in political, economic, and cultural life

In light of the Synod Fathers' recommendations and his own passion for the Church's social teaching, John Paul treats the laity's mission to build communion in the political, economic, and cultural spheres of contemporary society. Concerned lest the lay faithful neglect their responsibility to society, the Holy Father is particularly exhortatory. He urges lay men and women not to flee from the world to the confines of the sanctuary: "The lay faithful *are never to relinquish their participation in 'public life,'* that is, in the many different economic, social, legislative, administrative and cultural areas, which are intended to promote organically and institutionally the *common good"* (§42.2). The Pope encourages the laity to bear fruit in the different realms of social life; they are to embrace their "right and duty to participate in public life, albeit in a diversity and complementarity of forms, levels, tasks and responsibilities" (§42.2).

Pope John Paul singles out two reasons which discourage people from entering the public square. First, "charges of careerism, idolatry of power, egoism and corruption" are frequently directed at those active in political life. Second, many today think that taking part in politics represents an "absolute moral danger" (§42.2). Despite these negative evaluations of public service, the Pope warns lay people not to become skeptical or abdicate responsibility for the political process. As a counterbalance, he offers a lofty view of the laity's mission in public life: they are to pursue the common good. Enlightened by the Church's social doctrine, politicians should exercise authority in a spirit of service. "The lay faithful," John Paul states, "must bear witness to those human and Gospel values that are intimately connected with political activity itself, such as liberty and justice, solidarity, faithful and unselfish dedication for the good of all, a simple lifestyle, and a preferential love for the poor" (§42.7). They ought as well to assume the task of being "peacemakers"

(Mt 5:9), striving at every level — from the local to the international — to build a culture free of hatred and conflict.

In the socioeconomic sphere, especially in the field of work, lay women and men have "the responsibility of being in the forefront in working out a solution to the very serious problems" (§43.5) of unemployment, exploitation, and injustice of all kinds. The Pope recommends that the laity approach their work honestly and with professional competence. Above all they should see it as a means of sanctification.

Always eager to ensure that the Gospel is embodied in culture, since "only from within and through culture does the Christian faith become a part of history and the creator of history" (§44.1), John Paul urges the lay faithful to take part in its creation and transmission. This involvement is all the more crucial in situations where a culture's Christian and human values are losing ground or where science and technology cannot respond adequately to people's pressing questions about meaning and truth. To meet these challenges, the Holy Father calls on the laity to purify the destructive elements in a culture and to enrich it with the light of the Gospel. Thus, he exhorts them "to be present as signs of courage and intellectual creativity in the privileged places of culture, that is, the world of education — school and university — in places of scientific and technological research, the areas of artistic creativity and work in the humanities" (§44.2). It is especially important, the Pope adds, that lay people be present in the area of social communications, the "new frontier for the mission of the Church" (§44.4).

Laborers in the vineyard

In chapter four, the Holy Father becomes even more exhortatory. He addresses the different groups of laborers in the Lord's vineyard, explains their particular contribution to the Church's mission, and recommends specific pastoral initiatives. In this way he deals with the various categories of the lay faithful: youth, children, the elderly, the sick and the suffering, and women.

Each member of the People of God — ordained minister, Religious, and lay person — is called "to work for the coming of the Kingdom of God according to the diversity of callings and situations, charisms and ministries" (§45.2). Their tasks are different yet complementary, "in the sense that each of them has a basic and unmistakable character which sets each apart, while at the same time each of them is seen in relation to the other and placed at each other's service" (§55.3). Although the states of life are different, all are ordered to the Church's mission. Moreover, the lay state itself manifests a rich variety in approaches to spirituality and the apostolate. But in every case the individual "is called by name, to make a special contribution to the coming of the Kingdom of God. No talent, no matter how small, is to be hidden or left unused" (§56.4, cf. §45.2).

Throughout his pontificate John Paul has shown a special concern for youth, who are "a *great challenge for the future of the Church*" (§46.1). Young people are more than an object of the Church's pastoral care. The Pope encourages them to "be active on behalf of the Church as *leading characters in evangelization and participants in the renewal of society*" (§46.3). Young Christians have much to offer the Church, and those involved with them must be willing to engage in a mutually enriching dialogue. The Church's path to the future passes by way of the young.

Children, too, play an active role in ecclesial life. First of all, they are "the eloquent symbol and exalted image of those moral and spiritual conditions that are essential for entering into the Kingdom of God and for living the logic of total confidence in the Lord" (§47.1). Second, children are a reminder that the Church's spiritual fruitfulness is an absolutely gratuitous gift of God, independent of any human calculation or merit. Third, because children contribute to the sanctification of family members, they strengthen this basic community of love and thus also build up society.

The Holy Father reminds the elderly that they are still laborers in the vineyard with an important contribution to make. Old age does not acquit them of their ecclesial mission. "They must always have a clear knowledge that one's role in the Church and society does not stop at a certain age at all," says the Pope, "but at such times knows only new ways of application" but calls for new forms of apostolate (§48.3). As living witnesses to tradition, teachers of the lessons of life, and workers of charity, older people are a gift to society and the Church.

After martyrs for the faith, John Paul believes that the sick and the suffering are the Church's greatest spiritual treasure. In the vineyard of the world, they "participate in the growth of the Kingdom of God in a *new and even more valuable manner*" (§53.3). Through suffering, people play an active part in evangelization and the work of salvation (cf. Col 1:24). The Pope also calls attention to the contribution that those who suffer can make in societies which censor any mention of suffering. By uniting themselves to Christ's Passion, they reveal that suffering can have "a positive meaning for the individual and for society" (§54.2). The Church then spiritually benefits from her suffering members. But she is also called to reenact the parable of the Good Samaritan in her pastoral activity *for* and *with* the sick and suffering.

By way of response to the Synod's recommendations, the Holy Father devotes a long section of *Christifideles Laici* to the dignity of women and their mission in the Church and society. He acknowledges their indispensable contribution to social and ecclesial life, takes a firm stand against all forms of discrimination and abuse of women, and urges greater awareness of women's "own specific vocation" in the Church (§49.5). This vocation is twofold: their task to safeguard and foster the dignity of married life and motherhood, and their responsibility to promote a social and cultural life more worthy of the person. The Pope also explores the anthropological and theological foundation of masculinity and femininity. This male-female complementarity is the basis for the coordinated cooperation of lay men and women as laborers in the vineyard.

Formation of the lay faithful

Chapter five of *Christifideles Laici* is devoted to lay formation. John Paul confirms the Synod Fathers' proposal that "the formation of the lay faithful must be placed *among the priorities of a Diocese*" (§57.5). He describes the purpose of formation, its content, the people and communities responsible for it, and where it takes place. Here the Pope again returns to the Gospel image of the vine and the branches, this time to highlight that the laity must mature if they wish to serve the Kingdom of God. Christian formation is the process which enables people to grow, develop, and "bear much fruit" (Jn 15:5).

Lay formation is aimed at awakening a clearer sense in each individual of his or her unique vocation and mission in the Church. But only in "the unfolding of the history of our lives and its events is the eternal plan of God revealed to us" (§58.3). The discerning of God's call is an ongoing process. Certainly an awareness of this call is an indispensable first step, but this knowledge requires carrying out in practice what God wants. The faithful following of God's will demands both "a *capability* for acting and *the developing of that capability*" (§58.6). Hence formation is necessary, ongoing, and relevant to every area of a person's life. It is not the privilege of a few, "but a right and duty of all" (§63.1). Moreover, the Holy Father stresses that formation is primarily God's work. It is totally dependent on the branches remaining engrafted on the vine: "For apart from me you can do nothing" (Jn 15:5).

According to *Christifideles Laici*, the laity should receive a complete and integrated formation, one which "bears its fruit in every sphere of existence and activity" (§59.2). What does such a formation program entail? First, John Paul mentions the primacy to be given to the spiritual formation of the laity. Their continual growth in communion with Christ is nourished by the help to holiness offered by the Church. Second, lay men and women require a doctrinal formation which will enable them to explain to the world the reason for their hope (cf. 1 Pet 3:15). Thus a systematic catechesis, geared to different ages and backgrounds, is also necessary. Third, the laity, especially those involved in public and social life, need "a proper formation of a social conscience, especially in the Church's social teaching" (§60.4). Lastly, an integrated program of formation cultivates the human values and skills necessary for the lay faithful's apostolic activities.

Who forms the laity? God is their first educator: "Just as the work of human education is intimately connected with fatherhood and motherhood, so Christian formation finds its origin and its strength in God the Father who loves and educates his children" (§61.2). The Father's work is fulfilled in Christ, the Teacher who instructs by reaching to the depths of the heart through the gift of the Spirit. For her part, the Church also takes part in forming the lay faithful: through the ministry of teaching and celebration of the sacraments. "It is thus," writes John Paul, "that *the lay faithful are formed by the Church and in the Church*" (§61.3). In the universal Church, the Successor of Peter has the primary role in forming the laity. In the local Churches the Bishop has the direct responsibility for their formation. Priests and Religious help in this endeavor; in turn, "the lay faithful themselves can and should help priests and Religious in the course of their spiritual and pastoral journey" (§61.8). Aside from the various external teachers, John Paul points out that each individual must develop "a personal responsibility for formation" (§63.4).

Where does lay formation take place? The domestic Church of the family is, of course, the first and fundamental school of formation in the faith. Helped by the grace of the Sacrament of Matrimony, parents educate their children, "before whom they bear witness and to whom they transmit both human and religious values" (§62.1). But formation is also an essential task of the parish. In the parish, especially if it is very large, basic ecclesial communities can help in formation "by providing a consciousness and an experience of ecclesial communion and mission" (§61.7). For their part, Catholic schools and universities, the increasing number of centers of spiritual renewal, and groups, associations, and movements of the lay faithful contribute significantly to their integral formation.

The Holy Father ends his post-synodal apostolic exhortation with an appeal and a prayer. He appeals to Bishops and laity alike to foster an ecclesial consciousness which is "ever mindful of what it means to be members of the Church of Jesus Christ, participants in her mystery of communion and in her dynamism in mission and the apostolate" (§64.3). The Pope's appeal then becomes a concluding prayer to Mary. He asks her to implore a renewed outpouring of the Holy Spirit "on all the faithful, men and women alike, so that they might more fully respond to their vocation and mission, as branches engrafted to the true vine, called to bear much fruit for the life of the world" (§64.9).

Key Themes

Even though *Christifideles Laici* is a summary of the Church's teaching on the laity, John Paul II pays particular attention to several themes which are key to his understanding of the dignity and mission of the lay faithful. I have selected four of these, each of which develops a specific aspect of his teaching: the secular character of the lay vocation, the new evangelization, "lay" ministry, and the dignity and mission of women.

Secular character of the lay vocation

In agreement with *Lumen Gentium* §31, *Christifideles Laici* repeatedly refers to the "secular character" of the lay vocation (cf. §§15.2, 15.3, 15.6, 15.9, 15.10, 36.5, 55.4, 64.5). Within the Body of Christ the gifts specific to the different states of life converge for its upbuilding, yet each state has a specific identity, vocation, and mission. What distinguishes the lay faithful from clergy and Religious is precisely their activity in the world. This activity specifies the "unique character of their vocation" (§9.2). To be sure, the whole People of God are "sharers in this secular dimension but in *different ways*" (§15.6). For lay Christians, this presence and activity in the world are central to their mission. It identifies their state of life in the Church, as Holy Orders specifies the clerical state and the profession of the evangelical counsels that of the consecrated life. Despite the exhortation's emphasis on activity in the world as characteristic of the lay state, it nonetheless insists that the lay faithful are *defined* by the newness of Christian life conferred by Baptism. *Being* Christian precedes *acting* as a Christian.

John Paul's understanding of the laity's "secular character" is closely connected with the meaning he gives to the "world" and its relation to the Church. The world is the vineyard: "*This* is the field in which the faithful are called to fulfill their mission" (§3.6). It is here that they are called to be the "salt of the earth" and the "light of the world" (cf. Mt 5:13-14). It is here that they provide for individual and family needs and work for the development of the wider social community. For the laity, the world is "the place in which they receive their call from God" (§15.7). Their baptismal consecration "does not take them from the world at all" (§15.8). Like the Church, which "lives in the world, even if she is not of the world" (§15.5), so, too, do the lay faithful.

But lay Christians do more than live *in* the world as a sphere of action. John Paul believes that they also have a mission *to* the world. "In their situation in the world," he writes, "God manifests his plan and communicates to them their particular vocation of 'seeking the Kingdom of God by engaging in temporal affairs and by ordering them according to the plan of God' [*Lumen Gentium,* §31]" (§15.8). This vineyard to which the laborers are sent "is to be transformed according to the plan of God in view of the final coming of the Kingdom of God" (§1.2). Here the laity are "the humble yet great builders of the Kingdom of God in history" (§17.2).

The Holy Father describes the secularity of the lay vocation in the full perspective of the saving plan of God and the mystery of the Church. The divine plan embraces the world so loved by God that he gave it his only Son (cf. Jn 3:16). John Paul highlights this positive meaning of the world: it is the realm where Christ's redeeming work brings God's plan to fulfillment. The world, then, is not essentially evil but "destined to glorify God the Father in Christ" (§15.8). Thus the Pope urges lay people "to restore to creation all its original value . . . [to order it] to the authentic well-being of humanity in an activity governed by the life of grace" (§14.8, cf. §15.9). By sharing in the royal mission of the Risen Christ, who draws all things to himself (cf. Jn 12:32), the lay faithful work to bring creation to completion. Thus they have a mission not only *in* the world but also *for* the world, acknowledging it "as a reality *destined to find in Jesus Christ the fullness of its meaning*" (§15.7). In the Pope's mind, the secularity of the lay vocation is not "worldly," in the sense of being divorced from God, but is intimately tied to the great mysteries of creation, Incarnation, and Redemption: all things are to be restored in Christ (cf. Eph 1:10).

John Paul carefully avoids setting up a false dichotomy between the mundane and the spiritual, and between the laity's activity in the world and the clergy's activity in the Church. Through Baptism all the faithful are incorporated into Christ's Mystical Body, and whatever activity they undertake they do so precisely as individuals indelibly marked by this consecration. Lay people engage in worldly activity precisely *as Church.* Indeed, in the memorable words of Pius XII cited by John Paul II, the laity *"are the Church"* (§9.3). Their mission to build communion extends beyond intra-ecclesial life to the whole world: "The Church knows that the communion received by her as a gift is destined for all people" (§32.4). While respecting "the autonomy of earthly realities properly understood" (§42.7), lay men and women strive to draw the world into divine communion. This communion can be brought about only through the Church, the Body of which Christ is the Head (cf. Col 1:17-18). Lay people therefore strive to transform the world with the gift of communion with the Triune God, which is always mediated through Christ and the Church. For this reason the Pope says that the laity's secular vocation "has the purpose of making everyone know and live the 'new' communion that the Son of God made man introduced into the history of the world" (§32.4).

New evangelization

With the publication of *Christifideles Laici,* John Paul launches his pressing appeal, which grows ever more insistent in subsequent papal documents, for "re-evangelization." This term was later replaced, at least for the most part, by "new evangelization," and as such has become a leitmotiv of his pontificate. The origins of the need for a new evangelization come from the Church's "more lively awareness of her missionary nature" (§2.3), an awareness that missionary activity involves all Christians. In recent years, a renewed commitment to proclaiming the Gospel has taken root. The Good News is to be preached not only to people who have not yet heard it but also to those who have lost a living sense of the Christian faith, have ceased to practice it, or no longer consider themselves members of the Church. This latter situation, found in nations and cultures which once absorbed Gospel principles and values, challenges the ecclesial community to commit its energies to a new evangelization. The Pope specifically invites the lay faithful "to regard themselves as an active and responsible part of this venture" (§64.8). He also insists that the beginning of the new evangelization is the witness of life given by lay people in everyday circumstances. A rekindling of the freshness and timeless novelty of the Christian faith "gains credibility when it is not simply voiced in words, but passes into a testimony of life" (§54.3).

Missionary activity is therefore needed today where Christianity has long been known but is now sporadically practiced. "The *present situation,* not only of the world but also of many parts of the Church," John Paul affirms, "*absolutely demands that the word of Christ receive a more ready and generous obedience*" (§33.5). Quite simply, the hour has come for re-evangelization. This new evangelization of formerly Christian nations and societies "is directed not only to individual persons but also to entire portions of populations in the variety of their situations, surroundings and cultures" (§34.9, cf. §§27.5, 44.2). Lay men and women are the primary protagonists of this vast effort of reopening the doors to Christ.

In *Christifideles Laici,* the Holy Father repeats the impassioned cry made at the beginning of his papal ministry: *"Do not be afraid! Open, indeed, open wide the doors to Christ!* Open to his saving power the confines of States, and systems political and economic, as well as the vast fields of culture, civilization, and development" (§34.5). New social and cultural factors have brought about a situation which calls for a fresh proclamation of the Gospel in areas where Christianity once flourished. Secularism, indifference to religion, and atheism are taking their toll. In the wealthy nations of the First World, largely Christian in their religious tradition, the situation is particularly acute. Prosperity and consumerism, although they often coexist with poverty and misery, lead many to live "as if God did not exist" (§34.1). Furthermore, even in regions or nations where popular forms of Christian religiosity continue to exist, "this moral and spiritual patrimony runs the risk of being dispersed under the impact of a multiplicity of processes, including secularization and the spread of sects" (§34.2). These situations call for a new evangelization.

Re-evangelization involves the cooperation of every lay individual and every lay group. Because of the secular character of their vocation, the lay faithful are well suited to bringing the Gospel to the world, to awakening everyone "to a full sense of human existence, that is, to communion with God and with all people" (§28.5). Now more than ever each lay man and woman must proclaim the Good News in the neighborhoods of the world: "Woe to me if I do not preach the Gospel!" (1 Cor 9:16). The Pope also urges parishes to play their part. They are "to reawaken *missionary zeal* toward non-believers and believers themselves who have abandoned the faith or grown lax in the Christian life" (§27.5). Furthermore, he exhorts every lay association, movement, and group "to have a missionary zeal which will increase their effectiveness as participants in a re-evangelization" (§30.5). For the new evangelization to be successful, John Paul believes that the first step is "to *first remake the Christian fabric of the ecclesial community itself*" in societies where the faith is waning.

The message of the new evangelization is as simple as the Gospel itself: humanity is loved by God! The Holy Father writes: "Each Christian's words and life must make this proclamation resound: God loves you, Christ came for you, Christ is for you 'the way, the truth and the life!' (Jn 14:6)" (§34.8).

"Lay" ministry

Among the positive fruits of the Second Vatican Council the Pope mentions "the new manner of active collaboration among priests, Religious and the lay faithful" (§2.8). Both doctrinal reflection and practical organization have unleashed the energies of the laity to proclaim the Gospel and build up the Body of Christ. More than ever before their apostolate work should be carried out with a profound ecclesial spirit. This sense of communion unites lay people to clergy and consecrated men and women in accomplishing the Church's mission.

Again and again the Holy Father points to Baptism as "the source of being a Christian in the mystery of the Church . . . [which] serves as the basis for all the vocations and dynamism of the Christian life of the lay faithful" (§9.5, cf. §§9.6, 10, 14.9, 15.1, 23.1, 23.2, 23.7, 29.7, 51.1, 64.4). This sacrament confers on all the faithful a common dignity which is "the source of equality for all members of the Church" (§17.7). By reaffirming the universal call to holiness, the Pope also emphasizes the teaching that the "commonly shared Christian dignity" (§55.3) is rooted in Baptism. Christ's followers, because of their baptismal consecration, are all equally obliged to "the common vocation to holiness" incumbent on members of the Church (§16.4). Through the sacrament of spiritual rebirth, all the faithful share in the one priesthood of Jesus Christ, inasmuch as they offer themselves to God as a "living sacrifice" (Rom 12:1). Moreover, the common priesthood and the ministerial priesthood are meant to support each other. The laity acknowledge that "the ministerial priesthood is totally necessary for their participation in the mission in the Church" (§22.3), and the clergy acknowledge that their ministry has "the royal priesthood of all the faithful as its aim and is ordered to it" (§22.2, cf. §22.3).

But Pope John Paul also thinks that certain theological and pastoral problems have arisen in the wake of the post-conciliar emphasis on the faithful's "royal priesthood" (1 Pet 2:9). Theologically, the major difficulty comes from those who attenuate "the essential difference between the ministerial priesthood and the common priesthood, and the difference between the ministries derived from the Sacrament of Orders and those derived from the Sacraments of Baptism and Confirmation" (§23.12, cf. §§22.2, 22.7, 23.6, 23.9). Several reasons can be offered to explain why belief in this doctrine has weakened: a misunderstanding of the equality of every member of the Church, one which fails to respect the sacramentally based distinctions based on different roles; a decline in the conviction about priestly identity; the laity's taking on certain "ministerial" responsibilities traditionally associated with the clergy; and a "functionalist" theology of pastoral activity, one which rejects or obscures the teaching that the ministerial priest receives "the authority and sacred power to serve the Church, acting *in persona Christi Capitis*" (§22.1).

To clear up this doctrinal confusion, John Paul, while always respecting the equal dignity of all Christians created by Baptism, affirms the complementarity of the different states of life. He thus studiously avoids any theory or practice that would "clericalize" the lay faithful or "laicize" the clergy. Fidelity to the Church's constitution as willed by Christ and guided through history by the Holy Spirit leads the Pope to distinguish "the substantial *diversity of the ministry* of pastors which is rooted in the Sacrament of Orders . . . [from] the other ministries, offices and roles in the Church, which are rooted in the Sacraments of Baptism and Confirmation" (§23.7). Far from creating divisions in the community, the distinction between ordained and baptismal ministries builds up ecclesial communion.

Whereas the essential difference between the common and ministerial priesthood is doctrinally certain, some pastoral practices have developed which obscure this difference. John Paul addresses specific problems which arise when lay men and women share in pastoral and liturgical ministry. The first issue raised focuses on the terminology of "ministry." The Synod, he observes, voiced a critical judgment about "a too-indiscriminate use of the word 'ministry' . . . and the risk of creating, in reality, an ecclesial structure of parallel service to that founded on the Sacrament of Orders" (§23.6). Some Fathers wanted to restrict the term almost exclusively to the ordained ministry. Others defended the use of "ministry" in reference to certain lay tasks, though without agreeing on a more precise usage. At least occasionally *Christifideles Laici* reflects the use of "ministry" common in some quarters to refer to certain tasks carried out by the laity (cf. §§22.3, 23.2). For the most part, however, the exhortation prefers terms such as "offices," "roles," or "tasks." The Holy Father seems to favor a restricted use of the term "ministry" to refer to tasks carried out by the lay faithful.

John Paul distinguishes between functions and tasks ("ministries") which the laity assume by way of exception and those proper to the lay vocation. In line with the 1983 Code of Canon Law, the Pope holds that lay people can carry out "certain offices and roles that are connected to their [pastors'] pastoral ministry but do not require the character of Orders" (§23.3). These offices include presiding at liturgical prayer, conferring Baptism, and distributing Holy Communion. This new situation, however, calls for a doctrinal and pastoral clarification. Doctrinally, the Holy Father asserts that *"the exercise of such tasks does not make pastors of the lay faithful"* (§23.3). Any "ministry" they perform is rooted exclusively in the common priesthood conferred at Baptism. There can be no partial or gradual sharing in Holy Orders. Pastorally, the Pope sets out two conditions for their rightful exercise. The lay faithful exercise these ministries lawfully only "when necessity and expediency in the Church require it" and with the "official deputation" of the pastor (§23.3). Moreover, he admonishes pastors to "guard against a facile yet abusive recourse to a presumed 'situation of emergency' or to 'supply by necessity,' where objectively this does not exist or where alternative possibilities could exist through better pastoral planning" (§23.8). The coupling of these conditions with the exhortation's emphasis on the laity's secular character is yet another indication of John Paul's desire to safeguard the specificity of the lay vocation.

The Pope's tone in discussing the laity's participation in liturgical ministries is, however, far less cautious. Indeed, in this realm it is "natural that the tasks not proper to the ordained ministers are fulfilled by the lay faithful" (§23.5). These liturgical functions are *not* linked to the pastoral ministry, and hence are not *per se* subject to the same papal admonitions. Furthermore, John Paul agrees with the Synod Fathers that the liturgical ministries of lector and acolyte, while open to lay men since 1972, need further study. To this end he established a Commission which met but never published its results.

Ecclesial communion is fostered when everyone respects the specific contribution of the different states of life. To be sure, ecclesial life is "characterized by a *diversity* and a *complementarity* of vocations and states in life, of ministries, of charisms and responsibilities" (§20.1, cf. §23.7). Collaboration between the lay faithful and the clergy is rooted in their shared baptismal dignity and call to holiness. But it is also founded on the complementarity of their roles, which allows each one to carry out the service proper to the sacraments he or she has received.

Christifideles Laici mentions three places or structures where cooperation between the laity and the clergy already takes place but needs further encouragement. In the particular Church, Diocesan Pastoral Councils, Diocesan Synods, and Local Councils are structures which invite the collaboration of clerics and the lay faithful. In the parish, the Pope encourages ecclesial authorities to promote "participation by the lay faithful in pastoral responsibilities" (§26.4), especially in Parish Councils. Everywhere greater cooperation needs to be nourished between members of lay associations and ecclesial authorities (cf. §§30.3, 30.4, 31.5).

Dignity and mission of lay women

More so than any previous Assembly, the 1987 Synod turned its attention to "the place and role of women both in the Church and in society" (§2.10) — a theme especially dear to Pope John Paul II. Questions dealing with women had already attracted his interest as an ethics professor at Lublin, and later, as Pope, he continued to pursue this interest: in the long catechesis, at the beginning of his Pontificate, devoted to the "theology of the body"; in his encyclical on Mary, *Redemptoris Mater* (1987); in his apostolic letter *Mulieris Dignitatem* (1988), "On the Dignity and Vocation of Women on the Occasion of the Marian Year"; in his Letter to Women (1995); and in his many interventions in preparation for the Beijing Conference in 1995. This papal concern for women's dignity and vocation coincides with the Synod's intention. The Fathers wanted to acknowledge "the contribution" which women make to society and the Church, and "to work on a more specific analysis of women's participation in the life and mission of the Church" (§49.1).

"Through committing herself to a reflection on the anthropological and theological basis of femininity," writes the Holy Father, "the Church enters the historic process of the various movements for the promotion of woman" (§50.2). *Christifideles Laici* makes a significant contribution to these movements by means of its brief but incisive summary of the Church's teaching on women. While much of what the exhortation says also applies to consecrated women, it gives primary attention to lay women.

According to the Pope, contemporary women's movements owe their origins to the widespread lack of respect for the personal dignity of women. Despite the beneficial changes that have been introduced, much remains to be done to end "the various forms of discrimination and marginalization to which women are subjected simply because they are women" (§49.2). The dignity of women as persons is wounded whenever they are dominated, treated as objects, or denied basic human rights. At the source of this discrimination is an "unjust and deleterious mentality which considers the human being as a thing, as an object to buy and sell, as an instrument for selfish interests or for pleasure only" (§49.3). John Paul roundly condemns all forms of discrimination which victimize women. For him, it undermines the equality of all people willed by the Creator, confirmed by Jesus' attitude to women, and taught by the apostolic community (cf. Gal 3:28).

Although the Holy Father recognizes the positive role of social movements which promote women, he is convinced that the Church, with Christian women as the protagonists, has her own "most precious contribution" to offer to this cause (§50.2). Her wisdom is based on revelation. He invites every woman to discern with the light of faith "what truly responds to her dignity as a person and to her vocation from all that, under the pretext of this 'dignity' and in the name of 'freedom' and 'progress,' militates against true values" (§51.7). Christian women participate in the prophetic mission of Christ and the Church when they engage in such discernment.

For the Pope, this process of evaluation has a particular point of departure, one which involves a decisively Christian perspective: "God's plan for woman . . . is to be read within the context of the faith of the Church" (§50.2). He contends that the discussion of women's roles and mission should begin with a study of "her make-up and meaning as a person" (§50.1). This starting point involves a meditation on God's creation of man and woman "in his image" (Gen 1:27). From the very beginning, the divine plan "has been indelibly imprinted in the very being of the human person — men and women — and, therefore, in the make-up, meaning and deepest workings of the individual" (§50.2). The Holy Father teaches that a woman's social and ecclesial mission can properly be grasped only in light of her feminine originality, identity, or genius.

Respect for women's personal dignity entails acknowledging not only "her equality with man" (§49.2) but also her "complementarity" (§50.1) in relation to him. In the plan of creation, God "willed the human being to be a 'unity of the two'" (§52.3), the first communion between persons. There is equality and complementarity — a partnership — between the sexes. This equality in diversity, willed by God at the very dawn of creation, has significant consequences for the identity and roles of men and women. The Pope urges "the coordinated presence of both men and women . . . so that the participation of the lay faithful in the salvific mission of the Church might be rendered more rich, complete and harmonious" (§52.2).

One sign of the times mentioned at the beginning of *Christifideles Laici* is the desire of women for greater participation "not only in areas of family and academic life, but also in cultural, economic, social and political areas" (§5.7). John Paul encourages them, precisely as women, to assume an increasingly responsible role in social life. At the same time, he recognizes the obstacles which they still face in fully expressing their womanhood. The Holy Father counsels that, in the various spheres of human endeavor, "the personal dignity of woman and her specific vocation ought to be respected and promoted" (§51.12).

The Pope mentions two great tasks that are entrusted to women. First, they have the responsibility of "*bringing full dignity to the conjugal life and to motherhood*" (§51.10). Indeed, women's decisive contributions to family life are necessary if this community of persons is to realize its vocation to be the domestic Church and basic cell of society. Second, because of their feminine identity, women have the task of "*assuring the moral dimension of culture,* the dimension, namely of *a culture worthy of the person,* of an individual yet social life" (§51.11). Women are uniquely capable of guaranteeing this moral dimension because "in a special way the human being is entrusted to woman." In virtue of their "special experience of motherhood," women have "a *specific sensitivity* toward the human person and all that constitutes the individual's true welfare" (§51.13). This entrusting and sensitivity determine women's particular sharing in the royal mission of Christ and the Church.

Pope John Paul accompanies his call for women's increased role in society with an equally urgent appeal for their *"active and responsible participation in the life and mission of the Church"* (§49.4, cf. §§50.4, 51.4). Before describing their ecclesial contributions as partners in the apostolate, he clarifies the Church's teaching on reserving priestly ordination to men. "In her participation in the life and mission of the Church," the Holy Father writes, "a woman cannot receive the *Sacrament of Orders,* and therefore cannot fulfill the proper function of the ministerial priesthood" (§51.2, cf. §49.6). Very carefully he points out that the reason for this teaching does not proceed from sociological or cultural motives peculiar to a particular time. Instead, it is "the expressed will of Christ, totally free and sovereign, who called only men to be his Apostles" (§51.2). To this will the Church must remain obedient.

While not called to the apostolate of the Twelve, Jesus' attitude to women confirmed the "newness of life" in which they fully share. Women accompanied Jesus in his public ministry, were in the forefront at the foot of the Cross, assisted at his burial, and were the first witnesses and messengers of the Resurrection. The early Christian community followed Christ's liberating example: it "called women to tasks connected with spreading the Gospel" (§49.7). In her internal life today's Church must likewise make efforts to enhance the role given to feminine gifts. According to John Paul, the conviction that women are called to share ever more completely in the Church's mission still needs to be carried out in practice. He calls attention to the relevant provisions of the Code of Canon Law which "must be more commonly known and, according to the diverse sensibilities of culture and opportuneness in a pastoral situation, be realized with greater timeliness and determination" (§51.4). The feminine presence in the Church should penetrate all areas of her life: from taking part in diocesan and parochial Pastoral Councils, Diocesan Synods, and particular Councils to catechesis, works of evangelization, and appropriate "ministries." Every woman is called to work in these apostolates with "the 'gifts' which are properly hers: first of all, the gift that is her very dignity as a person exercised in word and testimony of life; gifts, therefore, connected with her vocation as a woman" (§51.1).

* * *

Selected Bibliography

Beauchesne, Richard J. "Heeding the Early Congar Today, and Two Recent Roman Catholic Issues." *Journal of Ecumenical Studies,* 27 (1990), 535-560.

Brown, Susan. "The Most Precious Fruit Desired: the Synod on the Laity and the Apostolic Exhortation." *The Canadian Catholic Review,* 7 (1989), 370-378.

Coughlan, Peter J. *The Hour of the Laity — Their Expanding Role: Exploring "Christifideles Laici" — the Pope's Key Document on the Laity.* Philadelphia: E. J. Dwyer, 1989.

Eyt, Pierre. "Summary of the Definitive Propositions of the Synod." *L'Osservatore Romano,* 45 (1987), 8.

Leckey, Dolores R. "*Christifideles Laici:* An Unfinished Four-Act Play." *Church,* 6 (Spring 1990), 11-18.

Lucas, Brian Joseph. *The Laity Today: A Commentary on "Christifideles Laici."* Homebush, Australia: St. Paul, 1991.

O'Grady, Desmond. "No Idlers in the Vineyard." *Columbia,* 69 (June 1989), 6-9.

Pontifical Council for the Laity. *Christifideles Laici: Comments and Reflections = The Laity Today,* 32/33 (1989/1990). Vatican City: Vatican Press, 1990.

Synod of Bishops, Seventh Ordinary General Assembly. "*Instrumentum Laboris.*" *Origins,* 17 (1987), 1, 3-19.

Synod of Bishops, Seventh Ordinary General Assembly. "*Lineamenta.*" *Origins,* 14 (1985), 624-634.

Synod of Bishops, Seventh Ordinary General Assembly. "Message to the People of God." *L'Osservatore Romano,* 44 (1987), 1, 11; and *Origins,* 17 (1987), 385, 387-389.

Synod of Bishops, Seventh Ordinary General Assembly. "The Synod Propositions." *Origins,* 17 (1987), 499-509.

"Working in the Lord's Vineyard." Editorial. *The Tablet,* 243 (1989), 115.

POST-SYNODAL

APOSTOLIC EXHORTATION

CHRISTIFIDELES LAICI

OF

HIS HOLINESS

JOHN PAUL II

ON

THE VOCATION AND THE MISSION

OF THE LAY FAITHFUL

IN THE CHURCH AND IN THE WORLD

Christifideles Laici

To Bishops
To Priests and Deacons
To Women and Men Religious
and to All the Lay Faithful

Introduction

1.1 The lay members of Christ's faithful people *(Christifideles laici),* whose "Vocation and Mission in the Church and in the World Twenty Years after the Second Vatican Council" was the topic of the 1987 Synod of Bishops, are those who form that part of the People of God which might be likened to the laborers in the vineyard mentioned in Matthew's Gospel: "For the Kingdom of heaven is like a householder who went out early in the morning to hire laborers for his vineyard. After agreeing with the laborers for a denarius a day, he sent them into his vineyard" (Mt 20:1-2).

1.2 The Gospel parable sets before our eyes the Lord's vast vineyard and the multitude of persons, both women and men, who are called and sent forth by him to labor in it. The vineyard is the whole world (cf. Mt 13:38), which is to be transformed according to the plan of God in view of the final coming of the Kingdom of God.

You Go into My Vineyard Too

2.1 "And going out about the third hour he saw others standing idle in the marketplace; and he said to them, 'You go into the vineyard too'"(Mt 20:3-4).

2.2 From that distant day the call of the Lord Jesus, "You go into my vineyard too," never fails to resound in the course of history: it is addressed to every person who comes into this world.

2.3 In our times, the Church after Vatican II, in a renewed outpouring of the Spirit of Pentecost, has come to a more lively awareness of her missionary nature and has listened again to the voice of her Lord who sends her forth into the world as "the universal sacrament of salvation."[1]

2.4 *You go too.* The call is a concern not only of Pastors, clergy, and men and women Religious. The call is addressed to everyone: lay people as well are

---

[1] Second Vatican Ecumenical Council, Dogmatic Constitution on the Church *Lumen Gentium,* 48.

personally called by the Lord, from whom they receive a mission on behalf of the Church and the world. In preaching to the people, Saint Gregory the Great recalls this fact and comments on the parable of the laborers in the vineyard: "Keep watch over your manner of life, dear people, and make sure that you are indeed the Lord's laborers. Each person should take into account what he does and consider if he is laboring in the vineyard of the Lord."[2]

2.5 The Council, in particular, with its rich doctrinal, spiritual and pastoral patrimony, has written as never before on the nature, dignity, spirituality, mission and responsibility of the lay faithful. And the *Council Fathers, reechoing the call of Christ, have summoned all the lay faithful, both women and men, to labor in the vineyard:* "The Council, then, makes an earnest plea in the Lord's name that all lay people give a glad, generous, and prompt response to the impulse of the Holy Spirit and to the voice of Christ, who is giving them an especially urgent invitation at this moment. Young people should feel that this call is directed to them in particular, and they should respond to it eagerly and magnanimously. The Lord himself renews his invitation to all the lay faithful to come closer to him every day, and with the recognition that what is his is also their own (cf. Phil 2:5), they ought to associate themselves with him in his saving mission. Once again he sends them into every town and place where he himself is to come (cf. Lk 10:1)."[3]

2.6 *You go into my vineyard too.* During the *Synod of Bishops,* held in Rome, October 1-30, 1987, these words were reechoed in spirit once again. Following the path marked out by the Council and remaining open to the light of the experience of persons and communities from the whole Church, the Fathers, enriched by preceding Synods, treated in a specific and extensive manner the topic of the vocation and mission of the lay faithful in the Church and in the world.

2.7 In this Assembly of Bishops there was not lacking a qualified representation of the lay faithful, both women and men, which rendered a valuable contribution to the Synod proceedings. This was publicly acknowledged in the concluding homily: "We give thanks that during the course of the Synod we have not only rejoiced in the participation of the lay faithful (both men and women auditors), but even more so in that the progress of the synodal discussions has enabled us to listen to those whom we invited, representatives of the lay faithful from all parts of the world, from different countries, and to profit

---

[2] *Homiliae in Evangelium,* I, 19, 2: PL 76, 1155.
[3] Second Vatican Ecumenical Council, Decree on the Apostolate of the Laity *Apostolicam Actuositatem,* 33.

from their experience, their advice and the suggestions they have offered out of love for the common cause."[4]

2.8 In looking over the years following the Council, the Synod Fathers have been able to verify how the Holy Spirit continues to renew the youth of the Church and how he has inspired new aspirations toward holiness and the participation of so many lay faithful. This is witnessed, among other ways, in the new manner of active collaboration among priests, Religious and the lay faithful; the active participation in the liturgy, in the proclamation of the word of God and catechesis; the multiplicity of services and tasks entrusted to the lay faithful and fulfilled by them; the flourishing of groups, associations and spiritual movements as well as a lay commitment in the life of the Church; and in the fuller and meaningful participation of women in the development of society.

2.9 At the same time, the Synod has pointed out that the post-conciliar path of the lay faithful has not been without its difficulties and dangers. In particular, two temptations can be cited which they have not always known how to avoid: the temptation of being so strongly interested in Church services and tasks that some fail to become actively engaged in their responsibilities in the professional, social, cultural and political world; and the temptation of legitimizing the unwarranted separation of faith from life, that is, a separation of the Gospel's acceptance from the actual living of the Gospel in various situations in the world.

2.10 In the course of its work, the Synod made constant reference to the Second Vatican Council, whose teaching on the lay faithful, after twenty years, has taken on a surprisingly contemporary character and at times has carried prophetic significance: such teaching has the capacity to enlighten and guide the responses which today must be given to new situations. In reality, the challenge embraced by the Synod Fathers has been that of indicating the concrete ways through which this rich "theory" on the lay state expressed by the Council can be translated into authentic Church "practice." Some situations have made themselves felt because of a certain "novelty" that they have, and in this sense they can be called post-conciliar, at least chronologically: to these the Synod Fathers have rightly given a particular attention in the course of their discussion and reflection. Among those situations to be recalled are those regarding the ministries and Church services entrusted at present and in the future to the lay faithful, the growth and spread of new "movements"

[4] John Paul II, Homily at the Solemn Eucharistic Concelebration for the Closing of the Synod of Bishops, Seventh Ordinary General Assembly (October 30, 1987), 3: *AAS* 80 (1988), 598.

alongside other group forms of lay involvement, and the place and role of women both in the Church and in society.

2.11 At the conclusion of their work, which proceeded with great commitment, competence and generosity, the Synod Fathers made known to me their desires and requested that, at an opportune time, a conclusive papal document on the topic of the lay faithful be offered to the universal Church.[5]

2.12 This Post-Synodal Apostolic Exhortation intends to take into account all the richness of the Synod work, from the *Lineamenta* to the *Instrumentum Laboris*, from the introductory report, the presentations of individual Bishops and lay persons to the summary reports after discussion in the Synod Hall, from the discussions and reports of the "small groups" to the final "Propositions" and the concluding "Message." For this reason the present document is not something in contradistinction to the Synod, but is meant to be a faithful and coherent expression of it, a fruit of collegiality. As such, the Council of the General Secretariat of the Synod of Bishops and the Secretariat itself have contributed to its final form.

2.13 This Exhortation intends to stir and promote a deeper awareness among all the faithful of the gift and responsibility they share, both as a group and as individuals, in the communion and mission of the Church.

The Pressing Needs of the World Today: "Why Do You Stand Here Idle All Day?"

3.1 The basic meaning of this Synod and the most precious fruit desired as a result of it, is the *lay faithful's hearkening to the call of Christ the Lord to work in his vineyard,* to take an active, conscientious and responsible part in the mission of the Church *in this great moment in history,* made especially dramatic by occurring on the threshold of the third millennium.

3.2 A new state of affairs today, both in the Church and in social, economic, political and cultural life, calls with a particular urgency for the action of the lay faithful. If lack of commitment is always unacceptable, the present time renders it even more so. *It is not permissible for anyone to remain idle.*

3.3 We continue in our reading of the Gospel parable: "And about the eleventh hour he went out and found others standing; and he said to them, 'Why do you stand here idle all day?' They said to him, 'Because no one has hired us.' He said to them, 'You go into the vineyard too'" (Mt 20:6-7).

3.4 Since the work that awaits everyone in the vineyard of the Lord is so great, there is no place for idleness. With even greater urgency the "householder" repeats his invitation: "you go into my vineyard too."

---

[5] Cf. *Propositio* 1.

3.5 The voice of the Lord clearly resounds in the depths of each of Christ's followers who, through faith and the sacraments of Christian initiation, is made like to Jesus Christ, is incorporated as a living member in the Church and has an active part in her mission of salvation. The voice of the Lord also comes to be heard through the historic events of the Church and humanity, as the Council reminds us: "The People of God believes that it is led by the Spirit of the Lord, who fills the whole world. Moved by this faith it tries to discern authentic signs of God's presence and purpose in the events, the needs, and the longings which it shares with other people of our time. For faith throws a new light on all things and makes known the full ideal to which God has called each individual, and thus guides the mind toward solutions which are fully human."[6]

3.6 It is necessary, then, to keep a watchful eye on this our world, with its problems and values, its unrest and hopes, its defeats and triumphs: a world whose economic, social, political and cultural affairs pose problems and grave difficulties in light of the description provided by the Council in the Pastoral Constitution, *Gaudium et Spes*.[7] *This,* then, is the vineyard; *this* is the field in which the faithful are called to fulfill their mission. Jesus wants them, as he wants all his disciples, to be the "salt of the earth" and the "light of the world" (cf. Mt 5:13-14). But what is the *actual state of affairs* of the "earth" and the "world," for which Christians ought to be "salt" and "light"?

3.7 The variety of situations and problems that exist in our world is indeed great and rapidly changing. For this reason it is all the more necessary to guard against generalizations and unwarranted simplifications. It is possible, however, to highlight *some trends that are emerging in present-day society.* The Gospel records that the weeds and the good grain grew together in the farmer's field. The same is true in history, where in everyday life there often exist contradictions in the exercise of human freedom, where there is found side by side and at times closely intertwined, evil and good, injustice and justice, anguish and hope.

---

[6] Pastoral Constitution on the Church in the Modern World *Gaudium et Spes,* 11.

[7] The Fathers of the Extraordinary Synod of 1985, after affirming "the great importance and timeliness of the Pastoral Constitution, *Gaudium et Spes,*" continue: "Nevertheless, at the same time, they perceive that the signs of our times are in part different from those at the time of the Council with its problems and major trials. In fact, hunger, oppression, injustice and war, suffering, terrorism and forms of various kinds of violence are growing everywhere in the world today" (Final Report *Ecclesia sub Verbo Dei Mysteria Christi Celebrans pro Salute Mundi* [December 7, 1985], II, D, 1: *L'Osservatore Romano* [English-language edition], December 16, 1985, 9).

Secularism and the need for religion

4.1 How can one not notice the ever-growing existence of *religious indifferentism* and *atheism* in its more varied forms, particularly in its perhaps most widespread form of *secularism?* Adversely affected by the impressive triumphs of continuing scientific and technological development and above all, fascinated by a very old and yet new temptation, namely, that of wishing to become like God (cf. Gen 3:5) through the use of a liberty without bounds, individuals cut the religious roots that are in their hearts; they forget God, or simply retain him without meaning in their lives, or outrightly reject him, and begin to adore various "idols" of the contemporary world.

4.2 The present-day phenomenon of secularism is truly serious, not simply as regards the individual, but in some ways as regards whole communities, as the Council has already indicated: "Growing numbers of people are abandoning religion in practice."[8] At other times I myself have recalled the phenomenon of de-Christianization which strikes long-standing Christian people and which continually calls for a re-evangelization.

4.3 *Human longing and the need for religion,* however, are not able to be totally extinguished. When persons in conscience have the courage to face the more serious questions of human existence — particularly questions related to the purpose of life, to suffering and to dying — they are unable to avoid making their own the words of truth uttered by Saint Augustine: "You have made us for yourself, O Lord, and our hearts are restless until they rest in you."[9] In the same manner the present-day world bears witness to this as well, in ever-increasing and impressive ways, through an openness to a spiritual and transcendent outlook toward life, the renewed interest in religious research, the return to a sense of the sacred and to prayer, and the demand for freedom to call upon the name of the Lord.

The human person: a dignity violated and exalted

5.1 We furthermore call to mind the *violations* to which the *human person* is subjected.

5.2 When the individual is not recognized and loved in the person's dignity as the living image of God (cf. Gen 1:26), the human being is exposed to more humiliating and degrading forms of "manipulation," that most assuredly reduce the individual to a slavery to those who are stronger. "Those who are stronger" can take a variety of names: an ideology, economic power, political and inhumane systems, scientific technocracy or the intrusiveness of the mass

---

[8] Pastoral Constitution on the Church in the Modern World *Gaudium et Spes,* 7.
[9] *Confessions,* I, 1: CCL 27, 1.

media. Once again we find ourselves before many persons, our sisters and brothers, whose fundamental rights are being violated, owing to their exceedingly great capacity for endurance and to the clear injustice of certain civil laws: the right to life and to integrity, the right to a house and to work, the right to a family and responsible parenthood, the right to participation in public and political life, the right to freedom of conscience and the practice of religion.

5.3 Who is able to count the number of babies unborn because they have been killed in their mothers' wombs, children abandoned and abused by their own parents, children who grow up without affection and education? In some countries entire populations are deprived of housing and work, lacking the means absolutely essential for leading a life worthy of a human being, and are deprived even of those things necessary for their subsistence. There are great areas of poverty and of misery, both physical and moral, existing at this moment on the periphery of great cities. Entire groups of human beings have been seriously afflicted.

5.4 But the *sacredness of the human person* cannot be obliterated, no matter how often it is devalued and violated, because it has its unshakable foundation in God as Creator and Father. The sacredness of the person always keeps returning, again and again.

5.5 The *sense of the dignity of the human person* must be pondered and reaffirmed in stronger terms. A beneficial trend is advancing and permeating all peoples of the earth, making them ever more aware of the dignity of the individual: the person is not at all a "thing" or an "object" to be used, but primarily a responsible "subject," one endowed with conscience and freedom, called to live responsibly in society and history, and oriented toward spiritual and religious values.

5.6 It has been said that ours is the time of "humanism": paradoxically, some of its atheistic and secularistic forms arrive at a point where the human person is diminished and annihilated; other forms of humanism, instead, exalt the individual in such a manner that these forms become a veritable and real idolatry. There are still other forms, however, in line with the truth, which rightly acknowledge the greatness and misery of individuals and manifest, sustain and foster the total dignity of the human person.

5.7 The sign and fruit of this trend toward humanism is the growing need for *participation* which is undoubtedly one of the distinctive features of present-day humanity, a true "sign of the times" that is developing in various fields and in different ways: above all the growing need for participation regarding women and young people, not only in areas of family and academic life, but also in cultural, economic, social and political areas. To be leading characters in this development, in some ways to be creators of a new, more humane culture, is a requirement both for the individual and for peoples as a whole.[10]

Conflict and peace

6.1 Finally, we are unable to overlook another phenomenon that is quite evident in present-day humanity: perhaps as never before in history, humanity is daily buffeted by *conflict*. This is a phenomenon which has many forms, displayed in a legitimate plurality of mentalities and initiatives, but manifested in the fatal opposition of persons, groups, categories, nations and blocs of nations. This opposition takes the form of violence, of terrorism, and of war. Once again, but with proportions enormously widespread, diverse sectors of humanity today, wishing to show their "omnipotence," renew the futile experience of constructing the "tower of Babel" (cf. Gen 11:1-9), which spreads confusion, struggle, disintegration and oppression. The human family is thus in itself dramatically convulsed and wounded.

6.2 On the other hand, totally unsuppressible is that human longing experienced by individuals and whole peoples for the inestimable good of *peace* in justice. The Gospel Beatitude "Blessed are the peacemakers" (Mt 5:9) finds in the people of our time a new and significant resonance: entire populations today live, suffer and labor to bring about peace and justice. The *participation* by so many persons and groups in the life of society is increasingly pursued today as the way to make a desired peace become a reality. On this road we meet many lay faithful generously committed to the social and political field, working in a variety of institutional forms and those of a voluntary nature in service to the least.

Jesus Christ, the Hope of Humanity

7.1 This, then, is the vast field of labor that stands before the laborers sent forth by the "householder" to work in his vineyard.

7.2 In this field the Church is present and working, every one of us, Pastors, priests, deacons, Religious and lay faithful. The adverse situations here mentioned deeply affect the Church: they in part condition the Church, but they do not crush her, nor even less overcome her, because the Holy Spirit, who gives her life, sustains her in her mission.

7.3 Despite every difficulty, delay and contradiction caused by the limits of human nature, by sin and by the Evil One, the Church knows that all the

---

[10] Cf. *Instrumentum Laboris,* "The Vocation and Mission of the Lay Faithful in the Church and in the World Twenty Years after the Second Vatican Council," 5-10.

forces that humanity employs for communion and participation find a full response in the intervention of Jesus Christ, the Redeemer of man and of the world.

7.4 The Church knows that she is sent forth by him as a "sign and instrument of intimate union with God and of the unity of all the human race."[11]

7.5 Despite all this, then, humanity is able to hope. Indeed it must hope: the living and personal Gospel, *Jesus Christ himself, is the "Good News" and the bearer of joy* that the Church announces each day, and to whom the Church bears testimony before all people.

7.6 The lay faithful have an essential and irreplaceable role in this announcement and in this testimony: through them the Church of Christ is made present in the various sectors of the world, as a sign and source of hope and of love.

I

I Am the Vine and You Are the Branches

The Dignity of the Lay Faithful in the Church as Mystery

The Mystery of the Vine

8.1. The Sacred Scriptures use the image of the vine in various ways. In a particular case, the vine serves to express the *mystery of the People of God.* From this perspective which emphasizes the Church's internal nature, the lay faithful are seen not simply as laborers who work in the vineyard, but as themselves being a part of the vineyard. Jesus says, "I am the vine, you are the branches" (Jn 15:5).

8.2 The Prophets in the Old Testament used the image of the vine to describe the chosen people. Israel is God's vine, the Lord's own work, the joy of his heart: "I have planted you a choice vine" (Jer 2:21); "Your mother was like a vine in a vineyard transplanted by the water, fruitful and full of branches by reason of abundant water" (Ezek 19:10); "My beloved had a vineyard on a very fertile hill. He dug it and cleared it of stones and planted it with choice vines" (Is 5:1-2).

---

[11] Second Vatican Ecumenical Council, Dogmatic Constitution on the Church *Lumen Gentium,* 1.

8.3 Jesus himself once again takes up the symbol of the vine and uses it to illustrate various aspects of the Kingdom of God: "A man planted a vineyard, and set a hedge around it, and dug a pit for the winepress, and built a tower and let it out to tenants and went into another country" (Mk 12:1; cf. Mt 21:33-46).

8.4 John the Evangelist invites us to go further and leads us to discover *the mystery of the vine:* it is the figure and symbol not only of the People of God, but of *Jesus himself.* He is the vine and we, his disciples, are the branches. He is the "true vine," to which the branches are engrafted to have life (cf. Jn 15:1ff.).

8.5 The Second Vatican Council, making reference to the various biblical images that help to reveal the mystery of the Church, proposes again the image of the vine and the branches: "Christ is the true vine who gives life and fruitfulness to the branches, that is, to us. Through the Church we abide in Christ, without whom we can do nothing (Jn 15:1-5)."[12] The Church herself, then, is the vine in the Gospel. She is *mystery* because the very life and love of the Father, Son and Holy Spirit are the gift gratuitously offered to all those who are born of water and the Holy Spirit (cf. Jn 3:5), and called to relive the very *communion* of God and to manifest it and communicate it in history (mission): "In that day," Jesus says, "you will know that I am in my Father and you in me, and I in you" (Jn 14:20).

8.6 Only *from inside the Church's mystery of communion is the "identity" of the lay faithful made known,* and their fundamental dignity revealed. Only within the context of this dignity can their vocation and mission in the Church and in the world be defined.

Who Are the Lay Faithful?

9.1 The Synod Fathers have rightly pointed to the need for a definition of the lay faithful's vocation and mission in *positive terms* through an in-depth study of the teachings of the Second Vatican Council in light of both recent documentation from the Magisterium and the lived experience of the Church, guided as she is by the Holy Spirit.[13]

9.2 In giving a response to the question "Who are the lay faithful?" the Council went beyond previous interpretations which were predominantly negative. Instead it opened itself to a decidedly positive vision and displayed a basic intention of asserting *the full belonging of the lay faithful to the Church and to her mystery. At the same time it insisted on the unique character of their*

---

[12] Dogmatic Constitution on the Church *Lumen Gentium,* 6.

[13] Cf. *Propositio* 3.

vocation, which is in a special way to "seek the Kingdom of God by engaging in temporal affairs and ordering them according to the plan of God."[14] "The term 'lay faithful' " — we read in the Constitution on the Church, *Lumen Gentium* — "is here understood to mean all the faithful except those in Holy Orders and those who belong to a religious state sanctioned by the Church. Through Baptism the lay faithful are made one body with Christ and are established among the People of God. They are in their own way made sharers in the priestly, prophetic and kingly office of Christ. They carry out their own part in the mission of the whole Christian people with respect to the Church and the world."[15]

9.3 Pius XII once stated: "The faithful, more precisely the lay faithful, find themselves on the front lines of the Church's life; for them the Church is the animating principle for human society. Therefore, they, in particular, ought to have an ever-clearer consciousness *not only of belonging to the Church, but of being the Church,* that is to say, the community of the faithful on earth under the leadership of the Pope, the head of all, and of the Bishops in communion with him. These *are the Church.*"[16]

9.4 According to the biblical image of the vineyard, the lay faithful, together with all the other members of the Church, are branches engrafted to Christ the true vine, and from him derive their life and fruitfulness.

9.5 Incorporation into Christ through faith and Baptism is the source of being a Christian in the mystery of the Church. This mystery constitutes the Christian's most basic "features" and serves as the basis for all the vocations and dynamism of the Christian life of the lay faithful (cf. Jn 3:5). In Christ who died and rose from the dead, the baptized become a "new creation" (Gal 6:15; 2 Cor 5:17), washed clean from sin and brought to life through grace.

9.6 Therefore, only through accepting the richness in mystery that God gives to the Christian in Baptism is it possible to come to a basic description of the lay faithful.

Baptism and the "Newness" of Christian Life

10 It is no exaggeration to say that the entire existence of the lay faithful has as its purpose to lead a person to a knowledge of the radical newness of the Christian life that comes from Baptism, the sacrament of faith, so that this knowledge can help that person live the responsibilities which arise from that vocation received from God. In arriving at a basic description of the lay

[14] Dogmatic Constitution on the Church *Lumen Gentium,* 31.
[15] Ibid.
[16] Address to the New Cardinals (February 20, 1946): *AAS* 38 (1946), 149.

faithful we now more explicitly and directly consider among others the following three fundamental aspects: *Baptism regenerates us in the life of the Son of God; unites us to Christ and to his Body, the Church; anoints us in the Holy Spirit, making us spiritual temples.*

Children in the Son

11.1 We here recall Jesus' words to Nicodemus: "Truly, truly, I say to you, unless one is born of water and the Spirit, he cannot enter the Kingdom of God" (Jn 3:5). Baptism, then, is a rebirth, a regeneration.

11.2 In considering this aspect of the gift which comes from Baptism, the Apostle Peter breaks out into song: "Blessed be the God and Father of our Lord Jesus Christ! By his great mercy we have been born anew to a living hope through the Resurrection of Jesus Christ from the dead and to an inheritance which is imperishable, undefiled and unfading" (1 Pet 1:3-4). And he calls Christians those who have been "born anew, not of perishable seed but of imperishable, through the living and abiding word of God" (1 Pet 1:23).

11.3 With Baptism we become *children of God in his only-begotten Son, Jesus Christ.* Rising from the waters of the baptismal font, every Christian hears again the voice that was once heard on the banks of the Jordan River: "You are my beloved Son; with you I am well pleased" (Lk 3:22). From this comes the understanding that one has been brought into association with the beloved Son, becoming a child of adoption (cf. Gal 4:4-7) and a brother or sister of Christ. In this way the eternal plan of the Father for each person is realized in history: "For those whom he foreknew he also predestined to be conformed to the image of his Son, in order that he might be the first-born among many brethren" (Rom 8:29).

11.4 It is the *Holy Spirit* who constitutes the baptized as children of God and members of Christ's Body. Saint Paul reminds the Christians of Corinth of this fact: "For by one Spirit we are all baptized into one body" (1 Cor 12:13), so that the Apostle can say to the lay faithful: "Now you are the Body of Christ and individually members of it" (1 Cor 12:27); "And because you are sons, God has sent the Spirit of his Son into our hearts" (Gal 4:6; cf. Rom 8:15-16).

We are one body in Christ

12.1 Regenerated as "children in the Son," the baptized are inseparably joined together as *"members of Christ and members of the body of the Church,"* as the Council of Florence teaches.[17]

---

[17] *Decretum pro Armeniis: DS* 1314.

12.2 Baptism symbolizes and brings about a mystical but real incorporation into the crucified and glorious body of Christ. Through the sacrament Jesus unites the baptized to his death so as to unite the recipient to his Resurrection (cf. Rom 6:3-5). The "old man" is stripped away for a reclothing with "the new man," that is, with Jesus himself: "For as many of you as were baptized into Christ have put on Christ" (Gal 3:27; cf. Eph 4:22-24; Col 3:9-10). The result is that "we, though many, are one body in Christ" (Rom 12:5).

12.3 In the words of Saint Paul we find again the faithful echo of the teaching of Jesus himself, which reveals *the mystical unity of Christ with his disciples and the disciples with each other,* presenting it as an image and extension of that mystical *communion* that binds the Father to the Son and the Son to the Father in the bond of love, the Holy Spirit (cf. Jn 17:21). Jesus refers to this same unity in the image of the vine and the branches: "I am the vine, you the branches" (Jn 15:5), an image that sheds light not only on the deep intimacy of the disciples with Jesus but on the necessity of a vital communion of the disciples with each other: all are branches of a single vine.

Holy and living temples of the Spirit

13.1 In another comparison, using the image of a building, the Apostle Peter defines the baptized as "living stones" founded on Christ, the "cornerstone," and destined to "be raised up into a spiritual building" (1 Pet 2:5ff.). The image introduces us to another aspect of the newness of Christian life coming from Baptism and described by the Second Vatican Council: "By regeneration and the anointing of the Holy Spirit, the baptized are consecrated into a spiritual house."[18]

13.2 The Holy Spirit "anoints" the baptized, sealing each with an indelible character (cf. 2 Cor 1:21-22), and constituting each as a spiritual temple, that is, he fills this temple with the holy presence of God as a result of each person's being united and likened to Jesus Christ.

13.3 With this spiritual "unction," Christians can repeat in an individual way the words of Jesus: "The Spirit of the Lord is upon me, because he has anointed me to preach the good news to the poor. He has sent me to proclaim release to captives and recovery of sight to the blind, to set at liberty those who are oppressed to proclaim the acceptable year of the Lord" (Lk 4:18-19; cf. Is 61:1-2). Thus with the outpouring of the Holy Spirit in Baptism and Confirmation, the baptized share in the same mission of Jesus as the Christ, the Savior-Messiah.

---

[18] Dogmatic Constitution on the Church *Lumen Gentium,* 10.

Sharers in the Priestly, Prophetic and Kingly Mission of Jesus Christ

14.1 Referring to the baptized as "newborn babes," the Apostle Peter writes: "Come to him, to that living stone, rejected by men but in God's sight chosen and precious; and like living stones be yourselves built into a spiritual house, to be a holy priesthood to offer spiritual sacrifices acceptable to God through Jesus Christ. . . . You are a chosen race, a royal priesthood, a holy nation, God's own people, that you may declare the wonderful deeds of him who called you out of darkness into his marvelous light" (1 Pet 2:4-5, 9).

14.2 A new aspect to the grace and dignity coming from Baptism is here introduced: the lay faithful participate, for their part, in the threefold mission of Christ as Priest, Prophet and King. This aspect has never been forgotten in the living Tradition of the Church, as exemplified in the explanation which Saint Augustine offers for Psalm 26: "David was anointed king. In those days only a king and a priest were anointed. These two persons prefigured the one and only priest and king who was to come, Christ (the name 'Christ' means 'anointed'). Not only has our head been anointed but we, his Body, have also been anointed . . . therefore *anointing* comes to all Christians, even though in Old Testament times it belonged only to two persons. Clearly we are the Body of Christ because we are all 'anointed' and in him are 'christs,' that is, 'anointed ones,' as well as Christ himself, 'the Anointed One.' In a certain way, then, it thus happens that with head and body the whole Christ is formed."[19]

14.3 In the wake of the Second Vatican Council,[20] at the beginning of my pastoral ministry, my aim was to emphasize forcefully the priestly, prophetic and kingly dignity of the entire People of God in the following words: "He who was born of the Virgin Mary, the carpenter's Son — as he was thought to be — Son of the living God (confessed by Peter), has come to make us 'a Kingdom of priests.' The Second Vatican Council has reminded us of the mystery of this power and of the fact that the mission of Christ — Priest, Prophet-Teacher, King — continues in the Church. Everyone, the whole People of God, shares in this threefold mission."[21]

14.4 With this Exhortation the lay faithful are invited to take up again and reread, meditate on and assimilate with renewed understanding and love, the rich and fruitful teaching of the Council which speaks of their participation in

[19] *Enarratio in Psalmum XXVI*, II, 2: *CCL*, 38, 154ff.

[20] Cf. Dogmatic Constitution on the Church *Lumen Gentium*, 10.

[21] Homily at the Beginning of his Pastoral Ministry as Supreme Shepherd of the Church (October 22, 1978), 4: *AAS* 70 (1978), 946.

the threefold mission of Christ.[22] Here in summary form are the essential elements of this teaching.

14.5 The lay faithful are sharers in the *priestly mission,* for which Jesus offered himself on the Cross and continues to be offered in the celebration of the Eucharist for the glory of God and the salvation of humanity. Incorporated in Jesus Christ, the baptized are united to him and to his sacrifice in the offering they make of themselves and their daily activities (cf. Rom 12:1-2). Speaking of the lay faithful the Council says: "For their work, prayers and apostolic endeavors, their ordinary married and family life, their daily labor, their mental and physical relaxation, if carried out in the Spirit, and even the hardships of life if patiently borne — all of these become spiritual sacrifices acceptable to God through Jesus Christ (cf. 1 Pet 2:5). During the celebration of the Eucharist these sacrifices are most lovingly offered to the Father along with the Lord's Body. Thus as worshipers whose every deed is holy, the lay faithful consecrate the world itself to God."[23]

14.6 Through their participation in the *prophetic mission* of Christ, "who proclaimed the Kingdom of his Father by the testimony of his life and by the power of his word,"[24] the lay faithful are given the ability and responsibility to accept the Gospel in faith and to proclaim it in word and deed, without hesitating to courageously identify and denounce evil. United to Christ, the "great Prophet" (Lk 7:16), and in the Spirit made "witnesses" of the risen Christ, the lay faithful are made sharers in the appreciation of the Church's supernatural faith, that "cannot err in matters of belief"[25] and sharers as well in the grace of the word (cf. Acts 2:17-18; Rev 19:10). They are also called to allow the newness and the power of the Gospel to shine out everyday in their family and social life, as well as to express patiently and courageously in the contradictions of the present age their hope of future glory even "through the framework of their secular life."[26]

14.7 Because the lay faithful belong to Christ, Lord and King of the Universe, they share in his *kingly mission* and are called by him to spread that Kingdom in history. They exercise their kingship as Christians, above all in the spiritual combat in which they seek to overcome in themselves the king-

---

[22] Cf. the renewed proposal of this teaching in the 1987 Synod's *Instrumentum Laboris,* "The Vocation and the Mission of the Lay Faithful in the Church and in the World Twenty Years after the Second Vatican Council," 25.

[23] Dogmatic Constitution on the Church *Lumen Gentium,* 34.

[24] Ibid., 35.

[25] Ibid., 12.

[26] Ibid., 35.

dom of sin (cf. Rom 6:12), and then to make a gift of themselves so as to serve, in justice and in charity, Jesus, who is himself present in all his brothers and sisters, above all in the very least (cf. Mt 25:40).

14.8 But in particular the lay faithful are called to restore to creation all its original value. In ordering creation to the authentic well-being of humanity in an activity governed by the life of grace, they share in the exercise of the power with which the Risen Christ draws all things to himself and subjects them along with himself to the Father, so that God might be everything to everyone (cf. 1 Cor 15:28; Jn 12:32).

14.9 The participation of the lay faithful in the threefold mission of Christ as Priest, Prophet and King finds its source in the anointing of Baptism, its further development in Confirmation and its realization and dynamic sustenance in the Holy Eucharist. It is a participation given to each member of the lay faithful *individually,* inasmuch as each is one of the *many* who form the *one Body* of the Lord: in fact, Jesus showers his gifts upon the Church which is his Body and his Spouse. In such a way individuals are sharers in the threefold mission of Christ in virtue of their being members of the Church, as Saint Peter clearly teaches when he defines the baptized as "a chosen race, a royal priesthood, a holy nation, God's own people" (1 Pet 2:9). Precisely because it derives *from* Church *communion,* the sharing of the lay faithful in the threefold mission of Christ requires that it be lived and realized *in communion* and *for the increase of communion itself.* Saint Augustine writes: "As we call everyone 'Christians' in virtue of a mystical anointing, so we call everyone 'priests' because all are members of only one priesthood."[27]

The Lay Faithful and Their Secular Character

15.1 The newness of the Christian life is the foundation and title for equality among all the baptized in Christ, for all the members of the People of God: "As members, they share a common dignity from their rebirth in Christ, they have the same filial grace and the same vocation to perfection. They possess in common one salvation, one hope and one undivided charity."[28] Because of the one dignity flowing from Baptism, each member of the lay faithful, together with ordained ministers and men and women Religious, shares a responsibility for the Church's mission.

15.2 But among the lay faithful this one baptismal dignity takes on *a manner of life which sets a person apart, without, however, bringing about a*

---

[27] *De Civitate Dei,* XX, 10: CCL 48, 720.

[28] Second Vatican Ecumenical Council, Dogmatic Constitution on the Church *Lumen Gentium,* 32.

separation from the ministerial priesthood or from men and women Religious. The Second Vatican Council has described this manner of life as the "secular character": "The secular character is properly and particularly that of the lay faithful."[29]

15.3 To understand properly the lay faithful's position in the Church in a complete, adequate and specific manner it is necessary to come to a deeper theological understanding of their secular character in light of God's plan of salvation and in the context of the mystery of the Church.

15.4 Pope Paul VI said the Church "has an authentic secular dimension, inherent to her inner nature and mission, which is deeply rooted in the mystery of the Word Incarnate, and which is realized in different forms through her members."[30]

15.5 The Church, in fact, lives in the world, even if she is not of the world (cf. Jn 17:16). She is sent to continue the redemptive work of Jesus Christ, which "by its very nature concerns the salvation of humanity, and also involves the renewal of the whole temporal order."[31]

15.6 Certainly *all the members* of the Church are sharers in this secular dimension but *in different ways.* In particular the sharing of the *lay faithful* has its own manner of realization and function, which, according to the Council, is "properly and particularly" theirs. Such a manner is designated with the expression "secular character."[32]

15.7 In fact the Council, in describing the lay faithful's situation in the secular world, points to it, above all, as the place in which they receive their call from God: "There they are called by God."[33] This "place" is treated and presented in dynamic terms: the lay faithful "live in the world, that is, in every one of the secular professions and occupations. They live in the ordinary circumstances of family and social life, from which the very fabric of their existence is woven."[34] They are persons who live an ordinary life in the world: they study, they work, they form relationships as friends, professionals, members of society, cultures, etc. However, the Council considers their condition not simply an external and environmental framework, but as a reality *destined to find in Jesus Christ the fullness of its meaning.*[35] Indeed it

---

[29] Ibid., 31.

[30] Address to the Members of Secular Institutes (February 2, 1972): *AAS* 64 (1972), 208.

[31] Second Vatican Ecumenical Council, Decree on the Apostolate of the Laity *Apostolicam Actuositatem,* 5.

[32] Dogmatic Constitution on the Church *Lumen Gentium,* 31.

[33] Ibid.

[34] Ibid.

[35] Cf. ibid., 48.

leads to the affirmation that "the Word made flesh willed to share in human fellowship. . . . He sanctified those human ties, especially family ones, from which social relationships arise, willingly submitting himself to the laws of his country. He chose to lead the life of an ordinary craftsman of his own time and place."[36]

15.8 *The "world" thus becomes the place and the means for the lay faithful to fulfill their Christian vocation,* because the world itself is destined to glorify God the Father in Christ. The Council is able then to indicate the proper and special sense of the divine vocation which is directed to the lay faithful. They are not called to abandon the position that they have in the world. Baptism does not take them from the world at all, as the Apostle Paul points out: "So, brethren, in whatever state each was called, there let him remain with God" (1 Cor 7:24). On the contrary, he entrusts a vocation to them that properly concerns their situation in the world. The lay faithful, in fact, "are called by God so that they, led by the spirit of the Gospel, might contribute to the sanctification of the world, as from within like leaven, by fulfilling their own particular duties. Thus, especially in this way of life, resplendent in faith, hope and charity they manifest Christ to others."[37] Thus for the lay faithful, to be present and active in the world is not only an anthropological and sociological reality, but in a specific way, a theological and ecclesiological reality as well. In fact, in their situation in the world, God manifests his plan and communicates to them their particular vocation of "seeking the Kingdom of God by engaging in temporal affairs and by ordering them according to the plan of God."[38]

15.9 Precisely with this in mind the Synod Fathers said: "The secular character of the lay faithful is not therefore to be defined only in a sociological sense, but most especially in a theological sense. The term *secular* must be understood in light of the act of God the Creator and Redeemer, who has handed over the world to women and men, so that they may participate in the work of creation, free creation from the influence of sin and sanctify themselves in marriage or the celibate life, in a family, in a profession, and in the various activities of society."[39]

15.10 The lay faithful's *position in the Church,* then, comes to be funda-

---

[36] Pastoral Constitution on the Church in the Modern World *Gaudium et Spes,* 32.

[37] Second Vatican Ecumenical Council, Dogmatic Constitution on the Church *Lumen Gentium,* 31.

[38] Ibid.

[39] *Propositio* 4.

mentally defined by their *newness in Christian life* and distinguished by their *secular character.*[40]

15.11 The images taken from the Gospel of salt, light and leaven, although indiscriminately applicable to all Jesus' disciples, are specifically applied to the lay faithful. They are particularly meaningful images because they speak not only of the deep involvement and the full participation of the lay faithful in the affairs of the earth, the world and the human community, but also and above all, they tell of the radical newness and unique character of an involvement and participation which has as its purpose the spreading of the Gospel that brings salvation.

Called to Holiness

16.1 We come to a full sense of the dignity of the lay faithful if we consider *the prime and fundamental vocation* that the Father assigns to each of them in Jesus Christ through the Holy Spirit: the vocation to holiness, that is, the perfection of charity. Holiness is the greatest testimony of the dignity conferred on a disciple of Christ.

16.2 The Second Vatican Council has significantly spoken on the universal call to holiness. It is possible to say that this call to holiness is precisely the basic charge entrusted to all the sons and daughters of the Church by a Council which intended to bring a renewal of Christian life based on the Gospel.[41] This charge is not a simple moral exhortation, but an *undeniable requirement arising from the mystery of the Church: she is the choice vine,* whose branches live and grow with the same holy and life-giving energies that come from Christ; she is the Mystical Body whose members share in the same life of holiness of the Head who is Christ; she is the beloved Spouse of the Lord Jesus, who delivered himself up for her sanctification (cf. Eph 5:25-27). The Spirit that sanctified the human nature of Jesus in Mary's virginal womb (cf. Lk 1:35) is the same Spirit that is abiding and working in the Church to communicate to her the holiness of the Son of God made man.

16.3 It is ever more urgent that today all Christians take up again the way

[40] "Full members of the People of God and the Mystical Body, they participate, through Baptism, in the threefold priestly, prophetic and kingly mission of Christ; the lay faithful express and exercise the riches of their dignity through their living in the world. What can be an additional or exceptional task for those who belong to the ordained ministry is the typical mission of the lay faithful. Their proper vocation consists 'in seeking the Kingdom of God by engaging in temporal affairs and by ordering them according to the plan of God' (*Lumen Gentium,* 31)": John Paul II, Angelus (March 15, 1987), 1: *Insegnamenti* X/1 (1987), 561.

[41] See, in particular, the Dogmatic Constitution on the Church *Lumen Gentium,* 39-42, which treats the subject of "the universal call to holiness in the Church."

of Gospel renewal, welcoming in a spirit of generosity the invitation expressed by the Apostle Peter "to be holy in all conduct" (1 Pet 1:15). The 1985 Extraordinary Synod, twenty years after the Council, opportunely insisted on this urgency: "Since the Church in Christ is a mystery, she ought to be considered the sign and instrument of holiness. . . . Men and women saints have always been the source and origin of renewal in the most difficult circumstances in the Church's history. Today we have the greatest need of saints whom we must assiduously beg God to raise up."[42]

16.4 Everyone in the Church, precisely because they are members, receives and thereby shares in the common vocation to holiness. In the fullness of this title and on equal par with all other members of the Church, the lay faithful are called to holiness: "All the faithful of Christ of whatever rank or status are called to the fullness of Christian life and to the perfection of charity"[43]; "All of Christ's followers are invited and bound to pursue holiness and the perfect fulfillment of their own state of life."[44]

16.5 The call to holiness is *rooted in Baptism* and proposed anew in the other sacraments, principally in the *Eucharist.* Since Christians are reclothed in Christ Jesus and refreshed by his Spirit, they are "holy." They therefore have the ability to manifest this holiness and the responsibility to bear witness to it in all that they do. The Apostle Paul never tires of admonishing all Christians to live "as is fitting among saints" (Eph 5:3).

16.6 Life according to the Spirit, whose fruit is holiness (cf. Rom 8:5; Gal 5:22), stirs up every baptized person and requires each to *follow and imitate Jesus Christ* in embracing the Beatitudes, in listening and meditating on the word of God, in conscious and active participation in the liturgical and sacramental life of the Church, in personal, family and community prayer, in the hunger and thirst for justice, in the practice of the commandment of love in all circumstances of life and in service to the brethren, especially the least, the poor and the suffering.

[42] Synod of Bishops, Second Extraordinary General Assembly (1985), Final Report *Ecclesia sub Verbo Dei Mysteria Christi Celebrans pro Salute Mundi* (December 7, 1985), II, A, 4: *L'Osservatore Romano* (English-language edition), December 16, 1985, 7.

[43] Second Vatican Ecumenical Council, Dogmatic Constitution on the Church *Lumen Gentium,* 40.

[44] Ibid., 42. These solemn and unequivocal affirmations of the Council repropose a fundamental truth of the Christian faith. Thus, for example, Pius XI in the Encyclical Letter *Casti Connubii* (December 31, 1930) addressed Christian spouses in the following words: "In whatever state they might be and whatever upright way of life they might have chosen, all must imitate the most perfect example of holiness, proposed by God to humanity, namely, our Lord Jesus Christ, and with the help of God to even reach the highest stage of Christian perfection, shown in the example of many saints": *AAS* 22 (1930), 548.

The life of holiness in the world

17.1 The vocation of the lay faithful to holiness implies that life according to the Spirit expresses itself in a particular way in their *involvement in temporal affairs* and in their *participation in earthly activities.* Once again the Apostle admonishes us: "Whatever you do, in word or deed, do everything in the name of the Lord Jesus, giving thanks to God the Father through him" (Col 3:17). Applying the Apostle's words to the lay faithful, the Council categorically affirms: "Neither family concerns nor other secular affairs should be excluded from their religious program of life."[45] Likewise the Synod Fathers have said: "The unity of life of the lay faithful is of the greatest importance: indeed they must be sanctified in everyday professional and social life. Therefore, to respond to their vocation, the lay faithful must see their daily activities as an occasion to join themselves to God, fulfill his will, serve other people and lead them to communion with God in Christ."[46]

17.2 The vocation to holiness must be recognized and lived by the lay faithful, first of all as an undeniable and demanding obligation and as a shining example of the infinite love of the Father that has regenerated them in his own life of holiness. Such a vocation, then, ought to be called an *essential and inseparable element of the new life of Baptism,* and therefore an element which determines their dignity. At the same time the vocation to holiness is *intimately connected to mission* and to the responsibility entrusted to the lay faithful in the Church and in the world. In fact, that same holiness which is derived simply from their participation in the Church's holiness, represents their first and fundamental contribution to the building of the Church herself, which is the "Communion of Saints." The eyes of faith behold a wonderful scene: that of a countless number of lay people, both women and men, busy at work in their daily life and activity, oftentimes far from view and quite unacclaimed by the world, unknown to the world's great personages but nonetheless looked upon in love by the Father, untiring laborers who work in the Lord's vineyard. Confident and steadfast through the power of God's grace, these are the humble yet great builders of the Kingdom of God in history.

17.3 Holiness, then, must be called a fundamental presupposition and an irreplaceable condition for everyone in fulfilling the mission of salvation within the Church. The Church's holiness is the hidden source and the infallible measure of the works of the apostolate and of the missionary effort. Only in the measure that the Church, Christ's Spouse, is loved by him and she, in turn, loves him, does she become a Mother fruitful in the Spirit.

[45] Decree on the Apostolate of the Laity *Apostolicam Actuositatem,* 4.
[46] *Propositio* 5.

17.4 Again we take up the image from the Gospel: the fruitfulness and the growth of the branches depend on their remaining united to the vine. "As the branch cannot bear fruit by itself, unless it abides in the vine, neither can you, unless you abide in me. I am the vine, you are the branches. He who abides in me, and I in him, he it is that bears much fruit, for apart from me you can do nothing" (Jn 15:4-5).

17.5 It is appropriate to recall here the solemn proclamation of beatification and canonization of lay men and women which took place during the month of the Synod. The entire People of God, and the lay faithful in particular, can find at this moment new models of holiness and new witnesses of heroic virtue lived in the ordinary everyday circumstances of human existence. The Synod Fathers have said: "Particular Churches, especially the so-called younger Churches, should be attentive to recognizing among their members men and women who have given witness to holiness in such conditions (everyday secular conditions and the conjugal state) and who can be an example for others, so that, if the case calls for it, they (the Churches) might propose them to be beatified and canonized."[47]

17.6 At the end of these reflections intended to define the lay faithful's position in the Church, the celebrated admonition of Saint Leo the Great comes to mind: "Acknowledge, O Christian, your dignity!"[48] Saint Maximus, Bishop of Turin, in addressing those who had received the holy anointing of Baptism, repeats the same sentiments: "Ponder the honor that has made you sharers in this mystery!"[49] All the baptized are invited to hear once again the words of Saint Augustine: "Let us rejoice and give thanks; we have not only become Christians, but Christ himself. . . . Stand in awe and rejoice: we have become Christ."[50]

17.7 The dignity as a Christian, the source of equality for all members of the Church, guarantees and fosters the spirit of *communion* and fellowship, and, at the same time, becomes the hidden dynamic force in the lay faithful's apostolate and mission. It is a *dignity*, however, *which brings demands,* the dignity of laborers called by the Lord to work in his vineyard: "Upon all the lay faithful, then, rests the exalted duty of working to assure that each day the divine plan of salvation is further extended to every person, of every era, in every part of the earth."[51]

---

[47] *Propositio 8.*
[48] *Sermo 31, 3: SCh 22a, 72.*
[49] *Tractatus III de Baptismo: PL 57, 779.*
[50] *In Ioannis Evangelium Tractatus,* 21, 8: *CCL 36, 216.*
[51] Dogmatic Constitution on the Church *Lumen Gentium,* 33.

II

All Branches of a Single Vine

The Participation of the Lay Faithful in the Life of the Church as Communion

The Mystery of Church Communion

18.1 Again we turn to the words of Jesus: "I am the true vine and my Father is the vinedresser. . . . *Abide in me and I in you*" (Jn 15:1, 4).

18.2 These simple words reveal the mystery of communion that serves as the unifying bond between the Lord and his disciples, between Christ and the baptized: a living and life-giving communion through which Christians no longer belong to themselves but are the Lord's very own, as the branches are one with the vine.

18.3 The communion of Christians with Jesus has the communion of God as Trinity, namely, the unity of the Son with the Father in the gift of the Holy Spirit, as its model and source, and is itself the means to achieve this communion: united to the Son in the Spirit's bond of love, Christians are united to the Father.

18.4 Jesus continues: *"I am the vine, you are the branches"* (Jn 15:5). From the communion that Christians experience in Christ there immediately flows the communion which they experience with one another: all are branches of a single vine, namely, Christ. In this communion is the wonderful reflection and participation in the mystery of the intimate life of love in God as Trinity, Father, Son and Holy Spirit as revealed by the Lord Jesus. For this *communion* Jesus prays: "that they may all be one; even as you, Father, are in me, and I in you, that they also may be in us, so that the world may believe that you have sent me" (Jn 17:21).

18.5 *Such communion is the very mystery of the Church,* as the Second Vatican Council recalls in the celebrated words of Saint Cyprian: "The Church shines forth as 'a people made one with the unity of the Father, Son and Holy Spirit.' "[52] We are accustomed to recall this mystery of Church *communion* at the beginning of the celebration of the Eucharist when the priest welcomes all with the greeting of the Apostle Paul: "The grace of the Lord Jesus Christ, the

---

[52] Second Vatican Ecumenical Council, Dogmatic Constitution on the Church *Lumen Gentium*, 4.

love of God and the fellowship of the Holy Spirit be with you all" (2 Cor 13:13).

18.6 After having described the distinguishing features of the lay faithful on which their dignity rests, we must at this moment reflect on their mission and responsibility in the Church and in the world. A proper understanding of these aspects, however, can be found only in the living context of the Church as *communion*.

Vatican II and the ecclesiology of communion

19.1 At the Second Vatican Council the Church again proposed this central idea about herself, as the 1985 Extraordinary Synod recalls: "The ecclesiology of *communion* is a central and fundamental concept in the conciliar documents. *Koinonia-communion,* finding its source in Sacred Scripture, was a concept held in great honor in the early Church and in the Oriental Churches, and this teaching endures to the present day. Much was done by the Second Vatican Council to bring about a clearer understanding of the Church as *communion* and its concrete application to life. What, then, does this complex word *'communion'* mean? Its fundamental meaning speaks of the union with God brought about by Jesus Christ, in the Holy Spirit. The opportunity for such *communion* is present in the word of God and in the sacraments. Baptism is the door and the foundation of *communion* in the Church. The Eucharist is the source and summit of the whole Christian life (cf. *Lumen Gentium,* 11). The Body of Christ in the Holy Eucharist sacramentalizes this communion, that is, it is a sign and actually brings about the intimate bonds of *communion* among all the faithful in the Body of Christ which is the Church (cf. 1 Cor 10:16)."[53]

19.2 On the day after the conclusion of the Council, Pope Paul VI addressed the faithful in the following words: "The Church is a *communion*. In this context what does *communion* mean? We refer to the paragraph in the Catechism that speaks of the *sanctorum communionem,* 'the Communion of Saints.' The meaning of the Church is a Communion of Saints. *'Communion'* speaks of a double, life-giving participation: the incorporation of Christians into the life of Christ, and the communication of that life of charity to the entire body of the faithful, in this world and in the next, union with Christ and in Christ, and union among Christians, in the Church."[54]

19.3 Vatican Council II has invited us to contemplate the mystery of the

[53] Synod of Bishops, Second Extraordinary General Assembly (1985), Final Report *Ecclesia sub Verbo Dei Mysteria Christi Celebrans pro Salute Mundi* (December 7, 1985), II, C, 1: *L'Osservatore Romano* (English-language edition), December 16, 1985, 7.

[54] Address at the General Audience (June 8, 1966): *Insegnamenti* IV (1966), 794.

Church through biblical images which bring to light the reality of the Church as a communion with its inseparable dimensions: the communion of each Christian with Christ and the communion of all Christians with one another. There is the sheepfold, the flock, the vine, the spiritual building, the holy city.[55] Above all, there is the image of the *Body* as set forth by the Apostle Paul. Its doctrine finds a pleasing expression once again in various passages of the Council's documents.[56] In its turn, the Council has looked again at the entire history of salvation and has reposed the image of the Church as the *People of God:* "It has pleased God to make people holy and to save them, not merely as individuals without any mutual bonds, but by making them into a single people, a people which acknowledges him in truth and serves him in holiness."[57] From its opening lines, the Constitution *Lumen Gentium* summarizes this doctrine in a wonderful way: "The Church in Christ is a kind of sacrament, that is, a sign and instrument of intimate union with God and of the unity of all the human race."[58]

19.4 *The reality of the Church as communion is,* then, the integrating aspect, indeed *the central content of the "mystery,"* or rather, the divine plan for the salvation of humanity. For this purpose ecclesial communion cannot be interpreted in a sufficient way if it is understood as simply a sociological or a psychological reality. The Church as *communion* is the "new" People, the "messianic" People, the People that "has for its head, Christ . . . as its heritage, the dignity and freedom of God's children . . . for its law, the new commandment to love as Christ loved us . . . for its goal, the Kingdom of God . . . established by Christ as a communion of life, love and truth."[59] The bonds that unite the members of the New People among themselves — and first of all with Christ — are not those of "flesh and blood," but those of the spirit, more precisely those of the Holy Spirit, whom all the baptized have received (cf. Joel 3:1).

19.5 In fact, that Spirit is the One who from eternity unites the one and undivided Trinity, that Spirit who "in the fullness of time" (Gal 4:4) forever unites human nature to the Son of God, that same identical Spirit who in the course of Christian generations is the constant and never-ending source of communion in the Church.

---

[55] Cf. Second Vatican Ecumenical Council, Dogmatic Constitution on the Church *Lumen Gentium,* 6.

[56] Cf. ibid., 7 and *passim.*

[57] Ibid., 9.

[58] Ibid., 1.

[59] Ibid., 9.

An organic communion: diversity and complementarity

20.1 Ecclesial communion is more precisely likened to an "organic" communion, analogous to that of a living and functioning body. In fact, at one and the same time it is characterized by a *diversity* and a *complementarity* of vocations and states in life, of ministries, of charisms and responsibilities. Because of this diversity and complementarity every member of the lay faithful is seen *in relation to the whole body* and offers a *totally unique contribution* on behalf of the whole body.

20.2 Saint Paul insists in a particular way on the organic communion of the Mystical Body of Christ. We can hear his rich teaching echoed in the following synthesis from the Council: "Jesus Christ" — we read in the Constitution *Lumen Gentium* — "by communicating his spirit to his brothers and sisters, called together from all peoples, made them mystically into his own Body. In that Body, the life of Christ is communicated to those who believe. . . . As all the members of the human body, though they are many, form one body, so also are the faithful in Christ (cf. 1 Cor 12:12). Also, in the building up of Christ's Body there is a diversity of members and functions. There is only one Spirit who, according to his own richness and the necessities of service, distributes his different gifts for the welfare of the Church (cf. 1 Cor 12:1-11). Among these gifts comes in the first place the grace given to the Apostles to whose authority the Spirit himself subjects even those who are endowed with charisms (cf. 1 Cor 14). Furthermore it is this same Spirit, who through his power and through the intimate bond between the members, produces and urges love among the faithful. Consequently, if one member suffers anything, all the members suffer it too, and if one member is honored, all members together rejoice (cf. 1 Cor 12:26)."[60]

20.3 *One and the same Spirit is always the dynamic principle of diversity and unity* in the Church. Once again we read in the Constitution *Lumen Gentium*: "In order that we might be unceasingly renewed in him (cf. Eph 4:23), he has shared with us his Spirit who, existing as one and the same being in the head and in the members, gives life to, unifies and moves the whole Body. This he does in such a way that his work could be compared by the Fathers to the function which the soul as the principle of life fulfills in the human body."[61] And in another particularly significant text, which is helpful in understanding not only the organic nature proper to ecclesial communion but also its aspect of growth toward perfect communion, the Council writes: "The Spirit dwells in the Church and in the hearts of the faithful, as in a temple (cf. 1 Cor 3:16,

---

[60] Ibid., 7.
[61] Ibid., 7.

6:19). In them he prays and bears witness that they are adopted sons (cf. Gal 4:6; Rom 8:15-16, 26). Guiding the Church in the way of all truth (cf. Jn 16:13) and unifying her in communion and in the works of service, he bestows upon her varied hierarchical and charismatic gifts and adorns her with the fruits of his grace (cf. Eph 4:11-12; 1 Cor 12:4; Gal 5:22). By the power of the Gospel he makes the Church grow, perpetually renews her, and leads her to perfect union with her Spouse. The Spirit and the Bride both say to the Lord Jesus, 'Come!' (cf. Rev 22:17)."[62]

20.4 *Church communion then is a gift, a great gift of the Holy Spirit,* to be gratefully accepted by the lay faithful, and at the same time to be lived with a deep sense of responsibility. This is concretely realized through their participation in the life and mission of the Church, at whose service the lay faithful put their varied and complementary ministries and charisms.

20.5 A member of the lay faithful "can never remain in isolation from the community, but must live in a continual interaction with others, with a lively sense of fellowship, rejoicing in an equal dignity and common commitment to bring to fruition the immense treasure that each has inherited. The Spirit of the Lord gives a vast variety of charisms, inviting people to assume different ministries and forms of service and reminding them, as he reminds all people in their relationship in the Church, that what distinguishes persons is *not an increase in dignity,* but *a special and complementary capacity for service....* Thus, the charisms, the ministries, the different forms of service exercised by the lay faithful exist in communion and on behalf of communion. They are treasures that complement one another for the good of all and are under the wise guidance of their Pastors."[63]

Ministries and Charisms: the Spirit's Gifts to the Church

21.1 The Second Vatican Council speaks of the ministries and charisms as the gifts of the Holy Spirit which are given for the building up of the Body of Christ and for its mission of salvation in the world.[64] Indeed, the Church is directed and guided by the Holy Spirit, who lavishes diverse hierarchical and charismatic gifts on all the baptized, calling them to be, each in an individual way, active and coresponsible.

21.2 We now turn our thoughts to ministries and charisms as they directly

---

[62] Ibid., 4.

[63] John Paul II, Homily at the Solemn Eucharistic Concelebration for the Closing of the Synod of Bishops, Seventh Ordinary General Assembly (October 30, 1987), 6: *AAS* 80 (1988), 600.

[64] Cf. Dogmatic Constitution on the Church *Lumen Gentium,* 4.

relate to the lay faithful and to their participation in the life of Church-Communion.

Ministries, offices and roles

21.3 The ministries which exist and are at work at this time in the Church are all, even in their variety of forms, a participation in Jesus Christ's own ministry as the Good Shepherd who lays down his life for the sheep (cf. Jn 10:11), the humble servant who gives himself without reserve for the salvation of all (cf. Mk 10:45). The Apostle Paul is quite clear in speaking about the ministerial constitution of the Church in apostolic times. In his First Letter to the Corinthians he writes: "And God has appointed in the Church first Apostles, second prophets, third teachers . . ." (12:28). In his Letter to the Ephesians we read: "But the grace was given to each of us according to the measure of Christ's gift. . . . And his gifts were that some should be Apostles, some prophets, some evangelists, some pastors and teachers, to equip the saints for the work of ministry, for building up the Body of Christ until we all attain to the unity of the faith and of the knowledge of the Son of God, to mature manhood, to the measure of the stature of the fullness of Christ" (4:7, 11-13; cf. Rom 12:4-8). These and other New Testament texts indicate the diversity of ministries as well as of gifts and ecclesial tasks.

The ministries derived from Holy Orders

22.1 In a primary position in the Church are the *ordained ministries*, that is, the ministries *that come from the Sacrament of Orders*. In fact, with the mandate to make disciples of all nations (cf. Mt 28:19), the Lord Jesus chose and constituted the Apostles — seed of the People of the New Covenant and origin of the Hierarchy[65] — to form and to rule the priestly people. The mission of the Apostles, which the Lord Jesus continues to entrust to the Pastors of his people, is a true service, significantly referred to in Sacred Scripture as *"diakonia,"* namely, service or ministry. The ministries receive the charism of the Holy Spirit from the risen Christ in uninterrupted succession from the Apostles, through the Sacrament of Orders. From him they receive the authority and sacred power to serve the Church, acting *in persona Christi Capitis* (in the person of Christ, the Head),[66] and to gather her in the Holy Spirit through the Gospel and the sacraments.

[65] Cf. Second Vatican Ecumenical Council, Decree on the Church's Missionary Activity *Ad Gentes,* 5.

[66] Second Vatican Ecumenical Council, Decree on the Ministry and Life of Priests *Presbyterorum Ordinis,* 2; cf. Dogmatic Constitution on the Church *Lumen Gentium,* 10.

22.2 The ordained ministries, apart from the persons who receive them, are a grace for the entire Church. These ministries express and realize a participation in the priesthood of Jesus Christ that is different, not simply in degree but in essence, from the participation given to all the lay faithful through Baptism and Confirmation. On the other hand, the ministerial priesthood, as the Second Vatican Council recalls, essentially has the royal priesthood of all the faithful as its aim and is ordered to it.[67]

22.3 For this reason, so as to assure and to increase communion in the Church, particularly in those places where there is a diversity and complementarity of ministries, pastors must always acknowledge that their ministry is fundamentally ordered to the service of the entire People of God (cf. Heb 5:1). The lay faithful, in turn, must acknowledge that the ministerial priesthood is totally necessary for their participation in the mission in the Church.[68]

The ministries, offices and roles of the lay faithful

23.1 The Church's mission of salvation in the world is realized not only by the ministers in virtue of the Sacrament of Orders but also by all the lay faithful; indeed, because of their baptismal state and their specific vocation, in the measure proper to each person, the lay faithful participate in the priestly, prophetic and kingly mission of Christ.

23.2 The pastors, therefore, ought to acknowledge and foster the ministries, the offices and roles of the lay faithful that find their *foundation in the Sacraments of Baptism and Confirmation,* indeed, for a good many of them, *in the Sacrament of Matrimony.*

23.3 When necessity and expediency in the Church require it, the pastors, according to established norms from universal law, can entrust to the lay faithful certain offices and roles that are connected to their pastoral ministry but do not require the character of Orders. The Code of Canon Law states: "When the necessity of the Church warrants it and when ministers are lacking, lay persons, even if they are not lectors or acolytes, can also supply for certain of their offices, namely, to exercise the ministry of the word, to preside over liturgical prayers, to confer Baptism, and to distribute Holy Communion in accord with the prescriptions of the law."[69] However, *the exercise of such tasks does not make pastors of the lay faithful:* in fact, a person is not a

---

[67] Cf. Dogmatic Constitution on the Church *Lumen Gentium,* 10.

[68] Cf. John Paul II, Letter to Priests for Holy Thursday 1979 (April 8, 1979), 3-4: *AAS* 71 (1979), 396-400.

[69] Canon 230 § 3.

minister simply in performing a task, but through sacramental ordination. Only the Sacrament of Orders gives the ordained minister a particular participation in the office of Christ, the Shepherd and Head, and in his eternal Priesthood.[70] The task exercised in virtue of supply takes its legitimacy formally and immediately from the official deputation given by the pastors, as well as from its concrete exercise under the guidance of ecclesiastical authority.[71]

23.4 The recent Synodal Assembly has provided an extensive and meaningful overview of the situation in the Church on the ministries, offices and roles of the baptized. The Fathers have manifested a deep appreciation for the contribution of the lay faithful, both women and men, in the work of the apostolate, in evangelization, sanctification and the Christian animation of temporal affairs, as well as their generous willingness to supply in situations of emergency and chronic necessity.[72]

23.5 Following the liturgical renewal promoted by the Council, the lay faithful themselves have acquired a more lively awareness of the tasks that they fulfill in the liturgical assembly and its preparation, and have become more widely disposed to fulfill them: the liturgical celebration, in fact, is a sacred action not simply of the clergy, but of the entire assembly. It is, therefore, natural that the tasks not proper to the ordained ministers be fulfilled by the lay faithful.[73] In this way there is a natural transition from an effective involvement of the lay faithful in the liturgical action to that of announcing the word of God and pastoral care.[74]

---

[70] Cf. Second Vatican Ecumenical Council, Decree on the Ministry and Life of Priests *Presbyterorum Ordinis*, 2, 5.

[71] Cf. Second Vatican Ecumenical Council, Decree on the Apostolate of the Laity *Apostolicam Actuositatem*, 24.

[72] The Code of Canon Law lists a series of roles and tasks proper to the sacred ministers that, nevertheless for special and grave circumstances, and concretely in areas which lack priests or deacons, can temporarily be exercised by the lay faithful, with previous juridic faculty and mandated by competent ecclesiastical authority: cf. Canons 260 § 3, 517 § 2, 776, 861 § 2, 910 § 2, 943, 1112, etc.

[73] Cf. Second Vatican Ecumenical Council, Constitution on the Sacred Liturgy *Sacrosanctum Concilium*, 28; Code of Canon Law, Canon 230 § 2 states: "Lay persons can fulfill the function of lector during the liturgical actions by temporary deputation; likewise all lay persons can fulfill the functions of commentator or cantor or other functions, in accord with the norm of law."

[74] The Code of Canon Law presents diverse roles and tasks that the lay faithful can fulfill in the organized structure of the Church: cf. Canons 228, 229 § 3, 317 § 3, 463 § 1, 5 and § 2; 483, 494, 537, 759, 776, 784, 785, 1282, 1421.

23.6 In the same Synod Assembly, however, a critical judgment was voiced along with these positive elements, about a too-indiscriminate use of the word "ministry," the confusion and the equating of the common priesthood and the ministerial priesthood, the lack of observance of ecclesiastical laws and norms, the arbitrary interpretation of the concept of "supply," the tendency toward a "clericalization" of the lay faithful and the risk of creating, in reality, an ecclesial structure of parallel service to that founded on the Sacrament of Orders.

23.7 Precisely to overcome these dangers the Synod Fathers have insisted on the necessity to express with greater clarity, and with a more precise terminology,[75] both *the unity of the Church's mission* in which all the baptized participate, and the substantial *diversity of the ministry* of pastors which is rooted in the Sacrament of Orders, all the while respecting the other ministries, offices and roles in the Church, which are rooted in the Sacraments of Baptism and Confirmation.

23.8 In the first place, then, it is necessary that in acknowledging and in conferring various ministries, offices and roles on the lay faithful, the pastors exercise the maximum care to institute them on the basis of Baptism in which these tasks are rooted. It is also necessary that pastors guard against a facile yet abusive recourse to a presumed "situation of emergency" or to "supply by necessity," where objectively this does not exist or where alternative possibilities could exist through better pastoral planning.

23.9 The various ministries, offices and roles that the lay faithful can legitimately fulfill in the liturgy, in the transmission of the faith, and in the pastoral structure of the Church, ought to be exercised *in conformity with their specific lay vocation*, which is different from that of the sacred ministry. In this regard the Exhortation *Evangelii Nuntiandi*, that had such a great part in stimulating the varied collaboration of the lay faithful in the Church's life and mission of spreading the Gospel, recalls that "their own field of evangelizing activity is the vast and complicated world of politics, society and economics, as well as the world of culture, of the sciences and the arts, of international life, of the mass media. It also includes other realities which are open to evangelization, such as human love, the family, the education of children and adolescents, professional work, and suffering. The more Gospel-inspired lay people there are engaged in these realities, clearly involved in them, competent to promote them, and conscious that they must exercise to the full their Christian powers which are often repressed and buried, the more these realities will be at the service of the Kingdom of God and therefore at the service of salvation in Jesus Christ, without in any way losing or sacrificing their hu-

---

[75] Cf. *Propositio* 18.

man content but rather pointing to a transcendent dimension which is often disregarded."[76]

23.10 In the course of Synod work, the Fathers devoted much attention to the *Lectorate* and the *Acolythate*. While in the past these ministries existed in the Latin Church only as spiritual steps en route to the ordained ministry, with the *Motu Proprio* of Paul VI, *Ministeria Quaedam* (August 15, 1972), they assumed an autonomy and stability, as well as a possibility of their being given to the lay faithful, albeit only to men. The same fact is expressed in the new Code of Canon Law.[77] At this time the Synod Fathers expressed the desire that "the *Motu Proprio Ministeria Quaedam* be reconsidered, bearing in mind the present practice of local Churches and above all indicating criteria which ought to be used in choosing those destined for each ministry."[78]

23.11 In this regard a Commission was established to respond to this desire voiced by the Synod Fathers, specifically to provide an in-depth study of the various theological, liturgical, juridical and pastoral considerations which are associated with the great increase today of the ministries entrusted to the lay faithful.

23.12 While the conclusions of the Commission's study are awaited, a more ordered and fruitful ecclesial practice of the ministries entrusted to the lay faithful can be achieved if all the particular Churches faithfully respect the above mentioned theological principles, especially the essential difference between the ministerial priesthood and the common priesthood, and the difference between the ministries derived from the Sacrament of Orders and those derived from the Sacraments of Baptism and Confirmation.

Charisms

24.1 The Holy Spirit, while bestowing diverse ministries in the Church-Communion, enriches her still further with particular gifts or promptings of grace, called *charisms*. These can take a great variety of forms, both as a manifestation of the absolute freedom of the Spirit who abundantly supplies them, and as a response to the varied needs of the Church in history. The description and the classification given to these gifts in the New Testament are an indication of their rich variety. "To each is given the manifestation of the Spirit for the common good. To one is given through the Spirit the utterance of wisdom, and to another the utterance of knowledge according to the

---

[76] Paul VI, Apostolic Exhortation *Evangelii Nuntiandi* (December 8, 1975), 70: *AAS* 68 (1976), 60.

[77] Cf. Canon 230 § 1.

[78] *Propositio* 18.

same Spirit, to another faith by the same Spirit, to another gifts of healing by the one Spirit, to another the working of miracles, to another prophecy, to another the ability to distinguish between spirits, to another various kinds of tongues, to another the interpretation of tongues" (1 Cor 12:7-10; cf. 1 Cor 12:4-6, 28-31; Rom 12:6-8; 1 Pet 4:10-11).

24.2 Whether they be exceptional and great or simple and ordinary, the charisms are *graces of the Holy Spirit that have,* directly or indirectly, *a usefulness for the ecclesial community,* ordered as they are to the building up of the Church, to the well-being of humanity and to the needs of the world.

24.3 Even in our own times there is no lack of a fruitful manifestation of various charisms among the faithful, women and men. These charisms are given to individual persons and can even be shared by others in such ways as to continue in time a precious and effective heritage, serving as a source of a particular spiritual affinity among persons. In referring to the apostolate of the lay faithful the Second Vatican Council writes: "For the exercise of the apostolate the Holy Spirit who sanctifies the People of God through the ministry and the sacraments gives the faithful special gifts as well (cf. 1 Cor 12:7), 'allotting them to each one as he wills' (cf. 1 Cor 12:11), so that each might place 'at the service of others the grace received' and become 'good stewards of God's varied grace' (1 Pet 4:10), and build up thereby the whole body in charity (cf. Eph 4:16)."[79]

24.4 By a logic which looks to the divine source of this giving, as the Council recalls,[80] the gifts of the Spirit demand that those who have received them exercise them for the growth of the whole Church.

24.5 The charisms are *received in gratitude* both on the part of the one who receives them, and also on the part of the entire Church. They are in fact a singularly rich source of grace for the vitality of the apostolate and for the holiness of the whole Body of Christ, provided that they be gifts that come truly from the Spirit and are exercised in full conformity with the authentic promptings of the Spirit. In this sense the *discernment of charisms* is always necessary. Indeed, the Synod Fathers have stated: "The action of the Holy Spirit, who breathes where he will, is not always easily recognized and received. We know that God acts in all Christians, and we are aware of the

---

[79] Decree on the Apostolate of the Laity *Apostolicam Actuositatem,* 3.

[80] Ibid., 3: "From the reception of these charisms or gifts, even the most ordinary ones, there arises for each believer the right and duty to use them in the Church and in the world for the good of people and the building up of the Church. In doing so believers need to enjoy the freedom of the Holy Spirit who 'breathes where he wills' (Jn 3:8). At the same time they must act in communion with their brothers and sisters in Christ, especially with their pastors."

benefits which flow from charisms both for individuals and for the whole Christian community. Nevertheless, at the same time we are also aware of the power of sin and how it can disturb and confuse the life of the faithful and of the community."[81]

24.6 For this reason no charism dispenses a person from reference and submission to the *Pastors of the Church.* The Council clearly states: "Judgment as to their (charisms') genuineness and proper use belongs to those who preside over the Church, and to whose special competence it belongs, not indeed to extinguish the Spirit, but to test all things and hold fast to what is good (cf. 1 Thess 5:12, 19-21),"[82] so that all the charisms might work together, in their diversity and complementarity, for the common good.[83]

The Lay Faithful's Participation in the Life of the Church

25.1 The lay faithful participate in the life of the Church not only in exercising their tasks and charisms, but also in many other ways.

25.2 Such participation finds its first and necessary expression in the life and mission of the *particular Church,* in the Diocese in which "the Church of Christ, one, holy, catholic and apostolic, is truly present and at work."[84]

The particular Churches and the universal Church

25.3 For an adequate participation in ecclesial life the lay faithful absolutely need to have a clear and precise vision of *the particular Church with its primordial bond to the universal Church.* The particular Church does not come about from a kind of fragmentation of the universal Church, nor does the universal Church come about by a simple amalgamation of particular Churches. But there is a real, essential and constant bond uniting each of them and this is why the universal Church exists and is manifested in the particular Churches. For this reason the Council says that the particular Churches "are constituted after the model of the universal Church; it is in and from these particular Churches that there comes into being the one and unique Catholic Church."[85]

25.4 The same Council strongly encourages the lay faithful to live out

---

[81] *Propositio* 9.

[82] Dogmatic Constitution on the Church *Lumen Gentium,* 12.

[83] Cf. ibid., 30.

[84] Decree on the Bishops' Pastoral Office in the Church *Christus Dominus,* 11.

[85] Second Vatican Ecumenical Council, Dogmatic Constitution on the Church *Lumen Gentium,* 23.

actively their belonging to the particular Church, while at the same time assuming an ever-increasing "catholic" spirit: "Let the lay faithful constantly foster" — we read in the Decree on the Apostolate of the Laity — "a feeling for their own Diocese, of which the parish is a kind of cell, and be always ready at their Bishops' invitation to participate in diocesan projects. Indeed, if the needs of cities and rural areas are to be met, lay people should not limit their cooperation to the parochial or diocesan boundaries, but strive to extend it to interparochial, interdiocesan, national and international fields, the more so because the daily increase in population mobility, the growth of mutual bonds, and the ease of communication no longer allow any sector of society to remain closed in upon itself. Thus they should be concerned about the needs of the People of God scattered throughout the world."[86]

25.5 In this sense, the recent Synod has favored the creation of *Diocesan Pastoral Councils* as a recourse at opportune times. In fact, on a diocesan level this structure could be the principal form of collaboration, dialogue, and discernment as well. The participation of the lay faithful in these Councils can broaden resources in consultation and the principle of collaboration — and in certain instances also in decision-making — if applied in a broad and determined manner.[87]

25.6 The participation of the lay faithful in *Diocesan Synods* and in *Local Councils,* whether provincial or plenary, is envisioned by the Code of Canon Law.[88] These structures could contribute to Church communion and the mission of the particular Church, both in its own surroundings and in relation to the other particular Churches of the ecclesiastical province or Episcopal Conference.

25.7 Episcopal Conferences are called to evaluate the most opportune way of developing the consultation and the collaboration of the lay faithful, women and men, at a national or regional level, so that they may consider well the problems they share and manifest better the communion of the whole Church.[89]

The parish

26.1 The ecclesial community, while always having a universal dimension, finds its most immediate and visible expression in the *parish.* It is there that

---

[86] No.10.
[87] Cf. *Propositio* 10.
[88] Cf. Canons 443 § 4, 463 § 1, and § 2.
[89] Cf. *Propositio* 10.

the Church is seen locally. In a certain sense it is the *Church living in the midst of the homes of her sons and daughters.*[90]

26.2 It is necessary that in light of the faith all rediscover the true meaning of the parish, that is, the place where the very "mystery" of the Church is present and at work, even if at times it is lacking persons and means, even if at other times it might be scattered over vast territories or almost not to be found in crowded and chaotic modern sections of cities. The parish is not principally a structure, a territory, or a building, but rather, "the family of God, a fellowship afire with a unifying spirit,"[91] "a familial and welcoming home,"[92] the "community of the faithful."[93] Plainly and simply, the parish is founded on a theological reality because it is a *Eucharistic community.*[94] This means that the parish is a community properly suited for celebrating the Eucharist, the living source for its upbuilding and the sacramental bond of its being in full communion with the whole Church. Such suitableness is rooted in the fact that the parish is a *community of faith* and an *organic community,* that is, constituted by the ordained ministers and other Christians, in which the pastor — who represents the diocesan Bishop[95] — is the hierarchical bond with the entire particular Church.

26.3 Since the Church's task in our day is so great, its accomplishment cannot be left to the parish alone. For this reason the Code of Canon Law provides for forms of collaboration among parishes in a given territory[96] and recommends to the Bishop's care the various groups of the Christian faithful, even the unbaptized who are not under his ordinary pastoral care.[97] There are many other places and forms of association through which the Church can be present and at work. All are necessary to carry out the word and grace of the

---

[90] The Council documents read: "Because it is impossible for the Bishop always and everywhere to preside over the whole flock in his Church, he must of necessity establish groupings of the faithful. Among these, parishes set up locally under a pastor who takes the place of the Bishop are the most important: for in a certain way they represent the visible Church as it is established throughout the world" (Constitution on the Sacred Liturgy *Sacrosanctum Concilium,* 42).

[91] Second Vatican Ecumenical Council, Dogmatic Constitution on the Church *Lumen Gentium,* 28.

[92] John Paul II, Apostolic Exhortation *Catechesi Tradendae* (October 16, 1979), 67: *AAS* 71 (1979), 1333.

[93] Code of Canon Law, Canon 515 § 1.

[94] Cf. *Propositio* 10.

[95] Cf. Second Vatican Ecumenical Council, Constitution on the Sacred Liturgy *Sacrosanctum Concilium,* 42.

[96] Cf. Canon 555 § 1.1.

[97] Cf. Canon 383 § 1.

Gospel and to correspond to the various circumstances of life in which people find themselves today. In a similar way there exist in the areas of culture, society, education, professions, etc., many other ways for spreading the faith and other settings for the apostolate which cannot have the parish as their center and origin. Nevertheless, in our day the parish still enjoys a new and promising season. At the beginning of his Pontificate, Paul VI addressed the Roman clergy in these words: "We believe simply that this old and venerable structure of the parish has an indispensable mission of great contemporary importance: to create the basic community of the Christian people; to initiate and gather the people in the accustomed expression of liturgical life; to conserve and renew the faith in the people of today; to serve as the school for teaching the salvific message of Christ; to practice in thought and in deed the humble charity of good and fraternal works."[98]

26.4 The Synod Fathers for their part have given much attention to the present state of many parishes and have called for a *greater effort in their renewal:* "Many parishes, whether established in regions affected by urban progress or in missionary territory, cannot do their work effectively because they lack material resources or ordained men or are too big geographically or because of the particular circumstances of some Christians (for example, exiles and migrants). So that all parishes of this kind may be truly communities of Christians, local ecclesial authorities ought to foster the following: a) adaptation of parish structures according to the full flexibility granted by canon law, especially in promoting participation by the lay faithful in pastoral responsibilities; b) small, basic or so-called "living" communities, where the faithful can communicate the word of God and express it in service and love to one another; these communities are true expressions of ecclesial communion and centers of evangelization, in communion with their pastors."[99] For the renewal of parishes and for a better assurance of their effectiveness in work, various forms of cooperation, even on the institutional level, ought to be fostered among diverse parishes in the same area.

The apostolic commitment in the parish

27.1 It is now necessary to look more closely at the communion and participation of the lay faithful in parish life. In this regard all lay men and women are called to give greater attention to a particularly meaningful, stirring and incisive passage from the Council: "Their activity within Church communities

[98] Paul VI, Address to the Roman Clergy (June 24, 1963): *AAS* 55 (1963) 1979, 674.
[99] *Propositio* 11.

is so necessary that without it the apostolate of the pastors is generally unable to achieve its full effectiveness."[100]

27.2 This is indeed a particularly important affirmation which evidently must be interpreted in light of the "ecclesiology of communion." Ministries and charisms, being diverse and complementary, are — each in their own way — all necessary for the Church to grow.

27.3 The lay faithful ought to be ever more convinced of the special meaning that their commitment to the apostolate takes on in their parish. Once again the Council authoritatively places it in relief: "The parish offers an outstanding example of the apostolate on the community level inasmuch as it brings together the many human differences found within its boundaries, and draws them into the universality of the Church. The lay faithful should accustom themselves to working in the parish in close union with their priests, bringing to the Church community their own and the world's problems as well as questions concerning human salvation, all of which need to be examined together and solved through general discussion. As far as possible the lay faithful ought to collaborate in every apostolic and missionary undertaking sponsored by their own ecclesial family."[101]

27.4 The Council's mention of examining and solving pastoral problems "by general discussion" ought to find its adequate and structured development through a more convinced, extensive and decided appreciation for *Parish Pastoral Councils,* on which the Synod Fathers have rightly insisted.[102]

27.5 In the present circumstances the lay faithful have the ability to do very much and, therefore, ought to do very much toward the growth of an authentic *ecclesial communion* in their parishes in order to reawaken *missionary zeal* toward non-believers and believers themselves who have abandoned the faith or grown lax in the Christian life.

27.6 If indeed, the parish is the Church placed in the neighborhoods of humanity, it lives and is at work through being deeply inserted in human society and intimately bound up with its aspirations and its dramatic events. Oftentimes the social context, especially in certain countries and environments, is violently shaken by elements of disintegration and dehumanization. The individual is lost and disoriented, but there always remains in the human heart the desire to experience and cultivate caring and personal relationships. The response to such a desire can come from the parish, when, with the lay

---

[100] Decree on the Apostolate of the Laity *Apostolicam Actuositatem,* 10.
[101] Ibid., 10.
[102] Cf. *Propositio* 10.

faithful's participation, it adheres to its fundamental vocation and mission, that is, to be a "place" in the world for the community of believers to gather together as a "sign" and "instrument" of the vocation of all to communion; in a word, to be a house of welcome to all and a place of service to all, or, as Pope John XXIII was fond of saying, to be the *village fountain* to which all would have recourse in their thirst.

The Forms of Participation in the Life of the Church

28.1 The lay faithful, together with the clergy and women and men Religious, make up the one People of God and the Body of Christ.

28.2 Being "members" of the Church takes nothing away from the fact that each Christian as an individual is "unique and unrepeatable." On the contrary, this belonging guarantees and fosters the profound sense of that uniqueness and unrepeatability, insofar as these very qualities are the source of variety and richness for the whole Church. Therefore, God calls the individual in Jesus Christ, each one personally by name. In this sense the Lord's words "You go into my vineyard too," directed to the Church as a whole, are specially addressed to each member individually.

28.3 Because of each member's unique and unrepeatable character, that is, one's identity and actions as a person, each individual is placed at the service of the growth of the ecclesial community while, at the same time, singularly receiving and sharing in the common richness of all the Church. This is the "Communion of Saints" which we profess in the Creed. *The good of all becomes the good of each one, and the good of each one becomes the good of all.* "In the holy Church," writes Saint Gregory the Great, "all are nourished by each one and each one is nourished by all."[103]

Individual forms of participation

28.4 Above all, each member of the lay faithful should always be *fully aware of being a "member of the Church"* yet entrusted with a unique task which cannot be done by another and which is to be fulfilled for the good of all. From this perspective the Council's insistence on the *absolute necessity of an apostolate exercised by the individual* takes on its full meaning: "The apostolate exercised by the individual — which flows abundantly from a truly Christian life (cf. Jn 4:14) — is the origin and condition of the whole lay apostolate, even in its organized expression, and admits no substitute. Regardless of circumstance, all lay persons (including those who have no oppor-

---

[103] *Homiliae in Ezechielem,* II, I, 5: *CCL* 42, 211.

tunity or possibility for collaboration in associations) are called to this type of apostolate and obliged to engage in it. Such an apostolate is useful at all times and places, but in certain circumstances it is the only one available and feasible."[104]

28.5 In the apostolate exercised by the individual, great riches are waiting to be discovered through an intensification of the missionary effort of each of the lay faithful. Such an individual form of apostolate can contribute greatly to a *more extensive* spreading of the Gospel; indeed it can reach as many places as there are daily lives of individual members of the lay faithful. Furthermore, the spread of the Gospel will be *continual,* since a person's life and faith will be one. Likewise the spread of the Gospel will be particularly *incisive,* because in sharing fully in the unique conditions of the life, work, difficulties and hopes of their sisters and brothers, the lay faithful will be able to reach the hearts of their neighbors, friends, and colleagues, opening them to a full sense of human existence, that is, to communion with God and with all people.

Group forms of participation

29.1 Church communion, already present and at work in the activities of the individual, finds its specific expression in the lay faithful's working together in groups, that is, in activities done with others in the course of their responsible participation in the life and mission of the Church.

29.2 In recent days the phenomenon of lay people associating among themselves has taken on a character of particular variety and vitality. In some ways lay associations have always been present throughout the Church's history as various confraternities, third orders and sodalities testify even today. However, in modern times such lay groups have received a special stimulus, resulting in the birth and spread of a multiplicity of group forms: associations, groups, communities, movements. We can speak of *a new era of group endeavors* of the lay faithful. In fact, "alongside the traditional forming of associations, and at times coming from their very roots, movements and new sodalities have sprouted with a specific feature and purpose, so great is the richness and the versatility of resources that the Holy Spirit nourishes in the ecclesial community, and so great is the capacity of initiative and the generosity of our lay people."[105]

29.3 Oftentimes these lay groups show themselves to be *very diverse* from one another in various aspects: in their external structures, in their proce-

---

[104] Decree on the Apostolate of the Laity *Apostolicam Actuositatem,* 16.
[105] John Paul II, Angelus (August 23, 1987), 2: *Insegnamenti* X/3 (1987), 240.

dures and training methods, and in the fields in which they work. However, they all come together in an all-inclusive and *profound convergence* when viewed from the perspective of their common purpose, that is, the responsible participation of all of them in the Church's mission of carrying forth the Gospel of Christ, the source of hope for humanity and the renewal of society.

29.4 The actual formation of groups of the lay faithful for spiritual purposes or for apostolic work comes from various sources and corresponds to different demands. In fact, their formation itself expresses the social nature of the person and for this reason leads to a more extensive and incisive effectiveness in work. In reality, a "cultural" effect can be accomplished through work done not so much by an individual alone but by an individual as "a social being," that is, as a member of a group, of a community, of an association or of a movement. Such work is, then, the source and stimulus leading to the transformation of the surroundings and society as well as the fruit and sign of every other transformation in this regard. This is particularly true in the context of a pluralistic and fragmented society — the case in so many parts of the world today — and in light of the problems which have become greatly complex and difficult. On the other hand, in a secularized world, above all, the various group forms of the apostolate can represent for many a precious help for the Christian life in remaining faithful to the demands of the Gospel and to the commitment to the Church's mission and the apostolate.

29.5 Beyond this, the profound reason that justifies and demands the lay faithful's forming of lay groups comes from a theology *based on ecclesiology,* as the Second Vatican Council clearly acknowledged in referring to the group apostolate as a "sign of communion and of unity of the Church of Christ."[106]

29.6 It is a "sign" that must be manifested in relation to "communion" both in the internal and external aspects of the various group forms and in the wider context of the Christian community. As mentioned, this reason based on ecclesiology explains, on the one hand, the "right" of lay associations to form, and on the other, the necessity of "criteria" for discerning the authenticity of the forms which such groups take in the Church.

29.7 First of all, the *freedom for lay people in the Church to form such groups* is to be acknowledged. Such liberty is a true and proper right that is not derived from any kind of "concession" by authority, but flows from the Sacrament of Baptism, which calls the lay faithful to participate actively in the Church's communion and mission. In this regard the Council is quite clear: "As long as the proper relationship is kept to Church authority, the lay

---

[106] Decree on the Apostolate of the Laity *Apostolicam Actuositatem,* 18.

faithful have the right to found and run such associations and to join those already existing."[107] A citation from the recently published Code of Canon Law affirms it as well: "The Christian faithful are at liberty to found and govern associations for charitable and religious purposes or for the promotion of the Christian vocation in the world; they are free to hold meetings to pursue these purposes in common."[108]

29.8 It is a question of a freedom that is to be acknowledged and guaranteed by ecclesial authority and always and only to be exercised in Church communion. Consequently, the right of the lay faithful to form groups is essentially in relation to the Church's life of communion and to her mission.

"Criteria of ecclesiality" for lay groups

30.1 It is always from the perspective of the Church's communion and mission, and not in opposition to the freedom to associate, that one understands the necessity of having *clear and definite criteria for discerning and recognizing* such lay groups, also called "criteria of ecclesiality."

30.2 The following basic criteria might be helpful in evaluating an association of the lay faithful in the Church:

— *The primacy given to the call of every Christian to holiness,* as it is manifested "in the fruits of grace which the spirit produces in the faithful"[109] and in a growth toward the fullness of Christian life and the perfection of charity.[110]

30.3 In this sense whatever association of the lay faithful there might be, it is always called to be more of an instrument leading to holiness in the Church, through fostering and promoting "a more intimate unity between the everyday life of its members and their faith."[111]

— *The responsibility of professing the Catholic faith,* embracing and proclaiming the truth about Christ, the Church and humanity, in obedience to the Church's Magisterium, as the Church interprets it. For this reason every association of the lay faithful must be a *forum* where the faith is proclaimed as well as taught in its total content.

— *The witness to a strong and authentic communion* in filial relationship to

---

[107] Ibid., 19; cf. also, ibid., 15; Second Vatican Ecumenical Council, Dogmatic Constitution on the Church *Lumen Gentium,* 37.

[108] Canon 215.

[109] Second Vatican Ecumenical Council, Dogmatic Constitution on the Church *Lumen Gentium,* 39.

[110] Cf. ibid., 40.

[111] Second Vatican Ecumenical Council, Decree on the Apostolate of the Laity *Apostolicam Actuositatem,* 19.

the Pope, in total adherence to the belief that he is the perpetual and visible center of unity of the universal Church,[112] and with the local Bishop, "the visible principle and foundation of unity"[113] in the particular Church, and in "mutual esteem for all forms of the Church's apostolate."[114]

30.4 The communion with Pope and Bishop must be expressed in loyal readiness to embrace the doctrinal teachings and pastoral initiatives of both Pope and Bishop. Moreover, Church communion demands both an acknowledgment of a legitimate plurality of forms in the associations of the lay faithful in the Church and, at the same time, a willingness to cooperate in working together.

— *Conformity to and participation in the Church's apostolic goals,* that is, "the evangelization and sanctification of humanity and the Christian formation of people's conscience, so as to enable them to infuse the spirit of the Gospel into the various communities and spheres of life."[115]

30.5 From this perspective, every one of the group forms of the lay faithful is asked to have a missionary zeal which will increase their effectiveness as participants in a re-evangelization.

— *A commitment to a presence in human society,* which, in light of the Church's social doctrine, places it at the service of the total dignity of the person.

30.6 Therefore, associations of the lay faithful must become fruitful outlets for participation and solidarity in bringing about conditions that are more just and loving within society.

30.7 The fundamental criteria mentioned at this time find their verification in the *actual fruits* that various group forms show in their organizational life and the works they perform, such as: the renewed appreciation for prayer, contemplation, liturgical and sacramental life; the reawakening of vocations to Christian marriage, the ministerial priesthood and the consecrated life; a readiness to participate in programs and Church activities at the local, national and international levels; a commitment to catechesis and a capacity for teaching and forming Christians; a desire to be present as Christians in various settings of social life and the creation and awakening of charitable, cultural and spiritual works; the spirit of detachment and evangelical poverty

---

[112] Cf. Second Vatican Ecumenical Council, Dogmatic Constitution on the Church *Lumen Gentium,* 23.

[113] Ibid.

[114] Second Vatican Ecumenical Council, Decree on the Apostolate of the Laity *Apostolicam Actuositatem,* 23.

[115] Ibid., 20.

leading to a greater generosity in charity toward all; conversion to the Christian life or the return to Church communion of those baptized members who have fallen away from the faith.

The Pastors in service to communion

31.1 The Pastors of the Church, even if faced with possible and understandable difficulties as a result of such associations and the process of employing new forms, cannot renounce the service provided by their authority, not simply for the well-being of the Church, but also for the well-being of the lay associations themselves. In this sense they ought to accompany their work of discernment with guidance and, above all, encouragement so that lay associations might grow in Church communion and mission.

31.2 It is exceedingly opportune that some new associations and movements receive *official recognition* and explicit approval from competent Church authority to facilitate their growth on both the national and international level. The Council has already spoken in this regard: "Depending on its various forms and goals, the lay apostolate provides for different types of relationships with the hierarchy. . . . Certain forms of the lay apostolate are given explicit recognition by the hierarchy, though in different ways. Because of the demands of the common good of the Church, moreover, ecclesial authority can select and promote in a particular way some of the apostolic associations and projects which have an immediately spiritual purpose, thereby assuming in them a special responsibility."[116]

31.3 Among the various forms of the lay apostolate which have a particular relationship to the hierarchy, the Synod Fathers have singled out various movements and associations of *Catholic Action* in which "indeed, in this organic and stable form, the lay faithful may freely associate under the movement of the Holy Spirit, in communion with their Bishop and priests, so that in a way proper to their vocation and with some special method they might be of service through their faithfulness and good works to promote the growth of the entire Christian community, pastoral activities and the infusion of every aspect of life with the Gospel spirit."[117]

31.4 The Pontifical Council for the Laity has the task of preparing a list of those associations which have received the official approval of the Holy See, and, at the same time, of drawing up, together with the Pontifical Council for Promoting Christian Unity, the basic conditions on which this approval might be given to ecumenical associations in which there is a majority of Catho-

---

[116] Ibid., 24.
[117] *Propositio* 13.

lics, and determining those cases in which such an approval is not possible.[118]

31.5 All of us, Pastors and lay faithful, have the duty to promote and nourish stronger bonds and mutual esteem, cordiality and collaboration among the various forms of lay associations. Only in this way can the richness of the gifts and charisms that the Lord offers us bear their fruitful contribution in building the common house: "For the sound building of a common house it is necessary, furthermore, that every spirit of antagonism and conflict be put aside and that the competition be in outdoing one another in showing honor (cf. Rom 12:10), in attaining a mutual affection, a will toward collaboration, with patience, farsightedness, and readiness to sacrifice which will at times be required."[119]

31.6 So as to render thanks to God for the great *gift* of Church communion which is the reflection in time of the eternal and ineffable communion of the love of God, Three in One, we once again consider Jesus' words: "I am the vine, you are the branches" (Jn 15:5). The awareness of the gift ought to be accompanied by a strong sense of *responsibility* for its use: it is, in fact, a gift that, like the talent of the Gospel parable, must be put to work in a life of ever-increasing communion.

31.7 To be responsible for the gift of communion means, first of all, to be committed to overcoming each temptation to division and opposition that works against the Christian life with its responsibility in the apostolate. The cry of Saint Paul continues to resound as a reproach to those who are "wounding the Body of Christ": "What I mean is that each one of you says, 'I belong to Paul,' or 'I belong to Cephas,' or 'I belong to Christ!' Is Christ divided?" (1 Cor 1:12-13). No, rather let these words of the Apostle sound a persuasive call: "I appeal to you, brethren, by the name of our Lord Jesus Christ, that all of you agree and that there be no dissensions among you, but that you be united in the same mind and the same judgment" (1 Cor 1:10).

31.8 Thus the life of Church communion will become a *sign* for all the world and a compelling *force* that will lead persons to faith in Christ: "that they may all be one; even as you, Father, are in me and I in you, that they also may be in us, so that the world may believe that you have sent me" (Jn 17:21). In such a way communion leads to *mission,* and mission itself to communion.

---

[118] Cf. *Propositio* 15.

[119] John Paul II, Address at a Meeting of the Italian Church, Loreto (April 11, 1985): *AAS* 77 (1985), 964.

III

I Have Appointed You To Go Forth and Bear Fruit

The Coresponsibility of the Lay Faithful in the Church as Mission

Mission to Communion

32.1 We return to the biblical image of the vine and the branches, which immediately and quite appropriately lends itself to a consideration of fruitfulness and life. Engrafted to the vine and brought to life, the branches are expected to bear fruit: "He who abides in me, and I in him, he it is that bears much fruit" (Jn 15:5). Bearing fruit is an essential demand of life in Christ and life in the Church. The person who does not bear fruit does not remain in communion: "Each branch of mine that bears no fruit, he (my Father) takes away" (Jn 15:2).

32.2 Communion with Jesus, which gives rise to the communion of Christians among themselves, is an indispensable condition for bearing fruit: "Apart from me you can do nothing" (Jn 15:5). And communion with others is the most magnificent fruit that the branches can give: in fact, it is the gift of Christ and his Spirit.

32.3 At this point *communion begets communion*: essentially it is likened to a *mission on behalf of communion*. In fact, Jesus says to his disciples: "You did not choose me, but I chose you and *appointed you that you should go and bear fruit* and that your fruit should abide" (Jn 15:16).

32.4 Communion and mission are profoundly connected with each other, they interpenetrate and mutually imply each other, to the point that *communion represents both the source and the fruit of mission: communion gives rise to mission and mission is accomplished in communion*. It is always the one and the same Spirit who calls together and unifies the Church and sends her to preach the Gospel "to the end of the earth" (Acts 1:8). On her part, the Church knows that the communion received by her as a gift is destined for all people. Thus the Church feels she owes to each individual and to humanity as a whole the gift received from the Holy Spirit that pours the charity of Jesus Christ into the hearts of believers, as a mystical force for internal cohesion and external growth. The mission of the Church flows from her own nature. Christ has willed it to be so: that of "sign and instrument . . . of unity of all the human race."[120] Such a mission has the purpose of making everyone know and live the "new" communion that the Son of God made man introduced into the history of the world. In this regard, then, the testimony of John the Evangelist defines in an irrevocable way the blessed end toward which the entire mission of the Church is directed: "That which we have seen and heard we proclaim also to you, so that you may have fellowship with us; and our fellowship is with the Father and with his Son Jesus Christ" (1 Jn 1:3).

32.5 In the context of Church mission, then, *the Lord entrusts a great part of the responsibility to the lay faithful, in communion with all other members of the People of God.* This fact, fully understood by the Fathers of the Second Vatican Council, recurred with renewed clarity and increased vigor in all the works of the Synod: "Indeed, Pastors know how much the lay faithful contribute to the welfare of the entire Church. They also know that they themselves were not established by Christ to undertake alone the entire saving mission of the Church toward the world, but they understand that it is their exalted office to be shepherds of the lay faithful and also to recognize the latter's services and charisms that all according to their proper roles may cooperate in this common undertaking with one heart."[121]

Proclaiming the Gospel

33.1 The lay faithful, precisely because they are members of the Church, have the vocation and mission of proclaiming the Gospel: they are prepared for this work by the sacraments of Christian initiation and by the gifts of the Holy Spirit.

33.2 In a very clear and significant passage from the Second Vatican Council we read: "As sharers in the mission of Christ, Priest, Prophet and King, the lay faithful have an active part to play in the life and activity of the Church. . . . Strengthened by their active participation in the liturgical life of their community, they are eager to do their share in apostolic works of that community. They lead to the Church people who are perhaps far removed from it; they earnestly cooperate in presenting the word of God, especially by means of catechetical instruction; and offer their special skills to make the care of souls and the administration of the temporal goods of the Church more efficient."[122]

33.3 The entire mission of the Church, then, is concentrated and manifested in *evangelization.* Through the winding passages of history the Church

---

[120] Second Vatican Ecumenical Council, Dogmatic Constitution on the Church *Lumen Gentium,* 1.

[121] Ibid., 30.

[122] Decree on the Apostolate of the Laity *Apostolicam Actuositatem,* 10.

has made her way under the grace and the command of Jesus Christ: "Go into all the world and preach the Gospel to the whole creation" (Mk 16:15) . . . "and lo, I am with you always, until the close of the age" (Mt 28:20). "To evangelize," writes Paul VI, "is the grace and vocation proper to the Church, her most profound identity."[123]

33.4 Through evangelization the Church is built up into a *community of faith:* more precisely, into a community that *confesses* the faith in full adherence to the word of God which is *celebrated* in the sacraments and *lived* in charity, the principle of Christian moral existence. In fact, the "Good News" is directed to stirring a person to a conversion of heart and life and a clinging to Jesus Christ as Lord and Savior; to disposing a person to receive Baptism and the Eucharist and to strengthen a person in the prospect and realization of new life according to the Spirit.

33.5 Certainly the command of Jesus "Go and preach the Gospel" always maintains its vital value and its ever-pressing obligation. Nevertheless, the *present situation,* not only of the world but also of many parts of the Church, *absolutely demands that the word of Christ receive a more ready and generous obedience.* Every disciple is personally called by name; no disciple can withhold making a response: "Woe to me if I do not preach the Gospel" (1 Cor 9:16).

The hour has come for a re-evangelization

34.1 Whole countries and nations where religion and the Christian life were formerly flourishing and capable of fostering a viable and working community of faith are now put to a hard test, and in some cases, are even undergoing a radical transformation as a result of a constant spreading of an indifference to religion, of secularism and atheism. This particularly concerns countries and nations of the so-called First World in which economic well-being and consumerism, even if coexistent with a tragic situation of poverty and misery, inspires and sustains a life lived "as if God did not exist." This indifference to religion and the practice of religion devoid of true meaning in the face of life's very serious problems are not less worrying and upsetting when compared with declared atheism. Sometimes the Christian faith as well, while maintaining some of the externals of its tradition and rituals, tends to be separated from those moments of human existence which have the most significance, such as birth, suffering and death. In such cases, the questions and formidable enigmas posed by these situations, if remaining without responses, expose contemporary people to an inconsolable delusion or to the

---

[123] Apostolic Exhortation *Evangelii Nuntiandi* (December 8, 1975), 14: *AAS* 68 (1976), 13.

temptation of eliminating the truly humanizing dimension of life implicit in these problems.

34.2 On the other hand, in other regions or nations many vital traditions of piety and popular forms of Christian religion are still conserved; but today this moral and spiritual patrimony runs the risk of being dispersed under the impact of a multiplicity of processes, including secularization and the spread of sects. Only a re-evangelization can assure the growth of a clear and deep faith, and serve to make these traditions a force for authentic freedom.

34.3 Without doubt a mending of the Christian fabric of society is urgently needed in all parts of the world. But for this to come about what is needed is to *first remake the Christian fabric of the ecclesial community itself* present in these countries and nations.

34.4 At this moment the lay faithful, in virtue of their participation in the prophetic mission of Christ, are fully part of this work of the Church. Their responsibility, in particular, is to testify how the Christian faith constitutes the only fully valid response — consciously perceived and stated by all in varying degrees — to the problems and hopes that life poses to every person and society. This will be possible if the lay faithful will know how to overcome in themselves the separation of the Gospel from life, to again take up in their daily activities in family, work and society, an integrated approach to life that is fully brought about by the inspiration and strength of the Gospel.

34.5 To all people of today, I once again repeat the impassioned cry with which I began my pastoral ministry: *"Do not be afraid! Open, indeed, open wide the doors to Christ!* Open to his saving power the confines of States, and systems political and economic, as well as the vast fields of culture, civilization, and development. Do not be afraid! Christ knows 'what is inside a person.' Only he knows! Today too often people do not know what they carry inside, in the deepest recesses of their soul, in their heart. Too often people are uncertain about a sense of life on earth. Invaded by doubts they are led into despair. Therefore — with humility and trust I beg and implore you — allow Christ to speak to the person in you. Only he has the words of life, yes, eternal life."[124]

34.6 Opening wide the doors to Christ, accepting him into humanity itself, poses absolutely no threat to persons; indeed it is the only road to take to arrive at the total truth and the exalted value of the human individual.

34.7 This vital synthesis will be achieved when the lay faithful know how to put the Gospel and their daily duties of life into a most shining and con-

---

[124] Homily at the Beginning of His Pastoral Ministry as Supreme Shepherd of the Church (October 22, 1978), 5: *AAS* 70 (1978), 947.

vincing testimony, where, not fear but the loving pursuit of Christ and adherence to him will be the factors determining how a person is to live and grow, and these will lead to new ways of living more in conformity with human dignity.

34.8 *Humanity is loved by God!* This very simple yet profound proclamation is owed to humanity by the Church. Each Christian's words and life must make this proclamation resound: God loves you, Christ came for you, Christ is for you "the way, the truth and the life!" (Jn 14:6).

34.9 This re-evangelization is directed not only to individual persons but also to entire portions of populations in the variety of their situations, surroundings and cultures. Its purpose is the *formation of mature ecclesial communities,* in which the faith might radiate and fulfill the basic meaning of adherence to the person of Christ and his Gospel, of an encounter and sacramental communion with him, and of an existence lived in charity and in service.

34.10 The lay faithful have their part to fulfill in the formation of these ecclesial communities, not only through an active and responsible participation in the life of the community, in other words, through a testimony that only they can give, but also through a missionary zeal and activity toward the many people who still do not believe and who no longer live the faith received at Baptism.

34.11 In the case of coming generations, the lay faithful must offer the very valuable contribution, more necessary than ever, of a *systematic work in catechesis.* The Synod Fathers have gratefully taken note of the work of catechists, acknowledging that they "have a task that carries great importance in animating ecclesial communities."[125] It goes without saying that Christian parents are the primary and irreplaceable catechists of their children, a task for which they are given the grace by the Sacrament of Matrimony. At the same time, however, we all ought to be aware of the "rights" that each baptized person has to being instructed, educated and supported in the faith and the Christian life.

Go into the whole world

35.1 While pointing out and experiencing the present urgency for a re-evangelization, the Church cannot withdraw from *her ongoing mission of bringing the Gospel to the multitudes — the millions and millions of men and women — who as yet do not know Christ the Redeemer of humanity.* In a specific way this is the missionary work that Jesus entrusted and again entrusts each day to his Church.

[125] *Propositio* 10.

35.2 The activity of the lay faithful, who are always present in these surroundings, is revealed in these days as increasingly necessary and valuable. As it stands, the command of the Lord "Go into the whole world" is continuing to find a generous response from lay persons who are ready to leave familiar surroundings, their work, their region or country, at least for a determined time, to go into mission territory. Even Christian married couples, in imitation of Aquila and Priscilla (cf. Acts 18; Rom 16:3-16), are offering a comforting testimony of impassioned love for Christ and the Church, through their valuable presence in mission lands. A true missionary presence is exercised even by those who for various reasons live in countries or surroundings where the Church is not yet established and bear witness to the faith.

35.3 However, at present the missionary concern is taking on such extensive and serious proportions for the Church that only a truly consolidated effort to assume responsibility by all members of the Church, both individuals and communities, can lead to the hope for a more fruitful response.

35.4 The invitation addressed by the Second Vatican Council to the particular Church retains all its value, even demanding at present a more extensive and more decisive acceptance: "Since the particular Churches are bound to mirror the universal Church as perfectly as possible, let them be fully aware that they have been sent also to those who do not believe in Christ."[126]

35.5 The Church today ought to take *a giant step forward* in her evangelization effort, and enter into *a new stage of history* in her missionary dynamism. In a world where the lessening of distance makes the world increasingly smaller, the Church community ought to strengthen the bonds among its members, exchange vital energies and means, and commit itself as a group to a unique and common mission of proclaiming and living the Gospel. "So-called younger Churches have need of the strength of the older Churches and the older ones need the witness and impulse of the younger, so that individual Churches receive the riches of other Churches."[127]

35.6 In this area, younger Churches are finding that an essential and undeniable element in the *founding of Churches*[128] is the formation not only of local clergy but also of a mature and responsible lay faithful: in this way the community which itself has been evangelized goes forth into a new region of the world so that it too might respond to the mission of proclaiming and bearing witness to the Gospel of Christ.

---

[126] Decree on the Church's Missionary Activity *Ad Gentes,* 20; cf. also, ibid., 37.

[127] *Propositio* 29.

[128] Cf. Second Vatican Ecumenical Council, Decree on the Church's Missionary Activity *Ad Gentes,* 21.

35.7 The Synod Fathers have mentioned that the lay faithful can favor the relations which ought to be established with followers of *various religions* through their example in the situations in which they live and in their activities: "Throughout the world today the Church lives among people of various religions. . . . All the faithful, especially the lay faithful who live among the people of other religions, whether living in their native region or in lands as migrants, ought to be for all a sign of the Lord and his Church, in a way adapted to the actual living situation of each place. Dialogue among religions has a preeminent part, for it leads to love and mutual respect, and takes away, or at least diminishes, prejudices among the followers of various religions and promotes unity and friendship among peoples."[129]

35.8 What is first needed for the evangelization of the world are *those who will evangelize.* In this regard everyone, beginning with the Christian family, must feel the responsibility to foster the birth and growth of *vocations,* both priestly and religious as well as in the lay state, *specifically directed to the missions.* This should be done by relying on every appropriate means, but without ever neglecting the privileged means of prayer, according to the very words of the Lord Jesus: "The harvest is plentiful, but the laborers are few; pray therefore the Lord of the harvest to send out laborers into his harvest!" (Mt 9:37-38).

To Live the Gospel: Serving the Person and Society

36.1 In both accepting and proclaiming the Gospel in the power of the Spirit, the Church becomes at one and the same time an "evangelizing and evangelized" community, and for this very reason she is made the *servant of all.* In her the lay faithful participate in the mission of service to the person and society. Without doubt the Church has the Kingdom of God as her supreme goal, of which "she on earth is its seed and beginning,"[130] and is therefore totally consecrated to the glorification of the Father. However, the Kingdom is the source of full liberation and total salvation for all people: with this in mind, then, the Church walks and lives, intimately bound in a real sense to their history.

36.2 Having received the responsibility of manifesting to the world the mystery of God that shines forth in Jesus Christ, *the Church likewise awakens one person to another,* giving a sense of one's existence, opening each

---

[129] *Propositio* 30 *bis.*
[130] Second Vatican Ecumenical Council, Dogmatic Constitution on the Church *Lumen Gentium,* 5.

to the whole truth about the individual and of each person's final destiny.[131] From this perspective the Church is called, in virtue of her very mission of evangelization, to serve all humanity. Such service is rooted primarily in the extraordinary and profound fact that "through the Incarnation the Son of God has united himself in some fashion to every person."[132]

36.3 For this reason the person "is the primary route that the Church must travel in fulfilling her mission: the individual is the *primary and fundamental way for the Church,* the way traced out by Christ himself, the way that leads invariably through the mystery of the Incarnation and Redemption."[133]

36.4 The Second Vatican Council, repeatedly and with a singular clarity and force, expressed these very sentiments in its documents. We again read a particularly enlightening text from the Constitution *Gaudium et Spes:* "Pursuing the saving purpose which is proper to her, the Church not only communicates divine life to all, but in some way casts the reflected light of that divine life over the entire earth. She does this most of all by her healing and elevating impact on the dignity of the human person, by the way in which she strengthens the bonds of human society, and imbues the daily activity of people with a deeper sense and meaning. Thus, through her individual members and the whole community, the Church believes she can contribute much to make the family of man and its history more human."[134]

36.5 In this work of contributing to the human family, for which the whole Church is responsible, a particular place falls to the lay faithful, by reason of their "secular character," obliging them, in their proper and irreplaceable way, to work toward the Christian animation of the temporal order.

Promoting the dignity of the person

37.1 *To rediscover and make others rediscover the inviolable dignity of every human person* makes up an essential task, in a certain sense, the central and unifying task of the service which the Church, and the lay faithful in her, are called to render to the human family.

37.2 Among all other earthly beings, *only a man or a woman is a "person,"*

---

[131] Cf. Second Vatican Ecumenical Council, Pastoral Constitution on the Church in the Modern World *Gaudium et Spes,* 22.

[132] Ibid.

[133] John Paul II, Encyclical Letter *Redemptor Hominis* (March 4, 1979), 14: *AAS* 71 (1979), 284-285.

[134] No. 40.

a conscious and free being and, precisely for this reason, the "center and summit" of all that exists on the earth.[135]

37.3 The dignity of the person is *the most precious possession* of an individual. As a result, the value of one person transcends all the material world. The words of Jesus "For what does it profit a man to gain the whole world and to forfeit his life?" (Mk 8:36) contain an enlightening and stirring statement about the individual: value comes not from what a person "has" — even if the person possessed the whole world! — as much as from what a person "is": the goods of the world do not count as much as the goods of the person, the good which is the person individually.

37.4 The dignity of the person is manifested in all its radiance when the person's origin and destiny are considered: created by God in his image and likeness as well as redeemed by the most precious blood of Christ, the person is called to be a "child in the Son" and a living temple of the Spirit, destined for the eternal life of blessed communion with God. For this reason every violation of the personal dignity of the human being cries out in vengeance to God and is an offense against the Creator of the individual.

37.5 In virtue of a personal dignity, the human being is *always a value as an individual,* and as such demands being considered and treated as a person and never, on the contrary, considered and treated as an object to be used, or as a means, or as a thing.

37.6 The dignity of the person constitutes *the foundation of the equality of all people among themselves.* As a result, all forms of discrimination are totally unacceptable, especially those forms which unfortunately continue to divide and degrade the human family, from those based on race or economics to those social and cultural, from political to geographic, etc. Each discrimination constitutes an absolutely intolerable injustice, not so much for the tensions and the conflicts that can be generated in the social sphere, as much as for the dishonor inflicted on the dignity of the person: not only to the dignity of the individual who is the victim of the injustice, but still more to the one who commits the injustice.

37.7 Just as personal dignity is the foundation of equality of all people among themselves, so it is also *the foundation of participation and solidarity of all people among themselves:* dialogue and communion are rooted ultimately in what people "are," first and foremost, rather than on what people "have."

37.8 The dignity of the person is the indestructible property of *every hu-*

---

[135] Cf. Second Vatican Ecumenical Council, Pastoral Constitution on the Church in the Modern World *Gaudium et Spes,* 12.

man being. The force of this affirmation is based on the *uniqueness and unrepeatability of every person.* From it flows that the individual can never be reduced by all that seeks to crush and to annihilate the person into the anonymity that comes from collectivity, institutions, structures and systems. As an individual, a person is not a number or simply a link in a chain, nor even less, an impersonal element in some system. The most radical and elevating affirmation of the value of every human being was made by the Son of God in his becoming man in the womb of a woman, as we continue to be reminded each Christmas.[136]

Respecting the inviolable right to life

38.1 In effect, the acknowledgment of the personal dignity of every human being demands *the respect, the defense and the promotion of the rights of the human person.* It is a question of inherent, universal and inviolable rights. No one, no individual, no group, no authority, no State, can change — let alone eliminate — them because such rights find their source in God himself.

38.2 The inviolability of the person, which is a reflection of the absolute inviolability of God, finds its primary and fundamental expression in the *inviolability of human life.* Above all, the common outcry, which is justly made on behalf of human rights — for example, the right to health, to home, to work, to family, to culture — is false and illusory if *the right to life,* the most basic and fundamental right and the condition for all other personal rights, is not defended with maximum determination.

38.3 The Church has never yielded in the face of all the violations that the right to life of every human being has received, and continues to receive, both from individuals and from those in authority. The human being is entitled to such rights, *in every phase of development,* from conception until natural death; and *in every condition,* whether healthy or sick, whole or handicapped, rich or poor. The Second Vatican Council openly proclaimed: "All offenses against life itself, such as every kind of murder, genocide, abortion, euthanasia and willful suicide; all violations of the integrity of the human person, such as mutilation, physical and mental torture, undue psychological pres-

---

[136] "If we celebrate so solemnly the birth of Jesus, we do it so as to bear witness to the fact that each person is someone, unique and unrepeatable. If humanity's statistics and arrangement, its political, economic and social systems as well as its simple possibilities, do not come about to assure man that he can be born, exist and work as a unique and unrepeatable individual, then bid 'farewell' to all assurances. For Christ and because of him, the individual is always unique and unrepeatable; someone eternally conceived and eternally chosen; someone called and given a special name" (John Paul II, First Christmas Radio Message to the World [December 25, 1978], 1: *AAS* 71 [1979], 66).

sures; all offenses against human dignity, such as subhuman living conditions, arbitrary imprisonment, deportation, slavery, prostitution, the selling of women and children, degrading working conditions where men are treated as mere tools for profit rather than free and responsible persons; all these and the like are certainly criminal: they poison human society; and they do more harm to those who practice them than those who suffer from the injury. Moreover, they are a supreme dishonor to the Creator."[137]

38.4 If, indeed, everyone has the mission and responsibility of acknowledging the personal dignity of every human being and of defending the right to life, some lay faithful are given a particular title to this task: such as *parents, teachers, health-care workers and the many who hold economic and political power.*

38.5 The Church today lives a fundamental aspect of her mission in lovingly and generously accepting every human being, especially those who are weak and sick. This is made all the more necessary as a "culture of death" threatens to take control. In fact, "the Church family believes that human life, even if weak and suffering, is always a wonderful gift of God's goodness. Against the pessimism and selfishness which casts a shadow over the world, the Church stands for life: in each human life she sees the splendor of that 'Yes,' that 'Amen,' which is Christ himself (cf. 2 Cor 1:19; Rev 3:14). To the 'No' which assails and afflicts the world, she replies with this living 'Yes,' this defending of the human person and the world from all who plot against life."[138] It is the responsibility of the lay faithful, who more directly through their vocation or their profession are involved in accepting life, to make the Church's "Yes" to human life concrete and efficacious.

38.6 The enormous development of *biological and medical science,* united to an amazing *power in technology,* today provides possibilities on the very frontier of human life which imply new responsibilities. In fact, today humanity is in the position not only of "observing" but even "exercising a control over" human life at its very beginning and in its first stages of development.

38.7 The *moral conscience* of humanity is not able to turn aside or remain indifferent in the face of these gigantic strides accomplished by a technology that is acquiring continually more extensive and profound dominion over the working processes that govern procreation and the first phases of human life. Today as perhaps never before in history or in this field, *wisdom shows itself to be the only firm basis of salvation,* in that persons engaged in scientific

---

[137] Pastoral Constitution on the Church in the Modern World *Gaudium et Spes,* 27.

[138] John Paul II, Apostolic Exhortation *Familiaris Consortio* (November 22, 1981), 30: *AAS* 74 (1982), 116.

research and in its application are always to act with intelligence and love, that is, respecting, even remaining in veneration of, the inviolable dignity of the personhood of every human being, from the first moment of life's existence. This occurs when science and technology are committed with licit means to the defense of life and the cure of disease in its beginnings, refusing on the contrary — even for the dignity of research itself — to perform operations that result in falsifying the genetic patrimony of the individual and of human generative power.[139]

38.8 The lay faithful, having responsibility in various capacities and at different levels of science as well as in the medical, social, legislative and economic fields, must *courageously accept the "challenge" posed by new problems in bioethics.* The Synod Fathers used these words: "Christians ought to exercise their responsibilities as masters of science and technology, and not become their slaves.... In view of the moral challenges presented by enormous new technological power endangering not only fundamental human rights but the very biological essence of the human species, it is of utmost importance that lay Christians — with the help of the universal Church — take up the task of calling culture back to the principles of an authentic humanism, giving a dynamic and sure foundation to the promotion and defense of the rights of the human being in one's very essence, an essence which the preaching of the Gospel reveals to all."[140]

38.9 Today maximum vigilance must be exercised by everyone in the face of the phenomenon of the concentration of power and technology. In fact, such a concentration has a tendency to manipulate not only the biological essence but the very content of people's consciences and lifestyles, thereby worsening the condition of entire peoples by discrimination and marginalization.

Free to call upon the name of the Lord

39.1 Respect for the dignity of the person, which implies the defense and promotion of human rights, demands the recognition of the religious dimension of the individual. This is not simply a requirement "concerning matters of faith," but a requirement that finds itself inextricably bound up with the very reality of the individual. In fact, the individual's relation to God is a constitutive element of the very "being" and "existence" of an individual: it is in God that we "live, move and have our being" (Acts 17:28). Even if not all believe

---

[139] Cf. Congregation for the Doctrine of the Faith, Instruction on Respect for Human Life in Its Origin and on the Dignity of Procreation *Donum Vitae* (March 11, 1987): *AAS* 80 (1988), 70-102.

[140] *Propositio* 36.

this truth, the many who are convinced of it have the right to be respected for their faith and for their life-choice, individual and communal, that flows from that faith. This is the *right of freedom of conscience and religious freedom,* the effective acknowledgment of which is among the highest goods and the most serious duties of every people that truly wishes to assure the good of the person and society. "Religious freedom, an essential requirement of the dignity of every person, is a cornerstone of the structure of human rights, and for this reason an irreplaceable factor in the good of individuals and of the whole of society, as well as of the personal fulfillment of each individual. It follows that the freedom of individuals and of communities to profess and practice their religion is an essential element for peaceful human coexistence. . . . The civil and social right to religious freedom, inasmuch as it touches the most intimate sphere of the spirit, is a point of reference for the other fundamental rights and in some way becomes a measure of them."[141]

39.2 The Synod did not forget the many brothers and sisters that still do not enjoy such a right and have to face difficulties, marginalization, suffering, persecution, and oftentimes death because of professing the faith. For the most part, they are brothers and sisters of the Christian lay faithful. The proclamation of the Gospel and the Christian testimony given in a life of suffering and martyrdom make up the summit of the apostolic life among Christ's disciples, just as the love for the Lord Jesus even to the giving of one's life constitutes a source of extraordinary fruitfulness for the building up of the Church. Thus the mystic vine bears witness to its earnestness in the faith, as expressed by Saint Augustine: "But that vine, as predicted by the Prophets and even by the Lord himself, spread its fruitful branches in the world, and becomes the more fruitful the more it is watered by the blood of martyrs."[142]

39.3 The whole Church is profoundly grateful for this example and this gift. These sons and daughters give reason for renewing the pursuit of a holy and apostolic life. In this sense the Fathers at the Synod have made it their special duty "to give thanks to those lay people who, despite their restricted liberty, live as tireless witnesses of faith in faithful union with the Apostolic See, although they may be deprived of sacred ministers. They risk everything, even life. In this way the lay faithful bear witness to an essential property of the Church: God's Church is born of God's grace which is expressed in an excellent way in martyrdom."[143]

---

[141] John Paul II, Message for the 1988 World Day of Peace, "Religious Freedom: Condition for Peace" (December 8, 1987), intro., 1: *AAS* 80 (1988), 278, 280.

[142] *De Catechizandis Rudibus,* XXIV, 44: *CCL* 46, 168.

[143] *Propositio* 32.

39.4 Without doubt, all that has been said until now on the subject of respect for personal dignity and the acknowledgment of human rights concerns the responsibility of each Christian, of each person. However, we must immediately recognize how such a problem today has a *world dimension:* in fact, it is a question which at this moment affects entire groups, indeed entire peoples, who are violently being denied their basic rights. Those forms of unequal development among the so-called different "Worlds" were openly denounced in the recent Encyclical *Sollicitudo Rei Socialis.*

39.5 Respect for the human person goes beyond the demands of individual morality. Instead, it is a basic criterion, an essential element in the very structure of society, since the purpose of the whole of society itself is geared to the human person.

39.6 Thus, intimately connected with the responsibility of *service to the person* is the responsibility to *serve society,* as the general task of that Christian animation of the temporal order to which the lay faithful are called as their proper and specific role.

The family: where the duty to society begins

40.1 The human person has an inherent social dimension which calls a person from the innermost depths of self to *communion* with others and to the *giving* of self to others: "God, who has fatherly concern for everyone has willed that all people should form one family and treat one another in a spirit of brotherhood."[144] Thus *society* as a fruit and sign of the *social nature* of the individual reveals its whole truth in being a *community of persons.*

40.2 Thus the result is an interdependence and reciprocity between the person and society: all that is accomplished in favor of the person is also a service rendered to society, and all that is done in favor of society redounds to the benefit of the person. For this reason the duty of the lay faithful in the apostolate of the temporal order is always to be viewed both from its meaning of service to the person founded on the individual's uniqueness and unrepeatability as well as on the meaning of service to all people which is inseparable from it.

40.3 The first and basic expression of the social dimension of the person, then, is *the married couple and the family:* "But God did not create man a solitary being. From the beginning 'male and female he created them' (Gen 1:27). This partnership of man and woman constitutes the first form of com-

---

[144] Second Vatican Ecumenical Council, Pastoral Constitution on the Church in the Modern World *Gaudium et Spes,* 24.

munion between persons."[145] Jesus is concerned to restore integral dignity to the married couple and solidity to the family (cf. Mt 19:3-9). Saint Paul shows the deep rapport between marriage and the mystery of Christ and the Church (cf. Eph 5:22–6:4; Col 3:18-21; 1 Pet 3:1-7).

40.4 The *lay faithful's duty to society primarily begins* in marriage and in the family. This duty can only be fulfilled adequately with the conviction of the unique and irreplaceable value that the family has in the development of society and the Church herself.

40.5 The family is the basic cell of society. It is the cradle of life and love, the place in which the individual "is born" and "grows." Therefore a primary concern is reserved for this community, especially in those times when human egoism, the anti-birth campaign, totalitarian politics, situations of poverty, material, cultural and moral misery, threaten to make these very springs of life dry up. Furthermore, ideologies and various systems, together with forms of uninterest and indifference, dare to take over the role in education proper to the family.

40.6 Required in the face of this is a vast, extensive and systematic work, sustained not only by culture but also by economic and legislative means, which will safeguard the role of the family in its task of being the *primary place of "humanization"* for the person and society.

40.7 It is above all the lay faithful's duty in the apostolate to make the family aware of its identity as the primary social nucleus, and its basic role in society, so that it might itself become always a more *active and responsible place* for proper growth and proper participation in social life. In such a way the family can and must require from all, beginning with public authority, the respect for those rights which in saving the family will save society itself.

40.8 All that is written in the Exhortation *Familiaris Consortio* about participation in the development of society,[146] and all that the Holy See, at the invitation of the 1980 Synod of Bishops, has formulated with the "Charter of Rights for the Family," represent a complete and coordinated working program for all those members of the lay faithful who, in various capacities, are interested in the values and the needs of the family. Such a program needs to be more opportunely and decisively realized as the threats to the stability and fruitfulness of the family become more serious and the attempt to reduce the value of the family and to lessen its social value become more pressing and coordinated.

40.9 As experience testifies, whole civilizations and the cohesiveness of

---

[145] Ibid., 12.
[146] Cf. Nos. 42:48: *AAS* 74 (1982), 134-140.

peoples depend above all on the human quality of their families. For this reason the duty in the apostolate toward the family acquires an incomparable social value. The Church, for her part, is deeply convinced of it, knowing well that "the path to the future passes through the family."[147]

Charity: the soul and sustenance of solidarity

41.1 Service to society is expressed and realized in the most diverse ways, from those spontaneous and informal to those more structured, from help given to individuals to those destined for various groups and communities of persons.

41.2 The whole Church as such is directly called to the service of charity: "In the very early days the Church added the *agape* to the Eucharistic Supper, and thus showed herself to be wholly united around Christ by the bond of charity. So too, in all ages, she is recognized by this sign of love, and while she rejoices in the undertakings of others, she claims works of charity as her own inalienable duty and right. For this reason, mercy to the poor and the sick, works of charity and mutual aid intended to relieve human needs of every kind, are held in special honor in the Church."[148] *Charity toward one's neighbor,* through contemporary forms of the traditional spiritual and corporal works of mercy, represent the most immediate, ordinary and habitual ways that lead to the Christian animation of the temporal order, the specific duty of the lay faithful.

41.3 Through charity toward one's neighbor, the lay faithful exercise and manifest their participation in the kingship of Christ, that is, in the power of the Son of man who "came not to be served but to serve" (Mk 10:45). They live and manifest such a kingship in a most simple yet exalted manner, possible for everyone at all times because charity is the highest gift offered by the Spirit for building up the Church (cf. 1 Cor 13:13) and for the good of humanity. In fact, *charity gives life and sustains the works of solidarity that look to the total needs of the human being.*

41.4 The same charity, realized not only by individuals but also in a joint way by groups and communities, is and will always be necessary. Nothing and no one will be able to substitute for it, not even the multiplicity of institutions and public initiatives forced to give a response to the needs — oftentimes today so serious and widespread — of entire populations. Paradoxically such

---

[147] John Paul II, Apostolic Exhortation *Familiaris Consortio* (November 22, 1981), 85: *AAS* 74 (1982), 188.

[148] Second Vatican Ecumenical Council, Decree on the Apostolate of the Laity *Apostolicam Actuositatem,* 8.

charity is made increasingly necessary the more that institutions become complex in their organization and pretend to manage every area at hand. In the end such projects lose their effectiveness as a result of an impersonal functionalism, an overgrown bureaucracy, unjust private interests and an all-too-easy and generalized disengagement from a sense of duty.

41.5 Precisely in this context various forms of *volunteer work* which express themselves in a multiplicity of services and activities continue to come about and to spread, particularly in organized society. If this impartial service be truly given for the good of all persons, especially the most in need and forgotten by the social services of society itself, then volunteer work can be considered an important expression of the apostolate in which lay men and women have a primary role.

Public life: "for" everyone and "by" everyone

42.1 A charity that loves and serves the person is never able to be separated from *justice*. Each in its own way demands the full, effective acknowledgment of the rights of the individual, to which society is ordered in all its structures and institutions.[149]

42.2 In order to achieve their task directed to the Christian animation of the temporal order, in the sense of serving persons and society, the lay faithful *are never to relinquish their participation in "public life,"* that is, in the many different economic, social, legislative, administrative and cultural areas, which are intended to promote organically and institutionally the *common good*. The Synod Fathers have repeatedly affirmed that every person has a right and duty to participate in public life, albeit in a diversity and complementarity of forms, levels, tasks and responsibilities. Charges of careerism, idolatry of power, egoism and corruption that are oftentimes directed at persons in government, parliaments, the ruling classes, or political parties, as well as the common opinion that participating in politics is an absolute moral danger, does not in the least justify either skepticism or an absence on the part of Christians in public life.

42.3 On the contrary, the Second Vatican Council's words are particularly significant: "The Church regards as worthy of praise and consideration the work of those who, as a service to others, dedicate themselves to the public good of the State and undertake the burdens of this task."[150]

42.4 Public life on behalf of the person and society finds its *basic standard*

---

[149] For the relationship between justice and mercy, see John Paul II, Encyclical Letter *Dives in Misericordia* (November 30, 1980), 12: *AAS* 72 (1980), 1215-1217.

[150] Pastoral Constitution on the Church in the Modern World *Gaudium et Spes,* 75.

in *the pursuit of the common good,* as the good of *everyone* and as the good of each person taken as a *whole,* which is guaranteed and offered in a fitting manner to people, both as individuals and in groups, for their free and responsible acceptance. "The political community" — we read in the Constitution *Gaudium et Spes* — "exists for that common good in which the community finds its full justification and meaning, and from which it derives its basic, proper and lawful arrangement. The common good embraces the sum total of all those conditions of social life by which individuals, families and organizations can achieve more thoroughly their own fulfillment."[151]

42.5 Furthermore, public life on behalf of the person and society finds its *continuous line of action* in *the defense and the promotion of justice,* understood to be a "virtue," an understanding which requires education, as well as a moral "force" that sustains the obligation to foster the rights and duties of each and everyone based on the personal dignity of each human being.

42.6 *The spirit of service* is a fundamental element in the exercise of political power. This spirit of service, together with the necessary competence and efficiency, can make "virtuous" or "above criticism" the activity of persons in public life which is justly demanded by the rest of the people. To accomplish this requires a full-scale battle and a determination to overcome every temptation, such as the recourse to disloyalty and to falsehood, the waste of public funds for the advantage of a few and those with special interests, and the use of ambiguous and illicit means for acquiring, maintaining and increasing power at any cost.

42.7 The lay faithful given a charge in public life certainly ought to respect the autonomy of earthly realities properly understood, as we read in the Constitution *Gaudium et Spes*: "It is of great importance, especially in a pluralistic society, to work out a proper vision of the relationship between the political community and the Church, and to distinguish clearly between the activities of Christians, acting individually or collectively in their own name as citizens guided by the dictates of a Christian conscience, and their activity in communion with their Pastors in the name of the Church. The Church, by reason of her role and competence, is not identified with any political community nor bound by ties to any political system. She is at once the sign and the safeguard of the transcendental dimension of the human person."[152] At the same time — and this is felt today as a pressing responsibility — the lay faithful must bear witness to those human and Gospel values that are intimately connected with political activity itself, such as liberty and justice, solidarity,

---

[151] Ibid., 74.
[152] Ibid., 76.

faithful and unselfish dedication for the good of all, a simple lifestyle, and a preferential love for the poor and the least. This demands that the lay faithful always be more animated by a real participation in the life of the Church and enlightened by her social doctrine. In this they can be supported and helped by the nearness of the Christian community and their Pastors.[153]

42.8 The manner and means for achieving a public life which has true human development as its goal is *solidarity.* This concerns the active and responsible *participation* of all in public life, from individual citizens to various groups, from labor unions to political parties. All of us, each and everyone, are the goal of public life as well as its leading participants. In this environment, as I wrote in the Encyclical *Sollicitudo Rei Socialis,* solidarity "is not a feeling of vague compassion or shallow distress at the misfortunes of so many people, both near and far. On the contrary, it is *a firm and persevering determination* to commit oneself to the *common good,* that is to say, to the good of all and of each individual because *we are all really responsible for all.*"[154]

42.9 Today political solidarity requires going beyond single nations or a single bloc of nations, to a consideration on a properly continental and world level.

42.10 The fruit of sound political activity, which is so much desired by everyone but always lacking in advancement, is *peace.* The lay faithful cannot remain indifferent or be strangers and inactive in the face of all that denies and compromises peace, namely, violence and war, torture and terrorism, concentration camps, militarization of public life, the arms race, and the nuclear threat. On the contrary, as disciples of Jesus Christ, "Prince of Peace" (Is 9:5) and "our Peace" (Eph 2:14), the lay faithful ought to take upon themselves the task of being "peacemakers" (Mt 5:9), both through a conversion of "heart," justice and charity, all of which are the undeniable foundation of peace.[155]

42.11 The lay faithful in working together with all those that truly seek peace, and themselves serving in specific organizations as well as national and international institutions, ought to promote an extensive work of education intended to defeat the ruling culture of egoism, hate, the vendetta and hostility, and thereby to develop the culture of solidarity at every level. Such solidarity, in fact, "is *the way to peace and at the same time to development.*"[156]

---

[153] Cf. *Propositio* 28.
[154] No. 38: *AAS* 80 (1988), 565-566.
[155] Cf. John XXIII, Encyclical Letter *Pacem in Terris* (April 11, 1963), I: *AAS* 55 (1963), 265-266.
[156] John Paul II, Encyclical Letter *Sollicitudo Rei Socialis* (December 30, 1987), 39: *AAS* 80 (1988), 568.

From this perspective the Synod Fathers have invited Christians to reject as unacceptable all forms of violence, to promote attitudes of dialogue and peace and to commit themselves to establish a just international and social order.[157]

Placing the individual at the center of socioeconomic life

43.1 Service to society on the part of the lay faithful finds its essence in the *socioeconomic question,* which depends on the organization of *work.*

43.2 Recently recalled in the Encyclical *Sollicitudo Rei Socialis* is the seriousness of present problems as they relate to the subject of development and a proposed solution according to the social doctrine of the Church. I warmly desire to again refer its contents to all, in particular, to the lay faithful.

43.3 The basis for the social doctrine of the Church is the principle of *the universal destination of goods.* According to the plan of God the goods of the earth are offered to all people and to each individual as a means toward the development of a truly human life. At the service of this destination of goods is *private property,* which — precisely for this purpose — possesses an *intrinsic social function.* Concretely the *work* of man and woman represents the most common and most immediate instrument for the development of economic life, an instrument that constitutes at one and the same time a right and a duty for every individual.

43.4 Once again, all of this comes to mind in a particular way in the mission of the lay faithful. The Second Vatican Council formulates in general terms the purpose and criterion of their presence and their action: "In the socioeconomic realm the dignity and total vocation of the human person must be honored and advanced along with the welfare of society as a whole, for man is the source, the center, and the purpose of all socioeconomic life."[158]

43.5 In the context of the transformations taking place in the world of economy and work which are a cause of concern, the lay faithful have the responsibility of being in the forefront in working out a solution to the very serious problems of growing unemployment; to fight for the most opportune overcoming of numerous injustices that come from organizations of work which lack a proper goal; to make the workplace become a community of persons respected in their uniqueness and in their right to participation; to develop new solidarity among those that participate in a common work; to raise up new forms of entrepreneurship and to look again at systems of commerce, finance and exchange of technology.

43.6 To such an end the lay faithful must accomplish their work with

---

[157] Cf. *Propositio* 26.
[158] Pastoral Constitution on the Church in the Modern World *Gaudium et Spes,* 63.

professional competence, with human honesty, with a Christian spirit, and especially as a way of their own sanctification,[159] according to the explicit invitation of the Council: "By work an individual ordinarily provides for self and family, is joined in fellowship to others, renders them service, and is enabled to exercise genuine charity and be a partner in the work of bringing divine creation to perfection. Moreover, we know that through work offered to God, an individual is associated with the redemptive work of Jesus Christ, whose labor with his hands at Nazareth greatly ennobled the dignity of work."[160]

43.7 Today in an ever-increasingly acute way, the *so-called "ecological" question* poses itself in relation to socioeconomic life and work. Certainly humanity has received from God himself the task of "dominating" the created world and "cultivating the garden" of the world. But this is a task that humanity must carry out in respect for the divine image received, and, therefore, with intelligence and with love, assuming responsibility for the gifts that God has bestowed and continues to bestow. Humanity has in its possession a gift that must be passed on to future generations, if possible, passed on in better condition. Even these future generations are the recipients of the Lord's gifts: "The dominion granted to humanity by the Creator is not an absolute power, nor can one speak of a freedom to 'use and misuse,' or to dispose of things as one pleases. The limitation imposed from the beginning by the Creator himself and expressed symbolically by the prohibition not to 'eat of the fruit of the tree' (cf. Gen 2:16-17) shows clearly enough that, when it comes to the natural world, we are subject not only to biological laws but also to moral ones, which cannot be violated with impunity. A true concept of development cannot ignore the use of the things of nature, the renewability of resources and the consequences of haphazard industrialization — three considerations which alert our consciences to the *moral dimension* of development."[161]

Evangelizing culture and the cultures of humanity

44.1 Service to the individual and to human society is expressed and finds its fulfillment through *the creation and the transmission of culture,* which especially in our time constitutes one of the more serious tasks of living together as a human family and of social evolution. In light of the Council, we mean by "culture" all those "factors which go to the refining and developing of humanity's diverse spiritual and physical endowments. It means the

---

[159] Cf. *Propositio* 24.

[160] Pastoral Constitution on the Church in the Modern World *Gaudium et Spes,* 67.

[161] John Paul II, Encyclical Letter *Sollicitudo Rei Socialis* (December 30, 1987), 34: *AAS* 80 (1988), 560.

efforts of the human family to bring the world under its control through its knowledge and its labor; to humanize social life both in the family and in the whole civic community through the improvement of customs and institutions; to express through its works the great spiritual experiences and aspirations of all peoples throughout the ages; finally, to communicate and to preserve them to be an inspiration for the progress of many, indeed of the whole human race."[162] In this sense, culture must be held as the common good of every people, the expression of its dignity, liberty and creativity, and the testimony of its course through history. In particular, only from within and through culture does the Christian faith become a part of history and the creator of history.

44.2 The Church is fully aware of a pastoral urgency that calls for an absolutely special concern for culture in those circumstances where the development of a culture becomes disassociated not only from Christian faith but even from human values,[163] as well as in those situations where science and technology are powerless in giving an adequate response to the pressing questions of truth and well-being that burn in people's hearts. For this reason the Church calls upon the lay faithful to be present as signs of courage and intellectual creativity in the privileged places of culture, that is, the world of education — school and university — in places of scientific and technological research, the areas of artistic creativity and work in the humanities. Such a presence is destined not only for the recognition and possible purification of the elements that critically burden existing culture, but also for the elevation of these cultures through the riches which have their source in the Gospel and the Christian faith. The extensive treatment by the Second Vatican Council of the rapport between the Gospel and culture represents a constant historic fact and at the same time serves as a working ideal of particular and immediate urgency. It is a challenging program given as a pastoral responsibility to the entire Church, but in a specific way to the lay faithful in her. "The Good News of Christ continually renews the life and culture of fallen humanity; it combats and removes the error and evil which flow from the attraction of sin which are a perpetual threat. She never ceases to purify and to elevate the morality of peoples. . . . In this way the Church carries out her mission and in that very act she stimulates and makes her contribution to human and civic culture. By her action, even in its liturgical forms, she leads people to interior freedom."[164]

[162] Pastoral Constitution on the Church in the Modern World *Gaudium et Spes,* 53.
[163] Cf. *Propositio* 35.
[164] Pastoral Constitution on the Church in the Modern World *Gaudium et Spes,* 58.

44.3 Some particularly significant citations from Paul VI's Exhortation *Evangelii Nuntiandi* merit recollection here: "The Church evangelizes when she seeks to convert, solely through the divine power of the message she proclaims (cf. Rom 1:16; 1 Cor 1:18, 2:4), both the personal and collective consciences of people, the activities in which they engage, and the lives and concrete milieux which are theirs. Strata of humanity are transformed: for the Church it is a question not only of preaching the Gospel in ever-wider geographic areas or to ever-greater numbers of people, but also of affecting and as it were challenging through the power of the Gospel, mankind's criteria of judgment, determining values, points of interest, lines of thought, sources of inspiration and models of life, which are in contrast with the word of God and the plan of salvation. All this could be expressed in the following words: What matters is to evangelize humanity's culture and the cultures of the human family. . . . The split between the Gospel and culture is without a doubt the drama of our time, just as it was of other times. Therefore, every effort must be made to ensure a full evangelization of culture, or more correctly of cultures."[165]

44.4 The privileged way at present for the creation and transmission of culture is the *means of social communications.*[166] The world of the mass media represents a new frontier for the mission of the Church, because it is undergoing a rapid and innovative development and has an extensive worldwide influence on the formation of mentality and customs. In particular, the lay faithful's responsibility as professionals in this field, exercised both by individual right and through community initiatives and institutions, demands a recognition of all its values, and demands that it be sustained by more adequate resource materials, both intellectual and pastoral.

44.5 The use of these instruments by professionals in communication and their reception by the public demand both a work of education in a critical sense, which is animated by a passion for the truth, and a work of defense of liberty, respect for the dignity of individuals, and the elevation of the authentic culture of peoples which occurs through a firm and courageous rejection of every form of monopoly and manipulation.

44.6 However, the pastoral responsibility among the lay faithful does not stop with this work of defense. It extends to everyone in the world of communications, even to those professional people of the press, cinema, radio, television and theater. These also are called to proclaim the Gospel that brings salvation.

[165] Nos. 18-20: *AAS* 68 (1976), 18-19.
[166] Cf. *Propositio* 37.

IV

Laborers in the Lord's Vineyard

Good Stewards of God's Varied Grace

The Variety of Vocations

45.1 According to the Gospel parable, the "householder" calls the laborers for his vineyard at *various* times during the day: some at dawn, others about nine in the morning, still others about midday and at three, the last, around five (cf. Mt 20:1-16). In commenting on these words of the Gospel, Saint Gregory the Great makes a comparison between the various times of the call and the different *stages in life:* "It is possible to compare the different hours," he writes, "to the various stages in a person's life. According to our analogy the morning can certainly represent childhood. The third hour, then, can refer to adolescence; the sun has now moved to the height of heaven, that is, at this stage a person grows in strength. The sixth hour is adulthood, the sun is in the middle of the sky, indeed at this age the fullness of vitality is obvious. Old age represents the ninth hour, because the sun starts its descent from the height of heaven, thus the youthful vitality begins to decline. The eleventh hour represents those who are most advanced in years. . . . The laborers, then, are called and sent forth into the vineyard at different hours, that is to say, one is led to a holy life during childhood, another in adolescence, another in adulthood and another in old age."[167]

45.2 We can make a further application of the comments of Saint Gregory the Great to the extraordinary variety of ways the Church becomes "present" in life; one and all are called to work for the coming of the Kingdom of God according to the diversity of callings and situations, charisms and ministries. This variety is not only linked to age, but also to the difference of sex and to the diversity of natural gifts, as well as to careers and conditions affecting a person's life. It is a variety that makes the riches of the Church more vital and concrete.

Young People, Children and Older People

Youth, the hope of the Church

46.1 The Synod wished to *give particular attention to the young.* And rightly so. In a great many countries of the world, they represent half of entire popu-

---

[167] Saint Gregory the Great, *Homiliae in Evangelium,* I, 19, 2: *PL* 76, 1155.

lations, and often constitute in number half of the People of God itself living in those countries. Simply from this aspect youth make up an exceptional potential and a *great challenge for the future of the Church.* In fact the Church sees her path toward the future in the youth, beholding in them a reflection of herself and her call to that blessed youthfulness which she constantly enjoys as a result of Christ's Spirit. In this sense the Council has defined youth as "the hope of the Church."[168]

46.2 In the Letter of March 31, 1985 to young men and women in the world we read: "The Church looks to the youth, indeed the Church in a special way *looks at herself in the youth,* in all of you and in each of you. It has been so from the beginning, from apostolic times. The words of Saint John in his *First Letter* can serve as special testimony: 'I am writing to you, *young people,* because *you have overcome the evil one.* I write to you, children, because *you know the Father. . . .* I write to you, *young people,* because *you are strong* and the word of God *abides in you'* (2:13-14). . . . In our generation, at the end of the second millennium after Christ, the Church also sees herself in the youth."[169]

46.3 Youth must not simply be considered as an object of pastoral concern for the Church: in fact, young people are and ought to be encouraged to be active on behalf of the Church as *leading characters in evangelization and participants in the renewal of society.*[170] Youth is a time of an especially intensive *discovery* of a "self" and a "choice of life." It is a time for growth which ought to progress "in wisdom, age and grace before God and people" (Lk 2:52).

46.4 The Synod Fathers have commented: "The sensitivity of young people profoundly affects their perceiving of the values of justice, non-violence and peace. Their hearts are disposed to fellowship, friendship and solidarity. They are greatly moved by causes that relate to the quality of life and the conservation of nature. But they are troubled by anxiety, deceptions, anguishes and fears of the world as well as by the temptations that come with their state."[171]

46.5 The Church must seek to rekindle the very special love displayed by Christ toward the young man in the Gospel: "Jesus, looking upon him, loved him" (Mk 10:21). For this reason the Church does not tire of proclaiming Jesus Christ, of proclaiming his Gospel as the unique and satisfying response to the most deep-seated aspirations of young people as illustrated in Christ's forceful and exalted personal call to discipleship ("Come and follow me" [Mk

---

[168] Declaration on Christian Education *Gravissimum Educationis,* 2.

[169] John Paul II, Apostolic Letter to the Young People of the World on the Occasion of the International Year of Youth *Parati Semper* (March 31, 1985), 15: *AAS* 77 (1985), 620-621.

[170] Cf. *Propositio* 52.

[171] *Propositio* 51.

10:21]) that brings about a sharing in the filial love of Jesus for his Father and the participation in his mission for the salvation of humanity.

46.6 *The Church has so much to talk about with youth, and youth have so much to share with the Church.* This mutual dialogue, by taking place with great cordiality, clarity and courage, will provide a favorable setting for the meeting and exchange between generations, and will be a source of richness and youthfulness for the Church and civil society. In its Message to Young People the Council said: "The Church looks to you with confidence and with love. . . . She is the real youthfulness of the world. . . . Look upon the Church and you will find in her the face of Christ."[172]

Children and the Kingdom of heaven

47.1 Children are certainly the object of the Lord Jesus' tender and generous love. To them he gave his blessing, and, even more, to them he promised the Kingdom of heaven (cf. Mt 19:13-15; Mk 10:14). In particular Jesus exalted the active role that little ones have in the Kingdom of God. They are the eloquent symbol and exalted image of those moral and spiritual conditions that are essential for entering into the Kingdom of God and for living the logic of total confidence in the Lord: "Truly I say to you, unless you turn and become like children, you will never enter the Kingdom of heaven. Whoever humbles himself like this child, he is the greatest in the Kingdom of heaven" (Mt 18:3-5; cf. Lk 9:48).

47.2 Children are a continual reminder that the missionary fruitfulness of the Church has its life-giving basis not in human means and merits, but in the absolute gratuitous gift of God. The life itself of innocence and grace of many children, and even the suffering and oppression unjustly inflicted upon them, are in virtue of the Cross of Christ a source of spiritual enrichment for them and for the entire Church. Everyone ought to be more conscious and grateful for this fact.

47.3 Furthermore, it must be acknowledged that valuable possibilities exist even in the stages of infancy and childhood, both for the building up of the Church and for making society more humane. How often the Council referred to the beneficial and constructive effects for the family, "the domestic Church," through the presence of sons and daughters: "Children as living members of the family contribute in their own way to the sanctification of their parents."[173] The Council's words must also be repeated about children in relation to the local and universal Church. John Gerson, a great theologian and educator of

---

[172] (December 8, 1965): *AAS* 58 (1966), 18.
[173] Pastoral Constitution on the Church in the Modern World *Gaudium et Spes*, 48.

the fifteenth century, had already emphasized this fact in stating that "children and young people are in no way a negligible part of the Church."[174]

Older people and the gift of wisdom

48.1 I now address older people, oftentimes unjustly considered as unproductive, if not directly an insupportable burden. I remind older people that the Church calls and expects them to continue to exercise their mission in the apostolic and missionary life. This is not only a possibility for them, but it is their duty even in this time in their life, when age itself provides opportunities in some specific and basic way.

48.2 The Bible delights in presenting the older person as the symbol of someone rich in wisdom and fear of the Lord (cf. Sir 25:4-6). In this sense the "gift" of older people can be specifically that of being the witness to tradition in the faith both in the Church and in society (cf. Ps 44:1; Ex 12:26-27), the teacher of the lessons of life (cf. Sir 6:34, 8:11-12), and the worker of charity.

48.3 At this moment the growing number of older people in different countries worldwide and the expected retirement of persons from various professions and the workplace provide older people with a new opportunity in the apostolate. Involved in the task is their determination to overcome the temptation of taking refuge in a nostalgia in a never-to-return past or fleeing from present responsibility because of difficulties encountered in a world of one novelty after another. They must always have a clear knowledge that one's role in the Church and society does not stop at a certain age at all, but at such times knows only new ways of application. As the Psalmist says: "They still bring forth fruit in old age, they are ever full of sap and green, to show that the Lord is upright" (Ps 92:14-15). I repeat all that I said during the celebration of the Older People's Jubilee: "Arriving at an older age is to be considered a privilege: not simply because not everyone has the good fortune to reach this stage in life, but also, and above all, because this period provides real possibilities for better evaluating the past, for knowing and living more deeply the Paschal Mystery, for becoming an example in the Church for the whole People of God. . . . Despite the complex nature of the problems you face: a strength that progressively diminishes, the insufficiencies of social organizations, official legislation that comes late, or the lack of understanding by a self-centered society, you are not to feel yourselves as persons underestimated in the life of the Church or as passive objects in a fast-paced world, but as participants at a time of life which is humanly and spiritually fruitful. You still have a mission to fulfill, a contribution to make. According to the divine plan, each individual

---

[174] *De Parvulis ad Christum Trahendis*: *Oeuvres Complètes*, Desclée, Paris, 1973, IX, 669.

human being lives a life of continual growth, from the beginning of existence to the moment at which the last breath is taken."[175]

Women and Men

49.1 The Synod Fathers gave special attention to the status and role of women, with two purposes in mind: to acknowledge themselves and to invite all others once again to acknowledge the indispensable contribution of women to the building up of the Church and the development of society. They wished as well to work on a more specific analysis of women's participation in the life and mission of the Church.

49.2 Making reference to Pope John XXIII, who saw women's greater consciousness of their proper dignity and their entrance into public life as signs of our times,[176] the Synod Fathers, when confronted with the various forms of discrimination and marginalization to which women are subjected simply because they are women, time and time again strongly affirmed the urgency to defend and to promote the *personal dignity of woman,* and consequently her equality with man.

49.3 If anyone has this task of advancing the dignity of women in the Church and society, it is women themselves, who must recognize their responsibility as leading characters. There is still much effort to be done, in many parts of the world and in various surroundings, to destroy that unjust and deleterious mentality which considers the human being as a thing, as an object to buy and sell, as an instrument for selfish interests or for pleasure only. Women themselves, for the most part, are the prime victims of such a mentality. Only through openly acknowledging the personal dignity of women is the first step taken to promote the full participation of women in Church life as well as in social and public life. A more extensive and decisive response must be given to the demands made in the Exhortation *Familiaris Consortio* concerning the many discriminations of which women are the victims: "Vigorous and incisive pastoral action must be taken by all to overcome completely these forms of discrimination so that the image of God that shines in all human beings without exception may be fully respected."[177] Along the same lines, the Synod Fathers stated: "As an expression of her mission, the Church must stand firmly against all forms of discrimination and abuse of women."[178] And

---

[175] Address to a Gathering of Older People from the Dioceses of Italy (March 23, 1984), 2-3: *Insegnamenti* VII/1 (1984), 744.

[176] Cf. Encyclical Letter *Pacem in Terris* (April 11, 1963), I: *AAS* 55 (1963), 267-268.

[177] No. 24: *AAS* 74 (1982), 109-110.

[178] *Propositio* 46.

again: "The dignity of women, gravely wounded in public esteem, must be restored through effective respect for the rights of the human person and by putting the teaching of the Church into practice."[179]

49.4 In particular when speaking of *active and responsible participation in the life and mission of the Church,* emphasis should be placed on what has already been stated and clearly urged by the Second Vatican Council: "Since in our days women are taking an increasingly active share in the whole life of society, it is very important that they participate more widely also in the various fields of the Church's apostolate."[180]

49.5 The awareness that women with their own gifts and tasks have *their own specific vocation* has increased and been deepened in the years following the Council and has found its fundamental inspiration in the Gospel and the Church's history. In fact, for the believer the Gospel, namely, the word and example of Jesus Christ, remains the necessary and decisive point of reference. In no other moment in history is this fact more fruitful and innovative.

49.6 Though not called to the apostolate of the Twelve, and thereby to the ministerial priesthood, many women, nevertheless, accompanied Jesus in his ministry and assisted the group of Apostles (cf. Lk 8:2-3), were present at the foot of the Cross (cf. Lk 23:49), assisted at the burial of Christ (cf. Lk 23:55), received and transmitted the message of Resurrection on Easter morn (cf. Lk 24:1-10), and prayed with the Apostles in the Cenacle awaiting Pentecost (cf. Acts 1:14).

49.7 From the evidence of the Gospel, the Church at her origin detached herself from the culture of the time and called women to tasks connected with spreading the Gospel. In his letters the Apostle Paul even cites by name a great number of women for their various functions in service of the primitive Christian community (cf. Rom 16:1-15; Phil 4:2-3; Col 4:15; 1 Cor 11:5; 1 Tim 5:16). "If the witness of the Apostles founds the Church," stated Paul VI, "the witness of women contributes greatly toward nourishing the faith of Christian communities."[181]

49.8 Both in her earliest days and in her successive development, the Church, albeit in different ways and with diverse emphases, has always known women who have exercised an oftentimes decisive role in the Church herself and accomplished tasks of considerable value on her behalf. History is marked by grand works, quite often lowly and hidden, but not for this reason any less

---

[179] *Propositio* 47.

[180] Decree on the Apostolate of the Laity *Apostolicam Actuositatem,* 9.

[181] Address to the Committee for the International Year of the Woman (April 18, 1975): *AAS* 67 (1975), 266.

decisive to the growth and the holiness of the Church. It is necessary that this history continue, indeed that it be expanded and intensified in the face of the growing and widespread awareness of the personal dignity of woman and her vocation, particularly in light of the urgency of a "re-evangelization" and a major effort toward "humanizing" social relations.

49.9 Gathering together the pronouncements of the Second Vatican Council, which reflect the Gospel's message and the Church's history, the Synod Fathers formulated, among others, this precise "recommendation": "It is necessary that the Church recognize all the gifts of men and women for her life and mission, and put them into practice."[182] And again, "This Synod proclaims that the Church seeks the recognition and use of all the gifts, experiences and talents of men and women to make her mission effective (cf. Congregation for the Doctrine of the Faith, Instruction on Christian Freedom and Liberation, 72)."[183]

Anthropological and theological foundations

50.1 The condition that will assure the rightful presence of woman in the Church and in society is a more penetrating and accurate consideration of the *anthropological foundation for masculinity and femininity* with the intent of clarifying woman's personal identity in relation to man, that is, a diversity yet mutual complementarity, not only as it concerns roles to be held and functions to be performed, but also, and more deeply, as it concerns her make-up and meaning as a person. The Synod Fathers have deeply felt this requirement, maintaining that "the anthropological and theological foundations for resolving questions about the true significance and dignity of each sex require deeper study."[184]

50.2 Through committing herself to a reflection on the anthropological and theological basis of femininity, the Church enters the historic process of the various movements for the promotion of woman, and, in going to the very basic aspect of woman as a personal being, provides her most precious contribution. But even before this the Church intends, in such a way, to obey God who created the individual "in his image," "male and female he created them" (Gen 1:27), and who intended that they would accept the call of God to come to know, reverence and live his plan. It is a plan that "from the beginning" has been indelibly imprinted in the very being of the human person — men and women — and, therefore, in the make-up, meaning and deepest workings of

---

[182] *Propositio* 46.
[183] *Propositio* 47.
[184] Ibid.

the individual. This most wise and loving plan must be explored to discover all its richness of content — a richness that "from the beginning" came to be progressively manifested and realized in the whole history of salvation, and was brought to completion in "the fullness of time," when "God sent his Son, born of a woman" (Gal 4:4). That "fullness" continues in history: God's plan for woman is read and is to be read within the context of the faith of the Church, and also, in the lives lived by so many Christian women today. Without forgetting the help that can come from different human sciences and cultures, researchers, because of an informed discernment, will be able to help gather and clarify the values and requirements that belong to the enduring essential aspects of women and those bound to evolve in history. The Second Vatican Council reminds us: "The Church maintains that beneath all changes there are many realities which do not change; these find their ultimate foundation in Christ who is the same yesterday, and today, and forever (cf. Heb 13:8)."[185] The Apostolic Letter on the Dignity and Vocation of Women gives much attention to the anthropological and theological foundation of woman's dignity as a person. The document seeks to again treat and develop the catechetical reflections of the Wednesday General Audiences devoted over a long period of time to the "theology of the body," while at the same time fulfilling a promise made in the Encyclical *Redemptoris Mater*[186] and serving as a response to the request of the Synod Fathers.

50.3 May the reading of the Apostolic Letter *Mulieris Dignitatem,* in particular, as a biblical-theological meditation, be an incentive for everyone, both women and men, and especially for those who devote their lives to the human sciences and theological disciplines, to pursue on the basis of the personal dignity of man and woman and their mutual relationship, a critical study to

---

[185] Pastoral Constitution on the Church in the Modern World *Gaudium et Spes,* 10.

[186] The Encyclical Letter *Redemptoris Mater,* after having recalled that the "Marian dimension of the Christian life takes on a particular importance in relation to women and their status," states: "In fact, femininity has a *unique relationship* with the Mother of the Redeemer, a subject which can be studied in greater depth elsewhere. Here I simply wish to note that the example of Mary of Nazareth sheds light on *womanhood as such* by the very fact that God, in the sublime event of the Incarnation of his Son, entrusted himself to the ministry, the free and active ministry, of a woman. It can thus be said that women, by looking to Mary, find in her the secret of living their femininity with dignity and of achieving their own true advancement. In the light of Mary, the Church sees in women the reflection of a beauty which mirrors the loftiest sentiments of which the human heart is capable: the totality of the gift of self in love; the strength that is capable of bearing the greatest sorrows; limitless fidelity and tireless devotion to work; the ability to combine penetrating intuition with words, support and encouragement" (No. 46: *AAS* 79 [1987], 424-425).

better and more deeply understand the values and specific gifts of femininity and masculinity, not only in the surroundings of social living but also and above all in living as Christians and as members of the Church.

50.4 This meditation on the anthropological and theological foundations of women ought to enlighten and guide the Christian response to the most frequently asked questions, oftentimes so crucial, on *the "place" that women can have and ought to have in the Church and in society.*

50.5 It is quite clear from the words and attitude of Christ, which are normative for the Church, that no discrimination exists on the level of an individual's relation to Christ, in which "there is neither male nor female; for you are all one in Christ Jesus" (Gal 3:28) and on the level of participation in the Church's life of grace and holiness, as Joel's prophecy fulfilled at Pentecost wonderfully attests: "I will pour out my spirit on all flesh: your sons and daughters shall prophesy" (Joel 3:1; cf. Acts 2:17-21). As the Apostolic Letter on the Dignity and Vocation of Women reads: "Both women and men . . . are equally capable of receiving the outpouring of divine truth and love in the Holy Spirit. Both receive his salvific and sanctifying 'visits.' "[187]

Mission in the Church and in the world

51.1 In speaking about participation in the apostolic mission of the Church, there is no doubt that in virtue of Baptism and Confirmation, a woman — as well as a man — is made a sharer in the threefold mission of Jesus Christ, Priest, Prophet and King, and is thereby charged and given the ability to fulfill the fundamental apostolate of the Church: *evangelization.* However, a woman is called to put to work in this apostolate the "gifts" which are properly hers: first of all, the gift that is her very dignity as a person exercised in word and testimony of life; gifts, therefore, connected with her vocation as a woman.

51.2 In her participation in the life and mission of the Church, a woman cannot receive the *Sacrament of Orders,* and therefore cannot fulfill the proper function of the ministerial priesthood. This is a practice that the Church has always found in the expressed will of Christ, totally free and sovereign, who called only men to be his Apostles[188]; a practice that can be understood from the rapport between Christ, the Spouse, and his Bride, the Church.[189] Here we

---

[187] John Paul II, Apostolic Letter *Mulieris Dignitatem* (August 15, 1988), 16: *AAS* 80 (1988), 1691.

[188] Cf. Congregation for the Doctrine of the Faith, Declaration on the Question of Admission of Women to the Ministerial Priesthood *Inter Insigniores* (October 15, 1976): *AAS* 69 (1977), 98-116.

[189] Cf. John Paul II, Apostolic Letter *Mulieris Dignitatem* (August 15, 1988), 26: *AAS* 80 (1988), 1715-1716.

are in the area of *function,* not of *dignity* and *holiness.* In fact, it must be maintained: "Although the Church possesses a 'hierarchical' structure, nevertheless this structure is totally ordered to the holiness of Christ's members."[190]

51.3 However, as Paul VI has already said: "We cannot change what our Lord did, nor his call to women; but we can recognize and promote the role of women in the mission of evangelization and in the life of the Christian community."[191]

51.4 Above all, the *acknowledgment in theory* of the active and responsible presence of women in the Church must be *realized in practice.* With this in mind this Exhortation addressed to the lay faithful, with its deliberate and repeated use of the terms "women and men," must be read. Furthermore the revised Code of Canon Law contains many provisions on the participation of women in the life and mission of the Church: they are provisions that must be more commonly known and, according to the diverse sensibilities of culture and opportuneness in a pastoral situation, be realized with greater timeliness and determination.

51.5 An example comes to mind in the participation of women on diocesan and parochial Pastoral Councils as well as Diocesan Synods and particular Councils. In this regard the Synod Fathers have written: "Without discrimination women should be participants in the life of the Church and also in consultation and the process of coming to decisions."[192] And again: "Women, who already hold places of great importance in transmitting the faith and offering every kind of service in the life of the Church, ought to be associated in the preparation of pastoral and missionary documents and ought to be recognized as cooperators in the mission of the Church in the family, in professional life and in the civil community."[193]

51.6 In the more specific area of evangelization and catechesis the particular work that women have in the transmission of the faith, not only in the

---

[190] Ibid., 27: loc. cit., 1718; "The Church is a differentiated body in which each individual has a role; the tasks are distinct and must not be confused; they do not favor the superiority of one over the other, nor do they provide an excuse for jealousy; the only better gift, which can and must be desired, is love (cf. 1 Cor 12-13). The greatest in the Kingdom of heaven are not the ministers but the saints" (Congregation for the Doctrine of the Faith, Declaration on the Question of Admission of Women to the Ministerial Priesthood *Inter Insigniores* [October 15, 1976], 6: *AAS* 69 [1977], 115).

[191] Address to the Committee for the International Women's Year (April 18, 1975): *AAS* 67 (1975), 266.

[192] *Propositio* 47.

[193] Ibid.

family but also in the various educational environments, is to be more strongly fostered. In broader terms, this should be applied in all that regards embracing the word of God, its understanding and its communication, as well as its study, research and theological teaching.

51.7 While she is to fulfill her duty to evangelize, woman is to feel more acutely her need to be evangelized. Thus, with her vision illumined by faith (cf. Eph 1:18), woman is to be able to distinguish what truly responds to her dignity as a person and to her vocation from all that, under the pretext of this "dignity" and in the name of "freedom" and "progress," militates against true values. On the contrary, these false values become responsible for the moral degradation of the person, the environment and society. This same "discernment," made possible and demanded from Christian women's participation in the prophetic mission of Christ and his Church, recurs with continued urgency throughout history. This "discernment," often mentioned by the Apostle Paul, is not only a matter of evaluating reality and events in the light of faith, but also involves a real decision and obligation to employ it, not only in Church life but also in human society.

51.8 It can be said that the problems of today's world already cited in the second part of the Council's Constitution *Gaudium et Spes,* which remain unresolved and not at all affected by the passage of time, must witness the presence and commitment of women with their irreplaceable and customary contributions.

51.9 In particular, two great tasks entrusted to women merit the attention of everyone.

51.10 First of all, the task of *bringing full dignity to the conjugal life and to motherhood.* Today new possibilities are opened to women for a deeper understanding and a richer realization of human and Christian values implied in the conjugal life and the experience of motherhood. Man himself — husband and father — can be helped to overcome forms of absenteeism and of periodic presence as well as a partial fulfillment of parental responsibilities — indeed he can be involved in new and significant relations of interpersonal communion — precisely as a result of the intelligent, loving and decisive intervention of woman.

51.11 Secondly, women have the task of *assuring the moral dimension of culture,* the dimension, namely of *a culture worthy of the person,* of an individual yet social life. The Second Vatican Council seems to connect the moral dimension of culture with the participation of the lay faithful in the kingly mission of Christ: "Let the lay faithful by their combined efforts remedy the institutions and conditions of the world when the latter are an inducement to sin, that all such things may be conformed to the norms of justice, and may favor the practice of virtue rather than hindering it. By so doing, they will infuse culture and human works with a moral value."[194]

51.12 As women increasingly participate more fully and responsibly in the activities of institutions which are associated with safeguarding the basic duty to human values in various communities, the words of the Council just quoted point to an important field in the apostolate of women: in all aspects of the life of such communities, from the socioeconomic to the sociopolitical dimension, the personal dignity of woman and her specific vocation ought to be respected and promoted. Likewise this should be the case in living situations not only affecting the individual but also communities, not only in forms left to personal freedom and responsibility, but even in those guaranteed by just civil laws.

51.13 "It is not good for man to be alone: let us make him a helper fit for him" (Gen 2:18). *God entrusted the human being to woman.* Certainly, every human being is entrusted to each and every other human being, but in a special way the human being is entrusted to woman, precisely because the woman in virtue of her special experience of motherhood is seen to have a *specific sensitivity* toward the human person and all that constitutes the individual's true welfare, beginning with the fundamental value of life. How great are the possibilities and responsibilities of woman in this area, at a time when the development of science and technology is not always inspired and measured by true wisdom, with the inevitable risk of "dehumanizing" human life, above all when it would demand a more intense love and a more generous acceptance.

51.14 The participation of woman in the life of the Church and society in the sharing of her gifts is likewise the path necessary for her personal fulfillment — on which so many justly insist today — and the basic contribution of woman to the enrichment of Church communion and the dynamism in the apostolate of the People of God.

51.15 From this perspective the presence also of men, together with women, ought to be considered.

The presence and collaboration of men together with women

52.1 Many voices were raised in the Synod Hall expressing the fear that excessive insistence given to the status and role of women would lead to an unacceptable omission, that, in point, regarding *men.* In reality, various sectors in the Church must lament the absence or the scarcity of the presence of

[194] Dogmatic Constitution on the Church *Lumen Gentium,* 36.

men, some of whom abdicate their proper Church responsibilities, allowing them to be fulfilled only by women. Such instances are participation in the liturgical prayer of the Church, education and, in particular, catechesis of their own sons and daughters and other children, presence at religious and cultural meetings, and collaboration in charitable and missionary initiatives.

52.2 Therefore, the coordinated presence of both men and women is to be pastorally urged so that the participation of the lay faithful in the salvific mission of the Church might be rendered more rich, complete and harmonious.

52.3 The fundamental reason that requires and explains the presence and the collaboration of both men and women is not only, as it was just emphasized, the major source of meaning and efficacy in the pastoral action of the Church, nor even less is it the simple sociological fact of sharing a life together as human beings, which is natural for man and woman. It is, rather, the original plan of the Creator who from the "beginning" willed the human being to be a "unity of the two," and willed man and woman to be the prime community of persons, source of every other community, and, at the same time, to be a "sign" of that interpersonal communion of love which constitutes the mystical, intimate life of God, One in Three.

52.4 Precisely for this reason, the most common and widespread way, and at the same time, fundamental way, to assure this coordinated and harmonious presence of men and women in the life and mission of the Church, is the fulfillment of the tasks and responsibilities of the couple and the Christian family, in which the variety of diverse forms of life and love is seen and communicated: conjugal, paternal and maternal, filial and familial. We read in the Exhortation *Familiaris Consortio*: "Since the Christian family is a community in which the relationships are renewed by Christ through faith and the sacraments, the family's sharing in the Church's mission should follow *a community pattern:* the spouses together *as a couple,* the parents and children *as a family,* must live their service to the Church and to the world. . . . The Christian family also builds up the Kingdom of God in history through the everyday realities that concern and distinguish its *state of life:* it is thus in the *love between husband and wife and between members of the family* — a love lived out in all its extraordinary richness of values and demands: totality, oneness, fidelity and fruitfulness — that the Christian family's participation in the prophetic, priestly and kingly mission of Jesus Christ and of his Church finds expression and realization."[195]

52.5 From this perspective, the Synod Fathers have recalled the meaning

---

[195] No. 50: *AAS* 74 (1982), 141-142.

that the Sacrament of Matrimony ought to assume in the Church and society in order to illuminate and inspire all the relations between men and women. In this regard they have emphasized an "urgent need for every Christian to live and proclaim the message of hope contained in the relation between man and woman. The Sacrament of Matrimony, which consecrates this relation in its conjugal form and reveals it as a sign of the relation of Christ with his Church, contains a teaching of great importance for the Church's life — a teaching that ought to reach today's world through the Church; all those relations between man and woman must be imbued by this spirit. The Church should even more fully rely on the riches found here."[196] These same Fathers have rightly emphasized that "the esteem for virginity and reverence for motherhood must be respectively restored,"[197] and still again they have called for the development of diverse and complementary vocations in the living context of Church communion and in the service of its continued growth.

The Sick and the Suffering

53.1 People are called to joy. Nevertheless, each day they experience many forms of suffering and pain. The Synod Fathers, in addressing men and women affected by these various forms of suffering and pain, used the following words in their final *Message:* "You who are the abandoned and pushed to the edges of our consumer society; you who are sick, people with disabilities, the poor and hungry, migrants and prisoners, refugees, unemployed, abandoned children and old people who feel alone; you who are victims of war and all kinds of violence: the Church reminds you that she shares your suffering. She takes it to the Lord who in turn associates you with his redeeming Passion. You are brought to life in the light of his Resurrection. We need you to teach the whole world what love is. We will do everything we can so that you may find your rightful place in the Church and in society."[198]

53.2 In the context of such a limitless world as human suffering, we now turn our attention to all those struck down by sickness in its various forms: sickness is indeed the most frequent and common expression of human suffering.

53.3 The Lord addresses his call to each and every one. *Even the sick are sent forth as laborers into the Lord's vineyard:* the weight that wearies the

---

[196] *Propositio* 46.

[197] *Propositio* 47.

[198] Synod of Bishops, Seventh Ordinary General Assembly, Message to the People of God: In the Path of the Council, 12: *L'Osservatore Romano* (English-language edition), November 2, 1987, 11.

body's members and dissipates the soul's serenity is far from dispensing a person from working in the vineyard. Instead the sick are called to live their human and Christian vocation and to participate in the growth of the Kingdom of God in a *new and even more valuable manner.* The words of the Apostle Paul ought to become their approach to life or, better yet, cast an illumination to permit them to see the meaning of grace in their very situation: "In my flesh I complete what is lacking in Christ's afflictions for the sake of his Body, that is, the Church" (Col 1:24). Precisely in arriving at this realization, the Apostle is raised up in joy: "I rejoice in my sufferings for your sake" (Col 1:24). In the same way many of the sick can become bearers of the "joy inspired by the Holy Spirit in much affliction" (1 Thess 1:6) and witnesses to Jesus' Resurrection. A handicapped person expressed these sentiments in a presentation in the Synod Hall: "It is very important to make clear that Christians who live in situations of illness, pain and old age are called by God not only to unite their suffering to Christ's Passion but also to receive in themselves now, and to transmit to others, the power of renewal and the joy of the risen Christ (cf. 2 Cor 4:10-11; 1 Pet 4:13; Rom 8:18-25)."[199]

53.4 On the Church's part — as it reads in the Apostolic Letter *Salvifici Doloris* — "Born in the mystery of Redemption in the Cross of Christ, the Church has to try to meet man in a special way on the path of suffering. In this meeting, man 'becomes the way for the Church,' and this is one of the most important ways."[200] At this moment *the suffering individual is the way of the Church* because that person is, first of all, the way of Christ himself who is the Good Samaritan who "does not pass by," but "has compassion on him, went to him . . . bound up his wounds . . . took care of him" (Lk 10:32-34).

53.5 From century to century the Christian community, in revealing and communicating its healing love and the consolation of Jesus Christ, has reenacted the Gospel parable of the Good Samaritan in caring for the vast multitude of persons who are sick and suffering. This came about through the untiring commitment of all those who have taken care of the sick and suffering as a result of science and the medical arts as well as the skilled and generous service of health-care workers. Today there is an increase in the presence of lay women and men in Catholic hospital and health-care institutions. At times the lay faithful's presence in these institutions is total and exclusive. It is to just such people — doctors, nurses, other health-care workers, volunteers — that the call becomes the living sign of Jesus Christ and his Church in showing love toward the sick and suffering.

[199] *Propositio* 53.
[200] No. 3: *AAS* 76 (1984), 203.

Renewed pastoral action

54.1 It is necessary that this most precious heritage which the Church has received from Jesus Christ, "Physician of the body and the spirit,"[201] must never diminish but must always come to be more valued and enriched through renewal and decisive initiatives of *pastoral activity for and with the sick and suffering.* This activity must be capable of sustaining and fostering attention, nearness, presence, listening, dialogue, sharing and real help toward individuals in moments when sickness and suffering sorely test not only faith in life but also faith in God and his love as Father.

54.2 One of the basic objectives of this renewed and intensified pastoral action, which must involve all components of the ecclesial community in a coordinated way, is an attitude which looks upon the sick person, the bearer of a handicap, or the suffering individual, not simply as an *object* of the Church's love and service, but as an *active and responsible participant in the work of evangelization and salvation.* From this perspective the Church has to let the Good News resound within a society and culture, which, having lost the sense of human suffering, "censors" all talk on such a hard reality of life. The Good News is the proclamation that suffering can even have a positive meaning for the individual and for society itself, since each person is called to a form of participation in the salvific suffering of Christ and in the joy of Resurrection, as well as, thereby, to become a force for the sanctification and building up of the Church.

54.3 The proclamation of this Good News gains credibility when it is not simply voiced in words, but passes into a testimony of life, both in the case of all those who lovingly care for the sick, the handicapped and the suffering, as well as the suffering themselves who are increasingly made more conscious and responsible of their place and task within and on behalf of the Church.

54.4 In order that "the civilization of love" can flourish and produce fruit in this vast world of human pain, I invite all to reread and meditate on the Apostolic Letter *Salvifici Doloris* from which I am pleased to again propose the lines from its conclusion: "There should come together in spirit beneath the Cross of Calvary all suffering people who believe in Christ, and particularly those who suffer because of their faith in him who is the Crucified and Risen One, so that the offering of their sufferings may hasten the fulfillment of the prayer of the Savior himself, that all may be one. Let there also gather beneath the Cross all people of good will, for on this Cross is the 'Redeemer of Man,' the Man of Sorrows, who has taken upon himself the physical and moral sufferings of the people of all times, so that *in love* they may find the salvific meaning of their sorrow and valid answers to all their questions."

---

[201] Saint Ignatius of Antioch, *Ad Ephesios*, VII, 2: SCh 10, 64.

54.5 *"Together with Mary,* Mother of Christ who *stood beneath the Cross,* we pause beside all the crosses of contemporary man and we ask all of you *who suffer* to support us. We ask precisely you who are weak to *become a source of strength* for the Church and humanity. In the terrible battle between the forces of good and evil revealed to our eyes by our modern world, may your sufferings in union with the Cross of Christ be victorious."[202]

The States of Life and Vocations

55.1 All the members of the People of God — clergy, men and women Religious, the lay faithful — are laborers in the vineyard. At one and the same time they are all the goal and subjects of Church communion as well as of participation in the mission of salvation. Every one of us possessing charisms and ministries, diverse yet complementary, works in one and the same vineyard of the Lord.

55.2 Simply in *being* Christians, even before actually *doing* the works of a Christian, all are branches of the one fruitful vine which is Christ. All are living members of the one Body of the Lord built up through the power of the Spirit. The significance of "being" a Christian does not come about simply from the life of grace and holiness, which is the primary and more productive source of the apostolic and missionary fruitfulness of Holy Mother Church. Its meaning also arises from the state of life that characterizes the clergy, men and women Religious, members of Secular Institutes and the lay faithful.

55.3 In Church communion the states of life, by being ordered one to the other, are thus bound together among themselves. They all share in a deeply basic meaning: that of being *the manner of living out the commonly shared Christian dignity and the universal call to holiness in the perfection of love.* They are *different yet complementary,* in the sense that each of them has a basic and unmistakable character which sets each apart, while at the same time each of them is seen in relation to the other and placed at each other's service.

55.4 Thus the *lay* state of life has its distinctive feature in its secular character. It fulfills an ecclesial service in bearing witness and, in its own way recalling for priests, women and men Religious, the significance of the earthly and temporal realities in the salvific plan of God. In turn, the *ministerial* priesthood represents, in different times and places, the permanent guarantee of the sacramental presence of Christ, the Redeemer. The religious state bears witness to the eschatological character of the Church, that is, the straining

---

[202] No. 31: *AAS* 76 (1984), 249-250.

toward the Kingdom of God that is prefigured and in some way anticipated and experienced even now through the vows of chastity, poverty and obedience.

55.5 All the states of life, whether taken collectively or individually in relation to the others, are at the service of the Church's growth. While different in expression, they are deeply united in the Church's "mystery of communion" and are dynamically coordinated in its unique mission.

55.6 Thus in the diversity of the states of life and the variety of vocations this same, unique mystery of the Church reveals and experiences anew *the infinite richness of the mystery of Jesus Christ.* The Fathers were fond of referring to the Church as a field of a pleasing and wonderful variety of herbs, plants, flowers and fruits. Saint Ambrose writes: "A field produces many fruits, but the one which has an abundance of both fruits and flowers is far better. The field of holy Church is fruitful in both one and the other. In this field there are the priceless buds of virginity blossoming forth; widowhood stands out boldly as the forest in the plain; elsewhere the rich harvest of weddings blessed by the Church fills the great granary of the world with abundant produce, and the wine-presses of the Lord Jesus overflow with the grapes of a productive vine, enriching Christian marriages."[203]

The various vocations in the lay state

56.1 The Church's rich variety is manifested still further from within each state of life. Thus *within the lay state diverse "vocations" are given,* that is, there are different paths in the spiritual life and the apostolate which are taken by individual members of the lay faithful. In the field of a "commonly shared" lay vocation, "special" lay vocations flourish. In this area we can also recall the spiritual experience of the flourishing of diverse forms of Secular Institutes that have developed recently in the Church. These offer the lay faithful, and even priests, the possibility of professing the evangelical counsels of poverty, chastity and obedience through vows or promises, while fully maintaining one's lay or clerical state.[204] In this regard the Synod Fathers have commented: "The Holy Spirit stirs up other forms of self-giving to which people who remain fully in the lay state devote themselves."[205]

56.2 We can conclude by reading a beautiful passage taken from Saint

---

[203] *De Virginitate,* VI, 34: *PL* 16, 288; cf. Saint Augustine, *Sermo* 304, III, 2: *PL* 38, 1396.

[204] Cf. Pius XII, Apostolic Constitution *Provida Mater* (February 2, 1947): *AAS* 39 (1947), 114-124; Code of Canon Law, Canon 573.

[205] *Propositio* 6.

Francis de Sales, who promoted lay spirituality so well.[206] In speaking of "devotion," that is, Christian perfection or "life according to the Spirit," he presents in a simple yet insightful way the vocation of all Christians to holiness while emphasizing the specific form with which individual Christians fulfill it: "In creation God commanded the plants to bring forth their fruits, each one after its kind. So does he command all Christians who are the living plants of his Church, to bring forth the fruits of devotion, each according to his character and vocation. Devotion must be exercised in different ways by the gentleman, the workman, the servant, the prince, the widow, the maiden and the married woman. Not only this, but the practice of devotion must also be adapted to the strength, the employment, and the duties of each one in particular. . . . It is an error, or rather a heresy, to try to banish the devout life from the regiment of soldiers, the shop of the mechanic, the court of princes, or the home of married folk. It is true, Philothea, that a purely contemplative, monastic and religious devotion cannot be exercised in such ways of life. But besides these three kinds of devotion, there are several others adapted to bring to perfection those who live in the secular state."[207]

56.3 Along the same line the Second Vatican Council states: "This lay spirituality should take its particular character from the circumstances of one's state in life (married and family life, celibacy, widowhood), from one's state of health and from one's professional and social activity. All should not cease to develop earnestly the qualities and talents bestowed on them in accord with these conditions of life and should make use of the gifts which they have received from the Holy Spirit."[208]

56.4 What has been said about the spiritual vocation can also be said — and to a certain degree with greater reason — of the infinite number of ways through which all members of the Church are employed as laborers in the vineyard of the Lord, building up the Mystical Body of Christ. Indeed as a person with a truly unique life story, each is called by name, to make a special contribution to the coming of the Kingdom of God. No talent, no matter how small, is to be hidden or left unused (cf. Mt 25:24-27).

56.5 In this regard the Apostle Peter gives us a stern warning: "As each has received a gift, employ it for one another, as good stewards of God's varied grace" (1 Pet 4:10).

---

[206] Cf. Paul VI, Apostolic Letter *Sabaudiae Gemma* (January 29, 1967): *AAS* 59 (1967), 113-123.

[207] Saint Francis de Sales, *Introduction to the Devout Life,* I, III.

[208] Decree on the Apostolate of the Laity *Apostolicam Actuositatem,* 4.

V

That You Bear Much Fruit

The Formation of the Lay Faithful

A Continual Process of Maturation

57.1 The Gospel image of the vine and the branches reveals to us another fundamental aspect of the lay faithful's life and mission: *the call to growth and a continual process of maturation, of always bearing much fruit.*

57.2 As a diligent vinedresser, the Father takes care of his vine. God's solicitude is so ardently called upon by Israel that she prays: "Turn again, O God of hosts! Look down from heaven, and see; have regard for this vine, the stock which your right hand has planted" (Ps 80:14-15). Jesus himself speaks of the Father's work: "I am the true vine, and my Father is the vinedresser. Every branch of mine that bears no fruit, he takes away, and every branch that does bear fruit he prunes, that it may bear more fruit" (Jn 15:1-2).

57.3 The vitality of the branches depends on their remaining attached to the vine, which is Jesus Christ: *"He who abides in me and I in him bears much fruit,* for apart from me you can do nothing" (Jn 15:5).

57.4 People are approached in liberty by God who calls everyone to grow, develop and bear fruit. A person cannot put off a response nor cast off personal responsibility in the matter. The solemn words of Jesus refer to this exalted and serious responsibility: "If a man does not abide in me, he is cast forth as a branch and withers; and the branches are gathered, thrown into the fire and burned" (Jn 15:6).

57.5 In this dialogue between God who offers his gifts, and the person who is called to exercise responsibility, there comes the possibility, indeed the necessity, of a total and ongoing formation of the lay faithful, as the Synod Fathers have rightly emphasized in much of their work. After having described Christian formation as "a continual process in the individual of maturation in faith, and a likening to Christ according to the will of the Father, under the guidance of the Holy Spirit," they have clearly affirmed that the formation of the lay faithful must be placed *among the priorities of a Diocese.* "It ought to be so placed within the *plan of pastoral action* that the efforts of the whole community (clergy, lay faithful and Religious) converge on this goal."[209]

---

[209] *Propositio* 40.

To Discover and Live One's Vocation and Mission

58.1 The fundamental objective of the formation of the lay faithful is an ever-clearer discovery of one's vocation and the ever-greater willingness to live it so as to fulfill one's mission.

58.2 *God calls me and sends me forth* as a laborer in his vineyard. He calls me and sends me forth to work for the coming of his Kingdom in history. This personal vocation and mission defines the dignity and the responsibility of each member of the lay faithful and makes up the focal point of the whole work of formation, whose purpose is the joyous and grateful recognition of this dignity and the faithful and generous living-out of this responsibility.

58.3 In fact, from eternity God has thought of us and has loved us as unique individuals. Every one of us he called by name, as the Good Shepherd "calls his sheep by name" (Jn 10:3). However, only in the unfolding of the history of our lives and its events is the eternal plan of God revealed to each of us. Therefore, it is a gradual process; in a certain sense, one that happens day by day.

58.4 To be able to discover the actual will of the Lord in our lives always involves the following: a receptive listening to the word of God and the Church, fervent and constant prayer, recourse to a wise and loving spiritual guide, and a faithful discernment of the gifts and talents given by God, as well as the diverse social and historic situations in which one lives.

58.5 Therefore, in the life of each member of the lay faithful there are *particularly significant and decisive moments* for discerning God's call and embracing the mission entrusted by him. Among these are the periods of *adolescence* and *young adulthood.* No one must forget that the Lord, as the master of the laborers in the vineyard, calls *at every hour* of life so as to make his holy will more precisely and explicitly known. Therefore, the fundamental and continuous attitude of the disciple should be one of vigilance and a conscious attentiveness to the voice of God.

58.6 It is not a question of simply *knowing* what God wants from each of us in the various situations of life. The individual must *do* what God wants, as we are reminded in the words that Mary, the Mother of Jesus, addressed to the servants at Cana: "Do whatever he tells you" (Jn 2:5). However, to act in fidelity to God's will requires a *capability* for acting and *the developing of that capability.* We can rest assured that this is possible through the free and responsible collaboration of each of us with the grace of the Lord which is never lacking. Saint Leo the Great says: "The one who confers the dignity will give the strength!"[210]

---

[210] "Dabit virtutem, qui contulit dignitatem!" (*Sermo* 2, 1: *SCh* 200, 248).

58.7 This, then, is the marvelous yet demanding task awaiting all the lay faithful and all Christians at every moment: to grow always in the knowledge of the richness of Baptism and faith as well as to live it more fully. In referring to birth and growth as two stages in the Christian life, the Apostle Peter makes the following exhortation: "Like newborn babes, long for the pure spiritual milk, that by it you may grow up to salvation" (1 Pet 2:2).

A Total Integrated Formation for Living an Integrated Life

59.1 In discovering and living their proper vocation and mission, the lay faithful must be formed according to the *union* which exists from their being *members of the Church and citizens of human society.*

59.2 There cannot be two parallel lives in their existence: on the one hand, the so-called "spiritual" life, with its values and demands; and on the other, the so-called "secular" life, that is, life in a family, at work, in social relationships, in the responsibilities of public life and in culture. The branch, engrafted to the vine which is Christ, bears its fruit in every sphere of existence and activity. In fact, every area of the lay faithful's lives, as different as they are, enters into the plan of God, who desires that these very areas be the "places in time" where the love of Christ is revealed and realized for both the glory of the Father and service of others. Every activity, every situation, every precise responsibility — as, for example, skill and solidarity in work, love and dedication in the family and the education of children, service to society and public life and the promotion of truth in the area of culture — are the occasions ordained by Providence for a "continuous exercise of faith, hope and charity."[211]

59.3 The Second Vatican Council has invited all the lay faithful to this *unity of life* by forcefully decrying the grave consequences in separating faith from life, and the Gospel from culture: "The Council exhorts Christians, as citizens of one city and the other, to strive to perform their earthly duties faithfully in response to the spirit of the Gospel. They are mistaken who, knowing that we have here no abiding city but seek one which is to come, think that they may therefore shirk their earthly responsibilities; for they are forgetting that by faith itself they are more than ever obliged to measure up to these duties, each according to one's vocation. . . . This split between the faith which many profess and their daily lives deserves to be counted among the more

---

[211] Second Vatican Ecumenical Council, Decree on the Apostolate of the Laity *Apostolicam Actuositatem,* 4.

serious errors of our age."[212] Therefore, I have maintained that a faith that does not affect a person's culture is a faith "not fully embraced, not entirely thought out, not faithfully lived."[213]

Various aspects of formation

60.1 The many interrelated aspects of a *totally integrated formation* of the lay faithful are situated within this unity of life.

60.2 There is no doubt that *spiritual* formation ought to occupy a privileged place in a person's life. Everyone is called to grow continually in intimate union with Jesus Christ, in conformity to the Father's will, in devotion to others in charity and justice. The Council writes: "This life of intimate union with Christ in the Church is nourished by spiritual helps available to all the faithful, especially by active participation in the liturgy. Lay people should so make use of these helps in such a way that, while properly fulfilling their secular duties in the ordinary conditions of life, they do not disassociate union with Christ from that life, but through the very performance of their tasks according to God's will, may they actually grow in it."[214]

60.3 The situation today points to an ever-increasing urgency for a *doctrinal* formation of the lay faithful, not simply in a better understanding which is natural to faith's dynamism but also in enabling them to "give a reason for their hoping" in view of the world and its grave and complex problems. Therefore, a systematic approach to *catechesis,* geared to age and the diverse situations of life, is an absolute necessity, as is a more decided Christian promotion of *culture,* in response to the perennial yet always new questions that concern individuals and society today.

60.4 This is especially true for the lay faithful who have responsibilities in various fields of society and public life. Above all, it is indispensable that they have a more exact knowledge — and this demands a more widespread and precise presentation — of the *Church's social doctrine,* as repeatedly stressed by the Synod Fathers in their presentations. They refer to the participation of

---

[212] Second Vatican Ecumenical Council, Pastoral Constitution on the Church in the Modern World *Gaudium et Spes,* 43; cf. also, Second Vatican Ecumenical Council, Decree on the Church's Missionary Activity *Ad Gentes,* 21; Paul VI, Apostolic Exhortation *Evangelii Nuntiandi* (December 8, 1975), 20: *AAS* 68 (1976), 19.

[213] Address to the Participants in the National Congress of Church Movements of Cultural Responsibility (January 16, 1982), 2: *Insegnamenti* V/1 (1982), 131; cf. Letter to Cardinal Agostino Casaroli, Secretary of State, Establishing the Pontifical Council for Culture (May 20, 1982): *AAS* 74 (1982), 685; Address to the Community of the University of Louvain (May 20, 1985), 2: *Insegnamenti* VIII/1 (1985), 1591.

[214] Decree on the Apostolate of the Laity *Apostolicam Actuositatem,* 4.

the lay faithful in public life in the following words: "But for the lay faithful to take up actively this noble purpose in political matters, it is not enough to exhort them. They must be offered a proper formation of a social conscience, especially in the Church's social teaching, which contains principles of reflection, criteria for judging and practical directives (cf. Congregation for the Doctrine of the Faith, Instruction on Christian Freedom and Liberation, 72), and which must be present in general catechetical instruction and in specialized gatherings, as well as in schools and universities. Nevertheless, this social doctrine of the Church is dynamic; that is, adapted to circumstances of time and place. It is the right and duty of Pastors to propose moral principles even concerning the social order, and of all Christians to apply them in defense of human rights. . . . Nevertheless, active participation in political parties is reserved to the lay faithful."[215]

60.5 The cultivation of *human values* finds a place in the context of a totally integrated formation, bearing a particular significance for the missionary and apostolic activities of the lay faithful. In this regard the Council wrote: "(the lay faithful) should also hold in high esteem professional skill, family and civic spirit, and the virtues related to social behavior, namely, honesty, a spirit of justice, sincerity, courtesy, moral courage; without them there is no true Christian life."[216]

60.6 In bringing their lives into an organic synthesis, which is, at one and the same time, the manifestation of the unity of "who they are" in the Church and society as well as the condition for the effective fulfillment of their mission, the lay faithful are to be guided interiorly and sustained by the Holy Spirit, who is the Spirit of unity and fullness of life.

Collaborators with God the Teacher

61.1 Where are the lay faithful formed? What are the means of their formation? Who are *the persons and the communities* called upon to assume the task of a totally integrated formation of the lay faithful?

61.2 Just as the work of human education is intimately connected with fatherhood and motherhood, so Christian formation finds its origin and its strength in God the Father who loves and educates his children. Yes, *God is the first and great teacher of his People,* as it states in the striking passage of the Song of Moses: "He found him in a desert land and in the howling waste of the wilderness; he encircled him, he cared for him, he kept him as the apple of

---

[215] *Propositio* 22; cf. also John Paul II, Encyclical Letter *Sollicitudo Rei Socialis* (December 30, 1987), 41: *AAS* 80 (1988), 570-572.

[216] Decree on the Apostolate of the Laity *Apostolicam Actuositatem,* 4.

his eye. Like an eagle that stirs up its nest, that flutters over its young, spreading out its wings, catching them, bearing them on its pinions, the Lord alone did lead him, and there was no foreign God with him" (Dt 32:10-12, cf. 8:5).

61.3 God's work in forming his people is revealed and fulfilled in Jesus Christ the Teacher, and reaches to the depths of every individual heart as a result of the living presence of the Spirit. *Mother Church* is called to take part in the divine work of formation, both through a sharing of her very life, and through her various pronouncements and actions. It is thus that *the lay faithful are formed by the Church and in the Church* in a mutual communion and collaboration of all her members: clergy, Religious and lay faithful. Thus the whole ecclesial community, in its diverse members, receives the fruitfulness of the Spirit and actively cooperates toward that end. With this in mind Methodius of Olympo wrote: "Those not yet perfected are carried and formed by those more perfect, as in the womb of a mother, until the time they are generated and brought forth for the greatness and beauty of virtue."[217] This happened with Saint Paul, who was carried and brought forth in the Church by those who were perfected (in the person of Ananias) and, then Paul in his turn, became perfected and fruitful in bringing forth many children.

61.4 First of all, the Church is a teacher, in which the Pope takes the "primary" role in the formation of the lay faithful. As Successor of Saint Peter, he has the ministry of "confirming his brothers in the faith," instructing all believers in the essential content of vocation and mission in light of the Christian faith and membership in the Church. Therefore, not simply the words coming directly from him, but also those transmitted by the various departments of the Holy See call for a loving and receptive hearing by the lay faithful.

61.5 The one and universal Church is present in various parts of the world, in and through the *particular Churches*. In each of them the Bishop in his person has a responsibility toward the lay faithful, in forming the animation and guidance of their Christian life through the proclamation of the word and the celebration of the Eucharist and the sacraments.

61.6 Situated and at work within the particular Church or Diocese is the *parish* which has the essential task of a more personal and immediate formation of the lay faithful. In fact, because it is in the position to reach more easily individual persons and singular groups, the parish is called to instruct its members in hearing God's word, in liturgical and personal dialogue with God, in the life of fraternal charity, and in allowing a more direct and concrete perception of the sense of ecclesial communion and responsibility in the Church's mission.

---

[217] *Symposion III*, 8: *SCh* 95, 110.

61.7 Internal to the parish, especially if vast and territorially extensive, *small Church communities,* where present, can be a notable help in the formation of Christians, by providing a consciousness and an experience of ecclesial communion and mission which are more extensive and incisive. The Synod Fathers have said that a post-baptismal catechesis in the form of a catechumenate can also be helpful by presenting again some elements from the Rite of Christian Initiation of Adults with the purpose of allowing a person to grasp and live the immense, extraordinary richness and responsibility received at Baptism.[218]

61.8 In the formation that the lay faithful receive from their Diocese and parish, especially concerning communion and mission, the help that diverse members of the Church can give to each other is particularly important. This mutual help also aids in revealing the mystery of the Church as Mother and Teacher. Priests and Religious ought to assist the lay faithful in their formation. In this regard the Synod Fathers have invited priests and candidates for Orders to "be prepared carefully so that they are ready to foster the vocation and mission of the lay faithful."[219] In turn, the lay faithful themselves can and should help priests and Religious in the course of their spiritual and pastoral journey.

Other places for formation

62.1 The *Christian family,* as the "domestic Church," also makes up a natural and fundamental school for formation in the faith: father and mother receive from the Sacrament of Matrimony the grace and the ministry of the Christian education of their children, before whom they bear witness and to whom they transmit both human and religious values. While learning their first words, children learn also the praise of God, whom they feel is near them as a loving and providential Father; while learning the first acts of love, children also learn to open themselves to others, and through the gift of self receive the sense of living as a human being. The daily life itself of a truly Christian family makes up the first "experience of Church," intended to find confirmation and development in an active and responsible process of the children's introduction into the wider ecclesial community and civil society. The more that Christian spouses and parents grow in the awareness that their "domestic Church" participates in the life and mission of the universal Church, so much the more will their sons and daughters be able to be formed in a "sense of the Church" and will perceive all the beauty of dedicating their energies to the service of the Kingdom of God.

[218] Cf. *Propositio* 11.
[219] *Propositio* 40.

62.2 *Schools and Catholic universities,* as well as centers of spiritual renewal which are becoming ever more widespread in these days, are also important places for formation. In the present social and historical context which is marked by an extensively deep cultural involvement, the Synod Fathers have emphasized that parents' participation in school life — besides being always necessary and without substitution — is no longer enough. What is needed is to prepare the lay faithful to dedicate themselves to the work of rearing their children as a true and proper part of Church mission. What is needed is to constitute and develop this "formation community" which is together comprised of parents, teachers, clergy, women and men Religious and representatives of youth. In order that the school can suitably fulfill its natural function in formation, the lay faithful ought to feel charged to demand from everyone and for everyone a true freedom in education, even through opportune civil legislation.[220]

62.3 The Synod Fathers expressed words of esteem and encouragement to all those lay faithful, both women and men, who with a civic and Christian spirit, fulfill a task which is involved in the education of children both in schools and institutes of formation. In addition they have emphasized the urgent need in various schools, whether Catholic or not, for teachers and professors among the lay faithful to be true witnesses of the Gospel, through their example of life, their professional competence and uprightness, their Christian inspired teaching, preserving always — as is obvious — the autonomy of various sciences and disciplines. It is of singular importance that scientific and technological research done by the faithful be correct from the standpoint of service to an individual in the totality of the context of one's values and needs: to these lay faithful the Church entrusts the task of allowing all to better understand the intimate bond that exists between faith and science, between the Gospel and human culture.[221]

62.4 "This Synod" — we read in the proposition — "appeals to the prophetic task of Catholic schools and universities, and praises teachers and professors, now lay people for the most part, for their dedication to maintaining institutes of Catholic education that can form men and women in whom the new commandment is enfleshed. The simultaneous presence of clergy, the lay faithful and men and women Religious, offers students a vivid image of the Church and makes recognition of its riches easier" (cf. Congregation for Catholic Education, Concerning the Lay Educator, Witness of Faith in the Schools).[222]

---

[220] Cf. *Propositio* 44.
[221] Cf. *Propositio* 45.
[222] *Propositio* 44.

62.5 *Groups, associations and movements* also have their place in the formation of the lay faithful. In fact they have the possibility, each with its own method, of offering a formation through a deeply shared experience in the apostolic life, as well as having the opportunity to integrate, to make concrete and specific the formation that their members receive from other persons and communities.

The Reciprocal Formation Received and Given by All

63.1 Formation is not the privilege of a few, but a right and duty of all. In this regard the Synod Fathers have said: "Possibilities of formation should be proposed to all, especially the poor, who can also be a source of formation for all"; and they added: "Suitable means to help each person fulfill a full, human and Christian vocation should be applied to formation."[223]

63.2 For the purpose of a truly incisive and effective pastoral activity, the *formation of those who will form others* is to be developed through appropriate courses or suitable schools. Forming those who in turn will be given the responsibility for the formation of the lay faithful, constitutes a basic requirement of assuring the general and widespread formation of all the lay faithful.

63.3 According to the explicit invitation of the Synod Fathers, special attention ought to be devoted to the local culture in the work of formation: "The formation of Christians will take the greatest account of local human culture which contributes to formation itself, and will help to discern the value, whether implanted in tradition or proposed in modern affairs. Attention should be paid to diverse cultures which can exist in one and the same people or nation at the same time. The Church, the Mother and Teacher of peoples, should strive to safeguard, where the need exists, the culture of a less numerous people living in large nations when the situation exists."[224]

63.4 In the work of formation some convictions reveal themselves as particularly necessary and fruitful. First of all, there is the conviction that one cannot offer a true and effective formation to others if the individual has not taken on or developed a personal responsibility for formation: this, in fact, is essentially a "formation of self."

63.5 In addition, there is the conviction that at one and the same time each of us is the goal and principle of formation: the more we are formed and the more we feel the need to pursue and deepen our formation, still more will we be formed and be rendered capable of forming others.

63.6 It is particularly important to know that the work of formation, while

---

[223] *Propositio* 41.
[224] *Propositio* 42.

having intelligent recourse to the means and methods available from human science, is made more effective the more it is open to the *action of God.* Only the branch which does not fear being pruned by the heavenly vinedresser can bear much fruit for the individual and for others.

An Appeal and a Prayer

64.1 At the conclusion of this post-synodal document I once again put forward the invitation of "the householder" proposed in the Gospel: *You go into my vineyard too.* It can be said that the significance of the Synod on the vocation and mission of the lay faithful might very well consist in this *call of the Lord which he addresses to everyone,* yet, in a particular way to the lay faithful, both women and men.

64.2 The happenings at the Synod have been a great spiritual experience for all the participants. The experience has been that of a Church under the light and the power of the Spirit, intent on discerning and embracing the renewed call of her Lord so that she can again propose to today's world, the mystery of her communion and the dynamism of her mission of salvation, especially by centering on the specific place and role of the lay faithful. This Exhortation, then, intends to urge the most abundant possible fruitfulness from this Synod in every part of the Church worldwide. This will come about as a result of an effective hearkening to the Lord's call by the entire People of God, in particular, by the lay faithful.

64.3 Therefore I make a strong appeal to one and all, Pastors and faithful, never to become tired of maintaining — indeed always taking an active part to fix deeply in one's mind, heart and life — an *ecclesial consciousness,* which is ever mindful of what it means to be members of the Church of Jesus Christ, participants in her mystery of communion and in her dynamism in mission and the apostolate.

64.4 It is of particular importance that all Christians be aware that through Baptism they have received an *extraordinary dignity:* through grace we are called to be children loved by the Father, members incorporated into Christ and his Church, living and holy temples of the Spirit. With deep emotion and gratitude, we again hear the words of John the Evangelist: "See what love the Father has given us, that we should be called children of God; and so we are" (1 Jn 3:1).

64.5 While this "Christian *newness of life*" given to the members of the Church constitutes for all the basis of their participation in the priestly, prophetic and kingly mission of Christ and of their vocation to holiness in love, it receives expression and is fulfilled in the lay faithful through the "secular character" which is "uniquely and properly" theirs.

64.6 Besides imparting an awareness of a commonly shared Christian dignity, an ecclesial consciousness brings a sense of belonging to *the mystery of the Church as communion*. This is a basic and undeniable aspect of the life and mission of the Church. For one and all, the earnest prayer of Jesus at the Last Supper, *"that all may be one"* (Jn 17:21), ought to become daily a required and undeniable program of life and action.

64.7 A real sense of Church communion, the gift of the Spirit that urges our free and generous response, will bring forth as its precious fruit, in the "one and catholic" Church the continuing value of the rich variety of vocations and conditions of life, charisms, ministries, works and responsibilities, as well as a more demonstrable and decisive collaboration of groups, associations and movements of the lay faithful in keeping with the accomplishment of the commonly shared salvific mission of the Church herself. This communion is already in itself the first great sign in the world of the presence of Christ, the Savior. At the same time, it promotes and stimulates the proper apostolic and missionary action of the Church.

64.8 The whole Church, Pastors and lay faithful alike, standing on the threshold of the third millennium, ought to feel more strongly the Church's responsibility to obey the command of Christ, "Go into all the world and preach the Gospel to the whole creation" (Mk 16:15), and take up anew the missionary endeavor. A great venture, both challenging and wonderful, is entrusted to the Church — that of a *re-evangelization,* which is so much needed by the present world. The lay faithful ought to regard themselves as an active and responsible part of this venture, called as they are to proclaim and to live the Gospel in service to the person and to society while respecting the totality of the values and needs of both.

64.9 Since the Synod of Bishops was celebrated last October during the Marian Year, its work was entrusted in a very special way to the intercession of the Most Blessed Virgin Mary, Mother of the Redeemer. I too entrust the spiritual fruitfulness of the Synod to her prayerful intercession. Therefore, along with the Synod Fathers, the lay faithful present at the Synod and all the other members of the People of God, I have recourse at the end of this post-synodal document to the Virgin Mary. At this moment this appeal becomes a prayer:

O Most Blessed Virgin Mary,
Mother of Christ and Mother of the Church,
With joy and wonder we seek to make our own your *Magnificat,*
joining you in your hymn of thankfulness and love.

With you we give thanks to God,
"whose mercy is from generation to generation,"
for the exalted vocation
and the many forms of mission
entrusted to the lay faithful.
God has called each of them by name
to live his own communion of love
and holiness
and to be one
in the great family of God's children.
He has sent them forth
to shine with the light of Christ
and to communicate the fire of the Spirit
in every part of society
through their life
inspired by the Gospel.

O Virgin of the *Magnificat,*
fill their hearts
with a gratitude and enthusiasm
for this vocation and mission.

With humility and magnanimity
you were the "handmaid of the Lord";
give us your unreserved willingness
for service to God
and the salvation of the world.
Open our hearts
to the great anticipation
of the Kingdom of God
and of the proclamation of the Gospel
to the whole of creation.
Your Mother's heart
is ever mindful of the many dangers
and evils which threaten
to overpower men and women
in our time.
At the same time your heart also takes notice
of the many initiatives

undertaken for good,
the great yearning for values,
and the progress achieved
in bringing forth
the abundant fruits of salvation.

O Virgin full of courage,
may your spiritual strength
and trust in God inspire us,
so that we might know
how to overcome all the obstacles
that we encounter
in accomplishing our mission.
Teach us to treat the affairs
of the world
with a real sense of Christian responsibility
and a joyful hope
of the coming of God's Kingdom, and
of "new heavens and a new earth."

You who were gathered in prayer
with the Apostles in the Cenacle,
awaiting the coming
of the Spirit at Pentecost,
implore his renewed outpouring
on all the faithful, men and women alike,
so that they might more fully respond
to their vocation and mission,
as branches engrafted to the true vine,
called to bear much fruit
for the life of the world.

O Virgin Mother,
guide and sustain us
so that we might always live
as true sons and daughters
of the Church of your Son.
Enable us to do our part
in helping to establish on earth

the civilization of truth and love,
as God wills it,
for his glory.

Amen.

Given in Rome, at Saint Peter's, on December 30, the Feast of the Holy Family of Jesus, Mary and Joseph, in the year 1988, the eleventh of my Pontificate.

Pastores Dabo Vobis

Editor's Introduction

Pope John Paul II's *Pastores Dabo Vobis,* dated March 25, 1992, is another link in the chain of his post-synodal apostolic exhortations aimed at implementing the teaching of the Second Vatican Council. It is the fruit of the Eighth Ordinary General Assembly of the Synod of Bishops which met in 1990 to discuss "the formation of priests in the circumstances of the present day." In the exhortation the Pope adds his authoritative voice to the Synod's deliberations on the identity, spirituality, and formation of priests. The result is a comprehensive treatment of Catholic teaching on the priesthood as the Church understands it and wishes to prepare men to live it. *Pastores Dabo Vobis* is a compendium for priestly formation in the third millennium.

From the beginning of his pontificate, the Pope has regularly dealt with theological and pastoral questions on the priesthood. Every Holy Thursday since 1979, he has addressed a special letter to his "brother priests" on different aspects of their ministry: from a meditation on the saintly Curé of Ars, to prayer, to the priest's relationship with women. *Pastores Dabo Vobis* reflects John Paul's lifelong interest in the theology of the priesthood and the formation of seminarians and priests. As the final document of the 1990 Synod, it also confirms the specific concerns voiced by the Fathers. During the Assembly they focused on "the increase of vocations to the priesthood and the formation of candidates in an attempt to help them come to know and follow Jesus. . . . At the same time, the Synod searched for forms of ongoing formation to provide realistic and effective means of support for priests in their spiritual life and ministry" (§3.7).

John Paul is indebted to the Fathers' collaboration in drawing up *Pastores Dabo Vobis.* In the exhortation he takes up "the rich legacy resulting from the reflections, endeavors and indications which were made during the Synod's preparation, as well as those which accompanied the work of the Synod Fathers" (§4.2). The *Lineamenta, Instrumentum Laboris,* interventions in the Synod Hall, and *propositiones,* or final proposals, furnished the Pope with material that he used in writing his exhortation.

When the Synod met in 1990, twenty-five years after the closing of the Second Vatican Council, it identified numerous problems about the state of the priesthood in the Church. Although the Holy Father does not dwell at length on these problems — it is not his practice to do so — four issues are of great concern to him. First, he notes the dramatic decrease in the number of candidates for the priesthood, particularly in many areas of Europe and North America, a situation which can be called a "crisis of priestly vocations" (§37.5). Despite the increase in seminarians in some areas, especially in Africa and Asia, there is still a "grave shortage" in certain parts of the world (§1.5), a "persisting scarcity of clergy" (§2.5). Indeed, "in many parts of the Church today it is still the scarcity of priests" which impedes evangelization (§7.5). The falling off in new candidates is aggravated by the large number of priests who have left the active ministry in recent years. This "great number of defections," the Pope says, "did serious harm to pastoral ministry and priestly vocations, especially missionary vocations" (§11.3).

A second problem which looms on the horizon is the crisis in priestly identity. This crisis entails "the very interpretation of the nature and significance of the ministerial priesthood" (§9.7, cf. §11.3). In the post-conciliar period, doubt and confusion have arisen concerning the specific nature of the ordained priesthood: its foundation in Scripture, its difference from the common priesthood of the faithful, and its relationship to sacramental ministry. Third, the lack of clarity about priestly identity has often brought in its wake a weakening of the spiritual life of priests. Influenced by secularism, they frequently forget that their call to holiness is unique and is to be lived out in a way determined by their particular state of life. Lastly, according to the Pope, both the initial formation of seminarians and the ongoing formation of priests need to be renewed. As he points out, lay people "asked that priests commit themselves to their formation so that they, the laity, could be suitably helped to fulfill their role in the ecclesial mission which is shared by all" (§3.8). In this exhortation, the Holy Father addresses the topics of priestly identity, spirituality, vocations, and formation.

Pastores Dabo Vobis is not only the longest document published by Pope John Paul II, it is arguably the lengthiest papal treatise ever penned. For all its comprehensiveness, which leads to occasional repetition, the exhortation's style is straightforward and relaxed. Moreover, despite the sobering facts to which the Holy Father alludes, it shows his unfailing trust in divine Providence. "Everyone," he writes, "is called upon to share complete trust in the unbroken fulfillment of God's promise" (§1.5). His call for a "total act of faith in the Holy Spirit" imbues *Pastores Dabo Vobis* with a strong sense of hope in the future (§1.6). At the same time, John Paul's confidence carries a note of urgency. He repeatedly exhorts his readers to accept their grave responsibility "to cooperate in the action of God who calls, and to contribute toward creating and preserving the conditions in which the good seed, sown by God, can take root and bring forth abundant fruit" (§2.2).

An exceptionally strong biblical tone permeates the post-synodal apostolic exhortation. From its title, "I Will Give You Shepherds," taken from the Prophet Jeremiah (3:15), through its five major chapters, each of which is introduced by a citation from Scripture, the document is studded with biblical quotations. More striking, however, is the Pope's reliance on several key scriptural images to which he frequently returns in his treatment of the different themes. His purpose is to ground his teaching on the priestly ministry in the revelation of the New Testament. First, he relies above all on the image of the shepherd to define the figure and mission of the priest. Christ is the Good Shepherd, and John Paul presents the ministry of priests in this "pastoral" light. Second, the Holy Father often refers to Jesus' reading of the Prophet Isaiah in the synagogue at Nazareth as recounted in Luke's Gospel (cf. 4:16-22). The image of Jesus as "anointed" by the Holy Spirit frames the Pope's discussion of the priest's identity, specific call to holiness, and mission. Third, John Paul frequently invokes the account of Christ's calling of the disciples. He uses Mark's account (cf. 3:13-15) to emphasize that the Church's work of priestly education continues Christ's formation of his disciples: it is a time of being with the Lord in order to develop a relationship of communion from which flows the priest's mission. Saint John's narrative of the call of Andrew and Peter, "which in some way is renewed constantly down the ages" (§34.4), serves to describe the dynamics of vocation: it involves a divine call and a human response. Throughout the exhortation, the Pope follows a clear strategy. He discusses the contemporary topic only after having sketched the relevant New Testament material which provides the model for today's Church.

As usual, in *Pastores Dabo Vobis* John Paul stresses the continuity between his view and the "rich and authoritative teaching" of the Second Vatican Council (§3.1). Like the Synod Fathers, he refers amply to the Council, citing it sixty-four times. He alludes most frequently to *Presbyterorum Ordinis,* the Decree on the Ministry and Life of Priests. The exhortation also contains many references to *Optatam Totius,* the Decree on Priestly Formation, and *Lumen Gentium,* the Dogmatic Constitution on the Church. *Pastores Dabo Vobis* confirms that the Pope regards his post-synodal apostolic exhortations as useful tools for keeping alive in the Church the wealth of the Council's teaching.

Another particularly rich documentary source which the Pope draws on are the Synod's *propositiones.* He refers to 38 of the Fathers' 41 recommendations, for a total of 82 citations. He also relies on material from the 1967 Synod of Bishops, which discussed the renewal of seminaries, the final document on the ministerial priesthood of the 1971 Synod, directives from various departments of the Roman Curia, and previous statements from his own teaching.

The exhortation's title page announces that the intended readers are the "Bishops, clergy and faithful" of the Church. *Pastores Dabo Vobis* is indeed directed to the whole Church. John Paul has this audience in mind especially when he exhorts the faithful to encourage and pray for priestly vocations, and to take an active part in the formation of candidates for the priesthood. But the Pope also has some specific recipients in mind. He addresses his document "in particular to each priest and to those involved in the important yet demanding ministry of their formation" (§4.2).

Summary

Pastores Dabo Vobis is divided into six chapters, to which are added an introduction and a conclusion. In the introduction (§§1-4), the Pope sets the stage; he comments on phenomena which influence the contemporary course of events, the Synod of Bishops' contribution to the exhortation, and the various sources from which he draws. Chapter one, "The Challenges Facing Priestly Formation at the Conclusion of the Second Millennium" (§§5-10), analyzes the bright spots and shadows of the present sociocultural situation in which vocations develop and formation takes place. In chapter two, "The Nature and Mission of the Ministerial Priesthood" (§§11-18), the Pope summarizes the Church's doctrine on the priesthood in light of the Church's faith, especially as it was presented at the Second Vatican Council. In chapter three, "The Spiritual Life of the Priest" (§§19-33), he describes the priest's particular call to holiness and manner of life in service to the People of God. Chapter four, "Priestly Vocation in the Church's Pastoral Work" (§§34-41), outlines the vital role played by the Church in discerning, fostering, and accompanying vocations to the priesthood. This is followed by the exhortation's longest chapter, "The Formation of Candidates for the Priesthood" (§§42-69). Here the Pope describes the different areas, various settings, and numerous agents of priestly formation. Chapter six, "The Ongoing Formation of Priests" (§§70-81), deals with the reasons, subjects, agents, and means for a complete and integral program of continuing formation for those already ordained. The Holy Father concludes his apostolic exhortation with a prayer to Mary, Mother and Teacher of Priests.

Lights and shadows of the current situation

John Paul begins *Pastores Dabo Vobis,* as he does many of his documents, with an analysis of the complex situation of the contemporary Church and the world. Briefly but precisely he sketches the positive and negative factors affecting vocations to the priesthood and the initial and continuing formation of priests. But the Holy Father does more than provide a descriptive analysis of the sociocultural and ecclesial state of affairs. He interprets the data, much of which the Synod Fathers handed over to him. In light of the Gospel, his primary interest is discerning the signs of the times in order to distinguish between "negative elements and reasons for hope, obstacles and alternatives, as in the field mentioned in the Gospel where good seed and weeds are both sown and 'coexist'" (§10.3). Evangelical discernment does not merely record facts but presents "a 'task,' a challenge to responsible freedom, both of the individual person and of the community" (§10.5). To accept this challenge wisely requires an appreciation of the ambivalence of the present-day situation, "where there is a mixture of difficulties and potentialities" (§10.3, cf. §9.7). Before pointing out the negative influences in the world and the Church, the Holy Father indicates the positive trends which can support pastoral work in the area of priestly spirituality, vocations, and formation.

Among the world's hopeful signs can be included an increased awareness of human dignity and openness to religious values, work for justice and peace, respect for creation and nature, commitment to solidarity and volunteer work. In the Church, there are "new and unexpected possibilities of evangelization and the rebirth of ecclesial life in many parts of the world" (§6.3). Indeed, the Holy Father is convinced that efforts to proclaim the Gospel can be successful because "the thirst for God and for an active meaningful relationship with him is so strong today" (§6.4, cf. §9.1). For many, especially among the young, "the question of religion and the need for spirituality are becoming more explicit" (§9.5).

However, as in the field containing good and bad seed, the current situation contains numerous negative factors as well. These trends have adverse repercussions, especially on young men who are considering a priestly vocation or who are living in seminaries, but also on priests who are active in the ministry. The breakup of the family, the distortion in the true meaning of human sexuality, and the lure of a consumer society exert a powerful influence on minds and hearts. Even more important than these phenomena are the dominant ideas that are shaping contemporary culture. John Paul points out four particularly dangerous ones. First, there is rationalism which "renders human reason insensitive to an encounter with revelation and with divine transcendence" (§7.2). Second, he notes a false kind of "personal *subjectivity*" which leads to a closed individualism "incapable of true human relationships" (§7.3, cf. §37.3-4). The resulting loneliness opens the door to hedonism, the frenetic pursuit of material well-being as the highest good, and the escape from responsibility. "The all-determining 'concern' for *having,*" writes the Pope, "supplants the primacy of *being,* and consequently personal and interpersonal values are interpreted and lived not according to the logic of giving and generosity but according to the logic of selfish possession and the exploitation of others" (§8.2, cf. §8.4). The third negative influence is the spread of "a sort of *practical and existential atheism* which coincides with a secularist outlook on life and human destiny" (§7.4). Lastly, a distorted sense of freedom lies at the root of many of the present-day's social ills. Ethical principles are eroded where freedom is lived out as the "individual's will to power" rather than as "obedience to objective and universal truth" (§8.4). When taken together, these adverse influences have a powerful hold on a culture.

According to the Pope, "there are also worrying and negative factors within the Church herself which have a direct influence on the lives and ministry of priests" (§7.6). Many of these phenomena are the result of cultural ideas that have contaminated ecclesial life. John Paul considers the root problem to be subjectivism in matters of faith. Such subjectivism entails a loss of "sensitivity to the universality and objectivity of the doctrine of the faith" (§7.8). This situation is particularly evident among young people (cf. §7.9). Subjectivism, in turn, leads people to identify with the Church in a partial and conditional way. The Holy Father also draws attention to some opinions in contemporary theology that exacerbate the situation: a misunderstood pluralism which compromises truth, a reduction of the Gospel message to "exclusively human and social liberation," and "a persistent diffidence" toward the Magisterium (§7.6, cf. §11.3). Undoubtedly these factors exert a negative influence on the pastoral care of vocations, the formation of seminarians, the spiritual life and continuing formation of priests. Nonetheless, the present situation also offers "new positive possibilities" (§9.7), which priests can take advantage of in carrying out their mission.

Nature and mission of the ministerial priesthood

As a necessary prelude to his treatment of initial and continuing formation, John Paul takes up the nature of the priesthood. Only if those in formation clearly grasp who the priest *is* will they run effective programs. Consequently, in *Pastores Dabo Vobis* the Pope focuses on priestly identity since the way in which it is understood will determine the kind of formation given to seminarians and priests.

John Paul begins his discussion of the ministerial priesthood with Luke's account of Jesus' being "consecrated with an anointing" (§11.1). Jesus Christ, "the one High Priest of the New and Eternal Covenant" (§12.4), fully revealed this new priesthood. In his very being Christ is the perfect mediator between God and humanity (cf. 1 Tim 2:5), who gives everyone immediate access to God. This mediation was accomplished through Jesus' definitive sacrifice on the Cross. Not the Old Testament priesthood, but "the priesthood of Christ, the expression of his absolute 'newness' in salvation history, constitutes the one source and essential model of the priesthood shared by all Christians and the priest in particular" (§12.4). According to the Holy Father, the "absolutely necessary key" for understanding the nature of the ministerial priesthood is the priesthood of Jesus.

The priest therefore finds "the full truth of his identity in being a derivation, a specific participation in and continuation of Christ," the one High Priest (§12.4, cf. §11.2). By virtue of their consecration through Holy Orders, ministerial priests share uniquely in the priesthood of Christ, to whom they are united in the very depths of their being. Through sacramental anointing, "the Holy Spirit configures them in a new and special way to Jesus Christ the Head and Shepherd" of the Church (§15.5, cf. §12.2). This configuration enables ministerial priests to share in Christ's own priestly consecration *"in a specific and authoritative way"* (§18.4, cf. §16.1). They prolong Christ's presence by making him visible in the midst of the Church. Every ordained priest is "a living and transparent image of Christ the Priest" (§12.4).

While priestly identity is secured primarily through his intense identification with Christ, it is also intimately related to the Church, the Body of Christ. This bond with the Church, writes the Pope, "is inscribed in the very relation which the priest has to Christ" (§16.1). So close is the relationship between the ministerial priesthood and the Church that one cannot exist without the other.

The priest's identity is closely linked to the ministry he discharges in and for the Church. This ecclesial mission has its origins in the "specific and authoritative mandate" that Christ bestowed on the Apostles (§14.1). When Jesus conferred upon them "a specific paschal outpouring of the Holy Spirit, the same messianic authority which he had received from the Father," he established a close relationship between his priesthood and the apostolic mission (§14.2). For their part, the Apostles were commissioned to "prolong throughout history to the end of time the same mission of Jesus on behalf of humanity" (§14.3). To carry out this mandate they appointed others, in various ways eventually differentiated by the Church, to help and succeed them. According to the Pope, "the ordained ministry arises with the Church and has in Bishops, and in priests who are related to and are in communion with them, a particular relation to the original ministry of the Apostles — to which it truly 'succeeds' — even though with regard to the latter it assumes different forms" (§16.3, cf. §15.1). Through ordination, priests today, in hierarchical communion with their Bishops, share in the original apostolic mission to the Church and the world.

Holiness and priestly ministry

After presenting the theological foundation of the priest's identity and mission, John Paul draws out some practical consequences for his life. The chapter devoted to the spiritual life of the priest also sheds light on the meaning of the priesthood and therefore on the kind of formation necessary for seminarians. The Pope's guiding principle is straightforward. Because the priest is specifically consecrated to Christ, Head and Shepherd of the Church, the spiritual life which nourishes his mission should reflect this consecration.

The same Spirit of God who anointed Jesus calls the whole People of God to holiness. Like all the faithful, priests are called to the perfection of charity in virtue of their Baptism. In addition, however, they have "a *'specific' vocation to holiness*" (§20.3). This call they are to pursue because they are priests, that is, "under a new title and in new and different ways deriving from the Sacrament of Holy Orders" (§19.4). *Who* the priest is determines the form of holiness appropriate to his state in life. Consequently, the Holy Father affirms, "the spiritual life of the priest is marked, molded and characterized by the way of thinking and acting proper to Jesus Christ, Head and Shepherd of the Church, and which are summed up in his pastoral charity" (§21.2).

John Paul reflects on the spiritual life of priests in light of their configuration to Christ as Head, Shepherd, and Bridegroom of the Church. Christ's headship of the Church is expressed in his being a servant, a service which "attains its fullest expression in his death on the Cross, that is, in his total gift of self in humility and love" (§21.3). As a minister of the Gospel, the priest's spiritual life should on that account be marked by the same attitude of service to the People of God. Like the Good Shepherd who feels compassion, gathers and protects his sheep, searches out the lost, and offers his life for his flock, so, too, the priest is called to imitate the "pastoral" charity of Jesus. Priestly holiness thus entails living this pastoral charity: it is the priest's *"gift of self, the total gift of self to the Church,* following the example of Christ" (§23.2).

Saint Paul depicts Christ as the Bridegroom of the Church, the Bride whom he loves and for whom he gave up his life (cf. Eph 5:21-32). For his part, the priest "is called to be the living image of Jesus Christ, the Spouse of the Church" (§22.3). Imitating the Bridegroom, the priest stands in a spousal relationship to the community he serves. His is an *amoris officium,* a ministry of love. The priest's life and ministry should radiate the same love which Christ has for the Church.

After describing the attitudes of a shepherd and a spouse which the priest should cultivate as proper to his holiness as one configured to Christ the High Priest, the Pope points out that "an intimate bond exists between the priest's spiritual life and the exercise of his ministry" (§24.3). The priest's consecration is for mission, a mission which permeates his spiritual life. When he fulfills his ministry according to the consecration received the priest grows in the love of Christ and the Church.

The Holy Father uses the traditional scheme of the priest's sharing in the prophetic, priestly, and kingly mission of Christ and the Church to describe some of the consequences for the priest's spiritual life that are determined by his ministry. First, as a minister of the word, the priest "ought first of all to develop a great personal familiarity with the word of God" (§26.2). He should study and contemplate it lovingly; he should receive it as one who constantly needs to be evangelized anew. Moreover, the priest should understand that "he is not the master of the word, but its servant" (§26.2). Thus he will transmit the Gospel in its fullness, with "a special sensitivity, love and docility to the living Tradition of the Church and to her Magisterium" (§26.2).

As a man of the sacraments and offering the public praise of the Church in the Liturgy of the Hours, "the priest is called to live and witness to the deep unity between the exercise of his ministry and his spiritual life" (§26.3). These actions sanctify the priest and the people whom he serves. In his ministry and spiritual life pride of place belongs to the Eucharist, the center and root of priestly holiness. For the Pope, "the priest's pastoral charity not only flows from the Eucharist but finds in the celebration of the Eucharist its highest realization, just as it is from the Eucharist that he receives the grace and obligation to give his whole life a 'sacrificial' dimension" (§23.6). Priests have the irreplaceable role of offering the Eucharist. They are, writes the Holy Father, "first and foremost ministers of the Sacrifice of the Mass" (§48.2). John Paul also recalls the importance of being witnesses to "God's mercy toward sinners" by receiving the Sacrament of Reconciliation of which they are ministers (§26.5).

In discharging their kingly mission priests express "the authority and service of Jesus Christ the Head and Priest of the Church" (§26.6). The mission of leading and building up the community entrusted to their pastoral care demands of priests "an intense spiritual life, filled with those qualities and virtues which are typical of a person who 'presides over' and 'leads' a community, of an 'elder' in the noblest and richest sense of the word" (§26.6).

Priestly life and Gospel radicalism

Besides discussing priestly spirituality in the light of Christ as Head, Shepherd, and Bridegroom of the Church, and the priest's mission as prophetic, priestly, and kingly, *Pastores Dabo Vobis* uses a third scheme to describe the specific spirituality of priests: the evangelical counsels of obedience, celibacy, and poverty in the priest's spiritual life. Like all the faithful, priests are called to embrace "the radicalism of the Gospel"; this is "a fundamental, undeniable demand flowing from the call of Christ to follow and imitate him by virtue of the intimate communion of life with him brought about by the Spirit" (§27.2). A particular expression of this radicalism is the life of the three evangelical counsels which Jesus proposes in the Sermon on the Mount. The Pope holds that every priest, and here he has diocesan priests particularly in mind, is called "to live these counsels in accordance with those ways and, more specifically, those goals and that basic meaning which derive from and express his own priestly identity" (§27.2).

According to the exhortation, the Christ-like obedience which must pervade the priest's spiritual life has three characteristics. First, it is apostolic; "it recognizes, loves and serves the Church in her hierarchical structure" (§28.2). The priest uses his freedom to accept the demands of organized ecclesial life and to give filial respect and obedience to the Successor of Peter, the Episcopal College, and especially his own Bishop. Only a priest who obeys without servility "is really able to require obedience from others in accordance with the Gospel" (§28.3). Second, priestly obedience has a community dimension; it is linked to his communion with the presbyterate and its mission. To be sure, the priest's spiritual life is enriched by his obedience to the Bishop, his sharing in the concerns of the presbyterate, "and his devotion to the evangelical care of the People of God in the specific historical and contextual conditions of a particular Church" (§31.2). This requires of him a strong sense of solidarity, a spirit of asceticism, and the setting aside of rivalry. Third, a priest's obedience is pastoral. "It is lived in an atmosphere of constant readiness," says the Pope, "to allow oneself to be taken up, as it were 'consumed,' by the needs and demands of the flock" (§28.6).

Priestly celibacy, the second of the evangelical counsels, enables the priest to enter more deeply into communion with the virginal Christ and his Church. It is part of his making a personal gift of himself to Jesus and others. "Priestly celibacy, then, is the gift of self *in* and *with* Christ *to* his Church and expresses the priest's service to the Church in and with the Lord" (§29.4). In his spiritual life the priest ought to consider celibacy as "a priceless gift from God" which stimulates his pastoral charity and the fruitfulness of his apostolic mission (§29.3).

Evangelical poverty in imitation of the poor Christ has significant repercussions on the priest's spiritual life as well as on the community he serves. The practice of poverty gives him the interior freedom that enables him to use and even, if the occasion should arise, to renounce material goods. Priestly poverty makes a man available for difficult tasks, ensures his honest administration of ecclesial goods, and inspires him "to stand beside the underprivileged, to practice solidarity with their efforts to create a more just society, to be more sensitive and capable of understanding and discerning realities involving the economic and social aspects of life, and to promote a preferential option for the poor" (§30.5). Imitating Christ, the model of the virtues of obedience, chastity, and poverty, the priest grows in holiness and the pastoral charity which the evangelical counsels inspire and develop.

Vocations to the priesthood

As elsewhere in *Pastores Dabo Vobis*, John Paul begins his discussion of priestly vocations with a Gospel scene to be contemplated, and one which he hopes will be repeated down through the years. Jesus' call of Andrew and Peter (cf. Jn 1:35-42) helps the Church to appreciate the priestly vocation as a gift which entails a dialogue between God and man, and is of concern to the community.

John Paul recognizes that the root of every vocation, including a priestly one, is "the history of an *inexpressible dialogue between God and human beings,* between the love of God who calls and the freedom of individuals who respond lovingly to him" (§36.1). It is always God who freely and graciously takes the initiative. Every call to the priesthood "bears unequivocal witness to the primacy of grace" (§36.4). The Pope stresses God's sovereignty. A vocation is his summons and command. A call to the priesthood is neither a human right nor a product of worldly ambition. At the same time, if the call is to bear fruit for the individual and the community, a man must respond to it freely. Like Christ's ready response to his Father's will, the priest must make a "free oblation, which constitutes the intimate and most precious core of a person's response to God who calls" (§36.8). God's initiative does not smother human freedom. Rather, when a man follows the Lord's call and entrusts himself to him this brings freedom to its fulfillment.

Like every Christian vocation, a priestly vocation is a gift of God. At the same time, "it always comes about in the Church and through the Church" (§35.2). A vocation to the priesthood is profoundly ecclesial. God's call reaches man through instruments that he has chosen; it is not merely interior. It is *through* the Church's mediation that a man is addressed. It is *in* the community, through the Bishop, that the call is discerned and ratified. It is in service *to* her that a priestly vocation is directed. Thus, the Church, herself "an *assembly of those who have been called*" (§34.6), is intimately involved in every priestly vocation.

The echo of God's call in the depths of a man's heart also resounds in the Church. She is invited to care for the birth and growth of vocations to the priesthood. Like the Apostle Andrew who brought Peter to Jesus (cf. Jn 1:41-42), so does the Church turn her heart to men open to a priestly vocation. Precisely as a priestly, prophetic, and kingly people the Church commits herself to fostering vocations. Her pastoral work begins with her priestly mission of prayer and the sacramental life. Prayer, both individual and liturgical, is "the pivot of all pastoral work for vocations" (§38.5). Moreover, by teaching people to pray and by celebrating the liturgy she offers men help in discerning their call. The Church carries out her prophetic role by preaching about the need "to appreciate life as a response to God's call" (§39.1). More specifically, however, she must attend to frequent and explicit catechesis and homilies on vocations to the priesthood. In his addresses and documents John Paul very often encourages vocations, and here he remarks: "The time has come to speak courageously about priestly life as a priceless gift and a splendid and privileged form of Christian living. Educators, and priests in particular, should not be afraid to set forth explicitly and forcefully the priestly vocation as a real possibility for those young people who demonstrate the necessary gifts and talents" (§39.2). The Christian community fulfills its kingly role on behalf of vocations by encouraging both spiritual direction for young men and teaching them that the service of love is fundamental to every vocation, including one to the priesthood.

Pastoral care to foster vocations is a major concern of the Pope's. He urges that this work "be taken up with a new vigor and more decisive commitment by all the members of the Church, in the awareness that it is not a secondary or marginal matter" (§34.5). Vocational initiatives cannot merely be delegated to some particular group in the community, even to priests. On the contrary, care for vocations is an essential part of the Church's pastoral work, a concern of every Catholic. John Paul urges everyone to embrace his conviction that "*all the members of the Church, without exception, have the grace and responsibility to look after vocations*" (§41.2). The entire People of God are to pray and work tirelessly for priestly vocations.

Within the Church, the chief responsibility for fostering vocations lies with the Bishop. It falls primarily to him "to be concerned about 'giving continuity' to the priestly charism and ministry" in his presbyterate (§41.3). Sharing his task are the priests united with him. They too are to seek out and encourage vocations. Christian families, schools, associations and movements, and groups specially devoted to the vocations apostolate all have an important role to play in promoting vocations to priestly life.

Human and spiritual formation

The long chapter on the formation of candidates for the priesthood — both diocesan and religious — takes up their human, spiritual, intellectual, and pastoral formation, the role of the major and minor seminary, and the agents of priestly training. John Paul begins with Jesus' call of the Twelve "to be with him" (Mk 3:14). Christ set aside this period of apostolic formation so that his disciples could "develop a relationship of deep communion and friendship with himself" (§42.2). For her part, the Church draws inspiration from Jesus' example in her work of accompanying men in their period of formation. Her role is to discern priestly vocations and prepare those who have been called, bringing them step by step to share in Jesus' life and mission of salvation.

The foundation of all priestly formation rests on a human formation "carried out in the context of an anthropology which is open to the full truth regarding the human person" (§45.1). Called to be a "living image" of Jesus Christ, the priest "should seek to reflect in himself, as far as possible, the human perfection which shines forth in the Incarnate Son of God" (§43.1). Human formation enables the candidate to mold his personality in such a way that his ministry is credible, a bridge leading people to Christ. Among the more important aspects of this training is fostering the capacity of candidates to relate to others and promoting their growth in affective maturity. In particular John Paul recalls that seminarians require "an education in true and responsible love" (§43.4), which includes its sexual dimension. They also need training in freedom, which will help them to gain self-mastery and prepare them to offer the sincere gift of self.

Candidates should receive a spiritual formation which takes into full account the priest's specific identity and ministry: "For every priest his spiritual formation is the core which unifies and gives life to his *being* a priest and his *acting* as a priest" (§45.3). Among the fundamental demands of this formation the Pope first mentions the candidate's need to live intimately united with Jesus; he is to search for him, imitate him, and share his life. To bring about this intimacy the Holy Father recommends the prayerful and meditative reading of the Scriptures. "A loving knowledge of the word of God and a prayerful familiarity with it," he says, "are specifically important for the prophetic ministry of the priest" (§47.3). This familiarity with the Bible must be accompanied by prayer, "which is without any doubt a primary value and demand of spiritual formation" (§47.4). If he is to be a teacher of prayer, the candidate must first be trained in the school of prayer. The spiritual formation of seminarians also pays careful attention to the liturgy. The Pope recommends that seminarians attend daily Mass and rediscover the beauty and joy of sacramental Reconciliation. Lastly, the candidates' spiritual formation should help them become men of charity, images of Christ the Good Shepherd. Consequently, "preparation for the priesthood must necessarily involve a proper training in charity and particularly in the preferential love for the 'poor' in whom our faith discovers Jesus (cf. Mt 25:40), and a merciful love for sinners" (§49.4).

Intellectual and pastoral formation

John Paul's treatment of the intellectual education of seminarians is lengthy and thorough. He discusses the reasons why it is necessary and stresses the importance of sound philosophy and theology to seminary formation.

The intellectual training of seminarians is necessary for personal and pastoral reasons. First, such formation is "a fundamental demand of the human intelligence" which seeks wisdom (§51.1). Second, the new evangelization demands that priests acquire a high level of intellectual maturity, who can make the Gospel "credible to the legitimate demands of human reason" (§51.2). To be pastorally effective such a formation must teach critical discernment in light of the faith and be integrated with a spirituality marked by a personal experience of God.

For John Paul, the study of philosophy as a preparation for theology is crucial for two reasons. First, there are profound links between "the great philosophical questions and the mysteries of salvation which are studied in theology under the guidance of the higher light of faith" (§52.1). Second, and equally important, is the contribution that a sound philosophy can make in confronting present-day currents of subjectivism and relativism. Rigorous philosophical training inspires a "*loving veneration of the truth,* which leads one to recognize that the truth is not created or measured by man but is given to man as a gift by the supreme Truth, God" (§52.2). By its nature, faith appeals to reason. Revealed truth is assisted by reason and philosophy in thinking through and seeking to understand the faith.

John Paul then turns to the study of theology, the heart of every program of intellectual formation. He holds that the effectiveness of theological training depends on "maintaining a scrupulous respect for the nature of theology" (§53.1). Above all, this means that professors of theology in seminaries should believe that faith is "as it were the *habitus* of theology, that is, its permanent principle of operation, and that the whole of theology is ordered to nourishing the faith" (§53.1). Above all they must be believers who are seeking a deeper understanding of it within the Church. Sound theology leads seminarians to *"a complete and unified vision* of the truths which God has revealed in Jesus Christ and of the Church's experience of faith" (§54.1).

The apostolic exhortation affirms that theological formation today should pay attention to three problem areas. First, seminary theology professors are called to cooperate with the Magisterium and not propose a "parallel" one at odds with the teaching of the Successor of Peter and the Episcopal College (cf. §55.1). Second, without sacrificing high academic standards, theological teaching in seminaries should enable future priests "to proclaim the Gospel message through the cultural modes of their age and to direct pastoral action according to an authentic theological vision" (§55.2). Third, seminary theology should equip students to evangelize their culture by inculturating the message of faith. This delicate process, however, must be "inspired by the Catholic principles of inculturation" which ensure that the Gospel penetrates culture, becomes incarnate in it, and purifies it of those elements incompatible with revelation (§55.3).

The human, spiritual, and intellectual formation of future priests is directed to "a specific pastoral end," which ensures the coordination of all formation and has "certain precise content and characteristics" (§57.2). Every aspect of formation is pastoral in preparing men "to enter into communion with the charity of Christ the Good Shepherd" (§57.1). Even so, a specific pastoral or practical theology is necessary. On the one hand, pastoral theology is "a true and genuine theological discipline" because faith provides its fundamental principles. It is not just "a set of exhortations, experiences and methods" (§57.4). On the other hand, pastoral theology also involves practical training. This field education cannot be "reduced to a mere apprenticeship" but seeks "to initiate the candidate into the sensitivity of being a shepherd, in the conscious and mature assumption of his responsibilities, in the interior habit of evaluating problems and establishing priorities and looking for solutions on the basis of honest motivations of faith and according to the theological demands inherent in pastoral work" (§58.1). For the Pope, the parish is the best place to receive this practical formation, "for it is a living cell of local and specialized pastoral work" (§58.3).

The seminary

In describing the places where formation take places, the Holy Father gives primary importance to the seminary and, by analogy, to the religious house of formation. More than a material space, the seminary is a period of preparation; it is "a spiritual place, a way of life, an atmosphere that fosters and ensures a process of formation" for those called to the priesthood (§42.3). Candidates for Holy Orders are to be trained in a way which embodies "the experience of formation which our Lord provided for the Twelve" (§60.2, §§60.3, 60.6). According to John Paul, the major seminary is "a *continuation in the Church of the apostolic community gathered about Jesus,* listening to his word, proceeding toward the Easter experience, awaiting the gift of the Spirit for the mission" (§60.3). Like the Apostles, seminarians receive a prolonged preparation which detaches them from their roots and frees them from ordinary work. This detachment enables the seminary to be "experienced as a community, a specifically ecclesial community, a community that relives the experience of the group of Twelve who were united to Jesus" (§60.6).

An essential element of being an ecclesial community is the major seminary's commitment to a definite program of priestly formation. This plan is "characterized by its being organized and unified, by its being in harmony or correspondence with the one aim which justifies the existence of the seminary: preparation of future priests" (§61.3). While the Holy Father urges Dioceses and Episcopal Conferences to draw up specific programs for their seminaries, he also asks that they pay attention to the individual candidates with their different problems, difficulties, and rates of progress. He calls for a "wise flexibility" in light of "a respect for the person who, in conditions which are very personal, is proceeding toward the priesthood" (§61.5). This same flexibility should also govern seminary programs given the different social and cultural contexts in which they operate.

John Paul also takes up the kind of preparation necessary for a candidate before he enters the major seminary. First of all, the Pope reaffirms the value of minor seminaries. He defends them on the grounds that long experience shows that "a priestly vocation tends to show itself in the preadolescent years or in the earliest years of youth" (§63.1). These high-school seminaries can give guidance in helping young men carefully discern a priestly vocation and can provide the human, intellectual, and spiritual formation necessary for the major seminary. Where minor seminaries are unavailable, the Pope encourages the formation of groups for adolescents and young people to help them discover and safeguard their vocation. For older candidates, he recommends "some kind of specific program to accompany them with formation" (§64.2) which differs from that of the major seminary.

But the Pope's most novel proposal follows a recommendation of the Synod. In earlier times candidates usually came to the major seminary after studying in the minor seminary and were sufficiently prepared for its full formation program. Often this is no longer the case. Today there is frequently a considerable discrepancy between candidates' way of life in the world and their cultural and catechetical preparation and "the style of life of the seminary with its formational demands" (§62.2). Consequently, before students begin the study of philosophy in the major study, John Paul calls for a "sufficient period of preparation prior to seminary formation" (§62.3). While this propaedeutic period is in place in some areas, it is still in the experimental stages. Thus the Holy Father proposes no fixed model for this year of "pre-theology." Nonetheless, a coordinated program should include formation in personal maturity, prayer and the spiritual life, and broad-based instruction in culture and the fundamentals of the Catholic faith.

Agents of priestly formation

After focusing on seminarians, *Pastores Dabo Vobis* then turns to those responsible for their formation. The primary agent of formation is, of course, the Holy Spirit. "It is the Spirit of Jesus," writes the Pope, "that throws light on and gives strength to vocational discernment and the journey to the priesthood" (§65.3, cf. §69.2). The Spirit of Christ charges the whole Church with the task of accompanying candidates to the priesthood. Nonetheless, within the Christian community, the Bishop, seminary faculty, family, parish, ecclesial movements, and the candidate himself have specific responsibilities.

The Bishop is "the first representative of Christ in priestly formation" (§65.4). He has the duty of judging the authenticity of the seminarian's interior call. To do this effectively, the Bishop should visit his seminarians and share with them "all that has to do with the pastoral progress of the particular Church" (§65.5).

On the spot, the seminary formation faculty represents and assists the Bishop in preparing men for the presbyterate. The Pope advices Bishops to select his assistants carefully, to encourage them, and see to their continuing formation. Those involved in formation should be exemplary priests who work well as a team and who, in the words of the Synod Fathers, bear witness to "a truly evangelical lifestyle and total dedication to the Lord" (§66.2). The Holy Father also notes that the laity should play a coordinated and integrated role in priestly formation. He draws special attention to "the charism of femininity in every educational itinerary," including the formation of candidates for the ministerial priesthood (§66.5). Also singled out for attention are the professors of theology, who often form a group distinct from the formation faculty. Seminary teachers ought to be distinguished by the soundness of their understanding of the nature of the priesthood and of theology, by their faith, and by their "total fidelity to the Magisterium" (§67.4).

The various communities which first nurtured a vocation to the priesthood continue to have an important role in the formation of seminarians. Despite the sacrifice frequently entailed, families "should accompany the formative journey with prayer, respect, the good example of the domestic virtues and spiritual and material help, especially in difficult moments" (§68.2). Loving family support often proves decisive for a candidate's perseverance. The seminarian's parish, too, should accompany his journey to ordination with its prayer, encouragement, and hospitality. In today's Church youth groups and ecclesial movements provide fertile soil for many vocations. Even after one of their members has entered the seminary, these associations and movements remain "a source of help and support on the path of formation toward the priesthood" (§68.4).

In keeping with his emphasis that individuals reach maturity through responsible action, John Paul affirms that every seminarian himself is "a necessary and irreplaceable agent in his own formation" (§69.1). The success of priestly formation depends on the candidate's readiness to assume its obligations. Not only is the seminarian to respond to the Spirit's interior call, he is also to welcome the "human 'mediating' forces which the Spirit employs" in the whole process of human, spiritual, intellectual, and pastoral formation (§69.2).

Ongoing formation: its necessity and meaning

Pastores Dabo Vobis is the first papal document which treats at length the ongoing formation of priests. Pope John Paul recognizes that priests today suffer from "an excessive loss of energy in their ever increasing pastoral activities" and that "feel compelled to reexamine their way of life and their pastoral priorities" (§3.6). By way of response to this situation he encourages a vast and comprehensive program of continuing priestly formation. Such a plan will help the priest "to *be* and *act* as a priest in the spirit and style of Jesus the Good Shepherd" (§73.1).

Thanks to his meditation on the biblical text, "I remind you to rekindle the gift of God that is within you" (2 Tim 1:6), the Pope can assert that the dynamism of God's gift in the Sacrament of Orders furnishes the most significant reason for the ongoing formation of priests. Throughout the priest's life, God himself "rekindles his own gift, so as better to release all the extraordinary riches of grace and responsibility contained in it" (§70.4). In other words, the priest's vocation continues *within* the priesthood. "God continues to call and send forth, revealing his saving plan in the historical development of the priest's life and the life of the Church and of society" (§70.10). Permanent formation is thus necessary if a priest is to discern and follow God's constant call faithfully in the course of his life. It is required by the process of continual conversion to the Lord. The Pope goes so far as to maintain that "ongoing formation is an intrinsic requirement of the gift and sacramental ministry received" (§70.13, cf. §82.7).

Other, less theological, reasons also call priests to continue their formation after ordination. Growth in personal maturity and pastoral effectiveness demand ongoing formation. According to the Holy Father, "there is no profession, job or work which does not require constant updating, if it is to remain current and effective" (§70.7). At the same time, however, continued growth in various areas helps the priest "to overcome the temptation to reduce his ministry to an activism which becomes an end in itself, to the provision of impersonal services, even if these are spiritual or sacred, or to a businesslike function which he carries out for the Church" (§72.10). Moreover, permanent formation is an act of justice to God's people. They have the "fundamental 'right' to receive the word of God, the sacraments and the service of charity" (§70.11). Ongoing formation ensures that the priest can suitably respond to this right of the faithful.

John Paul explains the profound meaning of permanent formation by considering it within the mystery of the Church as mystery, communion, and mission. As mystery, the Church is the continuing presence of God's grace in the midst of his people. The priest then must work unceasingly "to *safeguard and develop in faith his awareness of the total and marvelous truth of his being:* he is a minister of Christ and steward of the mysteries of God" (§73.4). Within the Church as communion, ongoing formation helps the priest to "grow in *awareness of the deep communion uniting him to the People of God*" (§74.2). It also inspires him to deepen his understanding of membership in the presbyterate, and his relation to the other particular Churches. Lastly, continuing formation increases *"the priest's awareness of his share in the Church's saving mission"* (§75.1). He is inspired to respond ever more fully to his obligation to preach the Gospel. Permanent formation serves to confirm "the priest in the essential and decisive element in his ministry, namely his faithfulness" (§75.2).

Dimensions, agents, and places of permanent formation

As "the natural and absolutely necessary continuation of the process of building priestly personality" (§71.1), ongoing formation is intrinsically linked to the whole process of seminary formation. It is, however, neither a review of seminary training nor merely professional renewal. Instead, the permanent formation of priests is a serious effort which guarantees the priest's process of constant growth in the human, spiritual, intellectual, and pastoral spheres.

Ongoing human formation is especially aimed at developing the priest's "human sensitivity," which enables him to grasp better the people's needs and to grow in love for them. Spiritual formation through the years also devotes special attention to the priest's prayer life. "Experience teaches," the Holy Father comments, "that in prayer one cannot live off past gains" (§72.5). The continued study of modern society and its challenges, and especially of theology, are required as well. Theological renewal is necessary "if the priest is to faithfully carry out the ministry of the word, proclaiming it clearly and without ambiguity, distinguishing it from mere human opinions, no matter how renowned and widespread these might be" (§72.7). The pastoral dimension of ongoing formation inspires priests to grow in pastoral charity and helps them "to seek the most suitable methods and the most useful forms for carrying out his ministry today" (§72.8).

According to the Pope, ongoing formation is "permanent"; it is part of a priest's life from the time he leaves the seminary until his death. Different programs of formation should be designed for the young, middle-aged, elderly, and sick and suffering. The primary promoter of this permanent formation is the particular Church, guided by its Bishop. He is to ensure that the priests of his presbyterate "are generously faithful to the gift and ministry received, that they are priests such as the People of God wishes to have and has a 'right' to" (§79.2). In order to meet his obligations, the Bishop, either by himself or working with other Bishops, is expected to establish a systematic program of ongoing formation. But the priest himself also has an irreplaceable role. Perhaps even more than in the case of seminarians, the individual priest is responsible for his own permanent formation. He must be "personally convinced of its need and is determined to make use of the opportunities, times and forms in which it comes" (§79.1).

The Pope ends the exhortation with some practical recommendations for implementing programs of permanent renewal. He notes the opportunities offered by meetings of the Bishop with his presbyterate, spiritual gatherings for priests, and study days and workshops. When priests live some form of common life or belong to a priestly association their ongoing formation is more likely to be fostered. John Paul especially urges priests to see in spiritual direction "a well-tried means" that "has lost none of its value" for permanent formation. Regular direction promotes faithfulness in carrying out the priestly ministry.

Pastores Dabo Vobis concludes with final appeals to the whole Church to pray for vocations and to assume responsibility for initial and ongoing priestly formation. The Holy Father ends with a prayer to Mary, Mother and Teacher of Priests. He asks her "to keep vigilant watch over the growth of vocations and priestly life in the Church" (§82.13).

Key Themes

Three particular themes stand out in this post-synodal apostolic exhortation: priestly identity, authority and ministry, and celibacy. Priestly identity and service are at the heart of the Pope's teaching. Celibacy will be taken up, not because it is the central issue in *Pastores Dabo Vobis,* but because the topic is frequently a matter of debate. Moreover, John Paul's presentation of celibacy in this document is the longest and most developed of his pontificate.

Priestly identity: configured to Christ in the Church

Although the 1990 Synod focused chiefly on priestly formation, the Fathers were convinced that a clear doctrinal understanding of the priesthood was needed in order to chart the course of a renewed formation and a secure priestly identity. According to John Paul, "knowledge of the nature and mission of the ministerial priesthood is an essential presupposition, and at the same time the surest guide and incentive toward the development of pastoral activities in the Church, for fostering and discerning vocations to the priesthood and training those called to the ordained ministry" (§11.2). He refers to this identity, rooted in faith of the Church, as "the permanent truth of the priestly ministry" (§5.6). Enlightened by this "truth of the priest" (§15.6, cf. §24.5), both candidates and those responsible for vocations and formation have sure guidelines for the process of discernment and priestly education. In *Pastores Dabo Vobis* the Holy Father does not present a complete theology of the priesthood. But he does describe its essential characteristics: the relationship of the ministerial priesthood to Christ's priesthood; the priest as a sacramental sign of Christ; his configuration to Christ as Head, Shepherd, and Spouse of the Church; the ontological bond established by ordination; and the ecclesial dimension of the priesthood.

A Christological focus is decisive for understanding the ministerial priesthood. "Reference to Christ," writes John Paul, "is thus the absolutely necessary key for understanding the reality of priesthood" (§12.4). Only from a Christological perspective can the ministry first conferred upon the Apostles be understood. According to the Scriptures (cf. Mt 10:40; Lk 10:16), Jesus himself "established a close relationship between the ministry entrusted to the Apostles and his own mission" (§14.3). This relationship to Jesus' mission continues in ordained priests who "are called to prolong the presence of Christ, the one High Priest, embodying his way of life and making him visible in the midst of the flock entrusted to their care" (§15.3). By themselves, of course, priests can "do nothing" (Jn 15:5). Their whole apostolic activity — from preaching to celebrating the sacraments, to leading God's People — is accomplished through the power of the Spirit.

At the Last Supper, which culminated in the Paschal Mystery, Christ revealed himself as the one and eternal High Priest. Here he "revealed in himself the perfect and definitive features of the priesthood of the New Covenant" (§13.1). All ministerial priesthood is rooted in this "one priesthood of Christ" (§15.5). It is "a participation, in the Church, in the very priesthood of Jesus Christ" (§11.2, cf. §12.4). The priest participates "in a specific and authoritative way in the 'consecration/anointing' and in the 'mission' of Christ" (§16.1).

Thanks to this participation the priest is "sacramental"; he is a sign of Christ. Priests are "a sacramental representation of Jesus Christ, the Head and Shepherd, authoritatively proclaiming his word, repeating his acts of forgiveness and his offer of salvation, particularly in Baptism, Penance and the Eucharist, showing his loving concern to the point of a total gift of self for the flock, which they gather into unity and lead to the Father through Christ and in the Spirit" (§15.4). Priests visibly prolong Christ's presence as Head of the Church and Redeemer of the world. John Paul expresses this sacramental role of the priest by calling him a "living image of Jesus Christ, Head and Shepherd of the Church" (§42.3, cf. §§22.3, 43.1, 72.9). Moreover, the priest is the "living instrument" of Christ (§25.2). In this way the Pope recalls that the priest's participation in Christ's priesthood is not inert or passive. Rather, "the exercise of his ministry deeply involves the priest himself as a conscious, free and responsible person" who, like Peter (cf. Jn 21:15-17), is called to respond lovingly to the charge he has been assigned (§25.3).

The Pope further conveys his strong Christocentricism by using the formula "in persona Christi" to describe the priest's most profound identity: the priest acts in the name and person of Christ. Sacramentally consecrated for his mission, the priest discharges it "in the name and in the person of Christ himself" (§20.4, cf. §§15.4, 31.5, 33.5, 35.6, 43.1). For the Holy Father, this traditional expression of Catholic theology emphasizes that the priest, chiefly but not exclusively in his sacramental actions, is an instrument of Christ's grace.

The priest's uniqueness is rooted in the ontological bond which unites him to Christ, the High Priest (cf. §§11.3, 25.2). Through sacramental ordination a man is changed in his very *being* (cf. §§16.5, 18.4, 70.5, 72.4). Holy Orders confers on him a new and specific relationship with Christ. John Paul describes this relationship as "an ontological and psychological bond, a sacramental and moral bond" (§72.4). John Paul's emphasis on the change in the priest's being brought about by ordination expresses the primacy which the Pope attributes to "being" over "doing." The priest's identity is anchored in who he *is*, not in what he *does*. Thus it is the presence of the Spirit of Christ at work in the priest's being who enables him to carry out his mission.

Repeatedly in *Pastores Dabo Vobis* the Holy Father describes the priest's mission in light of his being configured "to Christ the Head and Shepherd, the Servant and Spouse of the Church" (§3.7, cf. §§12.2, 15.5, 18.4, 20.1, 20.4, 21.1, 21.4, 22.2, 22.3, 23.1, 25.1, 27.1, 27.2, 29.4, 31.1, 35.6, 61.1, 69.2, 70.5, 72.4). Because the priest is configured to Jesus as "Head" of the Church, he makes present the authority of Christ. This divine authority, however, is that of a servant (cf. Mk 10:45). Indeed, the priest's configuration to Christ the Shepherd means that his whole life should be "a continual manifestation of his [Christ's] 'pastoral charity,' or rather, a daily enactment of it" (§22.1). Configured to Christ, Spouse of the Church, the priest stands "before" the Church. He is called "to live out Christ's spousal love toward the Church, his Bride" (§22.3). Like Christ, he is to cherish her, even to the point of giving up his life for her (cf. Eph 5:29).

While John Paul's theology of the priesthood is strongly Christological, he also considers its ecclesial dimension. His remarks are founded on the ecclesiology of communion which he so frequently draws on in his teaching. This ecclesiology, he believes, is "decisive for understanding the identity of the priest, his essential dignity, and his vocation and mission among the People of God and in the world" (§12.4). Christ's intimate relationship to the Church — she is his Body and Bride — is the model which the priest should strive to imitate. For the Pope, "the priest's relation to the Church is inscribed in the very relation which the priest has to Christ, such that the 'sacramental representation' to Christ serves as the basis and inspiration for the relation of the priest to the Church" (§16.1). Priestly ministry is to be carried out "totally at the service of the Church" (§16.4).

John Paul describes the priest as servant of the Church in three ways: he is servant of her mystery, of her communion, and of her mission. He is servant of the Church as mystery. With the eyes of faith he understands her as a divine work. The priest knows that the Church grows, thanks to the Spirit's gratuitous action, and that he himself is merely "a sign of the absolute priority and gratuitousness of the grace given to the Church by the risen Christ" (§16.6, cf. §59.2). Because of his ordination, the priest is *"in the forefront of the Church* as a visible continuation and sacramental sign of Christ in his own position before the Church and the world" (§16.6). The priest is servant of the Church as communion because, in sacramental union with the Bishop and his brother priests in the presbyterate and in a cooperation with the laity, he builds up the Body of Christ. His ministry is carried out in communion and for the increase of communion. The priest is servant of the Church as mission "because he makes the community a herald and witness of the Gospel" (§16.5).

Repeatedly and insistently the Holy Father teaches that the priest has a specific identity and mission that arises from Holy Orders. In turn, this specificity requires a unique priestly spirituality and formation. *Being* a priest and *acting* as a priest, these constitute a particular vocation in the Church.

Priestly service and pastoral charity

Lest his insistence on the priest's participation in Christ's ministry lead to triumphalism, John Paul explains the kind of authority that the priest is called to exercise in and for the community. Like Christ's, his authority is an authority of service. Jesus' pastoral charity is the key to the life and mission of every priest.

The Apostles shared in the messianic authority that Christ received from the Father (cf. Mt 28:18-20). This authority, however, was of a unique kind; it was the authority of the one who "came not to be served but to serve, and to give his life as a ransom for many" (Mk 10:45). Jesus exercised the authority of a servant. In the paschal action of the washing of the feet (cf. Jn 13:1-20), Jesus "leaves to his disciples a model of service" (§13.4). In him authority coincided "with his service, with his gift, with his total, humble and loving dedication on behalf of the Church" (§21.3). For his part, the priest who is configured to Christ must imitate his Master: "The spiritual existence of every priest receives its life and inspiration from exactly this type of authority" (§21.4). Priestly authority, then, is to be understood and exercised as a service to the community.

In order to describe in greater detail the authority belonging to the priesthood, the Pope looks to Christ as the Head and Shepherd of the Church. Christ expressed most fully this headship as Head of the Church on Calvary, where he made "his total gift of self in humility and love" (§21.3). Configured to Christ as Head of the Church, priests follow him by placing themselves completely at the service of the Gospel. Their service also entails a sacrifice. They make "*the gift of self,* the total gift of *self to the Church,* following the example of Christ" (§23.2, cf. §15.4). A priest's exercise of authority, then, is rooted in his gift of self to Christ and to the flock entrusted to his pastoral care.

In the Holy Father's description of Christ as Shepherd the meaning of priestly authority becomes even clearer. Jesus showed a shepherd's love for his flock, what the Pope refers to as his "pastoral charity." Priests are to imitate this pastoral charity of Christ. They are called "to live out, as radically as possible, the pastoral charity of Jesus, the love of the Good Shepherd" (§40.4), who gave up his life for his flock (cf. Jn 10:11). For priests, this giving up of their life is expressed by selfless and unstinting service to the Church and the world.

As a way of reinforcing his teaching on priestly service, the Pope warns against two mistaken views of authority. First, priestly authority should never be exercised in an overbearing manner. Priests should be free of "all presumption of desire of 'lording over' those in their charge" (§21.5). Instead, they ought to consider themselves as elders who carry out their mission as models to their flock (cf. 1 Pet 5:1-4). The Holy Father says that every priest is "to live out as a 'service' his own mission of 'authority' in the community, setting aside all attitudes of superiority or of exercising a power if it is not simply that which is justified by pastoral charity" (§58.4). Second, the humility which ought to accompany the exercise of priestly authority does not entail the elimination of different roles in the Church. Ministerial priests have a specific dignity and mission which belongs to them by virtue of sacramental ordination (cf. §3.8). Precisely because they are ordained, priests have received from Christ "a particular gift so that they can help the People of God to exercise faithfully and fully the common priesthood which it has received" (§17.4, cf. §§16.2, 37.4). Priestly authority is neither arrogant nor timid but takes as its model Christ, the Head and Shepherd of the Church.

The gift of celibacy

Controversy over the practice of the Latin Church and some Oriental Churches to confer "the order of presbyter only on men who have given proof that they have been called by God to the gift of chastity in absolute and perpetual celibacy" is long-standing (§29.2). At the 1990 Synod this discipline of celibacy was not as such debated. Nonetheless, some Bishops raised the question whether, in areas where priests were lacking, married men of mature age (*viri probati*) might be ordained to the priesthood. In his closing address to the Synod, Pope John Paul II replied directly to their suggestion. "This solution must not be taken into consideration; other responses must be found to this problem," he said. Consequently, *Pastores Dabo Vobis* makes no mention of the ordination of non-celibate *viri probati*. Instead, it urges making an act of faith in the grace of the Holy Spirit to provide sufficient vocations to meet the needs of particular Churches. In a positive light the exhortation reaffirms the gift of celibacy, gives reasons for the Church's practice, and discusses the formation of seminarians in celibacy.

The Pope wholeheartedly supports the Synod Fathers' unambiguous and forceful *propositio* that celibacy be maintained in the Latin Rite and some Eastern Rite Churches. At the same time he is careful not to call into question the tradition of married priests in other Eastern Churches and the exceptions given to married clergy who convert to Catholicism and receive ordination. According to John Paul, who cites the Synod Fathers, "the Synod does not wish to leave any doubts in the mind of anyone regarding the Church's firm will to maintain the law that demands perpetual and freely chosen celibacy for present and future candidates for priestly ordination in the Latin Rite" (§29.3). The Holy Father points out that this tradition is a law which expresses the Church's will. Its roots, however, are deeper than law; it depends on a "charism of the Spirit" which requires "a conscious and free response on the part of the receiver" (§50.2). Hence, celibacy "ought not to be considered and lived as an isolated or purely negative element, but as one aspect of the positive, specific and characteristic approach to being a priest" (§29.5). Far from being merely a legal norm or a condition imposed for ordination, celibacy expresses a candidate's "full and joyful availability in his heart for the pastoral ministry" (§50.2). It is a gift which the Church has received from Christ and a treasure she wishes to preserve.

In his exhortation the Holy Father provides four different reasons for maintaining the tradition of celibacy. He reaffirms this gift because of celibacy's link to the imitation of Christ, its ecclesial meaning, its prophetic and ecclesiological value, and its pastoral significance.

Out of keeping with the dominant culture of his day, Christ freely chose to live a celibate life. It was a sign of total commitment to his Father's will and to the service of others. The disciples, too, left "everything" to carry out their mission (cf. Lk 18:28-30). Priests likewise follow the example of Christ. Celibacy expresses their response to Jesus' call to radical discipleship for the Kingdom of God. The ultimate motivation for it is "the *link between celibacy and sacred ordination,* which configures the priest to Jesus Christ the Head and Spouse of the Church" (§29.4). According to the Pope, for the priest "holiness is intimacy with God; it is the imitation of Christ, who was poor, chaste and humble" (§33.3).

Christ's priestly oblation for the Church was carried out with spousal love (cf. Eph 5:25-26). Celibacy reflects Christ's virginal love for his Church. The ministerial priest, who sacramentally shares in Christ's priesthood, shows this same total love through his celibacy. Because ordination configures him to Christ, the Shepherd and Bridegroom of the Church, it asks of him an undivided love for Christ and his Bride. "The Church, as the Spouse of Jesus Christ, wishes to be loved by the priest in the total and exclusive manner in which Jesus Christ her Head and Spouse loved her" (§29.4, cf. §50.2). Celibacy is a sign of the priest's undivided love for God and for his People.

Besides these Christological and ecclesiological reasons, celibacy has an important eschatological and prophetic value. For Pope John Paul, priestly celibacy is a sign of contradiction for a society which needs to be called back to transcendent values. Celibacy entails "a personal gift to Jesus Christ and his Church which prefigures and anticipates the perfect and final communion and self-giving of the world to come" (§29.1). It anticipates the eschatological marriage of Christ and the Church. John Paul says that it is "a witness to the world of the eschatological Kingdom" (§29.5).

Finally, the exhortation points out the pastoral significance of celibacy. It makes the priest constantly available to serve his people: as celibate "the priest will be able to fulfill better his ministry on behalf of the People of God" (§50.3). The Pope especially notes that the priest's witness to evangelical celibacy will "aid Christian spouses to live fully the 'great sacrament' of the love of Christ the Bridegroom for his Spouse the Church, just as his own faithfulness to celibacy will help them to be faithful to each other as husband and wife" (§50.3). Celibacy is a sign of the pastoral charity which expresses a priest's selfless love for his flock.

Pastores Dabo Vobis pays considerable attention to the formation in celibacy for candidates to the priesthood. Their spiritual formation should help them to "know, appreciate, love and live celibacy according to its true nature and according to its real purposes, that is for evangelical, spiritual and pastoral motives" (§50.1). This careful preparation includes making seminarians aware of the value of celibacy and teaching them about its practice, so that they may "embrace priestly celibacy for the Kingdom of heaven with a free decision" (§50.4).

The seminary formation program is to present celibacy "clearly, without any ambiguities and in a positive fashion" (§50.4). In an age which often distorts the true meaning of human sexuality and reduces it "to nothing more than a consumer good" (§8.3), it is particularly important that candidates for the priesthood be helped in acquiring affective maturity. "Education for responsible love and the affective maturity of the person are totally necessary for those who, like the priest, are called to *celibacy*" (§44.4). Seminarians should be taught the importance of love and sexuality, and the beauty of marriage. They need to know that love "involves the entire person, in all his or her aspects, physical, psychic and spiritual" and that it is "expressed in the 'nuptial meaning' of the human body, thanks to which a person gives himself to another and takes the other to himself" (§44.2). Candidates for ordination will also benefit from receiving "a suitable education to true *friendship,* following the image of the bonds of fraternal affection which Christ himself lived on earth" (§44.5).

As well, John Paul offers some practical advice on celibacy. He maintains that there must be clarity about what it really entails and how it is to be safeguarded. Because a celibate man's "affections and instinctive impulses" remain intact, seminarians and priests must be "prudent, able to renounce anything that is a threat to it, vigilant over both body and spirit, and capable of esteem and respect in interpersonal relationships between men and women" (§44.5). More than anything else, the Pope reminds those who have embraced celibacy that the spiritual, moral, and pastoral demands of a celibate life make it "absolutely necessary that the priest pray humbly and trustingly . . . it is prayer, together with the Church's sacraments and ascetical practice, which will provide hope in difficulties, forgiveness in failings, and confidence and courage in resuming the journey" (§29.5, cf. §50.4). Besides an authentic life of prayer, recourse to spiritual direction is also necessary if the charism of celibacy is to be discerned and lived. The Holy Father states that "the spiritual director should help the seminarian so that he himself reaches a mature and free decision, which is built on esteem for priestly friendship and self-discipline, as well as on the acceptance of solitude and on a physically and psychologically sound personal state" (§50.4). Formation in priestly celibacy, therefore, includes helping candidates "to be aware of the 'precious gift of God,' which will lead to prayer and to vigilance in guarding the gift from anything which could put it under threat" (§50.2).

Pope John Paul concludes *Pastores Dabo Vobis* with a prayer to Mary: "Accept from the beginning those who have been called; protect their growth; in their life ministry accompany your sons, O Mother of Priests" (§82.14).

* * *

Selected Bibliography

Alphonso, Herbert. "Discernment and Careful Nurturing of the First Seeds of Priestly Vocation." *Seminarium,* 33 (1993), 322-333.

Atherton, John. "*Pastores Dabo Vobis* — Reflections on a Conference." *The Furrow,* 44 (1993), 440-443.

Bernardin, Joseph. "Relationships and Relational Life in Priestly Formation." *Seminarium,* 33 (1993), 334-340.

Bonnot, Bernard R. "St. Bernard, John Paul II, and Jean Vanier: On the Re-imaging of Priestly Life." *The Priest,* 50 (July 1994), 42-47.

Brom, Robert H. "Consecration, Ministry and Life Give Priests an Ecclesial Identity," *L'Osservatore Romano,* 31 (1992), 7.

Carey, Michael, and Cole, Basil. "*Pastores Dabo Vobis* and Priestly Formation." *The Priest,* 49 (July 1993), 10-18.

Conti, Luigi. "Seminary Has a Special Place at Heart of God's Plan of Salvation." *L'Osservatore Romano,* 44 (1992), 9-10.

Cordeiro, Joseph. "Bishops Gathered in 1990 Synod Focused on Priest and His Identity." *L'Osservatore Romano,* 17 (1992), 6-7.

Danneels, Godfried. "Priests for Our Time." *The Furrow,* 44 (1993), 331-340.

Dougherty, Jude P. "Superior Education Needed for Priest to Fulfill Teaching Office." *L'Osservatore Romano,* 35 (1992), 4.

Duffy, Eugene. "I Will Give You Shepherds — the Formation of Priests." *The Furrow,* 43 (1992), 597-606.

Giallanza, Joel. "The Ministry of Priesthood." *The Priest,* 51 (February 1995), 41-46.

Hillenbrand, Karl. "Seminary Trains Students for Life Shaped by Word and Sacrament." *L'Osservatore Romano,* 35 (1993), 3-4.

Hogan, William F. "Rooted in Christ the Priest." *Emmanuel,* 100 (1994), 414-416.

Laghi, Pio. "Formation Must Focus on Christ." *L'Osservatore Romano,* 33 (1993), 13-14.

Laghi, Pio. "Special Relationship with Christ Nourishes Priestly Spirituality." *L'Osservatore Romano,* 28 (1992), 9-10.

Malone, Richard. "On John Paul II's *Pastores Dabo Vobis.*" *Communio,* 20 (1993), 569-579.

Mulligan, James J. "The Presbyterate in *Pastores Dabo Vobis* [two parts]." *The Priest,* 49 (November 1993), 29-35; *The Priest,* 49 (December 1993), 30-35.

Murray, Daniel A. "Broad Consensus on Need for Propaedeutic Year in Seminaries." *L'Osservatore Romano,* 29 (1992), 7.

Murray, Daniel A. "Guidelines for the Formation of Seminary Educators." *Seminarium,* 34 (1994), 338-350.

Muszynski, Henryk. " 'Tria Munera' Provide the Theological Basis for Priest's Identity and Ministry." *L'Osservatore Romano,* 34 (1992), 6.

Pell, George. "Sound Training in Philosophy Is Essential to Priestly Formation." *L'Osservatore Romano,* 30 (1992), 6.

Schotte, Jan P. Presentation at the Press Conference for the Publication of *Pastores Dabo Vobis. L'Osservatore Romano,* 14 (1992), 1, 4.

Synod of Bishops, Eighth Ordinary General Assembly. *"Instrumentum Laboris." L'Osservatore Romano,* 30 (1990), 1-14; and *Origins,* 20 (1990), 149, 151-168.

Synod of Bishops, Eighth Ordinary General Assembly. *"Lineamenta." Origins,* 19 (1989), 33, 35-46.

Synod of Bishops, Eighth Ordinary General Assembly. "Message to the People of God." *L'Osservatore Romano,* 44 (1990), 1-2; and *Origins,* 20 (1990), 349, 351-355.

Synod of Bishops, Eighth Ordinary General Assembly. "Overview of Synod Proposals." *Origins,* 20 (1990), 353-355.

Viganò, Egidio. "Single Presbyterate Includes Priest Belonging to Religious Congregations." *L'Osservatore Romano,* 36 (1992), 4.

Woronieck, Michal. "Post-Communist Society Today Offers New Challenges to Priests." *L'Osservatore Romano,* 37 (1992), 7.

Zago, Marcello. "Future Priests Should Be Helped To Develop Missionary Consciousness." *L'Osservatore Romano,* 8 (1993),10-11.

POST-SYNODAL

APOSTOLIC EXHORTATION

PASTORES DABO VOBIS

OF HIS HOLINESS

JOHN PAUL II

TO THE BISHOPS

CLERGY AND FAITHFUL

ON THE FORMATION OF PRIESTS

IN THE CIRCUMSTANCES

OF THE PRESENT DAY

Pastores Dabo Vobis
Introduction

1.1 "I will give you shepherds after my own heart" (Jer 3:15).

1.2 In these words from the Prophet Jeremiah, God promises his people that he will never leave them without shepherds to gather them together and guide them: "I will set shepherds over them [my sheep] who will care for them, and they shall fear no more, nor be dismayed" (23:4).

1.3 The Church, the People of God, constantly experiences the reality of this prophetic message and continues joyfully to thank God for it. She knows that Jesus Christ himself is the living, supreme and definitive fulfillment of God's promise: "I am the Good Shepherd" (Jn 10:11). He, "the great Shepherd of the sheep" (Heb 13:20), entrusted to the Apostles and their successors the ministry of shepherding God's flock (cf. Jn 21:15-17; 1 Pet 5:2).

1.4 Without priests the Church would not be able to live that fundamental obedience which is at the very heart of her existence and her mission in history, an obedience in response to the command of Christ: "Go therefore and make disciples of all nations" (Mt 28:19) and "Do this in remembrance of me" (Lk 22:19; cf. 1 Cor 11:24), that is, an obedience to the command to announce the Gospel and to renew daily the sacrifice of the giving of his body and the shedding of his blood for the life of the world.

1.5 By faith we know that the Lord's promise cannot fail. This very promise is the reason and force underlying the Church's rejoicing at the growth and increase of priestly vocations now taking place in some parts of the world. It is also the foundation and impulse for a renewed act of faith and fervent hope in the face of the grave shortage of priests which is being felt in other parts of the world. Everyone is called upon to share complete trust in the unbroken fulfillment of God's promise, which the Synod Fathers expressed in clear and forceful terms: "The Synod, with complete trust in the promise of Christ who has said, 'Lo, I am with you always, to the close of the age' (Mt 28:20), and aware of the constant activity of the Holy Spirit in the Church, firmly believes that there will never be a complete lack of sacred ministers in the Church. . . . Even though in a number of regions there is a scarcity of clergy, the action of the Father, who raises up vocations, will nonetheless always be at work in the Church."[1]

1.6 At the conclusion of the Synod, I said that in the face of a crisis of

---

[1] *Propositio* 2.

priestly vocations "the first answer which the Church gives lies in a total act of faith in the Holy Spirit. We are deeply convinced that this trusting abandonment will not disappoint if we remain faithful to the graces we have received."[2]

2.1 To remain faithful to the grace received! This gift of God does not cancel human freedom; instead it gives rise to freedom, develops freedom and demands freedom.

2.2 For this reason, the total trust in God's unconditional faithfulness to his promise is accompanied in the Church by the grave responsibility to cooperate in the action of God who calls, and to contribute toward creating and preserving the conditions in which the good seed, sown by God, can take root and bring forth abundant fruit. The Church must never cease to pray to the Lord of the harvest that he send laborers into his harvest (cf. Mt 9:38). She must propose clearly and courageously to each new generation the vocational call, help people to discern the authenticity of their call from God and to respond to it generously, and give particular care to the formation of candidates for the priesthood.

2.3 The formation of future priests, both diocesan and Religious, and lifelong assiduous care for their personal sanctification in the ministry and for the constant updating of their pastoral commitment is considered by the Church one of the most demanding and important tasks for the future of the evangelization of humanity.

2.4 The Church's work of formation is a continuation in time of Christ's own work, which the Evangelist Mark illustrates in these words: "And he went up on the mountain, and called to him those whom he desired; and they came to him. And he appointed twelve, to be with him, and to be sent out to preach and have authority to cast out demons" (3:13-15).

2.5 It can be said that through her work of forming candidates to the priesthood and priests themselves, the Church throughout her history has continued to live this passage of the Gospel in various ways and with varying intensity. Today, however, the Church feels called to relive with a renewed commitment all that the Master did with his Apostles — urged on as she is by the deep and rapid transformations in the societies and culture of our age, by the multiplicity and diversity of contexts in which she announces the Gospel and witnesses to it, by the promising number of priestly vocations being seen in some Dioceses around the world, by the urgency of a new look at the contents and methods of priestly formation, by the concern of Bishops and their

[2] Address at the Closing of the Synod of Bishops, Eighth Ordinary General Assembly (October 27, 1990), 5: *AAS* 83 (1991), 496-497.

communities about a persisting scarcity of clergy, and by the absolute necessity that the "new evangelization" have priests as its initial "new evangelizers."

2.6 It is precisely in this cultural and historical context that the last Ordinary General Assembly of the Synod of Bishops took place. Dedicated to "the formation of priests in circumstances of the present day," its purpose was to put into practice the Council's teaching on this matter, making it more up-to-date and incisive in present circumstances, twenty-five years after the Council itself.[3]

3.1 Following the texts of the Second Vatican Council regarding the ministry of priests and their formation,[4] and with the intention of applying to various situations their rich and authoritative teaching, the Church has on various occasions dealt with the subject of the life, ministry and formation of priests.

3.2 She has done this in a more solemn way during the Synods of Bishops. Already in October 1967, the First General Ordinary Assembly of the Synod devoted five general congregations to the subject of the renewal of seminaries. This work gave a decisive impulse to the formulation of the document of the Congregation for Catholic Education entitled Fundamental Norms for Priestly Formation.[5]

3.3 The Second Ordinary General Assembly held in 1971 spent half its time on the ministerial priesthood. The fruit of the lengthy synodal discussion, incorporated and condensed in some "recommendations," which were submitted to my Predecessor Pope Paul VI and read at the opening of the 1974 Synod, referred principally to the teaching on the ministerial priesthood and to some aspects of priestly spirituality and ministry.

3.4 On many other occasions the Church's Magisterium has shown its concern for the life and ministry of priests. It may be said that in the years since the Council there has not been any subject treated by the Magisterium which has not in some way, explicitly or implicitly, had to do with the presence of priests in the community as well as their role and the need for them in the life of the Church and the world.

3.5 In recent years some have voiced a need to return to the theme of the priesthood, treating it from a relatively new point of view, one that was more

---

[3] Cf. *Propositio* 1.

[4] Cf. Dogmatic Constitution on the Church *Lumen Gentium,* 28; Decree on the Ministry and Life of Priests *Presbyterorum Ordinis;* Decree on Priestly Formation *Optatam Totius.*

[5] *Ratio Fundamentalis Institutionis Sacerdotalis* (January 6, 1970): *AAS* 62 (1970), 321-384.

adapted to present ecclesial and cultural circumstances. Attention has shifted from the question of the priest's identity to that connected with the process of formation for the priesthood and the quality of priestly life. The new generation of those called to the ministerial priesthood display different characteristics in comparison to those of their immediate predecessors. In addition, they live in a world which in many respects is new and undergoing rapid and continual evolution. All of this cannot be ignored when it comes to programming and carrying out the various phases of formation for those approaching the ministerial priesthood.

3.6 Moreover, priests who have been actively involved in the ministry for a more or less lengthy period of time seem to be suffering today from an excessive loss of energy in their ever increasing pastoral activities. Likewise, faced with the difficulties of contemporary culture and society, they feel compelled to reexamine their way of life and their pastoral priorities, and they are more and more aware of their need for ongoing formation.

3.7 The concern of the 1990 Synod of Bishops and its discussion focused on the increase of vocations to the priesthood and the formation of candidates in an attempt to help them come to know and follow Jesus, as they prepare to be ordained and to live the Sacrament of Holy Orders, which configures them to Christ the Head and Shepherd, the Servant and Spouse of the Church. At the same time, the Synod searched for forms of ongoing formation to provide realistic and effective means of support for priests in their spiritual life and ministry.

3.8 This same Synod also sought to answer a request which was made at the previous Synod on the vocation and mission of the laity in the Church and in the world. Lay people themselves had asked that priests commit themselves to their formation so that they, the laity, could be suitably helped to fulfill their role in the ecclesial mission which is shared by all. Indeed, "the more the lay apostolate develops, the more strongly is perceived the need to have well-formed holy priests. Thus the very life of the People of God manifests the teaching of the Second Vatican Council concerning the relationship between the common priesthood and the ministerial or hierarchical priesthood. For within the mystery of the Church the hierarchy has a ministerial character (cf. *Lumen Gentium,* 10). The more the laity's own sense of vocation is deepened, the more what is proper to the priest stands out."[6]

---

[6] John Paul II, Address at the Closing of the Synod of Bishops, Eighth Ordinary General Assembly (October 27, 1990), 3: *AAS* 83 (1991), 495-496.

4.1 In the ecclesial experience that is typical of the Synod (that is, "a unique experience on a universal basis of episcopal communion, which strengthens the sense of the universal Church and the sense of responsibility of the Bishops toward the universal Church and her mission, in affective and effective communion around Peter"[7]), *the voice of the various particular Churches* — and in this Synod, for the first time, the voices of some Churches from the East — were clearly heard and taken to heart. The Churches have proclaimed their faith in the fulfillment of God's promise: "I will give you shepherds after my own heart" (Jer 3:15), and they have renewed their pastoral commitment to care for vocations and for the formation of priests, aware that on this depends the future of the Church, her development and her universal mission of salvation.

4.2 In this Post-Synodal Apostolic Exhortation, I take up anew the rich legacy resulting from the reflections, endeavors and indications which were made during the Synod's preparation, as well as those which accompanied the work of the Synod Fathers, and as the Bishop of Rome and Successor of Peter I add my voice to theirs, addressing it to each and every one of the faithful, and in particular to each priest and to those involved in the important yet demanding ministry of their formation. Yes, in this Exhortation I wish to meet with *each and every priest,* whether diocesan or Religious.

4.3 Quoting from the Final Message of the Synod to the People of God, I make my own the words and the sentiments expressed by the Synod Fathers: "Brother priests, we want to express our appreciation to you, who are our most important collaborators in the apostolate. Your priesthood is absolutely vital. There is no substitute for it. You carry the main burden of priestly ministry through your day-to-day service of the faithful. You are ministers of the Eucharist and ministers of God's mercy in the Sacrament of Penance. It is you who bring comfort to people and guide them in difficult moments in their lives.

4.4 "We acknowledge your work and thank you once again, urging you to continue on your chosen path willingly and joyfully. No one should be discouraged as we are doing God's work; the same God who calls us, sends us and remains with us every day of our lives. We are ambassadors of Christ."[8]

---

[7] Ibid., 1: loc. cit., 494-495.

[8] Synod of Bishops, Eighth Ordinary General Assembly, Message to the People of God (October 28, 1990), III: *L'Osservatore Romano* (English-language edition), October 29, 1990, 1.

I

Chosen from among Men

The Challenges Facing Priestly Formation at the Conclusion of the Second Millennium

The priest in his time

5.1 "Every high priest chosen from among men is appointed to act on behalf of men in relation to God" (Heb 5:1).

5.2 The Letter to the Hebrews clearly affirms the *"human character" of God's minister:* he comes from the human community and is at its service, imitating Jesus Christ "who in every respect has been tempted as we are, yet without sin" (Heb 4:15).

5.3 God always calls his priests from specific human and ecclesial contexts, which inevitably influence them; and to these same contexts the priest is sent for the service of Christ's Gospel.

5.4 For this reason the Synod desired to "contextualize" the subject of priests, viewing it in terms of today's society and today's Church in preparation for the third millennium. This is indicated in the second part of the topic's formulation: "The formation of priests *in the circumstances of the present day."*

5.5 Certainly "there is an essential aspect of the priest that does not change: the priest of tomorrow, no less than the priest of today, must resemble Christ. When Jesus lived on this earth, he manifested in himself the definitive role of the priest, by establishing a ministerial priesthood with which the Apostles were the first to be invested. This priesthood is destined to last in endless succession throughout history. In this sense the priest of the third millennium will continue the work of the priests who, in the preceding millennia, have animated the life of the Church. In the third millennium the priestly vocation will continue to be the call to live the unique and permanent priesthood of Christ."[9] It is equally certain that the life and ministry of the priest must also "adapt to every era and circumstance of life. . . . For our part we must therefore seek to be as open as possible to light from on high from the Holy Spirit, in order to discover the tendencies of contemporary society, rec-

---

[9] John Paul II, Angelus (January 14, 1990), 2: *Insegnamenti* XIII/1 (1990), 84-85.

499

ognize the deepest spiritual needs, determine the most important concrete tasks and the pastoral methods to adopt, and thus respond adequately to human expectations."[10]

5.6 With the duty of bringing together the permanent truth of the priestly ministry and the characteristic requirements of the present day, the Synod Fathers sought to respond to *a few necessary questions:* What are the positive and negative elements in sociocultural and ecclesial contexts which affect boys, adolescents and young men who throughout their lives are called to bring to maturity a project of priestly life? What difficulties are posed by our times, and what new possibilities are offered for the exercise of a priestly ministry which corresponds to the gift received in the sacrament and the demands of the spiritual life which is consistent with it?

5.7 I now mention some comments taken from the Synod Fathers' analysis of the situation, fully aware that the great variety of sociocultural and ecclesial circumstances in different countries limits by necessity our treatment to only the most evident and widespread phenomena, particularly those relating to the question of education and priestly formation.

The Gospel today: hopes and obstacles

6.1 A number of factors seem to be working toward making people today more deeply aware of the dignity of the human person and more open to religious values, to the Gospel and to the priestly ministry.

6.2 Despite many contradictions, society is increasingly witnessing a powerful thirst for justice and peace, a more lively sense that humanity must care for creation and respect nature, a more open search for truth, a greater effort to safeguard human dignity, a growing commitment in many sectors of the world population to a more specific international solidarity and a new ordering of the world in freedom and justice. Parallel to the continued development of the potential offered by science and technology and the exchange of information and interaction of cultures, there is a new call for ethics, that is, a quest for meaning, and therefore for an objective standard of values which will delineate the possibilities and limits of progress.

6.3 In the more specifically religious and Christian sphere, ideological prejudice and the violent rejection of the message of spiritual and religious values are crumbling, and there are arising new and unexpected possibilities of evangelization and the rebirth of ecclesial life in many parts of the world. These are evident in an increased love of the Sacred Scriptures; in the vitality and growing vigor of many young Churches and their ever larger role in the defense and

---

[10] Ibid., 3: loc. cit., 85.

promotion of the values of human life and the person; and in the splendid witness of martyrdom provided by the Churches of Central and Eastern Europe as well as that of the faithfulness and courage of other Churches which are still forced to undergo persecution and tribulation for the faith.[11]

6.4 The thirst for God and for an active meaningful relationship with him is so strong today that, where there is a lack of a genuine and full proclamation of the Gospel of Christ, there is a rising spread of forms of religiosity without God and the proliferation of many sects. For all children of the Church, and for priests especially, the increase of these phenomena, even in some traditionally Christian environments, is not only a constant motive to examine our consciences as to the credibility of our witness to the Gospel but at the same time is a sign of how deep and widespread is the search for God.

7.1 Mingled with these and other positive factors, there are also, however, many problematic or negative elements.

7.2 *Rationalism* is still very widespread and, in the name of a reductive concept of "science," it renders human reason insensitive to an encounter with revelation and with divine transcendence.

7.3 We should take note also of a desperate defense of personal *subjectivity* which tends to close it off in individualism, rendering it incapable of true human relationships. As a result, many, especially children and young people, seek to compensate for this loneliness with substitutes of various kinds, in more or less acute forms of hedonism or flight from responsibility. Prisoners of the fleeting moment, they seek to "consume" the strongest and most gratifying individual experiences at the level of immediate emotions and sensations, inevitably finding themselves indifferent and "paralyzed" as it were when they come face to face with the summons to embark upon a life project which includes a spiritual and religious dimension and a commitment to solidarity.

7.4 Furthermore, despite the fall of ideologies which had made materialism a dogma and the refusal of religion a program, there is spreading in every part of the world a sort of *practical and existential atheism* which coincides with a secularist outlook on life and human destiny. The individual, "all bound up in himself, this man who makes himself not only the center of his every interest, but dares to propose himself as the principle and reason of all reality,"[12] finds himself ever more bereft of that "supplement of soul" which is all the more necessary to him in proportion as a wide availability of material

[11] Cf. *Propositio* 3.

[12] Paul VI, Homily at the Closing Session of the Second Vatican Ecumenical Council (December 7, 1965): *AAS* 58 (1966), 55.

goods and resources deceives him about his self-sufficiency. There is no longer a need to fight against God; the individual feels he is simply able to do without him.

7.5 In this context special mention should be made of *the breakup of the family and an obscuring or distorting of the true meaning of human sexuality.* These phenomena have a very negative effect on the education of young people and on their openness to any kind of religious vocation. Furthermore, one should mention the worsening of social injustices and the concentration of wealth in the hands of a few, the fruit of an inhuman capitalism[13] which increasingly widens the gap between affluent and indigent peoples. In this way tension and unrest are introduced into everyday life, deeply disturbing the lives of people and of whole communities.

7.6 There are also worrying and negative factors within the Church herself which have a direct influence on the lives and ministry of priests. For example: the lack of due knowledge of the faith among many believers; a catechesis which has little practical effect, stifled as it is by the mass media whose messages are more widespread and persuasive; an incorrectly understood pluralism in theology, culture and pastoral teaching which, though starting out at times with good intentions, ends up by hindering ecumenical dialogue and threatening the necessary unity of faith; a persistent diffidence toward and almost unacceptance of the Magisterium of the Hierarchy; the one-sided tendencies which reduce the richness of the Gospel message and transform the proclamation and witness to the faith into an element of exclusively human and social liberation or into an alienating flight into superstition and religiosity without God.[14]

7.7 A particularly important phenomenon, even though it is relatively recent in many traditionally Christian countries, is the presence within the same territory of large concentrations of people of different races and religions, thereby resulting in multiracial and multireligious societies. While on the one hand this can be an opportunity for a more frequent and fruitful exercise of dialogue, open-mindedness, good relations and a just tolerance, on the other hand the situation can also result in confusion and relativism, above all among people and populations whose faith has not matured.

7.8 Added to these factors, and closely linked with the growth of individualism, is the phenomenon of *subjectivism in matters of faith.* An increasing number of Christians seem to have a reduced sensitivity to the universality and objectivity of the doctrine of the faith, because they are subjectively at-

[13] Cf. *Propositio* 3.
[14] Ibid.

tached to what pleases them, to what corresponds to their own experience, and to what does not impinge on their own habits. In such a context, even the appeal to the inviolability of the individual conscience, in itself a legitimate appeal, may be dangerously marked by ambiguity.

7.9 This situation also gives rise to the phenomenon of *belonging to the Church* in ways which are ever more partial and conditional, with a resulting negative influence on the birth of new vocations to the priesthood, on the priest's own self-awareness and on his ministry within the community.

7.10 Finally, in many parts of the Church today it is still the scarcity of priests which creates the most serious problem. The faithful are often left to themselves for long periods, without sufficient pastoral support. As a result their growth as Christians suffers, not to mention their capacity to become better promoters of evangelization.

Young people: vocation and priestly formation

8.1 The many contradictions and potentialities marking our societies and cultures, as well as ecclesial communities, are perceived, lived and experienced by our young people with a particular intensity and have immediate and very acute repercussions on their personal growth. Thus, the emergence and development of priestly vocations among boys, adolescents and young men are continually under pressure and facing obstacles.

8.2 *The lure of the so-called "consumer society"* is so strong among young people that they become totally dominated and imprisoned by an individualistic, materialistic and hedonistic interpretation of human existence. Material "well-being," which is so intensely sought after, becomes the one ideal to be striven for in life, a well-being which is to be attained in any way and at any price. There is a refusal of anything that speaks of sacrifice and a rejection of any effort to look for and to practice spiritual and religious values. The all-determining "concern" for *having* supplants the primacy of *being*, and consequently personal and interpersonal values are interpreted and lived not according to the logic of giving and generosity but according to the logic of selfish possession and the exploitation of others.

8.3 This is particularly reflected in that *outlook on human sexuality* according to which sexuality's dignity in service to communion and to the reciprocal donation between persons becomes degraded and thereby reduced to nothing more than a consumer good. In this case, many young people undergo an affective experience which, instead of contributing to a harmonious and joyous growth in personality which opens them outward in an act of self-giving, becomes a serious psychological and ethical process of turning inward toward self, a situation which cannot fail to have grave consequences on them in the future.

8.4 In the case of some young people a *distorted sense of freedom* lies at the root of these tendencies. Instead of being understood as obedience to objective and universal truth, freedom is lived out as a blind acquiescence to instinctive forces and to an individual's will to power. Therefore, on the level of thought and behavior, it is almost natural to find an erosion of internal consent to ethical principles. On the religious level, such a situation, if it does not always lead to an explicit refusal of God, causes widespread indifference and results in a life which, even in its more significant moments and more decisive choices, is lived as if God did not exist. In this context it is difficult not only to respond fully to a vocation to the priesthood but even to understand its very meaning as a special witness to the primacy of "being" over "having," and as a recognition that the significance of life consists in a free and responsible giving of oneself to others, a willingness to place oneself entirely at the service of the Gospel and the Kingdom of God as a priest.

8.5 Often the world of young people is a "problem" in the Church community itself. In fact, if in them — more so than in adults — there is present a strong tendency to subjectivize the Christian faith and to belong only partially and conditionally to the life and mission of the Church, and if the Church community is slow for a variety of reasons to initiate and sustain an up-to-date and courageous pastoral care for young people, they risk being left to themselves, at the mercy of their psychological frailty, dissatisfied and critical of a world of adults who, in failing to live the faith in a consistent and mature fashion, do not appear to them as credible models.

8.6 Thus we see how difficult it is to present young people with a full and penetrating experience of Christian and ecclesial life and to educate them in it. So, the prospect of having a vocation to the priesthood is far from the actual everyday interests which young men have in life.

9.1 Nevertheless, there are positive situations and tendencies which bring about and nurture in the heart of adolescents and young men a new readiness, and even a genuine search, for ethical and spiritual values. These naturally offer favorable conditions for embarking on the journey of a vocation which leads toward the total gift of self to Christ and to the Church in the priesthood.

9.2 First of all, mention should be made of the decrease of certain phenomena which had caused many problems in the recent past, such as radical rebellion, libertarian tendencies, utopian claims, indiscriminate forms of socialization and violence.

9.3 It must be recognized, moreover, that today's young people, with the vigor and vitality typical of their age, are also bearers of ideals which are coming to the fore in history: the thirst for freedom, the recognition of the inestimable value of the person, the need for authenticity and sincerity, a new conception and style of reciprocity in the rapport between men and women, a convinced and earnest seeking after a more just, sympathetic and united world, openness and dialogue with all, and the commitment to peace.

9.4 The fruitful and active development among so many young people today of numerous and varied forms of voluntary service, directed toward the most forgotten and forsaken of our society, represents in these times a particularly important resource for personal growth. It stimulates and sustains young people in a style of life which is less self-interested and more open and sympathetic toward the poor. This way of life can help young men perceive, desire and accept a vocation to stable and total service of others, following the path of complete consecration to God as a priest.

9.5 The recent collapse of ideologies, the heavily critical opposition to a world of adults who do not always offer a witness of a life based on moral and transcendent values, and the experience of companions who seek escape through drugs and violence, contribute in no small fashion to making more keen and inescapable the fundamental question as to what values are truly capable of giving the fullest meaning to life, suffering and death. For many young people the question of religion and the need for spirituality are becoming more explicit. This is illustrated in the desire for "desert experiences" and for prayer, in the return to a more personal and regular reading of the word of God and in the study of theology.

9.6 As has happened in their involvement in the sphere of voluntary social service, young people are becoming more actively involved as leaders in the ecclesial community, above all through their membership in various groups — whether traditional but renewed ones or of more recent origin. Their experience of a Church challenged to undertake a "new evangelization" by virtue of her faithfulness to the Spirit who animates her and in response to the demands of a world far from Christ but in need of him, as well as their experience of a Church ever more united with individuals and peoples in the defense and promotion of the dignity of the person and of the human rights of each and every one — these experiences open the hearts and lives of the young to the exciting and demanding ideals which can find their concrete fulfillment in following Christ and in embracing the priesthood.

9.7 Naturally it is not possible to ignore this human and ecclesial situation, characterized by strong ambivalence, not only in the pastoral care of vocations and the formation of future priests, but also in the care of priests in their life and ministry and their ongoing formation. At the same time, while it is possible to detect various forms of "crisis" to which priests are subjected today in their ministry, in their spiritual life and indeed in the very interpretation of the nature and significance of the ministerial priesthood, mention must likewise be made, in a spirit of joy and hope, of the new positive possibilities which the present historical moment is offering to priests for the fulfillment of their mission.

Gospel discernment

10.1 The complex situation of the present day, briefly outlined above in general terms and examples, needs not only to be known but also and above all to be interpreted. Only in this way can an adequate answer be given to the fundamental question: How can we form priests who are truly able to respond to the demands of our times and capable of evangelizing the world of today?[15]

10.2 *Knowledge* of the situation is important. However, simply to provide data is not enough; what is needed is a "scientific" inquiry in order to sketch a precise and concrete picture of today's sociocultural and ecclesial circumstances.

10.3 Even more important is an *interpretation* of the situation. Such an interpretation is required because of the ambivalence, and at times contradictions, which are characteristic of the present situation where there is a mixture of difficulties and potentialities, negative elements and reasons for hope, obstacles and alternatives, as in the field mentioned in the Gospel where good seed and weeds are both sown and "coexist" (cf. Mt 13:24-30).

10.4 It is not always easy to give an interpretive reading capable of distinguishing good from evil, or signs of hope from threats. In the formation of priests it is not sufficient simply to welcome the positive factors and to counteract the negative ones. The positive factors themselves need to be subjected to a careful work of discernment, so that they do not become isolated and contradict one another, becoming absolutes and at odds with one another. The same is true for the negative factors, which are not to be rejected *en bloc* and without distinction, because in each one there may lie hidden some value which awaits liberation and restoration to its full truth.

10.5 For a believer the interpretation of the historical situation finds its principle for understanding and its criterion for making practical choices in a

---

[15] Cf. Synod of Bishops, Eighth Ordinary General Assembly, *Lineamenta,* "The Formation of Priests in the Circumstances of the Present Day," 5-6.

new and unique reality, that is, in a *Gospel discernment*. This interpretation is a work which is done in the light and strength provided by the true and living Gospel, which is Jesus Christ, and in virtue of the gift of the Holy Spirit. In such a way, Gospel discernment gathers from the historical situation, from its events and circumstances, not just a simple "fact" to be precisely recorded yet capable of leaving a person indifferent or passive, but a "task," a challenge to responsible freedom, both of the individual person and of the community. It is a "challenge" which is linked to a "call" which God causes to sound in the historical situation itself. In this situation, and also through it, God calls the believer, and first of all the Church, to ensure that "the Gospel of vocation and priesthood" expresses its perennial truth in the changing circumstances of life. In this case, the words of the Second Vatican Council are also applicable to the formation of priests: "The Church has always had the duty of scrutinizing the signs of the times and of interpreting them in the light of the Gospel, so that in a language intelligible to every generation, she can respond to the perennial questions which people ask about this present life and the life to come, and about the relationship of the one to the other. We must therefore recognize and understand the world in which we live, its expectations, its longings and its often dramatic characteristics."[16]

10.6 This Gospel discernment is based on trust in the love of Jesus Christ, who always and tirelessly cares for his Church (cf. Eph 5:29), he the Lord and Master, the Key, the Center and the Purpose of the whole of human history.[17] This discernment is nourished by the light and strength of the Holy Spirit, who evokes everywhere and in all circumstances obedience to the faith, the joyous courage of following Jesus, and the gift of wisdom, which judges all things and is judged by no one (cf. 1 Cor 2:15). It rests on the fidelity of the Father to his promises.

10.7 In this way the Church feels that she can face the difficulties and challenges of this new period of history and can also provide, in the present and in the future, priests who are well trained to be convinced and fervent ministers of the "new evangelization," faithful and generous servants of Jesus Christ and of the human family. We are not unmindful of difficulties in this regard; they are neither few nor insignificant. However, to surmount these difficulties we have at our disposal our hope, our faith in the unfailing love of Christ, and our certainty that the priestly ministry in the life of the Church and in the world knows no substitute.

---

[16] Pastoral Constitution on the Church in the Modern World *Gaudium et Spes*, 4.

[17] Cf. Synod of Bishops, Eighth Ordinary General Assembly, Message to the People of God (October 28, 1990), I: *L'Osservatore Romano* (English-language edition), October 29, 1990, 1.

II

He Has Anointed Me and Has Sent Me Forth

The Nature and Mission of the Ministerial Priesthood

A look at the priest

11.1 "The eyes of all in the synagogue were fixed on him" (Lk 4:20). What the Evangelist Luke says about the people in the synagogue at Nazareth that Sabbath, listening to Jesus' commentary on the words of the Prophet Isaiah which he had just read, can be applied to all Christians. They are always called to recognize in Jesus of Nazareth the definitive fulfillment of the message of the Prophets: "And he began to say to them, 'Today this Scripture has been fulfilled in your hearing'" (Lk 4:21). The "Scripture" he had read was this: "The Spirit of the Lord is upon me, because he has anointed me to preach good news to the poor. He has sent me to proclaim release to the captives and recovery of sight to the blind, to set at liberty those who are oppressed, to proclaim the acceptable year of the Lord" (Lk 4:18-19; cf. Is 61:1-2). Jesus thus presents himself as filled with the Spirit, "consecrated with an anointing," "sent to preach good news to the poor." He is the Messiah, the Messiah who is Priest, Prophet and King.

11.2 These are the features of Christ upon which the eyes of faith and love of Christians should be fixed. Using this "contemplation" as a starting point and making continual reference to it, the Synod Fathers reflected on the problem of priestly formation in present-day circumstances. This problem cannot be solved without previous reflection upon the goal of formation, that is, the ministerial priesthood, or, more precisely, the ministerial priesthood as a participation, in the Church, in the very priesthood of Jesus Christ. Knowledge of the nature and mission of the ministerial priesthood is an essential presupposition, and at the same time the surest guide and incentive toward the development of pastoral activities in the Church, for fostering and discerning vocations to the priesthood and training those called to the ordained ministry.

11.3 A correct and in-depth awareness of the nature and mission of the ministerial priesthood is the path which must be taken — and in fact the Synod did take it — in order to emerge from the crisis *of priestly identity*. In the Final Address to the Synod I stated: "This crisis arose in the years immediately following the Council. It was based on an erroneous understanding of

— and sometimes even a conscious bias against — the doctrine of the conciliar Magisterium. Undoubtedly, herein lies one of the reasons for the great number of defections experienced then by the Church, losses which did serious harm to pastoral ministry and priestly vocations, especially missionary vocations. It is as though the 1990 Synod, rediscovering, by means of the many statements which we heard in this Hall, the full depth of priestly identity, has striven to instill hope in the wake of these sad losses. These statements showed an awareness of the specific ontological bond which unites the priesthood to Christ the High Priest and Good Shepherd. This identity is built upon the type of formation which must be provided for priesthood, and then endure throughout the priest's whole life. This was the precise purpose of the Synod."[18]

11.4 For this reason the Synod considered it necessary to summarize the nature and mission of the ministerial priesthood, as the Church's faith has acknowledged them down the centuries of its history and as the Second Vatican Council has presented them anew to the people of our day.[19]

In the Church as mystery, communion and mission

12.1 "The priest's identity," as the Synod Fathers wrote, "like every Christian identity, has its source in the Blessed Trinity,"[20] which is revealed and is communicated to people in Christ, establishing, in him and through the Spirit, the Church as "the seed and the beginning of the Kingdom."[21] The Apostolic Exhortation *Christifideles Laici*, summarizing the Council's teaching, presents the Church as mystery, communion and mission: "She is mystery because the very life and love of the Father, Son and Holy Spirit are the gift gratuitously offered to all those who are born of water and the Spirit (cf. Jn 3:5) and called to relive the very *communion* of God and to manifest it and communicate it in history (mission)."[22]

---

[18] Address at the Closing of the Synod of Bishops, Eighth Ordinary General Assembly (October 27, 1990), 4: *AAS* 83 (1991), 496; cf. Letter to Priests for Holy Thursday 1991 (March 10, 1991): *AAS* 83 (1991), 463-468.

[19] Cf. Dogmatic Constitution on the Church *Lumen Gentium;* Decree on the Ministry and Life of Priests *Presbyterorum Ordinis;* Decree on Priestly Formation *Optatam Totius;* Sacred Congregation for Catholic Education, *Ratio Fundamentalis Institutionis Sacerdotalis* (January 6, 1970); Synod of Bishops, Second Ordinary General Assembly (1971).

[20] *Propositio* 7.

[21] Second Vatican Ecumenical Council, Dogmatic Constitution on the Church *Lumen Gentium,* 5.

[22] John Paul II, Post-Synodal Apostolic Exhortation *Christifideles Laici* (December 30, 1988), 8: *AAS* 81 (1989), 405; cf. Synod of Bishops, Second Extraordinary General Assembly (1985).

12.2 It is within the Church's mystery, as a mystery of Trinitarian communion in missionary tension, that every Christian identity is revealed, and likewise the specific identity of the priest and his ministry. Indeed, the priest, by virtue of the consecration which he receives in the Sacrament of Orders, is sent forth by the Father through the mediatorship of Jesus Christ, to whom he is configured in a special way as Head and Shepherd of his people, in order to live and work by the power of the Holy Spirit in service of the Church and for the salvation of the world.[23]

12.3 In this way the fundamentally "relational" dimension of priestly identity can be understood. Through the priesthood which arises from the depths of the ineffable mystery of God, that is, from the love of the Father, the grace of Jesus Christ and the Holy Spirit's gift of unity, the priest sacramentally enters into communion with the Bishop and with other priests,[24] in order to serve the People of God who are the Church and to draw all mankind to Christ in accordance with the Lord's prayer: "Holy Father, keep them in your name, which you have given me, that they may be one, even as we are one . . . even as you, Father, are in me, and I in you, that they also may be in us, so that the world may believe that you have sent me" (Jn 17:11, 21).

12.4 Consequently, the nature and mission of the ministerial priesthood cannot be defined except through this multiple and rich interconnection of relationships which arise from the Blessed Trinity and are prolonged in the communion of the Church, as a sign and instrument of Christ, of communion with God and of the unity of all humanity.[25] In this context the ecclesiology of communion becomes decisive for understanding the identity of the priest, his essential dignity, and his vocation and mission among the People of God and in the world. Reference to the Church is therefore necessary, even if not primary, in defining the identity of the priest. As a *mystery, the Church is essentially related to Jesus Christ.* She is his fullness, his Body, his Spouse. She is the "sign" and living "memorial" of his permanent presence and activity in our midst and on our behalf. The priest finds the full truth of his identity in being a derivation, a specific participation in and continuation of Christ himself, the one High Priest of the New and Eternal Covenant. The priest is a living and transparent image of Christ the Priest. The priesthood of Christ, the expression of his absolute "newness" in salvation history, constitutes the one source

---

[23] Cf. *Propositio* 7.

[24] Cf. Second Vatican Ecumenical Council, Decree on the Ministry and Life of Priests *Presbyterorum Ordinis,* 7-8.

[25] Cf. Second Vatican Ecumenical Council, Dogmatic Constitution on the Church *Lumen Gentium,* 1.

and essential model of the priesthood shared by all Christians and the priest in particular. Reference to Christ is thus the absolutely necessary key for understanding the reality of priesthood.

The fundamental relationship with Christ the Head and Shepherd

13.1 Jesus Christ has revealed in himself the perfect and definitive features of the priesthood of the New Covenant.[26] He did this throughout his earthly life, but especially in the central event of his Passion, Death and Resurrection.

13.2 As the author of the Letter to the Hebrews writes, Jesus, being a man like us and at the same time the only-begotten Son of God, is in his very being the perfect mediator between the Father and humanity (cf. Heb 8-9). Thanks to the gift of his Holy Spirit he gives us immediate access to God: "God has sent the Spirit of his Son into our hearts, crying, 'Abba! Father!' "(Gal 4:6; cf. Rom 8:15).

13.3 Jesus brought his role as mediator to complete fulfillment when he offered himself on the Cross, thereby opening to us, once and for all, access to the heavenly sanctuary, to the Father's house (cf. Heb 9:24-28). Compared with Jesus, Moses and all other "mediators" between God and his people in the Old Testament — kings, priests and prophets — are no more than "figures" and "shadows of the good things to come" instead of "the true form of these realities" (cf. Heb 10:1).

13.4 Jesus is the promised Good Shepherd (cf. Ezek 34), who knows each one of his sheep, who offers his life for them and who wishes to gather them together as one flock with one shepherd (cf. Jn 10:11-16). He is the Shepherd who has come "not to be served but to serve" (Mt 20:28), who in the paschal action of the washing of the feet (cf. Jn 13:1-20) leaves to his disciples a model of service to one another and who freely offers himself as the "innocent lamb" sacrificed for our Redemption (cf. Jn 1:36; Rev 5:6, 12).

13.5 With the one definitive sacrifice of the Cross, Jesus communicated to all his disciples the dignity and mission of priests of the New and Eternal Covenant. And thus the promise which God had made to Israel was fulfilled: "You shall be to me a kingdom of priests and a holy nation" (Ex 19:6). According to Saint Peter, the whole people of the New Covenant is established as "a spiritual house, a holy priesthood, to offer spiritual sacrifices acceptable to God through Jesus Christ" (1 Pet 2:5). The baptized are "living stones" who build the spiritual edifice by keeping close to Christ, "that living stone . . . in

---

[26] Cf. *Propositio 7*.

God's sight chosen and precious" (1 Pet 2:4). The new priestly people which is the Church not only has its authentic image in Christ, but also receives from him a real ontological share in his one eternal priesthood, to which she must conform every aspect of her life.

14.1 For the sake of this universal priesthood of the New Covenant Jesus gathered disciples during his earthly mission (cf. Lk 10:1-12), and with a specific and authoritative mandate he called and appointed the Twelve "to be with him, and to be sent out to preach and have authority to cast out demons" (Mk 3:14-15).

14.2 For this reason, already during his public ministry (cf. Mt 16:18), and then most fully after his Death and Resurrection (cf. Mt 28; Jn 20, 21), Jesus had conferred on Peter and the Twelve entirely special powers with regard to the future community and the evangelization of all peoples. After having called them to follow him, he kept them at his side and lived with them, imparting his teaching of salvation to them through word and example, and finally he sent them out to all mankind. To enable them to carry out this mission Jesus confers upon the Apostles, by a specific paschal outpouring of the Holy Spirit, the same messianic authority which he had received from the Father, conferred in its fullness in his Resurrection: "All authority in heaven and on earth has been given to me. Go therefore and make disciples of all nations, baptizing them in the name of the Father and of the Son and of the Holy Spirit, teaching them to observe all that I have commanded you; and lo, I am with you always, to the close of the age" (Mt 28:18-20).

14.3 Jesus thus established a close relationship between the ministry entrusted to the Apostles and his own mission: "He who receives you receives me, and he who receives me receives him who sent me" (Mt 10:40); "He who hears you hears me, and he who rejects you rejects me, and he who rejects me rejects him who sent me" (Lk 10:16). Indeed, in the light of the paschal event of the Death and Resurrection, the Fourth Gospel affirms this with great force and clarity: "As the Father has sent me, even so I send you" (Jn 20:21, cf. 13:20, 17:18). Just as Jesus has a mission which comes to him directly from God and makes present the very authority of God (cf. Mt 7:29, 21:23; Mk 1:27, 11:28; Lk 20:2, 24:19), so too the Apostles have a mission which comes to them from Jesus. And just as "the Son can do nothing of his own accord" (Jn 5:19) such that his teaching is not his own but the teaching of the One who sent him (cf. Jn 7:16), so Jesus says to the Apostles: "apart from me you can do nothing" (Jn 15:5). Their mission is not theirs but is the same mission of Jesus. All this is possible not as a result of human abilities, but only with the "gift" of Christ and his Spirit, with the "sacrament": "Receive the Holy Spirit. If you forgive the sins of any, they are forgiven; if you retain the sins of any, they are retained" (Jn 20:22-23). And so the Apostles, not by any special merit of their own, but only through a gratuitous participation in the grace of Christ, prolong throughout history to the end of time the same mission of Jesus on behalf of humanity.

14.4 The sign and presupposition of the authenticity and fruitfulness of this mission is the Apostles' unity with Jesus and, in him, with one another and with the Father, as the priestly prayer of our Lord, which sums up his mission, bears witness (cf. Jn 17:20-23).

15.1 In their turn, the Apostles, appointed by the Lord, progressively carried out their mission by calling, in various but complementary ways, other men as Bishops, as priests and as deacons in order to fulfill the command of the risen Jesus who sent them forth to all people in every age.

15.2 The writings of the New Testament are unanimous in stressing that it is the same Spirit of Christ who introduces these men chosen from among their brethren into the ministry. Through the laying on of hands (cf. Acts 6:6; 1 Tim 4:14, 5:22; 2 Tim 1:6) which transmits the gift of the Spirit, they are called and empowered to continue the same ministry of reconciliation, of shepherding the flock of God and of teaching (cf. Acts 20:28; 1 Pet 5:2).

15.3 Therefore, priests are called to prolong the presence of Christ, the one High Priest, embodying his way of life and making him visible in the midst of the flock entrusted to their care. We find this clearly and precisely stated in the First Letter of Peter: "I exhort the elders among you, as a fellow elder and a witness of the sufferings of Christ as well as a partaker in the glory that is to be revealed. Tend the flock of God that is your charge, not by constraint but willingly, not for shameful gain but eagerly, not as domineering over those in your charge but being examples to the flock. And when the chief Shepherd is manifested you will obtain the unfading crown of glory" (5:1-4).

15.4 In the Church and on behalf of the Church, priests are a sacramental representation of Jesus Christ, the Head and Shepherd, authoritatively proclaiming his word, repeating his acts of forgiveness and his offer of salvation, particularly in Baptism, Penance and the Eucharist, showing his loving concern to the point of a total gift of self for the flock, which they gather into unity and lead to the Father through Christ and in the Spirit. In a word, priests exist and act in order to proclaim the Gospel to the world and to build up the Church in the name and person of Christ the Head and Shepherd.[27]

---

[27] Ibid.

15.5 This is the ordinary and proper way in which ordained ministers share in the one priesthood of Christ. By the sacramental anointing of Holy Orders, the Holy Spirit configures them in a new and special way to Jesus Christ the Head and Shepherd; he forms and strengthens them with his pastoral charity; and he gives them an authoritative role in the Church as servants of the proclamation of the Gospel to every people and of the fullness of Christian life of all the baptized.

15.6 The truth of the priest as it emerges from the Word of God, that is, from Jesus Christ himself and from his constitutive plan for the Church, is thus proclaimed with joyful gratitude by the Preface of the Liturgy of the Chrism Mass: "By your Holy Spirit you anointed your only Son High Priest of the New and Eternal Covenant. With wisdom and love you have planned that this one priesthood should continue in the Church. Christ gives the dignity of a royal priesthood to the people he has made his own. From these, with a brother's love, he chooses men to share his sacred ministry by the laying on of hands. He appointed them to renew in his name the sacrifice of Redemption as they set before your family his paschal meal. He calls them to lead your holy people in love, nourish them by your word and strengthen them through the sacraments. Father, they are to give their lives in your service and for the salvation of your people as they strive to grow in the likeness of Christ and honor you by their courageous witness of faith and love."

Serving the Church and the world

16.1 The priest's fundamental relationship is to Jesus Christ, Head and Shepherd. Indeed, the priest participates in a specific and authoritative way in the "consecration/ anointing" and in the "mission" of Christ (cf. Lk 4:18-19). But intimately linked to this relationship is the priest's relationship with the Church. It is not a question of "relations" which are merely juxtaposed, but rather of ones which are interiorly united in a kind of mutual immanence. The priest's relation to the Church is inscribed in the very relation which the priest has to Christ, such that the "sacramental representation" to Christ serves as the basis and inspiration for the relation of the priest to the Church.

16.2 In this sense the Synod Fathers wrote: "Inasmuch as he represents Christ the Head, Shepherd and Spouse of the Church, the priest is placed not only *in the Church* but also *in the forefront of the Church*. The priesthood, along with the word of God and the sacramental signs which it serves, belongs to the constitutive elements of the Church. The ministry of the priest is entirely on behalf of the Church; it aims at promoting the exercise of the common priesthood of the entire People of God; it is ordered not only to the particular Church but also to the universal Church (cf. *Presbyterorum Ordinis,* 10), in communion with the Bishop, with Peter and under Peter. Through the priesthood of the Bishop, the priesthood of the second order is incorporated in the apostolic structure of the Church. In this way priests, like the Apostles, act as ambassadors of Christ (cf. 2 Cor 5:20). This is the basis of the missionary character of every priest."[28]

16.3 Therefore, the ordained ministry arises with the Church and has in Bishops, and in priests who are related to and are in communion with them, a particular relation to the original ministry of the Apostles — to which it truly "succeeds" — even though with regard to the latter it assumes different forms.

16.4 Consequently, the ordained priesthood ought not to be thought of as existing prior to the Church, because it is totally at the service of the Church. Nor should it be considered as posterior to the ecclesial community, as if the Church could be imagined as already established without this priesthood.

16.5 The relation of the priest to Jesus Christ, and in him to his Church, is found in the very *being* of the priest by virtue of his sacramental consecration/anointing and in his *activity,* that is, in his mission or ministry. In particular, "the priest minister is the servant of Christ present in the *Church as mystery, communion and mission.* In virtue of his participation in the 'anointing' and 'mission' of Christ, the priest can continue Christ's prayer, word, sacrifice and salvific action in the Church. In this way, the priest is a *servant of the Church as mystery* because he actuates the Church's sacramental signs of the presence of the risen Christ. He is a *servant of the Church as communion* because — in union with the Bishop and closely related to the presbyterate — he builds up the unity of the Church community in the harmony of diverse vocations, charisms and services. Finally, the priest is a *servant to the Church as mission* because he makes the community a herald and witness of the Gospel."[29]

16.6 Thus, by his very nature and sacramental mission, the priest appears in the structure of the Church as a sign of the absolute priority and gratuitousness of the grace given to the Church by the risen Christ. Through the ministerial priesthood the Church becomes aware in faith that her being comes not from herself but from the grace of Christ in the Holy Spirit. The Apostles and their successors, inasmuch as they exercise an authority which

---

[28] Ibid.

[29] Synod of Bishops, Eighth Ordinary General Assembly, *Instrumentum Laboris,* "The Formation of Priests in the Circumstances of the Present Day," 16; cf. *Propositio 7.*

comes to them from Christ, the Head and Shepherd, are placed — with their ministry — *in the forefront of the Church* as a visible continuation and sacramental sign of Christ in his own position before the Church and the world, as the enduring and ever new source of salvation, he "who is Head of the Church, his Body, and is himself its Savior" (Eph 5:23).

17.1 By its very nature, the ordained ministry can be carried out only to the extent that the priest is united to Christ through sacramental participation in the priestly order, and thus to the extent that he is in hierarchical communion with his own Bishop. The ordained ministry has a radical *"communitarian form"* and can only be carried out as "a collective work."[30] The Council dealt extensively with this communal aspect of the nature of the priesthood,[31] examining in succession the relationship of the priest with his own Bishop, with other priests and with the lay faithful.

17.2 The ministry of priests is above all communion and a responsible and necessary cooperation with the Bishop's ministry, in concern for the universal Church and for the individual particular Churches, for whose service they form with the Bishop a single presbyterate.

17.3 Each priest, whether diocesan or Religious, is united to the other members of this presbyterate on the basis of the Sacrament of Holy Orders and by particular bonds of apostolic charity, ministry and fraternity. All priests in fact, whether diocesan or Religious, share in the one priesthood of Christ the Head and Shepherd; "they work for the same cause, namely, the building up of the Body of Christ, which demands a variety of functions and new adaptations, especially at the present time,"[32] and is enriched down the centuries by ever new charisms.

17.4 Finally, because their role and task within the Church do not replace but promote the baptismal priesthood of the entire People of God, leading it to its full ecclesial realization, priests have a positive and helping relationship to the laity. Priests are there to serve the faith, hope and charity of the laity. They recognize and uphold, as brothers and friends, the dignity of the laity as children of God and help them to exercise fully their specific role in the overall context of the Church's mission.[33] The ministerial priesthood conferred by the

---

[30] John Paul II, Angelus (February 25, 1990), 1: *Insegnamenti* XIII/1 (1990), 523.

[31] Cf. Decree on the Ministry and Life of Priests *Presbyterorum Ordinis*, 7-9.

[32] Decree on the Ministry and Life of Priests *Presbyterorum Ordinis*, 8; cf. *Propositio* 7.

[33] Cf. Second Vatican Ecumenical Council, Decree on the Ministry and Life of Priests *Presbyterorum Ordinis*, 9.

Sacrament of Holy Orders and the common or "royal" priesthood of the faithful, which differ essentially and not only in degree,[34] are ordered one to the other, for each in its own way derives from the one priesthood of Christ. Indeed, the ministerial priesthood does not of itself signify a greater degree of holiness with regard to the common priesthood of the faithful; through it, Christ gives to priests, in the Spirit, a particular gift so that they can help the People of God to exercise faithfully and fully the common priesthood which it has received.[35]

18.1 As the Council points out, "the spiritual gift which priests have received in ordination does not prepare them merely for a limited and circumscribed mission, but for the fullest, in fact the universal, mission of salvation to the end of the earth. The reason is that every priestly ministry shares in the fullness of the mission entrusted by Christ to the Apostles."[36] By the very nature of their ministry they should therefore be penetrated and animated by a profound missionary spirit and "with that truly Catholic spirit which habitually looks beyond the boundaries of Diocese, country or rite to meet the needs of the whole Church, being prepared in spirit to preach the Gospel everywhere."[37]

18.2 Furthermore, precisely because within the Church's life the priest is a man of communion, in his relations with all people he must be a man of mission and dialogue. Deeply rooted in the truth and charity of Christ, and impelled by the desire and imperative to proclaim Christ's salvation to all, the priest is called to witness in all his relationships to fraternity, service and a common quest for the truth, as well as a concern for the promotion of justice and peace. This is the case above all with the brethren of other Churches and Christian denominations, but it also extends to the followers of other religions, to people of good will and in particular to the poor and the defenseless, and to all who yearn, even if they do not know it or cannot express it, for the truth and the salvation of Christ, in accordance with the words of Jesus who said: "Those who are well have no need of a physician, but those who are sick; I came not to call the righteous, but sinners" (Mk 2:17).

---

[34] Cf. Second Vatican Ecumenical Council, Dogmatic Constitution on the Church *Lumen Gentium,* 10.

[35] Cf. *Propositio 7.*

[36] Decree on the Ministry and Life of Priests *Presbyterorum Ordinis,* 10.

[37] Decree on Priestly Formation *Optatam Totius,* 20.

18.3 Today in particular, the pressing pastoral task of the new evangelization calls for the involvement of the entire People of God, and requires a new fervor, new methods and a new expression for the announcing and witnessing of the Gospel. This task demands priests who are deeply and fully immersed in the mystery of Christ and capable of embodying a new style of pastoral life, marked by a profound communion with the Pope, the Bishops and other priests, and a fruitful cooperation with the lay faithful, always respecting and fostering the different roles, charisms and ministries present within the ecclesial community.[38]

18.4 "Today this Scripture has been fulfilled in your hearing" (Lk 4:21). Let us listen once again to these words of Jesus in the light of the ministerial priesthood which we have presented in its nature and mission. The "today" to which Jesus refers, precisely because it belongs to and defines the "fullness of time," the time of full and definitive salvation, indicates the time of the Church. The consecration and mission of Christ, "the Spirit of the Lord . . . has anointed me and has sent me to preach good news to the poor" (cf. Lk 4:18), are the living branch from which bud the consecration and mission of the Church, the "fullness" of Christ (cf. Eph 1:23). In the rebirth of Baptism, the Spirit of the Lord is poured out on all believers, consecrating them as a spiritual temple and a holy priesthood and sending them forth to make known the marvels of him who out of darkness has called them into his marvelous light (cf. 1 Pet 2:4-10). *The priest shares in Christ's consecration and mission in a specific and authoritative way,* through the Sacrament of Holy Orders, by virtue of which he is configured in his being to Jesus Christ, Head and Shepherd, and shares in the mission of "preaching the good news to the poor" in the name and person of Christ himself.

18.5 In their Final Message the Synod Fathers summarized briefly but eloquently the "truth," or better the "mystery" and "gift" of the ministerial priesthood, when they stated: "We derive our identity ultimately from the love of the Father, we turn our gaze to the Son, sent by the Father as High Priest and Good Shepherd. Through the power of the Holy Spirit, we are united sacramentally to him in the ministerial priesthood. Our priestly life and activity continue the life and activity of Christ himself. Here lies our identity, our true dignity, the source of our joy, the very basis of our life."[39]

---

[38] Cf. *Propositio* 12.
[39] Cf. Synod of Bishops, Eighth Ordinary General Assembly, Message to the People of God (October 28, 1990), III: *L'Osservatore Romano* (English-language edition), October 29, 1990, 1.

III

The Spirit of the Lord Is upon Me

The Spiritual Life of the Priest

A "specific" vocation to holiness

19.1 "The Spirit of the Lord is upon me" (Lk 4:18). The Spirit is not simply "upon" the Messiah, but he "fills" him, penetrating every part of him and reaching to the very depths of all that he is and does. Indeed, the Spirit is the principle of the "consecration" and "mission" of the Messiah: "because he has anointed me, and sent me to preach good news to the poor" (cf. Lk 4:18). Through the Spirit, Jesus belongs totally and exclusively to God and shares in the infinite holiness of God, who calls him, chooses him and sends him forth. In this way the Spirit of the Lord is revealed as the source of holiness and of the call to holiness.

19.2 This name, "Spirit of the Lord," is "upon" the entire People of God, which becomes established as a People "consecrated" to God and "sent" by God to announce the Gospel of salvation. The members of the People of God are "inebriated" and "sealed" with the Spirit (cf. 1 Cor 12:13; 2 Cor 1:21-22; Eph 1:13, 4:30) and called to holiness.

19.3 In particular, *the Spirit reveals to us and communicates the fundamental calling* which the Father addresses to everyone from all eternity, the vocation to be *"holy* and blameless before him . . . in love," by virtue of our predestination to be his adopted children through Jesus Christ (cf. Eph 1:4-5). This is not all. By revealing and communicating this vocation to us, *the Spirit becomes within us the principle and wellspring of its fulfillment.* He, the Spirit of the Son (cf. Gal 4:6), configures us to Christ Jesus and makes us sharers in his life as Son, that is, sharers in his life of love for the Father and for our brothers and sisters. "If we live by the Spirit, let us also walk by the Spirit" (Gal 5:25). In these words the Apostle Paul reminds us that a Christian life is a "spiritual life," that is, a life enlivened and led by the Spirit toward holiness or the perfection of charity.

19.4 The Council's statement that "all Christians in any state or walk of life are called to the fullness of Christian life and to the perfection of charity"[40] applies in a special way to priests. They are called not only because they have

---

[40] Dogmatic Constitution on the Church *Lumen Gentium*, 40.

519

been baptized, but also and specifically because they are priests, that is, under a new title and in new and different ways deriving from the Sacrament of Holy Orders.

20.1 The Council's Decree on Priestly Life and Ministry gives us a particularly rich and thought-provoking synthesis of the priest's "spiritual life" and of the gift and duty to become "saints": "By the Sacrament of Orders priests are configured to Christ the Priest so that as ministers of the head and co-workers with the episcopal order they may build up and establish his whole Body which is the Church. Like all Christians they have already received in the consecration of Baptism the sign and gift of their great calling and grace, which enables and obliges them even in the midst of human weakness to seek perfection (cf. 2 Cor 12:9), according to the Lord's word: 'You, therefore, must be perfect, as your heavenly Father is perfect' (Mt 5:48). But priests are bound in a special way to strive for this perfection, since they are consecrated to God in a new way by their ordination. They have become living instruments of Christ the Eternal Priest, so that through the ages they can accomplish his wonderful work of reuniting the whole human race with heavenly power. Therefore, since every priest in his own way represents the person of Christ himself, he is endowed with a special grace. By this grace the priest, through his service of the people committed to his care and all the People of God, is able the better to pursue the perfection of Christ, whose place he takes. The human weakness of his flesh is remedied by the holiness of him who became for us a High Priest 'holy, innocent, undefiled, separated from sinners' (Heb 7:26)."[41]

20.2 The Council first affirms the *"common" vocation to holiness.* This vocation is rooted in Baptism, which characterizes the priest as one of the "faithful" *(Christifidelis),* as a "brother among brothers," a member of the People of God, joyfully sharing in the gifts of salvation (cf. Eph 4:4-6) and in the common duty of walking "according to the Spirit" in the footsteps of the one Master and Lord. We recall the celebrated words of Saint Augustine: "For you I am a Bishop, with you I am a Christian. The former title speaks of a task undertaken, the latter of grace; the former betokens danger, the latter salvation."[42]

20.3 With the same clarity the conciliar text also speaks of a *"specific" vocation to holiness,* or more precisely of a vocation based on the Sacrament of Holy Orders, as a sacrament proper and specific to the priest, and thus involving a new consecration to God through ordination. Saint Augustine also alludes to this specific vocation when, after the words, "For you I am a Bishop,

---

[41] Decree on the Ministry and Life of Priests *Presbyterorum Ordinis,* 12.
[42] *Sermo* 340, 1: *PL* 38, 1483.

with you I am a Christian," he goes on to say: "If therefore it is to me a greater cause for joy to have been rescued with you than to have been placed as your leader, following the Lord's command, I will devote myself to the best of my abilities to serve you, so as not to show myself ungrateful to him who rescued me with that price which has made me your fellow servant."[43]

20.4 The conciliar text goes on to point out some elements necessary for defining what constitutes the "specific quality" of the priest's spiritual life. These are elements connected with the priest's "consecration," which configures him to Christ the Head and Shepherd of the Church, with the "mission" or ministry peculiar to the priest, which equips and obliges him to be a "living instrument of Christ the Eternal Priest" and to act "in the name and in the person of Christ himself" and with his entire "life," called to manifest and witness in a fundamental way the "radicalism of the Gospel."[44]

Configuration to Christ, the Head and Shepherd, and pastoral charity

21.1 By sacramental consecration the priest is configured to Jesus Christ as Head and Shepherd of the Church, and he is endowed with a "spiritual power" which is a share in the authority with which Jesus Christ guides the Church through his Spirit.[45]

21.2 By virtue of this consecration brought about by the outpouring of the Spirit in the Sacrament of Holy Orders, the spiritual life of the priest is marked, molded and characterized by the way of thinking and acting proper to Jesus Christ, Head and Shepherd of the Church, and which are summed up in his pastoral charity.

21.3 Jesus Christ is *Head of the Church, his Body.* He is the "Head" in the new and unique sense of being a "servant," according to his own words: "The Son of Man came not to be served but to serve, and to give his life as a ransom for many" (Mk 10:45). Jesus' service attains its fullest expression in his death on the Cross, that is, in his total gift of self in humility and love. "He emptied himself, taking the form of a servant, being born in the likeness of men. And being found in human form, he humbled himself and became obedient unto death, even death on a Cross" (Phil 2:7-8). The authority of Jesus Christ as Head coincides then with his service, with his gift, with his total, humble and loving dedication on behalf of the Church. All this he did in perfect obedience

---

[43] Ibid.

[44] Cf. *Propositio* 8.

[45] Cf. Second Vatican Ecumenical Council, Decree on the Ministry and Life of Priests *Presbyterorum Ordinis*, 2, 12.

to the Father; he is the one true Suffering Servant of God, both Priest and Victim.

21.4 The spiritual existence of every priest receives its life and inspiration from exactly this type of authority, from service to the Church, precisely inasmuch as it is required by the priest's configuration to Jesus Christ, Head and Servant of the Church.[46] As Saint Augustine once reminded a Bishop on the day of his ordination: "He who is head of the people must in the first place realize that he is to be the servant of many. And he should not disdain being such; I say it once again, he should not disdain being the servant of many, because the Lord of Lords did not disdain to make himself our servant."[47]

21.5 The spiritual life of the ministers of the New Testament should therefore be marked by this fundamental attitude of service to the People of God (cf. Mt 20:24-28; Mk 10:43-44), freed from all presumption of desire of "lording over" those in their charge (cf. 1 Pet 5:2-3). The priest is to perform this service freely and willingly as God desires. In this way the priests, as the ministers, the "elders" of the community, will be in their person the "model" of the flock, which for its part is called to display this same priestly attitude of service toward the world, in order to bring to humanity the fullness of life and complete liberation.

22.1 The figure of Jesus Christ as *Shepherd of the Church,* his flock, takes up and re-presents in new and more evocative terms the same content as that of Jesus Christ as Head and Servant. Fulfilling the prophetic proclamation of the Messiah and Savior joyfully announced by the Psalmist and the Prophet Ezekiel (cf. Ps 23; Ezek 34:11-16), Jesus presents himself as "the Good Shepherd" (Jn 10:11, 14), not only of Israel but of all humanity (cf. Jn 10:16). His whole life is a continual manifestation of his "pastoral charity," or rather, a daily enactment of it. He feels compassion for the crowds because they were harassed and helpless, like sheep without a shepherd (cf. Mt 9:35-36). He goes in search of the straying and scattered sheep (cf. Mt 18:12-14) and joyfully celebrates their return. He gathers and protects them. He knows them and calls each one by name (cf. Jn 10:3). He leads them to green pastures and still waters (cf. Ps 23) and spreads a table for them, nourishing them with his own life. The Good Shepherd offers this life through his own Death and Resurrection, as the Church sings out in the Roman liturgy: "The Good Shepherd is risen! He who laid down his life for his sheep, who died for his flock, he is risen, alleluia."[48]

---

[46] Cf. *Propositio* 8.
[47] *Sermo Morin Guelferbytanus,* 32, 1: *PLS* 2, 637.
[48] Roman Missal, Communion Antiphon from the Mass of the Fourth Sunday of Easter.

22.2 The author of the First Letter of Peter calls Jesus the "chief Shepherd" (5:4) because his work and mission continue in the Church through the Apostles (cf. Jn 21:15-17) and their successors (cf. 1 Pet 5:1-4), and through priests. By virtue of their consecration, priests are configured to Jesus the Good Shepherd and are called to imitate and to live out his own pastoral charity.

22.3 Christ's gift of himself to his Church, the fruit of his love, is described in terms of that unique gift of self made by the Bridegroom to the Bride, as the sacred texts often suggest. *Jesus is the true Bridegroom* who offers to the Church the wine of salvation (cf. Jn 2:11). He who is "the Head of the Church, his Body, and is himself its Savior" (Eph 5:23) "loved the Church and gave himself up for her, that he might sanctify her, having cleansed her by the washing of water with the word, that he might present the Church to himself in splendor, without spot or wrinkle or any such thing, that she might be holy and without blemish" (Eph 5:25-27). The Church is indeed the Body in which Christ the Head is present and active, but she is also the Bride who proceeds like a new Eve from the open side of the Redeemer on the Cross. Hence Christ stands "before" the Church and "nourishes and cherishes her" (Eph 5:29), giving his life for her. The priest is called to be the living image of Jesus Christ, the Spouse of the Church.[49] Of course, he will always remain a member of the community as a believer alongside his other brothers and sisters who have been called by the Spirit, but in virtue of his configuration to Christ, the Head and Shepherd, the priest stands in this spousal relationship with regard to the community. "Inasmuch as he represents Christ, the Head, Shepherd and Spouse of the Church, the priest is placed not only in the Church but also in the forefront of the Church."[50] In his spiritual life, therefore, he is called to live out Christ's spousal love toward the Church, his Bride. Therefore, the priest's life ought to radiate this spousal character, which demands that he be a witness to Christ's spousal love and thus be capable of loving people with a heart which is new, generous and pure, with genuine self-detachment, with full, constant and faithful dedication and at the same time with a kind of "divine jealousy" (cf. 2 Cor 11:2), and even with a kind of maternal tenderness, capable of bearing "the pangs of birth" until "Christ be formed" in the faithful (cf. Gal 4:19).

23.1 The internal principle, the force which animates and guides the spiritual life of the priest inasmuch as he is configured to Christ the Head and

---

[49] Cf. John Paul II, Apostolic Letter *Mulieris Dignitatem* (August 15, 1988), 26: *AAS* 80 (1988), 1715-1716.

[50] *Propositio* 7.

Shepherd, is *pastoral charity,* as a participation in Jesus Christ's own pastoral charity, a gift freely bestowed by the Holy Spirit and likewise a task and a call which demand a free and committed response on the part of the priest.

23.2 The essential content of this pastoral charity is *the gift of self,* the total gift of *self to the Church,* following the example of Christ. "Pastoral charity is the virtue by which we imitate Christ in his self-giving and service. It is not just what we do, but our gift of self, which manifests Christ's love for his flock. Pastoral charity determines our way of thinking and acting, our way of relating to people. It makes special demands on us."[51]

23.3 The gift of self, which is the source and synthesis of pastoral charity, is directed toward the Church. This was true of Christ who "loved the Church and gave himself up for her" (Eph 5:25), and the same must be true for the priest. With pastoral charity, which distinguishes the exercise of the priestly ministry as an *amoris officium,*[52] "the priest, who welcomes the call to ministry, is in a position to make this a loving choice, as a result of which the Church and souls become his first interest, and with this concrete spirituality he becomes capable of loving the universal Church and that part of it entrusted to him with the deep love of a husband for his wife."[53] The gift of self has no limits, marked as it is by the same apostolic and missionary zeal of Christ, the Good Shepherd, who said: "And I have other sheep, that are not of this fold; I must bring them also, and they will heed my voice. So there shall be one flock, one shepherd" (Jn 10:16).

23.4 Within the Church community the priest's pastoral charity impels and demands in a particular and specific way his personal relationship with the presbyterate, united in and with the Bishop, as the Council explicitly states: "Pastoral charity requires that a priest always work in the bond of communion with the Bishop and with his brother priests, lest his efforts be in vain."[54]

23.5 The gift of self to the Church concerns her insofar as she is the Body and the *Bride of Jesus Christ.* In this way the primary point of reference of the priest's charity is Jesus Christ himself. Only in loving and serving Christ the Head and Spouse will charity become a source, criterion, measure and impetus for the priest's love and service to the Church, the Body and Spouse of

---

[51] John Paul II, Homily at Eucharistic Adoration, Seoul (October 7, 1989), 2: *Insegnamenti* XII/2 (1989), 785.

[52] Saint Augustine, *In Iohannis Evangelium Tractatus,* 123, 5: *CCL* 36, 678.

[53] John Paul II, Address to Priests Taking Part in an Assembly Organized by the Italian Episcopal Conference (November 4, 1980), 3: *Insegnamenti* III/2 (1980), 1055.

[54] Decree on the Ministry and Life of Priests *Presbyterorum Ordinis,* 14.

Christ. The Apostle Paul had a clear and sure understanding of this point. Writing to the Christians of the Church in Corinth, he refers to "ourselves as your servants for Jesus' sake" (2 Cor 4:5). Above all, this was the explicit and programmatic teaching of Jesus when he entrusted to Peter the ministry of shepherding the flock only after his threefold affirmation of love, indeed only after he had expressed a preferential love: "He said to him the third time, 'Simon, son of John, do you love me?' Peter . . . said to him, 'Lord, you know everything; you know that I love you.' Jesus said to him, 'Feed my sheep' " (Jn 21:17).

23.6 Pastoral charity, which has its specific source in the Sacrament of Holy Orders, finds its full expression and its supreme nourishment in the *Eucharist*. As the Council states: "This pastoral charity flows mainly from the Eucharistic Sacrifice, which is thus the center and root of the whole priestly life. The priestly soul strives thereby to apply to itself the action which takes place on the altar of sacrifice."[55] Indeed, the Eucharist re-presents, makes once again present, the sacrifice of the Cross, the full gift of Christ to the Church, the gift of his body given and his blood shed, as the supreme witness of the fact that he is Head and Shepherd, Servant and Spouse of the Church. Precisely because of this, the priest's pastoral charity not only flows from the Eucharist but finds in the celebration of the Eucharist its highest realization, just as it is from the Eucharist that he receives the grace and obligation to give his whole life a "sacrificial" dimension.

23.7 This same pastoral charity is the dynamic inner principle capable of unifying the many different activities of the priest. In virtue of this pastoral charity the essential and permanent demand for unity between the priest's interior life and all his external actions and the obligations of the ministry can be properly fulfilled, a demand particularly urgent in a sociocultural and ecclesial context strongly marked by complexity, fragmentation and dispersion. Only by directing every moment and every one of his acts toward the fundamental choice to "give his life for the flock" can the priest guarantee this unity which is vital and indispensable for his harmony and spiritual balance. The Council reminds us that "priests attain to the unity of their lives by uniting themselves with Christ whose food was to fulfill the will of him who sent him to do his work. . . . In this way, by assuming the role of the Good Shepherd they will find in the very exercise of pastoral charity the bond of priestly perfection which will unify their lives and activities."[56]

---

[55] Ibid.
[56] Ibid.

The spiritual life in the exercise of the ministry

24.1 The Spirit of the Lord anointed Christ and sent him forth to announce the Gospel (cf. Lk 4:18). The priest's mission is not extraneous to his consecration or juxtaposed to it, but represents its intrinsic and vital purpose: *consecration is for mission*. In this sense, not only consecration but *mission as well is under the seal of the Spirit and the influence of his sanctifying power.*

24.2 This was the case in Jesus' life. This was the case in the lives of the Apostles and their successors. This is the case for the entire Church and within her for priests: all have received the Spirit as a gift and call to holiness in and through the carrying out of the mission.[57]

24.3 Therefore, an intimate bond exists between the priest's spiritual life and the exercise of his ministry,[58] a bond which the Council expresses in this fashion: "And so it is that they are grounded in the life of the Spirit while they exercise the ministry of the Spirit and of justice (cf. 2 Cor 3:8-9), as long as they are docile to Christ's Spirit, who gives them life and guidance. For by their everyday sacred actions, as by the entire ministry which they exercise in union with the Bishop and their fellow priests, they are being directed toward perfection of life. Priestly holiness itself contributes very greatly to a fruitful fulfillment of the priestly ministry."[59]

24.4 *"Live the mystery that has been placed in your hands!"* This is the invitation and admonition which the Church addresses to the priest in the Rite of Ordination, when the offerings of the holy people for the Eucharistic Sacrifice are placed in his hands. The "mystery" of which the priest is a "steward" (cf. 1 Cor 4:1) is definitively Jesus Christ himself, who in the Spirit is the source of holiness and the call to sanctification. This "mystery" seeks expression in the priestly life. For this to be so, there is need for great vigilance and lively awareness. Once again, the Rite of Ordination introduces these words with this recommendation: "beware of what you will be doing." In the same way Paul had admonished Timothy, "Do not neglect the gift you have" (1 Tim 4:14; cf. 2 Tim 1:6).

24.5 The relation between a priest's spiritual life and the exercise of his ministry can also be explained on the basis of the pastoral charity bestowed by the Sacrament of Holy Orders. The ministry of the priest, precisely because of its participation in the saving ministry of Jesus Christ the Head and Shepherd, cannot fail to express and live out his pastoral charity which is both the

---

[57] Cf. Paul VI, Apostolic Exhortation *Evangelii Nuntiandi* (December 8, 1975), 75: *AAS* 68 (1976), 64-67.

[58] Cf. *Propositio* 8.

[59] Decree on the Ministry and Life of Priests *Presbyterorum Ordinis,* 12.

source and spirit of his service and gift of self. In its objective reality the priestly ministry is an *"amoris officium,"* according to the previously quoted expression of Saint Augustine. This objective reality itself serves as both the basis and requirement for a corresponding ethos, which can be none other than a life of love, as Saint Augustine himself points out: *"Sit amoris officium pascere dominicum gregem."*[60] This ethos, and as a result the spiritual life, is none other than embracing consciously and freely — that is to say in one's mind and heart, in one's decisions and actions — the "truth" of the priestly ministry as an *amoris officium.*

25.1 For a spiritual life that grows through the exercise of the ministry, it is essential that the priest should continually renew and deepen his *awareness of being a minister of Jesus Christ* by virtue of sacramental consecration and configuration to Christ the Head and Shepherd of the Church.

25.2 This awareness is not only in accordance with the very nature of the mission which the priest carries out on behalf of the Church and humanity, but it also provides a focus for the spiritual life of the priest who carries out that mission. Indeed, the priest is chosen by Christ not as an "object" but as a "person." In other words, he is not inert and passive, but rather is a "living instrument," as the Council states, precisely in the passage where it refers to the duty to pursue this perfection.[61] The Council also speaks of priests as "companions and helpers" of God who is "the holy one and sanctifier."[62]

25.3 In this way the exercise of his ministry deeply involves the priest himself as a conscious, free and responsible person. The bond with Jesus Christ assured by consecration and configuration to him in the Sacrament of Orders gives rise to and requires in the priest the further bond which comes from his "intention," that is, from a conscious and free choice to do in his ministerial activities what the Church intends to do. This bond tends by its very nature to become as extensive and profound as possible, affecting one's way of thinking, feeling and life itself: in other words, creating a series of moral and spiritual "dispositions" which correspond to the ministerial actions performed by the priest.

25.4 There can be no doubt that the exercise of the priestly ministry, especially in the celebration of the sacraments, receives its saving effects from the action of Christ himself who becomes present in the sacraments. But so as to emphasize the gratuitous nature of salvation which makes a person both

---

[60] *In Iohannis Evangelium Tractatus,* 123, 5: *CCL 36,* 678.
[61] Cf. Decree on the Ministry and Life of Priests *Presbyterorum Ordinis,* 12.
[62] Ibid., 5.

"saved" and a "savior" — always and only in Christ — God's plan has ordained that the efficacy of the exercise of the ministry is also conditioned by a greater or lesser human receptivity and participation.[63] In particular, the greater or lesser degree of the holiness of the minister has a real effect on the proclamation of the word, the celebration of the sacraments and the leadership of the community in charity. This was clearly stated by the Council: "The very holiness of priests is of the greatest benefit for the fruitful fulfillment of their ministry. While it is possible for God's grace to carry out the work of salvation through unworthy ministers, yet God ordinarily prefers to show his wonders through those men who are more submissive to the impulse and guidance of the Holy Spirit and who, because of their intimate union with Christ and their holiness of life, are able to say with Saint Paul: 'It is no longer I who live, but Christ who lives in me' (Gal 2:20)."[64]

25.5 The consciousness that one is a minister of Jesus Christ the Head and Shepherd also brings with it a thankful and joyful awareness that one has received a singular grace and treasure from Jesus Christ: the grace of having been freely chosen by the Lord to be a "living instrument" in the work of salvation. This choice bears witness to Jesus Christ's love for the priest. This love, like other loves and yet even more so, demands a response. After his Resurrection, Jesus asked Peter the basic question about love: "Simon, son of John, do you love me more than these?" And following his response Jesus entrusts Peter with the mission: "Feed my lambs" (Jn 21:15). Jesus first asks Peter if he loves him so as to be able to entrust his flock to him. However, in reality it was Christ's own love, free and unsolicited, which gave rise to his question to Peter and to his act of entrusting "his" sheep to Peter. Therefore, every ministerial action, while it leads to loving and serving the Church, provides an incentive to grow in ever greater love and service of Jesus Christ the Head, Shepherd and Spouse of the Church, a love which is always a response to the free and unsolicited love of God in Christ. Growth in the love of Jesus Christ determines in turn the growth of love for the Church: "We are your shepherds *(pascimus vobis),* with you we receive nourishment *(pascimur vobiscum).* May the Lord give us the strength to love you to the extent of dying for you, either in fact or in desire *(aut effectu aut affectu)."*[65]

---

[63] Cf. Ecumenical Council of Trent, Session VI, Decree on Justification *Cum Hoc Tempore,* Chapter 7: *Conciliorum Oecumenicorum Decreta,* Ed. Istituto per le Scienze Religiose, 3rd ed., Bologna, 1973, 708 (*DS* 1528-1531); Session VII, Decree on the Sacraments, Canon 6: loc. cit., 684 (*DS* 1604).

[64] Decree on the Ministry and Life of Priests *Presbyterorum Ordinis,* 12.

[65] Saint Augustine, *Sermo de Natale Sanctorum Apostolorum Petri et Pauli ex Evangelio in*

26.1 Thanks to the insightful teaching of the Second Vatican Council,[66] we can grasp the conditions and demands, the manifestations and fruits of the intimate bond between the priest's spiritual life and the exercise of his three-fold ministry of word, sacrament and pastoral charity.

26.2 The priest is first of all a *minister of the word of God*. He is conse-crated and sent forth to proclaim the Good News of the Kingdom to all, calling every person to the obedience of faith and leading believers to an ever increas-ing knowledge of and communion in the mystery of God, as revealed and communicated to us in Christ. For this reason, the priest himself ought first of all to develop a great personal familiarity with the word of God. Knowledge of its linguistic or exegetical aspects, though certainly necessary, is not enough. He needs to approach the word with a docile and prayerful heart so that it may deeply penetrate his thoughts and feelings and bring about a new out-look in him — "the mind of Christ" (1 Cor 2:16) — such that his words and his choices and attitudes may become ever more a reflection, a proclamation and a witness to the Gospel. Only if he "abides" in the word will the priest become a perfect disciple of the Lord. Only then will he know the truth and be set truly free, overcoming every conditioning which is contrary or foreign to the Gospel (cf. Jn 8:31-32). The priest ought to be the first "believer" in the word, while being fully aware that the words of his ministry are not "his," but those of the One who sent him. He is not the master of the word, but its servant. He is not the sole possessor of the word; in its regard he is in debt to the People of God. Precisely because he can and does evangelize, the priest, like every other mem-ber of the Church, ought to grow in awareness that he himself is continually in need of being evangelized.[67] He proclaims the word in his capacity as "min-ister," as a sharer in the prophetic authority of Christ and the Church. As a result, in order that he himself may possess and give to the faithful the guar-antee that he is transmitting the Gospel in its fullness, the priest is called to develop a special sensitivity, love and docility to the living Tradition of the Church and to her Magisterium. These are not foreign to the word, but serve its proper interpretation and preserve its authentic meaning.[68]

26.3 It is above all in the *celebration of the sacraments* and in the celebra-

---

quo ait: Simon Iohannis diligis me?: Bibliotheca Casinensis, in "Miscellanea Augustiniana," vol. 1, ed. G. Morin, O.S.B., Rome, Vatican Polyglot Press, 1930, 404.

[66] Cf. Decree on the Ministry and Life of Priests *Presbyterorum Ordinis,* 4-6, 13.

[67] Cf. Paul VI, Apostolic Exhortation *Evangelii Nuntiandi* (December 8, 1975), 15: *AAS* 68 (1976), 13-15.

[68] Cf. Second Vatican Ecumenical Council, Dogmatic Constitution on Divine Revelation *Dei Verbum,* 8, 10.

tion of the Liturgy of the Hours that the priest is called to live and witness to the deep unity between the exercise of his ministry and his spiritual life. The gift of grace offered to the Church becomes the principle of holiness and a call to sanctification. For the priest as well, the truly central place, both in his ministry and spiritual life, belongs to the Eucharist, since in it is contained "the whole spiritual good of the Church, namely Christ himself our Pasch and the living bread which gives life to men through his flesh — that flesh which is given life and gives life through the Holy Spirit. Thus people are invited and led to offer themselves, their works and all creation with Christ."[69]

26.4 From the various sacraments, and in particular from the specific grace proper to each of them, the priest's spiritual life receives certain features. It is built up and molded by the different characteristics and demands of each of the sacraments as he celebrates them and experiences them.

26.5 I would like to make special mention of the Sacrament of Penance, of which priests are the ministers, but ought also to be its beneficiaries, becoming themselves witnesses of God's mercy toward sinners. Once again, I would like to set forth what I wrote in the Exhortation *Reconciliatio et Paenitentia:* "The priest's spiritual and pastoral life, like that of his brothers and sisters, lay and Religious, depends, for its quality and fervor, on the frequent and conscientious personal practice of the Sacrament of Penance. The priest's celebration of the Eucharist and administration of the other sacraments, his pastoral zeal, his relationship with the faithful, his communion with his brother priests, his collaboration with his Bishop, his life of prayer — in a word, the whole of his priestly existence, suffers an inexorable decline if by negligence or for some other reason he fails to receive the Sacrament of Penance at regular intervals and in a spirit of genuine faith and devotion. If a priest were no longer to go to confession or properly confess his sins, his *priestly being* and his *priestly action* would feel its effects very soon, and this would also be noticed by the community of which he was the pastor."[70]

26.6 Finally, the priest is called to express in his life the authority and service of Jesus Christ the Head and Priest of the Church by *encouraging and leading the ecclesial community,* that is, by gathering together "the family of God as a fellowship endowed with the spirit of unity" and by leading it "in Christ through the Spirit to God the Father."[71] This *munus regendi* represents

[69] Second Vatican Ecumenical Council, Decree on the Ministry and Life of Priests *Presbyterorum Ordinis,* 5.

[70] Post-Synodal Apostolic Exhortation *Reconciliatio et Paenitentia* (December 2, 1984), 31: *AAS* 77 (1985), 265-266.

[71] Second Vatican Ecumenical Council, Decree on the Ministry and Life of Priests *Presbyterorum Ordinis,* 6.

a very delicate and complex duty which, in addition to the attention which must be given to a variety of persons and their vocations, also involves the ability to coordinate all the gifts and charisms which the Spirit inspires in the community, to discern them and to put them to good use for the upbuilding of the Church in constant union with the Bishops. This ministry demands of the priest an intense spiritual life, filled with those qualities and virtues which are typical of a person who "presides over" and "leads" a community, of an "elder" in the noblest and richest sense of the word: qualities and virtues such as faithfulness, integrity, consistency, wisdom, a welcoming spirit, friendliness, goodness of heart, decisive firmness in essentials, freedom from overly subjective viewpoints, personal disinterestedness, patience, an enthusiasm for daily tasks, confidence in the value of the hidden workings of grace as manifested in the simple and the poor (cf. Tit 1:7-8).

Priestly life and the radicalism of the Gospel

27.1 "The Spirit of the Lord is upon me" (Lk 4:18). The Holy Spirit poured out in the Sacrament of Holy Orders is a source of holiness and a call to sanctification. This is the case not only because it configures the priest to Christ, the Head and Shepherd of the Church, entrusting him with a prophetic, priestly and royal mission to be carried out in the name and person of Christ, but also because it inspires and enlivens his daily existence, enriching it with gifts and demands, virtues and incentives which are summed up in pastoral charity. This charity is a synthesis which unifies the values and virtues contained in the Gospel and likewise a power which sustains their development toward Christian perfection.[72]

27.2 For all Christians without exception, the radicalism of the Gospel represents a fundamental, undeniable demand flowing from the call of Christ to follow and imitate him by virtue of the intimate communion of life with him brought about by the Spirit (cf. Mt 8:18-20, 10:37-39; Mk 8:34-38, 10:17-21; Lk 9:57-62). This same demand is made anew to priests, not only because they are "in" the Church, but because they are "in the forefront" of the Church, inasmuch as they are configured to Christ, the Head and Shepherd, equipped for and committed to the ordained ministry, and inspired by pastoral charity. Within and as a manifestation of the radicalism of the Gospel one can find a blossoming of many virtues and ethical demands which are decisive for the pastoral and spiritual life of the priest, such as faith, humility in relation to the mystery of God, mercy and prudence. A particularly significant expres-

---

[72] Cf. Second Vatican Ecumenical Council, Dogmatic Constitution on the Church *Lumen Gentium*, 42.

sion of the radicalism of the Gospel is seen in the different "evangelical counsels" which Jesus proposes in the Sermon on the Mount (cf. Mt 5–7), and among them the intimately related counsels of obedience, chastity and poverty.[73] The priest is called to live these counsels in accordance with those ways and, more specifically, those goals and that basic meaning which derive from and express his own priestly identity.

28.1 "Among the virtues most necessary for the priestly ministry must be named that disposition of soul by which priests are always ready to seek not their own will, but the will of him who sent them (cf. Jn 4:34, 5:30, 6:38)."[74] It is in the spiritual life of the priest that obedience takes on certain special characteristics.

28.2 First of all, obedience is *"apostolic"* in the sense that it recognizes, loves and serves the Church in her hierarchical structure. Indeed, there can be no genuine priestly ministry except in communion with the Supreme Pontiff and the Episcopal College, especially with one's own diocesan Bishop, who deserves that "filial respect and obedience" promised during the Rite of Ordination. This "submission" to those invested with ecclesial authority is in no way a kind of humiliation. It flows instead from the responsible freedom of the priest who accepts not only the demands of an organized and organic ecclesial life, but also that grace of discernment and responsibility in ecclesial decisions which was assured by Jesus to his Apostles and their successors, for the sake of faithfully safeguarding the mystery of the Church and serving the structure of the Christian community along its common path toward salvation.

28.3 Authentic Christian obedience, when it is properly motivated and lived without servility, helps the priest to exercise in accordance with the Gospel the authority entrusted to him for his work with the People of God: an authority free from authoritarianism or demagoguery. Only the person who knows how to obey in Christ is really able to require obedience from others in accordance with the Gospel.

28.4 Priestly obedience has also a *"community" dimension:* it is not the obedience of an individual who alone relates to authority, but rather an obedience which is deeply a part of the unity of the presbyterate, which as such is called to cooperate harmoniously with the Bishop and, through him, with Peter's Successor.[75]

---

[73] Cf. *Propositio* 9.

[74] Second Vatican Ecumenical Council, Decree on the Ministry and Life of Priests *Presbyterorum Ordinis,* 15.

[75] Cf. ibid.

28.5 This aspect of the priest's obedience demands a marked spirit of asceticism, both in the sense of a tendency not to become too bound up in one's own preferences or points of view, and in the sense of giving brother priests the opportunity to make good use of their talents, and abilities, setting aside all forms of jealousy, envy and rivalry. Priestly obedience should be one of solidarity, based on belonging to a single presbyterate. Within the presbyterate, this obedience is expressed in coresponsibility regarding directions to be taken and choices to be made.

28.6 Finally, priestly obedience has a particular *"pastoral" character.* It is lived in an atmosphere of constant readiness to allow oneself to be taken up, as it were "consumed," by the needs and demands of the flock. These last ought to be truly reasonable and at times they need to be evaluated and tested to see how genuine they are. But it is undeniable that the priest's life is fully "taken up" by the hunger for the Gospel and for faith, hope and love for God and his mystery, a hunger which is more or less consciously present in the People of God entrusted to him.

29.1 Referring to the evangelical counsels, the Council states that "preeminent among these counsels is that precious gift of divine grace given to some by the Father (cf. Mt 19:11; 1 Cor 7:7) in order more easily to devote themselves to God alone with an undivided heart (cf. 1 Cor 7:32-34) in virginity or celibacy. This perfect continence for love of the Kingdom of heaven has always been held in high esteem by the Church as a sign and stimulus of love, and as a singular source of spiritual fertility in the world."[76] In virginity and celibacy, chastity retains its original meaning, that is, of human sexuality lived as a genuine sign of and precious service to the love of communion and gift of self to others. This meaning is fully found in virginity which makes evident, even in the renunciation of marriage, the "nuptial meaning" of the body through a communion and a personal gift to Jesus Christ and his Church which prefigures and anticipates the perfect and final communion and self-giving of the world to come: "In virginity or celibacy, the human being is awaiting, also in a bodily way, the eschatological marriage of Christ with the Church, giving himself or herself completely to the Church in the hope that Christ may give himself to the Church in the full truth of eternal life."[77]

29.2 In this light one can more easily understand and appreciate the reasons behind the centuries-old choice which the Western Church has made

[76] Dogmatic Constitution on the Church *Lumen Gentium,* 42.
[77] John Paul II, Apostolic Exhortation *Familiaris Consortio* (November 22, 1981), 16: *AAS* 74 (1982), 98.

and maintained — despite all the difficulties and objections raised down the centuries — of conferring the order of presbyter only on men who have given proof that they have been called by God to the gift of chastity in absolute and perpetual celibacy.

29.3 The Synod Fathers clearly and forcefully expressed their thought on this matter in an important proposal which deserves to be quoted here in full: "While in no way interfering with the discipline of the Oriental Churches, the Synod, in the conviction that perfect chastity in priestly celibacy is a charism, reminds priests that celibacy is a priceless gift of God for the Church and has a prophetic value for the world today. This Synod strongly reaffirms what the Latin Church and some Oriental Rites require, that is, that the priesthood be conferred only on those men who have received from God the gift of the vocation to celibate chastity (without prejudice to the tradition of some Oriental Churches and particular cases of married clergy who convert to Catholicism, which are admitted as exceptions in Pope Paul VI's Encyclical on priestly celibacy, No. 42). The Synod does not wish to leave any doubts in the mind of anyone regarding the Church's firm will to maintain the law that demands perpetual and freely chosen celibacy for present and future candidates for priestly ordination in the Latin Rite. The Synod would like to see celibacy presented and explained in the fullness of its biblical, theological and spiritual richness, as a precious gift given by God to his Church and as a sign of the Kingdom which is not of this world, a sign of God's love for this world and of the undivided love of the priest for God and for God's people, with the result that celibacy is seen as a positive enrichment of the priesthood."[78]

29.4 It is especially important that the priest understand the theological motivation of the Church's law on celibacy. Inasmuch as it is a law, it expresses *the Church's will,* even before the will of the subject expressed by his readiness. But the will of the Church finds its ultimate motivation in the *link between celibacy and sacred ordination,* which configures the priest to Jesus Christ the Head and Spouse of the Church. The Church, as the Spouse of Jesus Christ, wishes to be loved by the priest in the total and exclusive manner in which Jesus Christ her Head and Spouse loved her. Priestly celibacy, then, is the gift of self *in* and *with* Christ *to* his Church and expresses the priest's service to the Church in and with the Lord.

29.5 For an adequate priestly spiritual life, celibacy ought not to be considered and lived as an isolated or purely negative element, but as one aspect of the positive, specific and characteristic approach to being a priest. Leaving father and mother, the priest follows Jesus the Good Shepherd in an apostolic

---

[78] *Propositio* 11.

communion, in the service of the People of God. Celibacy, then, is to be welcomed and continually renewed with a free and loving decision as a priceless gift from God, as an "incentive to pastoral charity,"[79] as a singular sharing in God's fatherhood and in the fruitfulness of the Church, and as a witness to the world of the eschatological Kingdom. To put into practice all the moral, pastoral and spiritual demands of priestly celibacy it is absolutely necessary that the priest pray humbly and trustingly, as the Council points out: "In the world today, many people call perfect continence impossible. The more they do so, the more humbly and perseveringly priests should join with the Church in praying for the grace of fidelity. It is never denied to those who ask. At the same time let priests make use of all the supernatural and natural helps which are now available to all."[80] Once again it is prayer, together with the Church's sacraments and ascetical practice, which will provide hope in difficulties, forgiveness in failings, and confidence and courage in resuming the journey.

30.1 On the subject of *evangelical poverty,* the Synod Fathers gave a concise yet important description, presenting it as "the subjection of all goods to the supreme good of God and his Kingdom."[81] In reality, only the person who contemplates and lives the mystery of God as the one and supreme good, as the true and definitive treasure, can understand and practice poverty, which is certainly not a matter of despising or rejecting material goods, but of a loving and responsible use of these goods and at the same time an ability to renounce them with great interior freedom, that is, with reference to God and his plan.

30.2 Poverty for the priest, by virtue of his sacramental configuration to Christ, the Head and Shepherd, takes on specific "pastoral" connotations which the Synod Fathers took up from the Council's teaching[82] and further developed. Among other things, they wrote: "Priests, following the example of Christ who rich though he was became poor for love of us (cf. 2 Cor 8:9), should consider the poor and the weakest as people entrusted in a special way to them and they should be capable of witnessing to poverty with a simple and austere lifestyle, having learned the generous renunciation of superfluous things (cf. *Optatam Totius,* 9; *Code of Canon Law,* Canon 282)."[83]

---

[79] Second Vatican Ecumenical Council, Decree on the Ministry and Life of Priests *Presbyterorum Ordinis,* 16.

[80] Ibid., 16.

[81] *Propositio* 8.

[82] Cf. Decree on the Ministry and Life of Priests *Presbyterorum Ordinis,* 17.

[83] *Propositio* 10.

30.3 It is true that "the workman deserves his wages" (Lk 10:7) and that "the Lord commanded that those who proclaim the Gospel should get their living by the Gospel" (1 Cor 9:14), but it is no less true that this right of the apostle can in no way be confused with attempts of any kind to condition service to the Gospel and the Church upon the advantages and interests which can derive from it. Poverty alone ensures that the priest remains available to be sent wherever his work will be most useful and needed even at the cost of personal sacrifice. It is a condition and essential premise of the apostle's docility to the Spirit, making him ready to "go forth," without traveling bag or personal ties, following only the will of the Master (cf. Lk 9:57-62; Mk 10:17-22).

30.4 Being personally involved in the life of the community and being responsible for it, the priest should also offer the witness of a total "honesty" in the administration of the goods of the community, which he will never treat as if they were his own property, but rather something for which he will be held accountable by God and his brothers and sisters, especially the poor. Moreover, his awareness of belonging to the one presbyterate will be an incentive for the priest to commit himself to promoting both a more equitable distribution of goods among his fellow priests and a certain common use of goods (cf. Acts 2:42-47).

30.5 The interior freedom which is safeguarded and nourished by evangelical poverty will help the priest to stand beside the underprivileged, to practice solidarity with their efforts to create a more just society, to be more sensitive and capable of understanding and discerning realities involving the economic and social aspects of life, and to promote a preferential option for the poor. The latter, while excluding no one from the proclamation and gift of salvation, will assist him in gently approaching the poor, sinners, and all those on the margins of society, following the model given by Jesus in carrying out his prophetic and priestly ministry (cf. Lk 4:18).

30.6 Nor should the prophetic significance of priestly poverty be forgotten, so urgently needed in affluent and consumeristic societies: "A truly poor priest is indeed a specific sign of separation from, disavowal of and non-submission to the tyranny of a contemporary world which puts all its trust in money and in material security."[84]

30.7 Jesus Christ, who brought his pastoral charity to perfection on the Cross with a complete exterior and interior emptying of self, is both the model and source of the virtues of obedience, chastity and poverty which the priest is called to live out as an expression of his pastoral charity for his brothers

---

[84] Ibid.

and sisters. In accordance with Saint Paul's words to the Christians at Philippi, the priest should have "the mind which was in Christ Jesus," emptying himself of his own "self," so as to discover, in a charity which is obedient, chaste and poor, the royal road of union with God and unity with his brothers and sisters (cf. 2:5).

Membership in and dedication to the particular Church

31.1 Like every authentically Christian spiritual life, the spiritual life of the priest has an *essential and undeniable ecclesial dimension* which is a sharing in the holiness of the Church herself, which we profess in the *Creed* to be a "Communion of Saints." The holiness of the Christian has its source in the holiness of the Church; it expresses that holiness and at the same time enriches it. This ecclesial dimension takes on special forms, purposes and meanings in the spiritual life of the priest by virtue of his specific relation to the Church, always as a result of his configuration to Christ the Head and Shepherd, his ordained ministry and his pastoral charity.

31.2 In this perspective, it is necessary to consider the priest's membership in and dedication to a particular Church. These two factors are not the result of purely organizational and disciplinary needs. On the contrary, the priest's relationship with his Bishop in the one presbyterate, his sharing in the Bishop's ecclesial concern, and his devotion to the evangelical care of the People of God in the specific historical and contextual conditions of a particular Church are elements which must be taken into account in sketching the proper configuration of the priest and his spiritual life. In this sense, "incardination" cannot be confined to a purely juridical bond, but also involves a set of attitudes as well as spiritual and pastoral decisions which help to fill out the specific features of the priestly vocation.

31.3 The priest needs to be aware that his "being in a particular Church" constitutes by its very nature a significant element in his living a Christian spirituality. In this sense, the priest finds precisely in his belonging to and dedication to the particular Church a wealth of meaning, criteria for discernment and action which shape both his pastoral mission and his spiritual life.

31.4 Other insights or reference to other traditions of spiritual life can contribute to the priest's journey toward perfection, for these are capable of enriching the life of individual priests as well as enlivening the presbyterate with precious spiritual gifts. Such is the case with many old and new Church associations which welcome priests into their spiritual family: from Societies of Apostolic Life to priestly Secular Institutes, and from various forms of spiritual communion and sharing to ecclesial movements. Priests who belong to

Religious Orders and Congregations represent a spiritual enrichment for the entire diocesan presbyterate, to which they contribute specific charisms and special ministries, stimulating the particular Church by their presence to be more intensely open to the Church throughout the world.[85]

31.5 The priest's membership in a particular Church and his dedication — even to the gift of his life — to the upbuilding of the Church, "in the person" of Christ the Head and Shepherd, in service of the entire Christian community and in a generous and filial relationship with the Bishop, must be strengthened by every charism which becomes part of his priestly life or surrounds it.[86]

31.6 For the abundance of the Spirit's gifts to be welcomed with joy and allowed to bear fruit for the glory of God and the good of the entire Church, each person is required first to have a knowledge and discernment of his or her own charisms and those of others, and always to use these charisms with Christian humility, with firm self-control and with the intention, above all else, to help build up the entire community which each particular charism is meant to serve. Moreover, all are required to make a sincere effort to live in mutual esteem, to respect others and to hold in esteem all the positive and legitimate diversities present in the presbyterate. This too constitutes part of the priest's spiritual life and continual practice of asceticism.

32.1 Membership in and dedication to a particular Church does not limit the activity and life of the presbyterate to that Church: a restriction of this sort is not possible, given the very nature both of the particular Church[87] and of the priestly ministry. In this regard the Council teaches that "the spiritual gift which priests received at their ordination prepares them not for any limited or narrow mission but for the widest scope of the universal mission of salvation 'to the end of the earth' (Acts 1:8). For every priestly ministry shares in the universality of the mission entrusted by Christ to his Apostles."[88]

32.2 It thus follows that the spiritual life of the priest should be profoundly marked by a missionary zeal and dynamism. In the exercise of their ministry

---

[85] Cf. Congregation for Religious and Secular Institutes and Congregation for Bishops, Directives for Mutual Relations Between Bishops and Religious in the Church *Mutuae Relationes* (May 14, 1978), 18: *AAS* 70 (1978), 484-485.

[86] Cf. *Propositiones* 25, 38.

[87] Cf. Second Vatican Ecumenical Council, Dogmatic Constitution on the Church *Lumen Gentium*, 23.

[88] Decree on the Ministry and Life of Priests *Presbyterorum Ordinis*, 10; cf. *Propositio* 12.

and the witness of their lives, priests have the duty to form the community entrusted to them as a truly missionary community. As I wrote in the Encyclical *Redemptoris Missio:* "all priests must have the mind and heart of missionaries open to the needs of the Church and the world, with concern for those farthest away and especially for the non-Christian groups in their own area. They should have at heart, in their prayers and particularly at the Eucharistic Sacrifice, the concern of the whole Church for all of humanity."[89]

32.3 If the lives of priests are generously inspired by this missionary spirit, it will be easier to respond to that increasingly serious demand of the Church today which arises from the unequal distribution of the clergy. In this regard, the Council was both quite clear and forceful: "Let priests remember then that they must have at heart the care of all the Churches. Hence priests belonging to Dioceses which are rich in vocations should show themselves willing and ready, with the permission or at the urging of their own Bishop, to exercise their ministry in other regions, missions or activities which suffer from a shortage of clergy."[90]

"Renew in them the outpouring of your Spirit of holiness"

33.1 "The Spirit of the Lord is upon me, because he has anointed me to preach good news to the poor" (Lk 4:18). Even today Christ makes these words which he proclaimed in the synagogue of Nazareth echo in our priestly hearts. Indeed, our faith reveals to us the presence of the Spirit of Christ at work in our being, in our acting and in our living, just as the Sacrament of Orders has configured, equipped and molded it.

33.2 *Yes, the Spirit of the Lord is the principal agent in our spiritual life.* He creates our "new heart," inspires it and guides it with the "new law" of love, of pastoral charity. For the development of the spiritual life it is essential to be aware that the priest will never lack the grace of the Holy Spirit as a totally gratuitous gift and as a task which he is called to undertake. Awareness of this gift is the foundation and support of the priest's unflagging trust amid the difficulties, temptations and weaknesses which he will meet along his spiritual path.

33.3 Here I would repeat to all priests what I said to so many of them on another occasion: "The priestly vocation is essentially a call to holiness in the form which derives from the Sacrament of Orders. Holiness is intimacy with God; it is the imitation of Christ, who was poor, chaste and humble; it is unreserved love for souls and a giving of oneself on their behalf and for their

---

[89] Encyclical Letter *Redemptoris Missio* (December 7, 1990), 67: *AAS* 83 (1991), 315-316.
[90] Decree on the Ministry and Life of Priests *Presbyterorum Ordinis,* 10.

true good; it is love for the Church which is holy and wants us to be holy, because this is the mission that Christ entrusted to her. Each one of you should also be holy in order to help your brothers and sisters to pursue their vocation to holiness.

33.4 "How can we fail to reflect on . . . the essential role that the Holy Spirit carries out in this particular call to holiness which is proper to the priestly ministry? Let us remember the words of the Rite of Priestly Ordination which are considered to be central in the sacramental formula: 'Almighty Father, give these your sons the dignity of the priesthood. Renew in them the outpouring of your Spirit of holiness. O Lord, may they fulfill the ministry of the second degree of priesthood received from you, and by their example may they lead all to upright conduct of life.'

33.5 "Beloved, through ordination, you have received the same Spirit of Christ, who makes you like him, so that you can act in his name and so that his very mind and heart might live in you. This intimate communion with the Spirit of Christ, while guaranteeing the efficacy of the sacramental actions which you perform *in persona Christi*, seeks to be expressed in fervent prayer, in integrity of life, in the pastoral charity of a ministry tirelessly spending itself for the salvation of the brethren. In a word, it calls for your personal sanctification."[91]

IV

Come and See

Priestly Vocation in the Church's Pastoral Work

Seek, follow, abide

34.1 *"Come, and see"* (Jn 1:39). This was the reply Jesus gave to the two disciples of John the Baptist who asked him where he was staying. In these words we find the meaning of vocation.

34.2 This is how the Evangelist relates the call of Andrew and Peter: "The next day again John was standing with two of his disciples; and he looked at Jesus as he walked, and said, 'Behold, the Lamb of God!' The two disciples

[91] Homily to 5,000 Priests from throughout the World (October 9, 1984), 2: *Insegnamenti* VII/2 (1984), 839.

heard him say this, and they followed Jesus. Jesus turned, and saw them following, and said to them, 'What do you seek?' And they said to him, 'Rabbi' (which means Teacher), 'Where are you staying?' He said to them, 'Come and see.' They came and saw where he was staying; and they stayed with him that day, for it was about the tenth hour.

34.3 "One of the two who heard John speak, and followed him, was Andrew, Simon Peter's brother. He first found his brother, Simon, and said to him, 'We have found the Messiah' (which means Christ). He brought him to Jesus. Jesus looked at him, and said, 'So you are Simon the son of John? You shall be called Cephas' (which means Peter)" (Jn 1:35-42).

34.4 This Gospel passage is one of many in the Bible where the "mystery" of vocation is described, in our case the mystery of the vocation to be Apostles of Jesus. This passage of John, which is also significant for the Christian vocation as such, has a particular value with regard to the priestly vocation. As the community of Jesus' disciples, the Church is called to contemplate this scene which in some way is renewed constantly down the ages. The Church is invited to delve more deeply into the original and personal meaning of the call to follow Christ in the priestly ministry and the unbreakable bond between divine grace and human responsibility which is contained and revealed in these two terms which we find more than once in the Gospel: *come, follow me* (cf. Mt 19:21). She is asked to discern and to live out the proper dynamism of vocation, its gradual and concrete development in the phases of *seeking Christ, finding him* and *staying with him*.

34.5 The Church gathers from this *"Gospel of vocation"* the paradigm, strength and impulse behind her pastoral work of promoting vocations, of her mission to care for the birth, discernment and fostering of vocations, particularly those to the priesthood. By the very fact that "the lack of priests is certainly a sad thing for any Church,"[92] pastoral work for vocations needs, especially today, to be taken up with a new vigor and more decisive commitment by all the members of the Church, in the awareness that it is not a secondary or marginal matter, or the business of one group only, as if it were but a "part," no matter how important, of the entire pastoral work of the Church. Rather, as the Synod Fathers frequently repeated, it is an essential part of the overall pastoral work of each Church,[93] a concern which demands to be integrated into and fully identified with the ordinary "care of souls,"[94] a connatural

---

[92] John Paul II, Address at the Closing of the Synod of Bishops, Eighth Ordinary General Assembly (October 27, 1990), 5: *AAS* 83 (1991), 497.

[93] Cf. *Propositio* 6.

[94] Cf. *Propositio* 13.

and essential dimension of the Church's pastoral work, of her very life and mission.[95]

34.6 Indeed, *concern for vocations is a connatural and essential dimension of the Church's pastoral work.* The reason for this is that vocation, in a certain sense, defines the very being of the Church, even before her activity. In the Church's very name, *Ecclesia,* we find its deep vocational aspect, for the Church is a "convocation," an *assembly of those who have been called:* "All those who in faith look toward Jesus, the author of salvation and the principle of unity and peace, God has gathered together and established as the Church, that she may be for each and everyone the visible sacrament of this saving unity."[96]

34.7 A genuinely theological assessment of priestly vocation and pastoral work in its regard can only arise from an assessment of the mystery of the Church as a *mysterium vocationis.*

The Church and the gift of vocation

35.1 Every Christian vocation finds its foundation in the gratuitous and prevenient choice made by the Father "who has blessed us in Christ with every spiritual blessing in the heavenly places, even as he chose us in him before the foundation of the world, that we should be holy and blameless before him. He destined us in love to be his sons through Jesus Christ, according to the purpose of his will" (Eph 1:3-5).

35.2 Each Christian vocation comes from God and is God's gift. However, it is never bestowed outside of or independently of the Church. Instead it always comes about in the Church and through the Church because, as the Second Vatican Council reminds us, "God has willed to make men holy and save them, not as individuals without any bond or link between them, but rather to make them into a people who might acknowledge him and serve him in holiness."[97]

35.3 The Church not only embraces in herself all the vocations which God gives her along the path to salvation, but she herself appears as a mystery of vocation, a luminous and living reflection of the mystery of the Blessed Trinity. In truth, the Church, a "people made one by the unity of the Father, the Son and the Holy Spirit,"[98] carries within her the mystery of the Father, who, being neither called nor sent by anyone (cf. Rom 11:33-35), calls all to hallow his name and do his will; she guards within herself the mystery of the Son,

---

[95] Cf. *Propositio* 4.

[96] Second Vatican Ecumenical Council, Dogmatic Constitution on the Church *Lumen Gentium,* 9.

[97] Ibid.

[98] Saint Cyprian, *De Dominica Oratione,* 23: *CCL* 3/A, 105.

who is called by the Father and sent to proclaim the Kingdom of God to all and who calls all to follow him; and she is the trustee of the mystery of the Holy Spirit, who consecrates for mission those whom the Father calls through his Son Jesus Christ.

35.4 The Church, being by her very nature a "vocation," is also a *begetter and educator of vocations.* This is so because she is a "sacrament," a "sign" and "instrument" in which the vocation of every Christian is reflected and lived out. And she is so in her activity, in the exercise of her ministry of proclaiming the word, in her celebration of the sacraments and in her service and witness to charity.

35.5 We can now see the *essential dimension of the Christian vocation:* not only does it derive "from" the Church and her mediation, not only does it come to be known and find fulfillment "in" the Church, but it also necessarily appears — in fundamental service to God — as a service "to" the Church. Christian vocation, whatever shape it takes, is a gift whose purpose is to build up the Church and to increase the Kingdom of God in the world.[99]

35.6 What is true of every vocation is true specifically of the priestly vocation: the latter is a call, by the Sacrament of Holy Orders received in the Church, to place oneself at the service of the People of God with a particular belonging and configuration to Jesus Christ and with the authority of acting "in the name and in the person" of him who is Head and Shepherd of the Church.

35.7 From this point of view, we understand the statement of the Synod Fathers: "The vocation of each priest exists in the Church and for the Church: through her this vocation is brought to fulfillment. Hence we can say that every priest receives his vocation from our Lord through the Church as a gracious gift, a grace *gratis data (charisma).* It is the task of the Bishop or the competent superior not only to examine the suitability and the vocation of the candidate but also to recognize it. This ecclesiastical element is inherent in a vocation to the priestly ministry as such. The candidate to the priesthood should receive his vocation not by imposing his own personal conditions, but accepting also the norms and conditions which the Church herself lays down, in the fulfillment of her responsibility."[100]

The vocational dialogue: divine initiative and human response

36.1 The history of every priestly vocation, as indeed of every Christian vocation, is the history of an *inexpressible dialogue between God and human*

---

[99] Cf. Second Vatican Ecumenical Council, Decree on the Apostolate of the Laity *Apostolicam Actuositatem,* 3.

[100] *Propositio* 5.

beings, between the love of God who calls and the freedom of individuals who respond lovingly to him. These two indivisible aspects of vocation, God's gratuitous gift and man's responsible freedom, are reflected in a splendid and very effective way in the brief words with which the Evangelist Mark presents the calling of the Twelve: Jesus "went up into the hills, and *called* to him those *whom he desired;* and *they came* to him" (3:13). On the one hand, we have the completely free decision of Jesus; on the other, the "coming" of the Twelve, their "following" Jesus.

36.2 This is the constant paradigm, the fundamental datum of every vocation: whether of Prophets, Apostles, priests, Religious, the lay faithful — of everyone.

36.3 First of all, indeed in a prevenient and decisive way, comes *the free and gracious intervention of God who calls.* It is God who takes the initiative in the call. This was, for example, the experience of the Prophet Jeremiah: "Now the word of the Lord came to me saying, 'Before I formed you in the womb I knew you, and before you were born I consecrated you; I appointed you prophet to the nations'" (Jer 1:4-5). The same truth is presented by the Apostle Paul, who roots every vocation in the eternal election in Christ, made "before the foundation of the world" and "according to the purpose of his will" (Eph 1:4-5). The absolute primacy of grace in vocation is most perfectly proclaimed in the words of Jesus: "You did not choose me, but I chose you and appointed you that you should go and bear fruit and that your fruit should abide" (Jn 15:16).

36.4 If the priestly vocation bears unequivocal witness to the primacy of grace, God's free and sovereign decision to call man calls for total respect. It cannot be forced in the slightest by any human ambition, and it cannot be replaced by any human decision. Vocation is a gift of God's grace and never a human right, such that "one can never consider priestly life as a simply human affair, nor the mission of the minister as a simply personal project."[101] Every claim or presumption on the part of those called is thus radically excluded (cf. Heb 5:4-10). Their entire heart and spirit should be filled with an amazed and deeply felt gratitude, an unshakable trust and hope, because those who have been called know that they are rooted not in their own strength but in the unconditional faithfulness of God who calls.

36.5 "He called to him those whom he desired; and they came to him" (Mk 3:13). This "coming," which is the same as "following" Jesus, expresses the free response of the Twelve to the Master's call. We see it in the case of Peter and Andrew: "And he said to them, 'Follow me and I will make you fishers of

---

[101] John Paul II, Angelus (December 3, 1989), 2: *Insegnamenti* XII/2 (1989), 1417.

men.' Immediately they left their nets and followed him" (Mt 4:19-20). The experience of James and John was exactly the same (cf. Mt 4:21-22). And so it is always: in vocation there shine out at the same time God's gracious love and the highest possible exaltation of human freedom: the freedom of following God's call and entrusting oneself to him.

36.6 In effect, grace and freedom are not opposed. On the contrary, grace enlivens and sustains human freedom, setting it free from the slavery of sin (cf. Jn 8:34-36), healing it and elevating it in its ability to be open to receiving God's gift. And if we cannot in any way minimize the absolutely gratuitous initiative of God who calls, neither can we in any way minimize the serious responsibility which man faces in the challenge of his freedom. And so when he hears Jesus' invitation to "Come, follow me" the rich young man refuses, a sign — albeit only a negative sign — of his freedom: "At that saying his countenance fell, and he went away sorrowful; for he had great possessions" (Mk 10:22).

36.7 *Freedom,* therefore, *is essential to vocation,* a freedom which, when it gives a positive response, appears as a deep personal adherence, as a loving gift, or rather as a gift given back to the Giver who is God who calls, an oblation: "The call" — Paul VI once said — "is as extensive as the response. There cannot be vocations unless they be free; that is, unless they be spontaneous offerings of oneself, conscious, generous, total. . . . Oblations, we call them: here lies in practice the heart of the matter. . . . It is the humble and penetrating voice of Christ who says, today, as yesterday, and even more than yesterday: come. Freedom reaches its supreme foundation: precisely that of oblation, of generosity, of sacrifice."[102]

36.8 The free oblation, which constitutes the intimate and most precious core of a person's response to God who calls, finds its incomparable model, indeed its living root, in the most free oblation which Jesus Christ, the first of those called, made to the Father's will: "Consequently, when Christ came into the world, he said, 'Sacrifices and offerings you have not desired, but a body have you prepared for me; . . . Then I said, lo, I have come to do your will, O God' " (Heb 10:5, 7).

36.9 The creature who more than any other has lived the full truth of vocation is Mary the Virgin Mother, and she did so in intimate communion with Christ: no one has responded with a love greater than hers to the immense love of God.[103]

---

[102] Message for the 5th World Day of Prayer for Priestly Vocations (April 19, 1968): *Insegnamenti* VI (1968), 134-135.
[103] Cf. *Propositio* 5.

37.1 "At that saying his countenance fell, and he went away sorrowful; for he had great possessions" (Mk 10:22). The rich young man in the Gospel who did not follow Jesus' call reminds us of the obstacles preventing or eliminating one's free response: material goods are not the only things that can shut the human heart to the values of the Spirit and the radical demands of the Kingdom of God; certain social and cultural conditions of our day can also present many threats and can impose distorted and false visions about the true nature of vocation, making it difficult, if not impossible, to embrace or even to understand it.

37.2 Many people have such a general and confused idea of God that their religiosity becomes a religiosity without God, where God's will is seen as an immutable and unavoidable fate to which one has to bend and resign oneself in a totally passive manner. But this is not the face of God which Jesus Christ came to reveal to us: God is truly a Father who with an eternal and prevenient love calls human beings and opens up with them a marvelous and permanent dialogue, inviting them, as his children, to share his own divine life. It is true that if human beings have an erroneous vision of God they cannot even recognize the truth about themselves, and thus they will be unable to perceive or live their vocation in its genuine value: vocation will be felt only as a crushing burden imposed upon them.

37.3 Certain distorted ideas regarding human nature, sometimes backed up by specious philosophical or "scientific" theories, also sometimes lead people to consider their own existence and freedom as totally determined and conditioned by external factors of an educational, psychological, cultural or environmental type. In other cases, freedom is understood in terms of total autonomy, the sole and indisputable basis for personal choices, and effectively as self-affirmation at any cost. But these ways of thinking make it impossible to understand and live one's vocation as a free dialogue of love, which arises from the communication of God to man and ends in the sincere gift of self.

37.4 In the present context there is also a certain tendency to view the bond between human beings and God in an individualistic and self-centered way, as if God's call reached the individual by a direct route, without in any way passing through the community. Its purpose is held to be the benefit, or the very salvation, of the individual called and not a total dedication to God in the service of the community. We thus find another very deep and at the same time subtle threat which makes it impossible to recognize and accept joyfully the ecclesial dimension which naturally marks every Christian vocation, and the priestly vocation in particular: as the Council reminds us, priestly ministry acquires its genuine meaning and attains to its fullest truth in serving and in fostering the growth of the Christian community and the common priesthood of the faithful.[104]

37.5 The cultural context which we have just recalled, and which affects Christians themselves and especially young people, helps us to understand the spread of the crisis of priestly vocations, a crisis that is rooted in and accompanied by even more radical crises of faith. The Synod Fathers made this very point when recognizing that the crisis of vocations to the priesthood has deep roots in the cultural environment and in the outlook and practical behavior of Christians.[105]

37.6 Hence the urgent need that the Church's pastoral work in promoting vocations be aimed decisively and primarily toward restoring a "Christian mentality," one built on faith and sustained by it. More than ever, what is now needed is an evangelization which never tires of pointing to the true face of God, the Father who calls each one of us in Jesus Christ, and to the genuine meaning of human freedom as the principal driving force behind the responsible gift of oneself. Only thus will the indispensable foundations be laid, so that every vocation, including the priestly vocation, will be perceived for what it really is, loved in its beauty and lived out with total dedication and deep joy.

Content and methods of pastoral work for promoting vocations

38.1 Certainly a vocation is a fathomless mystery involving the relationship established by God with human beings in their absolute uniqueness, a mystery perceived and heard as a call which awaits a response in the depths of one's conscience, which is "man's most secret core and sanctuary. There he is alone with God whose voice echoes in his depths."[106] But this does not eliminate the communitarian and in particular the ecclesial dimension of vocation. The Church is also truly present and at work in the vocation of every priest.

38.2 In her service to the priestly vocation and its development, that is, in the birth, discernment and care of each vocation, the Church can look for her model to Andrew, one of the first two disciples who set out to follow Jesus. Andrew himself told his brother what had happened to him: " 'We have found the Messiah' (which means Christ)" (Jn 1:41). His account of this "discovery" opened the way to a meeting: *"He brought him to Jesus"* (Jn 1:42). There can

---

[104] Cf. Dogmatic Constitution on the Church *Lumen Gentium,* 10; Decree on the Ministry and Life of Priests *Presbyterorum Ordinis,* 12.

[105] Cf. *Propositio* 13.

[106] Second Vatican Ecumenical Council, Pastoral Constitution on the Church in the Modern World *Gaudium et Spes,* 16.

be no doubt about the absolutely free initiative nor about the sovereign decision of Jesus. It is Jesus who calls Simon and gives him a new name: "Jesus looked at him, and said, 'So you are Simon the son of John? You shall be called Cephas' (which means Peter)" (Jn 1:42). But Andrew also acted with initiative: he arranged his brother's meeting with Jesus.

38.3 *"He brought him to Jesus."* In a way, this is the heart of all the Church's pastoral work on behalf of vocations, in which she cares for the birth and growth of vocations, making use of the gifts and responsibilities, of the charisms and ministry she has received from Christ and his Spirit. The Church, as a priestly, prophetic and kingly people, is committed to foster and to serve the birth and maturing of priestly vocations through her prayer and sacramental life, by her proclamation of the word and by education in the faith, by her example and witness of charity.

38.4 The Church, in her dignity and responsibility as a priestly people, possesses in *prayer* and in the celebration of the *liturgy the essential and primary stages of her pastoral work for vocations.* Indeed, Christian prayer, nourished by the word of God, creates an ideal environment where each individual can discover the truth of his own being and the identity of the personal and unrepeatable life project which the Father entrusts to him. It is therefore necessary to educate boys and young men so that they will become faithful to prayer and meditation on God's word: in silence and listening, they will be able to perceive the Lord who is calling them to the priesthood, and be able to follow that call promptly and generously.

38.5 The Church should daily take up Jesus' persuasive and demanding invitation to "pray the Lord of the harvest to send out laborers into his harvest" (Mt 9:38). Obedient to Christ's command, the Church first of all makes a humble profession of faith: in praying for vocations, conscious of her urgent need of them for her very life and mission, she acknowledges that they are a gift of God and, as such, must be asked for by a ceaseless and trusting prayer of petition. This prayer, the pivot of all pastoral work for vocations, is required not only of individuals but of entire ecclesial communities. There can be no doubt about the importance of individual initiatives of prayer, of special times set apart for such prayer, beginning with the World Day of Prayer for Vocations, and of the explicit commitment of persons and groups particularly concerned with the problem of priestly vocations. Today the prayerful expectation of new vocations should become an ever more continual and widespread habit within the entire Christian community and in every one of its parts. Thus it will be possible to relive the experience of the Apostles in the Upper Room who, in union with Mary, prayerfully awaited the outpouring of the

Spirit (cf. Acts 1:14), who will not fail to raise up once again in the People of God "worthy ministers for the altar, ardent but gentle proclaimers of the Gospel."[107]

38.6 In addition, the liturgy, as the summit and source of the Church's existence[108] and in particular of all Christian prayer, plays an influential and indispensable role in the pastoral work of promoting vocations. The liturgy is a living experience of God's gift and a great school for learning how to respond to his call. As such, every liturgical celebration, and especially the Eucharist, reveals to us the true face of God and grants us a share in the Paschal Mystery, in the "hour" for which Jesus came into the world and toward which he freely and willingly made his way in obedience to the Father's call (cf. Jn 13:1). It shows us the Church as a priestly people and a community structured in the variety and complementarity of its charisms and vocations. The redemptive sacrifice of Christ, which the Church celebrates in mystery, accords a particular value to suffering endured in union with the Lord Jesus. The Synod Fathers invited us never to forget that "through the offering of sufferings, which are so frequent in human life, the Christian who is ill offers himself as a victim to God, in the image of Christ, who has consecrated himself for us all (cf. Jn 17:19)" and that "the offering of sufferings for this intention is a great help in fostering vocations."[109]

39.1 In carrying out her prophetic role, the Church feels herself irrevocably committed to the task of *proclaiming and witnessing to the Christian meaning of vocation,* or as we might say, to "the Gospel of vocation." Here too, she feels the urgency of the Apostle's exclamation: "Woe to me if I do not preach the Gospel!" (1 Cor 9:16). This admonishment rings out especially for us who are pastors but, together with us, it touches all educators in the Church. Preaching and catechesis must always show their intrinsic vocational dimension: the word of God enlightens believers to appreciate life as a response to God's call and leads them to embrace in faith the gift of a personal vocation.

39.2 But all this, however important and even essential, is not enough: we need a "direct preaching on the mystery of vocation in the Church, on the value of the ministerial priesthood, on God's people's urgent need of it."[110] A

---

[107] Roman Missal, Collect of the Mass for Vocations to Holy Orders.
[108] Cf. Second Vatican Ecumenical Council, Constitution on the Sacred Liturgy *Sacrosanctum Concilium,* 10.
[109] *Propositio* 15.
[110] Ibid.

properly structured catechesis, directed to all the members of the Church, in addition to dissipating doubts and countering one-sided or distorted ideas about priestly ministry, will open believers' hearts to expect the gift and create favorable conditions for the birth of new vocations. The time has come to speak courageously about priestly life as a priceless gift and a splendid and privileged form of Christian living. Educators, and priests in particular, should not be afraid to set forth explicitly and forcefully the priestly vocation as a real possibility for those young people who demonstrate the necessary gifts and talents. There should be no fear that one is thereby conditioning them or limiting their freedom; quite the contrary, a clear invitation, made at the right time, can be decisive in eliciting from young people a free and genuine response. Besides, the history of the Church and that of many individual priests whose vocations blossomed at a young age bear ample witness to how providential the presence and conversation of a priest can be: not only his words, but his very presence, a concrete and joyful witness which can raise questions and lead to decisions, even definitive ones.

40.1 As a kingly people, the Church sees herself rooted in and enlivened by "the law of the Spirit of life" (Rom 8:2), which is essentially the royal law of charity (cf. Jas 2:8) or the perfect law of freedom (cf. Jas 1:25). Therefore, the Church fulfills her mission when *she guides every member of the faithful to discover and live his or her own vocation in freedom and to bring it to fulfillment in charity.*

40.2 In carrying out her educational role, the Church aims with special concern at developing in children, adolescents and young men a desire and a will to follow Jesus Christ in a total and attractive way. This educational work, while addressed to the Christian community as such, must also be aimed at the individual person: indeed, God with his call reaches the heart of each individual, and the Spirit, who abides deep within each disciple (cf. 1 Jn 3:24), gives himself to each Christian with different charisms and special signs. Each one, therefore, must be helped to embrace the gift entrusted to him as a completely unique person, and to hear the words which the Spirit of God personally addresses to him.

40.3 From this point of view, the pastoral work of promoting vocations to the priesthood will also be able to find expression in a firm and encouraging invitation to *spiritual direction.* It is necessary to rediscover the great tradition of personal spiritual guidance which has always brought great and precious fruits to the Church's life. In certain cases and under precise conditions this work can be assisted, but not replaced, by forms of analysis or psychological help.[111] Children, adolescents and young men are invited to discover and appreciate the gift of spiritual direction, to look for it and experience it, and to ask for it with trusting insistence from those who are their educators in the faith. Priests, for their part, should be the first to devote time and energies to this work of education and personal spiritual guidance: they will never regret having neglected or put in second place so many other things which are themselves good and useful, if this proved necessary for them to be faithful to their ministry as cooperators of the Spirit in enlightening and guiding those who have been called.

40.4 The aim of education for a Christian is to attain the "stature of the fullness of Christ" (Eph 4:13) under the influence of the Spirit. This happens when, imitating and sharing Christ's charity, a person turns his entire life into an act of loving service (cf. Jn 13:14-15), offering to God a spiritual worship acceptable to him (cf. Rom 12:1) and giving himself to his brothers and sisters. *The service of love is the fundamental meaning of every vocation,* and it finds a specific expression in the priestly vocation. Indeed, a priest is called to live out, as radically as possible, the pastoral charity of Jesus, the love of the Good Shepherd who "lays down his life for the sheep" (Jn 10:11).

40.5 Consequently, an authentic pastoral work on behalf of vocations will never tire of training boys, adolescents and young men to appreciate commitment, the meaning of free service, the value of sacrifice and unconditional self-giving. In this context it is easy to see the great value of forms of volunteer work, which so many young people are growing to appreciate. If volunteer work is inspired by the Gospel values, capable of training people to discern true needs, lived with dedication and faithfulness each day, open to the possibility of a total commitment in consecrated life and nourished in prayer, then it will be more readily able to sustain a life of disinterested and free commitment and will make the one involved in it more sensitive to the voice of God who may be calling him to the priesthood. Unlike the rich young man, the person involved in volunteer work would be able to accept the invitation lovingly addressed to him by Jesus (cf. Mk 10:21); and he would be able to accept it because his only wealth now consists in giving himself to others and in "losing" his life.

We are all responsible for priestly vocations

41.1 The priestly vocation is a gift from God. It is undoubtedly a great good for the person who is its first recipient. But it is also a gift to the Church as a whole, a benefit to her life and mission. The Church, therefore, is called to

---

[111] Cf. Code of Canon Law, Canon 220: "It is not lawful for anyone . . . to violate the right which each person has of defending his own privacy"; cf. Canon 642.

safeguard this gift, to esteem it and love it. She is responsible for the birth and development of priestly vocations. Consequently, the pastoral work of promoting vocations has as its active agents, as its protagonists, the ecclesial community as such, in its various expressions: from the universal Church to the particular Church and, by analogy, from the particular Church to each of its parishes and to every part of the People of God.

41.2 There is an urgent need, especially nowadays, for a more widespread and deeply felt conviction that *all the members of the Church, without exception, have the grace and responsibility to look after vocations.* The Second Vatican Council was quite explicit in this regard: "The duty of fostering vocations falls on the whole Christian community, and they should discharge it principally by living full Christian lives."[112] Only on the basis of this conviction will pastoral work on behalf of vocations be able to show its truly ecclesial aspect, develop a harmonious plan of action, and make use of specific agencies and appropriate instruments of communion and coresponsibility.

41.3 The first responsibility for the pastoral work of promoting priestly vocations lies with the *Bishop,*[113] who is called to be the first to exercise this responsibility, even though he can and must call upon many others to cooperate with him. As the father and friend of his presbyterate, it falls primarily to the Bishop to be concerned about "giving continuity" to the priestly charism and ministry, bringing it new forces by the laying on of hands. He will be actively concerned to ensure that the vocational dimension is always present in the whole range of ordinary pastoral work, and that it is fully integrated and practically identified with it. It is his duty to foster and coordinate various initiatives on behalf of vocations.[114]

41.4 The Bishop can rely above all on the cooperation of his presbyterate. All its *priests* are united to him and share his responsibility in seeking and fostering priestly vocations. Indeed, as the Council states, "it is the priests' part as instructors of the people in the faith to see to it that each member of the faithful shall be led in the Holy Spirit to the full development of his own vocation."[115] "This duty belongs to the very nature of the priestly ministry which makes the priest share in the concern of the whole Church lest laborers should ever be wanting to the People of God here on earth."[116] The very life of

[112] Decree on Priestly Formation *Optatam Totius,* 2.
[113] Cf. Second Vatican Ecumenical Council, Decree on the Bishops' Pastoral Office in the Church *Christus Dominus,* 15.
[114] Cf. Second Vatican Ecumenical Council, Decree on Priestly Formation *Optatam Totius,* 2.
[115] Decree on the Ministry and Life of Priests *Presbyterorum Ordinis,* 6.
[116] Ibid., 11.

priests, their unconditional dedication to God's flock, their witness of loving service to the Lord and to his Church — a witness marked by free acceptance of the Cross in the spirit of hope and Easter joy — their fraternal unity and zeal for the evangelization of the world are the first and most convincing factor in the growth of vocations.[117]

41.5 A very special responsibility falls upon the *Christian family,* which by virtue of the Sacrament of Matrimony shares in its own unique way in the educational mission of the Church, Teacher and Mother. As the Synod Fathers wrote: "The Christian family, which is truly a 'domestic Church' (*Lumen Gentium,* 11), has always offered and continues to offer favorable conditions for the birth of vocations. Since the reality of the Christian family is endangered nowadays, much importance should be given to pastoral work on behalf of the family, in order that the families themselves, generously accepting the gift of human life, may be 'as it were, a first seminary' (*Optatam Totius,* 2) in which children can acquire from the beginning an awareness of piety and prayer and love for the Church."[118] Following upon and in harmony with the work of parents and the family, is the *school,* which is called to live its identity as an "educating community," also by providing a correct understanding of the dimension of vocation as an innate and fundamental value of the human person. In this sense, if it is endowed with a Christian spirit (either by a significant presence of members of the Church in State schools, following the laws of each country, or above all in the case of the Catholic school), it can infuse "in the hearts of boys and young men a desire to do God's will in that state in life which is most suitable to each person, and never excluding the vocation to the priestly ministry."[119]

41.6 The *lay faithful* also, and particularly catechists, teachers, educators and youth ministers, each with his or her own resources and style, have great importance in the pastoral work of promoting priestly vocations: the more they inculcate a deep appreciation of young people's vocation and mission in the Church, the more they will be able to recognize the unique value of the priestly vocation and mission.

41.7 With regard to diocesan and parish communities, special appreciation and encouragement should be given to *groups which promote vocations,* whose members make an important contribution by prayer and sufferings offered up for priestly and religious vocations, as well as by moral and material support.

---

[117] Cf. Second Vatican Ecumenical Council, Decree on Priestly Formation *Optatam Totius,* 2.
[118] *Propositio* 14.
[119] *Propositio* 15.

41.8 We should also remember the numerous *groups, movements and associations of lay faithful* whom the Holy Spirit raises up and fosters in the Church with a view to a more missionary Christian presence in the world. These various groupings of lay people are proving a particularly fertile field for the manifestation of vocations to consecrated life, and are truly environments in which vocations can be encouraged and can grow. Many young people, in and through these groupings, have heard the Lord's call to follow him along the path of priestly ministry[120] and have responded with a generosity that is reassuring. These groupings, therefore, are to be utilized well, so that in communion with the whole Church and for the sake of her growth they may make their proper contribution to the development of the pastoral work of promoting vocations.

41.9 The various elements and members of the Church involved in the pastoral work of promoting vocations will make their work more effective insofar as they stimulate the ecclesial community as such, starting with the parish, to sense that the problem of priestly vocations cannot in any way be delegated to some "official" group (priests in general and the priests working in the seminary in particular), for inasmuch as it is "a vital problem which lies at the very heart of the Church,"[121] it should be at the heart of the love which each Christian feels for the Church.

V

He Appointed Twelve To Be with Him

The Formation of Candidates for the Priesthood

Following Christ as the Apostles did

42.1 "And he went up on the mountain, and called to him those whom he desired; and they came to him. And he appointed twelve, to be with him, and to be sent out to preach and have authority to cast out demons" (Mk 3:13-15).

42.2 *"To be with him"*: it is not difficult to find in these words a reference to Jesus' "accompanying" the Apostles for the sake of their vocation. After calling them and before he sends them out, indeed in order to be able to send them

---

[120] Cf. *Propositio* 16.
[121] John Paul II, Message for the 22nd World Day of Prayer for Priestly Vocations (April 13 1985), 1: *AAS* 77 (1985), 982.

out to preach, Jesus asks them to set aside a "period of time" for formation. The aim of this time is to develop a relationship of deep communion and friendship with himself. In this time they receive the benefit of a catechesis that is deeper than the teaching he gives to the people (cf. Mt 13:11); also he wishes them to be witnesses of his silent prayer to the Father (cf. Jn 17:1-26; Lk 22:39-45).

42.3 In her care for priestly vocations the Church in every age draws her inspiration from Christ's example. There have been, and to some extent there still are, *many different practical forms* according to which the Church has been involved in the pastoral care of vocations. Her task is not only to discern but also to "accompany" priestly vocations. But *the spirit* which must inspire and sustain her *remains the same:* that of bringing to the priesthood only those who have been called, and to bring them adequately trained, namely, with a conscious and free response of adherence and involvement of their whole person with Jesus Christ who calls them to intimacy of life with him and to share in his mission of salvation. In this sense, the "seminary" in its different forms, and analogously the "house" of formation for Religious priests, more than a place, a material space, should be a spiritual place, a way of life, an atmosphere that fosters and ensures a process of formation, so that the person who is called to the priesthood by God may become, with the Sacrament of Orders, a living image of Jesus Christ, Head and Shepherd of the Church. In their *Final Message* the Synod Fathers have grasped in a direct and deep way the original and specific meaning of the formation of candidates for the priesthood, when they say that "to live in the seminary, which is a school of the Gospel, means to follow Christ as the Apostles did. You are led by Christ into the service of God the Father and of all people, under the guidance of the Holy Spirit. Thus you become more like Christ the Good Shepherd in order better to serve the Church and the world as a priest. In preparing for the priesthood we learn how to respond from the heart to Christ's basic question: 'Do you love me?' (Jn 21:15). For the future priest the answer can only mean total self-giving."[122]

42.4 What needs to be done is to transfer this spirit, which can never be lacking in the Church, to the social, psychological, political and cultural conditions of the world today, conditions which are so varied and complex, as the Synod Fathers have confirmed, bearing in mind the different particular Churches. The Fathers, with words expressing thoughtful concern but at the same time great hope, have shown awareness of and reflected at length on the

---

[122] Message to the People of God (October 28, 1990), IV: *L'Osservatore Romano* (English-language edition), October 29, 1990, 2.

efforts going on in all their Churches to identify and update methods of training candidates for the priesthood.

42.5 This present Exhortation seeks to gather the results of the work of the Synod, setting out some *established points,* indicating some *essential goals,* making available to all the *wealth of experiences and training programs* which have already been tried and found worthwhile. In this Exhortation we consider *"initial" formation* and *"ongoing" formation* separately, but without forgetting that they are closely linked and that as a result they should become one sole organic journey of Christian and priestly living. The Exhortation looks at the different *areas of formation* — the *human, spiritual, intellectual and pastoral* areas — as well as the *settings* and the *persons responsible* for the formation of candidates for the priesthood.

1. The Areas of Priestly Formation

Human formation, the basis of all priestly formation

43.1 "The whole work of priestly formation would be deprived of its necessary foundation if it lacked a suitable human formation."[123] This statement by the Synod Fathers expresses not only a fact which reason brings to our consideration every day and which experience confirms, but a requirement which has a deeper and specific motivation in the very nature of the priest and his ministry. The priest, who is called to be a "living image" of Jesus Christ, Head and Shepherd of the Church, should seek to reflect in himself, as far as possible, the human perfection which shines forth in the Incarnate Son of God and which is reflected with particular liveliness in his attitudes toward others as we see narrated in the Gospels. The ministry of the priest is, certainly, to proclaim the word, to celebrate the sacraments, to guide the Christian community in charity "in the name and in the person of Christ," but all this he does dealing always and only with individual human beings: "Every high priest chosen from among men is appointed to act on behalf of men in relation to God" (Heb 5:1). So we see that the human formation of the priest shows its special importance when related to the receivers of the mission: in order that his ministry may be humanly as credible and acceptable as possible, it is important that the priest should mold his human personality in such a way that it becomes a bridge and not an obstacle for others in their meeting with Jesus Christ the Redeemer of man. It is necessary that, following the example of Jesus who "knew what was in man" (Jn 2:25, cf. 8:3-11), the priest should be able to know the depths of the human heart, to perceive difficulties and

---

[123] *Propositio* 21.

problems, to make meeting and dialogue easy, to create trust and coopera-tion, to express serene and objective judgments.

43.2 Future priests should therefore cultivate a series of human qualities, not only out of proper and due growth and realization of self, but also with a view to the ministry. These qualities are needed for them to be balanced people, strong and free, capable of bearing the weight of pastoral responsibilities. They need to be educated to love the truth, to be loyal, to respect every person, to have a sense of justice, to be true to their word, to be genuinely compas-sionate, to be men of integrity and, especially, to be balanced in judgment and behavior.[124] A simple and demanding program for this human formation can be found in the words of the Apostle Paul to the Philippians: "whatever is true, whatever is honorable, whatever is just, whatever is pure, whatever is lovely, whatever is gracious, if there is any excellence, if there is anything worthy of praise, think about these things" (4:8). It is interesting to note that Paul, pre-cisely in these profoundly human qualities, presents himself as a model to his faithful, for he goes on to say: "What you have learned and received and heard and seen in me, do" (4:9).

43.3 Of special importance is the capacity to relate to others. This is truly fundamental for a person who is called to be responsible for a community and to be a "man of communion." This demands that the priest not be arrogant, or quarrelsome, but affable, hospitable, sincere in his words and heart,[125] pru-dent and discreet, generous and ready to serve, capable of opening himself to clear and brotherly relationships and of encouraging the same in others, and quick to understand, forgive and console (cf. 1 Tim 3:1-5; Tit 1:7-9). People today are often trapped in situations of standardization and loneliness, espe-cially in large urban centers, and they become ever more appreciative of the value of communion. Today this is one of the most eloquent signs and one of the most effective ways of transmitting the Gospel message.

43.4 In this context affective maturity, which is the result of an education in true and responsible love, is a significant and decisive factor in the forma-tion of candidates for the priesthood.

44.1 *Affective maturity* presupposes an awareness that love has a central role in human life. In fact, as I have written in the Encyclical *Redemptor Hominis*:

---

[124] Cf. Second Vatican Ecumenical Council, Decree on Priestly Formation *Optatam Totius,* 11; Decree on the Ministry and Life of Priests *Presbyterorum Ordinis,* 3; Sacred Congregation for Catholic Education, *Ratio Fundamentalis Institutionis Sacerdotalis* (January 6, 1970), 51: *AAS* 62 (1970), 356-357.

[125] Cf. *Propositio* 21.

"Man cannot live without love. He remains a being that is incomprehensible for himself; his life is meaningless, if love is not revealed to him, if he does not encounter love, if he does not experience it and make it his own, if he does not participate intimately in it."[126]

44.2 We are speaking of a love that involves the entire person, in all his or her aspects, physical, psychic and spiritual, and which is expressed in the "nuptial meaning" of the human body, thanks to which a person gives himself to another and takes the other to himself. A properly understood sexual education leads to understanding and realizing this "truth" about human love. We need to be aware that there is a widespread social and cultural atmosphere which "largely reduces human sexuality to the level of something commonplace, since it interprets and lives it in a reductive and impoverished way by linking it solely with the body and with selfish pleasure."[127] Sometimes the very family situations in which priestly vocations arise will display not a few weaknesses and at times even serious failings.

44.3 In such a context, an *education for sexuality* becomes more difficult but also more urgent. It should be truly and fully personal and therefore should present chastity in a manner that shows appreciation and love for it as a "virtue that develops a person's authentic maturity and makes him or her capable of respecting and fostering the 'nuptial meaning' of the body."[128]

44.4 Education for responsible love and the affective maturity of the person are totally necessary for those who, like the priest, are called to *celibacy,* that is, to offer with the grace of the Spirit and the free response of one's own will the whole of one's love and care to Jesus Christ and to his Church. In view of the commitment to celibacy, affective maturity should bring to human relationships of serene friendship and deep brotherliness a strong, lively and personal love for Jesus Christ. As the Synod Fathers have written: "A love for Christ, which overflows into a dedication to everyone, is of the greatest importance in developing affective maturity. Thus the candidate, who is called to celibacy, will find in affective maturity a firm support to live chastity in faithfulness and joy."[129]

44.5 Since the charism of celibacy, even when it is genuine and has proved itself, leaves one's affections and instinctive impulses intact, candidates to the priesthood need an affective maturity which is prudent, able to renounce

---

[126] No. 10: *AAS* 71 (1979), 274.

[127] John Paul II, Apostolic Exhortation *Familiaris Consortio* (November 22, 1981), 37: *AAS* 74 (1982), 128.

[128] Ibid.

[129] *Propositio* 21.

anything that is a threat to it, vigilant over both body and spirit, and capable of esteem and respect in interpersonal relationships between men and women. A precious help can be given by a suitable education to true *friendship,* following the image of the bonds of fraternal affection which Christ himself lived on earth (cf. Jn 11:5).

44.6 Human maturity, and in particular affective maturity, requires a clear and strong *training in freedom* which expresses itself in convinced and heartfelt obedience to the "truth" of one's own being, to the "meaning" of one's own existence, that is to the "sincere gift of self" as the way and fundamental content of the authentic realization of self.[130] Thus understood, freedom requires the person to be truly master of himself, determined to fight and overcome the different forms of selfishness and individualism which threaten the life of each one, ready to open out to others, generous in dedication and service to one's neighbor. This is important for the response that will have to be given to the vocation, and in particular to the priestly vocation, and for faithfulness to it and to the commitments connected with it, even in times of difficulty. On this educational journey toward a mature, responsible freedom, the community life of the seminary can provide help.[131]

44.7 Intimately connected with formation to responsible freedom is *education of the moral conscience.* Such education calls from the depths of one's own "self" obedience to moral obligations and at the same time reveals the deep meaning of such obedience. It is a conscious and free response, and therefore a loving response, to God's demands, to God's love. "The human maturity of the priest" — the Synod Fathers write — "should include especially the formation of his conscience. In order that the candidate may faithfully meet his obligations with regard to God and the Church and wisely guide the consciences of the faithful, he should become accustomed to listening to the voice of God, who speaks to him in his heart, and to adhere with love and constancy to his will."[132]

Spiritual formation: in communion with God and in search of Christ

45.1 Human formation, when it is carried out in the context of an anthropology which is open to the full truth regarding the human person, leads to and finds its completion in spiritual formation. Every man, as God's creature

---

[130] Cf. Second Vatican Ecumenical Council, Pastoral Constitution on the Church in the Modern World *Gaudium et Spes,* 24.

[131] Cf. *Propositio* 21.

[132] *Propositio* 22.

who has been redeemed by Christ's blood, is called to be reborn "of water and the Spirit" (Jn 3:5) and to become a "son in the Son." In this wonderful plan of God is to be found the basis of the essentially religious dimension of the human person, which moreover can be grasped and recognized by reason itself: the human individual is open to transcendence, to the absolute; he has a heart which is restless until it rests in the Lord.[133]

45.2 The educational process of a spiritual life, seen as a relationship and communion with God, derives and develops from this fundamental and irrepressible religious need. In the light of revelation and Christian experience, spiritual formation possesses the unmistakable originality which derives from evangelical "newness." Indeed, it "is the work of the Holy Spirit and engages a person in his totality. It introduces him to a deep communion with Jesus Christ, the Good Shepherd, and leads to the total submission of one's life to the Spirit, in a filial attitude toward the Father and a trustful attachment to the Church. Spiritual formation has its roots in the experience of the Cross, which in deep communion leads to the totality of the Paschal Mystery."[134]

45.3 Spiritual formation, as we have just seen, is applicable to all the faithful. Nevertheless, it should be structured according to the meanings and connotations which derive from the identity of the priest and his ministry. And just as for all the faithful spiritual formation is central and unifies their being and living as Christians, that is, as new creatures in Christ who walk in the Spirit, so too for every priest his spiritual formation is the core which unifies and gives life to his *being* a priest and his *acting* as a priest. In this context, the Synod Fathers state that "without spiritual formation pastoral formation would be left without foundation"[135] and that spiritual formation is "an extremely important element of a priest's education."[136]

45.4 The essential content of spiritual formation specifically leading toward the priesthood is well expressed in the Council's Decree *Optatam Totius:* "Spiritual formation . . . should be conducted in such a way that the students may learn to live in intimate and unceasing union with God the Father through his Son Jesus Christ, in the Holy Spirit. Those who are to take on the likeness of Christ the Priest by sacred ordination should form the habit of drawing close to him as friends in every detail of their lives. They should live his Paschal Mystery in such a way that they will know how to initiate into it the

[133] Cf. Saint Augustine, *Confessions*, I, 1: *CSEL* 33, 1.

[134] Synod of Bishops, Eighth Ordinary General Assembly, *Instrumentum Laboris,* "The Formation of Priests in the Circumstances of the Present Day," 30.

[135] *Propositio* 22.

[136] *Propositio* 23.

people committed to their charge. They should be taught to seek Christ in faithful meditation on the word of God and in active participation in the sacred mysteries of the Church, especially the Eucharist and the Divine Office, to seek him in the Bishop by whom they are sent and in the people to whom they are sent, especially the poor, little children, the weak, sinners and unbelievers. With the confidence of sons they should love and reverence the most Blessed Virgin Mary, who was given as a Mother to the disciple by Jesus Christ as he was dying on the Cross."[137]

46.1 This text from the Council deserves our careful and loving meditation, out of which we will easily be able to outline some fundamental values and demands of the spiritual path trodden by the candidate for the priesthood.

46.2 First, there is the value and demand of *"living intimately united"* to Jesus Christ. Our union with the Lord Jesus, which has its roots in Baptism and is nourished with the Eucharist, has to express itself and be radically renewed each day. Intimate communion with the Blessed Trinity, that is, the new life of grace which makes us children of God, constitutes the "novelty" of the believer, a novelty which involves both his being and his acting. It constitutes the "mystery" of Christian existence which is under the influence of the Spirit: it should, as a result, constitute the ethos of Christian living. Jesus has taught us this marvelous reality of Christian living, which is also the heart of spiritual life, with his allegory of the vine and the branches: "I am the true vine, and my Father is the vinedresser. . . . Abide in me, and I in you. As the branch cannot bear fruit by itself, unless it abides in the vine, neither can you, unless you abide in me. I am the vine, you are the branches. He who abides in me, and I in him, he it is that bears much fruit, for apart from me you can do nothing" (Jn 15:1, 4-5).

46.3 There are spiritual and religious values present in today's culture, and man, notwithstanding appearances to the contrary, cannot help but hunger and thirst for God. However, the Christian religion is often regarded as just one religion among many or reduced to nothing more than a social ethic at the service of man. As a result, its amazing novelty in human history is quite often not apparent. It is a "mystery," the event of the coming of the Son of God who becomes man and gives to those who welcome him the "power to become children of God" (Jn 1:12). It is the proclamation, nay the gift of a personal covenant of love and life between God and man. Only if future priests,

---

[137] No. 8.

through a suitable spiritual formation, have become deeply aware and have increasingly experienced this "mystery" will they be able to communicate this amazing and blessed message to others (cf. 1 Jn 1:1-4).

46.4 The Council text, while taking account of the absolute transcendence of the Christian mystery, describes the communion of future priests with Jesus in *terms of friendship.* And indeed it is not an absurdity for a person to aim at this, for it is the priceless gift of Christ, who said to his Apostles: "No longer do I call you servants, for the servant does not know what the master is doing; but I have called you friends, for all that I have heard from my Father I have made known to you" (Jn 15:15).

46.5 The Council text then points out a second great spiritual value: *the search for Jesus.* "They should be taught to seek Christ." This, along with the *quaerere Deum* (the search for God), is a classical theme of Christian spirituality. It has a specific application in the context of the calling of the Apostles. When John tells the story of the way the first two disciples followed Christ, he highlights this "search." It is Jesus himself who asks the question: "What do you seek?" And the two reply: "Rabbi, where are you staying?" The Evangelist continues: "He said to them, 'Come and see.' They came and saw where he was staying; and they stayed with him that day" (1:37-39). In a certain sense, the spiritual life of the person who is preparing for the priesthood is dominated by this search: by it and by the "finding" of the Master, to follow him, to be in communion with him. So inexhaustible is the mystery of the imitation of Christ and the sharing in his life, that this "seeking" will also have to continue throughout the priest's life and ministry. Likewise this "finding" the Master will have to continue, in order to bring him to others, or rather in order to excite in others the desire to seek out the Master. But all this becomes possible if it is proposed to others as a living "experience," an experience that is worthwhile sharing. This was the path followed by Andrew to lead his brother Simon to Jesus. The Evangelist John writes that Andrew "first found his brother Simon, and said to him, 'We have found the Messiah' (which means Christ)" and brought him to Jesus (1:41-42). And so Simon too will be called, as an Apostle, to follow the Messiah: "Jesus looked at him and said, 'So you are Simon the son of John? You shall be called Cephas' (which means Peter)" (Jn 1:42).

46.6 But what does to seek Christ signify in the spiritual life? And where is he to be found? "Rabbi, where are you staying?" The Decree *Optatam Totius* would seem to indicate a triple path to be covered: a faithful meditation on the word of God, active participation in the Church's holy mysteries and the service of charity to the "little ones." These are three great values and demands which further define the content of the spiritual formation of the candidate to the priesthood.

47.1 An essential element of spiritual formation is *the prayerful and meditated reading of the word of God (lectio divina),* a humble and loving listening of him who speaks. It is in fact by the light and with the strength of the word of God that one's own vocation can be discovered and understood, loved and followed, and one's own mission carried out. So true is this that the person's entire existence finds its unifying and radical meaning in being the terminus of God's word which calls man and the beginning of man's word which answers God. Familiarity with the word of God will make conversion easy, not only in the sense of detaching us from evil so as to adhere to the good, but also in the sense of nourishing our heart with the thoughts of God, so that the faith (as a response to the word) becomes our new basis for judging and evaluating persons and things, events and problems.

47.2 Provided that we approach the word of God and listen to it as it really is, it brings us into contact with God himself, God speaking to man. It brings us into contact with Christ, the Word of God, the Truth, who is at the same time both the Way and the Life (cf. Jn 14:6). It is a matter of reading the "Scriptures" by listening to the "words," "the word" of God, as the Council reminds us: "The Sacred Scriptures contain the word of God, and because they are inspired, are truly the word of God."[138] The Council also states: "By this revelation, then, the invisible God (cf. Col 1:15; 1 Tim 1:7), from the fullness of his love, addresses men as his friends (cf. Ex 33:11; Jn 15:14-15), and moves among them (cf. Bar 3:38), in order to invite and receive them into his own company."[139]

47.3 A loving knowledge of the word of God and a prayerful familiarity with it are specifically important for the prophetic ministry of the priest. They are a fundamental condition for such a ministry to be carried out suitably, especially if we bear in mind the "new evangelization" which the Church today is called to undertake. The Council tells us: "All clerics, particularly priests of Christ and others who, as deacons or catechists, are officially engaged in the ministry of the word, should immerse themselves in the Scriptures by constant sacred reading and diligent study. For it must not happen that anyone becomes 'an empty preacher of the word of God to others, not being a hearer of the word of God in his own heart' (Saint Augustine, *Sermon* 179, 1: PL 8, 966)."[140]

[138] Dogmatic Constitution on Divine Revelation *Dei Verbum,* 24.
[139] Ibid., 2.
[140] Ibid., 25.

47.4 The first and fundamental manner of responding to the word is *prayer,* which is without any doubt a primary value and demand of spiritual formation. Prayer should lead candidates for the priesthood to get to know and have experience of *the genuine meaning of Christian prayer,* as a living and personal meeting with the Father through the only-begotten Son under the action of the Spirit, a dialogue that becomes a sharing in the filial conversation between Jesus and the Father. One aspect of the priest's mission, and certainly by no means a secondary aspect, is that he is to be a "teacher of prayer." However, the priest will only be able to train others in this school of Jesus at prayer, if he himself has been trained in it and continues to receive its formation. This is what people ask of the priest: "The priest is *the man of God,* the one who belongs to God and makes people think about God. When the *Letter to the Hebrews* speaks of Christ it presents him as 'merciful and faithful high priest in the service of God' (2:17). . . . Christians expect to find in the priest not only a man who welcomes them, who listens to them gladly and shows a real interest in them, but also and above all *a man who will help them to turn to God,* to rise up to him. And so the priest needs to be trained to have a deep intimacy with God. Those who are preparing for the priesthood should realize that their whole priestly life will have value inasmuch as they are able to give themselves to Christ and, through Christ, to the Father."[141]

47.5 A necessary training in prayer in a context of noise and agitation like that of our society is an education in the deep human meaning and religious value of *silence,* as the spiritual atmosphere vital for perceiving God's presence and for allowing oneself to be won over by it (cf. 1 Kings 19:11-12).

48.1 The high point of Christian prayer is the *Eucharist,* which in its turn is to be seen as the *"summit and source" of the sacraments and the Liturgy of the Hours.* A totally necessary aspect of the formation of every Christian, and in particular of every priest, is *liturgical formation,* in the full sense of becoming inserted in a living way in the Paschal Mystery of Jesus Christ, who died and rose again, and is present and active in the Church's sacraments. Communion with God, which is the hinge on which the whole of the spiritual life turns, is the gift and fruit of the sacraments. At the same time it is a task and responsibility which the sacraments entrust to the freedom of the believer, so that one may live this same communion in the decisions, choices, attitudes and actions of daily existence. In this sense, the "grace" which "renews" Christian living is the grace of Jesus Christ, who died and rose again, and continues to pour out his holy and sanctifying Spirit in the sacraments. In the same

---

[141] John Paul II, Angelus (March 4, 1990), 2-3: *Insegnamenti* XIII/1 (1990), 594-595.

way, the "new law" which should guide and govern the life of the Christian is written by the sacraments in the "new heart." And it is a law of charity toward God and the brethren, as a response and prolonging of the charity of God toward man signified and communicated by the sacraments. It is thus possible to understand at once the value of a "full, conscious and active participation"[142] in sacramental celebrations for the gift and task of that "pastoral charity" which is the soul of the priestly ministry.

48.2 This applies above all to sharing in the Eucharist, the memorial of the sacrificial Death of Christ and of his glorious Resurrection, the "sacrament of piety, sign of unity, bond of charity,"[143] the paschal banquet "in which Christ is received, the soul is filled with grace and we are given a pledge of the glory that is to be ours."[144] For priests, as ministers of sacred things, are first and foremost ministers of the Sacrifice of the Mass:[145] the role is utterly irreplaceable, because without the priest there can be no Eucharistic offering.

48.3 This explains the essential importance of the Eucharist for the priest's life and ministry and, as a result, in the spiritual formation of candidates for the priesthood. To be utterly frank and clear, I would like to say once again: "It is fitting that seminarians take part *every day* in the Eucharistic celebration, in such a way that afterward they will take up as a rule of their priestly life this daily celebration. They should, moreover, be trained to consider the Eucharistic celebration as the *essential moment of their day,* in which they will take an active part and at which they will never be satisfied with a merely habitual attendance. Finally, candidates to the priesthood will be trained to share in the *intimate* dispositions which the Eucharist fosters: *gratitude* for heavenly benefits received, because the Eucharist is thanksgiving; *an attitude of self-offering* which will impel them to unite the offering of themselves to the Eucharistic offering of Christ; *charity* nourished by a sacrament which is a sign of unity and sharing; *the yearning to contemplate and bow in adoration* before Christ who is really present under the Eucharistic species."[146]

48.4 It is necessary and very urgent to rediscover, within spiritual formation, *the beauty and joy of the Sacrament of Penance.* In a culture which, through renewed and more subtle forms of self-justification, runs the fatal

---

[142] Second Vatican Ecumenical Council, Constitution on the Sacred Liturgy *Sacrosanctum Concilium,* 14.

[143] Saint Augustine, *In Iohannis Evangelium Tractatus*, 26, 13: *CCL* 36, 266.

[144] Liturgy of the Hours, Magnificat Antiphon of Second Vespers of the Solemnity of the Body and Blood of Christ.

[145] Cf. Second Vatican Ecumenical Council, Decree on the Ministry and Life of Priests *Presbyterorum Ordinis,* 13.

[146] Angelus (July 1, 1990), 3: *Insegnamenti* XIII/2 (1990), 7.

risk of losing the "sense of sin" and, as a result, the consoling joy of the plea for forgiveness (cf. Ps 51:14) and of meeting God who is "rich in mercy" (Eph 2:4), it is vital to educate future priests to have the virtue of penance, which the Church wisely nourishes in her celebrations and in the seasons of the liturgical year, and which finds its fullness in the Sacrament of Reconciliation. From it flow the sense of asceticism and interior discipline, a spirit of sacrifice and self-denial, the acceptance of hard work and of the Cross. These are elements of the spiritual life which often prove to be particularly arduous for many candidates for the priesthood who have grown up in relatively comfortable and affluent circumstances and have been made less inclined and open to these very elements by the models of behavior and ideals transmitted by the mass media; but this also happens in countries where the conditions of life are poorer and young people live in more austere situations. For this reason, but above all in order to put into practice the "radical self-giving" proper to the priest following the example of Christ the Good Shepherd, the Synod Fathers wrote: "It is necessary to inculcate the meaning of the Cross, which is at the heart of the Paschal Mystery. Through this identification with Christ crucified, as a slave, the world can rediscover the value of austerity, of suffering and also of martyrdom within the present culture, which is imbued with secularism, greed and hedonism."[147]

49.1 Spiritual formation also involves seeking Christ in people.

49.2 The spiritual life is, indeed, an interior life, a life of intimacy with God, a life of prayer and contemplation. But this very meeting with God, and with his fatherly love for everyone, brings us face to face with the need to meet our neighbor, to give ourselves to others, to serve in a humble and disinterested fashion, following the example which Jesus has proposed to everyone as a program of life when he washed the feet of the Apostles: "I have given you an example, that you also should do as I have done to you" (Jn 13:15).

49.3 Formation which aims at giving oneself generously and freely, which is something helped also by the communal structure which preparation to the priesthood normally takes, is a necessary condition for one who is called to be a manifestation and image of the Good Shepherd, who gives life (cf. Jn 10:11, 15). From this point of view, spiritual formation has and should develop its own inherent pastoral and charitable dimension, and can profitably make use of a proper devotion to the Sacred Heart of Jesus, one that is both strong and tender. This is a point made by the Synod Fathers: "When we speak of forming

---

[147] *Propositio* 23.

future priests in the spirituality of the heart of the Lord, we mean they should lead lives that are a response to the love and affection of Christ the Priest and Good Shepherd: to his love for the Father in the Holy Spirit, and to his love toward men that was so great as to lead him to give his life in sacrifice for them."[148]

49.4 The priest is, therefore, a *man of charity,* and is called to educate others according to Christ's example and the new commandment of brotherly love (cf. Jn 15:12). But this demands that he allow himself to be constantly trained by the Spirit in the charity of Christ. In this sense preparation for the priesthood must necessarily involve a proper training in charity and particularly in the preferential love for the "poor" in whom our faith discovers Jesus (cf. Mt 25:40), and a merciful love for sinners.

49.5 In the general context of charity, which consists in the loving gift of oneself, is to be found, in the program of spiritual formation of the future priest, *education in obedience, celibacy* and *poverty.*[149] The Council offers this invitation: "Students must clearly understand that it is not their lot in life to lord it over others and enjoy honors, but to devote themselves completely to the service of God and the pastoral ministry. With special care they should be trained in priestly obedience, poverty and a spirit of self-denial, that they may accustom themselves to living in conformity with the crucified Christ and to give up willingly even those things which are lawful, but not expedient."[150]

50.1 The spiritual formation of one who is called to live celibacy should pay particular attention to preparing the future priest so that he may *know, appreciate, love and live celibacy according to its true nature* and according to its real purposes, that is for evangelical, spiritual and pastoral motives. The virtue of chastity is a premise for this preparation and is its content. It colors all human relations and leads "to experiencing and showing . . . a sincere, human, fraternal and personal love, one that is capable of sacrifice, following Christ's example, a love for all and for each person."[151]

50.2 The celibacy of priests brings with it certain characteristics, thanks to which they "renounce marriage for the sake of the Kingdom of heaven (cf. Mt 19:12) and hold fast to their Lord with that undivided love which is profoundly in harmony with the New Covenant; they bear witness to the resur-

---

[148] Ibid.

[149] Cf. ibid.

[150] Decree on Priestly Formation *Optatam Totius,* 9.

[151] Sacred Congregation for Catholic Education, *Ratio Fundamentalis Institutionis Sacerdotalis* (January 6, 1970), 48: *AAS* 62 (1970), 354.

rection in a future life (cf. Lk 20:36) and obtain the most useful assistance toward the constant exercise of that perfect charity by which they can become all things to all men in their priestly ministry."[152] And so priestly celibacy should not be considered just as a legal norm, or as a totally external condition for admission to ordination, but rather as a value that is profoundly connected with ordination, whereby a man takes on the likeness of Jesus Christ, the Good Shepherd and Spouse of the Church, and therefore as a choice of a greater and undivided love for Christ and his Church, as a full and joyful availability in his heart for the pastoral ministry. Celibacy is to be considered as a special grace, as a gift, for "not all men can receive this saying, but only those to whom it is given" (Mt 19:11). Certainly it is a grace which does not dispense with, but counts most definitely on, a conscious and free response on the part of the receiver. This charism of the Spirit also brings with it the grace for the receiver to remain faithful to it for all his life and be able to carry out generously and joyfully its concomitant commitments. Formation in priestly celibacy should also include helping people to be aware of the "precious gift of God,"[153] which will lead to prayer and to vigilance in guarding the gift from anything which could put it under threat.

50.3 Through his celibate life, the priest will be able to fulfill better his ministry on behalf of the People of God. In particular, as he witnesses to the evangelical value of virginity, he will be able to aid Christian spouses to live fully the "great sacrament" of the love of Christ the Bridegroom for his Spouse the Church, just as his own faithfulness to celibacy will help them to be faithful to each other as husband and wife.[154]

50.4 The importance of a careful preparation for priestly celibacy, especially in the social and cultural situations that we see today, led the Synod Fathers to make a series of requests which have a permanent value, as the wisdom of our Mother the Church confirms. I authoritatively set them down again as criteria to be followed in formation for chastity in celibacy: "Let the Bishops together with the rectors and spiritual directors of the seminaries establish principles, offer criteria and give assistance for discernment in this matter. Of the greatest importance for formation for chastity in celibacy are the Bishop's concern and fraternal life among priests. In the seminary, that is, in the program of formation, celibacy should be presented clearly, without any ambiguities and in a positive fashion. The seminarian should have a suf-

---

[152] Second Vatican Ecumenical Council, Decree on Priestly Formation *Optatam Totius,* 10.
[153] Ibid., 10.
[154] Cf. John Paul II, Letter to Priests for Holy Thursday 1979 (April 8, 1979): *AAS* 71 (1979), 393-417.

ficient degree of psychological and sexual maturity as well as an assiduous and authentic life of prayer, and he should put himself under the direction of a spiritual father. The spiritual director should help the seminarian so that he himself reaches a mature and free decision, which is built on esteem for priestly friendship and self-discipline, as well as on the acceptance of solitude and on a physically and psychologically sound personal state. Therefore, seminarians should have a good knowledge of the teaching of the Second Vatican Council, of the Encyclical *Sacerdotalis Coelibatus* and the Instruction for Formation in Priestly Celibacy published by the Congregation for Catholic Education in 1974. In order that the seminarian may be able to embrace priestly celibacy for the Kingdom of heaven with a free decision, he needs to know the Christian and truly human nature and purpose of sexuality in marriage and in celibacy. It is necessary also to instruct and educate the lay faithful regarding the evangelical, spiritual and pastoral reasons proper to priestly celibacy, so that they will help priests with their friendship, understanding and cooperation."[155]

Intellectual formation: understanding the faith

51.1 Intellectual formation has its own characteristics, but it is also deeply connected with, and indeed can be seen as a necessary expression of, both human and spiritual formation: it is a fundamental demand of the human intelligence by which one "participates in the light of God's mind"[156] and seeks to acquire a wisdom which in turn opens to and is directed toward knowing and adhering to God.

51.2 The intellectual formation of candidates for the priesthood finds its specific justification in the very nature of the ordained ministry, and the challenge of the "new evangelization" to which our Lord is calling the Church on the threshold of the third millennium shows just how important this formation is. "If we expect every Christian" — the Synod Fathers write — "to be prepared to make a defense of the faith and to account for the hope that is in us (cf. 1 Pet 3:15), then all the more should candidates for the priesthood and priests have diligent care of the quality of their intellectual formation in their education and pastoral activity. For the salvation of their brothers and sisters they should seek an ever deeper knowledge of the divine mysteries."[157] The present situation is heavily marked by religious indifference, by a widespread

---

[155] *Propositio* 24.

[156] Second Vatican Ecumenical Council, Pastoral Constitution on the Church in the Modern World *Gaudium et Spes,* 15.

[157] *Propositio* 26.

mistrust regarding the real capacity of reason to reach objective and universal truth, and by fresh problems and questions brought up by scientific and technological discoveries. It strongly demands a high level of intellectual formation, such as will enable priests to proclaim, in a context like this, the changeless Gospel of Christ and to make it credible to the legitimate demands of human reason. Moreover, there is the present phenomenon of pluralism, which is very marked in the field not only of human society but also of the community of the Church herself. It demands special attention to critical discernment: it is a further reason showing the need for an extremely rigorous intellectual formation.

51.3 These "pastoral" reasons for intellectual formation reconfirm what has been said above concerning the unity of the educational process in its diverse aspects. The commitment to study, which takes up no small part of the time of those preparing for the priesthood, is not in fact an external and secondary dimension of their human, Christian, spiritual and vocational growth. In reality, through study, especially the study of theology, the future priest assents to the word of God, grows in his spiritual life and prepares himself to fulfill his pastoral ministry. This is the many-sided and unifying scope of the theological study indicated by the Council[158] and reproposed by the Synod's *Instrumentum Laboris:* "To be pastorally effective, intellectual formation is to be integrated with a spirituality marked by a personal experience of God. In this way a purely abstract approach to knowledge is overcome in favor of that intelligence of heart which knows how 'to look beyond,' and then is in a position to communicate the mystery of God to the people."[159]

52.1 A crucial stage of intellectual formation is the study of *philosophy*, which leads to a deeper understanding and interpretation of the person, and of the person's freedom and relationships with the world and with God. A proper philosophical training is vital, not only because of the links between the great philosophical questions and the mysteries of salvation which are studied in theology under the guidance of the higher light of faith,[160] but also vis-à-vis an extremely widespread cultural situation which emphasizes subjectivism as a criterion and measure of truth: only a sound philosophy can help candidates for the priesthood to develop a reflective awareness of the fundamental relationship that exists between the human spirit and truth,

[158] Cf. Decree on Priestly Formation *Optatam Totius,* 16.
[159] No. 39.
[160] Cf. Congregation for Catholic Education, Letter to Bishops *De Necessitate Philosophiae Studia in Seminariis Impensius Promovendi* (January 20, 1972): *AAS* 64 (1972), 583-586.

that truth which is revealed to us fully in Jesus Christ. Nor must one underestimate the importance of philosophy as a guarantee of that "certainty of truth" which is the only firm basis for a total giving of oneself to Jesus and to the Church. It is not difficult to see that some very specific questions, such as that concerning the priest's identity and his apostolic and missionary commitment, are closely linked to the question about the nature of truth, which is anything but an abstract question: if we are not certain about the truth, how can we put our whole life on the line, how can we have the strength to challenge others' way of living?

52.2 Philosophy greatly helps the candidate to enrich his intellectual formation in the "cult of truth," namely, in a kind of *loving veneration of the truth,* which leads one to recognize that the truth is not created or measured by man but is given to man as a gift by the supreme Truth, God; that, albeit in a limited way and often with difficulty, human reason can reach objective and universal truth, even that relating to God and the radical meaning of existence; and that faith itself cannot do without reason and the effort of "thinking through" its contents, as that great mind Augustine bore witness: "I wished to see with my mind what I have believed, and I have argued and labored greatly."[161]

52.3 For a deeper understanding of man and the phenomena and lines of development of society, in relation to a pastoral ministry which is as "incarnate" as possible, the so-called *"human sciences"* can be of considerable use, sciences such as sociology, psychology, education, economics and politics, and the science of social communication. Also in the precise field of the positive or descriptive sciences, these can help the future priest prolong the living "contemporaneousness" of Christ. As Paul VI once said: "Christ became the contemporary of some men and spoke their language. Our faithfulness to him demands that this contemporaneousness should be maintained."[162]

53.1 The intellectual formation of the future priest is based and built above all on the study of *sacred doctrine,* of theology. The value and genuineness of this theological formation depend on maintaining a scrupulous respect for the nature of theology. The Synod Fathers summarized this as follows: "True theology proceeds from the faith and aims at leading to the faith."[163] This is

[161] "Desideravi intellectu videre quod credidi, et multum disputavi et laboravi": *De Trinitate* XV, 28: *CCL* 50/A, 534.

[162] Address to the Participants in the 21st Italian Biblical Week (September 25, 1970): *AAS* 62 (1970), 618.

[163] *Propositio* 26.

the conception of theology which has always been put forward by the Church and, specifically, by her Magisterium. This is the line followed by the great theologians who have enriched the Church's thinking down the ages. Saint Thomas is extremely clear when he affirms that the faith is as it were the *habitus* of theology, that is, its permanent principle of operation,[164] and that the whole of theology is ordered to nourishing the faith.[165]

53.2 The theologian is therefore, first and foremost, a believer, a man of faith. But the theologian is a believer who asks himself questions about his own faith *(fides quaerens intellectum)*, with the aim of reaching a deeper understanding of the faith itself. The two aspects (of faith and mature reflection) are intimately connected, intertwined: their intimate coordination and interpenetration are what make for true theology, and as a result decide the contents, modalities and spirit according to which the sacred doctrine *(sacra doctrina)* is elaborated and studied.

53.3 Moreover, since the faith, which is the point of departure and the point of arrival of theology, brings about a personal relationship between the believer and Jesus Christ in the Church, theology also has intrinsic Christological and ecclesial connotations, which the candidate to the priesthood should take up consciously, not only because of what they imply for his personal life but also inasmuch as they affect his pastoral ministry. If our faith truly welcomes the word of God, it will lead to a radical "yes" on the part of the believer to Jesus Christ, who is the full and definitive Word of God to the world (cf. Heb 1:1-4). As a result, theological reflection is centered on adherence to Jesus Christ, the Wisdom of God: mature reflection has to be described as a sharing in the "thinking" of Christ (cf. 1 Cor 2:16) in the human form of a science *(scientia fidei)*. At the same time, faith inserts believers in the Church and makes them partake in the life of the Church as a community of faith. Hence theology has an ecclesial dimension, because it is a mature reflection on the faith of the Church by the theologian who is a member of the Church.[166]

53.4 These Christological and ecclesial dimensions which are connatural to theology, while they help candidates for the priesthood grow in scientific precision, will also help them develop a great and living love for Jesus Christ and for his Church. This love will both nourish their spiritual life and guide

---

[164] "Fides, quae est quasi habitus theologiae": *In Librum Boethii de Trinitate,* V, 4, ad 8.

[165] Cf. *In Primum Librum Sententiarum,* Prologue, q. 1, aa. 1-5.

[166] Cf. Congregation for the Doctrine of the Faith, Instruction on the Ecclesial Vocation of the Theologian *Donum Veritatis* (May 24, 1990), 11, 40: *AAS* 82 (1990), 1554-1555, 1568-1569.

them to carry out their ministry with a generous spirit. This was what the Second Vatican Council had in mind when it called for a revision of ecclesiastical studies, with a view to "a more effective coordination of philosophy and theology so that they supplement one another in revealing to the minds of the students with ever increasing clarity the mystery of Christ, which affects the whole course of human history, exercises an unceasing influence on the Church and operates mainly through the ministry of the priest."[167]

53.5 Intellectual formation in theology and formation in the spiritual life, in particular the life of prayer, meet and strengthen each other, without detracting in any way from the soundness of research or from the spiritual tenor of prayer. Saint Bonaventure reminds us: "Let no one think that it is enough for him to read if he lacks devotion, or to engage in speculation without spiritual joy, or to be active if he has no piety, or to have knowledge without charity, or intelligence without humility, or study without God's grace, or to expect to know himself if he is lacking the infused wisdom of God."[168]

54.1 Theological formation is both complex and demanding. It should lead the candidate for the priesthood to *a complete and unified vision* of the truths which God has revealed in Jesus Christ and of the Church's experience of faith. Hence the need both to know "all" the Christian truths, without arbitrarily selecting among them, and to know them in an orderly fashion. This means the candidate needs to be helped to build a synthesis which will be the result of the contributions of the different theological disciplines, the specific nature of which acquires genuine value only in their profound coordination.

54.2 In reflecting maturely upon the faith, theology moves in two directions. The first is that of the *study of the word of God:* the word set down in Holy Writ, celebrated and lived in the living Tradition of the Church, and authoritatively interpreted by the Church's Magisterium. Hence the importance of studying Sacred Scripture — "which should be the soul, as it were, of all theology,"[169] the Fathers of the Church, the liturgy, the history of the Church and the teachings of the Magisterium. The second direction is that of *man, who converses with God:* man who is called "to believe," "to live," "to communicate" to others the *Christian faith* and *outlook.* Hence the study of dogmatic and moral theology, of spiritual theology, of canon law and of pastoral theology.

54.3 Because of its relationship to the believer, theology is led to pay particular attention both to the fundamental and permanent question of the rela-

---

[167] Decree on Priestly Formation *Optatam Totius,* 14.
[168] *Itinerarium Mentis in Deum,* Prologue, 4: *Opera Omnia,* Ad Aquas Claras (1891), V, 296.
[169] Second Vatican Ecumenical Council, Decree on Priestly Formation *Optatam Totius,* 16.

tionship between faith and reason and to a number of requirements more closely related to the social and cultural situation of today. In regard to the first we have the study of fundamental theology, whose object is the fact of Christian revelation and its transmission in the Church. In regard to the second we have disciplines which have been and are being developed as responses to problems strongly felt nowadays. This is true of the study of the Church's social doctrine which "belongs to the field . . . of theology and, in particular, of moral theology"[170] and is to be counted among the "essential components" of the "new evangelization," of which it is an instrument.[171] This is likewise true of the study of missiology, ecumenism, Judaism, Islam and other religions.

55.1 Theological formation nowadays should pay attention to *certain problems* which not infrequently raise difficulties, tensions and confusion within the life of the Church. One can think of the *relationship between statements issued by the Magisterium and theological discussion,* a relationship which does not always take the shape it ought to have, that is, within a framework of cooperation. It is indeed true that the "living Magisterium of the Church and theology, while having different gifts and functions, ultimately have the same goal: preserving the People of God in the truth which sets free and thereby making them 'a light to the nations.' This service to the ecclesial community brings the theologian and the Magisterium into a mutual relationship. The latter authentically teaches the doctrine of the Apostles. And, benefitting from the work of theologians, it refutes objections to and distortions of the faith, and promotes, with the authority received from Jesus Christ, new and deeper comprehension, clarification and application of revealed doctrine. Theology, for its part, gains, by way of reflection, an ever deeper understanding of the word of God found in the Scripture and handed on faithfully by the Church's living Tradition under the guidance of the Magisterium. Theology strives to clarify the teaching of revelation with regard to reason and gives it finally an organic and systematic form."[172] When, for a number of reasons, this cooperation is lacking, one needs to avoid misunderstandings and confusion, and to know how to distinguish carefully "the common teaching of the Church from the opinions of theologians and from tendencies which quickly pass (the so-

---

[170] John Paul II, Encyclical Letter *Sollicitudo Rei Socialis* (December 30, 1987), 41: *AAS* 80 (1988), 571.

[171] Cf. John Paul II, Encyclical Letter *Centesimus Annus* (May 1, 1991), 54: *AAS* 83 (1991), 859-860.

[172] Congregation for the Doctrine of the Faith, Instruction on the Ecclesial Vocation of the Theologian *Donum Veritatis* (May 24, 1990), 21: *AAS* 82 (1990), 1559.

called 'trends')."[173] There is no "parallel" Magisterium, for the one Magisterium is that of Peter and the Apostles, the Pope and the Bishops.[174]

55.2 Another problem, which is experienced especially when seminary studies are entrusted to academic institutions, is that of the *relationship between high scientific standards in theology and its pastoral aim*. This raises the issue of the pastoral nature of theology. It is a question, really, of two characteristics of theology and how it is to be taught, which are not only not opposed to each other, but which work together, from different angles, in favor of a more complete "understanding of the faith." In fact the pastoral nature of theology does not mean that it should be less doctrinal or that it should be completely stripped of its scientific nature. It means, rather, that it enables future priests to proclaim the Gospel message through the cultural modes of their age and to direct pastoral action according to an authentic theological vision. Hence, on the one hand, a respectful study of the genuine scientific quality of the individual disciplines of theology will help provide a more complete and deeper training of the pastor of souls as a teacher of faith. And, on the other hand, an appropriate awareness that there is a pastoral goal in view will help the serious and scientific study of theology be more formative for future priests.

55.3 A further problem that is strongly felt these days is the demand for the *evangelization of cultures* and the *inculturation of the message of faith*. An eminently pastoral problem, this should enter more broadly and carefully into the formation of the candidates to the priesthood: "In the present circumstances in which, in a number of regions of the world, the Christian religion is considered as something foreign to cultures (be they ancient or modern), it is very important that in the whole intellectual and human formation the dimension of inculturation be seen as necessary and essential."[175] But this means we need a genuine theology, inspired by the Catholic principles on inculturation. These principles are linked with the mystery of the Incarnation of the Word of God and with Christian anthropology and thus illumine the authentic meaning of inculturation. In the face of all the different and at times contrasting cultures present in the various parts of the world, inculturation seeks to obey Christ's command to preach the Gospel to all nations even unto the ends of the earth. Such obedience does not signify either syncretism or a simple ad-

---

[173] *Propositio* 26.

[174] For example, Saint Thomas Aquinas wrote: "We have to be more on the side of the authority of the Church than on that of Augustine or Jerome, or any other Doctor" (*Summa Theologiae*, II-II, q. 10, a. 12). And again: "No one can shield himself with the authority of Jerome or Augustine or any other Doctor against the authority of Peter" (*Summa Theologiae*, I-II, q.11, a. 2, ad 3).

[175] *Propositio* 32.

aptation of the announcement of the Gospel, but rather the fact that the Gospel penetrates the very life of cultures, becomes incarnate in them, overcoming those cultural elements that are incompatible with the faith and Christian living, and raising their values to the mystery of salvation which comes from Christ.[176] The problem of inculturation can have a particularly great interest when the candidates to the priesthood are themselves coming from indigenous cultures. In that case, they will need to find suitable ways of formation, both to overcome the danger of being less demanding and to make proper use of the good and genuine elements of their own cultures and traditions.[177]

56.1 Following the teaching and the indications of the Second Vatican Council and their application in the *Ratio Fundamentalis Institutionis Sacerdotalis,* the Church decided upon a vast updating of the teaching of the philosophical and especially theological disciplines in seminaries. This updating, which in some cases still needs amendments and developments, has on the whole helped to make the education available a more effective medium for intellectual formation. In this respect "the Synod Fathers have confirmed once again, frequently and clearly, the need — indeed the urgency — to put the basic study plan (both the general one which applies to the Church worldwide, and those of the individual nations or Episcopal Conferences) into effect in seminaries and in houses of formation."[178]

56.2 It is necessary to oppose firmly the tendency to play down the seriousness of studies and the commitment to them. This tendency is showing itself in certain spheres of the Church, also as a consequence of the insufficient and defective basic education of students beginning the philosophical and theological curriculum. The very situation of the Church today demands increasingly that teachers be truly able to face the complexity of the times and that they be in a position to face competently, with clarity and deep reasoning, the questions about meaning which are put by the people of today, questions which can only receive a full and definitive reply in the Gospel of Jesus Christ.

Pastoral formation: communion with the charity of Jesus Christ the Good Shepherd

57.1 The whole formation imparted to candidates for the priesthood aims at preparing them to enter into communion with the charity of Christ the

---

[176] Cf. John Paul II, Encyclical Letter *Redemptoris Missio* (December 7, 1990), 67: *AAS* 83 (1991), 315-316.

[177] Cf. *Propositio* 32.

[178] *Propositio* 27.

Good Shepherd. Hence, their formation in its different aspects must have a fundamentally pastoral character. The Council's Decree *Optatam Totius* states so clearly when speaking of major seminaries: "The whole training of the students should have as its object to make them *true shepherds of souls after the example of our Lord Jesus Christ, Teacher, Priest and Shepherd.* Hence, they should be trained for the ministry of the word, so that they may gain an ever increasing understanding of the revealed word of God, making it their own by meditation and giving it expression in their speech and in their lives. They should be trained for the ministry of worship and sanctification so that by prayer and the celebration of the sacred liturgical functions they may carry on the work of salvation through the Eucharistic Sacrifice and the sacraments. They should be trained to undertake the ministry of the shepherd, that they may know how to represent Christ to humanity, Christ who 'did not come to have service done to him but to serve others and to give his life as a ransom for the lives of many' (Mk 10:45; cf. Jn 13:12-17), and that they may win over many by becoming the servants of all (cf. 1 Cor 9:19)."[179]

57.2 The Council text insists upon the coordination of the different aspects of human, spiritual and intellectual formation. At the same time it stresses that they are all directed to a specific pastoral end. This pastoral aim ensures that the human, spiritual and intellectual formation has certain precise content and characteristics; it also unifies and gives specificity to the whole formation of future priests.

57.3 Like all other branches of formation, pastoral formation develops by means of mature reflection and practical application, and it is rooted in a spirit, which is the hinge of all and the force which stimulates it and makes it develop.

57.4 It needs to be studied therefore as the true and genuine theological discipline that it is: *pastoral or practical theology.* It is a scientific reflection on the Church as she is built up daily, by the power of the Spirit, in history; on the Church as the "universal sacrament of salvation,"[180] as a living sign and instrument of the salvation wrought by Christ through the word, the sacraments and the service of charity. Pastoral theology is not just an art. Nor is it a set of exhortations, experiences and methods. It is theological in its own right, because it receives from the faith the principles and criteria for the pastoral action of the Church in history, a Church that each day "begets" the Church herself, to quote the felicitous expression of the Venerable Bede: "*Nam*

---

[179] No. 4.

[180] Second Vatican Ecumenical Council, Dogmatic Constitution on the Church *Lumen Gentium*, 48.

et Ecclesia quotidie gignit Ecclesiam. "[181] Among these principles and criteria, one that is specially important is that of the evangelical discernment of the sociocultural and ecclesial situation in which the particular pastoral action has to be carried out.

57.5 The study of pastoral theology should throw light upon its *practical application* through involvement in certain pastoral services which the candidates to the priesthood should carry out, with a necessary progression and always in harmony with their other educational commitments. It is a question of pastoral "experiences," which can come together in a real program of "pastoral training," which can last a considerable amount of time and the usefulness of which will itself need to be checked in an orderly manner.

57.6 Pastoral study and action direct one to an inner source, which the work of formation will take care to guard and make good use of: this is the *ever deeper communion with the pastoral charity of Jesus,* which, just as it was the principal and driving force of his salvific action, likewise, thanks to the outpouring of the Holy Spirit in the Sacrament of Orders, should constitute the principal and driving force of the priestly ministry. It is a question of a type of formation meant not only to ensure scientific, pastoral competence and practical skill, but also and especially a *way of being* in communion with the very sentiments and behavior of Christ the Good Shepherd: "Have this mind among yourselves, which is yours in Christ Jesus" (Phil 2:5).

58.1 And so pastoral formation certainly cannot be reduced to a mere apprenticeship, aiming to make the candidate familiar with some pastoral techniques. The seminary which educates must seek really and truly to initiate the candidate into the sensitivity of being a shepherd, in the conscious and mature assumption of his responsibilities, in the interior habit of evaluating problems and establishing priorities and looking for solutions on the basis of honest motivations of faith and according to the theological demands inherent in pastoral work.

58.2 Thanks to an initial and gradual experience of ministry, future priests will be able to be inserted into the living pastoral tradition of their particular Church. They will learn to open the horizon of their mind and heart to the missionary dimension of the Church's life. They will get practice in some initial forms of cooperation with one another and with the priests alongside whom they will be sent to work. These priests have a considerably important role, in union with the seminary program, in showing the candidates how they should go about pastoral work.

[181] *Explanatio Apocalypsis,* Book II, 12: *PL* 93, 166.

58.3 When it comes to choosing places and services in which candidates can obtain their pastoral experience, the parish should be given particular importance,[182] for it is a living cell of local and specialized pastoral work, in which they will find themselves faced with the kind of problems they will meet in their future ministry. The Synod Fathers have proposed a number of concrete examples, such as visits to the sick; caring for immigrants, refugees and nomads; and various social works which can be expressions of charitable zeal. Specifically, they write: "The priest must be a witness of the charity of Christ himself who 'went about doing good' (Acts 10:38). He must also be a visible sign of the solicitude of the Church who is Mother and Teacher. And given that man today is affected by so many hardships, especially those who are sunk in inhuman poverty, blind violence and unjust power, it is necessary that the man of God, who is to be equipped for every good work (cf. 2 Tim 3:17), should defend the rights and dignity of man. Nevertheless, he should be careful not to adopt false ideologies, nor should he forget, as he strives to promote its perfecting, that the only Redemption of the world is that effected by the Cross of Christ."[183]

58.4 These and other pastoral activities will teach the future priest to live out as a "service" his own mission of "authority" in the community, setting aside all attitudes of superiority or of exercising a power if it is not simply that which is justified by pastoral charity.

58.5 If the training is to be suitable, the different experiences which candidates for the priesthood have should assume a clear "ministerial" character, and should be intimately linked with all the demands that befit preparation to the priesthood and (certainly not neglecting their studies) in relation to the services of the proclamation of the word, of worship and of leadership. These services can become a specific way of experiencing the ministries of lector, acolyte and deacon.

59.1 Since pastoral action is destined by its very nature to enliven the Church, which is essentially "mystery," "communion" and "mission," pastoral formation should be aware of and should live these ecclesial aspects in the exercise of the ministry.

59.2 Of fundamental importance is awareness that the *Church* is a *"mystery,"* that is, a divine work, fruit of the Spirit of Christ, an effective sign of grace, the presence of the Trinity in the Christian community. This awareness, while never lessening the pastor's genuine sense of responsibility, will

---

[182] Cf. *Propositio* 28.
[183] *Propositio* 28.

convince him that the Church grows, thanks to the gratuitous work of the Spirit and that his service — thanks to the very grace of God that is entrusted to the free responsibility of man — is the Gospel service of the "unworthy servant" (cf. Lk 17:10).

59.3 Awareness of the *Church* as *"communion"* will prepare the candidate for the priesthood to carry out his pastoral work with a community spirit, in heartfelt cooperation with the different members of the Church: priests and Bishop, diocesan and Religious priests, priests and lay people. Such a cooperation presupposes a knowledge and appreciation of the different gifts and charisms, of the diverse vocations and responsibilities which the Spirit offers and entrusts to the members of Christ's Body. It demands a living and precise consciousness of one's own identity in the Church and of the identity of others. It demands mutual trust, patience, gentleness and the capacity for understanding and expectation. It finds its roots above all in a love for the Church that is deeper than love for self and the group or groups one may belong to. It is particularly important to prepare future priests for *cooperation with the laity.* The Council says: "They should be willing to listen to lay people, give brotherly consideration to their wishes and recognize their experience and competence in the different fields of human activity. In this way they will be able to recognize with them the signs of the times."[184] The recent Synod too has insisted upon pastoral solicitude for the laity: "The student should become capable of proposing and introducing the lay faithful, the young especially, to the different vocations (marriage, social services, apostolate, ministries and other responsibilities in pastoral activity, the consecrated life, involvement in political and social leadership, scientific research, teaching). Above all it is necessary that he be able to teach and support the laity in their vocation to be present in and to transform the world with the light of the Gospel, by recognizing this task of theirs and showing respect for it."[185]

59.4 Lastly, awareness of the Church as a *"missionary"* communion will help the candidate for the priesthood to love and live the essential missionary dimension of the Church and her different pastoral activities. He should be open and available to all the possibilities offered today for the proclamation of the Gospel, not forgetting the valuable service which can and should be given by the media.[186] He should prepare himself for a ministry which may mean in

---

[184] Decree on the Ministry and Life of Priests *Presbyterorum Ordinis,* 9; cf. John Paul II, Post-Synodal Apostolic Exhortation *Christifideles Laici* (December 30, 1988), 61: *AAS* 81 (1989), 512-514.

[185] *Propositio* 28.

[186] Cf. ibid.

practice that his readiness to follow the indications of the Holy Spirit and of his Bishop will lead him to be sent to preach the Gospel even beyond the frontiers of his own country.[187]

2. The Setting of Priestly Formation

The major seminary — a formation community

60.1 The need for the major seminary — and by analogy for the religious house — for the formation of candidates for priesthood, was affirmed with authority by the Second Vatican Council[188] and has been *reaffirmed by the Synod* as follows: "The institution of the major seminary, as the best place for formation, is to be certainly reaffirmed as the normal place, in the material sense as well, for a community and hierarchical life, indeed as the proper home for the formation of candidates for the priesthood, with superiors who are truly dedicated to this service. This institution has produced many good results down the ages and continues to do so all over the world."[189]

60.2 The seminary can be seen as a place and a period in life. But it is above all an *educational community in progress:* it is a community established by the Bishop to offer to those called by the Lord to serve as apostles the possibility of reliving the experience of formation which our Lord provided for the Twelve. In fact, the Gospels present a prolonged and intimate sharing of life with Jesus as a necessary premise for the apostolic ministry. Such an experience demands of the Twelve the practice of detachment in a particularly clear and specific fashion, a detachment that in some way is demanded of all the disciples, a detachment from their roots, from their usual work, from their nearest and dearest (cf. Mk 1:16-20, 10:28; Lk 9:23, 9:57-62, 14:25-27). On several occasions we have referred to the Marcan tradition which stresses the deep link that unites the Apostles to Christ and to one another: before being sent out to preach and to heal, they are called "to be with him" (Mk 3:14).

60.3 In its deepest identity the seminary is called to be, in its own way, a *continuation in the Church of the apostolic community gathered about Jesus,* listening to his word, proceeding toward the Easter experience, awaiting the gift of the Spirit for the mission. Such an identity constitutes the normative ideal which stimulates the seminary, in the many diverse forms and varied aspects which it assumes historically as a *human institution,* to find a con-

---

[187] Cf. John Paul II, Encyclical Letter *Redemptoris Missio* (December 7, 1990), 67-68: *AAS* 83 (1991), 315-316.

[188] Cf. Decree on Priestly Formation *Optatam Totius,* 4.

[189] *Propositio* 20.

crete realization, faithful to the Gospel values from which it takes its inspiration, and able to respond to the situations and needs of the times.

60.4 The seminary is, in itself, *an original experience of the Church's life.* In it the Bishop is present through the ministry of the rector and the service of coresponsibility and communion fostered by him with the other teachers, for the sake of the pastoral and apostolic growth of the students. The various members of the seminary community, gathered by the Spirit into a single brotherhood, cooperate, each according to his own gift, in the growth of all in faith and charity, so that they may prepare suitably for the priesthood and so prolong in the Church and in history the saving presence of Jesus Christ, the Good Shepherd.

60.5 From the human point of view, the major seminary should strive to become "a community built on deep friendship and charity, so that it can be considered a true family living in joy."[190] As a Christian institution, the seminary should become — as the Synod Fathers continue — an "ecclesial community," a "community of the disciples of the Lord in which the one same liturgy (which imbues life with a spirit of prayer) is celebrated, a community molded daily in the reading and meditation of the word of God and with the Sacrament of the Eucharist and in the practice of fraternal charity and justice, a community in which, as its life and the life of each of its members progresses, there shine forth the Spirit of Christ and love for the Church."[191] This ecclesial aspect of the seminary is confirmed and concretized by the Fathers when they add: "As an ecclesial community, be it diocesan or interdiocesan, or even religious, the seminary should nourish the meaning of communion between the candidates and their Bishop and presbyterate, in such a way that they share in their hopes and anxieties and learn to extend this openness to the needs of the universal Church."[192]

60.6 It is essential for the formation of candidates for the priesthood and the pastoral ministry, which by its very nature is ecclesial, that the seminary should be experienced not as something external and superficial, or simply a place in which to live and study, but in an interior and profound way. It should be experienced as a community, a specifically ecclesial community, a community that relives the experience of the group of Twelve who were united to Jesus.[193]

[190] Ibid.

[191] Ibid.

[192] Ibid.

[193] Cf. John Paul II, Address to the Students and Former Students of the Almo Collegio Capranica (January 21, 1983): *Insegnamenti* VI/1 (1983), 173-178.

61.1 The seminary is, therefore, an *educational ecclesial community,* indeed a particular educating community. And it is the specific goal which determines its physiognomy: the vocational accompanying of future priests, and therefore discernment of a vocation, the help to respond to it and the preparation to receive the Sacrament of Orders with its own graces and responsibilities, by which the priest is configured to Jesus Christ Head and Shepherd and is enabled and committed to share the mission of salvation in the Church and in the world.

61.2 Inasmuch as it is an educating community, the seminary and its entire life, in all its different expressions, is *committed to formation,* the human, spiritual, intellectual and pastoral formation of future priests. Although this formation has many aspects in common with the human and Christian formation of all the members of the Church, it has, nevertheless, contents, modalities and characteristics which relate specifically to the aim of preparation for the priesthood.

61.3 The content and form of the educational work require that the seminary should have a precise *program,* a program of life characterized by its being organized and unified, by its being in harmony or correspondence with the one aim which justifies the existence of the seminary: preparation of future priests.

61.4 In this regard, the Synod Fathers write: "As an educational community, (the seminary) should follow a clearly defined program which will have, as a characteristic, a unity of leadership expressed in the figure of the rector and his cooperators, a consistency in the ordering of life, formational activity and the fundamental demands of community life, which also involves the essential aspects of the task of formation. This program should be at the service of the specific finality which alone justify the existence of the seminary, and it should do so without hesitation or ambiguity. That aim is the formation of future priests, pastors of the Church."[194] And in order to ensure that the programming is truly apt and effective, the fundamental outlines of the program will have to be translated into more concrete details, with the help of particular norms that are aimed at regulating community life, establishing certain precise instruments and timetables.

61.5 A further aspect is to be stressed here: the educational work is by its nature an accompanying of specific individual persons who are proceeding to a choice of and commitment to precise ideals of life. For this very reason, the work of education should be able to bring together into a harmonious whole a clear statement of the goal to be achieved, the requirement that candidates

---

[194] *Propositio* 20.

proceed seriously toward the goal, and third, attention to the "journeyer," that is, the individual person who is embarked on this adventure, and therefore attention to a series of situations, problems, difficulties and different rates of progress and growth. This requires a wise flexibility. And this does not mean compromising, either as regards values or as regards the conscious and free commitment of the candidates. What it does mean is a true love and a sincere respect for the person who, in conditions which are very personal, is proceeding toward the priesthood. This applies not only to individual candidates, but also to the diverse social and cultural contexts in which seminaries exist and to the different life histories which they have. In this sense *the educational work requires continual renewal.* The Synod Fathers have brought this out forcefully also when speaking about the structure of seminaries: "Without questioning the validity of the classical forms of seminaries, the Synod desires that the work of consultation of the Episcopal Conferences on the present-day needs of formation should proceed as is established in the Decree *Optatam Totius* (No. 1), and in the 1967 Synod. The *Rationes* of the different nations or rites should be revised where opportune whether on the occasion of requests made by the Episcopal Conferences or in relation to apostolic visitations of the seminaries of different countries, in order to bring into them diverse forms of formation that have proved successful, as well as to respond to the needs of people with so-called indigenous cultures, the needs of the vocations of adult men and the needs of vocations for the missions, etc."[195]

62.1 The purpose and specific educational form of the major seminary demand that candidates for the priesthood have *a certain prior preparation* before entering it. Such preparation, at least until a few decades ago, did not create particular problems. In those days most candidates to the priesthood came from minor seminaries, and the Christian life of the community offered all, in general, a suitable Christian instruction and education.

62.2 The situation in many places has changed. There is a considerable discrepancy between, on the one hand, the style of life and basic preparation of boys, adolescents and young men, even when they are Christians and at times have been involved in Church life, and, on the other hand, the style of life of the seminary with its formational demands.

62.3 In this context, together with the Synod Fathers I ask that there be a sufficient period of preparation prior to seminary formation: "It is a good thing that there be a period of human, Christian, intellectual and spiritual preparation for the candidates to the major seminary. These candidates should, how-

---

[195] Ibid.

ever, have certain qualities: a right intention, a sufficient degree of human maturity, a sufficiently broad knowledge of the doctrine of the faith, some introduction into the methods of prayer and behavior in conformity with Christian tradition. They should also have attitudes proper to their regions, through which they can express their effort to find God and the faith (cf. *Evangelii Nuntiandi*, 48)."[196]

62.4 The "sufficiently broad knowledge of the doctrine of the faith" which the Synod Fathers mention is a primary condition for theology. It simply is not possible to develop an *"intelligentia fidei"* (an understanding of the faith), if the content of the *"fides"* is not known. Such a gap can be filled more easily when the forthcoming *Universal Catechism* appears.

62.5 While there is increasing consensus regarding the need for preparation prior to the major seminary, there are different ideas as to what such preparation should contain and what its characteristics should be: should it be directed mainly to spiritual formation to discern the vocation or to intellectual and cultural formation? On the other hand, we cannot overlook the many and deep diversities that exist, not only among the individual candidates, but also in the different regions and countries. This implies the need for a period of study and experimentation in order to define as clearly and suitably as possible the different elements of this prior preparation or *"propaedeutic period"*: the duration, place, form, subject matter of this period, all of which will have to be coordinated with the subsequent years of formation offered by the seminary.

62.6 In this sense I take up and propose to the Congregation for Catholic Education a request expressed by the Synod Fathers: "The Synod asks that the Congregation for Catholic Education gather all the information on experiments of such initial formation that have been done or are being done. At a suitable time, the Congregation is requested to communicate its findings on this matter to the Episcopal Conferences."[197]

The minor seminary and other forms of fostering vocations

63.1 As long experience shows, a priestly vocation tends to show itself in the preadolescent years or in the earliest years of youth. Even in people who decide to enter the seminary later on it is not infrequent to find that God's call had been perceived much earlier. The Church's history gives constant witness of calls which the Lord directs to people of tender age. Saint Thomas, for example, explains Jesus' special love for Saint John the Apostle "because of

---

[196] *Propositio* 19.
[197] Ibid.

his tender age" and draws the following conclusion: "This explains that God loves in a special way those who give themselves to his service from their earliest youth."[198]

63.2 The Church looks after these seeds of vocations sown in the hearts of children by means of the institution of minor seminaries, providing a careful though preliminary discernment and accompaniment. In a number of parts of the world, these seminaries continue to carry out a valuable educational work, the aim of which is to protect and develop the seeds of a priestly vocation, so that the students may more easily recognize it and be in a better position to respond to it. The educational goal of such seminaries tends to favor in a timely and gradual way the human, cultural and spiritual formation which will lead the young person to embark on the path of the major seminary with an adequate and solid foundation. *"To be prepared to follow Christ the Redeemer with generous souls and pure hearts"*: this is the purpose of the minor seminary as indicated by the Council in the Decree *Optatam Totius,* which thus outlines its educational aspect: the students "under the fatherly supervision of the superiors, the parents too playing their appropriate part, should lead lives suited to the age, mentality and development of young people. Their way of life should be fully in keeping with the standards of sound psychology and should include suitable experience of the ordinary affairs of daily life and contact with their own families."[199]

63.3 The minor seminary can also be in the Diocese a reference point for vocation work, with suitable forms of welcome and the offering of opportunities for information to adolescents who are looking into the possibility of a vocation or who, having already made up their mind to follow their vocation, have to delay entry into the seminary for various family or educational reasons.

64.1 In those cases where it is not possible to run minor seminaries (which "in many regions seem necessary and very useful"), other "institutions" need to be provided, as for example *vocational groups* for adolescents and young people.[200] While they lack the quality of permanence, such groups can offer a systematic guide, in a community context, with which to check the existence and development of vocations. While such young people live at home and take part in the activities of the Christian community which helps them along the path of formation, they should not be left alone. They need a particular group

[198] *In Iohannem Evangelistam Expositio,* c. 21, lect. V, 2.
[199] No. 3.
[200] Cf. *Propositio* 17.

or community to refer to, and where they can find support to follow through the specific vocational journey which the gift of the Holy Spirit has initiated in them.

64.2 We should also mention the phenomenon of *priestly vocations* arising among people *of adult age* after some years of experience of lay life and professional involvement. This phenomenon, while not new in the Church's history, at present appears with some novel features and with a certain frequency. It is not always possible and often it is not even convenient to invite adults to follow the educative itinerary of the major seminary. Rather, after a careful discernment of the genuineness of such vocations, what needs to be provided is some kind of specific program to accompany them with formation in order to ensure, bearing in mind all the suitable adaptations, that such persons receive the spiritual and intellectual formation they require. A suitable relationship with other candidates to the priesthood and periods spent in the community of the major seminary can be a way of guaranteeing that these vocations are fully inserted in the one presbyterate and are in intimate and heartfelt communion with it.[201]

3. The Agents of Priestly Formation

The Church and the Bishop

65.1 Given that the formation of candidates for the priesthood belongs to the Church's pastoral care of vocations, it must be said that *the Church as such is the communal subject* which has the grace and responsibility to accompany those whom the Lord calls to become his ministers in the priesthood.

65.2 In this sense the appreciation of the mystery of the Church helps us to establish more precisely the place and role which her different members have — be it individually or as members of a body — in the formation of candidates for the priesthood.

65.3 The Church is by her very nature the "memorial" or "sacrament" of the presence and action of Jesus Christ in our midst and on our behalf. The call to the priesthood depends on his saving presence: not only the call, but also the accompanying so that the person called can recognize the Lord's grace and respond to it freely and lovingly. It is the Spirit of Jesus that throws light on and gives strength to vocational discernment and the journey to the priesthood. So we can say that *there cannot exist any genuine*

---

[201] Cf. Sacred Congregation for Catholic Education, *Ratio Fundamentalis Institutionis Sacerdotalis* (January 6, 1970), 19: *AAS* 62 (1970), 342.

formational work for the priesthood without the influence of the Spirit of Christ. Everyone involved in the work of formation should be fully aware of this. How can we fail to appreciate this utterly gratuitous and completely effective "resource," which has its own decisive "weight" in the effort to train people for the priesthood? How can we not rejoice when we consider the dignity of every human being involved in formation, who for the candidate to the priesthood becomes, as it were, the visible representative of Christ? If training for the priesthood is, as it should be, essentially the preparation of future "shepherds" in the likeness of Jesus Christ the Good Shepherd, who better than Jesus himself, through the outpouring of his Spirit, can give them and fully develop in them that pastoral charity which he himself lived to the point of total self-giving (cf. Jn 15:13, 10:11) and which he wishes all priests to live in their turn?

65.4 The first representative of Christ in priestly formation is the Bishop. What Mark the Evangelist tells us, in the text we have already quoted more than once, can be applied to the Bishop, to every Bishop: "He called to him those whom he desired; and *they came to him.* And he appointed twelve *to be with him,* and to be sent out" (3:13-14). The truth is that the interior call of the Spirit needs to be recognized as the authentic call of the Bishop. Just as all can *"go" to the Bishop,* because he is shepherd and father to all, his priests who share with him the one priesthood and ministry can do so in a special way: the Bishop, the Council tells us, should consider them and treat them as "brothers and friends."[202] By analogy the same can be said of those who are preparing for the priesthood. As for "being with him," with the Bishop, the Bishop should make a point of visiting them often and in some way "being" with them as a way of giving significant expression to his responsibility for the formation of candidates for the priesthood.

65.5 The presence of the Bishop is especially valuable, not only because it helps the seminary community live its insertion in the particular Church and its communion with the Pastor who guides it, but also because it verifies and encourages the pastoral purpose which is what specifies the entire formation of candidates for the priesthood. In particular, with his presence and by his sharing with candidates for the priesthood all that has to do with the pastoral progress of the particular Church, the Bishop offers a fundamental contribution to formation in the *sensus Ecclesiae,* as a central spiritual and pastoral value in the exercise of the priestly ministry.

---

[202] Decree on the Ministry and Life of Priests *Presbyterorum Ordinis,* 7.

The seminary as an educational community

66.1 The educational community of the seminary is built around the various people involved in formation: *the rector, the spiritual father or spiritual director, the superiors and professors.* These people should feel profoundly united to the Bishop, whom they represent in their different roles and in various ways. They should also maintain among themselves a frank and genuine communion. The unity of the educators not only helps the educational program to be put into practice properly, but also and above all it offers candidates for the priesthood a significant example and a practical introduction to that ecclesial communion which is a fundamental value of Christian living and of the pastoral ministry.

66.2 It is evident that much of the effectiveness of the training offered depends on the maturity and strength of personality of those entrusted with formation, both from the human and from the Gospel points of view. And so it is especially important both *to select them carefully* and to encourage them to become ever *more suitable for carrying out the task entrusted to them.* The Synod Fathers were very aware that the future of the preparation of candidates for the priesthood depends on the choice and formation of those entrusted with the work of formation, and so they describe at length the qualities sought for in them. Specifically they wrote: "The task of formation of candidates for the priesthood requires not only a certain special preparation of those to whom this work is entrusted, one that is professional, pedagogical, spiritual, human and theological, but also a spirit of communion and of cooperating together to carry out the program, so that the unity of the pastoral action of the seminary is always maintained under the leadership of the rector. The body of formation personnel should witness to a truly evangelical lifestyle and total dedication to the Lord. It should enjoy a certain stability and its members as a rule should live in the seminary community. They should be intimately joined to the Bishop, who is the first one responsible for the formation of the priests."[203]

66.3 The Bishops first of all should feel their grave responsibility for the formation of those who have been given the task of educating future priests. For this ministry, priests of exemplary life should be chosen, men with a number of qualities: "human and spiritual maturity, pastoral experience, professional competence, stability in their own vocation, a capacity to work with others, serious preparation in those human sciences (psychology especially) which relate to their office, a knowledge of how to work in groups."[204]

---

[203] *Propositio* 29.
[204] Ibid.

66.4 While safeguarding the distinctions between internal and external forum, and maintaining a suitable freedom in the choice of confessors and the prudence and discretion which should be a feature of the ministry of the spiritual director, the priestly community of teachers should feel united in the responsibility of educating candidates for the priesthood. It is their duty, always with regard to the authoritative evaluation made by the Bishop and the rector together, to foster and verify in the first place the suitability of the candidates in regard to their spiritual, human and intellectual endowments, above all in regard to their spirit of prayer, their deep assimilation of the doctrine of the faith, their capacity for true fraternity and the charism of celibacy.[205]

66.5 Bearing in mind (as the Synod Fathers have indeed done) the indications of the Exhortation *Christifideles Laici* and of the Apostolic Letter *Mulieris Dignitatem*,[206] which stress the suitability of a healthy influence of lay spirituality and of the charism of femininity in every educational itinerary, it is worthwhile to involve, in ways that are prudent and adapted to the different cultural contexts, the cooperation also of *lay faithful, both men and women,* in the work of training future priests. They are to be selected with care, within the framework of Church laws and according to their particular charisms and proven competence. We can expect beneficial fruits from their cooperation, provided it is suitably coordinated and integrated in the primary educational responsibilities of those entrusted with the formation of future priests, fruits for a balanced growth of the sense of the Church and a more precise perception of what it is to be a priest on the part of the candidates to the priesthood.[207]

The professors of theology

67.1 Those who by their teaching of theology introduce future priests to *sacred doctrine* and accompany them in it have a particular educational responsibility. Experience teaches that they often have a greater influence on the development of the priest's personality than other educators.

67.2 The responsibility of the *teachers of theology* will lead them, even before they consider the teaching relationship they are to establish with candidates for the priesthood, to look into the concept they themselves should

[205] Cf. *Propositio* 23.

[206] Cf. John Paul II, Post-Synodal Apostolic Exhortation *Christifideles Laici* (December 30, 1988), 61, 63: *AAS* 81 (1989), 512-514, 517-518; Apostolic Letter *Mulieris Dignitatem* (August 15, 1988), 29-31: *AAS* 80 (1988), 1721-1729.

[207] Cf. *Propositio* 29.

have of the nature of theology and the priestly ministry, and also of the spirit and style in which they should carry out their teaching of theology. In this sense the Synod Fathers have rightly affirmed that "the theologian must never forget that as a teacher he is not presenting his personal doctrines but opening to and communicating to others the understanding of the faith, in the last analysis in the name of the Lord and his Church. In such a way, the theologian, using all the methods and techniques provided by his science, carries out his task at the mandate of the Church and cooperates with the Bishop in his task of teaching. Since theologians and Bishops are at the service of the Church herself in promoting the faith, they should develop and foster trust in each other and, in this spirit, overcome tensions and conflicts (for fuller treatment, cf. Congregation for the Doctrine of the Faith, Instruction on the Ecclesial Vocation of the Theologian)."[208]

67.3 The teacher of theology, like any other teacher, should remain in communion and sincerely cooperate with all the other people who are involved in the formation of future priests, and offer with scientific precision, generosity, humility and enthusiasm his own original and expert contribution, which is not simply the communication of doctrine — even though it be *sacred doctrine* — but is above all the presentation of the point of view which unifies, in the plan of God, all the different branches of human knowledge and the various expressions of life.

67.4 In particular, the formative effect of the teachers of theology will depend, above all, on whether they are "men of faith who are full of love for the Church, convinced that the one who really knows the Christian mystery is the Church as such and, therefore, that their task of teaching is really and truly an ecclesial ministry, men who have a richly developed pastoral sense which enables them to discern not only content but forms that are suitable for the exercise of their ministry. In particular, what is expected of the teachers is total fidelity to the Magisterium; for they teach in the name of the Church, and because of this they are witnesses to the faith."[209]

Communities of origin and associations and youth movements

68.1 The communities from which the candidate for the priesthood comes continue, albeit with the necessary detachment which is involved by the choice of a vocation, to bear considerable influence on the formation of the future priest. They should therefore be aware of their specific share of responsibility.

68.2 Let us mention first of all the *family:* Christian parents, as also broth-

---

[208] *Propositio* 30.
[209] Ibid.

ers and sisters and the other members of the family, should never seek to call back the future priest within the narrow confines of a too human (if not worldly) logic, no matter how supported by sincere affection that logic may be (cf. Mk 3:20-21, 31-35). Instead, driven by the same desire "to fulfill the will of God," they should accompany the formative journey with prayer, respect, the good example of the domestic virtues and spiritual and material help, especially in difficult moments. Experience teaches that, in so many cases, this multiple help has proved decisive for candidates for the priesthood. Even in the case of parents or relatives who are indifferent or opposed to the choice of a vocation, a clear and calm facing of the situation and the encouragement which derives from it can be a great help to the deeper and more determined maturing of a priestly vocation.

68.3 Closely linked with the families is the *parish community*. Both it and the family are connected in education in the faith. Often, afterward, the parish, with its specific pastoral care for young people and vocations, supplements the family's role. Above all, inasmuch as it is the most immediate local expression of the mystery of the Church, the parish offers an original and especially valuable contribution to the formation of a future priest. The parish community should continue to feel that the young man on his way to the priesthood is a living part of itself; it should accompany him with its prayer, give him a cordial welcome during the holiday periods, respect and encourage him to form himself in his identity as a priest, and offer him suitable opportunities and strong encouragement to try out his vocation for the priestly mission.

68.4 *Associations and youth movements,* which are a sign and confirmation of the vitality which the Spirit guarantees to the Church, can and should contribute also to the formation of candidates for the priesthood, in particular of those who are the product of the Christian, spiritual and apostolic experience of these groups. Young people who have received their basic formation in such groups and look to them for their experience of the Church should not feel they are being asked to uproot themselves from their past or to break their links with the environment which has contributed to their decision to respond to their vocation, nor should they erase the characteristic traits of the spirituality which they have learned and lived there in all that they contain that is good, edifying and rich.[210] For them too, this environment from which they come continues to be a source of help and support on the path of formation toward the priesthood.

---

[210] Cf. *Propositio* 25.

68.5 The Spirit offers to many young people opportunities to be educated in the faith and to grow as Christians and as members of the Church through many kinds of groups, movements and associations inspired in different ways by the Gospel message. These should be felt and lived as a nourishing gift of a soul within the institution and at its service. A movement or a particular spirituality "is not an alternative structure to the institution. It is rather a source of a presence which constantly regenerates the existential and historical authenticity of the institution. The priest should therefore find within a movement the light and warmth which make him capable of fidelity to his Bishop and which make him ready for the duties of the institution and mindful of ecclesiastical discipline, thus making the reality of his faith more fertile and his faithfulness more joyful."[211]

68.6 It is therefore necessary, in the new community of the seminary in which they are gathered by the Bishop, that young people coming from associations and ecclesial movements should learn "respect for other spiritual paths and a spirit of dialogue and cooperation," should take in genuinely and sincerely the indications for their training imparted by the Bishop and the teachers in the seminary, abandoning themselves with real confidence to their guidance and assessments.[212] Such an attitude will prepare and in some way anticipate a genuine priestly choice to serve the entire People of God in the fraternal communion of the presbyterate and in obedience to the Bishop.

68.7 The fact that seminarians and diocesan priests take part in particular spiritualities or ecclesial groupings is indeed, in itself, a factor which helps growth and priestly fraternity. Such participation, however, should not be an obstacle, but rather a help to the ministry and spiritual life which are proper to the diocesan priest, who "will always remain the shepherd of all. Not only is he a 'permanent' shepherd, available to all, but he presides over the gathering of all so that all may find the welcome which they have a right to expect in the community and in the Eucharist that unites them, whatever be their religious sensibility or pastoral commitment."[213]

The candidate himself

69.1 Lastly, we must not forget that the candidate himself is a necessary and irreplaceable agent in his own formation: all formation, priestly forma-

---

[211] John Paul II, Address to Priests connected with the Communion and Liberation Movement (September 12, 1985), 3: *AAS* 78 (1986), 256.

[212] Cf. *Propositio* 25.

[213] John Paul II, Meeting with Members of the Swiss Clergy, Einsiedeln (June 15, 1984), 10: *Insegnamenti* VII/1 (1984), 1798.

tion included, is ultimately a self-formation. No one can replace us in the responsible freedom that we have as individual persons.

69.2 And so the future priest also, and in the first place, must grow in his awareness that the Agent *par excellence* of his formation is the Holy Spirit, who, by the gift of a new heart, configures and conforms him to Jesus Christ the Good Shepherd. In this way the candidate to the priesthood will affirm in the most radical way possible his freedom to welcome the molding action of the Spirit. But to welcome this action implies also, on the part of the candidate, a welcome for the human "mediating" forces which the Spirit employs. As a result, the actions of the different teachers become truly and fully effective only if the future priest offers his own convinced and heartfelt cooperation to this work of formation.

VI

I Remind You To Rekindle the Gift of God That Is within You

The Ongoing Formation of Priests

Theological reasons behind ongoing formation

70.1 "I remind you to rekindle the gift of God that is within you" (2 Tim 1:6).

70.2 The words of Saint Paul to Timothy can appropriately be applied to the ongoing formation to which all priests are called by virtue of the "gift of God" which they have received at their ordination. The passage helps us to grasp the full truth, the absolute uniqueness of the permanent formation of priests. Here we are also helped by another text of Saint Paul, who once more writes to Timothy: "Do not neglect the gift you have, which was given you by prophetic utterance when the elders laid their hands upon you. Practice these duties, devote yourself to them, so that all may see your progress. Take heed to yourself and to your teaching; hold to that, for by so doing you will save both yourself and your hearers" (1 Tim 4:14-16).

70.3 Paul asks Timothy to "rekindle," or stir into flame, the divine gift he has received, much as one might do with the embers of a fire, in the sense of welcoming it and living it out without ever losing or forgetting that "permanent novelty" which is characteristic of every gift from God, who makes all things new (cf. Rev 21:5), and thus living it out in its unfading freshness and original beauty.

70.4 But this "rekindling" is not only the outcome of a task entrusted to the personal responsibility of Timothy, nor only the result of his efforts to use his mind and will. It is also the effect of a dynamism of grace intrinsic to God's gift. God himself, in other words, rekindles his own gift, so as better to release all the extraordinary riches of grace and responsibility contained in it.

70.5 With the sacramental outpouring of the Holy Spirit who consecrates and sends forth, the priest is configured to the likeness of Jesus Christ, Head and Shepherd of the Church, and is sent forth to carry out a pastoral ministry. In this way the priest is marked permanently and indelibly in his inner being as a minister of Jesus and of the Church. He comes to share in a permanent and irreversible way of life and is entrusted with a pastoral ministry which, because it is rooted in his being and involves his entire life, is itself permanent. The Sacrament of Holy Orders confers upon the priest sacramental grace which gives him a share not only in Jesus' saving "power" and "ministry" but also in his pastoral "love." At the same time it ensures that the priest can count on all the actual graces he needs, whenever they are necessary and useful for the worthy and perfect exercise of the ministry he has received.

70.6 We thus see that the proper foundation and original motivation for ongoing formation is contained in the dynamism of the Sacrament of Holy Orders.

70.7 Certainly there are also *purely human reasons* which call for the priest to engage in ongoing formation. This formation is demanded by his own continuing personal growth. Every life is a constant path toward maturity, a maturity which cannot be attained except by constant formation. It is also demanded by the priestly ministry seen in a general way and taken in common with other professions, that is, as a service directed to others. There is no profession, job or work which does not require constant updating, if it is to remain current and effective. The need to "keep pace" with the path of history is another human reason justifying ongoing formation.

70.8 But these and other motivations are taken up and become even clearer by the *theological motivations* mentioned previously and which demand further reflection.

70.9 The *Sacrament of Holy Orders,* by its nature (common to all the sacraments) as a "sign," may be considered, and truly is, a *word of God.* It is a word of God which *calls and sends forth.* It is the strongest expression of the priest's vocation and mission. By the Sacrament of Holy Orders, *God calls the candidate "to" the priesthood "coram Ecclesia."* The "come, follow me" of Jesus is proclaimed fully and definitively in the sacramental celebration of his Church. It is made manifest and communicated by the Church's voice, which is heard in the words of the Bishop who prays and imposes his hands. The priest then gives his response, in faith, to Jesus' call: "I am coming, to follow you." From this moment there begins that response which, as a fundamental choice, must be expressed anew and reaffirmed through the years of his priesthood in countless other responses, all of them rooted in and enlivened by that "yes" of Holy Orders.

70.10 In this sense one can speak of a *vocation "within" the priesthood.* The fact is that God continues to call and send forth, revealing his saving plan in the historical development of the priest's life and the life of the Church and of society. It is in this perspective that the meaning of ongoing formation emerges. Permanent formation is necessary in order to discern and follow this constant call or will of God. Thus the Apostle Peter is called to follow Jesus even after the risen Lord has entrusted his flock to him: "Jesus said to him, 'Feed my sheep. Truly, truly, I say to you, when you were young, you girded yourself and walked where you would; but when you are old, you will stretch out your hands, and another will gird you and carry you where you do not wish to go.' (This he said to show by what kind of death he was to glorify God.) And after this he said to him, 'Follow me' " (Jn 21:17-19). Consequently there is a "follow me" which accompanies the apostle's whole life and mission. It is a "follow me" in line with the call and demand of *faithfulness unto death* (cf. Jn 21:22), a "follow me" which can signify a *sequela Christi* to the point of total self-giving in martyrdom.[214]

70.11 The Synod Fathers explained the reason justifying the need for ongoing formation, while at the same time revealing its deep nature as *"faithfulness"* to the *priestly ministry* and as a *"process of continual conversion."*[215] It is the Holy Spirit, poured out in the sacrament, who sustains the priest in this faithfulness and accompanies him and encourages him along this path of unending conversion. The gift of the Spirit does not take away the freedom of the priest. It calls on the priest to make use of his freedom in order to cooperate responsibly and accept permanent formation as a task entrusted to him. Thus permanent formation is a requirement of the priest's own faithfulness to his ministry, to his very being. It is love for Jesus Christ and fidelity to oneself. But it is also an *act of love for the People of God,* at whose service the priest is placed. Indeed, an act of *true and proper justice:* the priest owes it to God's people, whose fundamental "right" to receive the word of God, the sacraments and the service of charity, the original and irreplaceable content of the priest's

---

[214] Cf. Saint Augustine, *In Iohannis Evangelium Tractatus,* 123, 5: *CCL* 36, 678-680.
[215] Cf. *Propositio* 31.

own pastoral ministry, he is called to acknowledge and foster. Ongoing formation is necessary to ensure that the priest can properly respond to this right of the People of God.

70.12 *The heart and form of the priest's ongoing formation is pastoral charity:* the Holy Spirit, who infuses pastoral charity, introduces and accompanies the priest to an ever deeper knowledge of the mystery of Christ, which is unfathomable in its richness (cf. Eph 3:14-19) and, in turn, to a knowledge of the mystery of Christian priesthood. Pastoral charity itself impels the priest to an ever deeper knowledge of the hopes, the needs, the problems, the sensibilities of the people to whom he ministers, taken in their specific situations, as individuals, in their families, in society, and in history.

70.13 All this constitutes the object of ongoing formation, understood as a conscious and free decision to live out the dynamism of pastoral charity and of the Holy Spirit who is its first source and constant nourishment. In this sense, ongoing formation is an intrinsic requirement of the gift and sacramental ministry received; and it proves necessary in every age. It is particularly urgent today, not only because of rapid changes in the social and cultural conditions of individuals and peoples among whom priestly ministry is exercised, but also because of that "new evangelization" which constitutes the essential and pressing task of the Church at the end of the second millennium.

Different dimensions of ongoing formation

71.1 The ongoing formation of priests, whether diocesan or Religious, is the natural and absolutely necessary continuation of the process of building priestly personality which began and developed in the seminary or the religious house with the training program which aimed at ordination.

71.2 It is particularly important to be aware of and to respect the intrinsic *link between formation before ordination to the priesthood and formation after ordination.* Should there be a break in continuity, or worse a complete difference between these two phases of formation, there would be serious and immediate repercussions on pastoral work and fraternal communion among priests, especially those in different age groups. Ongoing formation is not a repetition of the formation acquired in the seminary, simply reviewed or expanded with new and practical suggestions. Ongoing formation involves relatively new content and especially methods; it develops as a harmonious and vital process which — rooted in the formation received in the seminary — calls for adaptations, updating and modifications, but without sharp breaks in continuity.

71.3 On the other hand, long-term preparation for ongoing formation should take place in the major seminary, where encouragement needs to be given to future priests to look forward to it, seeing its necessity, its advantages and the spirit in which it should be undertaken, and appropriate conditions for its realization need to be ensured.

71.4 By the very fact that ongoing formation is a continuation of the formation received in the seminary, its aim cannot be the inculcation of a purely "professional" approach, which could be acquired by learning a few new pastoral techniques. Instead its aim must be that of promoting a general and integral process of constant growth, deepening each of the aspects of formation — human, spiritual, intellectual and pastoral — as well as ensuring their active and harmonious integration, based on pastoral charity and in reference to it.

72.1 Fuller development is first required in the *human aspect* of priestly formation. Through his daily contact with people, his sharing in their daily lives, the priest needs to develop and sharpen his human sensitivity so as to understand more clearly their needs, respond to their demands, perceive their unvoiced questions, and share the hopes and expectations, the joys and burdens which are part of life: thus he will be able to meet and enter into dialogue with all people. In particular, through coming to know and share, through making his own the human experience of suffering in its many different manifestations, from poverty to illness, from rejection to ignorance, loneliness, and material or moral poverty, the priest can cultivate his own humanity and make it all the more genuine and clearly apparent by his increasingly ardent love for his fellow man.

72.2 In this task of bringing his human formation to maturity, the priest receives special assistance from the grace of Jesus Christ. The charity of the Good Shepherd was revealed not only by his gift of salvation to mankind, but also by his desire to share our life: thus, the Word who became "flesh" (cf. Jn 1:14) desired to know joy and suffering, to experience weariness, to share feelings, to console sadness. Living as a man among and with men, Jesus Christ offers the most complete, genuine and perfect expression of what it means to be human. We see him celebrating at the wedding feast of Cana, visiting a friend's family, moved by the hungry crowd who follow him, giving sick or even dead children back to their parents, weeping for the death of Lazarus, and so on.

72.3 The People of God should be able to say about the priest, who has increasingly matured in human sensitivity, something similar to what we read about Jesus in the Letter to the Hebrews: "For we have not a high priest who is unable to sympathize with our weaknesses, but one who in every respect has been tempted as we are, yet without sinning" (4:15).

72.4 The formation of the priest in its *spiritual dimension* is required by the new Gospel life to which he has been called in a specific way by the Holy Spirit, poured out in the Sacrament of Holy Orders. The Spirit, by consecrating the priest and configuring him to Jesus Christ, Head and Shepherd, creates a bond which, located in the priest's very being, demands to be assimilated and lived out in a personal, free and conscious way through an ever richer communion of life and love and an ever broader and more radical sharing in the feelings and attitudes of Jesus Christ. In this bond between the Lord Jesus and the priest, an ontological and psychological bond, a sacramental and moral bond, is the foundation and likewise the power for that "life according to the Spirit" and that "radicalism of the Gospel" to which every priest is called today and which is fostered by ongoing formation in its spiritual aspect. This formation proves necessary also for the priestly ministry to be genuine and spiritually fruitful. "Are you exercising the care of souls?" Saint Charles Borromeo once asked in a talk to priests. And he went on to say: "Do not thereby neglect yourself. Do not give yourself to others to such an extent that nothing is left of yourself for yourself. You should certainly keep in mind the souls whose pastor you are, but without forgetting yourself. My brothers, do not forget that there is nothing so necessary to all churchmen than the meditation which precedes, accompanies and follows all our actions: I will sing, says the Prophet, and I will meditate (cf. Ps 101:1). If you administer the sacraments, my brother, meditate upon what you are doing. If you celebrate Mass, meditate on what you are offering. If you recite the Psalms in choir, meditate to whom and of what you are speaking. If you are guiding souls, meditate in whose blood they have been cleansed. And let all be done among you in charity (cf. 1 Cor 16:14). Thus we will be able to overcome the difficulties we meet, countless as they are, each day. In any event, this is what is demanded of us by the task entrusted to us. If we act thus, we will find the strength to give birth to Christ in ourselves and in others."[216]

72.5 The priest's prayer life in particular needs to be continually "re-formed." Experience teaches that in prayer one cannot live off past gains. Every day, we need not only to renew our external fidelity to times of prayer, especially those devoted to the celebration of the Liturgy of the Hours and those left to personal choice and not reinforced by fixed times of liturgical service, but also

---

[216] *Acta Ecclesiae Mediolanensis,* Milan, 1599, 1178.

to strive constantly for the experience of a genuine personal encounter with Jesus, a trusting dialogue with the Father, and a deep experience of the Spirit.

72.6 What the Apostle Paul says of all Christians, that they must attain "to mature manhood, to the measure of the stature of the fullness of Christ" (Eph 4:13), can be applied specifically to priests, who are called to the perfection of charity and therefore to holiness, even more so because their pastoral ministry itself demands that they be living models for all the faithful.

72.7 The *intellectual dimension* of formation likewise needs to be continually fostered through the priest's entire life, especially by a commitment to study and a serious and disciplined familiarity with modern culture. As one who shares in the prophetic mission of Jesus and is part of the mystery of the Church, the Teacher of truth, the priest is called to reveal to others, in Jesus Christ, the true face of God, and as a result the true face of man.[217] This demands that the priest himself seek God's face and contemplate it with loving veneration (cf. Ps 27:8, 42:2). Only thus will he be able to make others know him. In particular, continuing theological study is necessary if the priest is to faithfully carry out the ministry of the word, proclaiming it clearly and without ambiguity, distinguishing it from mere human opinions, no matter how renowned and widespread these might be. Thus he will be able to stand at the service of the People of God, helping them to give an account, to all who ask, of their Christian hope (cf. 1 Pet 3:15). Furthermore, the priest "in applying himself conscientiously and diligently to theological study is in a position to assimilate the genuine richness of the Church in a sure and personal way. Therefore, he can faithfully discharge the mission which is incumbent on him when responding to difficulties about authentic Catholic doctrine, and overcome the inclination, both in himself and others, which leads to dissent and negative attitudes toward the Magisterium and sacred Tradition."[218]

72.8 The *pastoral aspect* of ongoing formation is well expressed by the words of the Apostle Peter: "As each has received a gift, employ it for one another, as good stewards of God's varied grace" (1 Pet 4:10). If he is to live daily according to the graces he has received, the priest must be ever more open to accepting the pastoral charity of Jesus Christ granted him by Christ's Spirit in the sacrament he has received. Just as all the Lord's activity was the fruit and sign of pastoral charity, so should the priest's ministerial activity be. Pastoral charity is a gift, but it is likewise a task, a grace and a responsibility

---

[217] Cf. Second Vatican Ecumenical Council, Pastoral Constitution on the Church in the Modern World *Gaudium et Spes,* 22.

[218] Synod of Bishops, Eighth Ordinary General Assembly, *Instrumentum Laboris,* "The Formation of Priests in the Circumstances of the Present Day," 55.

to which we must be faithful. We have, therefore, to welcome it and live out its dynamism even to its most radical demands. This pastoral charity, as has been said, impels the priest and stimulates him to become ever better acquainted with the real situation of the men and women to whom he is sent, to discern the call of the Spirit in the historical circumstances in which he finds himself, and to seek the most suitable methods and the most useful forms for carrying out his ministry today. Thus pastoral charity encourages and sustains the priest's human efforts for pastoral activity that is relevant, credible and effective. But this demands some kind of permanent pastoral formation.

72.9 The path toward maturity does not simply demand that the priest deepen the different aspects of his formation. It also demands above all that he be able to combine ever more harmoniously all these aspects, gradually achieving their *inner unity*. This will be made possible by pastoral charity. Indeed, pastoral charity not only coordinates and unifies the diverse aspects, but it makes them more specific, marking them out as aspects of the formation of the priest as such, that is, of the priest as a clear and living image, a minister of Jesus the Good Shepherd.

72.10 Ongoing formation helps the priest to overcome the temptation to reduce his ministry to an activism which becomes an end in itself, to the provision of impersonal services, even if these are spiritual or sacred, or to a businesslike function which he carries out for the Church. Only ongoing formation enables the priest to *safeguard with vigilant love the "mystery" which he bears within his heart for the good of the Church and of mankind.*

The profound meaning of ongoing formation

73.1 The different and complementary dimensions of ongoing formation help us to grasp its profound meaning. Ongoing formation helps the priest to *be* and *act* as a priest in the spirit and style of Jesus the Good Shepherd.

73.2 Truth needs to be put into practice! Saint James tells us as much: "Be doers of the word, and not hearers only, deceiving yourselves" (1:22). Priests are called to "live the truth" of their being, that is to live "in love" (cf. Eph 4:15) their identity and ministry in the Church and for the Church. They are called to become ever more aware of the gift of God, and to live it out constantly. This is the invitation Paul makes to Timothy: "Guard the truth that has been entrusted to you by the Holy Spirit which dwells within us" (2 Tim 1:14).

73.3 In the ecclesiological context which we have recalled more than once, we can consider the profound meaning of ongoing priestly formation in relation to the priest's presence and activity in the Church as *mysterium, communio et missio.*

73.4 *Within the Church as "mystery"* the priest is called, by his ongoing formation, to *safeguard and develop in faith his awareness of the total and marvelous truth of his being:* he is a minister of Christ and steward of the mysteries of God (cf. 1 Cor 4:1). Paul expressly asks Christians to consider him in this way. But even before that, he himself lives in the awareness of the sublime gift he has received from the Lord. This should be the case with every priest, if he wishes to remain true to his being. But this is possible only in faith, only by looking at things through the eyes of Christ.

73.5 In this sense it can be said that ongoing formation has as its aim that *the priest become a believer and ever more of one:* that he grow in understanding of who he truly is, seeing things with the eyes of Christ. The priest must safeguard this truth with grateful and joyful love. He must renew his faith when he exercises his priestly ministry; he must feel himself a minister of Christ, a sacrament of the love of God for mankind, every time that he is the means and the living instrument for conferring God's grace upon men. He must recognize this same truth in his fellow priests, for this is the basis of his respect and love for other priests.

74.1 Ongoing formation helps priests, *within the Church as "communion,"* to deepen their awareness that their ministry is ultimately aimed at gathering together the family of God as a brotherhood inspired by charity and to lead it to the Father through Christ in the Holy Spirit.[219]

74.2 The priest should grow in *awareness of the deep communion uniting him to the People of God:* he is not only "in the forefront of" the Church, but above all "in" the Church. He is a brother among brothers. By Baptism, which marks him with the dignity and freedom of the children of God in the only-begotten Son, the priest is a member of the one Body of Christ (cf. Eph 4:16). His consciousness of this communion leads to a need to awaken and deepen *coresponsibility* in the one common mission of salvation, with a prompt and heartfelt esteem for all the charisms and tasks which the Spirit gives believers for the building up of the Church. It is above all in the exercise of the pastoral ministry, directed by its very nature to the good of the People of God, that the priest must live and give witness to his profound communion with all. As Pope Paul VI wrote: "We must become brothers to all at the very same time as we wish to be their shepherds, fathers and teachers. The climate of dialogue is friendship. Indeed it is service."[220]

---

[219] Cf. Second Vatican Ecumenical Council, Decree on the Ministry and Life of Priests *Presbyterorum Ordinis,* 6.

[220] Encyclical Letter *Ecclesiam Suam* (August 6, 1964), III: *AAS* 56 (1964), 647.

74.3 More specifically, the priest is called to deepen his awareness of being a *member of the particular Church* in which he is incardinated, joined by a bond that is juridical, spiritual and pastoral. This awareness presupposes a particular love for his own Church and it makes that love grow. This is truly the living and permanent goal of the pastoral charity which should accompany the life of the priest and lead him to share in the history or life experience of this same particular Church, in its riches and in its weaknesses, in its difficulties and in its hopes, working in it for its growth. And thus to feel himself both enriched by the particular Church and actively involved in building it up, carrying on — as an individual and together with other priests — that pastoral involvement typical of his brother priests who have gone before him. A necessary requirement of this pastoral charity toward one's own particular Church and its future ministry is the concern which the priest should have to find, so to speak, someone to replace him in the priesthood.

74.4 The priest must grow in his awareness of the *communion existing between the various particular Churches,* a communion rooted in their very being as Churches which make present in various places Christ's one universal Church. This awareness of the communion of the particular Churches will foster an *"exchange of gifts,"* beginning with living and personal gifts, such as priests themselves. There should be a readiness, indeed a generous commitment, to provide for a fair distribution of clergy.[221] Among these particular Churches, those should be kept in mind which, because they are "deprived of freedom, cannot have their own vocations," as well as those "Churches which have emerged recently from persecution and poor Churches which have been given help already for many years and from many sources with great-hearted brotherliness and still receive help."[222]

74.5 Within the ecclesial communion, the priest is called in particular to *grow,* thanks to his ongoing formation, *in and with his own presbyterate in union with his Bishop.* The presbyterate, in the fullness of its truth, is a *mysterium:* it is in fact a supernatural reality because it is rooted in the Sacrament of Holy Orders. This is its source and origin. This is its "place" of birth and of its growth. Indeed, "priests by means of the Sacrament of Orders are tied with a personal and indissoluble bond to Christ the one priest. The Sacrament of Holy Orders is conferred upon each of them as individuals, but they

---

[221] Cf. Congregation for the Clergy, Directives for the Promotion of Mutual Cooperation between Particular Churches and Especially for a More Suitable Distribution of the Clergy *Postquam Apostoli* (March 25, 1980): *AAS* 72 (1980), 343-364.

[222] *Propositio* 39.

are inserted into the communion of the presbyterate united with the Bishop (*Lumen Gentium,* 28; *Presbyterorum Ordinis,* 7, 8)."[223]

74.6 This sacramental origin is reflected and continued in the sphere of priestly ministry: from *mysterium* to *ministerium.* "Unity among the priests with the Bishop and among themselves is not something added from the outside to the nature of their service, but expresses its essence inasmuch as it is the care of Christ the Priest for the People gathered in the unity of the Blessed Trinity."[224] This unity among priests, lived in a spirit of pastoral charity, makes priests witnesses of Jesus Christ, who prayed to the Father "that they may all be one" (Jn 17:21).

74.7 The presbyterate thus appears as a *true family,* as a fraternity whose ties do not arise from flesh and blood but from the grace of Holy Orders. This grace takes up and elevates the human and psychological bonds of affection and friendship, as well as the spiritual bonds which exist between priests. It is a grace that grows ever greater and finds expression in the most varied forms of mutual assistance, spiritual and material as well. Priestly fraternity excludes no one. However, it can and should have its preferences, those of the Gospel, reserved for those who have greatest need of help and encouragement. This fraternity "takes special care of the young priests, maintains a kind and fraternal dialogue with those of the middle and older age groups, and with those who for whatever reasons are facing difficulties; as for those priests who have given up this way of life or are not following it at this time, this brotherhood does not forget them but follows them all the more with fraternal solicitude."[225]

74.8 *Religious clergy* who live and work in a particular Church also belong to the one presbyterate, albeit under a different title. Their presence is a source of enrichment for all priests. The different particular charisms which they live, while challenging all priests to grow in the understanding of the priesthood itself, help to encourage and promote ongoing priestly formation. The gift of religious life, in the framework of the Diocese, when accompanied by genuine esteem and rightful respect for the particular features of each Institute and each spiritual tradition, broadens the horizon of Christian witness and contributes in various ways to an enrichment of priestly spirituality, above all with regard to the proper relationship and interplay between the values of the particular Church and those of the whole People of God. For their part, Religious will be concerned to ensure a spirit of true ecclesial communion, a

[223] *Propositio* 34.
[224] Ibid.
[225] Ibid.

genuine participation in the progress of the Diocese and the pastoral decisions of the Bishop, generously putting their own charism at the service of building up everyone in charity.[226]

74.9 Finally, it is in the context of the Church as communion and in the context of the presbyterate that we can best discuss the problem of *priestly loneliness* treated by the Synod Fathers. There is a loneliness which all priests experience and which is completely normal. But there is another loneliness which is the product of various difficulties and which in turn creates further difficulties. With regard to the latter, "active participation in the diocesan presbyterate, regular contact with the Bishop and with the other priests, mutual cooperation, common life or fraternal dealings between priests, as also friendship and good relations with the lay faithful who are active in parish life are very useful means to overcome the negative effects of loneliness which the priest can sometimes experience."[227]

74.10 Loneliness does not, however, create only difficulties; it can also offer positive opportunities for the priestly life: "When it is accepted in a spirit of oblation and is seen as an opportunity for greater intimacy with Jesus Christ the Lord, solitude can be an opportunity for prayer and study, as also a help for sanctification and also for human growth."[228]

74.11 It should be added that a certain type of solitude is a necessary element in ongoing formation. Jesus often went off alone to pray (cf. Mt 14:23). The ability to handle a healthy solitude is indispensable for caring for one's interior life. Here we are speaking of a solitude filled with the presence of the Lord who puts us in contact with the Father, in the light of the Spirit. In this regard, concern for silence and looking for places and times of "desert" are necessary for the priest's permanent formation, whether in the intellectual, spiritual or pastoral areas. In this regard too, it can be said that those unable to have a positive experience of their own solitude are incapable of genuine and fraternal fellowship.

75.1 Ongoing formation aims at *increasing the priest's awareness of his share in the Church's saving mission.* In the Church's "mission," the priest's

---

[226] Cf. *Propositio* 38; Second Vatican Ecumenical Council, Decree on the Ministry and Life of Priests *Presbyterorum Ordinis,* 1; Decree on Priestly Formation *Optatam Totius,* 1; Sacred Congregation for Religious and Secular Institutes and Sacred Congregation for Bishops, Directives for Mutual Relations between Bishops and Religious in the Church *Mutuae Relationes* (May 14, 1978), 2, 10: *AAS* 70 (1978), 475, 479-480.

[227] *Propositio* 35.

[228] Ibid.

permanent formation appears not only as a necessary condition but also as an indispensable means for constantly refocusing on the *meaning* of his mission and for ensuring that he is carrying it out with fidelity and generosity. By this formation, the priest is helped to become aware of the seriousness and yet the splendid grace of an obligation which cannot let him rest, so that, like Paul, he must be able to say: "If I preach the Gospel, that gives me no ground for boasting. For necessity is laid upon me. Woe to me if I do not preach the Gospel!" (1 Cor 9:16). At the same time, he also becomes aware of a demand, whether explicit or implicit, which insistently comes from all those whom God is unceasingly calling to salvation.

75.2 Only a suitable ongoing formation will succeed in confirming the priest in the essential and decisive element in his ministry, namely his faithfulness. The Apostle Paul writes: "It is required of stewards [of the mysteries of God] that they be found trustworthy" (1 Cor 4:2). The priest must be faithful no matter how many and varied the difficulties he meets, even in the most uncomfortable situations or when he is understandably tired, expending all his available energy until the end of his life. Paul's witness should be both an example and an incentive for every priest: "We put no obstacle" — he writes to the Christians at Corinth — "in anyone's way, so that no fault may be found with our ministry, but as servants of God we commend ourselves in every way: through great endurance, in afflictions, hardships, calamities, beatings, imprisonments, tumults, labors, watching, hunger; by purity, knowledge, forbearance, kindness, the Holy Spirit, genuine love, truthful speech and the power of God; with the weapons of righteousness for the right hand and for the left; in honor and dishonor, in ill repute and good repute. We are treated as impostors, and yet are true; as unknown, and yet well known; as dying, and behold, we live; as punished, and yet not killed; as sorrowful, yet always rejoicing; as poor, yet making many rich; as having nothing, and yet possessing everything" (2 Cor 6:3-10).

At every age and in all conditions of life

76.1 Permanent or ongoing formation, precisely because it is "permanent," should *always* be a part of the priest's life. In every phase and condition of his life, at every level of responsibility he has in the Church, he is undergoing formation. Clearly then, the possibilities for formation and the different kinds of formation are connected with the variety of ages, conditions of life and duties one finds among priests.

76.2 Ongoing formation is a duty, in the first instance, for *young priests*. They should have frequent and systematic meetings which, while they continue the sound and serious formation they have received in the seminary, will gradually lead young priests to grasp and incarnate the unique wealth of God's gift which is the priesthood and to express their capabilities and ministerial attitude, also through an ever more convinced and responsible insertion in the presbyterate, and therefore in communion and coresponsibility with all their brethren.

76.3 With priests who have just come out of the seminary, a certain sense of "having had enough" is quite understandable, when faced with new times of study and meeting. But the idea that priestly formation ends on the day one leaves the seminary is false and dangerous, and needs to be totally rejected.

76.4 Young priests who take part in meetings for ongoing formation will be able to help one another by exchanging experiences and reflecting on how to put into practice the ideals of the priesthood and of ministry which they have imbibed during their seminary years. At the same time, their active participation in the formational meetings of the presbyterate can be an example and stimulus to other priests who are ahead of them in years. They can thus show their love for all those making up the presbyterate and how much they care for their particular Church, which needs well-formed priests.

76.5 In order to accompany the young priests in this first delicate phase of their life and ministry, it is very opportune, and perhaps even absolutely necessary nowadays, to create a *suitable support structure,* with appropriate guides and teachers. Here priests can find, in an organized way that continues through their first years of ministry, the help they need to make a good start in their priestly service. Through frequent and regular meetings — of sufficient duration and held within a community setting, if possible — they will be assured of having times for rest, prayer, reflection and fraternal exchange. It will then be easier for them, right from the beginning, to give a balanced approach, based on the Gospel, to their priestly life. And in those cases where individual local Churches are not in a position to offer this service to their own young priests, it will be a good idea for neighboring Churches to pool resources and draw up suitable programs.

77.1 Ongoing formation is a duty also for *priests of middle age.* They can face a number of risks precisely because of their age, as for example an exaggerated activism or a certain routine approach to the exercise of their ministry. As a result, the priest can be tempted to presume he can manage on his own, as if his own personal experience, which has seemed trustworthy to that point, needs no contact with anything or anyone else. Often enough, the older priest has a sort of interior fatigue which is dangerous. It can be a sign of a resigned disillusionment in the face of difficulties and failures. Such situations find an answer in ongoing formation, in a continued and balanced checking of oneself and one's activity, constantly looking for motivation and aids which will enable one to carry on one's mission. As a result the priest will maintain a vigilant spirit, ready to face the perennial yet ever new demands of salvation which people keep bringing to him as the "man of God."

77.2 Ongoing formation should also involve those *priests* who by their advanced years can be called *elderly* and who in some Churches make up the greater part of the presbyterate. The presbyterate should show them gratitude for the faithful service they have performed on behalf of Christ and his Church, and also practical solidarity to help them in their condition. Ongoing formation for these priests will not be a matter so much of study, updating and educational renewal, but rather a calm and reassuring confirmation of the part which they are still called upon to play in the presbyterate, not only inasmuch as they continue, perhaps in different ways, their pastoral ministry, but also because of the possibilities they themselves have, thanks to their experience of life and apostolate, of becoming effective teachers and trainers of other priests.

77.3 Also those priests who, because of the burden of work or illness, find themselves in a *condition of physical weakness or moral fatigue* can be helped by an ongoing formation which will encourage them to keep up their service to the Church in a calm and sustained fashion, and not to isolate themselves either from the community or from the presbyterate. However, they should reduce their external activities and dedicate themselves to those pastoral contacts and that personal spirituality which can help them keep up their motivation and priestly joy. Ongoing formation will help such priests to keep alive the conviction, which they themselves have inculcated in the faithful, that they continue to be active members for the building up of the Church, especially by virtue of their union with the suffering Christ and with so many other brothers and sisters in the Church who are sharing in the Lord's Passion, reliving Paul's spiritual experience when he said: "I rejoice in my sufferings for your sake, and in my flesh I complete what is lacking in Christ's afflictions for the sake of his Body, that is, the Church" (Col 1:24).[229]

The agents of ongoing formation

78.1 The conditions in which the ministry of priests — often and in many places — has to be carried out nowadays do not make it easy to undertake a serious commitment to formation. The multiplication of responsibilities and

---

[229] Cf. *Propositio* 36.

services, the complexity of human life in general and the life of the Christian communities in particular, the activism and anxiety that are features of vast areas of society today often deprive priests of the time and energies they need to "take heed of themselves" (cf. 1 Tim 4:16).

78.2 This should increase the responsibility of priests to overcome these difficulties and see them as a challenge to plan and carry out a permanent formation which will respond appropriately to the greatness of God's gift and to the urgency of the demands and requirements of our time.

78.3 Those responsible for the ongoing formation of priests are to be found in the Church as "communion." In this sense, the *entire particular Church* has the responsibility, under the guidance of the Bishop, to develop and look after the different aspects of its priests' permanent formation. Priests are not there to serve themselves but the People of God. So, ongoing formation, in ensuring the human, spiritual, intellectual and pastoral maturity of priests, is doing good to the People of God itself. Besides, the very exercise of the pastoral ministry leads to a constant and fruitful mutual exchange between the priest's life of faith and that of the laity. Indeed *the very relationship and sharing of life between the priest and the community,* if it is wisely conducted and made use of, will be a *fundamental contribution* to permanent formation, which cannot be reduced to isolated episodes or initiatives, but covers the whole ministry and life of the priest.

78.4 The truth is that the Christian experience of persons who are simple and humble, the spiritual enthusiasm of people who truly love God, the courageous application of the faith to practical life by Christians involved in all kinds of social and civil tasks — all these things are embraced by the priest who, while illuminating them with his priestly service, at the same time draws from them a precious spiritual nourishment. Even the doubts, crises and hesitations in the face of all kinds of personal or social situations, the temptation to rejection or despair at times of pain, illness, death: all the difficult circumstances which people find in their path as Christians are fraternally lived and sincerely suffered in the priest's heart. And he, in seeking answers for others, is constantly spurred on to find them first of all for himself.

78.5 And so the entire People of God, in each and every one of its members, can and should offer precious assistance to the ongoing formation of its priests. In this sense the people should see that priests are allowed time for study and prayer. They should ask of them that for which Christ has sent them and not require anything else. They should offer to help in the various aspects of the pastoral mission, especially in those related to human development and works of charity. They should establish cordial and brotherly relations with them, helping priests to remember that they are not "to lord it over" the faithful, but rather "work with them for their joy" (cf. 2 Cor 1:24).

78.6 The particular Church's responsibility for the formation of its priests is specific and depends on its different members, starting with the priest himself.

79.1 In a certain sense, it is the priest himself, *the individual priest, who is the person primarily responsible in the Church for ongoing formation.* Truly each priest has the duty, rooted in the Sacrament of Holy Orders, to be faithful to the gift God has given him and to respond to the call for daily conversion which comes with the gift itself. The regulations and norms established by Church authority, as also the example given by other priests, are not enough to make permanent formation attractive unless the individual priest is personally convinced of its need and is determined to make use of the opportunities, times and forms in which it comes. Ongoing formation keeps up one's "youthfulness" of spirit, which is something that cannot be imposed from without. Each priest must continually find it within himself. Only those who keep ever alive their desire to learn and grow can be said to enjoy this "youthfulness."

79.2 The responsibility of the *Bishop* and, with him, of the *presbyterate,* is fundamental. The Bishop's responsibility is based on the fact that priests receive their priesthood from him and share his pastoral solicitude for the People of God. He is responsible for ongoing formation, the purpose of which is to ensure that all his priests are generously faithful to the gift and ministry received, that they are priests such as the People of God wishes to have and has a "right" to. This responsibility leads the Bishop, in communion with the presbyterate, to outline a project and establish a program which can ensure that ongoing formation is not something haphazard but a systematic offering of subjects, which unfold by stages and take on precise forms. The Bishop will live up to his responsibility not only by seeing to it that his presbyterate has places and times for its ongoing formation, but also by being present in person and taking part in an interested and friendly way. Often it will be suitable, or indeed necessary, for Bishops of neighboring Dioceses or of an ecclesiastical region to come together and join forces to be able to offer initiatives for permanent formation that are better organized and more interesting, such as in-service training courses in biblical, theological and pastoral studies, residential weeks, conference series and times to reflect on and examine how, from the pastoral point of view, the affairs of the presbyterate and the ecclesial community are progressing.

79.3 To fulfill his responsibility in this field, the Bishop will also ask for help from theological and pastoral faculties or institutes, seminaries, offices and federations that bring together people — priests, Religious and lay faithful — who are involved in priestly formation.

79.4 In the context of the particular Churches, *families* have a significant role to play. The life of ecclesial communities, led and guided by priests, looks to families inasmuch as they are "domestic Churches." In particular the role of the family into which the priest is born needs to be stressed. By being one with their son in his aims, the family can offer him its own important contribution to his mission. The plan of Providence chose the priest's family to be the place in which his vocation was planted and nourished, an indispensable help for the growth and development of his vocation. Now the family, with the greatest respect for their son who has chosen to give himself to God and neighbor, should always remain as a faithful and encouraging witness of his mission, supporting that mission and sharing in it with devotion and respect. In this way the family will help bring God's providential plan to completion.

Times, forms and means for ongoing formation

80.1 While every moment can be an "acceptable time" (2 Cor 6:2) for the Holy Spirit to lead the priest to a direct growth in prayer, study and an awareness of his own pastoral responsibilities, nevertheless there are certain "privileged" moments for this, even though they may be common and prearranged.

80.2 Let us recall, in the first place, *the meetings of the Bishop with his presbyterate,* whether they be liturgical (in particular the concelebration of the Chrism Mass on Holy Thursday), or pastoral and educational, related to pastoral activity or to the study of specific theological problems.

80.3 There are also *spiritual gatherings for priests,* such as spiritual exercises, days of recollection and spirituality, etc. These are opportunities for spiritual and pastoral growth, in which one can devote more time to pray in peace; opportunities to get back to what it means deep down to be a priest, to find fresh motives for faithfulness and pastoral endeavor.

80.4 *Study workshops and sessions for reflection in common* are also important. They help to prevent cultural impoverishment or getting entrenched in one's ways, even in the pastoral field, as a result of mental laziness. They help to foster a greater synthesis between the various elements of the spiritual, intellectual and apostolic life. They open minds and hearts to the new challenges of history and to the new appeals which the Spirit addresses to the Church.

81.1 Many ways and means are at hand to make ongoing formation an ever more precious living experience for priests. Among them, let us recall the different *forms of common life* among priests, which have always existed, though they have appeared in different ways and with different degrees of intensity, in the life of the Church: "Today, it is impossible not to recommend them, especially among those who live together or are pastorally involved in the same place. Besides the advantage which comes to the apostolate and its activities, this common life of priests offers to all, to fellow priests and lay faithful alike, a shining example of charity and unity."[230]

81.2 Another help can be given by *priestly associations,* in particular by priestly Secular Institutes — which have as their characteristic feature their being diocesan — through which priests are more closely united to their Bishop, and which constitute "a state of consecration in which priests by means of vows or other sacred bonds consecrate themselves to incarnate in their life the evangelical counsels."[231] All the forms of "priestly fraternity" approved by the Church are useful not only for the spiritual life but also for the apostolic and pastoral life.

81.3 *Spiritual direction* too contributes in no small way to the ongoing formation of the priests. It is a well-tried means and has lost none of its value. It ensures spiritual formation. It fosters and maintains faithfulness and generosity in the carrying out of the priestly ministry. As Pope Paul VI wrote before his election to the Pontificate: "Spiritual direction has a wonderful purpose. We could say it is indispensable for the moral and spiritual education of young people who want to find what their vocation in life is and follow it wherever it may lead, with utter loyalty. It retains its beneficial effect at all stages of life, when in the light and affection of a devout and prudent counsel one asks for a check on one's own right intention and for support in the generous fulfillment of one's own duties. It is a very delicate but immensely valuable psychological means. It is an educational and psychological art calling for deep responsibility in the one who practices it. Whereas for the one who receives it, it is a spiritual act of humility and trust."[232]

Conclusion

82.1 "I will give you shepherds after my own heart" (Jer 3:15).

82.2 Today, this promise of God is still living and at work in the Church.

---

[230] Synod of Bishops, Eighth Ordinary General Assembly, *Instrumentum Laboris,* "The Formation of Priests in the Circumstances of the Present Day," 60: cf. Second Vatican Ecumenical Council, Decree on the Bishops' Pastoral Office in the Church *Christus Dominus,* 30; Decree on the Ministry and Life of Priests *Presbyterorum Ordinis,* 8; Code of Canon Law, Canon 550 § 2.

[231] *Propositio* 37.

[232] G. B. Montini, Pastoral Letter on the Moral Sense, 1961.

At all times, she knows she is the fortunate receiver of these prophetic words. She sees them put into practice daily in so many parts of the world, or rather, in so many human hearts, young hearts in particular. On the threshold of the third millennium, and in the face of the serious and urgent needs which confront the Church and the world, she yearns to see this promise fulfilled in a new and richer way, more intensely and effectively: she hopes for an extraordinary outpouring of the Spirit of Pentecost.

82.3 The Lord's promise calls forth from the heart of the Church a prayer, that is a confident and burning petition in the love of the Father, who, just as he has sent Jesus the Good Shepherd, the Apostles, their successors and a countless host of priests, will continue to show to the people of today his faithfulness, his goodness.

82.4 And the Church is ready to respond to this grace. She feels in her heart that God's gift begs for a united and generous reply: the entire People of God should pray and work tirelessly for priestly vocations. Candidates for the priesthood should prepare themselves very conscientiously to welcome God's gift and put it into practice, knowing that the Church and the world have an absolute need of them. They should deepen their love for Christ the Good Shepherd, pattern their hearts on his, be ready to go out as his image into the highways of the world to proclaim to all mankind Christ the Way, the Truth and the Life.

82.5 I appeal especially to families. May parents, mothers in particular, be generous in giving their sons to the Lord when he calls them to the priesthood. May they cooperate joyfully in their vocational journey, realizing that in this way they will be increasing and deepening their Christian fruitfulness in the Church and that, in a sense, they will experience the blessedness of Mary, the Virgin Mother: "Blessed are you among women, and blessed is the fruit of your womb!" (Lk 1:42).

82.6 To today's young people I say: be more docile to the voice of the Spirit, let the great expectations of the Church, of mankind, resound in the depths of your hearts. Do not be afraid to open your minds to Christ the Lord who is calling. Feel his loving look upon you and respond enthusiastically to Jesus when he asks you to follow him without reserve.

82.7 The Church responds to grace through the commitment which priests make to receive that ongoing formation which is required by the dignity and responsibility conferred on them by the Sacrament of Holy Orders. All priests are called to become aware how especially urgent it is for them to receive formation at the present time: the new evangelization needs new evangelizers, and these are the priests who are serious about living their priesthood as a specific path toward holiness.

82.8 God promises the Church not just any sort of shepherds, but shepherds "after his own heart." And God's "heart" has revealed itself to us fully in the heart of Christ the Good Shepherd. Christ's heart continues today to have compassion for the multitudes and to give them the bread of truth, the bread of love, the bread of life (cf. Mk 6:30-44), and it pleads to be allowed to beat in other hearts — priests' hearts: "You give them something to eat" (Mk 6:37). People need to come out of their anonymity and fear. They need to be known and called by name, to walk in safety, along the paths of life, to be found again if they have become lost, to be loved, to receive salvation as the supreme gift of God's love. All this is done by Jesus, the Good Shepherd — by himself and by his priests with him.

82.9 Now, as I bring this Exhortation to a close, I turn my thoughts to all aspirants to the priesthood, to seminarians and to priests who in all parts of the world — even in the most difficult and dramatic conditions, but always with the joyous struggle to be faithful to the Lord and to serve his flock unswervingly — are offering their lives daily in order that faith, hope and charity may grow in human hearts and in the history of the men and women of our day.

82.10 Dear brother priests, you do this because our Lord himself, with the strength of his Spirit, has called you to incarnate in the earthen vessels of your simple lives the priceless treasure of his Good Shepherd's love.

82.11 In communion with the Synod Fathers and in the name of all the Bishops of the world and of the entire community of the Church I wish to express all the gratitude which your faithfulness and service deserve.[233]

82.12 And while I wish for all of you the grace to rekindle daily the gift of God you have received with the laying on of hands (cf. 2 Tim 1:6), to feel the comfort of the deep friendship which binds you to Jesus and unites you with one another, the comfort of experiencing the joy of seeing the flock of God grow in an ever greater love for him and for all people, of cultivating the tranquil conviction that the one who began in you the good work will bring it to completion at the day of Jesus Christ (cf. Phil 1:6), I turn with each and every one of you in *prayer to Mary, Mother and Teacher of our priesthood.*

82.13 Every aspect of priestly formation can be referred to Mary, the human being who has responded better than any other to God's call. Mary became both the servant and the disciple of the Word to the point of conceiving, in her heart and in her flesh, the Word made man, so as to give him to mankind. Mary was called to educate the one Eternal Priest, who became docile and subject to her motherly authority. With her example and intercession the

---

[233] Cf. *Propositio* 40.

Blessed Virgin keeps vigilant watch over the growth of vocations and priestly life in the Church.

82.14 And so we priests are called to have an ever firmer and more tender devotion to the Virgin Mary and to show it by imitating her virtues and praying to her often.

O Mary,
Mother of Jesus Christ and Mother of Priests,
accept this title which we bestow on you
to celebrate your motherhood
and to contemplate with you the priesthood
of your Son and of your sons,
O Holy Mother of God.

O Mother of Christ,
to the Messiah-Priest you gave a body of flesh
through the anointing of the Holy Spirit
for the salvation of the poor and the contrite of heart;
guard priests in your heart and in the Church,
O Mother of the Savior.

O Mother of Faith,
you accompanied to the Temple the Son of Man,
the fulfillment of the promises given to the fathers;
give to the Father for his glory
the priests of your Son,
O Ark of the Covenant.

O Mother of the Church,
in the midst of the disciples in the Upper Room
you prayed to the Spirit
for the new people and their shepherds;
obtain for the Order of Presbyters
a full measure of gifts,
O Queen of the Apostles.

O Mother of Jesus Christ,
you were with him at the beginning
of his life and mission,

you sought the Master among the crowd,
you stood beside him when he was lifted up from the earth
consumed as the one eternal sacrifice
and you had John, your son, near at hand;
accept from the beginning
those who have been called,
protect their growth,
in their life ministry
accompany your sons,
O Mother of Priests.
Amen.

Given in Rome, at Saint Peter's, on March 25, the Solemnity of the Annunciation of the Lord, in the year 1992, the fourteenth of my Pontificate.

Vita Consecrata

Editor's Introduction

"The Church needs the spiritual and apostolic contribution of a renewed and revitalized consecrated life" (§13.3). In *Vita Consecrata,* signed on March 25, 1996, Pope John Paul II inspires the more than one million consecrated men and women in the Church to take up the path of renewal. As the final act of the Ninth Ordinary General Assembly of the Synod of Bishops, this document completes his trilogy of post-synodal apostolic exhortations on "the distinctive features of the states of life willed by the Lord Jesus for his Church" (§4.2): the laity, the priesthood, and the consecrated life. It clarifies the specific identity, vocation, and mission of consecrated persons. The exhortation also praises their "glorious history" and encourages them to look to the future, where the Spirit is sending them "to do even greater things" (§110.1).

In October 1994, the Synod of Bishops met in Rome to discuss the theme chosen by the Pope: "The Consecrated Life and Its Role in the Church and in the World." In view of the approaching third millennium, the Assembly studied the significance and future prospects of the consecrated life. No previous Synod elicited such a high percentage of responses to the *Lineamenta* nor occasioned such intense preparation. This interest continued right up through the Synodal Assembly, at whose sessions many consecrated men and women took part. The Holy Father followed the events closely. He made a point of being present at the meetings. Moreover, during and after the Synod he delivered a number of systematic talks on the consecrated life. *Vita Consecrata* is thus the fruit of the Pope's "heartfelt openness toward the Synod Fathers" (§13.4). It gives the whole Church "the results of the Synod process" (§4.1), which John Paul describes as *"a stimulating exchange,* guided by the Holy Spirit with his gifts of truth and love" (§13.1).

Whereas much of the pre-synodal discussion focused on the problems of the consecrated life, the exhortation pays little attention to contemporary difficulties. It prefers instead the path of encouragement. *Vita Consecrata* provides reasons why the consecrated life continues to be vitally important to the Church. The Holy Father recognizes that, despite its flourishing in many areas, "in some parts of the world Institutes of Consecrated Life seem to be experiencing a period of difficulty" (§2.4, cf. §3.2). This crisis, he thinks, stems in some way from the misguided renewal attempted after the Second Vatican Council. While these post-conciliar years have seen efforts which have invigorated the consecrated life, it has also been "a time of tension and struggle, in which well-meaning endeavors have not always met with positive results" (§13.2). Indeed, the consecrated life in many regions, especially in Europe and North America, is facing a decrease in vocations and an aging membership, both of which require a reassessment of current apostolic works. Yet even when the Pope adverts to these serious concerns, he strikes a reassuring note: "The various difficulties stemming from the decline in personnel and apostolates *must in no way lead to a loss of confidence in the evangelical vitality of the consecrated life*" (§63.3). John Paul's trust in Providence leads him to present the consecrated life in an almost idealized way. He prefers to describe its beauty rather than its problems.

Vita Consecrata is a song of thanksgiving and praise for the consecrated life. Neither a tough call to order nor an admonition against abuses, it is full of hope for the "gift of the consecrated life in the variety of its charisms and institutions" (§2.2, cf. §§1.1, 13.3, 48.3, 105.3, 109.2, 111.2). The exhortation aims at inspiring the same enthusiasm in consecrated persons as the letter sent by the Council of Jerusalem to the Christians in Antioch: "When they read it, they rejoiced at the encouragement which it gave" (Acts 15:31).

John Paul addresses his exhortation to "the whole Church" (§13.1) and, indirectly, "to any others who might be interested" (§4.1). In the first place, he intends it for religious communities and consecrated persons. But the Pope also hopes that his document will "increase the joy of the whole People of God," as they become better acquainted with the consecrated life (§13.3). This state of life is "a reality which affects the whole Church . . . something which concerns us all" (§3.1, cf. §§13.1, 49.1). The Holy Father also addresses men and women of good will, expressing the desire that they will recognize in the lives of consecrated persons "sure paths for those who seek God with a sincere heart" (§108.2).

The document's style, while characteristically dense, is remarkably contemplative. More than the other post-synodal apostolic exhortations, *Vita Consecrata* reflects the Oriental tradition of theology and spirituality. This Eastern flavor is evident in its numerous references to divine beauty and its emphasis on the mystery of the Transfiguration. God is "the infinite beauty which alone can fully satisfy the human heart" (§16.2), the "sublime beauty" (§16.4, cf. §§20.2, 24.1, 28.1). The Pope also refers to the spiritual path of "*philokalia, or love of the divine beauty*" (§19.3, cf. §§66.1, 75.4, 111.4). Most typically Eastern, however, is his use of the Transfiguration as a kind of icon to describe the consecrated life. A biblical account of this mystery opens and focuses the presentation of chapter one and sheds its light on the rest of the document. By fixing his readers' "gaze on Christ's radiant face in the mystery of the Transfiguration" (§14.3), the Holy Father impresses his treatment of the consecrated life with a marked Trinitarian and Christological imprint. Looking on Jesus' face opens the way to his discussion of the consecrated life in the Church.

With 186 scriptural references, *Vita Consecrata* relies on the Bible more than any other source. John Paul prefers John and Matthew among the Evangelists and, in the rest of the New Testament, the First Letter to the Corinthians and Acts. Especially noteworthy are the different biblical images or "icons" which the Pope uses to emphasize specific aspects of the consecrated life. Most important of these is the icon of the Transfiguration. It vividly portrays the contemplative life as linked to Jesus' prayer "on the mountain," and the active life to his "coming down the mountain" on the road to Golgotha (§14.3). Other icons include Mary's anointing of Jesus at Bethany, which expresses "a sign of *unbounded generosity,* as expressed in a life spent in loving and serving the Lord, in order to devote oneself to his person and his Mystical Body" (§104.3); the Virgin Mary and the Apostle John at the foot of the Cross, where "John, together with Mary, is among the first in a long line of men and women who, from the beginning of the Church until the end, are touched by God's love and feel called to follow the Lamb" (§23.3); and Mary and Peter in the Cenacle, where Jesus' Mother represents the Church's "spousal receptivity," and Peter and the other Apostles stand for "the aspect of fruitfulness, as it is expressed in ecclesial ministry" (§34.2). These biblical images allow the Pope to express profound truths about the identity and mission of the consecrated life by way of expressive portraits.

The teaching of the Second Vatican Council, the Magisterium of Paul VI and John Paul II, and the post-conciliar documents of the Roman Curia are also important sources cited in *Vita Consecrata.* John Paul regards the Council's teachings on the consecrated life as "an enlightening point of reference for subsequent doctrinal developments" (§13.4, cf. §29.2). He refers very frequently to chapter six of *Lumen Gentium* (§§43-47) and to *Perfectae Caritatis,* the Decree on the Appropriate Renewal of the Religious Life. Since Vatican II, theological reflection on the nature of the consecrated life has deepened, and later magisterial teachings express these new insights. Most noteworthy among these documents are the apostolic exhortations *Evangelica Testificatio* (1971) and *Redemptionis Donum* (1984), and the following curial documents: *Mutuae Relationes* (1978), on the mutual relations between Bishops and Religious in the Church; the 1983 Instruction on the essential elements in the Church's teaching on religious life as applied to Institutes dedicated to works of the apostolate; *Potissimum Institutioni* (1990), on formation in Religious Institutes; and, most frequently, *Congregavit Nos in Unum Christi Amor* (1994), on fraternal life in community.

John Paul's desire to echo the Synod's decisions faithfully is evident in his abundant references to the Fathers' recommendations. In no other post-synodal apostolic exhortation does he cite directly or indirectly every *propositio* submitted to him. Also unique is *Vita Consecrata's* heavy reliance on the writings of the saints, especially consecrated men and women from the West and East, even though quotations from men representative of the Western tradition predominate. The chronological range of these sources is as wide as the geographical — from Ignatius of Antioch in the early second century to Blessed Elizabeth of the Trinity in the twentieth century. The numerous quotations from those who themselves professed the evangelical counsels reinforces the exhortation's spiritual reading-like style.

Summary

The Pope divides *Vita Consecrata* into three principal chapters, each of which contains three subsections. To these he adds an introduction and conclusion. Using a tone of gratitude and encouragement, the introduction (§§1-13) sets out the document's purpose, affirms its faithfulness to the 1994 meeting of the Synod of Bishops, and sketches the principal characteristics of the different forms of consecrated life. Chapter one, *"Confessio Trinitatis:* The Origins of the Consecrated Life in the Mystery of Christ and of the Trinity" (§§14-28), is theologically the richest and spiritually the most contemplative section. It examines the nature of the consecrated life. In chapter two, *"Signum Fraternitatis:* Consecrated Life as a Sign of Communion in the Church" (§§41-71), the Holy Father describes the fraternal life of consecrated persons who live in community. Besides providing a theological foundation for the common life, the Pope takes up specific questions on the relationship between the consecrated life and ecclesial communion. Chapter three, *"Servitium Caritatis:* Consecrated Life, Manifestation of God's Love in the World" (§§72-103), focuses primarily on apostolic work. Finally, in the conclusion (§§104-112), John Paul vigorously confirms the value of the consecrated life and appeals to young people, families, men and women of good will, and consecrated persons to deepen their appreciation of its inestimable worth.

Lest *Vita Consecrata's* description of the consecrated life might appear abstract and formless, the Holy Father briefly summarizes the different ways in which men and women in the West and the East have lived the evangelical counsels of chastity, poverty, and obedience. First he describes the life of monks. "By becoming bearers of the Cross (*staurophoroi*), they have striven to become bearers of the Spirit (*pneumatophoroi*), authentically spiritual men and women, capable of endowing history with hidden fruitfulness by unceasing praise and intercession, by spiritual counsels and works of charity" (§6.2). Then the Pope refers to the ancient Order of Virgins, which constitutes *"a special eschatological image of the Heavenly Bride and of the life to come"* (§7.1); to hermits, whose lives invite people to recall their fundamental destiny of being with God; and to consecrated widows and widowers, who "devote themselves to prayer and the service of the Church" (§7.3). On the one hand, contemplatives are "an image of Christ praying on the mountain" of Tabor (§32.4, cf. §8.1); "they offer the ecclesial community a singular testimony of the Church's love for her Lord" (§8.2). On the other hand, active Religious reflect Christ's coming down from the mountain. While publicly professing the evangelical counsels in a community, they carry out many different apostolic works. Secular Institutes contribute to the proclamation of God's Kingdom by uniting the profession of the evangelical counsels with life in the world. Their members strive to "transfigure the world from within by the power of the Beatitudes" (§10.2). Those belonging to Societies of Apostolic Life live a common life and pursue a specific apostolic or missionary purpose, without publicly professing the evangelical counsels. Lastly, John Paul alludes to recent forms of the consecrated life that are "inspired by new spiritual and apostolic impulses" (§12.1).

The apostolic exhortation thus addresses a broad audience which embraces all those who have chosen to follow more closely the chaste, poor, and obedient Jesus by living the evangelical counsels in some stable form of life. John Paul directs his words to those who make a public profession of the three vows and live in common, those in Secular Institutes who are not bound by the common life and live their consecrated life in the world, those in Societies of Apostolic Life who are obliged to the common life but do not publicly profess the evangelical counsels, and hermits and consecrated virgins who live their consecration without the help of a community life. While the Pope takes into account the various forms of the consecrated life, the exhortation reflects the fact that the majority of the world's consecrated men and women publicly profess the evangelical counsels and share a common life.

Origin and identity of the consecrated life

John Paul fixes his gaze on the radiant face of the transfigured Jesus to explain that the origin of the consecrated life lies in the mystery of the Trinity. Tabor reveals not only God's glory on the face of Christ, lovingly contemplated by the three disciples, but it also prepares them for following him to Golgotha. Today this same divine light illumines all the baptized. Even so, "those who are called to the consecrated life have *a special experience of the light which shines forth from the Incarnate Word"* (§15.4).

More than in any other papal document, *Vita Consecrata* clarifies that the different vocations and states of life in the Church are "like so many rays of the one light of Christ" (§16.2). While all Christians are equally called to holiness and mission, they carry out their vocation in diverse ways. There are, in fact, three states of life, each of which has a distinct identity that reflects a specific dimension of the mystery of Christ: laity, priesthood, and the consecrated life. The lay faithful mirror Christ insofar as he is "the Alpha and the Omega of the world, the foundation and measure of the value of all created things" (§16.2). By prolonging the apostolic ministry through time, priests are living images of Christ, the Head and Shepherd of the Church. Consecrated persons constitute a third state, which is neither lay nor clerical. They "receive a new and special consecration which, without being sacramental, commits them to making their own — in chastity, poverty and obedience — the way of life practiced personally by Jesus and proposed by him to his disciples" (§31.4). Those who profess the evangelical counsels proclaim that Christ is "the splendor before which every other light pales" (§16.2). He alone can satisfy the yearning of the human heart. He alone is the fulfillment of all things.

John Paul believes that the consecrated life, as a distinct and specific state, ultimately originates in the Trinity. Intimately linked to each of the divine Persons, the consecrated life proclaims the mystery of God's being. The initiative for embracing the life of the evangelical counsels comes "wholly from the Father (cf. Jn 15:16), who asks those whom he has chosen to respond with complete and exclusive devotion" (§17.2). Dedication to him makes of their life an exclusive and unconditional holocaust. For those called to the consecrated life, the Son asks for a total commitment, "one which involves leaving everything behind (cf. Mt 19:27) in order to live at his side and to follow him wherever he goes" (§18.1). They conform themselves to Christ by imitating his way of living in chastity, poverty, and obedience. The Holy Spirit awakens the desire to respond to the divine call, guides its growth, and sustains it in difficulty. This same Spirit "shapes and molds the hearts of those who are called, configuring them to Christ, the chaste, poor and obedient One, and prompting them to make his mission their own" (§19.2).

The consecrated life is, therefore, a *"confessio Trinitatis."* By living in this radical way the consecrated person proclaims "what the Father, through the

Son and in the Spirit, brings about by his love, his goodness and his beauty" (§20.1). The evangelical counsels belong to the consecrated life. They are "an expression of the love of the Son for the Father in the unity of the Holy Spirit" (§21.1). Through the practice of these counsels the consecrated person lives with particular intensity the mysteries of the Triune God, the Incarnation, and the Redemption. In the light of these truths, Pope John Paul describes the meaning of consecrated chastity, poverty, and obedience.

By means of consecrated chastity individuals devote themselves to God with an undivided heart (cf. 1 Cor 7:32-34). Their chastity reflects "the *infinite love* which links the three divine Persons in the mysterious depths of the life of the Trinity" (§21.2). At the same time, consecrated virginity prolongs the revelation of divine love shown in the Incarnation. As the Consecrated One, Jesus lived as a virgin and revealed *"the sublime excellence and mysterious spiritual fruitfulness of virginity"* (§22.2). Those called to the consecrated life likewise commit themselves to perfect chastity for the sake of the Kingdom. "By embracing *chastity,* they make their own the pure love of Christ and proclaim to the world that he is the only-begotten Son who is one with the Father" (§16.3).

Poverty, too, reflects the Trinity's inner life. It expresses the *"total gift of self* which the three divine Persons make to one another" (§21.3). In the Son, this complete gift of self entailed the assuming of a human nature. Though Christ was rich, he became poor for our sake (cf. 2 Cor 8:9). On the Cross he fully revealed the depth of his poverty by offering the perfect gift of self to the Father. Consecrated men and women, when they imitate Christ's poverty, profess that he is "the Son who receives everything from the Father, and gives everything back to the Father in love" (§16.3). Their choice proclaims that God alone is humanity's dearest treasure.

The obedience of consecrated persons mirrors "the *loving harmony* between the three divine Persons" (§21.4). Within the Trinity, the Son is the exemplar of all obedience. He came to do the Father's will (cf. Jn 6:38) and was himself obedient to death, even to death on the Cross (cf. Phil 2:8). His obedience was filial, trustful, and responsible. By professing obedience in imitation of Christ, consecrated men and women make a similar gift of self: they announce that Christ is "infinitely beloved and loving, as the One who delights only in the will of the Father (cf. Jn 4:34), to whom he is perfectly united and on whom he depends for everything" (§16.3). Thus the consecrated life is both a sign of the Trinity — making visible the depths of its inner life — and *"a living memorial of Jesus' way of living and acting* as the Incarnate Word in relation to the Father and in relation to the brethren" (§22.3).

Paschal and eschatological dimensions of the consecrated life

The consecrated life not only imitates Jesus' way of life but also finds its roots in the Paschal Mystery. The glory of Christ's face on Tabor gave way to the disfigured face of the Crucified on Calvary. According to John Paul, Jesus' gift of the consecrated life to the Church is revealed at the foot of the Cross. On Golgotha, Mary and John are seen as the first of those totally consecrated to Christ. Here they proclaim that *"the Cross is the superabundance of God's love poured out upon this world"* (§24.2). From the outset, therefore, the consecrated life has entailed a particular sharing in Christ's saving Death and Resurrection.

Very frequently in *Vita Consecrata* the Pope draws attention to the eschatological dimension of the consecrated life. In a special way consecrated men and women keep alive the Church's hope in the Lord's definitive coming. They recall that "the form of this world is passing away" (1 Cor 7:31) and that "here we have no lasting city" (Heb 13:14). The monastic life of East and West bear convincing witness to ardent expectation for the Kingdom. Having made God their treasure, consecrated persons proclaim "the future age, when the fullness of the Kingdom of heaven, already present in its first fruits and in mystery, will be achieved" (§32.2).

The consecrated life is an eschatological sign for the Church and the world; that is, it foreshadows on earth the life of the heavenly Kingdom. It anticipates this future fulfillment primarily "by means of *the vow of virginity,* which tradition has always understood as *an anticipation of the world to come,* already at work for the total transformation of man" (§26.3, cf. §§14.2, 16.2). By living the evangelical counsels, consecrated men and women proclaim the future age when the children of the resurrection will take neither husband nor wife but will be like the angels of God (cf. Mt 22:30).

While the consecrated life points directly to the life of heaven, enkindling among people keen hope for its fulfillment, it also inspires firm commitment to the Church's mission on earth. The Pope rejects any idea that this prayerful expectation leads to passivity. Rather, he asserts that the *"eschatological expectation becomes mission,* so that the Kingdom may become ever more fully established here and now" (§27.2). The fact that consecrated persons live in joyful hope of the future strengthens their zeal, impelling them "to care for the deformed image of God on the faces of their brothers and sisters" (§75.4). As heralds of the coming Kingdom, they are spiritually equipped to bring hope to a world so often discouraged and pessimistic about the future. Their witness of life expresses that humanity is moving toward "a new heaven and a new earth" (Rev 21:1). It testifies that God alone "gives full meaning and joy to human lives, because men and women are made for God, and their hearts are restless until they rest in him" (§27.4).

In the mystery of the Church

Precisely because the consecrated life is intimately connected with the mystery and life of Christ, it is likewise linked to his Body and Bride, the Church. Present in the Church from the very beginning, the consecrated life belongs integrally to her life, holiness, and mission. Hence this way of life must be considered one of the Church's "essential and characteristic elements, for it expresses her very nature" (§29.2). John Paul leaves no doubt that Christ willed the consecrated life. It did not originate with a decision of later community: "Jesus himself, by calling some men and women to abandon everything in order to follow him, established this type of life which, under the guidance of the Spirit, would gradually develop down the centuries into the various forms of the consecrated life" (§29.3).

According to Christ's will revealed in the New Testament, the Church is composed of laity, sacred ministers, and consecrated persons. Consequently, in the Church three distinct consecrations effect a profound change in a person: the consecration of Baptism, of Holy Orders, and of the consecrated life. All members of the Church share equally in the consecration of Baptism, but the consecrated life is a distinct vocation and has a particular mission. Profession of the evangelical counsels is, therefore, more than merely a deepening of baptismal consecration. Rather, it is a "further consecration" which "differs in a special way from baptismal consecration, of which it is not a necessary consequence" (§30.2). Without being sacramental, this further consecration is something new with respect to Baptism and Confirmation. It is a *specific gift of the Holy Spirit* (§30.3), "a specific form of consecration" (§31.3). Indeed, the consecrated life "presupposes a particular gift of God not given to everyone" (§30.2). Those who receive this gift constitute a distinct state of life in the Church.

The three ecclesial vocations complement one another in carrying out the Church's mission. Each state, with its own specific identity, manifests the one mystery of Christ in the Church. For the laity, this particular dimension is activity in the temporal sphere; for clergy, ministry; for consecrated men and women, "special conformity to Christ, chaste, poor and obedient" (§31.4).

Despite the risk of being misunderstood, the Holy Father reaffirms the Church's teaching of "the *objective superiority of the consecrated life*" (§18.3, cf. §§32.2, 105.3). This affirmation has nothing to do with consecrated persons being "holier" than priests or laity. Rather, he confirms the Christian tradition that the consecrated life is "the most radical way of living the Gospel on this earth, a way which may be called *divine,* for it was embraced by him, God and man, as the expression of his relationship as the only-begotten Son with the Father and with the Holy Spirit" (§18.3). As a state, the consecrated life mirrors most closely Christ's own way of life and best reflects "the Church's purpose, which is the sanctification of humanity" (§32.2). However, its objective excellence confers a specific responsibility on consecrated men and women. Their mission "is to remind their other brothers and sisters to keep their eyes fixed on the peace which is to come, and to strive for the definitive happiness found in God" (§33.2).

Commitment to holiness

All members of the Church are called to the holiness of life which consists in perfect charity. But this pressing call especially challenges consecrated men and women. The Pope recalls that "the vocation of consecrated persons to seek first the Kingdom of God is first and foremost a call to complete conversion, in self-renunciation, in order to live fully for the Lord" (§35.2, cf. §30.2). The Church regards the life of the evangelical counsels as "a special path to holiness": it is "the school of the Lord's service, the school of love and holiness, the way or state of perfection" (§35.4). Consecrated persons, then, have a specific obligation to pursue holiness, and they are given the means to achieve it. Among these means John Paul mentions faithfulness to the original charism of their Institute, prayer, and asceticism.

Fidelity to "the founding charism and subsequent spiritual heritage" of one's Institute fosters a consecrated person's path to holiness (§36.2). This charism leads him or her to a deeper Trinitarian life: to belonging wholly to the Father, to joyful communion of life with the Son, and to docility to the guidance of the Spirit. This fidelity to the charism of the founder or foundress should be creative and dynamic, "adapting forms, if need be, to new situations and different needs" (§37.1). But the Pope also reminds consecrated persons that their way to perfection should follow a tried and true path. Hence he insists that "there is a pressing need today for every Institute *to return to the Rule,* since the Rule and Constitutions provide a map for the whole journey of discipleship, in accordance with a specific charism confirmed by the Church" (§37.2). Consecrated persons are conformed to Christ according to their Institute's original charism and authentic tradition.

John Paul briefly mentions the chief spiritual helps available to the consecrated life for the sanctification of its members: mental prayer and contemplation, liturgical prayer, sacramental life, Eucharistic adoration, retreats, and spiritual exercises. In particular, he urges a renewal of "the *ascetic practices* typical of the spiritual tradition of the Church and of the individual's own Institute" as powerful helps in growth toward holiness (§38.2). Such asceticism is all the more necessary if consecrated men and women are to engage successfully in the spiritual combat necessary to overcome the grave temptations which today threaten individuals and communities. The Pope also points out that a consecrated person's commitment to holiness stimulates the desire of other Christians for perfection.

Fraternal life

For John Paul, consecrated men and women mirror the inner life of the Holy Trinity not only by professing the evangelical counsels but also by living the common life required by the majority of Institutes. This fraternal life in community is "a form of witness to the Trinity" (§41.2) because it reflects the communion of the three divine Persons. Furthermore, the consecrated life is meant to show that *"sharing in the Trinitarian communion can change human relationships* and create a new type of solidarity" (§41.2).

The fraternal life has marked the consecrated life from its origins. It began with the Apostles' experience of completely sharing Jesus' life and continued in the communities formed around them after Pentecost. Today Institutes need to strengthen the common life. The Pope exhorts consecrated men and women to follow "the example of the first Christians in Jerusalem who were assiduous in accepting the teaching of the Apostles, in common prayer, in celebrating the Eucharist, and in sharing whatever goods of nature and grace they had" (§45.1). The Holy Spirit continues to inspire and enable consecrated persons to share everything in common: "material goods and spiritual experiences, talents and inspirations, apostolic ideals and charitable service" (§42.2). Fraternal life is, therefore, more than an instrument aimed at carrying out apostolic works efficiently. It expresses the experience of communion rooted in the inner life of God and in the example of Christ and the early Church.

Ecclesial communion

As a shared life in common, the fraternal life is "an eloquent sign of ecclesial communion" (§42.1). In light of the ecclesiology of communion proposed by the Second Vatican Council, John Paul calls upon consecrated men and women to be "true experts of communion and to practice the spirituality of communion" (§46.1). Consequently, the consecrated life, as an experience of authentic fraternity, entails a way of thinking and acting which builds up ecclesial communion. The Pope describes how consecrated persons ought to further this cooperation with the Hierarchy and with the laity, as well as within their own Institutes and among different ones.

Founders and foundresses of Institutes are renowned because they cultivated a lively sense of the Church and showed a deep love for her. Drawing on their example, today's consecrated men and women are likewise called to foster ecclesial communion, resisting anything that undermines it. The Holy Father exhorts them to show "allegiance of mind and heart to the Magisterium of the Bishops, an allegiance which must be lived honestly and clearly testified to before the People of God" (§46.3). John Paul especially reminds consecrated persons of their *"particular bond of communion . . . with the Successor of Peter"* (§47.1). Down through the centuries the Petrine ministry of the Bishop of Rome has protected the identity of the consecrated life. Because of the supra-diocesan character of many Institutes, which is grounded in their special relationship to the Successor of Peter, they have a unique responsibility to foster communion at every level of ecclesial life.

In every particular Church where consecrated men and women carry out their mission they ought to cooperate with the Bishop "for the organic development of diocesan pastoral life" (§48.1). On the one hand, ever faithful to their own charism, they are to work *"in full communion with the Bishop in the* areas of evangelization, catechesis and parish life" (§49.1). On the other hand, in ways that vary according to their statutes, Institutes enjoy a rightful autonomy from local authority, a freedom which assures their discipline, spirituality, and apostolic work. The Pope asks Bishops to safeguard this autonomy, and exhorts them "to welcome and esteem the charisms of the consecrated life, and to give them a place in the pastoral plans of the Diocese" (§48.3, cf. §49.1). Such autonomy, "or even the exemption which a number of them enjoy," however, should not be used "in order to justify choices which actually conflict with the demands of organic communion" (§49.2).

Every effort must therefore be made to strengthen the bonds of communion between consecrated persons and the particular Church in which they are carrying out their apostolate. The Holy Father recommends four specific measures to further mutual understanding and cooperation between Bishops and consecrated men and women. First, at the local level, Superiors and Bishops should engage in dialogue as a way of promoting pastoral planning in a Diocese. Second, at the national level, delegates of the Conferences of Major Superiors should be invited to meetings of the Bishops' Conferences and, likewise, delegates of the Episcopal Conferences should attend meetings of the Conferences of Major Superiors. Third, mixed commissions of Bishops and Major Superiors are to be set up at the national level for the study of common problems. Fourth, the formation of diocesan priests should include study of the theology and spirituality of the consecrated life, just as the initial preparation of men and women for the consecrated life should encompass the theology of the particular Church and the spirituality of the diocesan clergy.

Besides willingly cooperating with the Hierarchy, consecrated persons are called to work closely with the laity in fostering ecclesial communion. Monastic or contemplative Institutes manifest this collaboration chiefly through the spiritual bonds established with lay people. In addition to these ties, Institutes with active apostolates have opportunities for joint apostolic cooperation. Today, in fact, many Institutes recognize that the laity can share intimately in their charism, spirituality, and mission. This development, according to the Pope, opens up "a new chapter, rich in hope" (§54.2). For three reasons he encourages greater collaboration between consecrated persons and the lay faithful. First, by sharing in the spirituality and apostolic works of an Institute, lay men and women can ensure that its charism will remain alive, especially where vocations are decreasing. Second, because of their close contact with the consecrated life, lay people are encouraged to live the Gospel more intensely. Third, because the laity often have profound insights into an Institute's specific charism, they can help foster new apostolic directions faithful to the founder's or foundress's original vision. Although John Paul stresses the advantages of working out innovative forms of cooperation, he also sounds a warning note. The Pope insists that collaboration between the lay faithful and consecrated men and women should always be carried out "in such a way that the identity of the Institute in its internal life is not harmed" (§56.1). As always, the Holy Father scrupulously safeguards the specific identity and mission of each state of life in the Church, wishing to avoid any confusion among them.

Vita Consecrata also aims at fostering ecclesial communion within individual Institutes and between different ones. Traditionally the consecrated life has considered the role of Superiors as an integral dimension of the evangelical counsel of obedience and of the common life. The Pope recognizes that in the years of experimentation after the Second Vatican Council, "the need to revise this office has sometimes been felt" (§43.1). On the positive side, a legitimate desire for participation in decision-making by community members has corrected certain abuses. On the negative side, the cultural atmosphere of individualism and anti-authoritarianism has sometimes led to undermining the Superior's rightful role.

Ideally the fraternal life furnishes the world with a convincing example of how individuals and communities can discern God's will in a spirit of harmony. Within Institutes, members should reach decisions through appropriate dialogue. At the same time, this dialogue cannot eliminate the spirit of obedience proper to the common life. Moreover, Superiors also need to be reminded of their grave responsibilities. John Paul teaches that their authority is "received from God" and is "at the service of discernment and communion" (§92.1). Furthermore, he affirms that "those who exercise authority *cannot renounce their obligation as those first responsible* for the community, as guides of their brothers and sisters in the spiritual and apostolic life" (§43.1). Accordingly, in communities of the common life *"the final word belongs to authority* and, consequently, that authority has the right to see that decisions taken are respected" (§43.2).

The Pope's concern for building up ecclesial communion also leads him to urge the different Institutes of Consecrated Life to strengthen their ties of mutual cooperation. Following the example of "the spiritual friendship which often united founders and foundresses during their lives, consecrated persons, while remaining faithful to the character of their own Institute, are called to practice a fraternity which is exemplary" (§52.1). The Holy Father mentions two practical ways of expressing and fostering these bonds of communion with the particular and universal Church. First, Conferences of Major Superiors are helpful coordinating bodies which promote the identity and mission of the consecrated life. Especially in situations where Institutes are tempted to withdraw into themselves, he encourages them to reach out and work together with other Institutes in their apostolic efforts. Second, John Paul exhorts the Conferences of Major Superiors and Episcopal Conferences to develop more trusting relationships with each other. Third, he recommends that Institutes are "to maintain frequent and regular contacts with the Congregation for Institutes of Consecrated Life and Societies of Apostolic Life, as a sign of their communion with the Holy See" (§53.3). At all levels of ecclesial life everything touching upon the consecrated life should be carried out in a spirit of communion and dialogue.

Special questions

Chapter two of *Vita Consecrata* also takes up some particular questions dealt with at the Synod: the specific mission of consecrated women, the enclosure of cloistered nuns, the structure of mixed Institutes, and new forms of the evangelical life.

As in many other documents, the Holy Father especially highlights women's mission in the Church. He repeats his hope that all discrimination against women will be overcome and describes the particular feminine genius of consecrated women. "By virtue of their dedication lived in fullness and in joy," he writes, "consecrated women are called in a very special way to be *signs of God's tender love toward the human race* and to be special witnesses to the mystery of the Church, Virgin, Bride and Mother" (§57.1). John Paul encourages their aspirations "to have their identity, ability, mission and responsibility more clearly recognized, both in the awareness of the Church and in everyday life" (§57.2). Consecrated women can help the whole Christian community to get rid of one-sided perspectives that neglect women's dignity and specific contribution to the Church's life and mission. In order to further the role of women, the Pope urges their Institutes to provide more intensive formation, especially in theology, pastoral action, and catechesis. Precisely as women, they have an irreplaceable ecclesial mission "in understanding the faith in all its dimensions" and in "new efforts in fostering Christian doctrine and morals, family and social life, and especially in everything that affects the dignity of women and respect for human life" (§58.3).

Like the Synod Fathers, the Pope expresses the highest esteem for the cloistered life. The enclosure of contemplative women is an eloquent sign of exclusive love for God and of living solely for him. Like cities set on a hilltop or lights on a lampstand (cf. Mt 5:14-15), cloistered communities "visibly represent the goal toward which the entire community of the Church travels" (§59.3). By accepting the discipline of the enclosure these women intimately share in Christ's self-emptying love. Theirs is a "renunciation not only of things but also of 'space,' of contacts, of so many benefits of creation" (§59.1). Some questions about the concrete discipline regulating the cloister, however, still remain unresolved. Despite the need for further discussion, the Holy Father promises that the Synod Fathers' desire that Major Superiors be given "more responsibility in the granting of dispensations from enclosure for just and grave reasons, will be carefully considered" (§59.5).

Vita Consecrata clearly distinguishes between Religious brothers in mixed Institutes, where the founding charism or legitimate tradition does not entail ordination, from brothers in clerical Institutes, where the sacred ministry is constitutive of the original charism and determines the Institute's nature, purpose, and spirit. The former have traditionally been called lay Institutes. John Paul accepts the Synod's proposal that these lay Institutes should be renamed Religious Institutes of Brothers, "in order to avoid ambiguity and confusion with the secular state of the lay faithful" (§60.4). This recommendation reflects the Pope's desire to affirm the distinct identity of the consecrated life as neither lay nor clerical.

Mixed Institutes of Religious men were founded as brotherhoods in which all the members, the ordained and the non-ordained, were considered as brothers having the same rights and responsibilities. Over time, this aspect of the founding charism was often overlooked, and distinctions originally not foreseen were introduced. In light of the Synod's wish that both ordained and non-ordained Religious "be recognized as having equal rights and obligations, with the exception of those which stem from Holy Orders" (§61.2), the Pope asks mixed Institutes to evaluate whether they consider it "appropriate and possible to return to their original inspiration" (§61.1). This request, too, reflects John Paul's insistence on the unique vocation constituted by professing the evangelical counsels.

The last special question that the Holy Father takes up deals with the many new foundations inspired by the Holy Spirit in recent years. While some of these are similar to traditional forms of the consecrated life, others have original traits. The foremost distinguishing characteristic of these new forms concerns the composition of its membership. Some of today's foundations "are composed of mixed groups of men and women, of clerics and lay persons, of married couples and celibates, all of whom pursue a particular style of life" (§62.2). Even though members are committed to living the evangelical counsels in different ways, they share fraternal life, simplicity, common prayer and, frequently, apostolic works. The charisms of these new associations of evangelical life require careful discernment at both the local and universal level. To help in this discernment process the Pope proposes to set up a Commission which will determine the criteria for evaluating the authenticity of these charisms and for recognizing them officially.

Vocations

The decrease in vocations in some areas of the world is a serious problem, especially in countries which traditionally had a wealth of them. According to John Paul, some Institutes "even run the risk of disappearing altogether" (§63.1). Others, because of fewer members, are being forced to curtail their apostolates. Because this personnel crisis often disheartens the Institutes concerned, the Pope reminds them that the consecrated life is essential to the Church's life, even though this conviction does not guarantee the survival of any particular Institute. He urges Institutes of Consecrated Life with few vocations not to yield to discouragement or to "the temptation to practice lax and unwise recruitment" (§64.5).

John Paul strongly recommends that consecrated men and women themselves take specific measures to promote vocations to their Institutes. Above all prayer for an increase in vocations to the consecrated life is required. Not just consecrated persons but the whole Christian community is called to "pray unceasingly to the Lord of the harvest, that he will send workers to his Church in order to meet the needs of the new evangelization" (§64.2). To fervent prayer must be added efforts aimed at explicitly encouraging vocations to the consecrated life. "A primary responsibility of all consecrated men and women is therefore to propose with courage, by word and example, the ideal of the following of Christ" (§64.3). This initial fostering of vocations needs to be complemented by concern for bringing them to maturity. Consecrated persons must continue to support those who are responding to God's call, especially by providing them with good spiritual direction. Furthermore, the Pope recommends that Institutes "invest their best resources generously in vocational work, especially by their serious involvement in working with youth" (§64.6). Lastly, he affirms that vocational promotion ought to form "an integral part of the overall pastoral plan of every particular Church" (§64.5).

Formation

Like the Synod Fathers, John Paul recognizes the decisive role played by good formation. If Institutes of Consecrated Life are to flourish, their formation must aim at helping individuals to conform themselves totally to Christ in the service of the Church. In a harmonious and balanced way, it furnishes a program of human, cultural, and spiritual preparation. Formation never ends. Marking every stage of the consecrated life, it constantly offers men and women "opportunities to grow in their commitment to the charism and mission of their Institute" (§65.3).

Initial formation extends from the first stages of association right up to final profession of the evangelical counsels. Suitably trained directors are needed to guide this process. The Holy Father describes them as human instruments in the hands of "the Father who, through the Spirit, fashions the inner attitudes of the Son in the hearts of young men and women" (§66.1). These directors must be spiritual, sensitive to the action of grace in others, eager to disclose the beauty of following Christ, capable of explaining the Institute's charism by which this close discipleship is lived out, and willing to make use of regular personal dialogue with candidates in formation. Moreover, "formators" should "combine the illumination of spiritual wisdom with the light shed by human means, which can be a help both in discerning the call and in forming the new man or woman" (§66.1). Formation in the common life and an Institute's apostolic work also directly involves many others, since it takes place in the framework of the community itself.

Initial preparation provides practical experiences of an Institute's apostolate.

These experiences, when prudently monitored, enable candidates "to test, in the context of the local culture, their skills for the apostolate, their ability to adapt and their spirit of initiative" (§67.1). Furthermore, so that formation will proceed in an orderly way, the Pope recommends that all Institutes of Consecrated Life and Societies of Apostolic Life "draw up as soon as possible a *ratio institutionis,* that is, a formation program inspired by their particular charism, presenting clearly and in all its stages the course to be followed in order to assimilate fully the spirituality of the respective Institute" (§68.2).

John Paul asks that each Institute's *ratio institutionis* include a precise and systematic plan for continuing formation. Every stage of life presents challenges that can be turned into opportunities for spiritual growth. Ongoing formation nurtures the human, apostolic, and cultural maturity of consecrated men and women. Human formation gives special importance to fostering an individual's interior freedom, affective maturity, communication skills, serenity of spirit, and compassion. Apostolic formation involves updating the methods and objectives of the apostolate. This renewal is always to be carried out in fidelity to an Institute's original charism and authentic traditions, but also in light of changing historical and cultural circumstances. Cultural formation entails a sound theological training which fosters the intellectual openness and adaptability necessary for the renewal of apostolic works. All continuing education, regardless of the field, aims at helping consecrated persons to deepen their special consecration according to their Institute's proper charism. "This means," says the Holy Father, "that each member should study diligently the spirit, history and mission of the Institute to which he or she belongs, in order to advance the personal and communal assimilation of its charism" (§71.5).

Mission to evangelization

Just as Jesus was "consecrated and sent into the world" (Jn 10:36), so, too, are consecrated persons, whether active or contemplative, entrusted with an apostolic mission. Following the example of Jesus' washing the feet of his disciples (cf. Jn 13:1-11), consecrated men and women serve God's plan for humanity by carrying out various apostolic works. For these apostolates to be effective, three conditions must be met. First, those who are consecrated need to be able to read the signs of the times. Building on their profound experience of God and immersion in the Gospel, the Holy Spirit leads them to discern apostolic choices "which are consistent with the original charism and which correspond to the demands of the concrete historical situation" (§73.2). Second, all apostolic initiatives are to safeguard ecclesial communion, especially with the local Bishop and the Successor of Peter. Third, Institutes must foster *"a solid spirituality of action,* seeing God in all things and all things in God" (§74.2). Difficult tasks can be accomplished only when contemplation feeds apostolic activity. When consecrated persons fix their gaze on the Lord's countenance, they are inspired "to free history from all that disfigures it" (§75.3).

Consecrated men and women contribute to the Church's mission primarily by "making Christ present to the world through personal witness" (§72.2, cf. §76). By virtue of their testimony they make visible "the loving and saving presence of Christ, the One consecrated by the Father, sent in mission" (§76). But consecrated persons also have a mission beyond giving personal witness. In *Vita Consecrata* John Paul describes some of the principal apostolic endeavors to which Institutes devote themselves: missionary activity *ad gentes,* the promotion of justice, the care of the sick, education, social communications, ecumenism, and interreligious dialogue.

Although some Institutes are specifically devoted to missionary work among those still awaiting the Good News, the Pope believes that all consecrated persons have a special role in spreading the faith. He urges every Institute, according to its charism, to contribute to the pressing task of proclaiming the Gospel *ad gentes.* Whatever form this mission takes, it "strengthens the consecrated life, gives it new enthusiasm and new motivation, and elicits faithfulness" (§78.2).

Effective proclamation of Christ to the whole world requires that the Gospel message be embodied in diverse cultural contexts. John Paul counts especially on consecrated persons to respond to this challenge of inculturating the Gospel. Their spiritual formation "accustoms them to being detached from things, even from many features of their culture" (§79.2), and so enables them to discern authentic values wherever they are found. Inculturation is successful whenever it is carried out by consecrated men and women who adhere faithfully "to the indispensable criteria of doctrinal orthodoxy, moral integrity and ecclesial communion" (§79.1). The consecrated life, too, must be inculturated if it is to flourish, especially in the younger Churches. The guarantee that efforts at inculturation are on the right path "is offered by the Holy See, whose task it is to encourage the evangelization of cultures, as well as to authenticate developments and to sanction results in the area of inculturation" (§80.2). Ultimately, however, it is the Holy Spirit's unifying action which ensures that an Institute's charism is being genuinely lived in new cultures.

Concern for the poor — expressed through prayer, practical assistance, and hospitality — has marked the consecrated life from its beginning. Work on behalf of the needy is "an act of evangelization" which today takes on new features (§82.4). Imitating Christ, consecrated men and women live individual and communal poverty in a way which enables them to embrace the cause of the poor. While John Paul cautions consecrated persons to maintain their independence from political ideologies, he encourages them to denounce injustice and to promote social justice. He hopes that present-day consecrated life will see "a renewal of that dedication which was characteristic of the founders and foundresses who spent their lives serving the Lord in the poor" (§82.2).

The Pope also praises the contribution of consecrated persons, especially women, to the field of health care, where they carry on Christ's ministry of mercy. He urges them to continue following in the footsteps of the "Divine Samaritan, physician of body and souls" and to give special attention in their apostolate to the neediest among the sick and the suffering (§83.2).

In a forceful section John Paul exhorts consecrated men and women to renew their commitment to the educational apostolate. He invites Institutes traditionally devoted to education "to be faithful to their founding charism and to their traditions," so that they can free people from "that grave form of poverty which is the lack of cultural and religious training" (§97.2). Guided by their Institutes' specific charism, consecrated persons are especially effective in providing an education "permeated by the Gospel spirit of freedom and charity, in which young people are helped to mature humanly under the action of the Spirit" (§96.2). The Holy Father reminds those working in institutions of higher learning of their responsibility to ensure "the preservation of their unique Catholic identity in complete fidelity to the Church's Magisterium" (§97.3).

Closely linked with the institutional presence of the consecrated life in the field of education is its mission to foster dialogue between culture and faith. John Paul encourages consecrated men and women to take up apostolic work in the media, so that they can "speak effectively of Christ to our contemporaries" (§99.1). He also invites them to transform society by participating in social and professional groups, and by engaging in dialogue with all men and women of good will. To combat incipient anti-intellectual tendencies in the Church, the Pope makes a specific proposal. Within Institutes, he says, "there is a need for a *renewed and loving commitment to the intellectual life,* for dedication to study as a means of integral formation and as a path of asceticism which is extraordinarily timely, in the face of present-day cultural diversity" (§98.3).

According to *Vita Consecrata,* ecumenical dialogue and interreligious dialogue are integral to the mission of the consecrated life. The common monastic heritage of Catholics and Orthodox and the profession of the evangelical counsels revived in the Anglican Communion and Ecclesial Communities of the Reformation make the consecrated life an ecumenical bridge which can help to heal "the wound of disunity still existing between believers in Christ" (§100.1). As helps toward restoring Christian unity the exhortation urges common prayer, cordial hospitality, mutual knowledge, and joint initiatives of service and witness.

John Paul also exhorts Institutes of Consecrated Life to become increasingly involved in interreligious dialogue, a task belonging to the Church's evangelizing mission. Because of their experience of the fraternal life, consecrated persons can promote sincere dialogue, especially with monastic communities of other religions. Moreover, there is considerable room for the "dialogue of action" through common efforts aimed at fostering respect for human life, commitment to justice and peace, the protection of creation, and the promotion of women's dignity (cf. §102.2-3).

Challenges of the evangelical counsels

Like the lay faithful and priests, consecrated persons share in a specific way in the prophetic mission of Christ and the Church. The consecrated life bears witness "to the primacy which God and the truths of the Gospel have in the Christian life" (§84.1, cf. §85.1). With particular intensity, this prophetic dimension shines forth in the fraternal life, which answers the world's "profound yearning for a brotherhood which knows no borders" (§85.1). The prophetic aspect is most clearly evident in the martyrdom by which so many "consecrated men and women have borne witness to Christ the Lord *with the gift of their own lives*" (§86.1).

According to John Paul II, contemporary society addresses three radical challenges to the Church. Each one directly calls into question the value of the evangelical counsels of chastity, poverty, and obedience. These challenges enable consecrated persons to testify to "the *profound anthropological significance* of the counsels" which, far from impoverishing truly human values, "leads instead to their transformation" (§87). Because the evangelical counsels affirm that God is the one absolute good, they relativize the created goods of sexuality, possession of material goods, and personal freedom. The prophetic witness of the three counsels provides "a spiritual 'therapy' for humanity" which is a blessing for the Church and the world of today (§87).

The first challenge comes from a hedonistic culture that idolizes sexuality, treating it as a consumer good divorced from all objective moral norms. In reply to this challenge, the evangelical counsel of chastity proclaims that "in

Christ it is possible to love God with all one's heart, putting him above every other love, and thus to love every creature with the freedom of God" (§88.1). The faithful living of the consecrated life bears witness to the power of God's grace to transform the fallen human condition.

Materialism and consumerism present the Church with a second challenge. The consecrated life replies to this unbridled craving for money and possessions by the witness of evangelical poverty. This counsel can contribute significantly to the renewal of society, especially in the developed world, which "risks losing the sense of proportion and the very meaning of things" (§90.1). Through their witness of self-denial, a fraternal life inspired by hospitality and the preferential love for the poor, consecrated men and women proclaim not only that "God is the true wealth of the human heart" (§90.1) but also that a simple lifestyle at the service of others brings true joy.

A third challenge to contemporary Church life comes from a distorted notion of freedom, one which separates freedom from its essential relationship to the truth. This misunderstanding of freedom, like mistaken ideas about human sexuality and material possessions, frequently leads to tragic consequences. The evangelical obedience of the consecrated life provides an effective response to freedom interpreted as license. Striving to imitate the Son's obedience to the Father, consecrated men and women proclaim a fundamental truth necessary for the survival of authentic individual and social liberty: *"There is no contradiction between obedience and freedom"* (§91.2). Indeed, obedience to God's will is the path to true freedom for everyone.

The spiritual life

John Paul echoes the Synod Fathers' concern that the consecrated life should be "nourished *from the well-spring of a sound and deep spirituality"* (§93.1). Every baptized person is called to seek the perfection of charity. This pursuit of holiness is all the more necessary for those who are consecrated. The consecrated life is "a particular covenant with God" and "a spousal covenant with Christ" (§93.2). This covenantal relationship gives rise to *"a specific spirituality,* that is, a concrete program of relations with God and one's surroundings, marked by specific spiritual emphases and choices of apostolate" (§93.4). When the Church officially approves an Institute, she confirms that its charism contains "all the objective elements necessary for achieving personal and communal perfection according to the Gospel" (§93.4). The two chief means of fostering a consecrated person's spiritual life are meditation on God's word in the Scriptures and taking part in the liturgy.

The Pope regards the word of God as "the first source of all Christian spirituality" (§94.1). Thus he recommends that consecrated persons devote themselves to *lectio divina,* the prayerful meditation on the Scriptures which opens them to bring God's word to bear on their life. This meditation, especially reflection on the mysteries of Christ, "gives rise to fervor in contemplation and the ardor of apostolic activity" (§94.3). Moreover, meditation on the Bible, when carried out in common, helps consecrated men and women to make progress together in the way of perfection.

The liturgy, above all the Sacraments of the Eucharist and Reconciliation, is an indispensable means for sustaining communion with Christ. At the heart of the consecrated life of individuals and communities is the Eucharist. The Holy Father urges consecrated persons to take part every day in Mass, "the daily viaticum and source of the spiritual life" (§95.2), and frequently to adore Christ present in the Blessed Sacrament. He also recommends that they regularly receive God's mercy in the Sacrament of Reconciliation. The joyful experience of sacramental forgiveness stimulates their ongoing conversion, and their faithfulness to the Gospel and the charism of their Institute.

Also of great help to the spiritual life is the Liturgy of the Hours, prayed individually or in community. This act of worship expresses "the call proper to consecrated persons to raise their hearts in praise and intercession" (§95.3). Spiritual direction, especially in the period of initial formation, also helps individuals in their growth toward holiness. Lastly, the Pope exhorts consecrated men and women to renew their "spiritual union with the Blessed Virgin Mary" by praying the rosary (§95.6).

The conclusion of the apostolic exhortation addresses the age-old question of the spiritual and social value of the consecrated life. Using the Gospel episode of Mary's anointing of Jesus' feet with costly ointment at Bethany, John Paul affirms that the consecrated life expresses the unbounded generosity and love of individuals "captivated in the depths of their heart by the beauty and goodness of the Lord" (§104.4). At the end of the document, he asks the Blessed Virgin Mary to obtain from her Son the grace that "all who have received the gift of following him in the consecrated life may be enabled to bear witness to that gift by their transfigured lives" (§112.3).

Key Themes

Despite the dense content of *Vita Consecrata,* four themes of great interest to the Pope stand out. Above all, he wishes to ensure that the consecrated life will be understood and lived in light of the Gospel, the Church's Tradition, and a supernatural discernment of the signs of the times. With this purpose in mind, he turns his attention to the foundation of the consecrated life in the

Gospel and its necessity to the Church, its relationship to the Kingdom of God, its prophetic dimension, and the importance of evangelical poverty.

In the heart of the Church

From the outset, the exhortation refers to the consecrated life as a "gift of God the Father to his Church" (§1.1), a "treasure" (§2.2), a "necessary gift for the present and future of the People of God" (§3.1). Throughout *Vita Consecrata* the Pope expresses gratitude and awe that God makes possible the life of the evangelical counsels. He firmly believes that the Church "is adorned and enriched by the presence of the consecrated life" (§104.3). Indeed, the consecrated life is *"at the very heart of the Church"* (§3.1).

Against those who maintain that the consecrated life is a post-apostolic development which is a structure *in* the Church, John Paul takes a strong stand. He teaches that the origins of the consecrated life lie in Christ's will. Consequently, the life of the evangelical counsels belongs to the structure *of* the Church. Without some form of the consecrated life the Church, if she is to remain faithful to her Lord, could not exist.

According to the New Testament, Jesus planted the seeds of the consecrated life during his earthly life. Jesus called some of his disciples to a special relationship with himself. He invited them "not only to welcome the Kingdom of God into their own lives, but also to put their lives at its service, leaving everything behind and closely imitating his own *way of life*" (§14.1). His was a virginal, poor, and obedient life. Others followed him. They imitated "the way of life practiced personally by Jesus and proposed by him to his disciples" (§31.4). This calling "established this type of life which, under the guidance of the Spirit, would gradually develop down the centuries into the various forms of the consecrated life" (§29.3). Consequently, the Holy Father teaches that the consecrated life was "present in the Church from the beginning" (§29.2). Consecrated virgins and widows, for instance, have been known in the Church "since apostolic times" (§§7.1, 7.3), and monasticism appeared "at the dawn of Christianity" (§6.1).

Because of its origin in Christ's design for his Church, the consecrated life belongs to her as a necessary element. It is "an intimate part of her life, her holiness and her mission" (§3.1, cf. §3.2). To be sure, the consecrated life "can never fail to be one of her essential and characteristic elements, for it expresses her very nature" (§29.2). Between the Church and the consecrated life there is, then, an indissoluble bond.

John Paul also points out a complementary truth. The consecrated life itself is a "permanent element in the Church" (§5.1), but any specific institutional form of it can be transitory. Certainly the "substance" of this way of life will always be present in the Church as a witness to her holiness and mission. Nonetheless, individual Institutes as such have no claim to permanence. According to the Pope, "it is necessary to distinguish the *historical destiny* of a specific Institute or form of consecrated life from the *ecclesial mission* of the consecrated life as such. The former is affected by changing circumstances; the latter is destined to perdure" (§63.3, cf. §3.2). Down through the centuries, many Institutes have contributed significantly to the Church and have then disappeared. At the same time, new forms which embody the permanent substance of the consecrated life have arisen. The Church has thus never been left without this indispensable witness.

For the glory of God

Throughout *Vita Consecrata* the Pope repeats that the consecrated life is especially linked to the presence and definitive coming of God's Kingdom. This way of life "acknowledges with wonder the sublime beauty of God, Father, Son and Holy Spirit, and bears joyful witness to his loving concern for every human being" (§16.4). Giving convincing testimony to the primacy of God in human affairs, not apostolic works, is its primary responsibility. Drawing from the Eastern tradition of spirituality, the Holy Father encourages consecrated men and women "to let themselves be captivated by the fascination of God and of his Son's Gospel" (§109.4). Not overwhelmed by everyday concerns but enthralled by God's beauty, they are to seek his Kingdom above all else, thereby inspiring and assisting all those who yearn for him and the joys of the spirit.

Through their contemplation of the crucified Christ, consecrated persons point to God's absolute transcendence over all creation and to the true meaning of love. On Calvary God fully reveals the beauty and power of his love. Consecrated men and women, like the Virgin Mary and the Apostle John, stand at the foot of the Cross, praising the splendor of this act of divine love. By their confession of this great mystery, the Church keeps before her the truth that *"the Cross is the superabundance of God's love poured out upon this world,* and that it is the great sign of Christ's saving presence" (§24.2).

Again and again the Holy Father mentions that the consecrated state illustrates that nothing in life is to be preferred to the love of God. Every person's supreme vocation "is always to be with the Lord" on whom he sets his gaze (§7.2). When Peter exclaims on Tabor, "Lord, it is well that we are here" (Mt 17:4), the Apostle's words proclaim the Christological focus of every believer's life. But they also express the radical vocation of the consecrated life: "How good it is for us to be with you, to devote ourselves to you, to make you the one focus of our lives!" (§15.4). Through their "all-encompassing commitment which foreshadows the eschatological perfection" of heaven (§16.2), consecrated men and women are called to conform their whole existence to Christ. They remind people that God asks from everyone an exclusive, unconditional, and total devotion. The life of the evangelical counsels is "a sign of the primacy of God and his Kingdom" (§80.1, cf. §85.1).

Because Christ is "the whole meaning of their lives" (§16.3), the witness of consecrated men and women leads others to see that their "commonwealth is in heaven" (Phil 3:20). John Paul affirms that "the consecrated person points to Christ who is to be loved above all things and to the mystery of the Trinity as the response to the profound longings of the human heart and the ultimate goal of every religious journey sincerely open to transcendence" (§103.2). The consecrated life joyfully proclaims "the possibility offered to every person and to the whole of humanity to live solely for God in Christ Jesus" (§59.2).

Consecrated life as prophetic

Since the Second Vatican Council, the prophetic dimension of the consecrated life has received considerable attention. In some quarters, the notion of prophecy has been accompanied by certain ideological or anti-hierarchical biases. Keeping these trends in mind, John Paul deals with the prophetic role of the consecrated life in a measured way.

Consecrated men and women can carry out their prophetic mission only if their witness is visible. Thus the Pope emphasizes that "by the profession of the evangelical counsels *the characteristic features of Jesus — the chaste, poor and obedient one — are made constantly 'visible' in the midst of the world"* (§1.1). Since the consecrated life belongs to the Church's nature, which is itself sacramental, consecrated persons are to be "true signs of Christ in the world" (§25.3). Indeed, the more they are conformed to him, "the more Christ is made present and active in the world for the salvation of all" (§72.2, cf. §76). Through the witness of their transfigured life, they make visible the marvels wrought by God for humanity. In the first place the consecrated life contributes to the Church by its clear affirmation of the primacy of God and eternal life.

The Holy Father very carefully avoids limiting the notion of prophecy to that of denunciation. Instead, he considers the prophetic dimension as part of the sign-value which comes from the profession of the evangelical counsels. In a specific way each of them rejects "the idolatry of anything created" (§87). Each of them is "a kind of sign and prophetic statement for the community of the brethren and for the world" (§15.4). The fraternal life, too, has a prophetic dimension, which is evident in two ways. First, life in common strengthens ecclesial communion by its witness to the freedom brought about by filial and responsible obedience. Second, it is a sign that *"dialogue is always possible and that communion can bring differences into harmony"* (§51.1). The Church holds up the model of communities "in which solitude is overcome through concern for one another, in which communication inspires in everyone a sense of shared responsibility, and in which wounds are healed through forgiveness, and each person's commitment to communion is strengthened" (§45.2). This convincing prophetic witness has never been more necessary to the Church and the world, and the Pope encourages consecrated men and women to strengthen the persuasive power of their testimony by ever greater fidelity to their calling.

Consecrated persons carry out their prophetic role of supporting the faithful on their journey in two other ways. First, by faithfully living their consecration, they *"remind the baptized of the fundamental values of the Gospel"* (§33.1, cf. §105.1). In the consecrated life "the proclamation of the Gospel to the whole world finds fresh enthusiasm and power" (§105.2). This reminder takes shape in bearing witness to "the inseparable unity of love of God and love of neighbor" (§63.4, cf. §5.1). Second, the consecrated life is a powerful incentive to holiness for everyone. John Paul is convinced that a renewed commitment to holiness by consecrated persons is *"a means of promoting and supporting every Christian's desire for perfection"* (§39.1, cf. §93.5). Only if the consecrated life is spiritually sound will it inspire people today. In exhorting consecrated men and women, he tells them: "Christians . . . need to discover in you purified hearts which in faith 'see' God, people docile to the working of the Holy Spirit who resolutely press on in fidelity to the charism of their call and mission" (§109.1).

In his presentation of the *"special form of sharing in Christ's prophetic office"* (§84.1) that belongs to the consecrated life, John Paul proposes the Prophet Elijah as its model. Immersed in contemplation, the Prophet spoke boldly in God's name. The Pope insists that *"true prophecy is born of God, from friendship with him, from attentive listening to his word in the different circumstances of history"* (§84.2). True prophetic witness will lead consecrated men and women to seek God's will in communion with the Church. The Church's history testifies that some consecrated men and women have received a special gift of the Holy Spirit to carry out "a genuinely prophetic ministry, speaking in the name of God to all, even to the Pastors of the Church" (§84.2). Such charismatic gifts are aimed at enriching all the faithful. Their authenticity is "guaranteed by *full harmony with the Church's Magisterium and discipline"* (§85.2).

Evangelical poverty

From the beginning of his pontificate, John Paul has demonstrated great solicitude for the world's poor. His social encyclicals, homilies, interventions in international affairs, and the practical help offered to the destitute and suffering reflect his desire to alleviate their plight and to foster greater justice and solidarity among all peoples. Not surprisingly, therefore, *Vita Consecrata* echoes this deeply felt concern. It describes the Trinitarian and Christological foundation of poverty, its meaning as an evangelical counsel, and the obligation of Institutes to serve the poor in their apostolic works.

John Paul recognizes that poverty has a positive meaning for Christ's disciples. Evangelical poverty, he says, is a value in itself, "since it recalls the first of the Beatitudes in the imitation of the poor Christ" (§90.1). In the Trinity's inner life, the Son expresses an attitude of poverty before the Father, from whom he receives everything, in order to give back everything to him in love (cf. Jn 17:7, 10). Moreover, by assuming a human nature the Son became poor for humanity's sake (cf. 2 Cor 8:9). In the created order, the Incarnation and Redemption express "that *total gift of self* which the three divine Persons make to one another" (§21.3). This poverty of Jesus, rooted in the Holy Trinity, is the exemplar which inspires consecrated persons who strive to imitate his way of life.

Living poorly is constitutive of the consecrated life. The imitation of Christ leads those who are consecrated "to live a life of poverty and to embrace the cause of the poor" (§82.2). Consequently, the members of each Institute, according to its charism, will lead *"a simple and austere way of life"* (§82.2). By placing a brake on consumption, the common life bears witness to self-denial, restraint, simplicity, and hospitality, and to "sharing the conditions of life of the most neglected" (§90.2).

Apart from its spiritual value for consecrated men and women themselves, the practice of evangelical poverty also impels them to make an option of preference for the poor. John Paul affirms that the Church shows this preferential option "to those who are *in situations of greater weakness,* and therefore in greater need . . . the oppressed, those on the margin of society, the elderly, the sick, the young, any and all who are considered and treated as 'the least'" (§82.1, cf. §75.5). Like Jesus, consecrated persons are to "join him in washing the feet of the poor" (§110.2, cf. §75.2) — the materially, culturally, and spiritually needy among their brothers and sisters. This preferential option for the poor, which the Pope refers to frequently in his social teaching, entails both the denunciation of justice and directly serving those in need.

Through their own experience of poverty, consecrated persons feel that "hunger and thirst for justice which God has promised to satisfy" (§36.3). Like Elijah the Prophet, consecrated men and women come "to the defense of the poor against the powerful of the world" (§84.2). Profession of evangelical poverty enables those consecrated "to denounce the injustices committed against so many sons and daughters of God, and commit themselves to the promotion of justice in the society where they work" (§82.2). Their work for justice is to be inspired by the Gospel and the principles of the Church's social teaching.

The Holy Father outlines a fundamental principle on the importance of evangelical poverty if the consecrated life is to flourish: "Serving the poor is an act of evangelization and, at the same time, a seal of Gospel authenticity and a catalyst for permanent conversion in the consecrated life" (§82.4). Repeatedly he mentions that every Institute must find ways to embrace the cause of the poor. The Pope teaches that whatever an Institute's apostolic work, it should serve "especially the poor and the outcast " (§5.1, cf. §§24.2, 75.1, 75.5, 82, 90). In the case of Institutes devoted to health care and education he is explicit. The former, he says, "should give a special place in their ministry to the poorest and most abandoned of the sick, such as the elderly, and those who are handicapped, marginalized, or terminally ill, and to the victims of drug abuse and new contagious diseases" (§83.2). To those in the apostolate of education, he urges that they practice the love of preference for the poor by working to free them from the consequences of all forms of ignorance. In the exhortation's closing prayer, John Paul asks that Mary support consecrated men and women "in their work for the poor, the hungry, those without hope, the little ones and all who seek [her] Son with a sincere heart" (§112.2).

* * *

Selected Bibliography

Balducci, Anna Maria. "Consecrated Persons Are Called To Restore Balance to Life and Culture." *L'Osservatore Romano,* 36 (1996), 10.

Billy, Dennis, J. "*Vita Consecrata* and the Spirituality of Communion." *Dominican Ashram,* 15 (1996), 172-185.

Bisignano, Sante. "Major Superiors Should Encourage Exchange between Religious Families." *L'Osservatore Romano,* 35 (1996), 6.

Brusco, Angelo. "Consecrated Persons Remind Us To See Christ's Face in the Sick." *L'Osservatore Romano,* 21 (1996), 10.

Cabra, Piergiordano. "All Consecration Is for Mission, and All Mission Stems from Consecration." *L'Osservatore Romano,* 19 (1996), 10-11.

Callam, Daniel. Editorial. *The Canadian Catholic* Review, 14 (September 1996), 2-3.

Cencini, Amedeo. "Goal of Formation Is Conformity to Jesus Christ's Total Self-giving." *L'Osservatore Romano,* 29 (1996), 10-11.

Ciardi, Fabio. "Fraternal Life in Community Is Eloquent Witness to the Trinity." *L'Osservatore Romano,* 18 (1996), 10-11.

Costa, Maurizio. "Prophetic Witness Is an Essential Task and Feature of Consecrated Life." *L'Osservatore Romano,* 28 (1996), 9-10.

Drouin, Pierre. "Societies of Apostolic Life Compared to the Institutes of Consecrated Life." *L'Osservatore Romano,* 25 (1996), 10-11.

Fleming, David L. Editorial. *Review for Religious,* 55 (1996), 452-453.

Fong, M. Ko Ha. "Mary's Presence and Example Is Indispensable to Consecrated Life." *L'Osservatore Romano,* 22 (1996), 10-11.

Galot, Jean. "Consecrated Life Is Father's Gift to His Church through the Spirit." *L'Osservatore Romano,* 17 (1996), 10-11.

Gambino, Vittorino. "Faith in Jesus Christ Sheds Light on Whole Educational Enterprise." *L'Osservatore Romano,* 32/33 (1996), 6.

Gentili, Antonio. "Spiritual Life Is a Most Precious Gift Which Should Be Cultivated." *L'Osservatore Romano,* 37 (1996), 14.

Ghirlanda, Gianfranco. "Profession of Evangelical Counsels Is Integral Part of Church's Life." *L'Osservatore Romano,* 20 (1996), 10-11.

Holland, Sharon. "*Vita Consecrata:* A First Reading," *Dominican Ashram,* 15 (1996), 155-164.

Johnston, John. "Consecration of Religious Brothers Is a State of Life Complete in Itself." *L'Osservatore Romano,* 34 (1996), 6-7.

Lara, Elías Royón. "Laity Are Invited To Share in Mission and Spirituality of Consecrated Life." *L'Osservatore Romano,* 23 (1996), 10-11.

McDermott, Rose. "*Vita Consecrata:* A Vocation for the Third Millennium." *Review for Religious,* 55 (1996), 454-461.

Mongillo, Dalmazio. "*Vita Consecrata*: 'A Great History Yet To Be Accomplished.'" *Dominican Ashram,* 15 (1996), 147-154.

O'Donnell, Desmond. "*Vita Consecrata* on Community." *Religious Life Review,* 35 (1996), 305-309.

Quaranta, Ciro. "Promotion of Religious Vocations Is a Task for the Whole Church." *L'Osservatore Romano,* 27 (1996), 10-11.

Rocchetta, Carlo. "Secular Institutes Seek To Imbue the World with Evangelical Spirit." *L'Osservatore Romano,* 26 (1996), 10-11.

Rosanna, Enrica. "Church Needs Consecrated Women To Foster Christian Doctrine and Morals." *L'Osservatore Romano,* 31 (1996), 6-7.

Stoppa, Chiara Cristiana. "Cloistered Communities Witness to the Possibility of Encountering God." *L'Osservatore Romano,* 24 (1996), 10.

Synod of Bishops, Ninth Ordinary General Assembly. *"Instrumentum Laboris."* *L'Osservatore Romano,* 27 (1994), i-xii, and 28 (1994), xiii-xxiv; and *Origins,* 24 (1994), 97, 99-138.

Synod of Bishops, Ninth Ordinary General Assembly. *"Lineamenta."* *L'Osservatore Romano,* 48 (1992), 5-16; and *Origins,* 22 (1992), 433, 435-454.

Synod of Bishops, Ninth Ordinary General Assembly. "Message to the People of God." *L'Osservatore Romano,* 44 (1994), 6; and *Origins,* 24 (1994), 369, 371-374.

Union of Superiors General. "The International Reception of *Vita Consecrata.*" *Catholic International,* 7 (1996), 424-437.

Valero, Urbano. "Religious Brothers Are a Special Gift of God to 'Clerical Institutes.'" *L'Osservatore Romano,* 38 (1996), 14-15.

Zago, Marcello. "Call to Mission *Ad Gentes* to Every Institute of Consecrated Life." *L'Osservatore Romano,* 30 (1996), 6-7.

POST-SYNODAL

APOSTOLIC EXHORTATION

VITA CONSECRATA

OF THE HOLY FATHER

JOHN PAUL II

TO THE BISHOPS AND CLERGY

RELIGIOUS ORDERS AND CONGREGATIONS

SOCIETIES OF APOSTOLIC LIFE

SECULAR INSTITUTES

AND ALL THE LAY FAITHFUL

ON THE CONSECRATED LIFE AND ITS MISSION

IN THE CHURCH AND IN THE WORLD

Vita Consecrata
Introduction

1.1 The consecrated life, deeply rooted in the example and teaching of Christ the Lord, is a gift of God the Father to his Church through the Holy Spirit. By the profession of the evangelical counsels *the characteristic features of Jesus* — the chaste, poor and obedient one — *are made constantly "visible" in the midst of the world* and the eyes of the faithful are directed toward the mystery of the Kingdom of God already at work in history, even as it awaits its full realization in heaven.

1.2 In every age there have been men and women who, obedient to the Father's call and to the prompting of the Spirit, have chosen this special way of following Christ, in order to devote themselves to him with an "undivided" heart (cf. 1 Cor 7:34). Like the Apostles, they too have left everything behind in order to be with Christ and to put themselves, as he did, at the service of God and their brothers and sisters. In this way, through the many charisms of spiritual and apostolic life bestowed on them by the Holy Spirit, they have helped to make the mystery and mission of the Church shine forth, and in doing so have contributed to the renewal of society.

Thanksgiving for the consecrated life

2.1 Because the role of consecrated life in the Church is so important, I decided to convene a Synod in order to examine in depth its significance and its future prospects, especially in view of the approaching new millennium. It was my wish that the Synodal Assembly should include, together with the Bishops, a considerable number of consecrated men and women, in order that they too might contribute to the common reflection.

2.2 We are all aware of the treasure which the gift of the consecrated life in the variety of its charisms and institutions represents for the ecclesial community. *Together let us thank God* for the Religious Orders and Institutes devoted to contemplation or the works of the apostolate, for Societies of Apostolic Life, for Secular Institutes and for other groups of consecrated persons, as well as for all those individuals who, in their inmost hearts, dedicate themselves to God by a special consecration.

2.3 The Synod was a tangible sign of the universal extension of the consecrated life, present in the local Churches throughout the world. The consecrated life inspires and accompanies the spread of evangelization in the different parts of the world, where Institutes from abroad are gratefully welcomed and new ones are being founded, in a great variety of forms and expressions.

2.4 Consequently, although in some parts of the world Institutes of Consecrated Life seem to be experiencing a period of difficulty, in other places they are prospering with remarkable vitality. This shows that the choice of total self-giving to God in Christ is in no way incompatible with any human culture or historical situation. Nor is the consecrated life flourishing within the Catholic Church alone. In fact, it is particularly vibrant in the monasticism of the Orthodox Churches, where it is an essential feature of their life. It is also taking root or re-emerging in the Churches and Ecclesial Communities which originated in the Reformation, and is the sign of a grace shared by all of Christ's disciples. This fact is an incentive to ecumenism, which fosters the desire for an ever fuller communion between Christians, "that the world may believe" (Jn 17:21).

The consecrated life: a gift to the Church

3.1 Its universal presence and the evangelical nature of its witness are clear evidence — if any were needed — that the consecrated life *is not something isolated and marginal,* but a reality which affects the whole Church. The Bishops at the Synod frequently reaffirmed this: *"de re nostra agitur,"* "this is something which concerns us all."[1] In effect, *the consecrated life is at the very heart of the Church* as a decisive element for her mission, since it "manifests the inner nature of the Christian calling"[2] and the striving of the whole Church as Bride toward union with her one Spouse.[3] At the Synod it was stated on several occasions that the consecrated life has not only proved a help and support for the Church in the past, but is also a precious and necessary gift for the present and future of the People of God, since it is an intimate part of her life, her holiness and her mission.[4]

3.2 The present difficulties which a number of Institutes are encountering in some parts of the world must not lead to a questioning of the fact that the profession of the evangelical counsels is *an integral part of the Church's life*

---

[1] Cf. *Propositio* 2.

[2] Second Vatican Ecumenical Council, Decree on the Church's Missionary Activity *Ad Gentes,* 18.

[3] Cf. Second Vatican Ecumenical Council, Dogmatic Constitution on the Church *Lumen Gentium,* 44; Paul VI, Apostolic Exhortation *Evangelica Testificatio* (June 29, 1971), 7: *AAS* 63 (1971), 501-502; Apostolic Exhortation *Evangelii Nuntiandi* (December 8, 1975), 69: *AAS* 68 (1976), 59.

[4] Cf. Second Vatican Ecumenical Council, Dogmatic Constitution on the Church *Lumen Gentium,* 44.

and a much-needed incentive toward ever greater fidelity to the Gospel.[5] The consecrated life may experience further changes in its historical forms, but there will be no change in the substance of a choice which finds expression in a radical gift of self for love of the Lord Jesus and, in him, of every member of the human family. *This certainty,* which has inspired countless individuals in the course of the centuries, *continues to reassure the Christian people,* for they know that they can draw from the contribution of these generous souls powerful support on their journey toward the heavenly home.

Gathering the fruits of the Synod

4.1 In response to the desire expressed by the Ordinary General Assembly of the Synod of Bishops which met to discuss the theme "The Consecrated Life and Its Mission in the Church and in the World," I intend to set forth in this Apostolic Exhortation the results of the Synod process[6] and to point out to all the faithful — Bishops, priests, deacons, consecrated persons and laity, and to any others who might be interested — the wondrous things which today too the Lord wishes to accomplish through the consecrated life.

4.2 This Synod, coming after the ones dedicated to the lay faithful and to priests, completes the treatment of the distinctive features of the states of life willed by the Lord Jesus for his Church. Whereas the Second Vatican Council emphasized the profound reality of ecclesial communion, in which all gifts converge for the building up of the Body of Christ and for the Church's mission in the world, in recent years there has been felt the need to clarify *the specific identity of the various states of life,* their vocation and their particular mission in the Church.

4.3 Communion in the Church is not uniformity, but a gift of the Spirit who is present in the variety of charisms and states of life. These will be all the more helpful to the Church and her mission the more their specific identity is respected. For every gift of the Spirit is granted in order to bear fruit for the Lord[7] in the growth of fraternity and mission.

The work of the Spirit in the various forms of the consecrated life

5.1 How can we not recall with gratitude to the Spirit *the many different forms of consecrated life* which he has raised up throughout history and which still

---

[5] Cf. John Paul II, Address at the General Audience (September 28, 1994), 5: *Insegnamenti* 17/2 (1994), 405.

[6] Cf. *Propositio* 1.

[7] Cf. Saint Francis de Sales, *Introduction to the Devout Life,* Part I, Chapter 3.

exist in the Church today? They can be compared to a plant with many branches[8] which sinks its roots into the Gospel and brings forth abundant fruit in every season of the Church's life. What an extraordinary richness! I myself, at the conclusion of the Synod, felt the need to stress this permanent element in the history of the Church: the host of founders and foundresses, of holy men and women who chose Christ by radically following the Gospel and by serving their brothers and sisters, especially the poor and the outcast.[9] Such service is itself a sign of how the consecrated life manifests the *organic unity of the commandment of love,* in the inseparable link between love of God and love of neighbor.

5.2 The Synod recalled this unceasing work of the Holy Spirit, who in every age shows forth the richness of the practice of the evangelical counsels through a multiplicity of charisms. In this way too he makes ever present in the Church and in the world, in time and space, the mystery of Christ.

Monastic life in the East and the West

6.1 The Synod Fathers from the Eastern Catholic Churches and the representatives of the other Churches of the East emphasized *the evangelical values of monastic life,*[10] which appeared at the dawn of Christianity and which still flourishes in their territories, especially in the Orthodox Churches.

6.2 From the first centuries of the Church, men and women have felt called to imitate the Incarnate Word who took on the condition of a servant. They have sought to follow him by living in a particularly radical way, through monastic profession, the demands flowing from baptismal participation in the Paschal Mystery of his Death and Resurrection. In this way, by becoming bearers of the Cross (*staurophoroi*), they have striven to become bearers of the Spirit (*pneumatophoroi*), authentically spiritual men and women, capable of endowing history with hidden fruitfulness by unceasing praise and intercession, by spiritual counsels and works of charity.

6.3 In its desire to transfigure the world and life itself in expectation of the definitive vision of God's countenance, Eastern monasticism gives pride of place to conversion, self-renunciation and compunction of heart, the quest for *hesychia* or interior peace, ceaseless prayer, fasting and vigils, spiritual combat and silence, paschal joy in the presence of the Lord and the expectation of

---

[8] Cf. Second Vatican Ecumenical Council, Dogmatic Constitution on the Church *Lumen Gentium,* 43.

[9] Cf. Homily at the Mass for the Closing of the Synod of Bishops, Ninth Ordinary General Assembly (October 29, 1994), 3: *AAS* 87 (1995), 580.

[10] Cf. Synod of Bishops, Ninth Ordinary General Assembly, Message of the Synod (October 27, 1994), VII: *L'Osservatore Romano* (English-language edition), November 2, 1994, 7.

his definitive coming, and the oblation of self and personal possessions, lived in the holy communion of the monastery or in the solitude of the hermitage.[11]

6.4 The West too from the first centuries of the Church has practiced the monastic life and has experienced a great variety of expressions of it, both cenobitic and eremetical. In its present form, inspired above all by Saint Benedict, Western monasticism is the heir of the great number of men and women who, leaving behind life in the world, sought God and dedicated themselves to him, "preferring nothing to the love of Christ."[12] The monks of today likewise strive to *create a harmonious balance between the interior life and work* in the evangelical commitment to conversion of life, obedience and stability, and in persevering dedication to meditation on God's word (*lectio divina*), the celebration of the Liturgy and prayer. In the heart of the Church and the world, monasteries have been and continue to be eloquent signs of communion, welcoming abodes for those seeking God and the things of the spirit, schools of faith and true places of study, dialogue and culture for the building up of the life of the Church and of the earthly city itself, in expectation of the heavenly city.

The Order of Virgins; hermits and widows

7.1 It is a source of joy and hope to witness in our time a new flowering of *the ancient Order of Virgins,* known in Christian communities ever since apostolic times.[13] Consecrated by the diocesan Bishop, these women acquire a particular link with the local Church, which they are committed to serve while remaining in the world. Either alone or in association with others, they constitute *a special eschatological image of the Heavenly Bride and of the life to come,* when the Church will at last fully live her love for Christ the Bridegroom.

7.2 *Men and women hermits,* belonging to ancient Orders or new Institutes, or being directly dependent on the Bishop, bear witness to the passing nature of the present age by their inward and outward separation from the world. By fasting and penance, they show that man does not live by bread alone but by the word of God (cf. Mt 4:4). Such a life "in the desert" is an invitation to their contemporaries and to the ecclesial community itself *never to lose sight of the supreme vocation,* which is to be always with the Lord.

7.3 Again being practiced today is the consecration of *widows,*[14] known

---

[11] Cf. *Propositio* 5, B.
[12] Cf. *Rule,* 4, 21 and 72, 11.
[13] Cf. *Propositio* 12.
[14] Cf. Code of Canons of the Eastern Churches, Canon 570.

since apostolic times (cf. 1 Tim 5:5, 9-10; 1 Cor 7:8), as well as the consecration of widowers. These women and men, through a vow of perpetual chastity as a sign of the Kingdom of God, consecrate their state of life in order to devote themselves to prayer and the service of the Church.

Institutes completely devoted to contemplation

8.1 Institutes completely devoted to contemplation, composed of either women or men, are for the Church a reason for pride and a source of heavenly graces. By their lives and mission, the members of these Institutes imitate Christ in his prayer on the mountain, bear witness to God's lordship over history and anticipate the glory which is to come.

8.2 In solitude and silence, by listening to the word of God, participating in divine worship, personal asceticism, prayer, mortification and the communion of fraternal love, they direct the whole of their lives and all their activities to the contemplation of God. In this way they offer the ecclesial community a singular testimony of the Church's love for her Lord, and they contribute, with hidden apostolic fruitfulness, to the growth of the People of God.[15]

8.3 Thus there is good reason to hope that the different forms of contemplative life will experience *continued growth in the younger Churches* as an evident sign that the Gospel has taken firm root, especially in those areas of the world where other religions predominate. This will make it possible to bear witness to the vitality of the traditions of Christian asceticism and mysticism and will contribute to interreligious dialogue.[16]

Apostolic religious life

9.1 The West has also known, down the centuries, a variety of other expressions of religious life, in which countless persons, renouncing the world, have consecrated themselves to God through the public profession of the evangelical counsels in accordance with a specific charism and in a stable form of common life,[17] *for the sake of carrying out different forms of apostolic service to the People of God.* Thus there arose the different families of Canons Regular, the Mendicant Orders, the Clerics Regular and in general the Religious Congregations of men and women devoted to apostolic and missionary activity and to the many different works inspired by Christian charity.

9.2 This is a splendid and varied testimony, reflecting the multiplicity of

[15] Cf. Second Vatican Ecumenical Council, Decree on the Appropriate Renewal of the Religious Life *Perfectae Caritatis,* 7; Decree on the Church's Missionary Activity *Ad Gentes,* 40.

[16] Cf. *Propositio 6.*

[17] Cf. *Propositio 4.*

gifts bestowed by God on founders and foundresses who, in openness to the working of the Holy Spirit, successfully interpreted the signs of the times and responded wisely to new needs. Following in their footsteps, many other people have sought by word and deed to embody the Gospel in their own lives, bringing anew to their own times the living presence of Jesus, the Consecrated One *par excellence*, the One sent by the Father. In every age consecrated men and women must continue to be images of Christ the Lord, fostering through prayer a profound communion of mind with him (cf. Phil 2:5-11), so that their whole lives may be penetrated by an apostolic spirit and their apostolic work with contemplation.[18]

Secular Institutes

10.1 The Holy Spirit, who wondrously fashions the variety of charisms, has given rise in our time to *new expressions of consecrated life*, which appear as a providential response to the new needs encountered by the Church today as she carries out her mission in the world.

10.2 One thinks in the first place of members of *Secular Institutes* seeking to *live out their consecration to God in the world* through the profession of the evangelical counsels in the midst of temporal realities; they wish in this way to be a leaven of wisdom and a witness of grace within cultural, economic and political life. Through their own specific blending of presence in the world and consecration, they seek *to make present in society the newness and power of Christ's Kingdom*, striving to transfigure the world from within by the power of the Beatitudes. In this way, while they belong completely to God and are thus fully consecrated to his service, their activity in the ordinary life of the world contributes, by the power of the Spirit, to shedding the light of the Gospel on temporal realities. Secular Institutes, each in accordance with its specific nature, thus help to ensure that the Church has an effective presence in society.[19]

10.3 A valuable role is also played by *Clerical Secular Institutes*, in which priests who belong to the diocesan clergy, even when some of them are recognized as being incardinated in the Institute, consecrate themselves to Christ through the practice of the evangelical counsels in accordance with a specific charism. They discover in the spiritual riches of the Institute to which they belong great help for living more deeply the spirituality proper to the priesthood and thus they are enabled to be a leaven of communion and apostolic generosity among their fellow clergy.

---

[18] Cf. *Propositio* 7.
[19] Cf. *Propositio* 11.

Societies of Apostolic Life

11 Also worthy of special mention are *Societies of Apostolic Life* or of common life, composed of men or women. These pursue, each in its own particular way, a specific apostolic or missionary end. In many of them an explicit commitment to the evangelical counsels is made through sacred bonds officially recognized by the Church. Even in this case, however, the specific nature of their consecration distinguishes them from Religious Institutes and Secular Institutes. The specific identity of this form of life is to be preserved and promoted; in recent centuries it has produced many fruits of holiness and of the apostolate, especially in the field of charity and in the spread of the Gospel in the missions.[20]

New expressions of consecrated life

12.1 The perennial youth of the Church continues to be evident even today. In recent years, following the Second Vatican Council, *new or renewed forms of the consecrated life* have arisen. In many cases, these are Institutes similar to those already existing, but inspired by new spiritual and apostolic impulses. Their vitality must be judged by the authority of the Church, which has the responsibility of examining them in order to discern the authenticity of the purpose for their foundation and to prevent the proliferation of institutions similar to one another, with the consequent risk of a harmful fragmentation into excessively small groups. In other cases it is a question of new experiments which are seeking an identity of their own in the Church and awaiting official recognition from the Apostolic See, which alone has final judgment in these matters.[21]

12.2 These new forms of consecrated life now taking their place alongside the older ones bear witness to the constant attraction which the total gift of self to the Lord, the ideal of the apostolic community and the founding charisms continue to exert, even on the present generation. They also show how the gifts of the Holy Spirit complement one another.

12.3 In this newness, however, the Spirit does not contradict himself. Proof of this is the fact that the new forms of consecrated life have not supplanted the earlier ones. Amid such wide variety the underlying unity has been successfully preserved, thanks to the one call to follow Jesus — chaste, poor and obedient — in the pursuit of perfect charity. This call, which is found in all the existing forms of consecrated life, must also mark those which present themselves as new.

[20] Cf. *Propositio* 14.

[21] Cf. Code of Canon Law, Canon 605; Code of Canons of the Eastern Churches, Canon 571; *Propositio* 13.

Purpose of the Apostolic Exhortation

13.1 Gathering together the fruits of the Synod's labors, in this Apostolic Exhortation I wish to address the whole Church in order to offer not only to consecrated persons but also to the Bishops and the faithful *the results of a stimulating exchange,* guided by the Holy Spirit with his gifts of truth and love.

13.2 During these years of renewal, the consecrated life, like other ways of life in the Church, has gone through a difficult and trying period. It has been a period full of hopes, new experiments and proposals aimed at giving fresh vigor to the profession of the evangelical counsels. But it has also been a time of tension and struggle, in which well-meaning endeavors have not always met with positive results.

13.3 The difficulties, however, must not lead to discouragement. Rather, we need to commit ourselves with fresh enthusiasm, for the Church needs the spiritual and apostolic contribution of a renewed and revitalized consecrated life. In this Post-Synodal Exhortation I wish to address religious communities and consecrated persons in the same spirit which inspired the letter sent by the Council of Jerusalem to the Christians of Antioch, and I am hopeful that it will meet with the same response: "When they read it, they rejoiced at the encouragement which it gave" (Acts 15:31). And not only this. I also hope to increase the joy of the whole People of God. As they become better acquainted with the consecrated life, they will be able with greater awareness to thank Almighty God for this great gift.

13.4 In an attitude of heartfelt openness toward the Synod Fathers, I have carefully considered the valuable contributions made during the intense work of the Assembly, at which I made a point of being present throughout. During the Synod, I also sought to offer the entire People of God a number of systematic talks on the consecrated life in the Church. In them I presented anew the teachings found in the texts of the Second Vatican Council, which was an enlightening point of reference for subsequent doctrinal developments and for the reflections of the Synod during the busy weeks of its work.[22]

13.5 I am confident that the sons and daughters of the Church, and consecrated persons in particular, will receive this Exhortation with open hearts. At the same time, I hope that reflection will continue and lead to a deeper understanding of the great gift of the consecrated life in its three aspects of consecration, communion and mission. I also hope that consecrated men and women, in full harmony with the Church and her Magisterium, will discover in this Exhortation further encouragement to face in a spiritual and apostolic manner the new challenges of our time.

---

[22] Cf. *Propositiones* 3, 4, 6, 7, 8, 10, 13, 28, 29, 30, 35, 48.

I

Confessio Trinitatis: The Origins of the Consecrated Life in the Mystery of Christ and of the Trinity

Icon of the transfigured Christ

14.1 The evangelical basis of consecrated life is to be sought in the special relationship which Jesus, in his earthly life, established with some of his disciples. He called them not only to welcome the Kingdom of God into their own lives, but also to put their lives at its service, leaving everything behind and closely imitating his own *way of life.*

14.2 Many of the baptized throughout history have been invited to live such a life "in the image of Christ." But this is possible only on the basis of a special vocation and in virtue of a particular gift of the Spirit. For in such a life baptismal consecration develops into a radical response in the following of Christ through acceptance of the evangelical counsels, the first and essential of which is the sacred bond of chastity for the sake of the Kingdom of heaven.[23] This special way of "following Christ," at the origin of which is always the initiative of the Father, has an essential Christological and pneumatological meaning: it expresses in a particularly vivid way the *Trinitarian* nature of the Christian life and it anticipates in a certain way that *eschatological* fulfillment toward which the whole Church is tending.[24]

14.3 In the Gospel, many of Christ's words and actions shed light on the meaning of this special vocation. But for an overall picture of its essential characteristics, it is singularly helpful to fix our gaze on Christ's radiant face in the mystery of the Transfiguration. A whole ancient spiritual tradition refers to this "icon" when it links the contemplative life to the prayer of Jesus "on the mountain."[25] Even the "active" dimensions of consecrated life can in a way be included here, for the Transfiguration is not only the revelation of

---

[23] Cf. *Propositio* 3, A and B.

[24] Cf. *Propositio* 3, C.

[25] Cf. Cassian: "Secessit tamen solus in monte orare, per hoc scilicet nos instruens suae secessionis exemplo . . . ut similiter secedamus" (*Collationes* 10, 6: *PL* 49, 827); Saint Jerome: "Et Christum quaeras in solitudine et ores solus in monte cum Iesu" (*Epistula ad Paulinum* 58, 4, 2: *PL* 22, 582); William of Saint-Thierry: "[Vita solitaria] ab ipso Domino familiarissime celebrata, ab eius discipulis ipso praesente concupita: cuius transfigurationis gloriam cum vidissent qui cum eo in monte sancto erant, continuo Petrus . . . optimum sibi iudicavit in hoc semper esse" (*Ad Fratres de Monte Dei,* I, 1: *PL* 184, 310).

Christ's glory but also a preparation for facing Christ's Cross. It involves both "going up the mountain" and "coming down the mountain." The disciples who have enjoyed this intimacy with the Master, surrounded for a moment by the splendor of the Trinitarian life and of the Communion of Saints, and as it were caught up in the horizon of eternity, are immediately brought back to daily reality, where they see "Jesus only," in the lowliness of his human nature, and are invited to return to the valley, to share with him the toil of God's plan and to set off courageously on the way of the Cross.

"And he was transfigured before them . . ."

15.1 *And after six days Jesus took with him Peter and James and John his brother, and led them up a high mountain apart. And he was transfigured before them, and his face shone like the sun, and his garments became white as light. And behold, there appeared to them Moses and Elijah, talking with him. And Peter said to Jesus, "Lord, it is well that we are here; if you wish, I will make three booths here, one for you and one for Moses and one for Elijah." He was still speaking, when lo, a bright cloud overshadowed them, and a voice from the cloud said, "This is my beloved Son, with whom I am well pleased; listen to him." When the disciples heard this, they fell on their faces, and were filled with fear. But Jesus came and touched them, saying, "Rise, and have no fear." And when they lifted up their eyes, they saw no one but Jesus only.*

15.2 *And as they were coming down the mountain, Jesus commanded them, "Tell no one the vision, until the Son of man is raised from the dead"* (Mt 17:1-9).

15.3 The event of the Transfiguration marks *a decisive moment in the ministry of Jesus.* It is a revelatory event which strengthens the faith in the disciples' hearts, prepares them for the tragedy of the Cross and prefigures the glory of the Resurrection. This mystery is constantly relived by the Church, the people on its way to the eschatological encounter with its Lord. Like the three chosen disciples, the Church contemplates the transfigured face of Christ in order to be confirmed in faith and to avoid being dismayed at his disfigured face on the Cross. In both cases, she is the Bride before her Spouse, sharing in his mystery and surrounded by his light.

15.4 This light shines on all the Church's children. *All are equally called to follow Christ,* to discover in him the ultimate meaning of their lives, until they are able to say with the Apostle: "For to me to live is Christ" (Phil 1:21). But those who are called to the consecrated life have *a special experience of the light which shines forth from the Incarnate Word.* For the profession of the evangelical counsels makes them *a kind of sign and prophetic statement* for the community of the brethren and for the world; consequently they can echo in a particular way the ecstatic words spoken by Peter: "Lord, it is well that we are here" (Mt 17:4). These words bespeak the Christocentric orientation of the whole Christian life. But they also eloquently express the *radical* nature of the vocation to the consecrated life: how good it is for us to be with you, to devote ourselves to you, to make you the one focus of our lives! Truly those who have been given the grace of this special communion of love with Christ feel as it were caught up in his splendor: he is "the fairest of the sons of men" (Ps 45:2), the One beyond compare.

"This is my beloved Son: listen to him!"

16.1 The three disciples caught up in ecstasy hear the Father's call to listen to Christ, to place all their trust in him, to make him the center of their lives. The words from on high give new depth to the invitation by which Jesus himself, at the beginning of his public life, called them to follow him, to leave their ordinary lives behind and to enter into a close relationship to him. It is precisely this special grace of intimacy which, in the consecrated life, makes possible and even demands the total gift of self in the profession of the evangelical counsels. The counsels, more than a simple renunciation, are *a specific acceptance of the mystery of Christ, lived within the Church.*

16.2 In the unity of the Christian life, the various vocations are like so many rays of the one light of Christ, whose radiance "brightens the countenance of the Church."[26] The *laity*, by virtue of the secular character of their vocation, reflect the mystery of the Incarnate Word particularly insofar as he is the Alpha and the Omega of the world, the foundation and measure of the value of all created things. *Sacred ministers,* for their part, are living images of Christ the Head and Shepherd who guides his people during this time of "already and not yet," as they await his coming in glory. It is the duty of the *consecrated life* to show that the Incarnate Son of God is *the eschatological goal toward which all things tend,* the splendor before which every other light pales, and the infinite beauty which alone can fully satisfy the human heart. In the consecrated life, then, it is not only a matter of following Christ with one's whole heart, of loving him "more than father or mother, more than son or daughter" (cf. Mt 10:37) — for this is required of every disciple — but of living and expressing this *by conforming one's whole existence to Christ* in an all-encompassing commitment which foreshadows the eschatological perfec-

---

[26] Second Vatican Ecumenical Council, Dogmatic Constitution on the Church *Lumen Gentium,* 1.

tion, to the extent that this is possible in time and in accordance with the different charisms.

16.3 By professing the evangelical counsels, consecrated persons not only make Christ the whole meaning of their lives but strive to reproduce in themselves, as far as possible, "that form of life which he, as the Son of God, accepted in entering this world."[27] By embracing *chastity,* they make their own the pure love of Christ and proclaim to the world that he is the only-begotten Son who is one with the Father (cf. Jn 10:30, 14:11). By imitating Christ's *poverty,* they profess that he is the Son who receives everything from the Father, and gives everything back to the Father in love (cf. Jn 17:7, 10). By accepting, through the sacrifice of their own freedom, the mystery of Christ's filial *obedience,* they profess that he is infinitely beloved and loving, as the One who delights only in the will of the Father (cf. Jn 4:34), to whom he is perfectly united and on whom he depends for everything.

16.4 By this profound "configuration" to the mystery of Christ, the consecrated life brings about in a special way that *confessio Trinitatis* which is the mark of all Christian life; it acknowledges with wonder the sublime beauty of God, Father, Son and Holy Spirit, and bears joyful witness to his loving concern for every human being.

1. In Praise of the Trinity

"A Patre ad Patrem": God's initiative

17.1 Contemplation of the glory of the Lord Jesus in the icon of the Transfiguration reveals to consecrated persons first of all the Father, the Creator and Giver of every good thing, who draws his creatures to himself (cf. Jn 6:44) with a special love and for a special mission. "This is my beloved Son: listen to him!" (cf. Mt 17:5). In response to this call and the interior attraction which accompanies it, those who are called entrust themselves to the love of God who wishes them to be exclusively at his service, and they consecrate themselves totally to him and to his plan of salvation (cf. 1 Cor 7:32-34).

17.2 This is the meaning of the call to the consecrated life: it is an initiative coming wholly from the Father (cf. Jn 15:16), who asks those whom he has chosen to respond with complete and exclusive devotion.[28] The experience of

---

[27] Ibid., 44.

[28] Cf. Congregation for Religious and Secular Institutes, Instruction on the Essential Elements in the Church's Teaching on Religious Life as Applied to Institutes Dedicated to Works of the Apostolate (May 31, 1983), 5: *L'Osservatore Romano* (English-language edition), July 18, 1983, 4.

this gracious love of God is so deep and so powerful that the person called senses the need to respond by unconditionally dedicating his or her life to God, consecrating to him all things present and future, and placing them in his hands. This is why, with Saint Thomas, we come to understand the identity of the consecrated person, beginning with his or her complete self-offering, as being comparable to a genuine holocaust.[29]

"Per Filium": in the footsteps of the Son

18.1 The Son, who is the way which leads to the Father (cf. Jn 14:6), calls all those whom the Father has given to him (cf. Jn 17:9) to make the following of himself the whole purpose of their lives. But of some, those called to the consecrated life, he asks a total commitment, one which involves leaving everything behind (cf. Mt 19:27) in order to live at his side[30] and to follow him wherever he goes (cf. Rev 14:4).

18.2 In the countenance of Jesus, the "image of the invisible God" (Col 1:15) and the reflection of the Father's glory (cf. Heb 1:3), we glimpse the depths of an eternal and infinite love which is at the very root of our being.[31] Those who let themselves be seized by this love cannot help abandoning everything to follow him (cf. Mk 1:16-20; 2:14; 10:21, 28). Like Saint Paul, they consider all else as loss "because of the surpassing worth of knowing Jesus Christ," by comparison with which they do not hesitate to count all things as "refuse," in order that they "may gain Christ" (Phil 3:8). They strive to become one with him, taking on his mind and his way of life. This leaving of everything and following the Lord (cf. Lk 18:28) is a worthy program of life for all whom he calls, in every age.

18.3 The evangelical counsels, by which Christ invites some people to share his experience as the chaste, poor and obedient One, call for and make manifest in those who accept them *an explicit desire to be totally conformed to him.* Living "in obedience, with nothing of one's own and in chastity,"[32] consecrated persons profess that Jesus is the model in whom every virtue comes to perfection. His way of living in chastity, poverty and obedience appears as the most radical way of living the Gospel on this earth, a way which may be called *divine,* for it was embraced by him, God and man, as the expression of his relationship as the only-begotten Son with the Father and with the Holy Spirit.

---

[29] Cf. *Summa Theologiae*, II-II, q. 186, a. 1.

[30] Cf. *Propositio* 16.

[31] Cf. John Paul II, Apostolic Exhortation *Redemptionis Donum* (March 25, 1984), 3: *AAS* 76 (1984), 515-517.

[32] Saint Francis of Assisi, *Regula Bullata*, I, 1.

This is why Christian Tradition has always spoken of the *objective superiority of the consecrated life*.

18.4 Nor can it be denied that the practice of the evangelical counsels is also a particularly profound and fruitful way of sharing in *Christ's mission,* in imitation of the example of Mary of Nazareth, the first disciple, who willingly put herself at the service of God's plan by the total gift of self. Every mission begins with the attitude expressed by Mary at the Annunciation: "Behold, I am the handmaid of the Lord; let it be done to me according to your word" (Lk 1:38).

"In Spiritu": *consecrated by the Holy Spirit*

19.1 "A bright cloud overshadowed them" (Mt 17:5). A significant spiritual interpretation of the Transfiguration sees this cloud as an image of the Holy Spirit.[33]

19.2 Like the whole of Christian life, the call to the consecrated life is closely linked to the working of the Holy Spirit. In every age, the Spirit enables new men and women to recognize the appeal of such a demanding choice. Through his power, they relive, in a way, the experience of the Prophet Jeremiah: "You have seduced me, Lord, and I have let myself be seduced" (Jer 20:7). It is the Spirit who awakens the desire to respond fully; it is he who guides the growth of this desire, helping it to mature into a positive response and sustaining it as it is faithfully translated into action; it is he who shapes and molds the hearts of those who are called, configuring them to Christ, the chaste, poor and obedient One, and prompting them to make his mission their own. By allowing themselves to be guided by the Spirit on an endless journey of purification, they become, day after day, *conformed to Christ,* the prolongation in history of a special presence of the risen Lord.

19.3 With penetrating insight, the Fathers of the Church have called this spiritual path *philokalia,* or *love of the divine beauty,* which is the reflection of the divine goodness. Those who by the power of the Holy Spirit are led progressively into full configuration to Christ reflect in themselves a ray of the unapproachable light. During their earthly pilgrimage, they press on toward the inexhaustible Source of light. The consecrated life thus becomes a particularly profound expression of the Church as the Bride who, prompted by the Spirit to imitate her Spouse, stands before him "in splendor, without spot or wrinkle or any such thing, that she might be holy and without blemish" (Eph 5:27).

19.4 The same Spirit, far from removing from the life of humanity those

---

[33] "Tota Trinitas apparuit: Pater in voce; Filius in homine; Spiritus in nube clara": Saint Thomas Aquinas, *Summa Theologiae,* III, q. 45, a. 4, ad 2.

whom the Father has called, puts them at the service of their brothers and sisters in accordance with their particular state of life, and inspires them to undertake special tasks in response to the needs of the Church and the world, by means of the charisms proper to the various Institutes. Hence many different forms of the consecrated life have arisen, whereby the Church is "adorned by the various gifts of her children ... like a bride made beautiful for her spouse (cf. Rev 21:2)"[34] and is enriched by the means necessary for carrying out her mission in the world.

The evangelical counsels, gift of the Trinity

20.1 The evangelical counsels are thus above all *a gift of the Holy Trinity*. The consecrated life proclaims what the Father, through the Son and in the Spirit, brings about by his love, his goodness and his beauty. In fact, "the religious state reveals the transcendence of the Kingdom of God and its requirements over all earthly things. To all people it shows wonderfully at work within the Church the surpassing greatness of the force of Christ the King and the boundless power of the Holy Spirit."[35]

20.2 The first duty of the consecrated life is *to make visible* the marvels wrought by God in the frail humanity of those who are called. They bear witness to these marvels not so much in words as by the eloquent language of a transfigured life, capable of amazing the world. To people's astonishment they respond by proclaiming the wonders of grace accomplished by the Lord in those whom he loves. To the degree that consecrated persons let themselves be guided by the Spirit to the heights of perfection they can exclaim: "I see the beauty of your grace, I contemplate its radiance, I reflect its light; I am caught up in its ineffable splendor; I am taken outside myself as I think of myself; I see how I was and what I have become. O wonder! I am vigilant, I am full of respect for myself, of reverence and of fear, as I would be were I before you; I do not know what to do, I am seized by fear, I do not know where to sit, where to go, where to put these members which are yours; in what deeds, in what works shall I use them, these amazing divine marvels!"[36] The consecrated life thus becomes one of the tangible seals which the Trinity impresses upon history, so that people can sense with longing the attraction of divine beauty.

---

[34] Second Vatican Ecumenical Council, Decree on the Appropriate Renewal of the Religious Life *Perfectae Caritatis*, 1.

[35] Second Vatican Ecumenical Council, Dogmatic Constitution on the Church *Lumen Gentium*, 44.

[36] Symeon the New Theologian, *Hymns*, II, verses 19-27: *SCh* 156, 178-179.

Reflection of Trinitarian life in the evangelical counsels

21.1 The deepest meaning of the evangelical counsels is revealed when they are viewed in relation to the Holy Trinity, the source of holiness. They are in fact an expression of the love of the Son for the Father in the unity of the Holy Spirit. By practicing the evangelical counsels, the consecrated person lives with particular intensity the Trinitarian and Christological dimension which marks the whole of Christian life.

21.2 The *chastity* of celibates and virgins, as a manifestation of dedication to God with *an undivided heart* (cf. 1 Cor 7:32-34), is a reflection of the *infinite love* which links the three divine Persons in the mysterious depths of the life of the Trinity, the love to which the Incarnate Word bears witness even to the point of giving his life, the love "poured into our hearts through the Holy Spirit" (Rom 5:5), which evokes a response of total love for God and the brethren.

21.3 *Poverty* proclaims that God is man's only real treasure. When poverty is lived according to the example of Christ who, "though he was rich . . . became poor" (2 Cor 8:9), it becomes an expression of that *total gift of self* which the three divine Persons make to one another. This gift overflows into creation and is fully revealed in the Incarnation of the Word and in his redemptive death.

21.4 *Obedience,* practiced in imitation of Christ, whose food was to do the Father's will (cf. Jn 4:34), shows the liberating beauty of a *dependence which is not servile but filial,* marked by a deep sense of responsibility and animated by mutual trust, which is a reflection in history of the *loving harmony* between the three divine Persons.

21.5 The consecrated life is thus called constantly to deepen the gift of the evangelical counsels with a love which grows ever more genuine and strong in the *Trinitarian* dimension: love *for Christ,* which leads to closeness with him; love *for the Holy Spirit,* who opens our hearts to his inspiration; love *for the Father,* the first origin and supreme goal of the consecrated life.[37] The consecrated life thus becomes a confession and a sign of the Trinity, whose mystery is held up to the Church as the model and source of every form of Christian life.

21.6 Even *fraternal life,* whereby consecrated persons strive to live in Christ with "one heart and soul" (Acts 4:32), is put forward as an eloquent witness to the Trinity. It proclaims *the Father,* who desires to make all of humanity one

---

[37] Cf. John Paul II, Address at the General Audience (November 9, 1994), 4: *Insegnamenti* 17/2 (1994), 654.

family. It proclaims *the Incarnate Son,* who gathers the redeemed into unity, pointing the way by his example, his prayer, his words and above all his death, which is the source of reconciliation for a divided and scattered humanity. It proclaims *the Holy Spirit* as the principle of unity in the Church, wherein he ceaselessly raises up spiritual families and fraternal communities.

Consecrated like Christ for the Kingdom of God

22.1 The consecrated life, through the prompting of the Holy Spirit, "constitutes a closer imitation and an abiding re-enactment in the Church"[38] of the way of life which Jesus, the supreme Consecrated One and missionary of the Father for the sake of his Kingdom, embraced and proposed to his disciples (cf. Mt 4:18-22; Mk 1:16-20; Lk 5:10-11; Jn 15:16). In the light of Jesus' consecration, we can see in the initiative of the Father, the source of all holiness, the ultimate origin of the consecrated life. Jesus is the One whom "God anointed . . . with the Holy Spirit and with power" (Acts 10:38), the One "whom the Father consecrated and sent into the world" (Jn 10:36). Accepting his consecration by the Father, the Son in turn consecrates himself to the Father for the sake of humanity (cf. Jn 17:19). His life of virginity, obedience and poverty expresses his complete filial acceptance of the Father's plan (cf. Jn 10:30, 14:11). His perfect offering confers an aspect of consecration upon all the events of his earthly existence.

22.2 Jesus is *the exemplar of obedience,* who came down from heaven not to do his own will but the will of the One who sent him (cf. Jn 6:38; Heb 10:5, 7). He places his way of living and acting in the hands of the Father (cf. Lk 2:49). In filial obedience, he assumes the condition of a servant: he "emptied himself, taking the form of a servant . . . and became obedient unto death, even death on a Cross" (Phil 2:7-8). In this attitude of submissiveness to the Father, Christ lives his life as a virgin, even while affirming and defending the dignity and sanctity of married life. He thus reveals *the sublime excellence and mysterious spiritual fruitfulness of virginity.* His full acceptance of the Father's plan is also seen in his detachment from earthly goods: "though he was rich, yet for your sake he became poor, so that by his poverty you might become rich" (2 Cor 8:9). *The depth of his poverty* is revealed in the perfect offering of all that is his to the Father.

22.3 The consecrated life truly constitutes *a living memorial of Jesus' way*

---

[38] Second Vatican Ecumenical Council, Dogmatic Constitution on the Church *Lumen Gentium,* 44.

of living and acting as the Incarnate Word in relation to the Father and in relation to the brethren. It is a living tradition of the Savior's life and message.

2. Between Easter and Fulfillment

From Tabor to Calvary

23.1 The dazzling event of the Transfiguration is a preparation for the tragic, but no less glorious, event of Calvary. Peter, James and John contemplate the Lord Jesus together with Moses and Elijah, with whom, according to the Evangelist Luke, Jesus speaks "of his departure, which he was to accomplish at Jerusalem" (9:31). The eyes of the Apostles are therefore fixed upon Jesus who is thinking of the Cross (cf. Lk 9:43-45). There his virginal love for the Father and for all mankind will attain its highest expression. His poverty will reach complete self-emptying, his obedience the giving of his life.

23.2 The disciples are invited to contemplate Jesus raised up on the Cross, where, in his silence and solitude, "the Word come forth from silence"[39] prophetically affirms the absolute transcendence of God over all created things; in his own flesh he conquers our sin and draws every man and every woman to himself, giving to all the new life of the Resurrection (cf. Jn 12:32; 19:34, 37). It is in the contemplation of the crucified Christ that all vocations find their inspiration. From this contemplation, all gifts, together with the primordial gift of the Spirit, and in particular the gift of the consecrated life, take their origin.

23.3 After Mary, the Mother of Jesus, it is John who receives this gift. John is the disciple whom Jesus loved, the witness who together with Mary stood at the foot of the Cross (cf. Jn 19:26-27). His decision to consecrate himself totally is the fruit of the divine love which envelops him, sustains him and fills his heart. John, together with Mary, is among the first in a long line of men and women who, from the beginning of the Church until the end, are touched by God's love and feel called to follow the Lamb, once sacrificed and now alive, wherever he goes (cf. Rev 14:1-5).[40]

The paschal dimension of the consecrated life

24.1 In the different forms of life inspired by the Spirit throughout history, consecrated persons discover that the more they stand at the foot of the Cross of Christ, the more immediately and profoundly they experience the truth of

---

[39] Saint Ignatius of Antioch, *Letter to the Magnesians*, 8, 2: *Patres Apostolici*, ed. F. X. Funk, II, 237.

[40] Cf. *Propositio* 3.

God who is love. It is precisely on the Cross that the One who in death appears to human eyes as disfigured and without beauty, so much so that the bystanders cover their faces (cf. Is 53:2-3), fully reveals the beauty and power of God's love. Saint Augustine says: "Beautiful is God, the Word with God. . . . He is beautiful in heaven, beautiful on earth; beautiful in the womb, beautiful in his parents' arms, beautiful in his miracles, beautiful in his sufferings; beautiful in inviting to life, beautiful in not worrying about death, beautiful in giving up his life and beautiful in taking it up again; he is beautiful on the Cross, beautiful in the tomb, beautiful in heaven. Listen to the song with understanding, and let not the weakness of the flesh distract your eyes from the splendor of his beauty."[41]

24.2 The consecrated life reflects the splendor of this love because, by its fidelity to the mystery of the Cross, it confesses that it believes and lives by the love of the Father, Son and Holy Spirit. In this way it helps the Church to remain aware that *the Cross is the superabundance of God's love poured out upon this world,* and that it is the great sign of Christ's saving presence, especially in the midst of difficulties and trials. This is the testimony given constantly and with deeply admirable courage by a great number of consecrated persons, many of whom live in difficult situations, even suffering persecution and martyrdom. Their fidelity to the one Love is revealed and confirmed in the humility of a hidden life, in the acceptance of sufferings for the sake of completing in their own flesh "what is lacking in Christ's afflictions" (Col 1:24), in silent sacrifice and abandonment to God's holy will, and in serene fidelity even as their strength and personal authority wane. Fidelity to God also inspires devotion to neighbor, a devotion which consecrated persons live out not without sacrifice by constantly interceding for the needs of their brothers and sisters, generously serving the poor and the sick, sharing the hardships of others and participating in the concerns and trials of the Church.

Witnesses to Christ in the world

25.1 The Paschal Mystery is also the wellspring of the Church's *missionary nature,* which is reflected in the whole of the Church's life. It is expressed in a distinctive way in the consecrated life. Over and above the charisms proper to those Institutes which are devoted to the mission *ad gentes* or which are engaged in ordinary apostolic activity, it can be said that *the sense of mission is at the very heart of every form of consecrated life.* To the extent that consecrated persons live a life completely devoted to the Father (cf. Lk 2:49; Jn 4:34), held fast by Christ (cf. Jn 15:16; Gal 1:15-16) and animated by the

---

[41] *Expositions on the Book of Psalms,* 44, 3: PL 36, 495-496.

Spirit (cf. Lk 24:49; Acts 1:8, 2:4), they cooperate effectively in the mission of the Lord Jesus (cf. Jn 20:21) and contribute in a particularly profound way to the renewal of the world.

25.2 The first missionary duty of consecrated persons is to themselves, and they fulfill it by opening their hearts to the promptings of the Spirit of Christ. Their witness helps the whole Church to remember that the most important thing is to serve God freely, through Christ's grace which is communicated to believers through the gift of the Spirit. Thus they proclaim to the world the peace which comes from the Father, the dedication witnessed to by the Son, and the joy which is the fruit of the Holy Spirit.

25.3 Consecrated persons will be missionaries above all by continually deepening their awareness of having been called and chosen by God, to whom they must therefore direct and offer everything that they are and have, freeing themselves from the obstacles which could hinder the totality of their response. In this way they will become *true signs of Christ in the world.* Their lifestyle too must clearly show the ideal which they profess, and thus present itself as a living sign of God and as an eloquent, albeit often silent, proclamation of the Gospel.

25.4 The Church must always seek *to make her presence visible in everyday life,* especially in contemporary culture, which is often very secularized and yet sensitive to the language of signs. In this regard the Church has a right to expect a significant contribution from consecrated persons, called as they are in every situation to bear clear witness that they belong to Christ.

25.5 Since the habit is a sign of consecration, poverty and membership in a particular religious family, I join the Fathers of the Synod in strongly recommending to men and women Religious that they wear their proper habit, suitably adapted to the conditions of time and place.[42] Where valid reasons of their apostolate call for it, Religious, in conformity with the norms of their Institute, may also dress in a simple and modest manner, with an appropriate symbol, in such a way that their consecration is recognizable.

25.6 Institutes which from their origin or by provision of their Constitutions do not have a specific habit should ensure that the dress of their members corresponds in dignity and simplicity to the nature of their vocation.[43]

Eschatological dimension of the consecrated life

26.1 Since the demands of the apostolate today are increasingly urgent, and since involvement in temporal affairs risks becoming ever more absorb-

---

[42] Cf. *Propositio* 25; Second Vatican Ecumenical Council, Decree on the Appropriate Renewal of the Religious Life *Perfectae Caritatis,* 17.

[43] Cf. *Propositio* 25.

ing, it is particularly opportune to draw attention once more to the *eschatological nature of the consecrated life.*

26.2 "Where your treasure is, there will your heart be also" (Mt 6:21). The unique treasure of the Kingdom gives rise to desire, anticipation, commitment and witness. In the early Church, the expectation of the Lord's coming was lived in a particularly intense way. With the passing of the centuries, the Church has not ceased to foster this attitude of hope: she has continued to invite the faithful to look to the salvation which is waiting to be revealed, "for the form of this world is passing away" (1 Cor 7:31; cf. 1 Pet 1:3-6).[44]

26.3 It is in this perspective that we can understand more clearly *the role* of consecrated life as an *eschatological sign.* In fact it has constantly been taught that the consecrated life is a foreshadowing of the future Kingdom. The Second Vatican Council proposes this teaching anew when it states that consecration better "foretells the resurrected state and the glory of the heavenly Kingdom."[45] It does this above all by means of *the vow of virginity,* which tradition has always understood as *an anticipation of the world to come,* already at work for the total transformation of man.

26.4 Those who have dedicated their lives to Christ cannot fail to live in the hope of meeting him, in order to be with him for ever. Hence the ardent expectation and desire to "be plunged into the Fire of Love which burns in them and which is none other than the Holy Spirit,"[46] an expectation and desire sustained by the gifts which the Lord freely bestows on those who yearn for the things that are above (cf. Col 3:1).

26.5 Immersed in the things of the Lord, the consecrated person remembers that "here we have no lasting city" (Heb 13:14), for "our commonwealth is in heaven" (Phil 3:20). The one thing necessary is to seek God's "Kingdom and his righteousness" (Mt 6:33), with unceasing prayer for the Lord's coming.

Active expectation: commitment and watchfulness

27.1 "Come, Lord Jesus!" (Rev 22:20). This expectation is *anything but passive:* although directed toward the future Kingdom, it expresses itself in work and mission, that the Kingdom may become present here and now through the spirit of the Beatitudes, a spirit capable of giving rise in human society to effective aspirations for justice, peace, solidarity and forgiveness.

[44] Cf. Second Vatican Ecumenical Council, Dogmatic Constitution on the Church *Lumen Gentium,* 42.

[45] Ibid., 44.

[46] Blessed Elizabeth of the Trinity, *Le ciel dans la foi. Traité Spirituel,* I, 14: *Oeuvres Complètes* (Paris, 1991), 106.

27.2 This is clearly shown by the history of the consecrated life, which has always borne abundant fruit even for this world. By their charisms, consecrated persons become signs of the Spirit pointing to a new future enlightened by faith and by Christian hope. *Eschatological expectation becomes mission,* so that the Kingdom may become ever more fully established here and now. The prayer "Come, Lord Jesus!" is accompanied by another: "Thy Kingdom come!" (Mt 6:10).

27.3 Those who vigilantly await the fulfillment of Christ's promises are able to bring hope to their brothers and sisters who are often discouraged and pessimistic about the future. Theirs is a hope founded on God's promise contained in the revealed word: the history of humanity is moving toward "a new heaven and a new earth" (Rev 21:1), where the Lord "will wipe away every tear from their eyes, and death shall be no more, neither shall there be mourning nor crying nor pain any more, for the former things have passed away" (Rev 21:4).

27.4 The consecrated life is at the service of this definitive manifestation of the divine glory, when all flesh will see the salvation of God (cf. Lk 3:6; Is 40:5). The Christian East emphasizes this dimension when it considers monks as *angels of God on earth* who proclaim the renewal of the world in Christ. In the West, monasticism is the celebration of memory and expectation: *memory* of the wonders God has wrought and *expectation* of the final fulfillment of our hope. Monasticism and the contemplative life are a constant reminder that the primacy of God gives full meaning and joy to human lives, because men and women are made for God, and their hearts are restless until they rest in him.[47]

The Virgin Mary, model of consecration and discipleship

28.1 Mary is the one who, from the moment of her Immaculate Conception, most perfectly reflects the divine beauty. "All beautiful" is the title with which the Church invokes her. "The relationship with Mary most holy, which for every believer stems from his or her union with Christ, is even more pronounced in the life of consecrated persons . . . Mary's presence is of fundamental importance both for the spiritual life of each consecrated person and for the solidity, unity and progress of the whole community."[48]

28.2 Mary in fact is the *sublime example of perfect consecration,* since she belongs completely to God and is totally devoted to him. Chosen by the Lord,

---

[47] Cf. Saint Augustine, *Confessions,* I, 1: *CCL* 27, 1.

[48] John Paul II, Address at the General Audience (March 29, 1995), 1: *L'Osservatore Romano* (English-language edition), April 5, 1995, 3.

who wished to accomplish in her the mystery of the Incarnation, she reminds consecrated persons of *the primacy of God's initiative.* At the same time, having given her assent to the divine Word, made flesh in her, Mary is the *model of the acceptance of grace* by human creatures.

28.3 Having lived with Jesus and Joseph in the hidden years of Nazareth, and present at her Son's side at crucial moments of his public life, the Blessed Virgin teaches unconditional discipleship and diligent service. In Mary, "the temple of the Holy Spirit,"[49] all the splendor of the new creation shines forth. Consecrated life looks to her as the sublime model of consecration to the Father, union with the Son and openness to the Spirit, in the knowledge that acceptance of the "virginal and humble life"[50] of Christ also means imitation of Mary's way of life.

28.4 In the Blessed Virgin Mary, consecrated persons also find a *Mother who is altogether unique.* Indeed, if the new motherhood conferred on Mary at Calvary is a gift for all Christians, it has a specific value for those who have completely consecrated their lives to Christ. "Behold your mother!" (Jn 19:27): Jesus' words to the disciple "whom he loved" (Jn 19:26) are particularly significant for the lives of consecrated persons. They, like John, are called to take the Blessed Virgin Mary to themselves (cf. Jn 19:27), loving her and imitating her in the radical manner which befits their vocation, and experiencing in return her special motherly love. The Blessed Virgin shares with them the love which enables them to offer their lives every day for Christ and to cooperate with him in the salvation of the world. Hence a filial relationship to Mary is the royal road to fidelity to one's vocation and a most effective help for advancing in that vocation and living it fully.[51]

3. In the Church and for the Church

"It is well that we are here": the consecrated life in the mystery of the Church

29.1 In the episode of the Transfiguration, Peter speaks on behalf of the other Apostles: "It is well that we are here" (Mt 17:4). The experience of Christ's glory, though completely filling his mind and heart, does not set him apart but rather unites him more closely to the "we" of the Apostles.

29.2 This dimension of "we" invites us to consider the place which the

---

[49] Second Vatican Ecumenical Council, Dogmatic Constitution on the Church *Lumen Gentium,* 53.

[50] Ibid., 46.

[51] Cf. *Propositio* 55.

consecrated life occupies in the *mystery of the Church*. In recent years, theological reflection on the nature of the consecrated life has deepened the new insights which emerged from the teaching of the Second Vatican Council. In the light of that teaching it has been recognized that the profession of the evangelical counsels *indisputably belongs to the life and holiness of the Church*.[52] This means that the consecrated life, present in the Church from the beginning, can never fail to be one of her essential and characteristic elements, for it expresses her very nature.

29.3 This is clearly seen from the fact that the profession of the evangelical counsels is intimately connected with the mystery of Christ, and has the duty of making somehow present the way of life which Jesus himself chose and indicated as an absolute eschatological value. Jesus himself, by calling some men and women to abandon everything in order to follow him, established this type of life which, under the guidance of the Spirit, would gradually develop down the centuries into the various forms of the consecrated life. The idea of a Church made up only of sacred ministers and lay people does not therefore conform to the intentions of her divine Founder, as revealed to us by the Gospels and the other writings of the New Testament.

New and special consecration

30.1 In the Church's tradition religious profession is considered to be *a special and fruitful deepening of the consecration received in Baptism,* inasmuch as it is the means by which the close union with Christ already begun in Baptism develops in the gift of a fuller, more explicit and authentic configuration to him through the profession of the evangelical counsels.[53]

30.2 This further consecration, however, differs in a special way from baptismal consecration, of which it is not a necessary consequence.[54] In fact, all those reborn in Christ are called to live out, with the strength which is the Spirit's gift, the chastity appropriate to their state of life, obedience to God and to the Church, and a reasonable detachment from material possessions: for all are called to holiness, which consists in the perfection of love.[55] But

---

[52] Cf. Second Vatican Ecumenical Council, Dogmatic Constitution on the Church *Lumen Gentium,* 44.

[53] Cf. John Paul II, Apostolic Exhortation *Redemptionis Donum* (March 25, 1984), 7: *AAS* 76 (1984), 522-524.

[54] Cf. Second Vatican Ecumenical Council, Dogmatic Constitution on the Church *Lumen Gentium,* 44; John Paul II, Address at the General Audience (October 26, 1994), 5: *Insegnamenti* 17/2 (1994), 549.

[55] Cf. Second Vatican Ecumenical Council, Dogmatic Constitution on the Church *Lumen Gentium,* 42.

Baptism in itself does not include the call to celibacy or virginity, the renunciation of possessions or obedience to a superior, in the form proper to the evangelical counsels. The profession of the evangelical counsels thus presupposes a particular gift of God not given to everyone, as Jesus himself emphasizes with respect to voluntary celibacy (cf. Mt 19:10-12).

30.3 This call is accompanied, moreover, by *a specific gift of the Holy Spirit,* so that consecrated persons can respond to their vocation and mission. For this reason, as the liturgies of the East and West testify in the rite of monastic or religious profession and in the consecration of virgins, the Church invokes the gift of the Holy Spirit upon those who have been chosen and joins their oblation to the sacrifice of Christ.[56]

30.4 The profession of the evangelical counsels is also *a development of the grace of the Sacrament of Confirmation,* but it goes beyond the ordinary demands of the consecration received in Confirmation by virtue of a special gift of the Spirit which opens the way to new possibilities and fruits of holiness and apostolic work. This can clearly be seen from the history of the consecrated life.

30.5 As for priests who profess the evangelical counsels, experience itself shows that *the Sacrament of Holy Orders finds a particular fruitfulness in this consecration,* inasmuch as it requires and fosters a closer union with the Lord. The priest who professes the evangelical counsels is especially favored in that he reproduces in his life the fullness of the mystery of Christ, thanks also to the specific spirituality of his Institute and the apostolic dimension of its proper charism. In the priest, in fact, the vocation to the priesthood and the vocation to the consecrated life converge in a profound and dynamic unity.

30.6 Also of immeasurable value is the contribution made to the Church's life by Religious priests completely devoted to contemplation. Especially in the celebration of the Eucharist they carry out an act of the Church and for the Church, to which they join the offering of themselves, in communion with Christ who offers himself to the Father for the salvation of the whole world.[57]

---

[56] Cf. Roman Ritual, *Rite of Religious Profession:* Solemn Blessing or Consecration of Professed Men, No. 67, and Solemn Blessing or Consecration of Professed Women, No. 72; Roman Pontifical, *Rite of Consecration to a Life of Virginity:* Solemn Blessing, No. 38; Eucologian sive Rituale Graecorum, *Officium Parvi Habitum Id Est Mandiae,* 384-385; Pontificale iuxta Ritum Ecclesiae Syrorum Occidentalium Id Est Antiochiae, *Ordo Rituum Monasticorum* (Vatican City: Vatican Polyglot Press, 1942), 307-309.

[57] Cf. Saint Peter Damian, *Liber qui appellatur "Dominus vobiscum" ad Leonem eremitam: PL* 145, 231-252.

Relationships between the different states of Christian life

31.1 The different ways of life which, in accordance with the plan of the Lord Jesus, make up the life of the Church have mutual relationships which merit consideration.

31.2 By virtue of their rebirth in Christ, all the faithful share a common dignity; all are called to holiness; all cooperate in the building up of the one Body of Christ, each in accordance with the proper vocation and gift which he or she has received from the Spirit (cf. Rom 12:3-8).[58] The equal dignity of all members of the Church is the work of the Spirit, is rooted in Baptism and Confirmation and is strengthened by the Eucharist. But diversity is also a work of the Spirit. It is he who establishes the Church as an organic communion in the diversity of vocations, charisms and ministries.[59]

31.3 The vocations to the lay life, to the ordained ministry and to the consecrated life can be considered paradigmatic, inasmuch as all particular vocations, considered separately or as a whole, are in one way or another derived from them or lead back to them, in accordance with the richness of God's gift. These vocations are also at the service of one another, for the growth of the Body of Christ in history and for its mission in the world. Everyone in the Church is consecrated in Baptism and Confirmation, but the ordained ministry and the consecrated life each presupposes a distinct vocation and a specific form of consecration, with a view to a particular mission.

31.4 For the mission of the *lay faithful,* whose proper task is to "seek the Kingdom of God by engaging in temporal affairs and by ordering them according to the plan of God,"[60] the consecration of Baptism and Confirmation common to all members of the People of God is a sufficient foundation. In addition to this basic consecration, *ordained ministers* receive the consecration of ordination in order to carry on the apostolic ministry in time. *Consecrated persons,* who embrace the evangelical counsels, receive a new and special consecration which, without being sacramental, commits them to making their own

---

[58] Cf. Second Vatican Ecumenical Council, Dogmatic Constitution on the Church *Lumen Gentium,* 32; Code of Canon Law, Canon 208; Code of Canons of the Eastern Churches, Canon 11.

[59] Cf. Second Vatican Ecumenical Council, Decree on the Church's Missionary Activity *Ad Gentes,* 4; Dogmatic Constitution on the Church *Lumen Gentium,* 4, 12, 13; Pastoral Constitution on the Church in the Modern World *Gaudium et Spes,* 32; Decree on the Apostolate of the Laity *Apostolicam Actuositatem,* 3; John Paul II, Post-Synodal Apostolic Exhortation *Christifideles Laici* (December 30, 1988), 20-21: *AAS* 81 (1989), 425-428; Congregation for the Doctrine of the Faith, Letter to the Bishops of the Catholic Church on Some Aspects of the Church Understood as Communion *Communionis Notio* (May 28, 1992), 15: *AAS* 85 (1993), 847.

[60] Second Vatican Ecumenical Council, Dogmatic Constitution *Lumen Gentium,* 31.

— in chastity, poverty and obedience — the way of life practiced personally by Jesus and proposed by him to his disciples. Although these different categories are a manifestation of the one mystery of Christ, the lay faithful have as their specific but not exclusive characteristic, activity in the world; the clergy, ministry; consecrated men and women, special conformity to Christ, chaste, poor and obedient.

The special value of the consecrated life

32.1 Within this harmonious constellation of gifts, each of the fundamental states of life is entrusted with the task of expressing, in its own way, one or other aspect of the one mystery of Christ. While *the lay life* has *a particular mission* of ensuring that the Gospel message is proclaimed in the temporal sphere, in the sphere of ecclesial communion *an indispensable ministry is carried out by those in Holy Orders,* and in a special way by Bishops. The latter have the task of guiding the People of God by the teaching of the word, the administration of the sacraments and the exercise of sacred power in the service of ecclesial communion, which is an organic communion, hierarchically structured.[61]

32.2 As a way of showing forth the Church's holiness, *it is to be recognized that the consecrated life,* which mirrors Christ's own way of life, *has an objective superiority.* Precisely for this reason, it is an especially rich manifestation of Gospel values and a more complete expression of the Church's purpose, which is the sanctification of humanity. The consecrated life proclaims and in a certain way anticipates the future age, when the fullness of the Kingdom of heaven, already present in its first fruits and in mystery,[62] will be achieved, and when the children of the resurrection will take neither wife nor husband, but will be like the angels of God (cf. Mt 22:30).

32.3 The Church has always taught the preeminence of perfect chastity for the sake of the Kingdom,[63] and rightly considers it the "door" of the whole consecrated life.[64] She also shows great esteem for the vocation to marriage, which makes spouses "witnesses to and cooperators in the fruitfulness of

[61] Cf. ibid., 12; John Paul II, Post-Synodal Apostolic Exhortation *Christifideles Laici* (December 30, 1988), 20-21: *AAS* 81 (1989), 425-428.

[62] Cf. Second Vatican Ecumenical Council, Dogmatic Constitution on the Church *Lumen Gentium,* 5.

[63] Cf. Ecumenical Council of Trent, Session XIV, *De Sacramento Paenitentiae,* Canon 10: *Conciliorum Oecumenicorum Decreta,* Ed. Istituto per le Scienze Religiose, 3rd ed., Bologna, 1973, 713 (*DS* 1810); Pius XII, Encyclical Letter *Sacra Virginitas* (March 25, 1954): *AAS* 46 (1954), 176.

[64] Cf. *Propositio* 17.

Holy Mother Church, who signify and share in the love with which Christ has loved his Bride and because of which he delivered himself up on her behalf."[65]

32.4 In this perspective, common to all consecrated life, there are many different but complementary paths. Men and women Religious *completely devoted to contemplation* are in a special way an image of Christ praying on the mountain.[66] Consecrated persons engaged in *the active life* manifest Christ "in his proclamation of the Kingdom of God to the multitudes, in his healing of the sick and the suffering, in his work of converting sinners to a better life, in his solicitude for youth and his goodness to all."[67] Consecrated persons in *Secular Institutes* contribute in a special way to the coming of the Kingdom of God; they unite in a distinctive synthesis the value of consecration and that of being in the world. As they live their consecration in the world and from the world,[68] "they strive to imbue everything with an evangelical spirit for the strengthening and growth of the Body of Christ."[69] For this purpose they share in the Church's evangelizing mission through their personal witness of Christian living, their commitment to ordering temporal affairs according to God's plan, and their cooperation in service of the ecclesial community, in accordance with the secular way of life which is proper to them.[70]

Bearing witness to the Gospel of the Beatitudes

33.1 A particular duty of the consecrated life is to *remind the baptized of the fundamental values of the Gospel,* by bearing "splendid and striking testimony that the world cannot be transfigured and offered to God without the spirit of the Beatitudes."[71] The consecrated life thus continually fosters in the People of God an awareness of the need to respond with holiness of life to the love of God poured into their hearts by the Holy Spirit (cf. Rom 5:5), by reflecting in their conduct the sacramental consecration which is brought about by God's power in Baptism, Confirmation or Holy Orders. In fact it is necessary to pass from the holiness communicated in the sacraments to the holiness of

---

[65] Second Vatican Ecumenical Council, Dogmatic Constitution on the Church *Lumen Gentium,* 41.

[66] Cf. ibid., 46.

[67] Ibid., 46.

[68] Cf. Pius XII, Motu Proprio *Primo Feliciter* (March 12, 1948), 6: *AAS* 40 (1948), 285.

[69] Code of Canon Law, Canon 713 § 1; cf. Code of Canons of the Eastern Churches, Canon 563 § 2.

[70] Cf. Code of Canon Law, Canon 713 § 2. "Clerical members" are specifically addressed in Canon 713 § 3.

[71] Second Vatican Ecumenical Council, Dogmatic Constitution on the Church *Lumen Gentium,* 31.

daily life. The consecrated life, by its very existence in the Church, seeks to serve the consecration of the lives of all the faithful, clergy and laity alike.

33.2 Nor must it be forgotten that consecrated persons themselves are helped by the witness of the other vocations to live fully and completely their union with the mystery of Christ and the Church in its many different dimensions. By virtue of this mutual enrichment, the mission of consecrated persons becomes more eloquent and effective: this mission is to remind their other brothers and sisters to keep their eyes fixed on the peace which is to come, and to strive for the definitive happiness found in God.

The living image of the Church as Bride

34.1 In the consecrated life, particular importance attaches to the spousal meaning, which recalls the Church's duty to be completely and exclusively devoted to her Spouse, from whom she receives every good thing. This spousal dimension, which is part of all consecrated life, has a particular meaning for women, who find therein their feminine identity and as it were discover the special genius of their relationship with the Lord.

34.2 A moving sign of this is seen in the New Testament passage which portrays Mary with the Apostles in the Upper Room, in prayerful expectation of the Holy Spirit (cf. Acts 1:13-14). We can see here a vivid image of the Church as Bride, fully attentive to her Bridegroom and ready to accept his gift. In Peter and the other Apostles there emerges above all the aspect of fruitfulness, as it is expressed in ecclesial ministry, which becomes an instrument of the Spirit for bringing new sons and daughters to birth through the preaching of the word, the celebration of the sacraments and the giving of pastoral care. In Mary the aspect of spousal receptivity is particularly clear; it is under this aspect that the Church, through her perfect virginal life, brings divine life to fruition within herself.

34.3 The consecrated life has always been seen primarily in terms of Mary — Virgin and Bride. This virginal love is the source of a particular fruitfulness which fosters the birth and growth of divine life in people's hearts.[72] Following in the footsteps of Mary, the New Eve, consecrated persons express their spiritual fruitfulness by becoming receptive to the Word, in order to contribute to the growth of a new humanity by their unconditional dedication and their living witness. Thus the Church fully reveals her motherhood both in the communication of divine grace entrusted to Peter and in the responsible acceptance of God's gift, exemplified by Mary.

---

[72] Saint Teresa of the Child Jesus, *Manuscrits autobiographiques* B, 2 v: "To be your bride, O Jesus . . . to be, in union with you, a mother of souls."

34.4 God's people, for their part, find in the ordained ministry the means of salvation, and in the consecrated life the incentive to make a full and loving response through all the different forms of Christian service.[73]

4. Guided by the Spirit of Holiness

A "transfigured" life: the call to holiness

35.1 "When the disciples heard this, they fell on their faces, and were filled with fear" (Mt 17:6). In the episode of the Transfiguration, the Synoptic Gospels, with varying nuances, point out the fear which overcomes the disciples. Their fascination at the transfigured face of Christ does not prevent them from being fearful before the divine Majesty which overshadows them. Whenever human beings become aware of the glory of God, they also become aware of their own insignificance and experience a sense of fear. Such fear is salutary. It reminds man of God's perfection, and at the same time urges him on with a pressing call to "holiness."

35.2 All the sons and daughters of the Church, called by God to "listen to" Christ, necessarily feel a *deep need for conversion and holiness.* But, as the Synod emphasized, this need in the first place challenges the consecrated life. In fact the vocation of consecrated persons to seek first the Kingdom of God is first and foremost a call to complete conversion, in self-renunciation, in order to live fully for the Lord, so that God may be all in all. Called to contemplate and bear witness to the transfigured face of Christ, consecrated men and women are also called to a "transfigured" existence.

35.3 The *Final Report* of the Second Extraordinary General Assembly of the Synod of Bishops made a significant observation in this regard: "Holy men and women have always been the source and origin of renewal in the most difficult circumstances throughout the Church's history. Today we have a tremendous need of saints, for whom we must assiduously implore God. The Institutes of Consecrated Life, through the profession of the evangelical counsels, must be conscious of their special mission in today's Church, and we must encourage them in that mission."[74] The Fathers of the Ninth Assembly of the Synod of Bishops echoed this conviction: "Throughout the Church's history, consecrated life has been a living presence of the Spirit's work, a kind of privileged milieu for absolute love of God and of neighbor, for witness to the

---

[73] Cf. Second Vatican Ecumenical Council, Decree on the Appropriate Renewal of the Religious Life *Perfectae Caritatis,* 8, 10, 12.

[74] Final Report *Ecclesia sub Verbo Dei Mysteria Christi Celebrans pro Salute Mundi* (December 7, 1985), II, A, 4: *L'Osservatore Romano* (English-language edition), December 16, 1985, 7.

divine plan of gathering all humanity into the civilization of love, the great family of the children of God."[75]

35.4 The Church has always seen in the profession of the evangelical counsels a special path to holiness. The very expressions used to describe it — the school of the Lord's service, the school of love and holiness, the way or state of perfection — indicate the effectiveness and the wealth of means which are proper to this form of evangelical life, and the particular commitment made by those who embrace it.[76] It is not by chance that there have been so many consecrated persons down the centuries who have left behind eloquent testimonies of holiness and have undertaken particularly generous and demanding works of evangelization and service.

Faithfulness to the charism

36.1 In Christian discipleship and love for the person of Christ there are a number of points concerning the growth of holiness in the consecrated life which merit particular emphasis today.

36.2 In the first place, there is the need for *fidelity to the founding charism* and subsequent spiritual heritage of each Institute. It is precisely in this fidelity to the inspiration of the founders and foundresses, an inspiration which is itself a gift of the Holy Spirit, that the essential elements of the consecrated life can be more readily discerned and more fervently put into practice.

36.3 Fundamental to every charism is a threefold orientation. First, charisms lead *to the Father,* in the filial desire to seek his will through a process of unceasing conversion, wherein obedience is the source of true freedom, chastity expresses the yearning of a heart unsatisfied by any finite love, and poverty nourishes that hunger and thirst for justice which God has promised to satisfy (cf. Mt 5:6). Consequently the charism of each Institute will lead the consecrated person to belong wholly to God, to speak with God or about God, as is said of Saint Dominic,[77] so that he or she can taste the goodness of the Lord (cf. Ps 34:8) in every situation.

36.4 Secondly, the charisms of the consecrated life also lead *to the Son,* fostering an intimate and joyful communion of life with him, in the school of his generous service of God and neighbor. Thus the attitude of consecrated

---

[75] Message of the Synod (October 27, 1994), IX: *L'Osservatore Romano* (English-language edition), November 2, 1994, 7.

[76] Cf. Saint Thomas Aquinas, *Summa Theologiae*, II-II, q. 184, a. 5, ad 2; II-II, q. 186, a. 2, ad 1.

[77] Cf. *Libellus de Principiis Ordinis Praedicatorum. Acta Canonizationis Sancti Dominici: Monumenta Ordinis Praedicatorum Historica* 16 (1935), 30.

persons "is progressively conformed to Christ; they learn detachment from externals, from the tumult of the senses, from all that keeps man from that freedom which allows him to be grasped by the Spirit."[78] As a result, consecrated persons are enabled to take up the mission of Christ, working and suffering with him in the spreading of his Kingdom.

36.5 Finally, every charism leads *to the Holy Spirit,* insofar as it prepares individuals to let themselves be guided and sustained by him, both in their personal spiritual journeys and in their lives of communion and apostolic work, in order to embody that attitude of service which should inspire the true Christian's every choice.

36.6 In fact it is this threefold relationship which emerges in every founding charism, though with the specific nuances of the various patterns of living. This is so because in every charism there predominates "a profound desire to be conformed to Christ to give witness to some aspect of his mystery."[79] This specific aspect is meant to take shape and develop according to the most authentic tradition of the Institute, as present in its Rule, Constitutions and Statutes.[80]

Creative fidelity

37.1 Institutes of Consecrated Life are thus invited courageously to propose anew the enterprising initiative, creativity and holiness of their founders and foundresses in response to the signs of the times emerging in today's world.[81] This invitation is first of all a call to perseverance on the path of holiness in the midst of the material and spiritual difficulties of daily life. But it is also a call to pursue competence in personal work and to develop a dynamic fidelity to their mission, adapting forms, if need be, to new situations and different needs, in complete openness to God's inspiration and to the Church's discernment. But all must be fully convinced that the quest for ever greater conformity to the Lord is the guarantee of any renewal which seeks to remain faithful to an Institute's original inspiration.[82]

37.2 In this spirit there is a pressing need today for every Institute *to return to the Rule,* since the Rule and Constitutions provide a map for the

---

[78] John Paul II, Apostolic Letter *Orientale Lumen* (May 2, 1995), 12: *AAS* 87 (1995), 758.

[79] Congregation for Religious and Secular Institutes and Congregation for Bishops, Directives for Mutual Relations between Bishops and Religious in the Church *Mutuae Relationes* (May 14, 1978), 51: *AAS* 70 (1978), 500.

[80] Cf. *Propositio* 26.

[81] Cf. *Propositio* 27.

[82] Cf. Second Vatican Ecumenical Council, Decree on the Appropriate Renewal of the Religious Life *Perfectae Caritatis,* 2.

whole journey of discipleship, in accordance with a specific charism confirmed by the Church. A greater regard for the Rule will not fail to offer consecrated persons a reliable criterion in their search for the appropriate forms of a witness which is capable of responding to the needs of the times without departing from an Institute's initial inspiration.

Prayer and asceticism: spiritual combat

38.1 The call to holiness is accepted and can be cultivated only *in the silence of adoration* before the infinite transcendence of God: "We must confess that we all have need of this silence, filled with the presence of him who is adored: in theology, so as to exploit fully its own sapiential and spiritual soul; in prayer, so that we may never forget that seeing God means coming down the mountain with a face so radiant that we are obliged to cover it with a veil (cf. Ex 34:33); in commitment, so that we will refuse to be locked in a struggle without love and forgiveness. All, believers and non-believers alike, need to learn a silence that allows the Other to speak when and how he wishes, and allows us to understand his words."[83] In practice this involves great fidelity to liturgical and personal prayer, to periods devoted to mental prayer and contemplation, to Eucharistic adoration, to monthly retreats and to spiritual exercises.

38.2 There is also a need to rediscover the *ascetic practices* typical of the spiritual tradition of the Church and of the individual's own Institute. These have been and continue to be a powerful aid to authentic progress in holiness. Asceticism, by helping to master and correct the inclinations of human nature wounded by sin, is truly indispensable if consecrated persons are to remain faithful to their own vocation and follow Jesus on the way of the Cross.

38.3 It is also necessary to recognize and overcome certain temptations which sometimes, by diabolical deceit, present themselves under the appearance of good. Thus, for example, the legitimate need to be familiar with today's society in order to respond to its challenges can lead to a surrender to passing fashions, with a consequent lessening of spiritual fervor or a succumbing to discouragement. The possibility of a deeper spiritual formation might lead consecrated persons to feel somehow superior to other members of the faithful, while the urgent need for appropriate and necessary training can turn into a frantic quest for efficiency, as if apostolic service depended primarily on human means rather than on God. The praiseworthy desire to become close to the men and women of our day, believers and non-believers, rich and poor, can lead to the adoption of a secularized lifestyle or the promotion of human

---

[83] John Paul II, Apostolic Letter *Orientale Lumen* (May 2, 1995), 16: *AAS* 87 (1995), 762.

values in a merely horizontal direction. Sharing in the legitimate aspirations of one's own nation or culture could lead to embracing forms of nationalism or accepting customs which instead need to be purified and elevated in the light of the Gospel.

38.4 The path to holiness thus involves *the acceptance of spiritual combat.* This is a demanding reality which is not always given due attention today. Tradition has often seen an image of this spiritual combat in Jacob's wrestling with the mystery of God, whom he confronts in order to receive his blessing and to see him (cf. Gen 32:23-31). In this episode from the beginnings of biblical history, consecrated persons can recognize a symbol of the asceticism which they need in order to open their hearts to the Lord and to their brothers and sisters.

Fostering holiness

39.1 Today a renewed commitment to holiness by consecrated persons is more necessary than ever, also *as a means of promoting and supporting every Christian's desire for perfection.* "It is therefore necessary to inspire in all the faithful a true longing for holiness, a deep desire for conversion and personal renewal in a context of ever more intense prayer and of solidarity with one's neighbor, especially the most needy."[84]

39.2 To the degree that they deepen their friendship with God, consecrated persons become better prepared to help their brothers and sisters through valuable spiritual activities such as schools of prayer, spiritual exercises and retreats, days of recollection, spiritual dialogue and direction. In this way people are helped to grow in prayer and will then be better able to discern God's will in their lives and to commit themselves to the courageous and sometimes heroic demands which faith makes of them. Consecrated persons "at the deepest level of their being . . . are caught up in the dynamism of the Church's life, which is thirsty for the divine Absolute and called to holiness. It is to this holiness that they bear witness."[85] The fact that all are called to become saints cannot fail to inspire more and more those who by their very choice of life have the mission of reminding others of that call.

"Rise, and have no fear": a renewed trust

40.1 "Jesus came and touched them, saying, 'Rise, and have no fear'" (Mt 17:7). Like the three Apostles in the episode of the Transfiguration, conse-

---

[84] John Paul II, Apostolic Letter *Tertio Millennio Adveniente* (November 10, 1994), 42: *AAS* 87 (1995), 32.

[85] Paul VI, Apostolic Exhortation *Evangelii Nuntiandi* (December 8, 1975), 69: *AAS* 68 (1976), 58.

crated persons know from experience that their lives are not always marked by the fervor which makes us exclaim: "It is well that we are here" (Mt 17:4). But it is always a life "touched" by the hand of Christ, a life where his voice is heard, a life sustained by his grace.

40.2 "Rise, and have no fear." Obviously, the Master's encouragement is addressed to every Christian. All the more does it apply to those called to "leave everything" and thus to "risk everything" for Christ. This is particularly true whenever one descends from the "mountain" with the Master and sets off on the road which leads from Tabor to Calvary.

40.3 When Luke relates that Moses and Elijah were speaking with Christ about his Paschal Mystery, it is significant that he uses the term "departure" (*éxodos*): "they spoke about his departure, which he was to accomplish at Jerusalem" (9:31). "Exodus" is a basic term in revelation; it evokes the whole of salvation history and expresses the deep meaning of the Paschal Mystery. It is a theme particularly dear to the spirituality of the consecrated life and well expresses its meaning. It inevitably includes everything that pertains to the *mysterium Crucis*. But this difficult "exodus journey," when viewed from the perspective of Tabor, is seen to be a road situated between two lights: the anticipatory light of the Transfiguration and the definitive light of the Resurrection.

40.4 From the standpoint of the Christian life as a whole, the vocation to the consecrated life is, despite its renunciations and trials, and indeed because of them, *a path "of light"* over which the Redeemer keeps constant watch: *"Rise, and have no fear."*

II

Signum Fraternitatis: Consecrated Life as a Sign of Communion in the Church

1. Permanent Values

In the image of the Trinity

41.1 During his earthly life, the Lord Jesus called those whom he wished in order to have them at his side and to train them to live, according to his example, for the Father and for the mission which he had received from the Father (cf. Mk 3:13-15). He thus inaugurated the new family which down the centuries would include all those ready to "do the will of God" (cf. Mk 3:32-35). After the Ascension, as a result of the gift of the Spirit, a fraternal community formed around the Apostles, gathered in the praise of God and in a concrete experience of communion (cf. Acts 2:42-47, 4:32-35). The life of that community and, even more, the experience of complete sharing with Christ lived out by the Twelve, have always been *the model to which the Church has looked* whenever she has sought to return to her original fervor and to resume with fresh evangelical vigor her journey through history.[86]

41.2 The Church is essentially a mystery of communion, "a people made one with the unity of the Father, the Son, and the Holy Spirit."[87] The fraternal life seeks to reflect the depth and richness of this mystery, taking shape as a human community in which the Trinity dwells, in order to extend in history the gifts of communion proper to the three divine Persons. Many are the settings and the ways in which fraternal communion is expressed in the life of the Church. The consecrated life can certainly be credited with having effectively helped to keep alive in the Church the obligation of fraternity as a form of witness to the Trinity. By constantly promoting fraternal love, also in the form of common life, the consecrated life has shown that *sharing in the Trinitarian communion can change human relationships* and create a new type of solidarity. In this way it speaks to people both of the beauty of fraternal communion and of the ways which actually lead to it. Consecrated persons live "for" God and "from" God, and precisely for this reason they are able to bear witness to the reconciling power of grace, which overcomes the divisive tendencies present in the human heart and in society.

Fraternal life in love

42.1 The fraternal life, understood as a life shared in love, is an eloquent sign of ecclesial communion. It is practiced with special care in Religious Institutes and in Societies of Apostolic Life, where community living acquires special significance.[88] Nor is the dimension of fraternal communion alien to Secular Institutes, or even to forms of the consecrated life lived individually. Hermits, in their profound solitude, do not withdraw from ecclesial communion but serve that communion by their specific charism of contemplation. Consecrated virgins in the world live out their consecration in a special relationship of communion with the particular and universal Church. The same is true of consecrated widows and widowers.

---

[86] Cf. Second Vatican Ecumenical Council, Decree on the Appropriate Renewal of the Religious Life *Perfectae Caritatis,* 15; Saint Augustine, *Regula ad Servos Dei,* 1, 1: *PL* 32, 1372.

[87] Saint Cyprian, *On the Lord's Prayer,* 23: *PL* 4, 553; cf. Second Vatican Ecumenical Council, Dogmatic Constitution on the Church *Lumen Gentium,* 4.

[88] Cf. *Propositio* 20.

42.2 All these people, by practicing evangelical discipleship, commit themselves to fulfilling the Lord's "new commandment," to love one another as he has loved us (cf. Jn 13:34). Love led Christ to the gift of self, even to the supreme sacrifice of the Cross. So too, among his disciples, *there can be no true unity without that unconditional mutual love* which demands a readiness to serve others generously, a willingness to welcome them as they are, without "judging" them (cf. Mt 7:1-2), and an ability to forgive up to "seventy times seven" (Mt 18:22). Consecrated persons, who become "of one heart and soul" (Acts 4:32) through the love poured into their hearts by the Holy Spirit (cf. Rom 5:5), experience an interior call *to share everything in common:* material goods and spiritual experiences, talents and inspirations, apostolic ideals and charitable service: "In community life, the power of the Holy Spirit at work in one individual passes at the same time to all. Here not only does each enjoy his own gift, but makes it abound by sharing it with others; and each one enjoys the fruits of the other's gift as if they were his own."[89]

42.3 In community life, then, it should in some way be evident that, more than an instrument for carrying out a specific mission, fraternal communion is *a God-enlightened space* in which to experience the hidden presence of the risen Lord (cf. Mt 18:20).[90] This comes about through the mutual love of all the members of the community, a love nourished by the word and by the Eucharist, purified in the Sacrament of Reconciliation, and sustained by prayer for unity, the special gift of the Spirit to those who obediently listen to the Gospel. It is the Spirit himself who leads the soul to the experience of communion with the Father and with his Son Jesus Christ (cf. 1 Jn 1:3), a communion which is the source of fraternal life. It is the Spirit who guides communities of the consecrated life in carrying out their mission of service to the Church and to all humanity, in accordance with their original inspiration.

42.4 In this perspective, special importance attaches to Chapters (or similar meetings), whether particular or general, at which Institutes are called to elect Superiors according to the norms set out in their Constitutions, and to discern, in the light of the Spirit, the best ways to preserve and adapt their charism and their spiritual patrimony to changing historical and cultural situations.[91]

---

[89] Saint Basil, *Long Rule,* Question 7: *PG* 31, 931.

[90] Cf. Saint Basil, *Short Rule,* Question 225: *PG* 31, 1231.

[91] Cf. Congregation for Religious and Secular Institutes, Instruction on the Essential Elements in the Church's Teaching as Applied to Institutes Dedicated to Works of the Apostolate (May 31, 1983), 51: *L'Osservatore Romano* (English-language edition), July 18, 1983, 7; Code of Canon Law, Canon 631 § 1; Code of Canons of the Eastern Churches, Canon 512 § 1.

The task of authority

43.1 In the consecrated life *the role of Superiors,* including local Superiors, has always been of great importance for the spiritual life and for mission. In these years of change and experimentation, the need to revise this office has sometimes been felt. But it should be recognized that those who exercise authority *cannot renounce their obligation as those first responsible* for the community, as guides of their brothers and sisters in the spiritual and apostolic life.

43.2 In an atmosphere strongly affected by individualism, it is not an easy thing to foster recognition and acceptance of the role which authority plays for the benefit of all. Nevertheless, its importance must be reaffirmed as essential for strengthening fraternal communion and in order not to render vain the obedience professed. While authority must be above all fraternal and spiritual, and while those entrusted with it must know how to involve their brothers and sisters in the decision-making process, it should still be remembered that *the final word belongs to authority* and, consequently, that authority has the right to see that decisions taken are respected.[92]

The role of the elderly

44.1 Caring for the elderly and the sick has an important place in the fraternal life, especially at times like the present, when in some parts of the world the percentage of elderly consecrated persons is increasing. The care and concern which these persons deserve arises not only from a clear obligation of charity and gratitude but also from an awareness that their witness greatly serves the Church and their own Institutes, and that their mission continues to be worthwhile and meritorious, even when for reasons of age or infirmity they have had to abandon their specific apostolate. *The elderly and the sick have a great deal to give* in wisdom and experience to the community, if only the community can remain close to them with concern and an ability to listen.

44.2 More than in any activity, the apostolate consists in the witness of one's own complete dedication to the Lord's saving will, a dedication nourished by the practice of prayer and of penance. The elderly are called in many ways to live out their vocation: by persevering prayer, by patient acceptance of their condition, and by their readiness to serve as spiritual directors, confessors or mentors in prayer.[93]

[92] Cf. Congregation for Institutes of Consecrated Life and for Societies of Apostolic Life, Instruction on Fraternal Life in Community *Congregavit Nos in Unum Christi Amor* (February 2, 1994), 47-53: Rome, 1994, 58-64; Code of Canon Law, Canon 618; *Propositio* 19.

[93] Cf. Congregation for Institutes of Consecrated Life and Societies of Apostolic Life, Instruction on Fraternal Life in Community *Congregavit Nos in Unum Christi Amor* (February 2, 1994), 68: Rome, 1994, 86-88; *Propositio* 21.

In the image of the apostolic community

45.1 The fraternal life plays a fundamental role in the spiritual journey of consecrated persons, both for their constant renewal and for the full accomplishment of their mission in the world. This is evident from the theological motivations which sustain it, and is amply confirmed by experience. I therefore exhort consecrated men and women to commit themselves to strengthening their fraternal life, following the example of the first Christians in Jerusalem who were assiduous in accepting the teaching of the Apostles, in common prayer, in celebrating the Eucharist, and in sharing whatever goods of nature and grace they had (cf. Acts 2:42-47). Above all I call upon men and women Religious and members of Societies of Apostolic Life to show generous mutual love, expressing it in ways which are in keeping with the nature of each Institute, so that every community will be revealed as a luminous sign of the new Jerusalem, "the dwelling of God with men" (Rev 21:3).

45.2 The whole Church greatly depends on the witness of communities filled "with joy and with the Holy Spirit" (Acts 13:52). She wishes to hold up before the world the example of communities in which solitude is overcome through concern for one another, in which communication inspires in everyone a sense of shared responsibility, and in which wounds are healed through forgiveness, and each person's commitment to communion is strengthened. The nature of the charism in communities of this kind directs their energies, sustains their fidelity and directs the apostolic work of all toward the one mission. If the Church is to reveal her true face to today's world, she urgently needs such fraternal communities, which, by their very existence, contribute to the new evangelization, inasmuch as they disclose in a concrete way the fruitfulness of the "new commandment."

"Sentire cum Ecclesia"

46.1 A great task also belongs to the consecrated life in the light of the teaching about the Church as communion, so strongly proposed by the Second Vatican Council. Consecrated persons are asked to be true experts of communion and to practice the spirituality of communion[94] as "witnesses and architects of the plan for unity which is the crowning point of human history in God's design."[95] The sense of ecclesial communion, developing into a *spirituality of communion,* promotes a way of thinking, speaking and acting which

---

[94] Cf. *Propositio* 28.

[95] Congregation for Religious and Secular Institutes, Document on Religious and Human Promotion (August 12, 1980), 24: *L'Osservatore Romano* (English-language edition), January 26, 1981, 11.

enables the Church to grow in depth and extension. The life of communion in fact "becomes a *sign* for all the world and a compelling *force* that leads people to faith in Christ. . . . In this way communion leads to *mission,* and itself becomes mission"; indeed, *"communion begets communion:* in essence it is a *communion that is missionary."*[96]

46.2 In founders and foundresses *we see a constant and lively sense of the Church,* which they manifest by their full participation in all aspects of the Church's life, and in their ready obedience to the Bishops and especially to the Roman Pontiff. Against this background of love toward Holy Church, "the pillar and bulwark of the truth" (1 Tim 3:15), we readily understand the devotion of Saint Francis of Assisi for "the Lord Pope,"[97] the daughterly outspokenness of Saint Catherine of Siena toward the one whom she called "sweet Christ on earth,"[98] the apostolic obedience and the *sentire cum Ecclesia* of Saint Ignatius Loyola,[99] and the joyful profession of faith made by Saint Teresa of Ávila: "I am a daughter of the Church."[100] We can also understand the deep desire of Saint Teresa of the Child Jesus: "In the heart of the Church, my mother, I will be love."[101] These testimonies are representative of the full ecclesial communion which the saints, founders and foundresses, have shared in diverse and often difficult times and circumstances. They are examples which consecrated persons need constantly to recall if they are to resist the particularly strong centrifugal and disruptive forces at work today.

46.3 A distinctive aspect of ecclesial communion is allegiance of mind and heart to the Magisterium of the Bishops, an allegiance which must be lived honestly and clearly testified to before the People of God by all consecrated persons, especially those involved in theological research, teaching, publishing, catechesis and the use of the means of social communication.[102] Because consecrated persons have a special place in the Church, their attitude in this regard is of immense importance for the whole People of God. Their witness of filial love will give power and forcefulness to their apostolic activity which, in the context of the prophetic mission of all the baptized, is generally distin-

---

[96] John Paul II, Post-Synodal Apostolic Exhortation *Christifideles Laici* (December 30, 1988), 31-32: *AAS* 81 (1989), 451-452.

[97] *Regula Bullata*, I, 1.

[98] *Letters* 109, 171, 196.

[99] Cf. *Rule* 13 at the end of the *Spiritual Exercises.*

[100] *Sayings*, No. 217.

[101] *Manuscrits autobiographiques*, B, 3 v.

[102] Cf. *Propositio* 30, A.

guished by special forms of cooperation with the Hierarchy.[103] In a specific way, through the richness of their charisms, consecrated persons help the Church to reveal ever more deeply her nature as the sacrament "of intimate union with God, and of the unity of all mankind."[104]

Fraternity in the universal Church

47.1 Consecrated persons are called to be a leaven of communion at the service of the mission of the universal Church by the very fact that the manifold charisms of their respective Institutes are granted by the Holy Spirit for the good of the entire Mystical Body, whose upbuilding they must serve (cf. 1 Cor 12:4-11). Significantly, "the more excellent way" (1 Cor 12:31), the "greatest of all" (cf. 1 Cor 13:13), as the Apostle says, is charity, which brings all diversity into one and strengthens everyone to support one another in apostolic zeal. This, precisely, is the scope of *the particular bond of communion* which the different Institutes of Consecrated Life and the Societies of Apostolic Life have *with the Successor of Peter in his ministry of unity and missionary universality.* The history of spirituality amply illustrates this bond and shows its providential function both in safeguarding the specific identity of the consecrated life and in advancing the missionary expansion of the Gospel. The vigorous spread of the Gospel message, the firm rooting of the Church in so many areas of the world, and the Christian springtime which the young Churches are experiencing today, would be unthinkable — as the Synod Fathers observed — without the contribution of numerous Institutes of Consecrated Life and Societies of Apostolic Life. Down the centuries they have maintained strong bonds of communion with the Successors of Peter, who found in them a generous readiness to devote themselves to the Church's missionary activity with an availability which, when necessary, went as far as heroism.

47.2 All this brings out *the character of universality and communion* proper to Institutes of Consecrated Life and to Societies of Apostolic Life. Because of their supra-diocesan character, grounded in their special relation to the Petrine ministry, they are also at the service of cooperation between the particular Churches,[105] since they can effectively promote an "exchange of gifts" among

---

[103] Cf. John Paul II, Apostolic Exhortation *Redemptionis Donum* (March 25, 1984), 15: *AAS* 76 (1984), 541-542.

[104] Second Vatican Ecumenical Council, Dogmatic Constitution on the Church *Lumen Gentium,* 1.

[105] Cf. Congregation for the Doctrine of the Faith, Letter to the Bishops of the Catholic Church on Some Aspects of the Church Understood as Communion *Communionis Notio* (May 28, 1992), 16: *AAS* 85 (1993), 847-848.

them, and thus contribute to an inculturation of the Gospel which purifies, strengthens and ennobles the treasures found in the cultures of all peoples.[106] Today too, the flowering of vocations to the consecrated life in the younger Churches demonstrates the ability of the consecrated life to make present in Catholic unity the needs of different peoples and cultures.

The consecrated life and the particular Church

48.1 Again, a significant role is played by consecrated persons *within the particular Churches.* On the basis of the Council's teaching on the Church as communion and mystery, and on the particular Churches as portions of the People of God in which "the one, holy, catholic and apostolic Church of Christ is truly present and operative,"[107] this aspect of the consecrated life has been systematically explored and codified in various post-conciliar documents. These texts bring out clearly the fundamental importance of cooperation between consecrated persons and Bishops for the organic development of diocesan pastoral life. The charisms of the consecrated life can greatly contribute to the building up of charity in the particular Churches.

48.2 The various ways of living the evangelical counsels are in fact the expression and fruit of spiritual gifts received by founders and foundresses. As such, they constitute an *"experience of the Spirit,* transmitted to their disciples to be lived, safeguarded, deepened and constantly developed by them, in harmony with the Body of Christ continually in the process of growth."[108] The identity of each Institute is bound up with a particular spirituality and apostolate, which takes shape in a specific tradition marked by objective elements.[109] For this reason the Church is concerned that Institutes should grow and develop in accordance with the spirit of their founders and foundresses, and their own sound traditions.[110]

48.3 Consequently, each Institute is recognized as having *a rightful autonomy,* enabling it to follow its own discipline and to keep intact its spiritual and apostolic patrimony. It is the responsibility of local Ordinaries to preserve

---

[106] Cf. Second Vatican Ecumenical Council, Dogmatic Constitution on the Church *Lumen Gentium,* 13.

[107] Second Vatican Ecumenical Council, Decree on the Bishops' Pastoral Office in the Church *Christus Dominus,* 11.

[108] Congregation for Religious and Secular Institutes and Congregation for Bishops, Directives for Mutual Relations between Bishops and Religious in the Church *Mutuae Relationes* (May 14, 1978), 11: *AAS* 70 (1978), 480.

[109] Cf. ibid.

[110] Cf. Code of Canon Law, Canon 576.

and safeguard this autonomy.[111] Thus, Bishops are asked to welcome and esteem the charisms of the consecrated life, and to give them a place in the pastoral plans of the Diocese. They should have a particular concern for Institutes of diocesan right, which are entrusted to the special care of the local Bishop. A Diocese which lacked the consecrated life would not only be deprived of many spiritual gifts, of suitable places for people to seek God, of specific apostolic activities and pastoral approaches, but it would also risk a great weakening of that missionary spirit which is characteristic of the majority of Institutes.[112] There is a duty then to respond to the gift of the consecrated life which the Spirit awakens in the particular Churches, by welcoming it with generosity and thanksgiving.

Fruitful and ordered ecclesial communion

49.1 The Bishop is the father and Pastor of the particular Church in its entirety. It is his task to discern and respect individual charisms, and to promote and coordinate them. In his pastoral charity he will therefore welcome the charism of the consecrated life as a grace which is not restricted to any one Institute, but which benefits the whole Church. Bishops will thus seek to support and help consecrated persons, so that, in communion with the Church, they open themselves to spiritual and pastoral initiatives responding to the needs of our time, while remaining faithful to their founding charism. For their part, consecrated persons will not fail to cooperate generously with the particular Churches as much as they can and with respect for their own charism, *working in full communion with the Bishop* in the areas of evangelization, catechesis and parish life.

49.2 It is helpful to recall that, in coordinating their service to the universal Church with their service to the particular Churches, Institutes may not invoke rightful autonomy, or even the exemption which a number of them enjoy,[113] in order to justify choices which actually conflict with the demands of organic communion called for by a healthy ecclesial life. Instead, the pastoral initiatives of consecrated persons should be determined and carried out in cordial and open dialogue between Bishops and Superi-

---

[111] Cf. Code of Canon Law, Canon 586; Congregation for Religious and Secular Institutes and Congregation for Bishops, Directives for the Mutual Relations between Bishops and Religious in the Church *Mutuae Relationes* (May 14, 1978), 13: *AAS* 70 (1978), 481-482.

[112] Cf. Second Vatican Ecumenical Council, Decree on the Church's Missionary Activity *Ad Gentes,* 18.

[113] Cf. Code of Canon Law, Canons 586 § 2, 591; Code of Canons of the Eastern Churches, Canon 412 § 2.

ors of the different Institutes. Special attention by Bishops to the vocation and mission of Institutes, and respect by the latter for the ministry of Bishops, with ready acceptance of their concrete pastoral directives for the life of the Diocese: these are two intimately linked expressions of that one ecclesial charity by which all work to build up the organic communion — charismatic and at the same time hierarchically structured — of the whole People of God.

A constant dialogue animated by charity

50.1 *Constant dialogue* between the Superiors of Institutes of Consecrated Life and Societies of Apostolic Life and Bishops is most valuable in order to promote mutual understanding, which is the necessary precondition for effective cooperation, especially in pastoral matters. Thanks to regular contacts of this kind, Superiors, both men and women, can inform Bishops about the apostolic undertakings which they are planning in Dioceses, in order to agree on the necessary practical arrangements. In the same way, it is helpful for delegates of the Conferences of Major Superiors to be invited to meetings of the Bishops' Conferences and, in turn, for delegates of the Episcopal Conferences to be invited to attend the Conferences of Major Superiors, following predetermined formats. It would be a great help if, where they do not yet exist, *mixed commissions of Bishops and Major Superiors*[114] were set up at the national level for the joint study of problems of common interest. Likewise, better reciprocal knowledge will result if the theology and the spirituality of the consecrated life are made part of the theological preparation of diocesan priests, and if adequate attention to the theology of the particular Church and to the spirituality of the diocesan clergy is included in the formation of consecrated persons.[115]

50.2 Finally, it is reassuring to mention that, at the Synod, not only were there many interventions on the doctrine of communion, but great satisfaction was expressed for the experience of dialogue conducted in a climate of mutual trust and openness between the Bishops and the men and women Religious present. This led to a desire that "this spiritual experience of communion and cooperation be extended to the whole Church," even after the Synod.[116] It is my hope too that all will grow in the understanding and spirituality of communion.

---

[114] Cf. *Propositio* 29, 4.
[115] Cf. *Propositio* 49, B.
[116] *Propositio* 54.

Fraternity in a divided and unjust world

51.1 The Church entrusts to communities of consecrated life the particular task of *spreading the spirituality of communion,* first of all in their internal life and then in the ecclesial community, and even beyond its boundaries, by opening or continuing a dialogue in charity, especially where today's world is torn apart by ethnic hatred or senseless violence. Placed as they are within the world's different societies — societies frequently marked by conflicting passions and interests, seeking unity but uncertain about the ways to attain it — communities of consecrated life, where persons of different ages, languages and cultures meet as brothers and sisters, are *signs that dialogue is always possible* and that communion can bring differences into harmony.

51.2 Consecrated men and women are sent forth to proclaim, by the witness of their lives, the value of Christian fraternity and the transforming power of the Good News,[117] which makes it possible to see all people as sons and daughters of God, and inspires a self-giving love toward everyone, especially the least of our brothers and sisters. Such communities are places of hope and of the discovery of the Beatitudes, where love, drawing strength from prayer, the wellspring of communion, is called to become a pattern of life and a source of joy.

51.3 In an age characterized by the globalization of problems and the return of the idols of nationalism, international Institutes especially are called to uphold and to bear witness to the sense of communion between peoples, races and cultures. In a climate of fraternity, an openness to the global dimension of problems will not detract from the richness of particular gifts, nor will the affirmation of a particular gift conflict with other gifts or with unity itself. International Institutes can achieve this effectively, inasmuch as they have to face in a creative way the challenge of inculturation, while at the same time preserving their identity.

Communion among different Institutes

52.1 Fraternal spiritual relations and mutual cooperation among different Institutes of Consecrated Life and Societies of Apostolic Life are sustained and nourished by the sense of ecclesial communion. Those who are united by a common commitment to the following of Christ and are inspired by the same Spirit cannot fail to manifest visibly, as branches of the one Vine, the fullness of the Gospel of love. Mindful of the spiritual friendship

---

[117] Cf. Congregation for Institutes of Consecrated Life and Societies of Apostolic Life, Instruction on Fraternal Life in Community *Congregavit Nos in Unum Christi Amor* (February 2, 1994), 56: Rome, 1994, 66.

which often united founders and foundresses during their lives, consecrated persons, while remaining faithful to the character of their own Institute, are called to practice a fraternity which is exemplary and which will serve to encourage the other members of the Church in the daily task of bearing witness to the Gospel.

52.2 Saint Bernard's words about the various Religious Orders remain ever timely: "I admire them all. I belong to one of them by observance, but to all of them by charity. We all need one another: the spiritual good which I do not own and possess, I receive from others. . . . In this exile, the Church is still on pilgrimage and is, in a certain sense, plural: she is a single plurality and a plural unity. All our diversities, which make manifest the richness of God's gifts, will continue to exist in the one house of the Father, which has many rooms. Now there is a division of graces; then there will be distinctions of glory. Unity, both here and there, consists in one and the same charity."[118]

Coordinating bodies

53.1 A significant contribution to communion can be made by the Conferences of Major Superiors and by the Conferences of Secular Institutes. Encouraged and regulated by the Second Vatican Council[119] and by subsequent documents,[120] these bodies have as their principal purpose the promotion of the consecrated life within the framework of the Church's mission.

53.2 By means of these bodies, Institutes express the communion which unites them, and they seek the means to reinforce that communion, with respect and esteem for the uniqueness of their different charisms, which reflect the mystery of the Church and the richness of divine wisdom.[121] I encourage Institutes of Consecrated Life to work together, especially in those countries where particularly difficult situations increase the temptation for them to withdraw into themselves, to the detriment of the consecrated life itself and of the Church. Rather, these Institutes should help one another in trying to discern God's plan in this troubled moment of history, in order better to re-

---

[118] *Apologia to William of Saint-Thierry,* IV, 8: *PL* 182, 903-904.

[119] Cf. Decree on the Appropriate Renewal of the Religious Life *Perfectae Caritatis,* 23.

[120] Cf. Congregation for Religious and Secular Institutes and Congregation for Bishops, Directives for Mutual Relationships between Bishops and Religious in the Church *Mutuae Relationes* (May 14, 1978), 21, 61: *AAS* 70 (1978), 486, 503-504; Code of Canon Law, Canons 708-709.

[121] Cf. Second Vatican Ecumenical Council, Decree on the Appropriate Renewal of the Religious Life *Perfectae Caritatis,* 1; Dogmatic Constitution on the Church *Lumen Gentium,* 46.

spond to it with appropriate works of the apostolate.[122] In the perspective of a communion open to the challenges of our time, Superiors, men and women, "working in harmony with the Bishops," should seek "to make use of the accomplishments of the best members of each Institute and to offer services which not only help to overcome eventual limits but which create a valid style of formation in consecrated life."[123]

53.3 I exhort the Conferences of Major Superiors and the Conferences of Secular Institutes to maintain frequent and regular contacts with the Congregation for Institutes of Consecrated Life and Societies of Apostolic Life, as a sign of their communion with the Holy See. An active and trusting relationship ought also to be maintained with the Episcopal Conference of each country. In the spirit of the document *Mutuae Relationes,* these contacts should be established on a stable basis, in order to provide for constant and timely coordination of initiatives as they come up. If all of this is done with perseverance and a spirit of faithful adherence to the directives of the Magisterium, the organizations which promote coordination and communion will prove to be particularly helpful in formulating solutions which avoid misunderstandings and tensions both on the theoretical and practical levels.[124] In this way they will make a positive contribution not only to the growth of communion between Institutes of Consecrated Life and the Bishops, but also to the advancement of the mission of the particular Churches.

Communion and cooperation with the laity

54.1 In recent years, one of the fruits of the teaching on the Church as communion has been the growing awareness that her members can and must unite their efforts, with a view to cooperation and exchange of gifts, in order to participate more effectively in the Church's mission. This helps to give a clearer and more complete picture of the Church herself, while rendering more effective the response to the great challenges of our time, thanks to the combined contributions of the various gifts.

54.2 Contacts with the laity, in the case of monastic or contemplative Institutes, take the form of a relationship that is primarily spiritual, while for

---

[122] Cf. Second Vatican Ecumenical Council, Pastoral Constitution on the Church in the Modern World *Gaudium et Spes,* 4.

[123] John Paul II, Message to the 14th Assembly of the Conference of Religious of Brazil (July 11, 1986), 4: *Insegnamenti* IX/2 (1986), 237; cf. *Propositio* 31.

[124] Cf. Congregation for Religious and Secular Institutes and Congregation for Bishops, Directives for Mutual Relationships between Bishops and Religious in the Church *Mutuae Relationes* (May 14, 1978), 63, 65: *AAS* 70 (1978), 504, 504-505.

Institutes involved in works of the apostolate these contacts also translate into forms of pastoral cooperation. Members of Secular Institutes, lay or clerical, relate to other members of the faithful at the level of everyday life. Today, often as a result of new situations, many Institutes have come to the conclusion that *their charism can be shared with the laity.* The laity are therefore invited to share more intensely in the spirituality and mission of these Institutes. We may say that, in the light of certain historical experiences such as those of the Secular or Third Orders, a new chapter, rich in hope, has begun in the history of relations between consecrated persons and the laity.

For a renewed spiritual and apostolic dynamism

55.1 These new experiences of communion and cooperation should be encouraged for various reasons. They can in fact give rise to the spread of a fruitful spirituality beyond the confines of the Institute, which will then be in a position to ensure the continuity in the Church of the services typical of the Institute. Another positive consequence will be to facilitate more intense cooperation between consecrated persons and the laity in view of the Institute's mission. Moved by the examples of holiness of the consecrated members, lay men and women will experience at first-hand the spirit of the evangelical counsels, and will thus be encouraged to live and bear witness to the spirit of the Beatitudes, in order to transform the world according to God's design.[125]

55.2 The participation of the laity often brings unexpected and rich insights into certain aspects of the charism, leading to a more spiritual interpretation of it and helping to draw from it directions for new activities in the apostolate. In whatever activity or ministry they are involved, consecrated persons should remember that before all else they must be expert guides in the spiritual life, and in this perspective they should cultivate "the most precious gift: the spirit."[126] For their part, the laity should offer Religious families the invaluable contribution of their "being in the world" and their specific service.

Associates and lay volunteers

56.1 A significant expression of lay people's sharing in the richness of the consecrated life is their participation in various Institutes under the new form of so-called associate members or, in response to conditions present in certain cultures, as people who share fully for a certain period of time the Institute's

---

[125] Cf. Second Vatican Ecumenical Council, Dogmatic Constitution on the Church *Lumen Gentium,* 31.

[126] Saint Anthony Mary Zaccaria, *Writings,* Sermon II (Rome, 1975), 129.

community life and its particular dedication to contemplation or the apostolate. This should always be done in such a way that the identity of the Institute in its internal life is not harmed.[127]

56.2 This voluntary service, which draws from the richness of the consecrated life, should be held in great esteem; it is, however, necessary to provide proper formation so that volunteers, besides being competent, always have supernaturally motivated intentions and, in their projects, a strong sense of community and of the Church.[128] Moreover, it should be borne in mind that initiatives involving lay persons at the decision-making level, in order to be considered the work of a specific Institute, must promote the ends of that Institute and be carried out under its responsibility. Therefore, if lay persons take on a directive role, they will be accountable for their actions to the competent Superiors. It is necessary for all this to be examined and regulated by special directives in each Institute, to be approved by higher authority; these directives should indicate the respective responsibilities of the Institute itself, of its communities, associate members and volunteers.

56.3 Consecrated persons, sent by their Superiors and remaining subject to them, can take part in *specific forms of cooperation in lay initiatives,* particularly in organizations and institutions which work with those on the margins of society and which have the purpose of alleviating human suffering. Such collaboration, if prompted and sustained by a clear and strong Christian identity and respectful of the particular character of the consecrated life, can make the radiant power of the Gospel shine forth brightly even in the darkest situations of human life.

56.4 In recent years, many consecrated persons have become members of one or other of the *ecclesial movements* which have spread in our time. From these experiences, those involved usually draw benefit, especially in the area of spiritual renewal. Nonetheless, it cannot be denied that in certain cases this involvement causes uneasiness and disorientation at the personal or community level, especially when these experiences come into conflict with the demands of the common life or of the Institute's spirituality. It is therefore necessary to take care that membership in these ecclesial movements does not endanger the charism or discipline of the Institute of origin,[129] and that all

---

[127] Cf. *Propositio* 33, A and C.

[128] Cf. *Propositio* 33, B.

[129] Cf. Congregation for Institutes of Consecrated Life and Societies of Apostolic Life, Instruction on Fraternal Life in Community *Congregavit Nos in Unum Christi Amor* (February 2, 1994), 62: Rome, 1994, 75-77; Directives on Formation in Religious Institutes *Potissimum Institutioni* (February 2, 1990), 92-93: *AAS* 82 (1990), 123-124.

is done with the permission of Superiors and with the full intention of accepting their decisions.

The dignity and role of consecrated women

57.1 The Church fully reveals her varied spiritual richness when she overcomes all discrimination and welcomes as a true blessing the gifts lavished by God upon both men and women, considering them in their equal dignity. By virtue of their dedication lived in fullness and in joy, consecrated women are called in a very special way to be *signs of God's tender love toward the human race* and to be special witnesses to the mystery of the Church, Virgin, Bride and Mother.[130] This mission of theirs was noted by the Synod, in which many consecrated women participated and made their voices heard. Those voices were listened to and appreciated. Thanks also to their contribution, useful directions for the Church's life and her evangelizing mission have emerged. Certainly, the validity of many assertions relating to the position of women in different sectors of society and of the Church cannot be denied. It is equally important to point out that women's new self-awareness also helps men to reconsider their way of looking at things, the way they understand themselves, where they place themselves in history and how they interpret it, and the way they organize social, political, economic, religious and ecclesial life.

57.2 Having received from Christ a message of liberation, the Church has the mission to proclaim this message prophetically, promoting ways of thinking and acting which correspond to the mind of the Lord. In this context the consecrated woman, on the basis of her experience of the Church and as a woman in the Church, can help eliminate certain one-sided perspectives which do not fully recognize her dignity and her specific contribution to the Church's life and pastoral and missionary activity. Consecrated women therefore rightly aspire to have their identity, ability, mission and responsibility more clearly recognized, both in the awareness of the Church and in everyday life.

57.3 Likewise, the future of the new evangelization, as of all other forms of missionary activity, is unthinkable without a renewed contribution from women, especially consecrated women.

New possibilities of presence and action

58.1 It is therefore urgently necessary to take certain concrete steps, beginning by *providing room for women to participate* in different fields and at all levels, including decision-making processes, above all in matters which concern women themselves.

---

[130] Cf. *Propositio* 9, A.

58.2 Moreover, the formation of consecrated women, no less than that of men, should be adapted to modern needs and should provide sufficient time and suitable institutional opportunities for a systematic education, extending to all areas, from the theological-pastoral to the professional. Pastoral and catechetical formation, always important, is particularly relevant in view of the new evangelization, which calls for new forms of participation also on the part of women.

58.3 Clearly, a more solid formation, while helping consecrated women to understand better their own gifts, cannot but encourage within the Church the reciprocity which is needed. In the field of theological, cultural and spiritual studies, much can be expected from the genius of women, not only in relation to specific aspects of feminine consecrated life, but also in understanding the faith in all its expressions. In this regard, the history of spirituality owes much to Saints like Teresa of Jesus and Catherine of Siena, the first two women to be given the title "Doctor of the Church," and to so many other mystics for their exploration of the mystery of God and their analysis of his action in believers! The Church depends a great deal on consecrated women for new efforts in fostering Christian doctrine and morals, family and social life, and especially in everything that affects the dignity of women and respect for human life.[131] In fact, "*women* occupy a place, in thought and action, which is unique and decisive. It depends on them to promote a 'new feminism' which rejects the temptation of imitating models of 'male domination,' in order to acknowledge and affirm the true genius of women in every aspect of the life of society, and overcome all discrimination, violence and exploitation."[132]

58.4 There is reason to hope that a fuller acknowledgment of the mission of women will provide feminine consecrated life with a heightened awareness of its specific role and increased dedication to the cause of the Kingdom of God. This will be expressed in many different works, such as involvement in evangelization, educational activities, participation in the formation of future priests and consecrated persons, animating Christian communities, giving spiritual support, and promoting the fundamental values of life and peace. To consecrated women and their extraordinary capacity for dedication, I once again express the gratitude and admiration of the whole Church, which supports them so that they will live their vocation fully and joyfully, and feel called to the great task of helping to educate the woman of today.

---

[131] Cf. *Propositio* 9.

[132] John Paul II, Encyclical Letter *Evangelium Vitae* (March 25, 1995), 99: *AAS* 87 (1995), 514.

2. Continuity in the Work of the Spirit: Faithfulness in the Course of Change

Cloistered nuns

59.1 The monastic life of women and the cloister deserve special attention because of the great esteem in which the Christian community holds this type of life, which is a sign of the exclusive union of the Church as Bride with her Lord, whom she loves above all things. Indeed, the life of cloistered nuns, devoted in a special way to prayer, to asceticism and diligent progress in the spiritual life, "is nothing other than a journey to the heavenly Jerusalem and an anticipation of the eschatological Church immutable in its possession and contemplation of God."[133] In the light of this vocation and ecclesial mission, the cloister responds to the need, felt as paramount, *to be with the Lord.* Choosing an enclosed space where they will live their lives, cloistered nuns share in Christ's emptying of himself by means of a radical poverty, expressed in their renunciation not only of things but also of "space," of contacts, of so many benefits of creation. This particular way of offering up the "body" allows them to enter more fully into the Eucharistic mystery. They offer themselves with Jesus for the world's salvation. Their offering, besides its elements of sacrifice and expiation, takes on the aspect of thanksgiving to the Father, by sharing in the thanksgiving of the beloved Son.

59.2 Rooted in this profound spiritual aspiration, the cloister is not only an ascetic practice of very great value but also *a way of living Christ's Passover.*[134] From being an experience of "death," it becomes a superabundance of life, representing a joyful proclamation and prophetic anticipation of the possibility offered to every person and to the whole of humanity to live solely for God in Christ Jesus (cf. Rom 6:11). The cloister brings to mind that *space in the heart* where every person is called to union with the Lord. Accepted as a gift and chosen as a free response of love, the cloister is the place of spiritual communion with God and with the brethren, where the limitation of space and contacts works to the advantage of interiorizing Gospel values (cf. Jn 13:34; Mt 5:3, 8).

59.3 Even in the simplicity of their life, cloistered communities, set like cities on a hilltop or lights on a lampstand (cf. Mt 5:14-15), visibly represent the goal toward which the entire community of the Church travels. "Eager to

---

[133] Congregation for Religious and Secular Institutes, Instruction on the Contemplative Life and on the Enclosure of Nuns *Venite Seorsum* (August 15, 1969), V: *AAS* 61 (1969), 685.

[134] Cf. ibid., I: loc. cit., 674.

act and yet devoted to contemplation,"[135] the Church advances down the paths of time with her eyes fixed on the future restoration of all things in Christ, when she will appear "in glory with her Spouse (cf. Col 3:1-4),"[136] and Christ will deliver "the Kingdom to God the Father after destroying every rule and every authority and power . . . that God may be everything to everyone" (1 Cor 15:24, 28).

59.4 To these dear Sisters, therefore, I extend my gratitude and I encourage them to remain faithful to the cloistered life according to their particular charism. Thanks to their example, this way of life continues to draw many vocations, attracting people by the radical nature of a "spousal" existence dedicated totally to God in contemplation. As an expression of pure love which is worth more than any work, the contemplative life generates an extraordinary apostolic and missionary effectiveness.[137]

59.5 The Synod Fathers expressed great esteem for the cloistered life, while at the same time giving attention to requests made by some with respect to its concrete discipline. The Synod's suggestions in this regard, and especially the desire that provision be made for giving Major Superiors more responsibility in the granting of dispensations from enclosure for just and grave reasons,[138] will be carefully considered, in the light of the path of renewal already undertaken since the Second Vatican Council.[139] In this way, the various forms and degrees of cloister — from papal and constitutional cloister to monastic cloister — will better correspond to the variety of contemplative Institutes and monastic traditions.

59.6 As the Synod itself emphasized, *associations* and *federations* of monasteries are to be encouraged, as already recommended by Pope Pius XII and the Second Vatican Council,[140] especially where there are no other effective forms of coordination or help, with a view to safeguarding and promoting the

---

[135] Second Vatican Ecumenical Council, Constitution on the Sacred Liturgy *Sacrosanctum Concilium,* 2.

[136] Second Vatican Ecumenical Council, Dogmatic Constitution on the Church *Lumen Gentium,* 6.

[137] Cf. Saint John of the Cross, *Spiritual Canticle,* 29, 1.

[138] Cf. Code of Canon Law, Canon 667 § 4; *Propositio* 22, 4.

[139] Cf. Paul VI, Motu Proprio *Ecclesiae Sanctae* (June 8, 1966), II, 30-31: *AAS* 58 (1966), 780; Second Vatican Ecumenical Council, Decree on the Appropriate Renewal of the Religious Life *Perfectae Caritatis,* 7, 16; Congregation for Religious and Secular Institutes, Instruction on the Contemplative Life and on the Enclosure of Nuns *Venite Seorsum* (August 15, 1969), VI: *AAS* 61 (1969), 686.

[140] Cf. Pius XII, Apostolic Constitution *Sponsa Christi* (November 21, 1950), VII: *AAS* 43 (1951), 18-19; Second Vatican Ecumenical Council, Decree on the Appropriate Renewal of the Religious Life *Perfectae Caritatis,* 22.

values of contemplative life. Such bodies, which must always respect the legitimate autonomy of monasteries, can in fact offer valuable help in adequately resolving common problems, such as appropriate renewal, initial and continuing formation, mutual economic support and even the reorganization of the monasteries themselves.

Religious brothers

60.1 According to the traditional doctrine of the Church, the consecrated life by its nature *is neither lay nor clerical.*[141] For this reason the "lay consecration" of both men and women constitutes a state which in its profession of the evangelical counsels is complete in itself.[142] Consequently, both for the individual and for the Church, it is a value in itself, apart from the sacred ministry.

60.2 Following the teaching of the Second Vatican Council,[143] the Synod expressed great esteem for the kind of consecrated life in which religious brothers provide valuable services of various kinds, inside or outside the community, participating in this way in the mission of proclaiming the Gospel and bearing witness to it with charity in everyday life. Indeed, some of these services can be considered *ecclesial ministries,* granted by legitimate authority. This requires an appropriate and integral formation: human, spiritual, theological, pastoral and professional.

60.3 According to the terminology currently in use, Institutes which, by reason of their founders' design or by legitimate tradition, have a character and purpose which do not entail the exercise of Holy Orders are called "Lay Institutes."[144] Nonetheless the Synod pointed out that this terminology does not adequately express the particular nature of the vocation of the members of these Religious Institutes. In fact, although they perform many works in common with the lay faithful, these men do so insofar as they are consecrated, and thereby express the spirit of total self-giving to Christ and the Church, in accordance with their specific charism.

60.4 For this reason the Synod Fathers, in order to avoid ambiguity and confusion with the secular state of the lay faithful,[145] proposed the term *Religious Institutes of Brothers.*[146] This proposal is significant, especially when we

---

[141] Cf. Code of Canon Law, Canon 588 § 1.

[142] Cf. Second Vatican Ecumenical Council, Decree on the Appropriate Renewal of the Religious Life *Perfectae Caritatis,* 10.

[143] Cf. ibid., 8, 10.

[144] Cf. ibid., 10; Code of Canon Law, Canon 588 § 3.

[145] Cf. Second Vatican Ecumenical Council, Dogmatic Constitution on the Church *Lumen Gentium,* 31.

[146] Cf. *Propositio* 8.

consider that the term "brother" suggests a rich spirituality. "These Religious are called to be brothers of Christ, deeply united with him, 'the firstborn among many brothers' (Rom 8:29); brothers to one another, in mutual love and working together in the Church in the same service of what is good; brothers to everyone, in their witness to Christ's love for all, especially the lowliest, the neediest; brothers for a greater brotherhood in the Church."[147] By living in a special way this aspect of Christian and consecrated life, Religious brothers are an effective reminder to Religious priests themselves of the fundamental dimension of brotherhood in Christ, to be lived among themselves and with every man and woman, and they proclaim to all the Lord's words: "And you are all brothers" (Mt 23:8).

60.5 In these Religious Institutes of Brothers nothing prevents certain members from receiving Holy Orders for the priestly service of the religious community, provided that this is approved by the General Chapter.[148] However, the Second Vatican Council does not give any explicit encouragement for this, precisely because it wishes Institutes of Brothers to remain faithful to their vocation and mission. The same holds true with regard to assuming the office of Superior, since that office reflects in a special way the nature of the Institute itself.

60.6 The vocation of brothers in what are known as "clerical" Institutes is different, since, according to the design of the founder or by reason of legitimate tradition, these Institutes presuppose the exercise of Holy Orders, are governed by clerics, and as such are approved by Church authority.[149] In these Institutes the sacred ministry is constitutive of the charism itself and determines its nature, purpose and spirit. The presence of brothers constitutes a different form of participation in an Institute's mission, through services rendered both within the community and in the apostolate, in collaboration with those who exercise the priestly ministry.

Mixed Institutes

61.1 Some Religious Institutes, which in the founder's original design were envisaged as a brotherhood in which all the members, priests and those who were not priests, were considered equal among themselves, have acquired a different form with the passing of time. It is necessary that these Institutes,

---

[147] John Paul II, Address at the General Audience (February 22, 1995), 6: *L'Osservatore Romano* (English-language edition), March 1, 1995, 11.

[148] Cf. Second Vatican Ecumenical Council, Decree on the Appropriate Renewal of the Religious Life *Perfectae Caritatis*, 10.

[149] Cf. Code of Canon Law, Canon 588 § 2.

known as "mixed," evaluate on the basis of a deeper understanding of their founding charism whether it is appropriate and possible to return to their original inspiration.

61.2 The Synod Fathers expressed the hope that in these Institutes all the Religious would be recognized as having equal rights and obligations, with the exception of those which stem from Holy Orders.[150] A special Commission has been established to examine and resolve the problems connected with this issue; it is necessary to await this Commission's conclusions before coming to suitable decisions in accordance with what will be authoritatively determined.

New forms of the evangelical life

62.1 The Spirit, who at different times has inspired numerous forms of consecrated life, does not cease to assist the Church, whether by fostering in already existing Institutes a commitment to renewed faithfulness to the founding charism, or by giving new charisms to men and women of our own day so that they can start institutions responding to the challenges of our times. A sign of this divine intervention is to be found in the so-called *new Foundations,* which display new characteristics compared to those of traditional Foundations.

62.2 The originality of the new communities often consists in the fact that they are composed of mixed groups of men and women, of clerics and lay persons, of married couples and celibates, all of whom pursue a particular style of life. These communities are sometimes inspired by one or other traditional form adapted to the needs of modern society. Their commitment to the evangelical life also takes on different forms, while, as a general rule, they are all characterized by an intense aspiration to community life, poverty and prayer. Both clerics and lay persons share in the duties according to the responsibilities assigned to them, and the apostolate focuses on the demands of the new evangelization.

62.3 If, on one hand, there is reason to rejoice at the Holy Spirit's action, there is, on the other, a need for *discernment regarding these charisms.* A fundamental principle, when speaking of the consecrated life, is that the specific features of the new communities and their styles of life must be founded on the essential theological and canonical elements proper to the consecrated life.[151] This discernment is necessary at both the local and universal level, in

---

[150] Cf. *Propositio* 10; Second Vatican Ecumenical Council, Decree on the Appropriate Renewal of the Religious Life *Perfectae Caritatis,* 15.

[151] Cf. Code of Canon Law, Canon 573; Code of Canons of the Eastern Churches, Canon 410.

order to manifest a common obedience to the one Spirit. In Dioceses, Bishops should examine the witness of life and the orthodoxy of the founders of such communities, their spirituality, the ecclesial awareness shown in carrying out their mission, the methods of formation and the manner of incorporation into the community. They should wisely evaluate possible weaknesses, watching patiently for the sign of results (cf. Mt 7:16), so that they may acknowledge the authenticity of the charism.[152] In a special way, Bishops are required to determine, according to clearly established criteria, the suitability of any members of these communities who wish to receive Holy Orders.[153]

62.4 Worthy of praise are those forms of commitment which some Christian married couples assume in certain associations and movements. They confirm by means of a vow the obligation of chastity proper to the married state and, without neglecting their duties toward their children, profess poverty and obedience.[154] They do so with the intention of bringing to the perfection of charity their love, already "consecrated" in the Sacrament of Matrimony.[155] This necessary clarification regarding the nature of such experiences in no way intends to underestimate this particular path of holiness, from which the action of the Holy Spirit, infinitely rich in gifts and inspirations, is certainly not absent.

62.5 In view of such a wealth of gifts and creative energies, it seems appropriate to *set up a Commission to deal with questions relating to new forms of consecrated life.* The purpose of this Commission will be to determine criteria of authenticity which will help discernment and decision-making.[156] Among its other tasks, this Commission will evaluate, in the light of the experience of recent decades, which new forms of consecration can, with pastoral prudence and to the advantage of all, be officially approved by Church authority, in order to be proposed to the faithful who are seeking a more perfect Christian life.

62.6 New associations of evangelical life *are not alternatives* to already existing institutions, which continue to hold the preeminent place assigned to them by tradition. Nonetheless, the new forms are also a gift of the Spirit, enabling the Church to follow her Lord in a constant outpouring of generosity, attentive to God's invitations revealed through the signs of the times. Thus the

---

[152] Cf. *Propositio* 13, B.

[153] Cf. *Propositio* 13, C.

[154] Cf. *Propositio* 13, A.

[155] Cf. Second Vatican Ecumenical Council, Pastoral Constitution on the Church in the Modern World *Gaudium et Spes,* 48.

[156] Cf. *Propositio* 13, B.

Church appears before the world with many forms of holiness and service, as "a kind of instrument or sign of intimate union with God, and of the unity of mankind."[157] The older Institutes, many of which have been tested by the severest of hardships, which they have accepted courageously down the centuries, can be enriched through dialogue and an exchange of gifts with the Foundations appearing in our own day.

62.7 In this way the vigor of the different forms of consecrated life, from the oldest to the most recent, as well as the vitality of the new communities, will renew faithfulness to the Holy Spirit, who is the source of communion and unceasing newness of life.

3. Looking to the Future

Difficulties and future prospects

63.1 The changes taking place in society and the decrease in the number of vocations are weighing heavily on the consecrated life in some regions of the world. The apostolic works of many Institutes and their very presence in certain local Churches are endangered. As has already occurred at other times in history, there are Institutes which even run the risk of disappearing altogether. The universal Church is profoundly grateful for the great contribution which these Institutes have made to building her up through their witness and service.[158] The trials of the present do not take away from their merits and the positive results of their efforts.

63.2 For other Institutes, there is the problem of reassessing their apostolate. This task, which is difficult and often painful, requires study and discernment in the light of certain criteria. For example, it is necessary to safeguard the significance of an Institute's own charism, to foster community life, to be attentive to the needs of both the universal and particular Church, to show concern for what the world neglects, and to respond generously and boldly to the new forms of poverty through concrete efforts, even if necessarily on a small scale, and above all in the most abandoned areas.[159]

63.3 The various difficulties stemming from the decline in personnel and apostolates *must in no way lead to a loss of confidence in the evangelical vital-*

---

[157] Second Vatican Ecumenical Council, Dogmatic Constitution on the Church *Lumen Gentium,* 1.

[158] Cf. *Propositio* 24.

[159] Cf. Congregation for Institutes of Consecrated Life and Societies of Apostolic Life, Instruction on Fraternal Life in Community *Congregavit Nos in Unum Christi Amor* (February 2, 1994), 67: Rome, 1994, 60-61.

ity of the consecrated life, which will always be present and active in the Church. While individual Institutes have no claim to permanence, the consecrated life itself will continue to sustain among the faithful the response of love toward God and neighbor. Thus it is necessary to distinguish the *historical destiny* of a specific Institute or form of consecrated life from the *ecclesial mission* of the consecrated life as such. The former is affected by changing circumstances; the latter is destined to perdure.

63.4 This is true of both the contemplative and apostolic forms of consecrated life. On the whole, under the ever creative guidance of the Spirit, the consecrated life is destined to remain a shining witness to the inseparable unity of love of God and love of neighbor. It appears as the living memory of the fruitfulness of God's love. New situations of difficulty are therefore to be faced with the serenity of those who know that what is required of each individual is *not success, but commitment to faithfulness.* What must be avoided at all costs is the actual breakdown of the consecrated life, a collapse which is not measured by a decrease in numbers but by a failure to cling steadfastly to the Lord and to personal vocation and mission. Rather, by persevering faithfully in the consecrated life, consecrated persons confess with great effectiveness before the world their unwavering trust in the Lord of history, in whose hands are the history and destiny of individuals, institutions and peoples, and therefore also the realization in time of his gifts. Sad situations of crisis invite consecrated persons courageously to proclaim their faith in Christ's Death and Resurrection, that they may become a visible sign of the passage from death to life.

Fresh efforts in the promotion of vocations

64.1 The mission of the consecrated life, as well as the vitality of Institutes, undoubtedly depend on the faithful commitment with which consecrated persons respond to their vocation. But they have a future to the extent that *still other men and women generously welcome the Lord's call.* The problem of vocations is a real challenge which directly concerns the various Institutes but also involves the whole Church. Great spiritual and material energies are being expended in the sphere of vocational promotion, but the results do not always match expectations and efforts. Thus, while vocations to the consecrated life are flourishing in the young Churches and in those which suffered persecution at the hands of totalitarian regimes, they are lacking in countries traditionally rich in vocations, including vocations for the missions.

64.2 This difficult situation puts consecrated persons to the test. Sometimes they ask themselves: Have we perhaps lost the capacity to attract new vocations? They must have confidence in the Lord Jesus, who continues to call men and women to follow him. They must entrust themselves to the Holy Spirit, who inspires and bestows the charisms of the consecrated life. Therefore, while we rejoice in the action of the Spirit, who rejuvenates the Bride of Christ by enabling the consecrated life to flourish in many nations, we must also pray unceasingly to the Lord of the harvest, that he will send workers to his Church in order to meet the needs of the new evangelization (cf. Mt 9:37-38). Besides promoting prayer for vocations, it is essential to act, by means of explicit presentation and appropriate catechesis, with a view to encouraging in those called to the consecrated life that free, willing and generous response which carries into effect the grace of vocation.

64.3 The invitation of Jesus, "Come and see" (Jn 1:39), is *the golden rule* of pastoral work for promoting vocations, even today. Following the example of founders and foundresses, this work aims at presenting *the attraction of the person of the Lord Jesus* and the beauty of the total gift of self for the sake of the Gospel. A primary responsibility of all consecrated men and women is therefore to propose with courage, by word and example, the ideal of the following of Christ, and then to support the response to the Spirit's action in the heart of those who are called.

64.5 After the enthusiasm of the first meeting with Christ, there comes the constant struggle of everyday life, a struggle which turns a vocation into a tale of friendship with the Lord. In view of this, the pastoral work of promoting vocations should make use of suitable help, such as *spiritual direction,* in order to nourish that personal response of love of the Lord which is the necessary condition for becoming disciples and apostles of his Kingdom. Moreover, if the flourishing of vocations evident in some parts of the world justifies optimism and hope, the lack of them in other areas must not lead either to discouragement or to the temptation to practice lax and unwise recruitment. The task of promoting vocations should increasingly express *a joint commitment of the whole Church.*[160] It calls for the active collaboration of pastors, Religious, families and teachers, as required in something which forms an integral part of the overall pastoral plan of every particular Church. In every Diocese there should be this *common endeavor,* which coordinates and promotes the efforts of everyone, not jeopardizing, but rather supporting, the vocational activity of each Institute.[161]

64.6 The effective cooperation of the whole People of God, with the support of Providence, cannot but give rise to an abundance of divine gifts. Christian

---

[160] Cf. *Propositio* 48, A.
[161] Cf. *Propositio* 48, B.

solidarity should abound in meeting the needs of vocational formation in countries which are economically poorer. The recruitment of vocations in these countries should be carried out by the various Institutes in full accord with the Churches of the region, and on the basis of an active and long-term involvement in their pastoral life.[162] The most authentic way to support the Spirit's action is for Institutes to invest their best resources generously in vocational work, especially by their serious involvement in working with youth.

Commitment to initial formation

65.1 The Synod Assembly paid special attention to the *formation* of those who wish to consecrate themselves to the Lord,[163] and recognized its decisive importance. The *primary objective* of the formation process is to prepare people for the total consecration of themselves to God in the following of Christ, at the service of the Church's mission. To say "yes" to the Lord's call by taking personal responsibility for maturing in one's vocation is the inescapable duty of all who have been called. One's whole life must be open to the action of the Holy Spirit, traveling the road of formation with generosity, and accepting in faith the means of grace offered by the Lord and the Church.[164]

65.2 Formation should therefore have a profound effect on individuals, so that their every attitude and action, at important moments as well as in the ordinary events of life, will show that they belong completely and joyfully to God.[165] Since the very purpose of consecrated life is conformity to the Lord Jesus in his *total self-giving,*[166] this must also be the principal objective of formation. Formation is a path of gradual identification with the attitude of Christ toward the Father.

65.3 If this is the purpose of the consecrated life, the manner of preparing for it should include and express *the character of wholeness.* Formation should involve the whole person,[167] in every aspect of the personality, in behavior and intentions. Precisely because it aims at the transformation of the whole person, it is clear that *the commitment to formation never* ends. Indeed, at every

---

[162] Cf. *Propositio* 48, C.

[163] Cf. *Propositio* 49, A.

[164] Cf. Congregation for Institutes of Consecrated Life and Societies of Apostolic Life, Directives on Formation in Religious Institutes *Potissimum Institutioni* (February 2, 1990), 29: *AAS* 82 (1990), 493.

[165] Cf. *Propositio* 49, B.

[166] Cf. Congregation for Religious and Secular Institutes, Instruction on the Essential Elements in the Church's Teaching as Applied to Institutes Dedicated to Works of the Apostolate (May 31, 1983), 45: *L'Osservatore Romano* (English-language edition), July 18, 1983, 7.

[167] Cf. Code of Canon Law, Canon 607 § 1.

stage of life, consecrated persons must be offered opportunities to grow in their commitment to the charism and mission of their Institute.

65.4 For formation to be complete, it must include every aspect of Christian life. It must therefore provide a human, cultural, spiritual and pastoral preparation which pays special attention to the harmonious integration of all its various aspects. Sufficient time should be reserved for initial formation, understood as a process of development which passes through every stage of personal maturity — from the psychological and spiritual to the theological and pastoral. In the case of those studying for the priesthood, this initial formation coincides with and fits well into a specific course of studies, as part of a broader formation program.

The work of those responsible for formation

66.1 God the Father, through the unceasing gift of Christ and the Spirit, is the educator *par excellence* of those who consecrate themselves to him. But in this work he makes use of human instruments, placing more mature brothers and sisters at the side of those whom he calls. Formation then is a sharing in the work of the Father who, through the Spirit, fashions the inner attitudes of the Son in the hearts of young men and women. Those in charge of formation must therefore be very familiar with the path of seeking God, so as to be able to accompany others on this journey. Sensitive to the action of grace, they will also be able to point out those obstacles which are less obvious. But above all they will disclose the beauty of following Christ and the value of the charism by which this is accomplished. They will combine the illumination of spiritual wisdom with the light shed by human means, which can be a help both in discerning the call and in forming the new man or woman, until they are genuinely free. The chief instrument of formation is personal dialogue, a practice of irreplaceable and commendable effectiveness which should take place regularly and with a certain frequency.

66.2 Because sensitive tasks are involved, the training of suitable directors of formation, who will fulfill their task in a spirit of communion with the whole Church, is very important. It will be helpful to establish appropriate structures for *the training of those responsible for formation,* preferably in places where they can be in contact with the culture in which their pastoral service will later be carried out. In the work of formation, the more solidly established Institutes should help those of more recent foundation by contributing some of their best members.[168]

---

[168] Cf. *Propositio* 50.

Formation in community and for the apostolate

67.1 Since formation must also have a *communal* dimension, the community is the chief place of formation in Institutes of Consecrated Life and Societies of Apostolic Life. Initiation into the hardships and joys of community life takes place in the community itself. Through the fraternal life each one learns to live with those whom God has put at his or her side, accepting their positive traits along with their differences and limitations. Each one learns to share the gifts received for the building up of all, because "to each is given the manifestation of the Spirit for the common good" (1 Cor 12:7).[169] At the same time, from the moment of initial formation, community life must disclose the essential missionary dimension of consecration. Thus, during the period of initial formation, Institutes of Consecrated Life do well to provide practical experiences which are prudently followed by the one responsible for formation, enabling candidates to test, in the context of the local culture, their skills for the apostolate, their ability to adapt and their spirit of initiative.

67.2 On the one hand, it is important for consecrated persons gradually to develop a critical judgment, based on the Gospel, regarding the positive and negative values of their own culture and of the culture in which they will eventually work. On the other hand, they must be trained in the difficult art of interior harmony, of the interaction between love of God and love of one's brothers and sisters; they must likewise learn that prayer is the soul of the apostolate, but also that the apostolate animates and inspires prayer.

The need for a complete and updated "ratio"

68.1 A definite period of formation extending up to final profession is recommended both for women's Institutes, and for men's Institutes as regards religious brothers. Essentially, this is also true for cloistered communities, which ought to set up suitable programs, aimed at imparting a genuine preparation for the contemplative life and its particular mission in the Church.

68.2 The Synod Fathers earnestly asked all Institutes of Consecrated Life and Societies of Apostolic Life to draw up as soon as possible a *ratio institutionis*, that is, a formation program inspired by their particular charism, presenting clearly and in all its stages the course to be followed in order to assimilate fully the spirituality of the respective Institute. The *ratio* responds to a pressing need today. On the one hand, it shows how to pass on the Institute's spirit so that it will be lived in its integrity by future generations, in different cul-

---

[169] Cf. Congregation for Institutes of Consecrated Life and Societies of Apostolic Life, Instruction on Fraternal Life in Community *Congregavit Nos in Unum Christi Amor* (February 2, 1994), 32-33: Rome, 1994, 39-42.

tures and geographical regions; on the other hand, it explains to consecrated persons how to live that spirit in the different stages of life on the way to full maturity of faith in Christ.

68.3 While it is true that the renewal of the consecrated life depends primarily on formation, it is equally certain that this training is, in turn, linked to the ability to establish a method characterized by spiritual and pedagogical wisdom, which will gradually lead those wishing to consecrate themselves to put on the mind of Christ the Lord. Formation is a dynamic process by means of which individuals are converted to the Word of God in the depths of their being and, at the same time, learn how to discover the signs of God in earthly realities. At a time when religious values are increasingly being ignored by society, this plan of formation is doubly important: as a result of it, consecrated persons will not only continue to "see" God with the eyes of faith in a world which ignores his presence, but will also be effective in making his presence in some way "perceptible" through the witness of their charism.

Continuing formation

69.1 Continuing formation, whether in Institutes of apostolic or contemplative life, is an intrinsic requirement of religious consecration. As mentioned above, the formation process is not limited to the initial phase. Due to human limitations, the consecrated person can never claim to have completely brought to life the "new creature" who, in every circumstance of life, reflects the very mind of Christ. *Initial* formation, then, should be closely connected with *continuing* formation, thereby creating a readiness on everyone's part to let themselves be formed every day of their lives.[170]

69.2 Consequently, it will be very important for every Institute to provide, as part of its *ratio institutionis,* a precise and systematic description of its plan of continuing formation. The chief purpose of this plan is to provide all consecrated persons with a program which encompasses their whole life. None are exempt from the obligation to grow humanly and as Religious; by the same token, no one can be overconfident and live in self-sufficient isolation. At no stage of life can people feel so secure and committed that they do not need to give careful attention to ensuring perseverance in faithfulness; just as there is no age at which a person has completely achieved maturity.

In a constant search for faithfulness

70.1 There is a youthfulness of spirit which lasts through time; it arises from the fact that at every stage of life a person seeks and finds a

---

[170] Cf. *Propositio* 51.

new task to fulfill, a particular way of being, of serving and of loving.[171]

70.2 In the consecrated life *the first years of full involvement in the apostolate* are a critical stage, marked by the passage from a supervised life to a situation of *full responsibility for one's work.* It is important that young consecrated persons be supported and accompanied by a brother or sister who helps them to live to the full the freshness of their love and enthusiasm for Christ.

70.3 The next stage can present *the risk of routine,* and the subsequent temptation to give in to disappointment because of meager results. Middle-aged consecrated persons must therefore be helped, in the light of the Gospel and the charism of their Institute, to renew their original decision, and not confuse the completeness of their dedication with the degree of good results. This will enable them to give a fresh impulse and new motivations to their decision. This is the time to search for what is essential.

70.4 *The stage of maturity,* while it brings personal growth, can also bring *the danger of a certain individualism,* accompanied either by a fear of not being in line with the times, or by forms of inflexibility, self-centeredness or diminished enthusiasm. At this point continuing formation is aimed at helping not only to bring back a higher level of spiritual and apostolic life, but also at discovering the special characteristics of this stage of life. For at this time, after refining certain features of the personality, the gift of self is made to God more genuinely and with greater generosity; it extends to others with greater serenity and wisdom, as well as with greater simplicity and richness of grace. This is the gift and experience of spiritual fatherhood and motherhood.

70.5 *Advanced age* poses new problems, which can be prepared for by a discerning program of spiritual support. The gradual withdrawal from activity, sometimes caused by sickness or forced immobility, can be a very formative experience. Often a time of suffering, advanced age nonetheless offers to elderly consecrated persons the chance to be transformed by the paschal experience,[172] by being configured to the crucified Christ who fulfills the Father's will in all things and abandons himself into the Father's hands, even to the surrendering of his spirit to him. This configuration represents a new way of living one's consecration, which is not tied to effectiveness in carrying out administrative responsibilities or apostolic work.

---

[171] Cf. Congregation for Institutes of Consecrated Life and Societies of Apostolic Life, Instruction on Fraternal Life in Community *Congregavit Nos in Unum Christi Amor* (February 2, 1994), 43-45: Rome, 1994, 52-57.

[172] Cf. Congregation for Institutes of Consecrated Life and Societies of Apostolic Life, Directives on Formation in Religious Institutes *Potissimum Institutioni* (February 2, 1990), 70: *AAS* 82 (1990), 513-514.

70.6 When *the moment finally comes for uniting oneself to the supreme hour of the Lord's Passion,* the consecrated person knows that the Father is now bringing to completion the mysterious process of formation which began many years before. Death will then be awaited and prepared for as the supreme act of love and self-offering.

70.7 It should be added that, independently of the different stages of life, any period can present critical situations due to external factors — such as a change of place or assignment, difficulties in work or lack of success in the apostolate, misunderstandings and feelings of alienation — or resulting from more directly personal factors such as physical or mental illness, spiritual aridity, deaths, difficulties in interpersonal relations, strong temptations, crises of faith or identity, or feelings of uselessness. When fidelity becomes more difficult, the individual must be offered the support of greater trust and deeper love, at both the personal and community levels. At such times, the sensitive closeness of the Superior is most essential. Great comfort can also come from the valuable help of a brother or sister, whose concerned and caring presence can lead to a rediscovery of the meaning of the covenant which God originally established, and which he has no intention of breaking. The person undergoing such a trial will then accept purification and hardship as essential to the following of Christ Crucified. The trial itself will appear as a providential means of being formed by the Father's hands, and as a struggle which is not only *psychological,* carried out by the "I" in relation to itself and its weaknesses, but also *religious,* touched each day by the presence of God and the power of the Cross!

Dimensions of continuing formation

71.1 If the subject of formation is the individual at every stage of life, the object of formation is the whole person, called to seek and love God "with all one's heart, and with all one's soul, and with all one's might" (cf. Dt 6:5), and one's neighbor as oneself (cf. Lev 19:18; Mt 22:37-39). Love of God and of the brethren is a powerful force which can ceaselessly inspire the process of growth and fidelity. *Life in the Spirit* is clearly of primary importance. Living in the Spirit, consecrated persons discover their own identity and find profound peace; they grow more attentive to the daily challenges of the word of God, and they allow themselves to be guided by the original inspiration of their Institute. Under the action of the Spirit, they resolutely keep times for prayer, silence and solitude, and they never cease to ask the Almighty for the gift of wisdom in the struggles of everyday life (cf. Wis 9:10).

71.2 *The human and fraternal dimensions* of the consecrated life call for self-knowledge and the awareness of personal limitations, so as to offer its members the inspiration and support needed on the path toward perfect freedom. In present-day circumstances, special importance must be given to the interior freedom of consecrated persons, their affective maturity, their ability to communicate with others, especially in their own community, their serenity of spirit, their compassion for those who are suffering, their love for the truth, and a correspondence between their actions and their words.

71.3 *The apostolic dimension* opens the hearts and minds of consecrated persons and prepares them for constant effort in the apostolate, as the sign that it is the love of Christ which urges them on (cf. 2 Cor 5:14). In practice, this will involve updating the methods and objectives of apostolic works in fidelity to the spirit and aims of the founder or foundress and to subsequently emerging traditions, with continuous attention to changing historical and cultural conditions, at the general and local levels where the apostolate is carried out.

71.4 *The cultural and professional dimensions,* based upon a solid theological training which provides the means for wise discernment, involve continual updating and special interest in the different areas to which each charism is directed. Consecrated persons must therefore keep themselves as intellectually open and adaptable as possible, so that the apostolate will be envisaged and carried out according to the needs of their own time, making use of the means provided by cultural progress.

71.5 Finally, all these elements are united *in the dimension of the charism* proper to each Institute, as it were in a synthesis which calls for a constant deepening of one's own special consecration in all its aspects, not only apostolic but also ascetical and mystical. This means that each member should study diligently the spirit, history and mission of the Institute to which he or she belongs, in order to advance the personal and communal assimilation of its charism.[173]

III

Servitium Caritatis: **Consecrated Life, Manifestation of God's Love in the World**

Consecrated for mission

72.1 In the image of Jesus, the beloved Son "whom the Father consecrated and sent into the world" (Jn 10:36), those whom God calls to follow him are

---

[173] Cf. ibid., 68: loc. cit., 512.

also consecrated and sent into the world to imitate his example and to continue his mission. Fundamentally, this is true of every disciple. In a special way, however, it is true of those who, in the manner that characterizes the consecrated life, are called to follow Christ "more closely," and to make him the "all" of their lives. The task of *devoting themselves wholly to "mission"* is therefore included in their call; indeed, by the action of the Holy Spirit who is at the origin of every vocation and charism, consecrated life itself is a mission, as was the whole of Jesus' life. The profession of the evangelical counsels, which makes a person totally free for the service of the Gospel, is important also from this point of view. It can therefore be said that *a sense of mission is essential to every Institute,* not only those dedicated to the active apostolic life, but also those dedicated to the contemplative life.

72.2 Indeed, more than in external works, the mission consists in making Christ present to the world through personal witness. This is the challenge, this is the primary task of the consecrated life! The more consecrated persons allow themselves to be conformed to Christ, the more Christ is made present and active in the world for the salvation of all.

72.3 Thus it can be said that consecrated persons are "in mission" by virtue of their very consecration, to which they bear witness in accordance with the ideal of their Institute. When the founding charism provides for pastoral activities, it is obvious that the witness of life and the witness of works of the apostolate and human development are equally necessary: both mirror Christ who is at one and the same time consecrated to the glory of the Father and sent into the world for the salvation of his brothers and sisters.[174]

72.4 Religious life, moreover, continues the mission of Christ with another feature specifically its own: *fraternal life in community for the sake of the mission.* Thus, men and women Religious will be all the more committed to the apostolate the more personal their dedication to the Lord Jesus is, the more fraternal their community life, and the more ardent their involvement in the Institute's specific mission.

At the service of God and humanity

73.1 The consecrated life has the prophetic task *of recalling and serving the divine plan for humanity,* as it is announced in Scripture and as it emerges from an attentive reading of the signs of God's providential action in history. This is the plan for the salvation and reconciliation of humanity (cf. Col 1:20-22). To carry out this service appropriately, consecrated per-

---

[174] Cf. Second Vatican Ecumenical Council, Dogmatic Constitution on the Church *Lumen Gentium,* 46.

sons must have a profound experience of God and be aware of the challenges of their time, understanding the profound theological meaning of these challenges through a discernment made with the help of the Spirit. In fact, it is often through historical events that we discern God's hidden call to work according to his plan by active and effective involvement in the events of our time.[175]

73.2 Discerning the signs of the times, as the Council affirms, must be done in the light of the Gospel, so as to "respond to the perennial questions which people ask about this present life and the life to come, and about the relationship of the one to the other."[176] It is necessary, therefore, to be open to the interior promptings of the Holy Spirit, who invites us to understand in depth the designs of Providence. He calls consecrated men and women to present new answers to the new problems of today's world. These are divine pleas which only souls accustomed to following God's will in everything can assimilate faithfully and then translate courageously into choices which are consistent with the original charism and which correspond to the demands of the concrete historical situation.

73.3 Faced with the many and pressing problems which sometimes seem to compromise or even overwhelm the consecrated life, those called to it cannot fail to feel the commitment to bear in their hearts and in their prayer the entire world's needs, while at the same time they work with zeal in the fields determined by the founding charism. Clearly, their dedication must be guided by *supernatural discernment,* which distinguishes what is of the Spirit from that which is contrary to him (cf. Gal 5:16-17, 22; 1 Jn 4:6). By means of fidelity to the Rules and Constitutions, this discernment safeguards full communion with the Church.[177]

73.4 In this way the consecrated life will not be limited to reading the signs of the times but will also contribute to elaborating and putting into effect *new initiatives of evangelization* for present-day situations. All this will be done in the certainty of faith that the Spirit can give satisfactory replies even to the most difficult questions. In this regard, we would do well to remember what the great champions of apostolic activity have always taught, namely, that we need to trust in God as if everything depended on him and, at the same time, to work generously as if everything depended on us.

[175] Cf. *Propositio* 35, A.

[176] Second Vatican Ecumenical Council, Pastoral Constitution on the Church in the Modern World *Gaudium et Spes,* 4.

[177] Cf. Second Vatican Ecumenical Council, Dogmatic Constitution on the Church *Lumen Gentium,* 12.

Ecclesial cooperation and apostolic spirituality

74.1 Everything must be done *in communion and dialogue* with all other sectors of the Church. The challenges of evangelization are such that they cannot be effectively faced without the cooperation, both in discernment and action, of all the Church's members. It is difficult for individuals to provide a definitive answer; but such an answer can arise from encounter and dialogue. In particular, effective communion among those graced with different charisms will ensure both mutual enrichment and more fruitful results in the mission in hand. The experience of recent years widely confirms that "dialogue is the new name of charity,"[178] especially charity within the Church. Dialogue helps us to see the true implications of problems and allows them to be addressed with greater hope of success. The consecrated life, by the very fact that it promotes the value of fraternal life, provides a privileged experience of dialogue. It can therefore contribute to creating a climate of mutual acceptance in which the Church's various components, feeling that they are valued for what they are, come together in ecclesial communion in a more convinced manner, ready to undertake the great universal mission.

74.2 Institutes involved in one or other form of the apostolate must therefore foster *a solid spirituality of action,* seeing God in all things and all things in God. In fact, "it is necessary to know that, just as a well-ordered life tends to pass from the active to the contemplative, so the soul generally returns with profit from the contemplative life to the active life, in order more perfectly to sustain the active life with the flame ignited in contemplation. Thus, the active life ought to lead to contemplation and, sometimes, from what we see interiorly, contemplation should more effectively call us back to action."[179] Jesus himself gave us the perfect example of how we can link communion with the Father to an intensely active life. Without a constant search for this unity, the danger of an interior breakdown, of confusion and discouragement, lurks always near. Today as yesterday, the close union between contemplation and action will allow the most difficult missions to be undertaken.

1. Love to the End

Loving with the heart of Christ

75.1 "Having loved his own who were in the world, he loved them to the end. And during supper ... Jesus rose ... and began to wash the disciples'

---

[178] Paul VI, Encyclical Letter *Ecclesiam Suam* (August 6, 1964), III: *AAS* 56 (1964), 639.

[179] Saint Gregory the Great, *Homilies on Ezekiel,* Book II, II, 11: *PL* 76, 954-955.

feet, and to wipe them with the towel with which he was girded" (Jn 13:1-2, 4-5).

75.2 In the washing of feet Jesus reveals the depth of God's love for humanity: in Jesus, God places himself at the service of human beings! At the same time, he reveals the meaning of the Christian life and, even more, of the consecrated life, which is a *life of self-giving love,* of practical and generous service. In its commitment to following the Son of Man, who "came not to be served but to serve" (Mt 20:28), the consecrated life, at least in the best periods of its long history, has been characterized by this "washing of feet," that is, by service directed in particular to the poorest and neediest. If, on the one hand, the consecrated life contemplates the sublime mystery of the Word in the bosom of the Father (cf. Jn 1:1), on the other hand it follows the Word who became flesh (cf. Jn 1:14), lowering himself, humbling himself in order to serve others. Even today, those who follow Christ on the path of the evangelical counsels intend to go where Christ went and to do what he did.

75.3 He continually calls new disciples to himself, both men and women, to communicate to them, by an outpouring of the Spirit (cf. Rom 5:5), the divine *agape,* his way of loving, and to urge them thus to serve others in the humble gift of themselves, far from all self-interest. Peter, overcome by the light of the Transfiguration, exclaims: "Lord, it is well that we are here" (Mt 17:4), but he is invited to return to the byways of the world in order to continue serving the Kingdom of God: "Come down, Peter! You wanted to rest up on the mountain: come down. Preach the word of God, be insistent both when it is timely and when it is not; reprove, exhort, give encouragement using all your forbearance and ability to teach. Work, spend yourself, accept even sufferings and torments, in order that, through the brightness and beauty of good works, you may possess in charity what is symbolized in the Lord's white garments."[180] The fact that consecrated persons fix their gaze on the Lord's countenance does not diminish their commitment on behalf of humanity; on the contrary, it strengthens this commitment, enabling it to have an impact on history, in order to free history from all that disfigures it.

75.4 The quest for divine beauty impels consecrated persons to care for the deformed image of God on the faces of their brothers and sisters, faces disfigured by hunger, faces disillusioned by political promises, faces humiliated by seeing their culture despised, faces frightened by constant and indiscriminate violence, the anguished faces of minors, the hurt and humiliated faces of women, the tired faces of migrants who are not given a warm wel-

---

[180] Saint Augustine, *Sermo* 78, 6: *PL* 38, 492.

come, the faces of the elderly who are without even the minimum conditions for a dignified life.[181] The consecrated life thus shows, with the eloquence of works, that divine charity is the foundation and stimulus of freely-given and active love. Saint Vincent de Paul was deeply convinced of this when he explained to the Daughters of Charity this program of life: "The spirit of the Society consists in giving yourselves to God in order to love our Lord and to serve him in the person of the materially and spiritually poor, in their houses and elsewhere, in order to teach poor young girls, children, in general anybody whom divine Providence sends you."[182]

75.5 Today, among the possible works of charity, certainly the one which in a special way shows the world this love "to the end" is the fervent proclamation of Jesus Christ to those who do not yet know him, to those who have forgotten him, and to the poor in a preferential way.

The specific contribution of the consecrated life to evangelization

76 The specific contribution of consecrated persons, both men and women, to evangelization is first of all the witness of a life given totally to God and to their brothers and sisters, in imitation of the Savior who, out of love for humanity, made himself a servant. In the work of salvation, in fact, everything comes from sharing in the divine *agape.* Consecrated persons make visible, in their consecration and total dedication, the loving and saving presence of Christ, the One consecrated by the Father, sent in mission.[183] Allowing themselves to be won over by him (cf. Phil 3:12), they prepare to become, in a certain way, a prolongation of his humanity.[184] The consecrated life eloquently shows that the more one lives in Christ, the better one can serve him in others, going even to the furthest missionary outposts and facing the greatest dangers.[185]

---

[181] Cf. Fourth General Conference of the Latin American Episcopate, *New Evangelization, Human Promotion and Christian Culture* (CELAM, 1992), 178.

[182] Conference "On the Spirit of the Society" (February 9, 1653): *Correspondance, Entretiens, Documents,* ed. Coste, Volume IX (Paris, 1923), 592.

[183] Cf. Congregation for Religious and Secular Institutes, Instruction on the Essential Elements in the Church's Teaching on Religious Life as Applied to Institutes Dedicated to Works of the Apostolate (May 31, 1983), 23-24: *L'Osservatore Romano* (English-language edition), July 18, 1983, 5.

[184] Cf. Blessed Elizabeth of the Trinity, *O mon Dieu, Trinité que j'adore:* Oeuvres Complètes (Paris, 1991), 199-200.

[185] Cf. Paul VI, Apostolic Exhortation *Evangelii Nuntiandi* (December 8, 1975), 69: *AAS* 68 (1976), 59.

The first evangelization: proclaiming Christ to the nations

77 Those who love God, the Father of all, cannot fail to love their fellow human beings, whom they recognize as brothers and sisters. Precisely for this reason, they cannot remain indifferent to the fact that many men and women do not know the full manifestation of God's love in Christ. The result, in obedience to Christ's commandment, is the missionary drive *ad gentes,* which every committed Christian shares with the Church which is missionary by nature. This drive is felt above all by the members of Institutes, whether of the contemplative or of the active life.[186] Consecrated persons, in fact, have the task of making present even among non-Christians[187] Christ who is chaste, poor, obedient, prayerful and missionary.[188] While remaining ever faithful to their charism, they must know that they have a special share in the Church's missionary activity, in virtue of their interior consecration made to God.[189] The desire so often expressed by Thérèse of Lisieux, "to love you and make you loved," the ardent longing of Saint Francis Xavier that many, "meditating on what the Lord God will expect from them and from the talents he has given them, would be converted, using the right means and the spiritual exercises to know and feel within themselves the divine will, and so, adapting themselves more to that will than to their own inclinations, they would say, 'Lord, here I am, what do you want me to do? Lead me wherever you will,' "[190] and other similar testimonies of countless holy men and women, manifest the unsuppressible missionary drive which distinguishes and ennobles the consecrated life.

Present in every part of the world

78.1 "The love of Christ impels us" (2 Cor 5:14): the members of every Institute should be able to repeat this truth with Saint Paul, because the task of the consecrated life is to work in every part of the world in order to consolidate and expand the Kingdom of Christ, bringing the proclamation of the

---

[186] Cf. *Propositio* 37, A.

[187] Cf. Second Vatican Ecumenical Council, Dogmatic Constitution on the Church *Lumen Gentium,* 46; Paul VI, Apostolic Exhortation *Evangelii Nuntiandi* (December 8, 1975), 69: *AAS* 68 (1976), 59.

[188] Cf. Second Vatican Ecumenical Council, Dogmatic Constitution on the Church *Lumen Gentium,* 44, 46.

[189] Cf. Second Vatican Ecumenical Council, Decree on the Church's Missionary Activity *Ad Gentes,* 18, 40.

[190] Letter from Cochin to Members of the Society in Rome (January 15, 1544): *Monumenta Historica Societatis Iesu* 67 (1944), 166-167.

Gospel even to the most far-off regions.[191] In fact, the history of the missions testifies to the great contribution made by consecrated men and women to the evangelization of peoples: from ancient monastic Families to recent Foundations committed exclusively to the mission *ad gentes,* from Institutes of active life to those devoted to contemplation.[192] Countless consecrated persons have given their whole lives in this primary activity of the Church, which is "essential and never-ending"[193] because it is addressed to the growing number of those who do not know Christ.

78.2 Today too this duty continues to present a pressing call to Institutes of Consecrated Life and Societies of Apostolic Life: they are expected to make the greatest possible contribution to the proclamation of the Gospel of Christ. Also those Institutes which are being established and are at work in the younger Churches are invited to open themselves to the mission among non-Christians, inside and outside their own countries of origin. Despite the understandable difficulties which some of them will meet, it is good to remind everyone that just as "faith is strengthened when it is given to others,"[194] so the mission strengthens the consecrated life, gives it new enthusiasm and new motivation, and elicits faithfulness. For its part, missionary activity offers ample room for all the different forms of the consecrated life.

78.3 The Church's mission *ad gentes* offers consecrated women, religious brothers and members of Secular Institutes special and extraordinary opportunities for a particularly fruitful apostolate. The members of Secular Institutes, by their presence in fields more suited to the lay vocation, can engage in the valuable work of evangelizing all sectors of society, as well as the structures and the very laws which regulate it. Moreover, they can bear witness to Gospel values, living in contact with those who do not yet know Jesus, thus making a specific contribution to the mission.

78.4 It should be emphasized that in countries where non-Christian religions are firmly established, the presence of the consecrated life is of great importance, whether through its educational, charitable and cultural activities, or through the witness of the contemplative life. For this reason the establishment of communities devoted to contemplation should be encouraged

---

[191] Cf. Second Vatican Ecumenical Council, Dogmatic Constitution on the Church *Lumen Gentium,* 44.

[192] Cf. John Paul II, Encyclical Letter *Redemptoris Missio* (December 7, 1990), 69: *AAS* 83 (1991), 317-318; *Catechism of the Catholic Church,* No. 927.

[193] John Paul II, Encyclical Letter *Redemptoris Missio* (December 7, 1990), 31: *AAS* 83 (1991), 277.

[194] Ibid., 2: loc. cit., 251.

in the new Churches, since "the contemplative life belongs to the fullness of the Church's presence."[195] It is necessary, then, to use appropriate means to foster an equitable distribution of the various forms of the consecrated life in order to give new momentum to evangelization, either by sending missionaries or by Institutes of Consecrated Life giving special help to poorer Dioceses.[196]

The proclamation of Christ and inculturation

79.1 The proclamation of Christ "is the permanent priority of mission"[197] and is directed toward conversion, that is, to full and sincere allegiance to Christ and his Gospel.[198] In the context of missionary activity the process of inculturation and interreligious dialogue have a role to play. The challenge of inculturation ought to be taken up by consecrated persons as a call to fruitful cooperation with grace in facing cultural diversity. This presupposes serious personal preparation, mature gifts of discernment, faithful adherence to the indispensable criteria of doctrinal orthodoxy, moral integrity and ecclesial communion.[199] Supported by the charism of their founders and foundresses, many consecrated persons have been able to approach cultures other than their own with the attitude of Jesus, who "emptied himself, taking the form of a servant" (Phil 2:7). With patient and courageous efforts to initiate dialogue, they have been successful in establishing contact with the most diverse peoples, proclaiming to all of them the way of salvation. Today too, many consecrated persons are looking for and are finding in the history of individuals and of entire peoples the traces of God's presence, a presence guiding all humanity toward the discernment of the signs of his saving will. Such a search proves to be advantageous for consecrated persons themselves: the values discovered in the different civilizations can in fact prompt them to deepen their own understanding of the Christian tradition of contemplation, community sharing, hospitality, respect for persons and attention to the environment.

79.2 A genuine inculturation requires attitudes similar to those of the Lord when he became man and walked among us in love and meekness. In this sense the consecrated life makes its members particularly well suited to face

---

[195] Second Vatican Ecumenical Council, Decree on the Church's Missionary Activity *Ad Gentes,* 18; cf. John Paul II, Encyclical Letter *Redemptoris Missio* (December 7, 1990), 69: *AAS* 83 (1991), 317-318.

[196] Cf. *Propositio* 38.

[197] John Paul II, Encyclical Letter *Redemptoris Missio* (December 7, 1990), 44: *AAS* 83 (1991), 290.

[198] Cf. ibid., 46: loc. cit., 292.

[199] Cf. ibid., 52-54: loc. cit., 299-302.

the complex work of inculturation, because it accustoms them to being detached from things, even from many features of their own culture. Applying themselves with these attitudes to the study and understanding of other cultures, consecrated persons can better discern the real values in them, and the best way to accept them and perfect them with the help of their own charism.[200] However, it should not be forgotten that in many ancient cultures religious expression is so deeply ingrained that religion often represents the transcendent dimension of the culture itself. In this case true inculturation necessarily entails a serious and open interreligious dialogue, which "is not in opposition to the mission *ad gentes*" and "does not dispense from evangelization."[201]

The inculturation of the consecrated life

80.1 For its part, the consecrated life itself is the bearer of Gospel values and, where it is authentically lived, it can make an innovative contribution in meeting the challenges of inculturation. As a sign of the primacy of God and his Kingdom, it can, through dialogue, elicit a positive reaction in people's consciences. If the consecrated life maintains its prophetic impact, it serves as a Gospel leaven within a culture, purifying and perfecting it. This is demonstrated by the lives of many saints who in different periods of history were able to immerse themselves in their time without being overcome by it, but opening new paths to the people of their generation. The Gospel way of life is an important source for proposing a new cultural model. A great many founders and foundresses, perceiving certain needs of their time, with all the limitations which they themselves recognized, have given these needs an answer which has become an innovative cultural proposal.

80.2 Communities of Religious Institutes and of Societies of Apostolic Life can, in fact, offer concrete and effective cultural proposals when they bear witness to the evangelical manner of practicing mutual acceptance in diversity and of exercising authority, and when they give an example of sharing material and spiritual goods, of being truly international, of cooperating with other Institutes, and of listening to the men and women of our time. The manner of thinking and acting of those who follow Christ more closely gives rise to *a true and proper point of reference for culture;* it serves to point out all that is inhuman; it bears witness that God alone strengthens and perfects

---

[200] Cf. *Propositio* 40, A.

[201] John Paul II, Encyclical Letter *Redemptoris Missio* (December 7, 1990), 55: *AAS* 83 (1991), 302; cf. Pontifical Council for Interreligious Dialogue and Congregation for the Evangelization of Peoples, Instruction *Dialogue and Proclamation: Reflections and Perspectives* (May 19, 1991), 45-46: *AAS* 84 (1992), 429-430.

values. In turn, a genuine inculturation will help consecrated persons to live the radical nature of the Gospel according to the charism of their Institute and the character of the people with whom they come into contact. This fruitful relationship can give rise to ways of life and pastoral approaches which can bring enrichment to the whole Institute, provided that they are consistent with the founding charism and with the unifying action of the Holy Spirit. In this process, which entails discernment, courage, dialogue and the challenge of the Gospel, a guarantee of being on the right path is offered by the Holy See, whose task it is to encourage the evangelization of cultures, as well as to authenticate developments and to sanction results in the area of inculturation.[202] This is "a difficult and delicate task, since it raises the question of the Church's fidelity to the Gospel and the apostolic Tradition amidst the constant evolution of cultures."[203]

The new evangelization

81.1 If the great challenges which modern history poses to the new evangelization are to be faced successfully, what is needed above all is a consecrated life which is continually open to challenge by the revealed word and the signs of the times.[204] The memory of the great evangelizers, both men and women, who were themselves profoundly evangelized, shows that in order to face the world of today it is necessary to have people who are lovingly dedicated to the Lord and his Gospel. "Consecrated persons, because of their specific vocation, are called to manifest the unity between self-evangelization and witness, between interior renewal and apostolic fervor, between being and acting, showing that dynamism arises always from the first element of each of these pairs."[205]

81.2 The new evangelization, like that of all times, will be effective if it proclaims from the rooftops what it has first lived in intimacy with the Lord. It calls for strong personalities, inspired by saintly fervor. The new evangelization demands that consecrated persons have *a thorough awareness of the theological significance of the challenges of our time.* These challenges must be weighed with careful joint discernment, with a view to renewing the mission.

---

[202] Cf. *Propositio* 40, B.

[203] John Paul II, Post-Synodal Apostolic Exhortation *Ecclesia in Africa* (September 14, 1995), 62: *AAS* 88 (1996), 39.

[204] Cf. Paul VI, Apostolic Exhortation *Evangelii Nuntiandi* (December 8, 1975), 15: *AAS* 68 (1976), 13-15.

[205] Synod of Bishops, Ninth Ordinary General Assembly, *Relatio ante Disceptationem,* 22: *L'Osservatore Romano* (English-language edition), October 12, 1994, 12.

Courage in proclaiming the Lord Jesus must be accompanied by trust in Providence, which is at work in the world and which "orders everything, even human differences, for the greater good of the Church."[206]

81.3 Important elements enabling Institutes to play a successful part in the new evangelization are fidelity to the founding charism, communion with all those who in the Church are involved in the same undertaking, especially the Bishops, and cooperation with all people of good will. All this requires a careful discernment of the calls which the Holy Spirit makes to each Institute, whether in areas where no great immediate progress is foreseen or in other areas where a consoling rebirth is anticipated. In every place and circumstance, consecrated persons should be zealous heralds of Jesus Christ, ready to respond with the wisdom of the Gospel to the questions posed today by the anxieties and the urgent needs of the human heart.

Preference for the poor and the promotion of justice

82.1 At the beginning of his ministry, in the synagogue at Nazareth, Jesus announces that the Spirit has consecrated him to preach good news to the poor, to proclaim release to captives, to give sight back to the blind, to set the oppressed free, to declare a year of favor from the Lord (cf. Lk 4:16-19). Taking up the Lord's mission as her own, the Church proclaims the Gospel to every man and woman, committing herself to their integral salvation. But with special attention, in a true "preferential option," she turns to those who are *in situations of greater weakness,* and therefore in greater need. "The poor," in varied states of affliction, are the oppressed, those on the margin of society, the elderly, the sick, the young, any and all who are considered and treated as "the least."

82.2 The option for the poor is inherent in the very structure of love lived in Christ. All of Christ's disciples are therefore held to this option; but those who wish to follow the Lord more closely, imitating his attitudes, cannot but feel involved in a very special way. The sincerity of their response to Christ's love will lead them to live a life of poverty and to embrace the cause of the poor. For each Institute, according to its charism, this involves *adopting a simple and austere way of life,* both as individuals and as a community. Strengthened by this living witness and in ways consistent with their choice of life, and maintaining their independence vis-à-vis political ideologies, consecrated persons will be able to denounce the injustices committed against so many sons and daughters of God, and commit themselves to the promotion of

---

[206] John XXIII, Opening Address to the Second Vatican Ecumenical Council (October 11, 1962): *AAS* 54 (1962), 789.

justice in the society where they work.[207] In this way, even in present circumstances, through the witness of countless consecrated persons, there will be a renewal of that dedication which was characteristic of the founders and foundresses who spent their lives serving the Lord in the poor. Christ "is poor on earth in the person of his poor. . . . As God he is rich, as man he is poor. With his humanity he has gone up to heaven and, prosperous, is seated at the right hand of the Father, and yet, here on earth, still poor, he suffers hunger, thirst and nakedness."[208]

82.3 The Gospel is made effective through charity, which is the Church's glory and the sign of her faithfulness to the Lord. This is demonstrated by the whole history of the consecrated life, which can be considered a living exegesis of Jesus' words: "As you did it to one of the least of these my brethren, you did it to me" (Mt 25:40). Many Institutes, especially in modern times, were established precisely to address one or other of the needs of the poor. But even when such a purpose was not the determining factor, concern and care for the needy — expressed in prayer, assistance and hospitality — was always a normal part of every form of the consecrated life, even of the contemplative life. And how could it be otherwise, since the Christ encountered in contemplation is the same who lives and suffers in the poor? In this sense, the history of the consecrated life is rich with marvelous and sometimes ingenious examples. Saint Paulinus of Nola, after distributing his belongings to the poor in order to consecrate himself fully to God, built the cells of his monastery above a hospice for the poor. He rejoiced at the thought of this singular "exchange of gifts": the poor, whom he helped, strengthened with their prayers the very "foundations" of his house, wholly dedicated to the praise of God.[209] Saint Vincent de Paul, for his part, loved to say that, when one is obliged to leave prayer to attend to a poor person in need, that prayer is not really interrupted, because "one leaves God to serve God."[210]

82.4 Serving the poor is an act of evangelization and, at the same time, a seal of Gospel authenticity and a catalyst for permanent conversion in the consecrated life, since, as Saint Gregory the Great says, "when charity lovingly stoops to provide even for the smallest needs of our neighbor, then does it suddenly surge upwards to the highest peaks. And when in great kindness

---

[207] Cf. *Propositio* 18.

[208] Saint Augustine, *Sermo* 123, 3-4: *PL* 38, 685-686.

[209] Cf. Poem XXI, 386-394: *PL* 61, 587.

[210] Conference "On the Rules" (May 30, 1647): *Correspondance, Entretiens, Documents*, ed. Coste, Volume IX (Paris, 1923), 319.

it bends to the most extreme needs, then with much vigor does it resume its soaring to the heights."[211]

Care of the sick

83.1 Following a glorious tradition, a great number of consecrated persons, above all women, carry out their apostolate in the field of health care, according to the charism of their respective Institutes. Down the centuries, many consecrated persons *have given their lives* in service to victims of contagious diseases, confirming the truth that dedication to the point of heroism belongs to the prophetic nature of the consecrated life.

83.2 The Church looks with admiration and gratitude upon the many consecrated persons who, by caring for the sick and the suffering, contribute in a significant way to her mission. They carry on the ministry of mercy of Christ, who "went about doing good and healing all" (Acts 10:38). In the footsteps of the Divine Samaritan, physician of souls and bodies,[212] and following the example of their respective founders and foundresses, those consecrated persons committed to this ministry by the charism of their Institute should persevere in their witness of love toward the sick, devoting themselves to them with profound understanding and compassion. They should give a special place in their ministry to the poorest and most abandoned of the sick, such as the elderly, and those who are handicapped, marginalized, or terminally ill, and to the victims of drug abuse and new contagious diseases. Consecrated persons should encourage the sick themselves to offer their sufferings in communion with Christ, crucified and glorified for the salvation of all.[213] Indeed they should strengthen in the sick the awareness of being able to *carry out a pastoral ministry of their own* through the specific charism of the Cross, by means of their prayer and their testimony in word and deed.[214]

83.3 Moreover, the Church reminds consecrated men and women that a part of their mission is *to evangelize the health-care centers* in which they work, striving to spread the light of Gospel values to the way of living, suffering and dying of the people of our day. They should endeavor to make the practice of medicine more human, and increase their knowledge of bioethics

---

[211] Saint Gregory the Great, *The Pastoral Rule* 2, 5: *PL* 77, 33.

[212] Cf. John Paul II, Apostolic Letter *Salvifici Doloris* (February 11, 1984), 28-30: *AAS* 76 (1984), 242-248.

[213] Cf. ibid., 18: loc. cit., 221-224; John Paul II, Post-Synodal Apostolic Exhortation *Christifideles Laici* (December 30, 1988), 52-53: *AAS* 81 (1989), 496-500.

[214] Cf. John Paul II, Post-Synodal Apostolic Exhortation *Pastores Dabo Vobis* (March 25, 1992), 77: *AAS* 84 (1992), 794-795.

at the service of the Gospel of life. Above all therefore they should respect for the person and for human life from conception to its natural end, in full conformity with the moral teaching of the Church.[215] For this purpose they should set up centers of formation[216] and cooperate closely with those ecclesial bodies entrusted with the pastoral ministry of health care.

2. A Prophetic Witness in the Face of Great Challenges

The prophetic character of the consecrated life

84.1 The prophetic character of the consecrated life was strongly emphasized by the Synod Fathers. It takes the shape of *a special form of sharing in Christ's prophetic office,* which the Holy Spirit communicates to the whole People of God. There is a prophetic dimension which belongs to the consecrated life as such, resulting from the radical nature of the following of Christ and of the subsequent dedication to the mission characteristic of the consecrated life. The sign value, which the Second Vatican Council acknowledges in the consecrated life,[217] is expressed in prophetic witness to the primacy which God and the truths of the Gospel have in the Christian life. Because of this preeminence nothing can come before personal love of Christ and of the poor in whom he lives.[218]

84.2 The patristic tradition has seen a model of monastic religious life in Elijah, courageous prophet and friend of God.[219] He lived in God's presence and contemplated his passing by in silence; he interceded for the people and boldly announced God's will; he defended God's sovereignty and came to the defense of the poor against the powerful of the world (cf. 1 Kg 18-19). In the history of the Church, alongside other Christians, there have been men and women consecrated to God who, through a special gift of the Holy Spirit, have carried out a genuinely prophetic ministry, speaking in the name of God to all, even to the Pastors of the Church. *True prophecy is born of God,* from friendship with him, from attentive listening to his word in the different circumstances of history. Prophets feel in their hearts a burning desire for the holiness of God and, having heard his word in the dialogue of prayer,

---

[215] Cf. John Paul II, Encyclical Letter *Evangelium Vitae* (March 25, 1995), 78-101: *AAS* 87 (1995), 490-518.

[216] Cf. *Propositio* 43.

[217] Cf. Dogmatic Constitution on the Church *Lumen Gentium*, 44.

[218] Cf. John Paul II, Homily at the Closing Liturgy of the Synod of Bishops, Ninth Ordinary General Assembly (October 29, 1994), 3: *AAS* 87 (1995), 580.

[219] Cf. Saint Athanasius, *Life of Saint Anthony*, 7: *PG* 26, 854.

they proclaim that word with their lives, with their lips and with their actions, becoming people who speak for God against evil and sin. Prophetic witness requires the constant and passionate search for God's will, for self-giving, for unfailing communion in the Church, for the practice of spiritual discernment and love of the truth. It is also expressed through the denunciation of all that is contrary to the divine will and through the exploration of new ways to apply the Gospel in history, in expectation of the coming of God's Kingdom.[220]

Significance for the contemporary world

85.1 In our world, where it often seems that the signs of God's presence have been lost from sight, a convincing prophetic witness on the part of consecrated persons is increasingly necessary. In the first place this should entail *the affirmation of the primacy of God and of eternal life,* as evidenced in the following and imitation of the chaste, poor and obedient Christ, who was completely consecrated to the glory of God and to the love of his brethren. The fraternal life is itself prophetic in a society which, sometimes without realizing it, has a profound yearning for a brotherhood which knows no borders. Consecrated persons are being asked to bear witness everywhere with the boldness of a prophet who is unafraid of risking even his life.

85.2 Prophecy derives a particularly persuasive power from *consistency between proclamation and life.* Consecrated persons will be faithful to their mission in the Church and the world, if they can renew themselves constantly in the light of the word of God.[221] Thus will they be able to enrich the other faithful with the charismatic gifts they have received and, in turn, let themselves be challenged by the prophetic stimulus which comes from other sectors of the Church. In this exchange of gifts, guaranteed by *full harmony with the Church's Magisterium and discipline,* there will shine forth the action of the Holy Spirit who "gives [the Church] a unity of fellowship and service; he furnishes and directs her with various gifts, both hierarchical and charismatic."[222]

Faithfulness to the point of martyrdom

86.1 In this century, as in other periods of history, consecrated men and women have borne witness to Christ the Lord *with the gift of their own lives.*

---

[220] Cf. *Propositio* 39, A.

[221] Cf. *Propositiones* 15, A and 39, C.

[222] Second Vatican Ecumenical Council, Dogmatic Constitution on the Church *Lumen Gentium,* 4; cf. Decree on the Ministry and Life of Priests *Presbyterorum Ordinis,* 2.

Thousands of them have been forced into the catacombs by the persecution of totalitarian regimes or of violent groups, or have been harassed while engaged in missionary activity, in action on behalf of the poor, in assisting the sick and the marginalized; yet they lived and continue to live their consecration in prolonged and heroic suffering, and often with the shedding of their blood, being perfectly configured to the crucified Lord. The Church has already officially recognized the holiness of some of these men and women, honoring them as martyrs for Christ. They enlighten us by their example, they intercede that we may be faithful, and they await us in glory.

86.2 There is a widespread desire that the memory of so many witnesses to the faith will remain in the consciousness of the Church as an invitation to celebrate and imitate them. The Institutes of Consecrated Life and the Societies of Apostolic Life can contribute to this endeavor by *gathering the names* of all those consecrated persons who deserve to be inscribed in the Martyrology of the twentieth century, and by *compiling testimonies about them.*[223]

The major challenges facing the consecrated life

87 The prophetic task of the consecrated life is brought into play by *three major challenges* addressed to the Church herself: they are the same challenges as ever, posed in new ways, and perhaps more radically, by contemporary society, at least in some parts of the world. These challenges relate directly to the evangelical counsels of chastity, poverty and obedience, impelling the Church, and consecrated persons in particular, to clarify and testify to the *profound anthropological significance* of the counsels. The decision to follow the counsels, far from involving an impoverishment of truly human values, leads instead to their transformation. The evangelical counsels should not be considered as a denial of the values inherent in sexuality, in the legitimate desire to possess material goods or to make decisions for oneself. Insofar as these inclinations are based on nature, they are good in themselves. Human beings, however, weakened as they are by original sin, run the risk of acting on them in a way which transgresses the moral norms. The profession of chastity, poverty and obedience is a warning not to underestimate the wound of original sin and, while affirming the value of created goods, it *relativizes them* by pointing to God as the absolute good. Thus, while those who follow the evangelical counsels seek holiness for themselves, they propose, so to

---

[223] Cf. *Propositio* 53; John Paul II, Apostolic Letter *Tertio Millennio Adveniente* (November 10, 1994), 37: *AAS* 87 (1995), 29-30.

speak, a spiritual "therapy" for humanity, because they reject the idolatry of anything created and in a certain way they make visible the living God. The consecrated life, especially in difficult times, is a blessing for human life and for the life of the Church.

The challenge of consecrated chastity

88.1 The *first challenge* is that of a *hedonistic culture* which separates sexuality from all objective moral norms, often treating it as a mere diversion and a consumer good and, with the complicity of the means of social communication, justifying a kind of idolatry of the sexual instinct. The consequences of this are before everyone's eyes: transgressions of every kind, with resulting psychic and moral suffering on the part of individuals and families. The *reply* of the consecrated life is above all in the *joyful living of perfect chastity,* as a witness to the power of God's love manifested in the weakness of the human condition. The consecrated person attests that what many have believed impossible becomes, with the Lord's grace, possible and truly liberating. Yes, in Christ it is possible to love God with all one's heart, putting him above every other love, and thus to love every creature with the freedom of God! This testimony is more necessary than ever today, precisely because it is so little understood by our world. It is offered to everyone — young people, engaged couples, husbands and wives and Christian families — in order to show that *the power of God's love can accomplish great things* precisely within the context of human love. It is a witness which also meets a growing need for interior honesty in human relationships.

88.2 The consecrated life must present to today's world examples of chastity lived by men and women who show balance, self-mastery, an enterprising spirit, and psychological and affective maturity.[224] Thanks to this witness, human love is offered a stable point of reference: the pure love which consecrated persons draw from the contemplation of Trinitarian love, revealed to us in Christ. Precisely because they are immersed in this mystery, consecrated persons feel themselves capable of a radical and universal love, which gives them the strength for the self-mastery and discipline necessary in order not to fall under the domination of the senses and instincts. Consecrated chastity thus appears as a joyful and liberating experience. Enlightened by faith in the risen Lord and by the prospect of the new heavens and the new earth (cf. Rev 21:1), it offers a priceless incentive in the task of educating to that chastity which corresponds to other states of life as well.

---

[224] Cf. Second Vatican Ecumenical Council, Decree on the Appropriate Renewal of the Religious Life *Perfectae Caritatis,* 12.

The challenge of poverty

89 *Another challenge* today is that of a *materialism which craves possessions,* heedless of the needs and sufferings of the weakest, and lacking any concern for the balance of natural resources. The *reply* of the consecrated life is found in the profession of *evangelical poverty,* which can be lived in different ways and is often expressed in an active involvement in the promotion of solidarity and charity. How many Institutes devote themselves to education, training and professional formation, preparing young people and those no longer young to become builders of their own future! How many consecrated persons give themselves without reserve in service of the most disadvantaged people on earth! How many of them work to train future educators and leaders of society, so that they in turn will be committed to eliminating structures of oppression and to promoting projects of solidarity for the benefit of the poor! Consecrated persons fight to overcome hunger and its causes; they inspire the activities of voluntary associations and humanitarian organizations; and they work with public and private bodies to promote a fair distribution of international aid. Nations truly owe a great deal to these enterprising agents of charity, whose tireless generosity has contributed and continues to contribute greatly to making the world more human.

Evangelical poverty at the service of the poor

90.1 Even before being a service on behalf of the poor, *evangelical poverty is a value in itself,* since it recalls the first of the Beatitudes in the imitation of the poor Christ.[225] Its primary meaning, in fact, is to attest that God is the true wealth of the human heart. Precisely for this reason evangelical poverty forcefully challenges the idolatry of money, making a prophetic appeal as it were to society, which in so many parts of the developed world risks losing the sense of proportion and the very meaning of things. Thus, today more than in other ages, the call of evangelical poverty is being felt also among those who are aware of the scarcity of the planet's resources and who invoke respect for and the conservation of creation by reducing consumption, by living more simply and by placing a necessary brake on their own desires.

90.2 Consecrated persons are therefore asked to bear a renewed and vigorous evangelical witness to self-denial and restraint, in a form of fraternal life inspired by principles of simplicity and hospitality, also as an example to those who are indifferent to the needs of their neighbor. This witness will of course be accompanied by *a preferential love for the poor* and will be shown especially by sharing the conditions of life of the most neglected. There are

[225] Cf. *Propositio* 18, A.

many communities which live and work among the poor and the marginalized; they embrace their conditions of life and share in their sufferings, problems and perils.

90.3 Outstanding pages in the history of evangelical solidarity and heroic dedication have been written by consecrated persons in these years of profound changes and great injustices, of hopes and disappointments, of striking victories and bitter defeats. And pages no less significant have been written and are still being written by very many other consecrated persons, who live to the full their life "hid with Christ in God" (Col 3:3) for the salvation of the world, freely giving of themselves, and spending their lives for causes which are little appreciated and even less extolled. In these various and complementary ways, the consecrated life shares in the radical poverty embraced by the Lord, and fulfills its specific role in the saving mystery of his Incarnation and redeeming Death.[226]

The challenge of freedom in obedience

91.1 The *third challenge* comes from those *notions of freedom* which separate this fundamental human good from its essential relationship to the truth and to moral norms.[227] In effect, the promotion of freedom is a genuine value, closely connected with respect for the human person. But who does not see the aberrant consequences of injustice and even violence, in the life of individuals and of peoples, to which the distorted use of freedom leads?

91.2 An effective *response* to this situation is the *obedience which marks the consecrated life.* In an especially vigorous way this obedience reproposes the obedience of Christ to the Father and, taking this mystery as its point of departure, testifies that *there is no contradiction between obedience and freedom.* Indeed, the Son's attitude discloses the mystery of human freedom as the path of obedience to the Father's will, and the mystery of obedience as the path to the gradual conquest of true freedom. It is precisely this mystery which consecrated persons wish to acknowledge by this particular vow. By obedience they intend to show their awareness of being children of the Father, as a result of which they wish to take the Father's will as their daily bread (cf. Jn 4:34), as their rock, their joy, their shield and their fortress (cf. Ps 18:2). Thus they show that they are growing in the full truth about themselves, remaining in touch with the source of their existence and therefore offering

---

[226] Cf. Second Vatican Ecumenical Council, Decree on the Appropriate Renewal of the Religious Life *Perfectae Caritatis,* 13.

[227] Cf. John Paul II, Encyclical Letter *Veritatis Splendor* (August 6, 1993), 31-35: *AAS* 85 (1993), 1158-1162.

this most consoling message: "The lovers of your law have great peace; they never stumble" (Ps 119:165).

Carrying out together the Father's will

92.1 This testimony of consecration takes on special meaning in religious life because of *the community dimension* which marks it. The fraternal life is the privileged place in which to discern and accept God's will, and to walk together with one mind and heart. Obedience, enlivened by charity, unites the members of an Institute in the same witness and the same mission, while respecting the diversity of gifts and individual personalities. In communal life as brothers or sisters, inspired by the Holy Spirit, each individual undertakes with the others a precious dialogue aimed at discovering the Father's will, and all together recognize in the one who presides an expression of the fatherhood of God and the exercise of authority received from God, at the service of discernment and communion.[228]

92.2 Life in community is thus the particular sign, before the Church and society, of the bond which comes from the same call and the common desire — notwithstanding differences of race and origin, language and culture — to be obedient to that call. Contrary to the spirit of discord and division, authority and obedience shine like a sign of that unique fatherhood which comes from God, of the brotherhood born of the Spirit, of the interior freedom of those who put their trust in God, despite the human limitations of those who represent him. Through this obedience, which some people make their rule of life, the happiness promised by Jesus to "those who hear the word of God and keep it" (Lk 11:28) is experienced and proclaimed for the good of all. Moreover, those who obey have the guarantee of truly taking part in the mission, of following the Lord and not pursuing their own desires or wishes. In this way we can know that we are guided by the Spirit of the Lord, and sustained, even in the midst of great hardships, by his steadfast hand (cf. Acts 20:22-23).

A decisive commitment to the spiritual life

93.1 One of the concerns frequently expressed at the Synod was that the consecrated life should be nourished *from the well-spring of a sound and deep spirituality*. This is a primary requirement, inscribed in the very essence of the consecrated life by the fact that, just as every other baptized person, and indeed even more so, those who profess the evangelical counsels must aspire

---

[228] Cf. *Propositio* 19, A; Second Vatican Ecumenical Council, Decree on the Appropriate Renewal of the Religious Life *Perfectae Caritatis,* 14.

with all their strength to the perfection of charity.[229] This commitment is clearly evidenced in the many examples of holy founders and foundresses, and of so many consecrated persons who have borne faithful witness to Christ to the point of martyrdom. To tend toward holiness: this is in summary the program of every consecrated life, particularly in the perspective of its renewal on the threshold of the third millennium. The starting point of such a program lies in leaving everything behind for the sake of Christ (cf. Mt 4:18-22, 19:21, 27; Lk 5:11), preferring him above all things, in order to share fully in his Paschal Mystery.

93.2 Saint Paul understood this well when he said: "Indeed I count everything as loss because of the surpassing worth of knowing Christ Jesus my Lord . . . that I may know him and the power of his Resurrection" (Phil 3:8, 10). This is the path marked out from the beginning by the Apostles, as testified to in the Christian tradition of the East and the West: "Those who now follow Jesus, leaving everything for his sake, remind us of the Apostles who, in answer to his invitation, gave up everything. As a result, it has become traditional to speak of religious life as *apostolica vivendi forma.*"[230] The same tradition has also emphasized in the consecrated life the aspect of a particular covenant with God, indeed of a spousal covenant with Christ, of which Saint Paul was a master by his example (cf. 1 Cor 7:7) and by his teaching, proposed under the Spirit's guidance (cf. 1 Cor 7:40).

93.3 We may say that the spiritual life, understood as life in Christ or life according to the Spirit, presents itself as a path of increasing faithfulness, on which the consecrated person is guided by the Spirit and configured by him to Christ, in full communion of love and service in the Church.

93.4 All these elements, which take shape in the different forms of the consecrated life, give rise to *a specific spirituality,* that is, a concrete program of relations with God and one's surroundings, marked by specific spiritual emphases and choices of apostolate, which accentuate and re-present one or another aspect of the one mystery of Christ. When the Church approves a form of consecrated life or an Institute, she confirms that in its spiritual and apostolic charism are found all the objective requisites for achieving personal and communal perfection according to the Gospel.

93.5 The spiritual life must therefore have first place in the program of Families of the consecrated life, in such a way that every Institute and community will be a school of true evangelical spirituality. Apostolic fruitfulness, gen-

---

[229] Cf. *Propositio* 15.

[230] John Paul II, Address at the General Audience (February 8, 1995), 2: *L'Osservatore Romano* (English-language edition), February 15, 1995, 11.

erosity in love of the poor, and the ability to attract vocations among the younger generation depend on this priority and its growth in personal and communal commitment. It is precisely *the spiritual quality of the consecrated life* which can inspire the men and women of our day, who themselves are thirsty for absolute values. In this way the consecrated life will become an attractive witness.

Listening to the word of God

94.1 The word of God is the first source of all Christian spirituality. It gives rise to a personal relationship with the living God and with his saving and sanctifying will. It is for this reason that from the very beginning of Institutes of Consecrated Life, and in a special way in monasticism, what is called *lectio divina* has been held in the highest regard. By its means the word of God is brought to bear on life, on which it projects the light of that wisdom which is a gift of the Spirit. Although the whole of Sacred Scripture is "profitable for teaching" (2 Tim 3:16), and is "the pure and perennial source of spiritual life,"[231] the writings of the New Testament deserve special veneration, especially the Gospels, which are "the heart of all the Scriptures."[232] It is therefore of great benefit for consecrated persons to meditate regularly on the Gospel texts and the New Testament writings which describe the words and example of Christ and Mary and the *apostolica vivendi forma.* Founders and foundresses were inspired by these texts in accepting their vocation and in discerning the charism and mission of their Institutes.

94.2 Meditation of the Bible *in common* is of great value. When practiced according to the possibilities and circumstances of life in community, this meditation leads to a joyful sharing of the riches drawn from the word of God, thanks to which brothers or sisters grow together and help one another to make progress in the spiritual life. Indeed it would be helpful if this practice were also encouraged among other members of the People of God, priests and laity alike. This will lead, in ways proper to each person's particular gifts, to setting up schools of prayer, of spirituality and of prayerful reading of the Scriptures, in which God "speaks to people as friends (cf. Ex 33:11; Jn 15:14-15) and lives among them (cf. Bar 3:38), so that he may invite and draw them into fellowship with himself."[233]

---

[231] Second Vatican Ecumenical Council, Dogmatic Constitution on Divine Revelation *Dei Verbum,* 21; cf. Decree on the Appropriate Renewal of the Religious Life *Perfectae Caritatis,* 6.

[232] *Catechism of the Catholic Church,* No. 125; cf. Second Vatican Ecumenical Council, Dogmatic Constitution on Divine Revelation *Dei Verbum,* 18.

[233] Second Vatican Ecumenical Council, Dogmatic Constitution on Divine Revelation *Dei Verbum,* 2.

94.3 As the Church's spiritual tradition teaches, meditation on God's word, and on the mysteries of Christ in particular, gives rise to fervor in contemplation and the ardor of apostolic activity. Both in contemplative and active religious life it has always been men and women of prayer, those who truly interpret and put into practice the will of God, who do great works. From familiarity with God's word they draw the light needed for that individual and communal discernment which helps them to seek the ways of the Lord in the signs of the times. In this way they acquire *a kind of supernatural intuition,* which allows them to avoid being conformed to the mentality of this world, but rather to be renewed in their own mind, in order to discern God's will about what is good, perfect and pleasing to him (cf. Rom 12:2).

In communion with Christ

95.1 An indispensable means of effectively sustaining communion with Christ is assuredly *the Sacred Liturgy,* and especially the celebration of the Eucharist and the Liturgy of the Hours.

95.2 In the first place, the *Eucharist* "contains the Church's entire spiritual wealth, that is, Christ himself, our Passover and living bread, who, through his very flesh, made vital and vitalizing by the Holy Spirit, offers life" to the human family.[234] This is the heart of the Church's life, and also of the consecrated life. How can those who are called, through the profession of the evangelical counsels, to choose Christ as the only meaning of their lives, not desire to establish an ever more profound communion with him by sharing daily in the Sacrament which makes him present, in the sacrifice which actualizes the gift of his love on Golgotha, the banquet which nourishes and sustains God's pilgrim people? By its very nature the Eucharist is at the center of the consecrated life, both for individuals and for communities. It is the daily viaticum and source of the spiritual life for the individual and for the Institute. By means of the Eucharist all consecrated persons are called to live Christ's Paschal Mystery, uniting themselves to him by offering their own lives to the Father through the Holy Spirit. Frequent and prolonged adoration of Christ present in the Eucharist enables us in some way to relive Peter's experience at the Transfiguration: "It is well that we are here." In the celebration of the mystery of the Lord's Body and Blood, the unity and charity of those who have consecrated their lives to God are strengthened and increased.

95.3 Alongside the Eucharist, and intimately connected with it, the *Liturgy of the Hours,* celebrated in union with the prayer of the Church, either in

---

[234] Second Vatican Ecumenical Council, Decree on the Life and Ministry of Priests *Presbyterorum Ordinis,* 5.

community or individually according to the nature of each Institute, expresses the call proper to consecrated persons to raise their hearts in praise and intercession.

95.4 The Eucharist is also closely connected with the commitment to continual conversion and necessary purification which consecrated persons bring to maturity in the *Sacrament of Reconciliation.* By their frequent encounter with God's mercy, they purify and renew their hearts, and through the humble recognition of their sins achieve openness in their relationship with him. The joyful experience of sacramental forgiveness, on the journey shared with one's brothers and sisters, makes the heart eager to learn and encourages growth in faithfulness.

95.5 Confident and humble recourse to *spiritual direction* is of great help on the path of fidelity to the Gospel, especially in the period of formation and at certain other times in life. Through it individuals are helped to respond with generosity to the movements of the Spirit, and to direct themselves resolutely toward holiness.

95.6 Finally, I exhort all consecrated persons, according to their own traditions, to renew daily their spiritual union with the Blessed Virgin Mary, reliving with her the mysteries of her Son, especially by saying the *Rosary.*

3. Some New Fields of Mission

Presence in the world of education

96.1 The Church has always recognized that *education is an essential dimension of her mission.* The Master of her inner life is the Holy Spirit, who penetrates the innermost depths of every human heart and knows the secret unfolding of history. The whole Church is enlivened by the Holy Spirit and with him carries out her educational work. Within the Church, however, consecrated persons have a specific duty. They are called to bring to bear on the world of education their radical witness to the values of the Kingdom, proposed to everyone in expectation of the definitive meeting with the Lord of history. Because of their special consecration, their particular experience of the gifts of the Spirit, their constant listening to the word of God, their practice of discernment, their rich heritage of pedagogical traditions built up since the establishment of their Institute, and their profound grasp of spiritual truth (cf. Eph 2:17), consecrated persons are able to be especially effective in educational activities and to offer a specific contribution to the work of other educators.

96.2 Equipped with this charism, consecrated persons can give life to educational undertakings permeated by the Gospel spirit of freedom and charity, in which young people are helped to mature humanly under the action of the Spirit.[235] In this way a community of learning becomes an experience of grace, where the teaching program contributes to uniting into a harmonious whole the human and the divine, the Gospel and culture, faith and life.

96.3 The history of the Church, from antiquity down to our own day, is full of admirable examples of consecrated persons who have sought and continue to seek holiness through their involvement in education, while at the same time proposing holiness as the goal of education. Indeed, many of them have achieved the perfection of charity through teaching. This is one of the most precious gifts which consecrated persons today can offer to young people, instructing them in a way that is full of love, according to the wise counsel of Saint John Bosco: "Young people should not only be loved, but should also know that they are loved."[236]

Need for a renewed commitment in the field of education

97.1 With respectful sensitivity and missionary boldness, consecrated men and women should show that faith in Jesus Christ enlightens the whole enterprise of education, never disparaging human values but rather confirming and elevating them. Thus do consecrated persons become witnesses and instruments of the power of the Incarnation and the vitality of the Spirit. This task of theirs is one of the most significant manifestations of that motherhood which the Church, in the image of Mary, exercises on behalf of all her children.[237]

97.2 It is for this reason that the Synod emphatically urged consecrated persons to take up again, wherever possible, the mission of education in schools of every kind and level, and in universities and institutions of higher learning.[238] Making my own the proposal of the Synod, I warmly invite members of Institutes devoted to education to be faithful to their founding charism and to their traditions, knowing that the preferential love for the poor finds a special application in the choice of means capable of freeing people from that grave form of poverty which is the lack of cultural and religious training.

97.3 Because of the importance that Catholic and ecclesiastical universities and faculties have in the field of education and evangelization, Institutes

---

[235] Cf. Second Vatican Ecumenical Council, Declaration on Christian Education *Gravissimum Educationis,* 8.

[236] *Scritti pedagogici e spirituali* (Rome, 1987), 294.

[237] Cf. John Paul II, Apostolic Constitution *Sapientia Christiana* (April 15, 1979), II: *AAS* 71 (1979), 471.

[238] Cf. *Propositio* 41.

which are responsible for their direction should be conscious of their responsibility. They should ensure the preservation of their unique Catholic identity in complete fidelity to the Church's Magisterium, all the while engaging in active dialogue with present-day cultural trends. Moreover, depending on the circumstances, the members of these Institutes and Societies should readily become involved in the educational structures of the State. Members of Secular Institutes in particular, because of their specific calling, are called to this kind of cooperation.

Evangelizing culture

98.1 Institutes of Consecrated Life have always had great influence in the formation and transmission of culture. This was true in the Middle Ages, when monasteries became places for the study of the cultural riches of the past, and for the development of a new humanistic and Christian culture. The same has happened every time the light of the Gospel has spread to new nations and peoples. Many consecrated persons have been promoters of culture, and frequently have studied and defended indigenous cultures. The need to contribute to the promotion of culture and to the dialogue between culture and faith is deeply felt in the Church today.[239]

98.2 Consecrated persons cannot fail to feel challenged by this pressing need. In their proclamation of the word of God, they too are called to discover the methods most suited to the needs of the different social groups and various professional categories, so that the light of Christ will penetrate all sectors of society and the leaven of salvation will transform society from within, fostering the growth of a culture imbued with Gospel values.[240] At the threshold of the third Christian millennium, such a commitment will enable consecrated men and women to renew their response to the will of God, who reaches out to all those who, knowingly or not, are searching for the Truth and the Life (cf. Acts 17:27).

98.3 But in addition to this service of others, within the consecrated life itself there is a need for a *renewed and loving commitment to the intellectual life,* for dedication to study as a means of integral formation and as a path of asceticism which is extraordinarily timely, in the face of present-day cultural diversity. A lessened commitment to study can have grave consequences for the apostolate, by giving rise to a sense of marginalization and inferiority, or encouraging superficiality and rash initiatives.

---

[239] Cf. John Paul II, Apostolic Constitution *Sapientia Christiana* (April 15, 1979), II: *AAS* 71 (1979), 470.

[240] Cf. *Propositio* 36.

98.4 With all respect for the diversity of charisms and the actual resources of individual Institutes, the commitment to study cannot be limited to initial formation or to the gaining of academic degrees and professional qualifications. Rather, study is an expression of the unquenchable desire for an ever deeper knowledge of God, the source of light and all human truth. Consequently, a commitment to study does not isolate consecrated persons in an abstract intellectualism, or confine them within a suffocating narcissism; rather, it is an incentive to dialogue and cooperation, a training in the capacity for judgment, a stimulus to contemplation and prayer in the constant quest for the presence and activity of God in the complex reality of today's world.

98.5 When they allow themselves to be transformed by the Holy Spirit, consecrated persons can broaden the horizons of narrow human aspirations and at the same time understand more deeply people and their life stories, going beyond the most obvious but often superficial aspects. Countless challenges are today emerging in the world of ideas, in new areas as well as those in which the consecrated life has traditionally been present. There is an urgent need to maintain fruitful contacts with all cultural realities, with a watchful and critical attitude, but also with confident attention to those who face the particular difficulties of intellectual work, especially when, in response to the unprecedented problems of our times, new efforts of analysis and synthesis have to be attempted.[241] A serious and effective evangelization of these new areas where culture is developed and transmitted cannot take place without active cooperation with the laity involved in them.

Presence in the field of social communications

99.1 Just as in the past consecrated persons successfully used all kinds of means at the service of evangelization and skillfully met difficulties, today too they are challenged anew by the need to bear witness to the Gospel through the communications media. The media, thanks to impressive developments in technology, have reached every corner of the earth. Consecrated persons, especially those who have the institutional charism of working in this field, have a duty to learn the language of the media, in order to speak effectively of Christ to our contemporaries, interpreting their "joys and hopes, their griefs and anxieties,"[242] and thus contributing to the building up of a society in which

---

[241] Cf. Second Vatican Ecumenical Council, Pastoral Constitution on the Church in the Modern World *Gaudium et Spes,* 5.

[242] Ibid., 1.

all people sense that they are brothers and sisters making their way to God.

99.2 Nevertheless, it is necessary to be vigilant with regard to the distorted use of the media, especially given their extraordinary power of persuasion. The problems which can result for the consecrated life should not be ignored; instead they should be faced with careful discernment.[243] The Church's response is above all educational: it aims at promoting a correct understanding of the dynamics underlying the media and a careful ethical assessment of their programs, as well as the development of healthy habits in their use.[244] In this work of education, aimed at training discerning listeners and expert communicators, consecrated persons are called to offer their specific witness regarding the relative nature of all created realities. In this way they help people to use the media wisely and in accordance with God's plan, but also to free themselves from an obsessive interest in "the form of this world which is passing away" (1 Cor 7:31).

99.3 All efforts in this important new field of the apostolate should be encouraged, so that the Gospel of Christ may be proclaimed also through these modern means. The various Institutes should be ready to cooperate, by contributing resources and personnel, in order to implement joint projects in all sectors of social communications. Furthermore, consecrated persons, especially members of Secular Institutes, should willingly lend their help, wherever pastorally appropriate, for the religious formation of leaders and workers in the field of public and private social communications. This should be done in order to offset the inappropriate use of the media and to promote higher quality programs, the contents of which will be respectful of the moral law and rich in human and Christian values.

4. Engaged in Dialogue with Everyone

At the service of Christian unity

100.1 Christ's prayer to the Father before his Passion, that his disciples may be one (cf. Jn 17:21-23), lives on in the Church's prayer and activity. How can those called to the consecrated life not feel themselves involved? The wound of disunity still existing between believers in Christ and the urgent need to pray and work for the promotion of Christian unity were deeply felt at

---

[243] Cf. Congregation for Institutes of Consecrated Life and Societies of Apostolic Life, Instruction on Fraternal Life in Community *Congregavit Nos in Unum Christi Amor* (February 2, 1994), 34: Rome, 1994, 30-31.

[244] Cf. John Paul II, Message for the 29th World Communications Day (January 24, 1994): *Insegnamenti,* 17/1 (1994), 183-188.

the Synod. The ecumenical sensitivity of consecrated persons is heightened also by the awareness that in other Churches and Ecclesial Communities monasticism has been preserved and is flourishing, as is the case in the Eastern Churches, and that there is a renewal of the profession of the evangelical counsels, as in the Anglican Communion and in the Communities of the Reformation.

100.2 The Synod emphasized the close connection between the consecrated life and the cause of ecumenism, and the urgent need for a more intense witness in this area. Since the soul of ecumenism is prayer and conversion,[245] Institutes of Consecrated Life and Societies of Apostolic Life certainly have a special duty to foster this commitment. There is an urgent need for consecrated persons to give more space in their lives to ecumenical prayer and genuine evangelical witness, so that by the power of the Holy Spirit the walls of division and prejudice between Christians can be broken down.

Forms of ecumenical dialogue

101.1 Sharing of the *lectio divina* in the search for the truth, a participation in common prayer, in which the Lord assures us of his presence (cf. Mt 18:20), the dialogue of friendship and charity which makes us feel how pleasant it is when brothers dwell in unity (cf. Ps 133), cordial hospitality shown to brothers and sisters of the various Christian confessions, mutual knowledge and the exchange of gifts, cooperation in common undertakings of service and of witness: these are among the many forms of ecumenical dialogue. They are actions pleasing to our common Father, which show the will to journey together toward perfect unity along the path of truth and love.[246] Likewise, the knowledge of the history, doctrine, liturgy, and charitable and apostolic activity of other Christians cannot but help to make ecumenical activity ever more fruitful.[247]

101.2 I wish to encourage those Institutes which, either because they were founded for this purpose or because of a later calling, are dedicated to promoting Christian unity and therefore foster initiatives of study and concrete action. Indeed, no Institute of Consecrated Life should feel itself dispensed from working for this cause. My thoughts likewise turn to the Eastern Catholic Churches with the hope that also through the monastic life of men and women — the flourishing of which is a grace constantly to be prayed for — they may help to bring about unity with the Orthodox Churches, through the

---

[245] Cf. John Paul II, Encyclical Letter *Ut Unum Sint* (May 25, 1995) 21: *AAS* 87 (1995), 934.
[246] Cf. ibid., 28: loc. cit., 938-939.
[247] Cf. *Propositio* 45.

dialogue of charity and the sharing of a common spirituality, itself the heritage of the undivided Church of the first millennium.

101.3 In a special way, I entrust to the monasteries of contemplative life the spiritual ecumenism of prayer, conversion of heart, and charity. To this end I encourage their presence wherever Christian communities of different confessions live side by side, so that their total devotion to the "one thing needful" (cf. Lk 10:42) — to the worship of God and to intercession for the salvation of the world, together with their witness of evangelical life according to their special charisms — will inspire everyone to abide, after the image of the Trinity, in that unity which Jesus willed and asked of the Father for all his disciples.

Interreligious dialogue

102.1 Because "interreligious dialogue is a part of the Church's evangelizing mission,"[248] Institutes of Consecrated Life cannot exempt themselves from involvement also in this field, each in accordance with its own charism and following the directives of ecclesiastical authority. The first form of evangelization in relation to our brothers and sisters of other religions should be the testimony of a life of poverty, humility and chastity, imbued with fraternal love for all. At the same time, the freedom of spirit proper to the consecrated life will favor that "dialogue of life"[249] which embodies a basic model of mission and of the proclamation of Christ's Gospel. In order to foster reciprocal knowledge, respect and charity, Religious Institutes can also promote *appropriate forms of dialogue,* marked by cordial friendship and mutual sincerity, with the monastic communities of other religions.

102.2 Another area for cooperation with men and women of different religious traditions is that of a shared *concern for human life,* extending from compassion for those who are suffering physically and spiritually to commitment to justice, peace and the protection of God's creation. In these areas, Institutes of active life especially will seek an understanding with members of other religions, through that "dialogue of action"[250] which prepares the way for more profound exchanges.

102.3 A particular field for successful common action with people of other

---

[248] John Paul II, Encyclical Letter *Redemptoris Missio* (December 7, 1990), 55: *AAS* 83 (1991), 302.

[249] Pontifical Council for Interreligious Dialogue and Congregation for the Evangelization of Peoples, Instruction *Dialogue and Proclamation: Reflections and Perspectives* (May 19, 1991), 42a: *AAS* 84 (1992), 428.

[250] Ibid., 42b: loc. cit., 428.

religious traditions is that of *efforts to promote the dignity of women.* In view of the equality and authentic complementarity of men and women, a valuable service can be rendered above all by consecrated women.[251]

102.4 These and other ways in which consecrated persons are engaged in the service of interreligious dialogue require an appropriate training, both in initial formation and in continuing formation. They require study and research,[252] since in this very delicate area a profound knowledge of Christianity and of other religions is needed, accompanied by solid faith and by spiritual and personal maturity.

Spirituality as a response to the search for the sacred and the desire for God

103.1 Because of the very nature of their choice, all who embrace the consecrated life, men and women alike, become privileged partners in the search for God which has always stirred the human heart and has led to the different forms of asceticism and spirituality. Today, in many places, this search is insistently emerging as a response to cultural forces which tend to marginalize the religious dimension of life, if not actually to deny it.

103.2 When consecrated persons live consistently and fully their freely assumed commitments, they are able to offer a response to the longings of their contemporaries, and can help to free them from solutions which are for the most part illusory and often involve a denial of the saving Incarnation of Christ (cf. 1 Jn 4:2-3), such as those proposed, for example, by the sects. By practicing a personal and communal asceticism which purifies and transfigures their entire existence, they bear witness, against the temptation to self-centeredness and sensuality, to the true nature of the search for God. They constitute a warning against confusing that search with a subtle search for self or a flight into gnosticism. Every consecrated person is committed to strengthening the interior life, which in no way involves withdrawal from reality or a turning in upon oneself. Listening in obedience to the word, of which the Church is the guardian and interpreter, the consecrated person points to Christ who is to be loved above all things and to the mystery of the Trinity as the response to the profound longings of the human heart and the ultimate goal of every religious journey sincerely open to transcendence.

103.3 For this reason, consecrated persons are in duty bound to offer a

---

[251] Cf. *Propositio* 46.

[252] Cf. Pontifical Council for Interreligious Dialogue and Congregation for the Evangelization of Peoples, Instruction *Dialogue and Proclamation: Reflections and Perspectives* (May 19, 1991), 42c: *AAS* 84 (1992), 428.

generous welcome and spiritual support to all those who, moved by a thirst for God and a desire to live the demands of faith, turn to them.[253]

Conclusion

Unbounded generosity

104.1 Many people today are puzzled and ask: What is the point of the consecrated life? Why embrace this kind of life, when there are so many urgent needs in the areas of charity and of evangelization itself, to which one can respond even without assuming the particular commitments of the consecrated life? Is the consecrated life not a kind of "waste" of human energies which might be used more efficiently for a greater good, for the benefit of humanity and the Church?

104.2 These questions are asked more frequently in our day, as a consequence of a utilitarian and technocratic culture which is inclined to assess the importance of things and even of people in relation to their immediate "usefulness." But such questions have always existed, as is eloquently demonstrated by the Gospel episode of the anointing at Bethany: "Mary took a pound of costly ointment of pure nard and anointed the feet of Jesus and wiped his feet with her hair; and the house was filled with the fragrance of the ointment" (Jn 12:3). When Judas, using the needs of the poor as an excuse, complained about such waste, Jesus replied: "Let her alone!" (Jn 12:7).

104.3 This is the perennially valid response to the question which many people, even in good faith, are asking about the relevance of the consecrated life: Could one not invest one's life in a more efficient and reasonable way for the betterment of society? This is how Jesus replies: "Let her alone!" Those who have been given the priceless gift of following the Lord Jesus more closely consider it obvious that he can and must be loved with an undivided heart, that one can devote to him one's whole life, and not merely certain actions or occasional moments or activities. The precious ointment poured out as a pure act of love, and thus transcending all "utilitarian" considerations, is a sign of *unbounded generosity,* as expressed in a life spent in loving and serving the Lord, in order to devote oneself to his person and his Mystical Body. From such a life "poured out" without reserve there spreads a fragrance which fills the whole house. The house of God, the Church, today no less than in the past, is adorned and enriched by the presence of the consecrated life.

104.4 What in people's eyes can seem a waste is, for the individuals capti-

---

[253] Cf. *Propositio* 47.

vated in the depths of their heart by the beauty and goodness of the Lord, an obvious response of love, a joyful expression of gratitude for having been admitted in a unique way to the knowledge of the Son and to a sharing in his divine mission in the world.

104.5 "If any of God's children were to know and taste divine love, the uncreated God, the incarnate God, the God who endured suffering, the God who is the supreme good, they would give themselves completely to him, they would withdraw not only from other creatures but even from their very selves, and with all their being would love this God of love, to the point of being completely transformed into the God-man, who is the supreme Beloved."[254]

The consecrated life in the service of the Kingdom of God

105.1 "What would become of the world if there were no Religious?"[255] Beyond all superficial assessments of its usefulness, the consecrated life is important precisely in its being *unbounded generosity and love,* and this all the more so in a world which risks being suffocated in the whirlpool of the ephemeral. "Without this concrete sign there would be a danger that the charity which animates the entire Church would grow cold, that the salvific paradox of the Gospel would be blunted, and that the 'salt' of faith would lose its savor in a world undergoing secularization."[256] The Church and society itself need people capable of devoting themselves totally to God and to others for the love of God.

105.2 The Church can in no way renounce the consecrated life, for it *eloquently expresses her inmost nature as "Bride."* In the consecrated life the proclamation of the Gospel to the whole world finds fresh enthusiasm and power. There is a need for people able to show the fatherly face of God and the motherly face of the Church, people who spend their lives so that others can have life and hope. The Church needs consecrated persons who, even before committing themselves to the service of this or that noble cause, allow themselves to be transformed by God's grace and conform themselves fully to the Gospel.

105.3 The whole Church finds in her hands this great gift and gratefully devotes herself to promoting it with respect, with prayer, and with the explicit

---

[254] Blessed Angela of Foligno, *Il libro della Beata Angela da Foligno* (Grottaferrata, 1985), 683.

[255] Saint Teresa of Ávila, *Autobiography,* Chapter 32, 11.

[256] Paul VI, Apostolic Exhortation *Evangelica Testificatio* (June 29, 1971), 3: *AAS* 63 (1971), 498.

invitation to accept it. It is important that Bishops, priests and deacons, convinced of the evangelical superiority of this kind of life, should strive to discover and encourage the seeds of vocation through preaching, discernment and wise spiritual guidance. All the faithful are asked to pray constantly for consecrated persons, that their fervor and their capacity to love may grow continually and thus contribute to spreading in today's society the fragrance of Christ (cf. 2 Cor 2:15). The whole Christian community — pastors, laity and consecrated persons — is responsible for the consecrated life, and for welcoming and supporting new vocations.[257]

To young people

106.1 To you, young people, I say: if you hear the Lord's call, do not reject it! Dare to become part of the great movements of holiness which renowned saints have launched in their following of Christ. Cultivate the ideals proper to your age, but readily accept God's plan for you if he invites you to seek holiness in the consecrated life. Admire all God's works in the world, but be ready to fix your eyes on the things destined never to pass away.

106.2 The third millennium awaits the contribution of the faith and creativity of great numbers of young consecrated persons, that the world may be made more peaceful and able to welcome God and, in him, all his sons and daughters.

To families

107.1 I address you, Christian families. Parents, give thanks to the Lord if he has called one of your children to the consecrated life. It is to be considered a great honor — as it always has been — that the Lord should look upon a family and choose to invite one of its members to set out on the path of the evangelical counsels! Cherish the desire to give the Lord one of your children so that God's love can spread in the world. What fruit of conjugal love could be more beautiful than this?

107.2 We must remember that if parents do not live the values of the Gospel, the young man or woman will find it very difficult to discern the calling, to understand the need for the sacrifices which must be faced, and to appreciate the beauty of the goal to be achieved. For it is in the family that young people have their first experience of Gospel values and of the love which gives itself to God and to others. They also need to be trained in the responsible use of their own freedom, so that they will be prepared to live, as their vocation demands, in accordance with the loftiest spiritual realities.

[257] Cf. *Propositio* 48.

107.3 I pray that you, Christian families, united with the Lord through prayer and the sacramental life, will create homes where vocations are welcomed.

To men and women of good will

108.1 To all the men and women who are willing to listen to my voice, I wish to address an invitation to seek the paths which lead to the living and true God, including the path marked out by the consecrated life. Consecrated persons bear witness to the fact that "whoever follows after Christ, the perfect man, becomes himself more of a man."[258] How many consecrated men and women have bent down, and continue to bend down, as Good Samaritans, over the countless wounds of the brothers and sisters whom they meet on their way!

108.2 Look at these people seized by Christ, who show that in self-mastery, sustained by grace and God's love, lies the remedy for the craving to possess, to seek pleasure, to dominate. Do not forget the charisms which have shaped remarkable "seekers of God" and benefactors of humanity, who have provided sure paths for those who seek God with a sincere heart. Consider the great number of saints who have flourished in this way of life; consider the good done to the world, in the past and in the present, by those who have devoted themselves to God! Does not this world of ours need joyful witnesses and prophets of the beneficent power of God's love? Does it not also need men and women who, by their lives and their work, are able to sow seeds of peace and fraternity?[259]

To consecrated persons

109.1 But it is above all to you, consecrated women and men, that at the end of this Exhortation I appeal with trust: live to the full your dedication to God, so that this world may never be without a ray of divine beauty to lighten the path of human existence. Christians, immersed in the cares and concerns of this world but also called to holiness, need to discover in you purified hearts which in faith "see" God, people docile to the working of the Holy Spirit who resolutely press on in fidelity to the charism of their call and mission.

109.2 You know well that you have set out on a journey of continual con-

---

[258] Second Vatican Ecumenical Council, Pastoral Constitution on the Church in the Modern World *Gaudium et Spes,* 41.

[259] Cf. Paul VI, Apostolic Exhortation *Evangelica Testificatio* (June 29, 1971), 53: *AAS* 63 (1971), 524; Apostolic Exhortation *Evangelii Nuntiandi* (December 8, 1975), 69: *AAS* 68 (1976), 59.

version, of exclusive dedication to the love of God and of your brothers and sisters, in order to bear ever more splendid witness to the grace which transfigures Christian life. The world and the Church seek authentic witnesses to Christ. And the consecrated life is a gift which God offers in order that everyone can recognize the "one thing necessary" (cf. Lk 10:42). To bear witness to Christ by one's life, works and words is the particular mission of the consecrated life in the Church and in the world.

109.3 You know the one in whom you have put your trust (cf. 2 Tim 1:12): give him everything! Young people will not be deceived: when they come to you, they want to see what they do not see elsewhere. An immense task awaits you in the future: in a special way young consecrated persons, by witnessing to their consecration, can lead their contemporaries to a renewal of their lives.[260] An impassioned love of Jesus Christ is a powerful attraction for those other young people whom Christ in his goodness is calling to follow him closely and for ever. Our contemporaries want to see in consecrated persons the joy which comes from being with the Lord.

109.4 Consecrated women and men, old and young alike, live faithfully your commitment to God, in mutual edification and mutual support! Despite the difficulties you may occasionally encounter, and despite the lessening of esteem for the consecrated life in certain quarters, you have the task of once more inviting the men and women of our time to lift their eyes, not to let themselves be overwhelmed by everyday things, to let themselves be captivated by the fascination of God and of his Son's Gospel. Do not forget that you, in a very special way, can and must say that you not only belong to Christ but that "you have become Christ"![261]

Looking to the future

110.1 You have not only a glorious history to remember and to recount, but also *a great history still to be accomplished!* Look to the future, where the Spirit is sending you in order to do even greater things.

110.2 Make your lives a fervent expectation of Christ; go forth to meet him like the wise virgins setting out to meet the Bridegroom. Be always ready, faithful to Christ, to the Church, to your Institute and to the men and women of our time.[262] In this way you will day by day be renewed in Christ, in order

---

[260] Cf. *Propositio* 16.

[261] Saint Augustine, *Treatise on Saint John's Gospel*, XXI, 8: *PL* 35, 1568.

[262] Cf. Congregation for Religious and Secular Institutes, Document on Religious and Human Promotion (August 12, 1980), 13-21: *L'Osservatore Romano* (English-language edition), January 26, 1981, 10-11.

with his Spirit to build fraternal communities, to join him in washing the feet of the poor, and to contribute in your own unique way to the transfiguration of the world.

110.3 As it enters the new millennium, may our world, entrusted to human hands, become ever more human and just, a sign and anticipation of the world to come, in which the Lord, humble and glorified, poor and exalted, will be the full and lasting joy for us and for our brothers and sisters, together with the Father and the Holy Spirit.

Prayer to the Holy Trinity

111.1 Most Holy Trinity, blessed and the source of all blessedness, bless your sons and daughters whom you have called to praise the greatness of your love, your merciful goodness and your beauty.

111.2 *Father Most Holy,* sanctify the sons and daughters who have consecrated themselves to you, for the glory of your name. Enfold them with your power, enabling them to bear witness that you are the Origin of all things, the one Source of love and freedom. We thank you for the gift of the consecrated life, which in faith seeks you and in its universal mission invites all people to draw near to you.

111.3 *Jesus our Savior,* Incarnate Word, as you have entrusted your own way of life to those whom you have called, continue to draw to yourself men and women who will be, for the people of our time, dispensers of mercy, heralds of your return, living signs of the Resurrection and of its treasures of virginity, poverty and obedience. May no tribulation separate them from you and from your love!

111.4 *Holy Spirit,* Love poured into our hearts, who grant grace and inspiration to our minds, the perennial Source of life, who bring to fulfillment the mission of Christ by means of many charisms, we pray to you for all consecrated persons. Fill their hearts with the deep certainty of having been chosen to love, to praise and to serve. Enable them to savor your friendship, fill them with your joy and consolation, help them to overcome moments of difficulty and to rise up again with trust after they have fallen; make them mirrors of the divine beauty. Give them the courage to face the challenges of our time and the grace to bring to all mankind the goodness and loving kindness of our Savior Jesus Christ (cf. Tit 3:4).

Invocation of the Blessed Virgin Mary

112.1 Mary, image of the Church, the Bride without spot or wrinkle, which by imitating you "preserves with virginal purity an integral faith, a firm hope and a sincere charity,"[263] sustain consecrated persons on their journey toward the sole and eternal Blessedness.

112.2 To you, Virgin of the Visitation, do we entrust them, that they may go forth to meet human needs, to bring help, but above all to bring Jesus. Teach them to proclaim the mighty things which the Lord accomplishes in the world, that all peoples may extol the greatness of his name. Support them in their work for the poor, the hungry, those without hope, the little ones and all who seek your Son with a sincere heart.

112.3 To you, our Mother, who desire the spiritual and apostolic renewal of your sons and daughters in a response of love and complete dedication to Christ, we address our confident prayer. You who did the will of the Father, ever ready in obedience, courageous in poverty and receptive in fruitful virginity, obtain from your divine Son that all who have received the gift of following him in the consecrated life may be enabled to bear witness to that gift by their transfigured lives, as they joyfully make their way with all their brothers and sisters toward our heavenly homeland and the light which will never grow dim.

112.4 We ask you this, that in everyone and in everything glory, adoration and love may be given to the Most High Lord of all things, who is Father, Son and Holy Spirit.

Given in Rome, at Saint Peter's, on March 25, the Solemnity of the Annunciation of the Lord, in the year 1996, the eighteenth of my Pontificate.

---

[263] Second Vatican Ecumenical Council, Dogmatic Constitution on the Church *Lumen Gentium,* 64.

Index of Scriptural Quotations

The references are to paragraph numbers in the encyclicals and post-synodal apostolic exhortations. Their titles are abbreviated in accordance with the list of abbreviations below. References to encyclicals precede those of the post-synodal apostolic exhortations. Within each category the references are listed in chronological order, based on the date of the document's publication.

Abbreviations

CA	*Centesimus Annus* (1991)
CL	*Christifideles Laici* (1988)
CT	*Catechesi Tradendae* (1979)
DM	*Dives in Misericordia* (1980)
DV	*Dominum et Vivificantem* (1986)
EV	*Evangelium Vitae* (1995)
FC	*Familiaris Consortio* (1981)
LE	*Laborem Exercens* (1981)
PDV	*Pastores Dabo Vobis* (1992)
RH	*Redemptor Hominis* (1979)
RM	*Redemptoris Missio* (1990)
RMA	*Redemptoris Mater* (1987)
RP	*Reconciliatio et Paenitentia* (1984)
SA	*Slavorum Apostoli* (1985)
SRS	*Sollicitudo Rei Socialis* (1987)
UUS	*Ut Unum Sint* (1995)
VC	*Vita Consecrata* (1996)
VS	*Veritatis Splendor* (1993)

OLD TESTAMENT

Genesis
1:2 • DV 12
1:10 • RH 8.1
1:26-27 • LE 6.2; DV 12, 34, 59.1; SRS 29:2-4, 30.5; CA 11.3; EV 34.2-4, 53.3; FC 11.1
1:26-30 • SRS 30.2
1:27 • FC 22.4
1:28 • RH 16.1; DM 2.3; LE 4.2-3, 6.2-3, 9.1-2; SRS 30.5; CA 31.2; VS 38.2; EV 34.3, 42.1-2, 52.3; FC 28.1
1:31 • SRS 47.2
2:2 • LE 25.2
2:3 • LE 25.2-3
2:15 • EV 9.2, 34.3, 42.3
2:15-17 • SRS 29.3, 30.2, 34.5

2:16 • VS 41.1
2:16-17 • DV 36.1; VS 35; CL 43.7
2:17 • VS 40
2:18 • FC 25.2; CL 51.13
2:18-20 • SRS 39.5
2:23 • EV 35.3; FC 25.2
2:24 • EV 43.2; FC 19.1
3:5 • DV 36, 37.2; RMA 11.1; VS 86.2, 102.2; RP 14.2; CL 4.1
3:15 • RMA 7.2, 11, 24.1-2
3:17-19 • LE 1.2, 9.2-3, 27.1; SRS 30.3
3:20 • EV 43.3
4:2-16 • EV 7-10, 18.1, 19.3, 21.2, 25.1, 39.1, 40.1; RP 31.15
6:5-7 • DV 39.2
9:1-17 • RM 12.2
9:5 • EV 39.1
9:6 • EV 39.1

13:52 • SA 20; CA 3.3
16:17-23 • UUS 91
16:18 • UUS 11.1
16:19 • CA 5.3
16:23 • UUS 91.2
16:26 • SRS 33.4
17:1-9 • VC 14-19, 23.1-2, 29.1, 35.1-2, 40, 75.3
18:19-20 • FC 59.2
18:20 • UUS 21.3
19:6 • VS 72.1; FC 19.1
19:8 • VS 22.2, 112.2; FC 20.4
19:10-12 • VS 22.2; PDV 29.1, 50.2; VC 30.2
19:13-15 • CL 47.1
19:16 • VS 6-8, 117.1
19:16-21 • VS 6-22
19:17 • VS 9-12, 72.1, 73.2, 117.2
19:17-18 • VS 52.2; EV 41.1, 52.1
19:18-19 • VS 13.1
19:19 • VS 97.1
19:20 • VS 16.1
19:21 • VS 16-19, 66.1
19:26 • VS 22
20:1-16 • CL 1, 2.1-4, 3.2-5, 45
20:25 • SRS 38.6; UUS 94.1
20:28 • RH 18.4, 21.1
22:30 • FC 16.3; VC 32.2
22:40 • VS 14.2
25:26-28 • SRS 30.7-8
25:31-46 • RH 16.9-10; SRS 13.2; CA 57.1; EV 44.5
25:40 • EV 87.2; PDV 49.4; VC 82.3
27:46 • RP 7.7
28:18-20 • RM 22-23, 47.2; PDV 14.2
28:19 • DV 9; RM 47.2; CL 22.1
28:20 • VS 25.1

Mark
1:15 • RH 20.5; RM 13.1-2; RP 1.1, 4.4, 26.4
3:5 • DV 47.1
3:13-15 • PDV 2.4-5, 4.1, 36.1-2, 36.5, 42.1-3, 65.4; VC 41.1
3:28-29 • DV 46-47
6:17-29 • VS 91.2
6:22-23 • VS 63.2
8:35 • EV 47.2
8:36 • CL 37.3
10:14 • CL 47.1
10:18 • VS 9
10:21 • CL 46.5
10:22 • PDV 37.1
10:42 • UUS 94.1
10:42-45 • CA 38.6; PDV 21.5
10:45 • PDV 21.4
12:31 • VS 13.2; EV 55.1
16:15 • FC 54.1

16:15-18 • RM 22-23

Luke
1:28 • RMA 8-9
1:32-33 • RMA 15.1
1:38 • DV 50.3; RMA 13.3-4, 15.2, 20.8, 39.1-2; VC 18.4
1:42 • RMA 8.2, 39.1-2
1:45 • DV 51.2; RMA 12.3, 13.1, 14.2, 17.1, 19, 27, 36.1
1:46-55 • RMA 35-37
1:49-54 • DM 5.1
1:50 • DM 9.1-2, 10.1
2:19 • RMA 26.4; VS 120.2
2:32-35 • RMA 16
2:34 • DV 55.1; RMA 16.2; EV 103.4
2:35 • RMA 16.2
2:51 • RMA 26.4
3:16 • DV 19.1-2, 23.1-2
3:21-22 • DV 19.3-4
4:16-21 • DV 18; RM 13.1, 14.2; PDV 11.1-2, 18.4, 19.1-2
4:18-19 • DM 3.1; SRS 47.6; CL 13.3; PDV 16.1, 24.1, 27.1, 33.1; VC 82.1
4:43 • RM 13.1
5:31-32 • EV 32.5
6:20 • RM 14.2
6:36 • VS 18.2
7:22 • EV 32.2
9:31 • VC 40.3
10:16 • VS 25.2
10:21-22 • DV 20
10:25-27 • VS 14.1
10:29-37 • VS 14; EV 27.2, 87.2; CL 53.4
11:3 • DV 65.1
11:27-28 • RMA 20
11:28 • VS 120.2
12:10 • DV 46-47
15:11-32 • DM 5-6; RP 5-6, 7.1, 10.3, 13.2, 26.4, 29.6, 31.15
16:19-31 • RH 16.4; SRS 33.7, 42.3
17:3-4 • RP 26.5
17:10 • RM 36.3
18:9-14 • VS 104.2-105.1
18:16 • FC 26.2
18:19 • VS 9
22:19 • PDV 1.4
22:25-27 • SRS 38.6
22:27 • UUS 88
22:31-32 • UUS 4, 91
22:32 • VS 115.2
24:46-49 • RM 22-23

John
1:14 • RH 1.1; DV 50.3

14:7-8 • EV 67.3
15:31 • VC 13.3
16:3-4 • FC 54.5; CL 35.2
16:26 • VS 66.1

1 Corinthians
1:12-13 • CL 31.7
2:10 • DV 32
2:10-11 • DV 35
2:16 • PDV 26.2
4:1 • PDV 24.4, 73.4
6:9-10 • VS 49, 81.1
7:7 • RH 21.3; PDV 29.1
7:31 • VC 99.2
7:32-35 • FC 16.5; VC 1.2, 17.1, 21.2
8:5-6 • RM 5.2
9:16 • RM 1.1-2; CL 33.5
9:22-23 • RM 88:3
11:24 • PDV 1.4
12:4-11 • CL 24.1-2
13:13 • CL 41.3
15:5 • UUS 91.1
15:22-23 • RMA 41.2
15:28 • CL 14.8

2 Corinthians
1:19 • CL 38.5
1:21-22 • CL 13.2
3:6 • RH 17.5
3:17 • DV 51.2, 60.2
5:14 • VC 78.1
5:20 • RP 10.6
5:21 • RH 9.2; DM 7.3, 8.1
8:9 • EV 33.2; VC 21.3, 22.2
11:28 • RM 89.4
12:7-10 • UUS 91.2, 92.1
13:11,13 • UUS 103.1
13:13 • DV 2.3; CL 18.6

Galatians
4:4 • DV 49.1, 51.1; RMA 1, 7.1
4:19 • RMA 43.1
5:1 • RH 21.5; VS 66.2
5:6 • VS 26.1
5:13 • VS 17.2, 66.2
5:16-26 • DV 55-57
5:22 • CL 16.6
5:25 • PDV 19.3

Ephesians
1:3-7 • RMA 7.1
2:4 • DM 2.2
2:14-16 • UUS 5.2; RP 10.7
3:14-16 • DV 58.2-3
3:15 • FC 14.3, 25.5

5:1-2 • VS 89.2
5:25 • RM 89.4; VS 89.2; PDV 23.3
5:25-29 • PDV 22.3
5:32-33 • FC 13.3

Philippians
2:5-11 • RMA 18.3; VC 79.1

Colossians
1:15-20 • DV 33.2; SRS 31.1-2, 31.5
1:24 • RM 78; CL 53.3
3:3 • VC 90.3
3:17 • CL 17.1

1 Thessalonians
2:2 • RM 45.2

2 Thessalonians
2:7 • RP 14.1

1 Timothy
2:4 • RM 9.2
2:5 • RM 5.4
3:15 • VS 27.3
3:16 • RP 19.2-20.3
6:13 • VS 91.3

2 Timothy
1:6 • PDV 70.1-4
4:2 • EV 82.2
4:3 • VS 29.4

Titus
1:7-8 • PDV 26.6

Hebrews
1:1-2 • RM 5.3
4:15 • RP 26.11; PDV 5.2
5:1 • CL 22.3; PDV 5.1-2, 43.1
5:7 • DV 65.1
5:7-8 • DV 40.3
9:13-14 • DV 40, 42.3
12:22, 24 • EV 25.1-2, 28.3

James
1:25 • VS 83.2
3:18 • SRS 39.9
4:1-2 • SRS 10.4

1 Peter
1:18-19 • EV 25.3
2:2 • CL 58.7
2:4-5 • PDV 13.5
2:5 • FC 56.5, 59.1
5:1-4 • PDV 15.2-3, 21.5

Index of Encyclicals and Post-Synodal Apostolic Exhortations

References are not just to official paragraph numbers but to paragraph divisions in the English text. If the reference is to the whole original paragraph, no subdivision reference is given. References to encyclicals are given in chronological order. They precede the references to the post-synodal apostolic exhortations which are also given in chronological order.

This is not a mere word search. Not every single reference to a word or theme is included, but only those judged to be sufficiently significant or developed to warrant inclusion in the index. If an earlier document is quoted in a later one, the later repetition is not usually mentioned.

and Holy Spirit VC 5.2, 9.2, 12.2-3, 19, 21.5-6, 30.3, 36, 62.7, 64.2, 72.1, 81.3, 84.2
as imitation of Christ VC 14.1, 18, 22
and inculturation VC 47.2, 48, 79-80
and initiative of Father VC 14.2, 17
as integral to Church VC 3, 5.1, 29.2-3, 63.3, 105.2
and intellectual life VC 98.3-4
and interreligious dialogue VC 8.3, 79, 102
as intimacy with Christ VC 16.1
and John, Saint VC 23.3
and justice, promotion of VC 82
and Kingdom of God VC 1.1, 14.1
and laity, cooperation with VC 54-56, 74.1
as living Tradition VC 22.3
and Magisterium, obedience to VC 13.5, 46.3, 85.2
and Mary, model of VC 18.4, 23.3, 28, 34.3, 112.3
and missionary institutes RM 66, 69-70
and mixed Institutes VC 61
and motherhood in the spirit RM 70
and new evangelization VC 45.2, 57.3, 58.2, 62.2, 81-83
new expressions of VC 10, 12, 62
origins of VC 1.2, 14.1, 22.1, 29.3
and Penance, sacrament of VC 95.4
and Paschal Mystery VC 6.2, 24, 25.1, 59.2, 70.6-7, 93.1
and poor, commitment to RM 60.3; VC 5.1, 82, 89-90, 110.2
and Pope VC 46.2, 47
and prayer VC 38.1
and presbyterate PDV 74.8
as prophetic VC 15.4, 20.2, 33, 45, 84-85
and Rule VC 37.2, 73.3
and spiritual life VC 35-40, 93-95
spousal meaning of VC 34
superiority of VC 18.3, 32.2. 105.3
superiors in VC 43, 70.7
and Trinity VC 16.3-4, 17-21, 41
as visible witness VC 20.2, 25.3-4, 72.2-3, 76, 87, 102.1
vocation to, as special VC 1.2, 14.2-3, 15.4
vocations to VC 63.1, 64, 105.3
of women in particular VC 57-58
in younger Churches VC 8.3
Consequentialism VS 74-77
Conspiracy against life EV 12, 17.2
see also Culture of death
Constantinople I, Council of (381) DV 2.2
Consumerism
and contraception FC 6.4, 30.2
description of RH 16.2-3; DM 11.4; SRS 28.2; CA 36.2, 41.2
effects of SRS 28.3-4
lure of PDV 8.2
and Marxism, defeat of CA 19.4
and values RM 59.2; CA 36.2-4
and young people CA 37.1; PDV 7.3, 8.2
Contemplation
and action VC 9.2, 74.2, 75.3, 94.3
and the Cross, source of all vocations VC 23.2

and mission RM 69, 91.2
and prayer of Jesus on Tabor VC 14.3, 32.4
and primacy of God VC 27.4
Contemplative outlook on life EV 83.2
Contraception
see also Contraceptive mentality; Natural family planning
and abortifacients EV 13.4
forced EV 17.2, 91.1; FC 30.2, 30.6
immorality of FC 32.3-4
pastoral attitude to FC 33-35
teaching on EV 13.2-4; FC 29.2, 31-33
and theologians FC 31.3-4, 73.5
Contraceptive mentality EV 13.2-4; FC 6.2, 6.4, 30.2-4
see also Contraception
Contrition
see also Conversion of heart; Penance, sacrament of; Reconciliation
and conversion of heart DV 45.1; RP 13.2-4, 31.8-9
as lost dignity, sense of DM 5.4-5
Conversion of heart
see also Contrition; Penance, sacrament of; Reconciliation
and Baptism RM 46-47
and contrition RP 31.8-9
and daily life RP 22.1
definition of RP 4.4-5, 26.4-6
and dialogue RM 56
and evangelization, purpose of RM 46
as gradual process FC 9, 34
and Holy Spirit, role in DV 31, 42.2-3, 48.2
and mercy DM 6.5, 13.6-7
need for FC 9.1
and non-religious persons SRS 38.3
personal aspect of RH 20.6; RP 4.11
and sin, awareness of DV 31.2-3, 45; RP 26.4
and socioeconomic change RH 16.7; SRS 38.3-4
and truth about self DM 6.3
Converts
force for ecclesial renewal RM 91
gift to Church RM 47.4
Cooperation, international see Solidarity, international
Corruption, political and economic RM 43.2; CA 48.1
Cosmos
see also Creation
interconnectedness of SRS 34.2
Councils of priests RH 5.3
Counseling, marriage EV 88.2
Courage
see also Fortitude
in preaching RM 45.2-3
and witness RM 24.1, 45.2, 87.3-4
Covenant
see also Decalogue; Law, Mosaic
Christ as link between Old and New VS 15.1
and creation LE 4.2; DV 34; FC 8.6
definitiveness from Calvary DM 7.5
fidelity to, by God DM 4.3